SKIING USA

THE GUIDE FOR SKIERS
AND SNOWBOARDERS

By Clive Hobson

THIRD EDITION

Fodor's Travel Publications, Inc.
New York • Toronto • London • Sydney • Auckland
www.fodors.com

Third Edition

ISBN 0–679–00324–X

ISSN 1525–6952

Fodor's Skiing USA: The Guide for Skiers and Snowboarders

EDITOR: Nancy van Itallie
Contributors: Mark Condon, Galen Crane, Gavin Ehringer, Clive Hobson, Brian Hurlbert, Moira McCarthy, Michael McCoy, Lolly Merrell, Effin Older, Jules Older, Eric Perlman, Kurt Repanshek, Robbe Stimson
Editorial Production: Linda K. Schmidt
Maps: Mapping Specialists, Inc., *cartographer*; Robert Blake, *map editor*
Design: Fabrizio La Rocca, *creative director*; Guido Caroti, *art director*; Jolie Novak, *photo editor*
Text Design: Teri McMahon
Cover Design: Allison Saltzman
Production/Manufacturing: Mike Costa
Cover Photograph: J. F. Causse/TSW

Special Sales

CONTENTS

INTRODUCTION

The best ski experiences (which are, after all, what you want, whether you plan to take just a one-week break from your local hills or to eschew all regular weekend skiing for a two-week extravaganza) can include anything from a breathtaking run on a perfect cloudless day, to a blissful moment luxuriating in a hot tub, a peerless view of snowcapped peaks, or an exquisite meal enjoyed in the company of newfound friends. For me it's memories like a two-week trip my family and I took one glorious Christmas. We drove from Salt Lake City to Jackson Hole, on to Big Sky, Montana, and finally Sun Valley, Idaho. Three different, superb resorts. But each one provided a distinct experience that is hard to forget and difficult to duplicate.

The same is true of the 30 resorts covered here. A decade or more of consolidation, modernization, and expansion has transformed the nation's ski resorts into the equal of any in the world. New technologies in lifts have provided dramatically faster, higher-capacity detachable quads and triples, surface lifts that serve high-alpine terrain and out-of-the way niches, and cable cars and telepheriques that rival those of the Alps. Similar advances in snowmaking and grooming have produced smoother, faster, superior, ego-soothing runs and virtually guaranteed snow conditions (witness the number of major mountains that are now covered top to bottom with sophisticated, computerized snowmaking systems); unbridled spending has created slopeside luxury comparable to that of the chicest spots anywhere.

This multibillion-dollar binge at resorts from Maine to California includes an emphasis on upscale and family-style accommodations, on-mountain village convenience, alternative activities as esoteric as guided fly fishing or hot-air ballooning, sybaritic health spas and fitness centers, and dining alternatives from haute to happening. Similarly, most resorts have accommodated snowboarders with open arms. Resorts offer separate runs, half-pipes, elaborate snowboard parks, and support services such as instruction, equipment rentals, and retail outlets.

When selecting the 30 best American ski areas, we looked for resorts that provided the complete resort experience, and we tried to provide balanced geographic representation. Obviously, Western resorts were more plentiful, with Colorado's embarrassment of riches yielding 10 resorts that meet the criteria. But the East is not without its champions, and Vermont is the leading contributor with five resorts. Overall though, these 30 resorts best represent the best of American skiing.

Even as we went to press with the third edition, we sensed a shifting in the lineup, with a number of new and improved resorts jockeying for a position in the top 30. In most cases they are close to resorts mentioned here and in some cases have interchangeable lift-ticket arrangements with them. Try the alternates when you're in their vicinity. Breckenridge, for example, is not only a fine ski town, but the nearby Breckenridge Resort is a definite option if you are skiing Copper Mountain or Keystone. Other resorts that deserve acknowledgment include: Purgatory, also in Colorado; Oregon's Mount Bachelor; Alpine Meadows and Kirkwood in California; and Utah's The Canyons.

CHOOSING THE RIGHT RESORT

So what's the right resort for you? If you have a limited amount of time in which to satisfy your skiing dreams, it's all the more important to make the right choice. Budget is usually the first consideration. This may dictate whether you fly or drive. Driving is your biggest personal cost saver, but if you're committed to getting behind the wheel, you have immediately reduced your list of possibles, depending on where you live. If flying fits your budget, you might then want to check other costs. Some resorts are just genetically expensive, and a one-bedroom condo two miles from the lifts might cost the same as a three-bedroom unit slopeside at another resort with less "cash-et." The prices in this book reflect a range from least expensive to "take my gold card" level, and you should compare carefully the high- and low-end prices. You may covet a slopeside three-bedroom condo at the Stein Erikson Lodge at Deer Valley for $2,000 a night, but you'll have just as good a ski experience if your budget is more suited to a similar size unit, without the Ralph Lauren sheets and exotic wall hangings, at a resort such as Winter Park.

Beyond price, there are other considerations: Not every ski resort is blessed with the most desirable focus, a nearby natural ski town. Nothing quite matches the atmosphere and feeling of a carefully preserved Victorian town in the shadow of great skiing. Telluride and Crested Butte in Colorado are classic examples, as are Park City, Jackson Hole, and Sun Valley. Resorts such as Snowbird, Squaw Valley, Snowmass (although the mother of all ski towns, Aspen, is but a shuttle bus ride away), or Stratton Mountain offer a more contained on-mountain experience. In most cases it's young families who prefer the slopeside convenience, while singles or couples tend to look for the expanded opportunity that a local town provides.

WHEN TO GO

If at all possible, avoid peak periods—Christmas, March break, and Easter. If you have no choice in the matter, the key is to book early—a year in advance is not too soon—to ensure a good choice in accommodation and the best prices for airfare.

WHERE TO STAY

Ski-resort accommodation is as varied as you'll find at any holiday resort setting. From multilevel slopeside suites with designer furnishings to snug period cabins tucked in the forest; from beautifully preserved Victorian hotels to modest motel rooms two miles down the highway from the lifts, the choice is abundant, and accommodating to most budgets.

Full-Service Hotels

These are usually the most expensive accommodation in the resort area, based on a per-person per-day rate. If convenience, unlimited creature comforts, and specialty services such as business centers or baby-sitting/day-care are what you need, hotels with all the amenities are your best bet. Rates can get a little silly for some of the top dogs in this category ($2,000 per day or even more), but in most cases you get what you pay for. And that's usually a full range of services and facilities from bellman to concierge to room service to valet parking to extensive dining, fitness, and spa amenities.

Condominium Suites

The word condo (referred to as "unit" in this book) has come to mean many things over time, and nowhere has it been more liberally represented than in ski country. It can cover everything from a tiny bachelor suite with fold-away furnishings to a magnificent five-bedroom townhouse-style layout with a heated garage and a private lap pool. Similarly, prices run the gamut, from $100 to $2,000 per day, but even at the high end, a condo unit is usually cheaper on a per-person basis than hotel rooms of comparable quality. The quality can vary wildly, and some of the older, less expensive units can be a little frayed around the edges, but for the most part they'll be comfortable and clean. At the other end of the scale, you'll find units with a fireplace in every room, hand-woven rugs, hot tubs, saunas, high-tech accessories such as satellite TV, and fully equipped kitchen and dining facilities. Besides price, the chief advantage to a condo unit is the availability of kitchen facilities, where you can prepare your own food, whether it's just breakfast and snacks or three meals a day. Family and other groups find condos the best choice. When considering what type of condo unit you should choose, bear in mind:

Location

In most cases, the closer the unit is to the lifts, the more expensive it will be. You can rationalize that if you don't want or need to rent a car. On the other hand, a car gives you the flexibility to see more of the area, and for the cost of a car for that 2-mile drive to and from the lifts you may get a larger, more upscale unit than a similarly priced unit slopeside.

Size

Never underestimate the space you need. Four college kids on March break may be perfectly comfortable splitting a bachelor unit with one pull-out bed, but almost anyone over the age of 20 wants a little more space. This is especially true if the group is new to communal living with each other, and hasn't overcome the inherent shyness of scrambling for the bathroom in longjohns or whatever skimpy attire passes for pajamas. If you value a little privacy, count bedrooms rather than beds when sizing up a unit's true capacity. One for every four people should be a guideline. Consider also whether you will be cooking and entertaining in your unit. Prepared breakfasts and dinners, plus slopeside lunch packages, can represent a big saving over daily restaurant dining, and the savings can often justify paying a little extra for the unit to get better kitchen and dining facilities. If that's the route you are going, make sure you clarify and identify shopping and cooking responsibilities in advance.

Amenities

Generally, condo buildings provide less service than traditional hotels, so it pays to ask in advance if you want specific services such as daily housekeeping (which is not standard in many condos), front desk attendants, or baby-sitting/day-care facilities. If fitness and spa facilities are important, make sure you know just what is available. The more amenities a condo building or complex offers, the higher its price is likely to be.

Small Inns, B&Bs, and Motels

This category can include a sumptuous $200 per-person per-night B&B with down comforters, epicurean meals, and distinctively decorated rooms, or a bare-bones motel room with a warm bed and a plug-in coffeemaker. In between are rustic cabins, convenience units with simple cooking facilities, or mom-and-pop B&Bs with small rooms and commu-

nal dining. Prices vary accordingly; keep in mind that many smaller establishments have a per-person rate rather than a per-room rate. Some will include breakfast and/or dinner in the basic rate, and some of the more expensive places provide afternoon or après-ski refreshments.

HOW TO GO

By Car

If your chosen destination is within driving distance—say 500 miles—the car is definitely your best bet. An alternative to loading up the family car is a rental car. Book well in advance for the best weekly rate; the couple of hundred dollars it costs to rent a car may well be worth paying to avoid wear and tear on your own vehicle.

If you're traveling to the resort by some other means but need a car once you get there, book well in advance for the best rate. Request a vehicle equipped with a ski rack and winter tires, and inquire about local chain regulations. Most airport rental locations provide a map to your destination, and many run special promotions with the resorts. Ask about special deals when booking. Sign at least two drivers on the vehicle registration, and make sure you understand the implications of the insurance waiver or surcharge.

By Plane

Booking early is the key to getting both your lowest fare and a flight that best fits your schedule. Schedule your arrival at the destination airport as early in the day as possible. In some places, like Salt Lake City, where the skiing is less than 30 minutes away, you might be able to sneak in an extra half day on the slopes, but even if that's not possible an early arrival makes driving to the resort easier, especially in bad conditions. Most airlines accept skis as a regular part of your luggage allotment, although at some airports skis have to be checked or retrieved at a special service desk. Make sure your bag is well secured and has identification tags. If possible, try to carry your boots on board, but if that is not convenient, make sure they are packed in a good, sturdy boot bag. Another alternative is to ship your equipment ahead by UPS or Federal Express to avoid having to carry it through aiports and ensure that it gets there by the time you do.

By Train
If you yearn to ride the rails, **Amtrak** (tel. 800/872–7245) is your best source for information on what major cities are served, along with resorts that are reachable by train.

On the Mountain
For every resort we have endeavored to provide each level of skier with a detailed guide to skiing the mountain, with specifics on certain runs, the best runs to ski when it's overcast, or the best route to take across the breadth of the area. As much as you may use this book to pick out your resort, the accommodations, and the restaurants, it's not convenient to take it skiing with you. Planning your day on the mountain, however, is just as important as picking the right hotel or the right dining spot. Whenever possible, obtain a trail map of the area in advance. Most resorts will send one by mail (use the toll-free number to ask for one), or you can look for it on the area's Web site. At the very least,

find a trail map the moment you arrive and give it a quick study before hitting the slopes.

The descriptions supplied here take into account several factors, but generally an effort is made to get you skiing in the sun—if it's shining—all day or to steer you to protected runs when the weather turns nasty. We also want you to start your day with easier runs, building toward the tougher ones by midafternoon, then tapering off for the final runs of the day, when you're running out of steam. Checking the descriptions in the book with the trail map will prepare you better for your day, especially if your group is destined to split up into different levels. Make sure your morning route leads you to a suitable lunch spot, where your group can meet, and by mid-afternoon make sure you are heading back to your starting point.

Remember also that runs can change by the hour or by the day, and one described as a "smooth cruiser" can change quickly with traffic and temperature increases into a gnarled mogul pit with choppy snow. Above all, never head out to the slopes without a trail map in your pocket.

THE WEB CONNECTION
Once you've made the resort choice, the Web is a great source of alternative information, including current ski conditions, local weather, special events, and trail maps. You can also book reservations on line, sometimes getting a better rate in the process. All the ski resorts in this book have Web sites, which are listed at the beginning of each chapter with the resort's telephone number and other vital statistics.

A FEW NOTES ON PACKING

Beyond the obvious need for the essentials of skiing, packing for a ski trip does require a little more planning than, say, throwing a few pairs of shorts and some assorted beach accessories into a bag for a vacation in the sun. Well-fitting boots and a warm ski suit top the list, but make sure you have a sufficient selection of other winter wear. Layering is the key to covering all your weather bases from mild and wet to warm to sub-zero, so pack plenty of sweaters, vests, T-necks and shirts. Fleece is the insulation of choice: It's light and warm, and it dries quickly, folds up into small places, and comes in every shape from sleeveless vests to car blankets.

Add accessories—gloves, goggles, neck warmers, hats—double up if you have spares, and try to observe the one-bag rule, especially if you are taking your own skis and boots. A boot bag is essential; a good-size one can take the overflow from your main bag; and you can also pack soft items in your ski bag. Consider also whether you'll be doing any other activities—hot tubbing, swimming, health clubbing, snowmobiling, cross-country skiing—and pack accordingly. Ski resorts are comfortably casual places, and it's extremely unlikely that you'll need anything more formal than dress casual attire.

Skis Are Optional

Unless you are a rank novice (in which case, renting boots is your best first step), it's asking for trouble to go skiing for a week without your own boots, but skis are another matter. Beyond the obvious advantage of not having to swing a fully loaded ski bag through crowded airports and in and out of ground transportation, renting skis at your destination is a good idea for a number of reasons. Today's on-mountain rental facilities stock excellent products in general, as well as offering high-end, high-performance models to those who prefer a little more swagger in their skis. Also ask about demo models, which manufacturers supply to ski shops as a try-before-you-buy strategy. It's a chance to try out new models with the very latest technology. Prices vary for different models, so check specifics with the resort before making your decision to leave your skis at home.

OTHER THAN SKIING

One of the least-noticed developments at U.S. ski resorts is the creation of diversions for the nonskier or the light skier in the family or group. The resorts in this book have a lineup of non-ski activities that would keep anyone occupied for a week without ever setting foot on a slope. Health clubs and health spas are as de rigueur as high-speed detachable quads, and more esoteric activities can include dog-sledding; nature walks; classes in astronomy, painting, gourmet cooking, or photography; hot-air ballooning; fly fishing; side trips to local points of physical or cultural interest; and cross-country skiing. If you enjoy skiing but really only care to spend 3 out of 7 days on the slopes you'll find no shortage of alternate activities.

SNOWBOARDING

Today, by most estimates, snowboarders easily account for 25% of all lift-ticket sales, and at some resorts more than half the people on the slopes will be riding boards. Moreover, boards are not just the ride of choice for 20-somethings, but more and more you'll see older boarders right up to, and including, grandparents. If the board's your thing, this guide will provide you with all the same information as for skiers, but for each resort we have paid specific attention to designated boarding runs and other facilities.

ABOUT PRICES

There's a tremendous range of prices at ski resorts, peaking during the key family-vacation periods such as Christmas and March break, and dropping lowest early in the season (pre-December 20) and toward the end (post-March 30). Packages that include transportation, accommodation, lifts, and even meals are generally cheaper than arranging everything à la carte–style. Certain types of packages can be even more cost-efficient if you book a small group or eschew separate bookings in favor of shared accommodation in larger multi-bedroom units.

Accommodations

All prices are based on a high-season, single-night, 1999 rate with no advance booking. Unless noted otherwise, all rooms have private bath, and all condo units have kitchens. Rates are per unit (standard double-room suite or condo) unless otherwise indicated; if extras such as meals are included, that is also noted. Accommodations are reviewed in three categories—expensive, moderate, and inexpensive. The ranges vary widely according to the amenities and facilities provided at each hotel or condo property. The actual price ranges are included in the service information for each lodging.

Dining

Restaurants are reviewed in three categories—expensive, moderate, and inexpensive. Specific prices are not quoted. As a guideline to price ranges, use the following:

Expensive: $100 plus for dinner for two people, including one medium-price bottle of wine.

Moderate: $50–$100 for dinner for two people, including one medium-price bottle of wine.

Inexpensive: $25–$50 for dinner for two people, including one cocktail or glass of wine.

Places to eat on the mountain and best bets for breakfast fall into the moderate price range unless otherwise noted.

In the restaurants reviewed here dress is casual and reservations are not required unless noted otherwise.

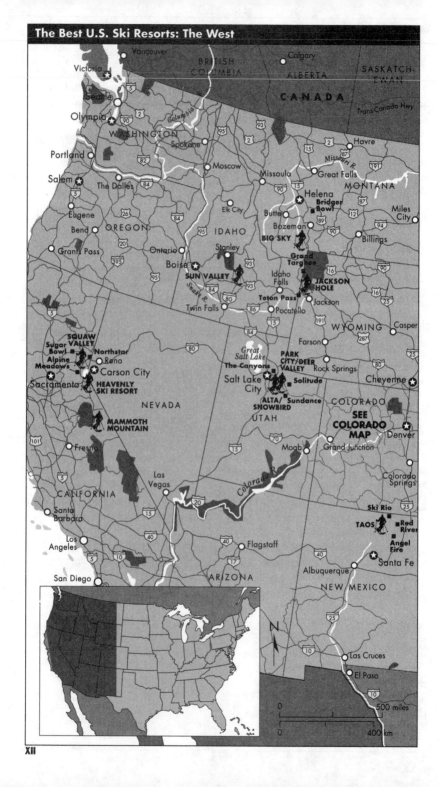

The Best U.S. Ski Resorts: The West

The Best U.S. Ski Resorts: Colorado

CANADA

Moosehead
Lake

15

MAINE

Plattsburgh
Lake
Champlain
Barton
STOWE
Smugglers'
Notch
Saddleback
Mt.
SUGARLOAF
16

Waterville

Saranac
Lake
WHITEFACE
MOUNTAIN
Burlington
Montpelier
St.
Johnsbury
91
Berlin
SUNDAY RIVER
Augusta

Lake
Placid
Big
Tupper
Mad
River
Glen
SUGARBUSH
89
Barre
Littleton
Cannon
Mt.
93
Loon Mt.
Mt. Abram
Lewiston
95

Connecticut River
Middlebury
VERMONT
NEW
HAMPSHIRE
WATERVILLE
VALLEY
Auburn
Brunswick

Gore
Mt.
87
White River
Junction
Rutland
Lebanon
Laconia
Sanford
Portland

NEW
YORK
91
Franklin
89
Kennebunk

Glens Falls
KILLINGTON
Okemo
Ascutney
Mt.
Concord
Dover
Kittery

Saratoga
Springs
STRATTON
Bromley Mt.
Manchester
Portsmouth

Bennington
7
Keene
Nashua
95

Schenectady
MT.
SNOW
Brattleboro
ATLANTIC
OCEAN

Albany
MASSACHUSETTS
Cambridge
Salem

Pittsfield
91
Worcester
495
Boston

Hudson River
90
Springfield
84
Providence
R.I.
3
Brockton
Provincetown

Kingston
Hartford
395
Cape
Cod

Poughkeepsie
Litchfield
CONNECTICUT
New
Bedford
Newport
6

87
Middletown
84
Norwich
Martha©s
Vineyard
Nantucket
Island

West Point
New Haven
95
New London
N

NEW
JERSEY
Stamford
Yonkers
495
Long Island

New York

Bridgeport

0   50 miles
0   80 km

F or a state that is most often associated with sun, surfing, and vineyards, California has an astonishing variety of skiing. The mighty Sierra Nevada range stretches north from Los Angeles to the Oregon state line, yielding more than 30 ski areas, which range from the glittering two-state sprawl of Heavenly Ski Resort, in both California and Nevada, to the more isolated locals-oriented slopes such as June Mountain and Bear Valley. The region that includes Heavenly and Squaw Valley is called the Lake Tahoe basin.

This 300-by-150-mile wilderness area dominated by the wall of rugged sky-punching peaks is little known outside California, but for the 55% of visitors to Lake Tahoe who are Californians, it is their winter playground. And as with most things Californian, nothing succeeds like excess. The resorts in this snow-blessed gift from the gods can variously lay claim as the biggest, the highest, the snowiest, the hippest, and the most star-studded resorts in America.

The Sierra Nevada—an unbroken monolith that is nearly as big as the Alps and boasts the highest peaks (many topping the 14,000-foot mark) outside Alaska, as well as the largest trees, the deepest valleys, and the highest waterfalls—is the most massive mountain block in North America. (Physically, the Rockies encompass a larger area, but they are a collection of ranges, separated by wide steppes and mesas.)

The ski resorts in this region are just as impressive: Heavenly—in the storied and striking Lake Tahoe basin—is the largest ski resort in the state, and maybe in the nation, depending on how you measure. Lofty Mammoth Mountain is annually smothered under more than 70 feet of snow; and Squaw Valley is one of only two U.S. resorts that have hosted the Winter Olympics. The skiing, weather, and snow conditions in the region certainly rival those found in Colorado and Utah.

GETTING TO CALIFORNIA RESORTS

By Plane

Reno-Tahoe International Airport, in Reno, Nevada, is the international facility closest to Lake Tahoe and Mammoth Mountain. **Alaska Airlines** (tel. 800/426–0333), **American** (tel. 800/433–7300), **America West** (tel. 800/235–9292), **Continental** (tel. 800/525–0280), **Delta** (tel. 800/221–1212), **Northwest** (tel. 800/225–2525), **Reno Air** (tel. 800/736–6247), **Sky West** (tel. 800/453–9417 in Nevada, Utah, Arizona, Idaho, and Wyoming only), **Southwest** (tel. 800/435–9792), **TWA** (tel. 800/221–2000), **United** (tel. 800/241–6522), and **US Airways** (tel. 800/428–4322) have direct or connecting service into Reno International from most major cities.

Car Rental

Avis (tel. 800/831–8000), **Budget** (tel. 800/527–0700), **Dollar** (tel. 702/739–8408), **Hertz** (tel. 800/654–3131), and **National** (tel. 702/541–7994) have counters at Reno-Tahoe International Airport. Most rent winterized vehicles—four-wheel-drive cars or front-wheel-drive cars equipped with chains. Be sure to reserve one of these vehicle types: in the event of a storm, if you don't have a four-wheel-drive car and chains are required, you may have to purchase them for an exorbitant amount of money from one of the few gas stations on the highway; or worse, you may end up stranded for several days.

Shuttle Service

From Reno-Tahoe International Airport look for the **Tahoe Casino Express** (tel. 702/785–2424 or 800/446–6128), which has an average of 18 round-trips daily; the cost is $30 round-trip.

By Bus

Greyhound Lines (tel. 916/541–2222 or 800/231–2222) serves South Lake Tahoe with daily nonstop service to and from the Sacramento and San Francisco areas (2½ and 4 hours, respectively). **Sierra Nevada Gray Line** (tel. 702/331–1147 or 800/822–6009) has regularly scheduled service from Reno to South Lake Tahoe.

By Train

The **Amtrak** (tel. 800/872–7245) *California Zephyr* bound for Chicago has daily service from the San Francisco/Oakland train station to both Reno and Truckee (20 miles from the north shore of Lake Tahoe and 60 miles from the south shore). It's a spectacular ride up the coast and over the Donner Pass, with stops in Richmond, Martinez, Fairfield, Davis, Sacramento, Roseville, and Colfax.

HEAVENLY SKI RESORT

HEAVENLY SKI RESORT

Box 2180
Stateline, NV 89449
Tel. 702/586–7000
www.skiheavenly.com

STATISTICALLY SPEAKING

Base elevation: 6,540 feet in California; 7,200 feet in Nevada

Summit elevation: 10,040 feet

Vertical drop: 3,500 feet

Skiable terrain: 4,800 acres

Number of trails: 82

Longest run: 5.5 miles

Lifts and capacity: 1 aerial tram, 5 high-speed quads, 8 triples, 5 doubles, 5 surface; 29,000 skiers per hour

Daily lift ticket: $52

Average annual snowfall: 340 inches

Number of skiing days 1997–98: 178

Snowmaking: 3,100 acres; 69%

Terrain mix: N 20%, I 45%, E 35%

Snowboarding: yes

Heavenly Ski Resort is the largest of seven such areas dotting the shore of the achingly aquamarine Lake Tahoe. The vision of the lake prompted Mark Twain to write, "I thought it must surely be the fairest picture the whole earth affords." The 22-by-12-mile blue glacial jewel, rimmed by a necklace of white peaks and fed by 63 streams, is circled by a 72-mile drive that is among the most stunning in America. Although its physical attributes are singularly spectacular, this is a resort of many contradictions. It is at once a gaudy, ostentatious casino and entertainment hot spot and a strikingly picturesque and diverse outdoor recreation nirvana. In fact, it is two towns divided by the state line between California and Nevada: butting up against this man-made boundary are the towns of South Lake Tahoe, California, and Stateline, Nevada.

Although they share a common boundary, they are strikingly different in character. The Nevada side is flush with major casino action led by some of the most familiar names in the business—Caesars, Harvey's, Harrah's—all presenting towering edifices reflecting their success at separating you from your money yet making you as comfortable as possible while doing so. On the California side you'll find a town in transition—a faded lady, if you will, attempting to redefine its character after the decline of its belle epoque in the '30s and '40s, when the blue bloods of southern California made Tahoe their retreat, much the way East Coast millionaires carved their place in the Adirondack wilderness around Lake Placid. The grand homes on the shoreline still stand, alongside new multimillion-dollar houses, but unfortunately so does a shantytown with run-down motels that embarrassingly sits slap in the middle of town. However, a 10-year revitalization of the area is under way, with a new regulation-size ice-skating rink, parks, shops, and hotels in the plans. A new gondola began construction in May '99 from the center of town to Heavenly ski area.

In the meantime, this curious coexistence continually draws record crowds because it provides visitors with virtually every conceivable experience—from high-stakes poker to high-alpine touring. The region is an entertainment mecca, perhaps second to none

Area code: 530 (CA); 702 (NV)

Children's services: Perfect Kids, tel. 702/586–7000

Snow phone: tel. (702) 786–7000, press 1

Police: tel. 530/542–6100 (CA)

Sheriff: tel. 702/586–7250 (NV)

California highway patrol: tel. 530/587–3510

Medical center: California Stateline Medical, tel. 702/588–3561; Tahoe Urgent Care, tel. 530/541–3277

Hospital: Barton Memorial Hospital, tel. 530/541–3420

South Lake Tahoe Chamber of Commerce: tel. 530/541–5255

Road conditions: tel. 916/445–1534 (CA); 702/793–1313 (NV)

Towing: Welcome's, tel. 916/541–8811

FIVE-STAR FAVORITES
Best run for vertical: Gunbarrel

Best run overall: Big Dipper Bowl to Stagecoach

Best bar/nightclub: Thirsty Duck

Best hotel: Embassy Suites

Best restaurant: Evan's

in ski country, with its natural wonders at times playing second fiddle to the man-made variety. Still, overall, it is a resort area that has something for everyone—from high rollers in limousines to families in station wagons.

HOW TO GET THERE

By Plane
The closest major airport is Reno's **Reno-Tahoe International Airport** (*see* Getting to California Resorts, *above*), 90 minutes by car.

By Car
From Reno-Tahoe International Airport, take Route 395 south to Carson City, where you take Route 50 west over Spooner Summit and down into South Lake Tahoe and then to Heavenly. During the day and in good weather, the 55-mile drive along winding mountain roads is easy and scenically spectacular, but if you arrive late in the day, it's best to stay in Reno overnight rather than tackle the highways in darkness. From the San Francisco area it's about a 200-mile (3½-hour) journey—east on I–80 for about 90 minutes to Sacramento and then east on Route 50 for about 100 miles (two hours) directly to Lake Tahoe. Regardless of where your travels begin, the weather changes fast—especially in the high passes—and police and highway department crews will move equally quickly to close roads when the snows come or stop those without chains or four-wheel-drive vehicles.

Avis and **Hertz** operate out of South Lake Tahoe Airport.

GETTING AROUND
A car is not really necessary in Tahoe unless you want to do some touring. Parking at the resort is limited, the roads to it are congested, and often you'll have to park as much as a half mile from the lifts on holidays and weekends. Heavenly operates a free ski shuttle from most South Lake Tahoe lodging properties; also most casinos provide on-request shuttle service to and from the ski area every half hour between 8 and 5:20. Finally, a number of taxi services, including **Yellow Cab** (tel. 530/544–5555) and **Paradise**

Cab (tel. 530/577–4708), cover the entire Heavenly and Lake Tahoe area.

THE SKIING

Heavenly is a vast, sprawling resort of nine peaks, two valleys, and three base-lodge areas straddling two states. It is by most measurements the largest ski area in the nation and has become one of my favorites. Like the resort area, the mountain has a little something for everyone, including some remarkable expert terrain. Curiously, when first seen from the base, the slopes on the California side look impossibly difficult, with the heart-stopping, unnerving view of mogul-choked Gunbarrel Run. What you see is not what you get, however, for Heavenly is an inverted mountain; the majority of the slopes are rated as intermediate and are located out of sight, on the top half.

This extensive intermediate terrain, combined with the prolific and reliable snow coverage and sunny weather, has always attracted large crowds of skiers, especially families. The world's largest snow-making system also guarantees good early and late-season coverage. The opening of the Mott and Killebrew canyon areas—with their steep chutes and thick-timbered slopes—has added a dimension that the resort admittedly had been missing. For the very few who relish the formidable, it's a reason to return to Heavenly, but for most of us, the 20 square miles of wide, well-groomed pistes present enough challenge.

Another knock against the sprawling Heavenly terrain is the number of flat traverses that must be negotiated between mountain sectors. It's true enough, and there's not too much you can do about it except to pay careful attention to the trail map and be prepared to carry some speed across the critical sections. The resort has made some effort to minimize this inconvenience with some well-placed signs and good grooming on the flat sections; overall, it's a small price to pay for the vastness and variety of the mountain.

Like the towns below the peaks, Heavenly can be busy and confusing, with three base lodges that help disperse the traffic on both sides of the resort. The California side is typically the most crowded in the morning; the tram used to be the fastest and most popular way to the midstation and the upper-mountain lifts. But the new Gunbarrel Express, a high-speed detachable quad, zips from the base lodge to the 8,240-foot elevation mark in just under 4 minutes. To avoid the crowds, you can set out from the slightly less busy Stagecoach or Boulder base lodges, on the Nevada side. Heading to the top from this side requires a three-lift ride from the Boulder base, but the new Stagecoach Express shortens the old 15-minute ride to just about 6 minutes.

Novices

If you start your day from the California side, be prepared for a jaw-to-the-chest gape when you feast your eyes on the bump-studded front face under the tram. Don't worry, though; you'll never have to ski the famed Gunbarrel because just as the lift will whisk you up to tamer territory, so it can bring you down at the end of the day. In fact, according to one veteran Heavenly skier, "Hardly anyone skis

Gunbarrel because in the morning most are not ready for it, and at the end of the day most are too tired." First-timers starting from the California base can tackle the Poma Trail and the Enchanted Forest first—two short, smooth, gentle runs served by their own West Bowl Poma. Once you get a few runs under your boots, take the tram to midstation, where two chairs—Powderbowl and Waterfall—take you to several wide, well-groomed boulevards that will surely increase your confidence level. The easiest way down is via Maggies, but you can reach it only from the Waterfall lift. If you take the Powderbowl lift, there's a short blue section, fairly steep, to tackle before you get to Maggies. Also from the top of the Waterfall lift you can cut off Maggies to Mombo Meadows, which winds back under both lifts. Powderbowl Run, the other trail accessible from the top of either chair, is marked blue, but it's wide and groomed, with a fairly gentle pitch and no surprises. Try it once you've had your warm-ups on the green trails.

To move up a notch but still stay on wide, groomed trails, take the Canyon, Sky Express, or Ridge lifts (go to the top of the Waterfall lift and then ski down Maggies to the bottom of the Ridge chair or tackle the short, not-too-steep right-hand side of Maggies and carry on down to the bottom of the Canyon or Sky Express lifts) and go right off the lift, along the winding Ridge Run. The lower half, where it turns into Powderbowl, gets a little steeper, but you can always bail out at Mombo Meadows.

If you're a first-timer or early novice, your options are a bit limited if you're skiing on the Nevada side. On the California side a new beginner lift, the Perfect Ride, almost doubles the Learn-to-Ski/Ride area. But novice-intermediates should be able to make the transition successfully from green to blue here. To warm up, head for the Edgewood Bowl run, at the Boulder base, reached from the Boulder lift. From here take the Northbowl lift to midmountain and a plethora of blue runs that any solid snowplower should be able to handle. Right off the lift you come to Upper North Bowl, which starts out on a good pitch but is wide and well groomed and tends not to be busy because most folks have gone farther up the mountain. When it widens out more below the initial pitch, make sure you turn hard right (looking down the mountain), or you could end up on the North Bowl, a black run with lots of moguls. After you pass under the North Bowl chair, you come to a three-way split: 075 is groomed but tends to get bumped early in the day; Way Home is a wide speed-controlled zone that takes you to the bottom of the North Bowl lift; and the lower part of the Olympic Downhill, wide and groomed, takes you to the bottom of the Stagecoach chair.

Intermediates
This is your mountain, with an endless selection of medium-to-high-end intermediate runs, no matter which side you set off from in the morning. From the California base take the tram and follow the long, flat traverse over to the Sky Express lift and turn right off the lift along the Ridge Run for a choice of a half dozen primo

intermediate cruisers. As you ski along the Ridge Run trail, you'll have easy access to all the blues. For your first run, however, you might want to skip Liz's and start on Canyon, or Betty's—a pair of fairly steep but wide and groomed leg warmers. Next time up the Sky Express lift try Liz's, which tends to be steeper than the others and is moguled.

Your next move from the top is to take the Skyline Trail, skirting the canyon to the Nevada side, and come down the mountain on Big Dipper, a long, high-speed cruiser. If you really want to burn your thighs and can carry some cautious speed, cut through the midstation day-lodge area and pick up Stagecoach, which will carry you all the way down to the Stagecoach base area. Another option is to cut left (looking down the mountain) instead of right just below midstation, get onto Pepi's to Upper North Bowl, and then take 075 down to the Boulder base area. If you see that traffic is heavy on the Stagecoach, North Bowl, or Dipper lifts, cut right at midstation and head for the less busy Galaxy lift, where you'll find a pair of medium-paced blue runs: Perimeter is a well-groomed cruiser with steady pitch and some speed-checking rolls and dips, while Galaxy has sections of ungroomed bumps.

Maybe it's time to try some bowl and chute skiing (without losing your dignity in the canyons) in the Milky Way Bowl, which is mostly above tree line except for the lower third of the area. Take the Dipper Express and cut a hard left off the lift to the cat track that runs along the edge of the bowl. Although it's steep here, it's easy to pick your way down, taking advan-tage of the open space as you pause and ponder your next move. When you reach the control gates to the expert terrain in the canyon, you'll be steered to a steep, narrow exit trail that spits you out on a blue run, just a short scoot from the Dipper chair. The signs are clear. Skiing with your eyes closed would be the only way to end up in expert terrain without knowing it, so relax. Keep in mind that if you are based on the California side, you must start heading back that way no later than 3 PM, or you risk being stuck in Nevada. If this happens, you'll have to take a shuttle bus, which only stops at the accommodations, back into town. Your only other choice is a $10 cab ride.

Experts

You'll most certainly want to head for the Mott and Killebrew canyons with their chutes and couloirs, but in your rush for vertical, don't ignore some of the challenging tree runs that lie partly concealed on the front face. On this side you'll find stepladder steepness, big-tree closeness, and some of the best untouched snow on the mountain. The chance to brush teeth with mountain pine does not appeal to everyone; hence the snow often lies still and preserved for even several days after a storm. The fastest route from the California side is on the tram and the Sky Express lift to the top. To warm up, turn left off the Sky Express lift to Ellie's, a satisfying blend of high-speed steeps, drop-offs, and a limitless number of excursions through the trees. Next time up follow the Skyline Trail to the Nevada side and take a few runs in the Big Dipper Bowl before heading for the wide-open spaces of the Milky Way Bowl, which is steep and wide and mostly above tree line, apart from some tasty and challenging little groves near the bottom.

You could easily explore the Milky Way for a half day, but when you crave just a little more steepness and fewer skiers, it's time to head for either Mott or Killibrew Canyon. There are a dozen or so designated runs, but this is really free-form skiing out of free-fall chutes and couloirs. Entry to the canyons is through clearly marked control gates, and once you pick your spot over the lip, recover your equilibrium, and restore your breathing to normal, you can fancy-dance your way down some of the sweetest tree-stuffed steeps you'll find anywhere. This is 800 acres of double-black-diamond terrain that's never groomed and features many hidden obstacles, tight knots of trees, and lots of untouched snow. Remember, if you're staying on the California side, head back by 3 PM and—if you dare—strut your stuff on Gunbarrel's school-bus-size moguls.

SNOWBOARDING

For snowboarders the entire mountain is a playground, particularly the Airport snowboard park on the Nevada side. Snowboard classes are offered for all levels, from novice to expert. The 1998–99 season saw the opening of a half-pipe and terrain park in each state. On the Nevada side on Comet there is a permanent boarder-cross run, the Shaun Palmer Boarder-X, which has banked turns, tabletops, whoop-de-doos, and lots of big air jumps. On the California side there's a huge half-pipe on Groove. A small terrain park on Cascade trail has jumps and spines and custom terrain features that change every few days, depending on the whims of the grooming-equipment operators.

NEARBY

Kirkwood (tel. 209/258–6000), a 40-minute drive southwest, gets massive amounts of snow on classic, high-sierra terrain with a mix of wide-open bowls, rocky chutes, and tree skiing. **Sierra-At-Tahoe** (tel. 530/659–7453), 30 minutes west, has some of the best tree skiing in California but very little open terrain. **Spooner Lake Cross Country** (tel. 775/887–8844), only 15 minutes away, has superbly groomed tracks and fabulous Lake Tahoe views. **Hope Valley Cross Country** (tel. 916/694–2203), 15 to 20 minutes away, offers the beautiful meadows and alpine forests of Luther Pass.

WHERE TO STAY

Reno is an option if you want to gamble more than ski or if you arrive on a late-evening flight and don't want to deal with the sometimes tricky route over Spooner Summit and down to South Lake Tahoe. The hotels and motels are numerous and somewhat indistinguishable, with the casinos claiming the high ground and a string of nondescript chain properties dominating the midrange choices. Rates are more than reasonable—most places aim to get your money some other way—and as winter tends to be low season in Reno, discount deals are available at most major hotels. This dusty Nevada gambling town is no Las Vegas, but it can amuse you for an evening.

If you're here to ski, your best bet is to stay closer to the slopes, in either Stateline or South Lake Tahoe, where many casino hotels have set up shop alongside the more traditional ski resort hotels and inns and altogether too many decidedly tacky motels. Yes, there are some truly awful motels and small hotels in this area, and although there is a possibility that many will be leveled in the near future, in the meantime they remain a blight on the town. Prices are very reasonable, especially package deals, and with some careful shopping you can get a three-, five-, or seven-day deal that works out to less than $50 a night.

In terms of access to Heavenly, it makes little difference whether you stay in Stateline, Nevada, or South Lake Tahoe, California, as shuttle buses run regularly from hotels to either the California or Nevada base lodges. Avoid using your car if possible, especially if you're going to the California side, where the traffic jams are fierce and some of the parking so far from the lifts that you need to take a shuttle bus back to the base area. When the new Gondola is finished in 1999, traffic jams should no longer be a problem. Accommodations can be booked through central reservations at 800/243-2836 or by writing to Box 2180, Stateline, NV 89449.

Expensive

Christiana Inn
Perhaps, when the much-talked-about renovation of the area takes place, some thought will be given to building more small, European-style lodges such as the Christiana. Within walking distance of the lifts on the Califor-

nia side, this delightful spot has rooms and suites tastefully decorated with custom furnishings and special touches like king-size beds and a complimentary decanter of brandy. The suites all have fireplaces—two even have a fireplace in the bedroom, and two others have an individual sauna and whirlpool bath. Although the suites will definitely handle a family of four, the inn is more suited to couples because of the generally low-key ambience. *3819 Saddle Rd., Box 18298, South Lake Tahoe, CA 96151, tel. 530/544-7337, fax 530/544-5342. 2 rooms, 4 suites. Facilities: restaurant, lounge, maid service, ski storage, laundry. MC, V. $75-$175, including Continental breakfast.*

Embassy Suites
A favorite full-service hotel in South Lake Tahoe for many reasons (including that it's *not* a gambling emporium), it sits just far enough away from the casino canyon and the tacky motel strip. Inside, the six-story atrium lobby gives you a sense of mountain-size space. The capacious feel is continued in all the extraspacious rooms, which are really two-room suites with minikitchens that include a fridge, a microwave, and a coffeemaker. A pullout couch expands sleeping capacity to four—ideal for small families. The daily rate includes an excellent buffet breakfast served in the atrium lobby along with a complimentary two-hour cocktail session each day. *4130 Lake Tahoe Blvd., South Lake Tahoe, CA 96150, tel. 530/544-5400 or 800/362-2779, fax 530/544-4900. 400 rooms. Facilities: restaurant, bar, lounge, exercise room, indoor pool, 24-hr desk service, maid*

service, ski storage, game room. AE, D, DC, MC, V. $198–$278.

Harvey's Resort Hotel & Casino

Harvey's—being a little more like a resort hotel than a gambling den—manages to rise above the casino hotel competition. When you check in, you don't have to maneuver your baggage around the slot machines, and the ambience is a bit more tasteful. The multitude of rooms and suites is definitely upscale, with elegant French-provincial furnishings and lots of luxury extras, such as multiple telephones and TVs, a bar, and a refrigerator. Rooms and suites on the lakeside have the added attraction of a spectacular view. A family or two couples would be more than comfortable in a two-room suite with a balcony, a Jacuzzi, and a marble bathroom. Excellent deals exist on two- and three-night packages that include accommodation, dinner for two, a pitcher of margaritas, a daily buffet breakfast, daily box lunches for skiers, and two lift tickets. *Rte. 50, Box 128, Stateline, NV 89449, tel. 702/588–2411 or 800/427–8397, fax 702/782–4889. 742 rooms. Facilities: 8 restaurants, 5 bars, hot tub, outdoor heated pool, health club, 24-hr desk service, 24-hr room service, maid service, ski storage, laundry, game room. AE, D, DC, MC, V. $99–$195.*

Ridge Tahoe Resort

Its private 10-passenger gondola connects this fairly exclusive enclave of deluxe one- and two-bedroom condos directly to the slopes on the Nevada side of Heavenly. The condo units are ultraluxurious, with designer furnishings and decorations, large bedrooms with king- and queen-size beds, a full kitchen, a fireplace, a wet bar, and a stereo. It's an ideal spot for families because of its self-contained isolation, away from the bright lights and gaming of downtown Tahoe. *400 Ridge Club Dr., Box 5790, Stateline, NV 89449, tel. 702/588–3553, fax 702/588–7099. 480 rooms. Facilities: 2 restaurants, bar, 14 hot tubs, indoor pool, health club, 24-hr desk service, maid service, ski storage, laundry, game room. AE, D, MC, V. $160–$455.*

Moderate

Best Western Station House Inn

This good midrange property is about 2 miles from the resort. Although its rooms are not luxurious, they are comfortable, roomy, and equipped with enough amenities to satisfy all but the most fussy visitor. There are also several two- and three-bedroom cabins that will suit families or groups. Ski packages include breakfast, dinner, and daily lift ticket. *901 Park Ave., South Lake Tahoe, CA 96157, tel. 530/542–1101 or 800/822–5953, fax 530/542–1714. 102 rooms. Facilities: restaurant, bar, hot tub, ski storage. AE, D, DC, MC, V. $108–$175, including full breakfast.*

Inn by the Lake

These two three-story brown wooden buildings linked by heated brick walkways are in a pretty lakeside location. The spacious, no-nonsense rooms that can sleep four, and larger suites that sleep more, make this an ideal family spot. The rooms, furnished in light oak and earth-tone patterned fabrics, come with various bed configurations ranging from one king-size to two doubles or queen-size beds. The suites—some with a lake view—can sleep 12 comfortably; some have a full kitchen. *3300 Lake Tahoe Blvd., South Lake Tahoe, CA 96150, tel. 530/ 542–0330 or 800/877–1466, fax 530/ 541–6596. 87 rooms, 13 suites. Facilities: pool, whirlpool, sauna, ski storage. AE, D, DC, MC, V. $84–$395, including Continental breakfast.*

Lakeland Village Beach & Ski Resort

This sprawling lakefront resort complex, about a mile from town and the lifts, has units in the main lodge that range from small, comfortable studios to larger one-bedrooms with a loft. There are also one- to four-bedroom town houses, some with a great lake view, that come complete with fireplace, deck, and kitchen and can sleep 10. *3535 Lake Tahoe Blvd., Box 1356, South Lake Tahoe, CA 96150, tel. 530/541–7711 or 800/822–5969, fax 530 /544–0193. 211 units. Facilities: pool, hot tub, sauna, ski storage. AE, MC, V. $89–$460.*

Tahoe Chalet Inn

This well-maintained hotel suits families, groups, or even couples, as units range from fairly spacious standard rooms to small suites with a kitchen to self-contained chalets and even elaborate theme suites. You can choose to stay in the opulent Marie Antoinette, the King Arthur, or the Cleopatra suites, among others. The standard suites are more contemporary in furnishings but just as comfortable. *3860 Lake Tahoe Blvd., Rte. 50, South Lake Tahoe, CA 96150, tel. 530/544–3311 or 800/821–2656, fax 530/544–4069. 67 units. Facilities: hot tub, sauna, ski storage, laundry, game room. AE, D, DC, MC, V. $58–$205.*

Inexpensive

Camp Richardson Resort

This 1906 logging camp became a resort in the '20s, during Lake Tahoe's heyday. The two lodges and 47 log cabins are nestled among 80 acres of pines bordering the lake. The cabins sleep eight, with fireplaces or wood stoves. The log-cabin-style lodge has a great room with a rock fireplace and a big-screen TV. Rooms in the newer Beach Inn are the only ones with phones and TVs. *1900 Jameson Beach, South Lake Tahoe, CA 96157, tel. 530/ 542–6550. 36 lodge rooms, 47 cabins. Facilities: restaurant, grocery, cross-country skiing, ski storage, sleigh rides, ski shuttle. AE, MC, V. $59–$180.*

Cedar Lodge Lake Tahoe

A standard two-story wood-and-painted-brick motor lodge, it's clean and comfortable and stands in a pleasant forest grove at the east end of Stateline/South Lake Tahoe. The quiet location is within walking distance of the bright lights and an easy shuttle-bus ride from the slopes. The rooms have a rustic feel, with dark pine furniture and brown tones; they contain either one or two queen-size beds. Ski packages include lift tickets and all meals. *4069 Cedar Ave., Box 4547, South Lake Tahoe, CA 96157, tel. 530/544–6453 or 800/222–1177. 34 rooms. Facilities: outdoor hot tub. D, MC, V. $36–$72.*

Lakeside Inn & Casino

If you don't want to spend the money for a room at one of the mainstream casinos, the Lakeside will give you a taste of the action for about half the price. The rooms may not be as lavish as those offered by the big guns up the street, but they are spacious and clean and come with either one king- or two queen-size beds. There are also a number of larger suites with a separate bedroom. All come with a TV, a coffeemaker, and little delights such as Belgian chocolates and French soap. *Rte. 50, Kingsbury Grade, Box 5640, Stateline, NV 89449, tel. 775/ 588-7777 or 800/624-7980, fax 702/ 588-4092. 124 rooms. Facilities: casino, games arcade, dining room, gift shop, bar. AE, D, DC, MC, V. $59-$79.*

Montgomery Inn

This wood-exterior motor inn in a pine grove not far from the action has green-and-white rooms with rustic wooden furniture. The two-bedroom cabin has a kitchen, a fireplace, a sleep sofa, and a hot tub. *966 Modesto Ave., South Lake Tahoe, CA 96105, tel. 530/544-3871 or 800/624-8224, fax 530/542-4385. 25 rooms, 1 cabin. Facilities: hot tub, ski storage. AE, D, MC, V. $30-$120.*

WHERE TO EAT

There are more than 100 restaurants in the Lake Tahoe area, and that's not including the multitude of dining rooms in the ubiquitous casino hotels. You can go for high cuisine or basic pub grub, and you can blast a hole in your credit card or feed a family of four for less than $20. Remember, some of the best deals in town are the casino buffets.

Expensive

Christiana Inn

The dining room in this inn is quiet and elegant, with impeccable service and an American/Continental menu. Particular favorites are the combina-

tion dishes such as quail and scallops on a tomato coulis or prawns and lamb served with a red onion confit. The more traditional solo offerings also get high marks, especially the beef dishes—Wellington, tournedos, and filet mignon—which are all cooked precisely to your liking. If you don't mind dining before 7, check out the early skier's special. *3819 Saddle Rd., South Lake Tahoe, CA, tel. 530/ 544-7337. MC, V.*

Evan's

Ask locals about the best upscale dining in town, and most will suggest this delightful family-owned-and-operated eatery. The vintage Tahoe cottage, nestled in the pine trees, is about 5 miles from the town center. Inside, it brims with a warm, woodsy atmosphere and faultless service. The menu is American, with a daily lineup that includes homemade soups and fish dishes. Try the carpaccio of peppered ahi tuna, the roast pepper venison steak with dried blueberries and black-currant glaze, or the baked salmon with smoked salmon crust served with asparagus and black caviar. *536 Emerald Bay Rd., South Lake Tahoe, CA, tel. 530/542-1990. MC, V.*

Fresh Ketch

In an upbeat bistro atmosphere, this is an excellent spot for a seafood potpourri of fresh dishes such as tuna, swordfish, sole, salmon, crab legs, and any other piscatorial pleasures the daily markets produce. All are prepared to your choosing—charred, panfried, sautéed, baked, or blackened—and can be enjoyed with a number of interesting sauces. There's also a good selection of charbroiled steaks and a rack of lamb basted in a tangy Dijon batter. *2433 Venice Dr., South Lake Tahoe, CA, tel. 530/541–5683. AE, D, DC, MC, V.*

Zackary's
This bright, stylish dining room manages to pull off—with no little panache—an unorthodox mix of wood-fired brick-oven pizzas and a smattering of upscale Continental cuisine. The pizzas are inventive, with an adventurous array of California-style toppings ranging from sprouts to goat cheese. The emphasis is mostly on light, nouvelle cooking, with a California twist, such as chicken tequila fettuccine. *Embassy Suites Hotel, 4130 Lake Tahoe Blvd., South Lake Tahoe, CA, tel. 530/543–2140. AE, D, DC, MC, V.*

Moderate

Beacon
This restaurant, in historic Camp Richardson Resort (*see* Lodging, *above*) offers the only lakeside dining on the South Shore. The decor is nautical, and the menu leans toward fish, although steaks and pastas are also well represented. It's a popular spot with locals. *1900 Jameson Beach, South Lake Tahoe, CA, tel. 530/541–0232. AE, MC, V.*

Cafe Fiore
If you're looking for a quiet, romantic atmosphere, and especially if you like Northern Italian food, then try this relaxed, friendly place. The low lighting, tiny candlelit tables, and attentive (but unobtrusive) service make it perfect for intimate evenings. The menu offers pastas, a selection of veal dishes including a divine parmigiana, rack of lamb, traditional European specialties such as scrumptious beef bourguignonne, and a daily fish special. *1169 Ski Run Blvd., South Lake Tahoe, CA, tel. 530/541–2908. AE, MC, V.*

The Met
This is a bit of a locals' hangout, as you'll see from the prices—particularly those in the bar during après-ski—and the reliable quality of the food. It's really an all-purpose menu that stars excellent burgers, a 20-item salad bar, and a variety of specialty pizzas, such as spinach and garlic or the Roundhill combo, stacked mountain-high with just about everything you can imagine. *Round Hill Mall, Zephyr Cove, NV, tel. 702/588–8220. AE, D, MC, V.*

Siam
If you're a fan of Thai food, you're likely to compare Siam's favorably with almost any you've tried elsewhere. Good preparation and delicate seasoning—with occasional power spicing—complement all the traditional dishes. Satay comes in numerous styles, and there are other choices such as *pad thai* (noodles with bean sprouts, egg, sugar, salt, and red onion in a sweet-and-sour spice mix). Numerous delicious soups are perked up with lemongrass, chicken is zesty with coconut, and fish dishes are delicately cooked. *2180 Rte. 50, South Lake Tahoe, CA, tel. 530/544–0370. AE, MC, V.*

Inexpensive

The Cantina
Good, spirited Mexican fare accompanies a great après-ski atmosphere that tends to linger here well into the evening after it spills over from the

dining room into the bar. The fajitas get high marks, but so do most of the traditional dishes. There are also crab enchiladas and *carnitas* (roast pork leg served with a soft taco). Portions are generous, and even larger appetites can opt for mesquite-barbecued steaks or chicken. *765 Emerald Bay Rd., South Lake Tahoe, CA, tel. 530/544–1233. MC, V.*

Dixon's Brew Pub
This place is fast, friendly, and thrifty, with the added attraction of more than a dozen brews on tap. The extensive menu relies on good, contemporary American dining, with a variety of salads, healthy pastas, and specialties from south of the border, including good chicken fajitas. *675 Emerald Bay Rd., South Lake Tahoe, CA, tel. 530/542–3389. AE, MC, V.*

Best Bets for Breakfast
Casino Buffets
No self-respecting casino is without a high-speed breakfast buffet (the faster you get through the first meal of the day, the faster you can get back to losing your money), and if volume and price are your chief criteria, check out the all-you-can-eat affairs at the major gambling emporiums.

Ernie's
The fast, friendly waitstaff in this diner has been here so long their portraits are framed and hanging above the kitchen. If you come often enough, you can get a coffee mug with your name on it. The selection of egg dishes is good, and the locally roasted Alpen Sierra Coffee will wake you up for a day on the slopes. *1146 Emerald Bay Rd., South Lake Tahoe, CA, tel. 530/541–2161. No credit cards.*

Jumpstart Jack's
The early (very early) morning crowd tends to be the mountain workers, so this is a great place to pick up some tips about weather and conditions. What attracts them, and everyone else, to this somewhat grungy little coffee hut is the best java in town, and that includes the cappuccino and espresso. A varied selection of pastries and bagels makes up most of the food menu. *4040 Lake Tahoe Blvd., South Lake Tahoe, CA, tel. 530/544–5522. No credit cards.*

NIGHTLIFE AND ENTERTAINMENT
Truly, there are few ski towns anywhere that can match the diversity and intensity of the nightlife and entertainment in South Lake Tahoe. Even if you eliminate the gambling from your après-ski activities, the lineup of headline acts, special events, and dozens of bars and nightclubs gives it the edge even over Aspen. The casinos want nothing more than to keep you happy by feeding you and entertaining you as they parade the temptation of the tables and the slots in front of your face. Thus bargains abound, with reduced drink prices, discount coupons by the bucket, and endless meal specials. For current live entertainment, check the local listings.

Après-Ski
California Bar
Make this bar your first stop after your last run. It's in the base lodge area on the California side, and it really cooks after skiing. You'll always find it packed with sun-flushed revelers, and the daily drink specials ensure that the glow doesn't fade. The

bar also has regular live entertainment. *Base lodge area, Wildwood Rd. and Saddle Rd., South Lake Tahoe, CA, tel. 702/586–7000. AE, D, DC, MC, V.*

Loud and Lively/Dancing

The Brewery

This good brew pub has a fine lineup of drafts, a lively atmosphere, and a good mix of locals and visitors. The crowd changes as it gets later, but for the better part of the evening it's mostly folks on the flusher side of 30. By midnight the younger partiers tend to gather in numbers. *3542 Lake Tahoe Blvd., South Lake Tahoe, CA, tel. 530/544–2739. AE, MC, V.*

Thirsty Duck

This place is not easy to find: Take Elk Point Road across from the Round Hill Mall, turn left at Dorla Court, and look for the building with the satellite dish on top. It's worth the search to discover this popular locals' hangout, with a friendly staff, a strong lineup of draft beers, and an upbeat atmosphere. The decor runs to sports paraphernalia and posters, multiple TVs providing nonstop sports viewing, and a pool table. *400 Dorla Ct., Zephyr Cove, NV, tel. 702/588–3899. D, MC, V.*

More Mellow

Peak Lounge

Getting away from the contrived cacophony of the casinos is not easy, but the Peak Lounge in Harvey's stands out like a welcome oasis. Deep chairs, low-key piano music, and a quiet, civilized atmosphere are all yours for the price of a drink. *Harvey's Hotel, Rte. 50, Stateline, NV, tel. 702/588–2411. AE, D, DC, MC, V.*

St. Moritz Bar

This is the perfect place to sip and relax right after skiing or later in the evening, and it may be one of the best-kept secrets in Tahoe. There's a delightful fireside bar, a large fireplace, and lots of cozy couches and well-stuffed chairs. It has live jazz on weekends. *Christiana Inn, 9819 Saddle Rd., South Lake Tahoe, CA, tel. 530/544–7337. MC, V.*

MAMMOTH MOUNTAIN SKI AREA

MAMMOTH MOUNTAIN SKI AREA

Box 24
Mammoth Lakes, CA 93546
Tel. 760/934–2571
www.mammoth-mtn.com

STATISTICALLY SPEAKING

Base elevation: 7,953 feet

Summit elevation: 11,053 feet

Vertical drop: 3,100 feet

Skiable terrain: 3,500 acres

Number of trails: 150

Longest run: 3 miles

Lifts and capacity: 7 express quads, 10 doubles, 7 triples, 3 quads, 2 gondolas, 1 surface lift; 53,000 skiers per hour

Daily lift ticket: $49

Average annual snowfall: 353 inches

Number of skiing days 1997–98: 241

Snowmaking: 370 acres; 20%

Terrain mix: N 30%, I 40%, E 30%

Snowboarding: yes

Mammoth says it all. Call it tautological, call it California size. Call it large, with a capital *L*. Mammoth is a monster, and if Heavenly can be compared to a Christmas cake, spiced with exotic and interesting ingredients, then Mammoth is best likened to a giant sundae, its conelike flanks smothered from November through June by some of the deepest snow in the Sierra Nevada. Such is the lure of this broad-shouldered conical peak that 10,000 to 12,000 skiers pack its slopes on some weekend days, most enduring a five- to six-hour drive from southern California and contributing to Mammoth's reputation as one of the busiest ski areas in America.

Mammoth, mind you, is more than up to the task of accommodating the crowds; its "dormant" volcanic mass, set against the craggy backdrop of the Minaret Peaks, consists of more than 3,500 acres of skiable terrain. At 11,000 feet, Mammoth is the highest resort in California and one of the highest in the country. It straddles the Sierra Crest in conical isolation, its north and south shoulders drooping down to 9,000 feet and its western and eastern slopes plunging more than 3,000 feet down to the San Joaquin Canyon on one side and the mountain village of Mammoth Lakes on the other.

Accommodations at the resort are limited, so the town of Mammoth Lakes is where the majority of people bunk. It's about a 4-mile drive between the main lodge and town—a route served by the Mammoth Area Shuttle—and like its namesake mountain, the town is a sprawling development that has often been referred to as the "condo city of the Sierra." It's an accurate appellation, given the preponderance of this type of accommodation. There's no real town center and few traditional hotels or gracious inns— just a gridwork of streets, many four lanes wide. Hotels, restaurants, shops, bars, and boutiques are strung out along a mile of Main Street, and at times the vehicular traffic can resemble Hollywood Boulevard at rush hour. In spite of this, Mammoth Lakes does have its charm, most of which comes from the stunning scenery that surrounds it and from the youthful vibrancy of its 5,000 permanent residents.

Children's services: day-care, tel. 760/934–0646; instruction, tel. 760/934–0658

Snow phone: tel. 760/934–6166, 888/766–9778

Police: tel. 911 or 760/934–2011

Medical center: tel. 760/934–2551

Hospital: Mammoth Hospital, tel. 760/934–3311

Mammoth Lakes Visitors Bureau: tel. 760/934–2712, 800/367–6572

National Forest Visitor Center: tel. 760/934–2505

Taxi: tel. 760/934–3030

Road conditions: tel. 800/427–7623

Towing: Bill's Towing & Recovery, tel. 760/934–4264; Mammoth Towing, tel. 760/934–3385

Weather conditions: tel. 760/873–3213

FIVE-STAR FAVORITES
Best run for vertical: Cornice Bowl

Best run overall: Roadrunner

Best bar/nightclub: Whiskey Creek

Best hotel: Mammoth Mountain Inn

Best restaurant: Restaurant at Convict Lake

HOW TO GET THERE
By Plane
Reno-Tahoe International Airport (*see* Getting to California Resorts, *above*), about 165 miles away, is the closest major airport. The **Mammoth Lakes Airport** (tel. 760/934–3825) is about 10 minutes from the resort and is served by Mountain Air Express (tel. 562/595–1011 or 800/788–4247) from Long Beach.

Shuttle Service
There is no shuttle between Reno and Mammoth. The free **Mammoth Area Shuttle** (760/934–2571) meets flights at Mammoth Lakes Airport and takes passengers to resort-owned accommodations in Mammoth. **Mammoth Shuttle Systems** (tel. 760/934–3030) runs from the airport to town.

By Car
The resort is 325 miles from Los Angeles and Orange County on U.S. 395 north to U.S. 203 at Mammoth Lakes Junction. From Reno it's 165 miles southwest on U.S. 395. It's a 360-mile drive east from the San Francisco area on U.S. 80 or U.S. 50 to U.S. 395 south. No matter which direction you're driving from, carrying chains is recommended.

Major car-rental firms have desks at the Reno-Tahoe airport (*see* Getting to California Resorts, *above*). There are no car rentals at Mammoth Lakes Airport.

By Bus
Greyhound Lines (tel. 800/231–2222) provides daily service between Mammoth and both Los Angeles and Reno. A number of charter bus companies also travel daily from Los Angeles to Mammoth for $40–$50 round-trip.

By Train
See Getting to California Resorts, *above*.

GETTING AROUND
A car can be useful for exploring the region, but if you are just commuting between town and the resort, the free **Mammoth Area Shuttle** (MAS; tel. 760/934–2571), which runs throughout the town of Mammoth and to the Main Lodge, Juniper Springs

Base Camp, and Canyon Lodge areas at the resort, is your best bet. Parking is limited at the resort, and the roads are often so snow-covered that chains are essential. **Mammoth Shuttle Systems** (tel. 760/934-3030) runs cars and small vans throughout the town and between the town and the lodge.

THE SKIING

Mammoth is so vast that even regulars who have been skiing the resort for years have not skied its entire Brobdingnagian mass, and for visitors it represents a confusing network of lifts numbered in the order in which they were built, which results, for example, in Chair 22 going to an entirely different point on the mountain from Chair 23. That idiosyncrasy aside, Mammoth is actually well laid out; most of the expert runs lace the top half of its sloping shoulders, and the intermediate and novice runs network the lower half of the mountain. Fortunately, the newest generation of high-speed or express quads now have names, and the rest of the lift network eventually will be named as improvements continue.

Mammoth began life in prehistoric times as a volcano, and now with half its girth so much geological dust, the remaining ridge gives access to a dozen wide bowls, the largest one—once the interior of the cone—a staggering 13,000 feet across. Below this vast expanse are the lower peaks of Lincoln Mountain, Gold Hill, and Hemlock Ridge, where you'll find a 6.5-mile-wide swath of groomed boulevards and moguled canyons.

It is those bowls that make it one of the most expansive ski resorts in America and that are the preoccupation of its owner, Dave McCoy, who first strapped on skis and explored the area more than 50 years ago. McCoy overcame considerable obstacles—isolation and lack of money, just two of them—to create his vision of a ski resort. There are only three other resorts in the country that can be said to bear such a personal stamp of their creators—Dick Bass's Snowbird in Utah, Alex Cushing's Squaw Valley, and the late Ernie Blake's Taos Ski Valley. Even today, as Mammoth enjoys its place among the great resorts of America, McCoy is still actively involved in running it.

Loosely speaking, there are three main staging areas for tackling the mountain. At the far east side, closest to the town, is Juniper Springs Base Camp, with a mix of runs ranging from bunny slopes to black-diamond plunges. Halfway up the access road to the resort is Canyon Lodge, with lifts that serve the Lincoln Mountain area. At the end of the access road is the main base lodge area, which serves the west side of the mountain. All three areas are linked by either trails or lifts that intermediates and up can handle. Each base area is progressively more crowded as you approach the main base area. The best way to avoid crowds and enjoy the morning sun is to start at Juniper Springs Base Camp, move to the Canyon Lodge area by midmorning, and then hit the main lodge area and the summit gondola by lunchtime, when the lifts in this area are slightly less busy. Just make sure you begin your return journey from the west to the east in time to catch all the required lifts.

Novices

You have three choices for starting your day: Juniper Springs Base Camp, the lift area closest to Mammoth Lakes; Canyon Lodge, which is halfway up the Mammoth entrance road; and the main base lodge area. Juniper Springs Base Camp gets the early morning sun and tends to be the least crowded, mainly because it has only two novice trails—Lupin and Sleepy Hollow—but once you grow bored with them, you can easily reach the Canyon Lodge area by traversing the Chickadee or Swell trails and ending up on Clover Leaf. Conversely, the main base lodge area gets no early morning sun and is typically the most crowded place on the mountain. Three lifts serve the novice terrain in this area. Runs such as Jill's Run, St. Moritz, and Gus's Pasture are wide open, meticulously groomed, and gently undulating. From Chairs 11 and 27 beginners can reach the most popular gentle slopes, Sesame Street and Road Runner.

A good compromise between the limited terrain and isolation of Juniper Springs Base Camp and the congestion of the Main Base lodge area is Canyon Lodge, where the sun makes an appearance by midmorning and two lifts (7 and 17) serve a mixture of green and gentle blue runs. Chair 7 lets you explore the novice trails of Hansel and Gretel—both wide and smooth—and Chair 17 will take you a little higher up the slope once you feel comfortable about tackling gentle blue runs such as Clover Leaf and Round Robin, both of which are well groomed and wide open—perfect for trying those first intermediate turns. Unfortunately, there are no novice runs on the upper half of the mountain, so until you can comfortably link turns and handle a little more steepness, you'll have to stay below.

Intermediates

If you want to catch the early morning sun and avoid the crowds, it's a good idea to start at Juniper Springs Base Camp. Take either Chair 15 or Chair 24, turn left, and scoot down Holiday to Chair 25, which carries you to a point just below the double-black-diamond bowls of the upper mountain. You can take Repeat 22, a moderately steep and wide cruiser, to get the legs warmed up.

When you are ready to move on, cut left onto Holiday about halfway down Repeat 22 and follow a combination of Swell and Clover Leaf that will take you down to the base area at Canyon Lodge. This is a good high-speed run with consistent pitch and a few interesting rolls and drop-offs; it's usually groomed. You can ride Chair 8 back up for a repeat shot or pick up Hully Gully (turn right off the lift) for a taste of some bumps. Your other choice is to take Chair 16, a high-speed quad, and follow Roller Coaster or Lost in the Woods, a pair of giant-slalom runs that let the skis track fast and smooth. A slightly steeper and narrower alternative is Wall Street. Roller Coaster takes you back to the bottom of Chair 16, but Wall Street and Lost in the Woods take you to the bottom of Stump Alley Express (Chair 2), which will take you high up into the sloping and wide-open bowl area just below the summit.

From here you can continue down Stump Alley or Broadway. Both are wide and well groomed but tend to be extremely busy, especially Broadway, which ends up in the main base lodge area. From either point you can ride back up to the Mid-Chalet or the top of the upper gondola. From there you can take Chair 1 up to the top of the Wall, a steep black run; skip that and head over the back side and pick up Silver Tip. Follow it down to the lower bowls of the western ridge. This is wide-open intermediate bowl cruising. From the main base lodge area you can also take Gondola 1 and Gondola 2 up to the summit and turn right to follow Road Runner, a long, wide, and varied green cruiser that skirts the western summit ridge and gives you a spectacular view of the surrounding Minarets.

Experts

You can start the day in the sun at Juniper Springs Base Camp by riding either Chair 24 or Chair 15 and then Chair 25 to the blue-black runs of Quicksilver, Back for More, or Haven't the Foggiest. When you're ready for more challenges, head over to the steep double-black terrain of Grizzly, Shaft, Viva, and Avalanche Chutes. These are all supersteep freefalls that slash through the trees like a frozen waterfall, and you can ski them intensely from Chair 22, which, to the amazement of locals, tends to be one of the least busy lifts on the mountain. From the top of Chair 22, you can turn left on Repeat 22, a blue run that takes you to the bottom of Chair 9, another relatively unbusy lift, which gets you to the upper bowls on the eastern fringe of the summit ridge. Another option is to turn right off the top of Chair 22 and ski down

to Chair 5. This lift—again, it tends to be relatively uncrowded—parallels the path of the gondola but stops short of the summit (on a different peak). From this point you get a taste of some ultrasteep chutes—Face of Five, Sanctuary, Silver, and Dry Creek. When you're ready to move on, ski down to the base of Stump Alley Express and ride it up to Mid-Chalet. The gondola gets very busy by mid-morning, so if you find yourself there at that time, a good alternative is to head for Chair 23—fed by Chair 19 from the main base area—which is usually less crowded. From either point (the gondola or Chair 23) you have the full expanse of Mammoth's bowls at your feet. The Cornice Bowl is a favorite for morning powder, but skiers later head either east to the Dragon's Back off Chair 9 or west to Hemlock Ridge off Chair 14.

SNOWBOARDING

For snowboarders Mammoth offers a huge terrain park called The Unbound, on Bowling Alley, with a half-pipe, quarter pipes, table tops, and lots of features designed for lift-off. The Unbound is also open for night skiing Friday and Saturday from 4 to 9 and during select holiday periods. The American Snowboard Tour and the National Snowboarding Championships are both held here.

WHERE TO STAY

For a small, somewhat isolated community in the mountains, Mammoth Lakes has an astonishingly large bed base of almost 11,000. Unfortunately, the town's nickname of "condo city of the Sierra Nevada," is accurate, and there is a real shortage of small lodges, full-service hotels, and even true slopeside accommodation.

Expensive

Mammoth Mountain Inn

Next to a tiny stream just a few hundred yards from the Mammoth day lodge and surrounded by forest, this full-service hotel complex has a choice of spacious hotel rooms and suites or one- and two-bedroom condo-style units. The decor is mountain modern, with lots of wood trim and well-crafted pine furniture offset by bright wall coverings and upholstery in warm colors. Both the rooms and the suites are flooded with light. *1 Minaret Rd., Box 353, Mammoth Lakes 93546, tel. 760/934–2581 or 800/228–4947, fax 760/934–0700. 213 units. Facilities: 2 restaurants, 2 bars, lounge, 3 whirlpools, 24-hr desk service, maid service, ski valet, ski storage, laundry, game room. AE, MC, V. $115–$485.*

Silver Bear

Just a few hundred yards from the lifts at Canyon Lodge, this condo complex combines traditional Euro-inn style with modern architecture and furnishings. The units are either two-bedroom or two plus a loft, making them perfect for families. Each unit has a dining area, a stone fireplace, and a combination of wood, wicker, and plush furnishings. *527 Lakeview Blvd., Box 7670, Mammoth Lakes 93546, tel. 760/934–5680 or 800/336–6543, fax 760/934–5306. 24 units. Facilities: sauna,whirlpool, indoor pool, ski storage, laundry, game room. No credit cards. $240–$350.*

Snowcreek Resort

A resort unto itself, on 335 acres about a five-minute drive from the mountain, this complex offers some of the more luxurious units available in Mammoth, especially the three- and four-bedroom town houses. The decor in both the condos and town houses is stylish and modern, with high, vaulted ceilings, acres of windows, and a pleasant blend of wood and rock. *1254 Old Mammoth Rd., Box 1647, Mammoth Lakes 93546, tel. 760/934–3333 or 800/544–6007, fax 760/934–1619. 160 units. Facilities: health club, whirlpool, indoor pool, steam room, sauna, ski storage. D, MC, V. $120–$620.*

Moderate

Krystal Villa East

Close to Juniper Springs Base Camp, this villa houses condo units in two sizes—one bedroom or one bedroom with loft, both roomy enough to handle groups of six. All have good, practical furnishings. The big, comfortable common area is decorated with a certain country charm. *137 Laurel Mountain Rd., Box 1132, Mammoth Lakes 93546, tel. 619/934–2669 or 800/237–6181, fax 760/934–1770. 24 units. Facilities: sauna, hot tub, maid service, ski storage, laundry. D, MC, V. $72–$175.*

Snowflower

These spacious three-story units right next to the Snow Creek golf course can sleep eight people and have a great view and comfortable, modern furnishings. They all have two bedrooms with baths downstairs, with a living room with fireplace, a dining room, a bathroom, and a full kitchen on the second floor, and a loft with queen-size bed. *Gateway Center, Box*

1608, Mammoth Lakes 93546, tel. 760/934–2528 or 800/527–6273, fax 760/934–2317. 88 units. Facilities: 2 saunas, 2 hot tubs, ski storage, ski shuttle. D, MC, V. $350.

Snowgoose Inn

Just off Main Street, this tidy little two-story lodge with a wood-plank exterior and a shingled roof is billed as a B&B, but it has a number of rooms and suites that come with kitchens. The well-furnished rooms are an ideal size for couples, while the suites—with one or two bedrooms—are a good bet for families or several couples. 57 Forest Trail, Box 387, Mammoth Lakes 93546, tel. 760/934–2660 or 800/874–7368, fax 760/934–5655. 19 units. Facilities: hot tub, maid service, ski storage, ski shuttle, games room. AE, D, DC, MC, V. $78–$208, including full breakfast and evening appetizers.

Tamarack Lodge

Tucked away on the edge of the John Muir Wilderness Area, this original 1924 log lodge was built by Mary Foy—mother of the famous vaudevillian family immortalized in the 1955 Bob Hope movie The Seven Little Foys. Whether you stay in the main lodge or in a cabin, you are guaranteed rustic solitude in a historic natural setting. Some of the rooms share bathroom facilities and can be fairly spartan in their furnishings. The cabins scattered around the resort's six acres range from rustic to luxurious and come in various sizes from smallish studio units all the way to large houses that sleep 10. They're comfortable and functional, and some come with a wood-burning stove. Twin Lakes Rd.,

Box 69, Mammoth Lakes 93546, tel. 760/934–2442 or 800/237–6879 in CA, fax 760/934–2281. 36 units. Facilities: restaurant, lounge, maid service, cross-country skiing, ski storage, shuttle (winter). D, MC, V. $85–$360.

White Horse Inn Bed & Breakfast

This delightful bed-and-breakfast is small and homey but maintains a high level of style and good taste. Each of its rooms is distinctive for its furnishings and ambience. They may have Chinese, Austrian, or Italian antiques. The Tribal Room, with artifacts of the region's earliest Indian inhabitants, has three single beds and is ideal for small families. 2180 Old Mammoth Rd., Box 2326, Mammoth Lakes 93456, tel. 760/924–3656 or 800/982–5657. 5 rooms. Facilities: ski storage. D, DC, MC, V. $115–$135, including full breakfast.

Inexpensive

Austria Hof

A tidy, tiny wood-and-stucco Austrian-style chalet a short distance from the lifts at Canyon Lodge, this place is clean, comfortable, modern, and convenient. Smaller rooms come with just a queen-size bed, while the larger ones have either two queens or a queen and two twins. 924 Canyon Blvd., Mammoth Lakes 93546, tel. 760/934–2764 or 800/922–2966 in CA, fax 760/934–1880. 22 units. Facilities: restaurant, bar, lounge, hot tub, maid service, ski storage. D, DC, MC, V. $78–$130.

Mammoth Travelodge

These small side-by-side motel-type accommodations have combined into a single lodging. Ideally situated just off Main Street, the lodge has studios, one- and two-bedroom suites, and two-bedroom cottages complete with kitchen. The decor is simple rec-room style, and the furnishings and amenities are minimal, but the place also has an indoor swimming pool—something of a rarity in Mammoth. *6209 Minaret Rd., Mammoth Lakes 93546, tel. 760/934–8526 or 800/228–4947, fax 760/934–8007. 123 units. Facilities: indoor pool, 2 hot tubs, 2 saunas, maid service, ski storage, ski shuttle. AE, MC, V. $99–$165.*

White Stag Inn
The simple stained wood-plank exterior looks cute, and all rooms in this clean, comfortable two-story motor lodge right in the middle of town are large enough for four people. Some rooms come with a small kitchenette. *Main St. and Minaret St., Box 45, Mammoth Lakes 93546, tel. 760/934–7507. 21 rooms. Facilities: sauna, maid service, ski storage, ski shuttle. AE, D, MC, V. $44–$84.*

WHERE TO EAT
The dining and nightlife scene is spread all around the Mammoth resort area, from the slopeside hotels to small inns and restaurants between the mountain and the town and into the town itself. The most varied selection is found in town, although there are some noteworthy spots in the vicinity that are worth making the effort to get to.

Expensive
The Lakefront
The 10-table dining room in the Tamarack Lodge is constructed completely of knotty pine—walls, floors, ceilings, and tables—with the exception of the oversize stone fireplace. The atmosphere is relaxed but definitely upscale, and celebrity-packed photographs of Mammoth's early glory days, in the 1930s and '40s, bedeck the walls. The menu is Continental, with specialties such as rack of lamb; roast duckling with raspberry–green peppercorn sauce; eggplant Wellington, with eggplant substituting for the meat; veal scallopini; and a selection of steak, fish, and chicken dishes. *Twin Lakes Rd., Mammoth Lakes, tel. 760/934–3534. AE, MC, V.*

Mountainside Grill
The Grill is a beautifully serene dining room, with a vaulted ceiling, large windows, and a warm, woodsy motif that both absorbs large groups and sequesters quiet couples. The menu is a mix of traditional American and classic Continental, with such entrées as sautéed Long Island duck breast served with mango sauce; Iowa-style pork chop, broiled or blackened, with jalapeño-pineapple compote; generous cuts of prime rib; grilled mahimahi; chicken Kiev; and pepper steak. *Mammoth Mountain Inn, 1 Minaret Rd., Mammoth Lakes, tel. 760/934–0601. AE, MC, V.*

Restaurant at Convict Lake
Just south of town is one of the more luxurious dining experiences in Mammoth. Here spectacular views of the surrounding countryside complement an atmosphere of rustic elegance and eclectic Californian cuisine. The decor is a mix of refined dark wood furniture and pale peach linen and crystal place settings. The menu offers a strong lineup of Continental dishes, such as steak Diane and oven-roasted

duck with berry confit. The fish dishes include seared tuna and mahimahi in chervil and butter sauce. *4 mi south of Mammoth Lakes off U.S. 395 at Convict Lake exit, tel. 760/934–3803. AE, D, MC, V.*

Skadi

A great high, oak-beamed ceiling dominates the dining room of this upscale restaurant, named for the Viking goddess of skiing. The decor is refined country, with dark wood tables and chairs, elegant wainscoting and other wood trim, and floral accents. The menu draws on mountain cuisines from around the world, with such offerings as pasta with smoked chicken and wild mushrooms or roast duck with kiln-dried cherries. Venison is a mainstay here; the restaurant has its own deer ranch in southern California. *587 Old Mammoth Rd., Mammoth Lakes, tel. 760/934–3902. AE, MC, V.*

Moderate

Austria Hof

This restaurant envelops you in a warm Old World Austrian atmosphere, the perfect setting for the best selection of schnitzels in town, including Wiener, chicken, and Jaeger, as well as sauerbraten, thick goulash soups, and plump German sausages with sauerkraut. *924 Canyon Blvd., by Canyon Lodge, Mammoth Lakes, tel. 760/934–2764. AE, D, DC, MC, V.*

Cervinos

This Italian bistro with modern decor gets away from the red-and-white-checked-tablecloth syndrome. It is both elegant—with linen and crystal place settings, stylish art, and low lighting—and casual. The menu is diverse: the veal piccata served with sun-dried tomato and chive sauce is feathery light and succulent; there's an excellent lineup of fish entrées including swordfish and calamari, both buttered and pan-seared, and a fine cioppino (fish stew), as well as pasta. *View Point Rd., Mammoth Lakes, tel. 760/934–4734. AE, D, DC, MC, V.*

Mogul Restaurant

In these four small dining rooms almost every table seems to have a secluded corner to itself. Landscapes by local artists hang on the mauve-painted walls, and the largest dining room has a great window looking out onto the mountain. It's a traditional steak house, with a grill in the center of the room. There's also excellent prime rib, lobster and other seafood, chicken, and rack of lamb. *1528 Tavern Rd., Mammoth Lakes, tel. 760/934–3039. AE, MC, V.*

Ocean Harvest

This is the place to go for seafood. A fresh, woody smell wafts from the rough-sawed cedar siding of the interior, and old photos of local fishing heroes adorn the walls. The daily specials vary depending on the catch, and you can take your choice of sauce—such as the béarnaise over peppered ahi or the cajun spices over catfish—as well as such dishes as Idaho rainbow trout (panfried), Canadian scallops on a skewer, and a delicious cioppino. *248 Old Mammoth Rd., Mammoth Lakes, tel. 760/934–8539. AE, D, DC, MC, V.*

Whiskey Creek

If you're looking for a light bite in a busy roadhouse atmosphere with a loud country/rock jukebox, try the oyster bar upstairs or just sample a few appetizers before heading down to the main dining room. It is larger and quieter, with a crackling fireplace and mellow background music. The menu relies heavily on grilled steaks and seafood with a variety of interesting homemade marinades and sauces. Among house specialties are shrimp and scallops Marguerite (sautéed in tequila-lime sauce) and New Zealand rack of lamb with jalapeño mint jelly. *Main St. and Minaret Rd., Mammoth Lakes, tel. 760/934–2555. AE, MC, V.*

Inexpensive

Angels
The antique decor and old wooden tables might give the place an upscale look, but this cheerful spot in the middle of town attracts a good number of locals because of its monster portions, friendly service, and reasonable prices. It has family-friendly food such as sandwiches and burgers—notably the avocado melt (a combo of tuna, avocado, and cheese)—and an excellent selection of giant salads, including an outstanding grilled Southwestern chicken. *20 Sierra Blvd., Mammoth Lakes, tel. 760/934–7427. AE, D, MC, V.*

Bergers
The simple decor—rough wooden tables and chairs, local artists' photos on walls, red carpeting—is modestly understated, allowing you to enjoy the beaming sunshine and glorious view of the Sherwin Mountains through the high windows up front. This place serves the best burgers in town, which come in a variety of flavors and sizes—try the jumbo buffalo burger. There's also a good selection

of meal-size sandwiches, including turkey, pastrami, chicken breast, and beef brisket, along with pork ribs, fresh fish, and venison steak dinners. *6118 Minaret Rd., Mammoth Lakes, tel. 760/934–6622. MC, V.*

Carl's Jr.
Fast and funky, this is an excellent fast-food spot—complete with plastic booths, Formica tables, wraparound mirrors, and wood paneling—offering standard favorites from hamburger platters to chicken and sandwiches. There's also a good lineup of salads and other low-fat and low-cholesterol options. *437 Old Mammoth Rd., Mammoth Lakes, tel. 760/934–8812. No credit cards.*

Best Bets for Breakfast

Schat's Bakery
Part restaurant, part bakery, and part community center, this family-run business serves everything from huge, superbly cooked omelets and other egg dishes to monster pancakes, awesome French toast, and a joyous selection of freshly baked breads and pastries. *Main St., Mammoth Lakes, tel. 760/934–6055. MC, V.*

The Stove
Leading the breakfast hit parade here—apart from the friendly service—are four-egg omelets, oversize pancakes, and cinnamon French toast. *644 Old Mammoth Rd., Mammoth Lakes, tel. 760/934–2821. AE, MC, V.*

NIGHTLIFE AND ENTERTAINMENT
Après-Ski

Dry Creek Bar
This bar is in a quiet spot in the Mammoth Mountain Inn. A guitarist

and/or pianist usually keeps the mood mellow, and bar snacks are served daily. *Mammoth Mountain Inn, 1 Minaret Rd., Mammoth Lakes, tel. 760/934–2581. AE, MC, V.*

Yodler Restaurant and Bar

This is a funky wooden chalet bar with several different rooms. It gets cheek to jowl around the bar area, but you can also spread out in front of the fireplace. There's music, occasionally a live entertainer, and a TV pumping out ski movies. *Mammoth Mountain Inn, 1 Minaret Rd., Mammoth Lakes, tel. 760/934–2581. AE, MC, V.*

Loud and Lively/Dancing

Goat's Bar

A good all-purpose hangout, this is the closest thing to a traditional neighborhood pub in Mammoth Lakes. It has a pool table, darts, and multiple TVs for tube junkies. *Red Rooster Mall, upstairs, Mono and Main Sts., Mammoth Lakes, tel. 760/934–4629.*

La Sierra's Cantina

A combination of live rock and blues acts, Mammoth's largest dance floor, and (at last count) at least 10 televisions explain the popularity of this spot. The numerous drink and food specials make it fun to part with your money. *3789 Main St., Mammoth Lakes, tel. 760/934–8083.*

The Ocean Club

Downstairs from Ocean Harvest Restaurant, the club typically attracts a younger crowd looking to dance. DJ's spin the latest hits and classic dance tunes to bump and grind the night away. *248 Old Mammoth Road, tel. 760/934–8539. AE, D, DC, MC, V.*

Whiskey Creek

Definitely your best choice for live entertainment, this place has an ever-changing lineup of club bands from across the state. You can count on large, youthful crowds on Friday and Saturday. *Main St. and Minaret Rd., Mammoth Lakes, tel. 760/934–2555. AE, MC, V.*

More Mellow

High Sierra House of Blues

The cigar bar adjacent to the restaurant of the same name offers a quiet place to relax in front of the fire. Jazz or blues is featured nightly and is live on weekends with a large dance floor. Appetizers are served in the bar. *202 Old Mammoth Rd., tel. 760/934–7019. AE, D, DC, MC, V.*

Looney Bean

This throwback to the days of coffee-house hippiedom has live acoustic and folk entertainers every weekend night. They don't serve beer or alcohol, but you will find the best selection of coffee in town. *Main St., Mammoth Lakes, tel. 760/934–1345. No credit cards.*

SQUAW VALLEY USA

Box 2007
Olympic Valley, CA 96146
Tel. 530/583–6955
www.squaw.com

STATISTICALLY SPEAKING

Base elevation: 6,200 feet

Summit elevation: 9,050 feet

Vertical drop: 2,850 feet

Lift-served terrain: 4,000 acres

Longest run: 3.2 miles

Lifts and capacity: 1 cable car, 1 Funitel, 4 high-speed quads, 1 quad, 9 triples, 10 doubles, 3 surface, 1 Pulse lift; 49,000 skiers per hour

Daily lift ticket: $49

Average annual snowfall: 450 inches

Number of skiing days 1997–98: 196

Snowmaking: 360 acres; 8%

Terrain mix: N 25%, I 45%, E 30%

Snowboarding: yes

Cross-country skiing: 18 kilometers

Squaw Valley is a big brute of a resort, its 4,000 lift-served acres competing well with its megasize California neighbors: Mammoth at 3,500 acres and Heavenly at 4,800. Still, Squaw seems more intimidating than even Heavenly, more daunting, more in-your-face, with arguably the toughest skiing and boarding of any of the 19 ski resorts that ring the cobalt blue waters of Lake Tahoe. In part, Squaw gained such notoriety from the famous Warren Miller films featuring extreme skiers taking on the chutes, cliffs, and steeps, including the infamous KT-22 Peak. Squaw's ferociousness has been oversold, though, for despite all its serious terrain, 45% of the mountain is considered intermediate, and 25% is novice.

The resort, which sits high in the Sierra Nevada on the north shore of Lake Tahoe, began in 1949 as a modest single chairlift. In 1960 it attracted the world's attention as the site of the VIII Winter Olympic Games, the first of the games to be televised daily. They were dubbed the "games of simplicity," reflecting Squaw's modest, close-knit community. From these humble beginnings, Squaw Valley has developed into a six-peak colossus, with one of the most advanced ski-lift networks in North America. The lift system's chairs, cable car, and 28-passenger Funitel can move 49,000 skiers an hour over 4,000 acres of open bowls in a layout of interconnected peaks and valleys similar to the broad resort expanses found in the Swiss Alps.

At the core of the resort is the Olympic House (a collection of restaurants, bars and shops), some condominiums in the immediate vicinity, and two remarkable midmountain complexes. One of the villages, the High Camp, at 8,200 feet, includes restaurants, bars, and a recreation complex with an Olympic-size ice pavilion, a swimming pool, a Jacuzzi, tennis courts, a bungee-jumping tower, and an Olympic Heritage museum. Nearby is the Gold Coast complex, with a smaller collection of restaurants and bars.

Tahoe City is a pretty lakefront town just 5 miles south of the resort; the larger and ever-expanding Truckee, 10 miles north of Squaw Valley, is similarly charming. Both are lively, with an abundance of restaurants, bars, shops, and services. Along a

USEFUL NUMBERS

Area code: 530 (CA);
775 (NV)

Children's services: day-care,
instruction, tel. 530/581–7225

Snow phone: tel. 530/583–
6955

Police: tel. 911

Hospital: Tahoe Forest Hospital, tel. 530/587–6011

North Lake Tahoe Resort
Association: tel. 530/581–
6900 or 800/824–6348

Cross-country skiing: tel. 530/
583–6300

Road conditions: tel. 530/
445–1534

Towing: Dependable Tow,
Truckee, tel. 916/587–5292;
Lakeside Towing, Tahoe, tel.
530/587–6000

FIVE-STAR FAVORITES

Best runs for vertical: Mose-
ley's of KT-22 and Headwall

Best run overall: Mountain
Run from top of Siberia lift

Best bar/nightclub: Bar One

Best hotel: Resort at Squaw
Creek

Best restaurant: Glissandi

10-mile stretch around the north end of the lake are strung the smaller residential communities of Tahoe Vista, Kings Beach, and Crystal Bay. The latter abuts the Nevada border, where the casino action lies. For more gaming, check out Incline Village—22 miles east of Squaw—just inside the Nevada state line—a tony enclave of high-priced houses and condos. These nearby towns provide accommodations choices within a short and straightforward drive from the mountain. There's plenty of day parking at the resort, though dispersion of skier traffic at 4 PM on sunny weekends can take as long as half an hour.

Splaying up from the base area, the Funitel and the cable car move intermediates and novices to the upper mountain for most of the green and blue slopes, while a pair of chairs sends experts to their proper chutes. In between are a plethora of lifts serving experienced intermediate, advanced, and expert skiers on a massive variety of terrain. As the only on-mountain lunch spots are the Gold Coast complex, in a valley between two of Squaw's six peaks, and High Camp, perched on the lip of a mountain ridge, meeting up midday with your whole group may be diffi- cult. The upper-mountain complexes are a long way from other parts of the resort, such as the expert ski- ing on KT-22, and even farther from the mostly inter- mediate runs of Snow King Peak, which is reached directly from the self-contained Resort at Squaw Creek, about a mile outside the Olympic House area, or from the base village by the Red Dog and Papoose chairs.

HOW TO GET THERE

By Plane

Reno-Tahoe International Airport (*see* Getting to Nevada Resorts, *above*), in Reno, Nevada, is 42 miles (about 60 minutes by car) from Squaw Valley.

By Shuttle

The once-a-day **Sierra Nevada Grey Line ski shuttle** (tel. 530/542–5930 for South Lake Tahoe, 530/583–5585 or 800/822–6009 for Reno) serves South Lake Tahoe hotels to Squaw Valley starting at 7 AM; the return shuttle bus leaves Squaw Valley at 4:30 PM for Reno. There is no charge with a lift ticket, otherwise it costs $20 round-trip. The Reno shuttle departs for Squaw Valley starting at 6:50 AM from Reno hotels; the return shuttle bus leaves Squaw Valley at 4:30 PM for Reno. Fare is $20 round-trip.

By Car

From Reno-Tahoe International Airport, take 395 north for about 5 miles to I–80 west. At Truckee, about 40 miles along I–80, take Route 89 for about 8 miles to Squaw Valley Road. From Sacramento, 96 miles away, take I–80 east for 88 miles to Truckee, then take Route 89 to Squaw Valley Road. From San Francisco, 196 miles from Squaw, take I–80 east for 188 miles to Truckee, then take Route 89 to Squaw Valley Road. From Los Angeles, 450 miles away, take Route 14 235 miles to Lone Pine, then take Route 395 to the Carson Valley. Take Route 50 out of Carson City and pick up Route 28 for 60 miles into Tahoe City. Take Route 89 to Squaw Valley Road.

By Ferry

If you're staying on the south shore, you can take the *Tahoe Queen* (tel. 530/541–3364 or 800/238–2463) across the lake to Squaw. The boat departs from the dock at the Ski Run Marina, at the bottom of Ski Run Boulevard, weekdays at 8 AM and reaches the Homewood dock at 10 AM; you can buy breakfast on board. The $18 round-trip fare includes a shuttle bus up to the Squaw Valley Resort.

GETTING AROUND

A car is preferable whether you are staying at the mountain or in the neighboring communities because it's the only way to explore the environs that contribute so much to the overall experience of skiing and vacationing here. Parking can be a nightmare on weekends; plan on leaving your car at your hotel and taking a shuttle to ski areas.

By Shuttle

Shuttle bus service from **TART** (Tahoe Area Rapid Transit; tel. 530/581–6365 or 800/736–6365) is available between the major hotels and the resort, as well as scheduled service from Truckee, Reno, and the south shore. The free **Resort at Squaw Creek shuttle** (tel. 530/583–6300) runs every half hour from 7 to 6:30 seven days a week. The driver will drop you pretty much anywhere you like. The **Squaw Valley Ski Corporation Shuttle** (tel. 530/583–6985) runs twice a day to and from a number of stops in the North Lake Tahoe area and is also free.

By Taxi

North Shore Taxi (tel. 530/546–9090), **Sierra Taxi** (tel. 530/577–8888), **Tahoe Truckee Taxi** (tel. 530/583–8294) and **Yellow Cabs** (tel. 530/546–9090), all based nearby, cover the Squaw Valley area.

THE SKIING

Most of the skiing at Squaw is in bowls, glades, and chutes where the trees grow sparsely, leaving wide-open slopes, without excessively defined and marked trails. Instead of trails, you count ski lifts or mountains—six of the latter and 29 of the former. The centerpiece of this mountain terrain is Squaw Peak, at 8,900 feet. It's flanked by Broken Arrow, to the northeast, at 8,200 feet; Emigrant, to the north, at 8,700 feet; and Granite Chief, to the northwest, at 9,050 feet. To the east are KT-22, at 8,200 feet, and Snow King, at 7,550 feet.

Each mountain offers distinct levels of terrain. Snow King has large expanses of intermediate terrain and most of the tree skiing found at the resort. Great black-diamond runs on Snow King include Poulsen's Gully and Rusty's Ridge. KT-22 is the radical peak, with its legendary chutes, steeps, and extreme skiing. Squaw Peak, Broken Arrow, and Emigrant also have intermediate terrain, with a unique high-altitude novice area that starts at High Camp and gives beginners and early intermediates a chance to experience the breathtaking views that are usually the monopoly of advanced skiers.

More than 70% of the terrain is free-form: it's find-your-own-way-down skiing, most of it beginning high on the ridges where the bowls are wind-scoured and wide-open. Although the layout might seem disconcerting at first, you'll quickly feel liberated at not having to abide by designated trails while skiing on the more than 450 inches (annual average snowfall) of snow cover. Take the skier's guide map with you as you explore the resort, but don't expect to find individual runs: it's simply a general mountain map identifying lifts as green, blue, or black and offering landmarks to help you get your bearings.

Novices

Nine of the 29 lifts at Squaw are designated green, with the majority at the High Camp area, although three are surface lifts (one at the base of Snow King, two at the base facility near Olympic House) for never-evers to get started on. From the main base area, you can take either the Funitel or the cable car to the green chairs off the High Camp lift (East Broadway, Belmont, Links, Bailey's Beach, or Riviera) and ski the wide-open expanse of gentle and groomed high-altitude slopes that are seldom visited by advanced skiers. You can play on these all day and then some, or take blue lifts, such as Gold Coast or High Camp, for more sustained pitch and length.

Intermediates

Squaw has much to offer intermediates, with 12 lifts serving the designated blue terrain, which includes all of Snow King Peak and the upper part of Emigrant. Siberia and Shirley Lake have some of the best intermediate skiing on the mountain. If you're ready to step up to black terrain, take the Siberia chair to the advanced but groomed slopes on the upper part of Squaw Peak or head over to Granite Chief for similar terrain. At the end of the day, ski the open terrain off the Mainline and Gold Coast lifts, then follow the broad, groomed Mountain Run (the route of the Olympic men's downhill race) or the parallel Home Run from the Gold Coast to the base village.

Experts

Only six of Squaw's lifts are designated black, with the majority serving the wild, untamed terrain of KT-22 or the upper limits of Squaw Peak. You can warm up on the steeps under the Cornice II or Headwall lifts—mostly ungroomed, pure fall-line adrenaline boosts with enough bowls, couloirs, and drops to tire you out. Try Granite Chief, Silverado, or Broken Arrow. The real test, though, is KT-22, with its extreme-level north faces. It's in this area that you'll find the cliffs, the gulp-and-go chutes, the curled cornice lips, and the biggest bumps. For truly world-class skiers and snowboarders the ultimate challenge is The Palisades. Ride either the Headwall lift or the Siberia lift to the top, then climb to the summit of flat-topped Squaw Peak. A series of progressively narrower and more harrowing chutes laces this northeast-facing cliff. On the far left is the National Chute, the take-off point for the Men's Downhill during the 1960 Olympics, and the easiest line on the cliff. After that it gets steeper, narrower, and crazier, depending on where the snow has blown in. If you want to know where the extreme snowboard and ski movies are filmed, this is it.

SNOWBOARDING

Squaw Valley was one of the first resorts in the west to embrace snowboarding and has some of the finest freeriding terrain in the country. Granite Chief is marked by terrific natural kickers, chutes, and rock jumps. Broken Arrow has the full menu, from wide-open bowls to narrow chutes—much of it south-facing for unbelievable corn snow in the spring. On a fresh snow day when most of the rest of the mountain has been slashed and burned, there's usu-

ally a bit of untouched powder still to be found off the horse trails on the the southeast side of Cornice 2 lift. Because the Central Park snowboard terrain park is illuminated, snowboarders can ride the half pipe 12 hours a day. The terrain park is one of the largest in the Sierra. Squaw Valley hosts the annual US Spring Ski and Board Fest, with live music, product demos, and snowboarding exhibitions.

Squaw Valley has two half-pipes and two terrain parks at the top of the Funitel in a complex known as Central Park. **Beginners** and **intermediates** can get twisted in the park and half-pipe under the Belmont lift. **Advanced** shredders favor the terrain under the Riviera lift. The park, open 12 hours a day, has lights and a sound system. True **experts** can attack the Palisades (*see above*).

NEARBY

Though Squaw Valley is the largest resort in North Tahoe, it is by no means the only game in town. If you're staying more than a few days and want some variety, try one of these. **Alpine Meadows** (tel. 530/583-4232), the next valley south of Squaw, has easy access and backcountry bowls. **Northstar** (tel. 530/562-1010), just south of Truckee, offers meticulously groomed tree skiing in a Colorado-style resort. **Sugar Bowl** (530/426-9000), on Donner Summit, was founded by Walt Disney in the 1930s. It is the oldest ski area in the region, boasts the most snowfall, and presents the same kind of skiing terrain as Squaw Valley in a more compact and tranquil setting.

WHERE TO STAY

Squaw Valley's base village area has about 2,000 beds, most of them moderately priced, plus several good restaurants, bars, and shops. High Camp (at the top of the cable car) is open until midnight with more bars, restaurants, bakeries, and lockers, not to mention a skating rink and swimming center.

An alternative to the higher-end village hotels is Truckee, a 10-mile drive north of the mountain. It's a bustling Sierra town of more than 10,000 with a variety of moderate and inexpensive inns, lodges, motels, and hotels. Five miles south of Squaw Valley is Tahoe City, a small lakeside community with more moderately priced accommodations plus the best choice of restaurants and nightlife. In addition, a number of small residential lakefront communities lie within a 20- to 25-minute drive from the mountain, including the upscale Incline Village, on the Nevada side of the state line. You can also stay on the South Shore (see Heavenly, above), with its well-established casino life. The drive takes about an hour, or you can take the ferry boat across the lake, but South Shore is only recommended as an overnight spot if you have a casino itch that you are desperate to scratch.

Expensive

Cal-Neva Lodge

One of the most storied of all the Tahoe lodges, this is also one of the oldest. Built in 1927 as a luxury retreat for celebrities and other high rollers, Cal-Neva prospered during Prohibition and thrived into the '50s. Frank Sinatra owned it in the 1960s, during which time it hosted gatherings for Hollywood moguls, the Mafia, and the upper-class elite. In decline in the 1970s and closed 1983–1986, it was then renovated and reopened. Its grand and striking nine-story log-and-stone facade at the edge of Crystal Bay stands precisely on the state line dividing California and Nevada. The vaulted Indian Room has massive exposed beams, an enormous fireplace, stone floors, and a score of big-game trophies. Next to it is the mesmerizing Crystal Bar, a circular extravaganza of wood paneling and mirrors topped by a cut-crystal dome overhead. You can choose a room, a suite with a balcony, a cottage with a small porch, or a chalet with a wraparound deck and a fireplace. All are decorated in French country style and offer views of the lake. *2 Stateline Rd., Box 368, Crystal Bay, NV 89402, tel. 775/832–4000 or 800/225–6382, fax 775/831–9007. 162 rooms, 18 suites, 20 chalets and cottages. Facilities: restaurant, spa, sauna, steam room, massage, casino. AE, D, DC, MC, V. $89–$289.*

Olympic Village Inn

This gorgeous replica of a Swiss A-frame mountain lodge, with stucco walls, towers, and wooden balconies, is ¼ mile from the main lift area. Built as part of the original Olympic Village, the inn stresses simple elegance but has the added appeal of being family oriented and slightly more relaxed than some other luxury accommodations. Some suites come with a fireplace; reserve these early. The decor is sophisticated Swiss/French country, with delicate floral-print wall coverings and curtains, light-amber furnishings, and wood trim. All rooms come with a queen-size bed, a queen-size sleeper sofa, and a kitchenette. Extra touches include eiderdown comforters and terry-cloth robes. *1909 Chamonix Pl., Olympic Valley, CA 96146, tel. 530/581–6000 or 800/845–5243, fax 530/583–3135. 90 units. Facilities: lounge, library/game room, 5 outdoor hot tubs. AE, MC, V. $175–$285.*

Resort at Squaw Creek

This vast, 650-acre resort-within-a-resort is the class act at Squaw: It has everything from penthouse suites to a towering man-made waterfall. The rooms and suites, impeccably turned out in modern West Coast decor, are bright, window-dominated aeries, with exceptional views, sleek and stylish furnishings, original artwork, plants, and just about every finishing touch imaginable. Each of the 18 deluxe penthouse suites provides two levels of luxurious living in plush, individual owner–decorated palaces. The standard rooms and suites all come with a king- or two queen-size beds. The resort sits on the perimeter of Squaw Valley, with direct access to the slopes from its own chairlift. *400 Squaw Creek Rd., Olympic Valley, CA 96146, tel. 530/583–6300 or 800/327–3353, fax 530/581–6647. 200 rooms, 205 suites. Facilities: 4 restaurants, deli, health club, heated outdoor pool, sand beach pool, ski lift, ski rentals, ski shop, cross-country ski lessons, ski storage, 3 hot tubs, children's programs, baby-sitting, laundry service, shuttle to slopes, skating pavilion. AE, D, DC, MC, V. $250–$1,900.*

Squaw Valley Lodge

Here's an upscale ski-in/ski-out condo hotel, excellently situated in the mountain village at the base of the Squaw 1 express lift and near many others. The stylish three-building enclave has a fitness and health center, maid service, a concierge, and a bell staff. Each unit is individually owned and styled. Decor ranges from contemporary European to Southwestern. Oddly, the units best suited for families have only a kitchenette rather than a full kitchen. *201 Squaw Peak Rd., Box 2364, Olympic Village, CA 96146, tel. 530/583–5500 or 800/922–9970, fax 530/583–0326. 85 units. Facilities: health club, outdoor pool, 5 hot tubs, laundry, ski shop. AE, DC, MC, V. $180–$725.*

Moderate

Hyatt Regency Lake Tahoe

In striking contrast to the serene, wooded setting near the waters of Lake Tahoe, the Hyatt is a large, sprawling casino hotel that looks like a transplant from the South Shore (*see* Heavenly, *above*), with round-the-clock opportunities to chance fate. There are all-you-can-eat buffet specials, discounted lift tickets, and complimentary drinks. Rooms have California mountain-lodge decor—big wooden beds, pine armoires, and overstuffed furniture—and large bathrooms. The cottages are lakeside and come with either a kitchen or a wet bar/kitchenette. A complimentary shuttle service runs to and from the resort. *Country Club Dr. and Lake Shore, Box 3239, Incline Village, NV 89450, tel. 775/832–1234 or 800/553–3288, fax 775/832–3222. 434 rooms, 24 suites/cottages. Facilities: 3 restaurants,*

2 lounges, health spa, outdoor heated pool. AE, D, DC, MC, V. $215–$850.

Mayfield House

This delightful stone-and-wood house was built in the 1930s by Norman Mayfield, one of the original development tycoons to work the Lake Tahoe area. A classic example of Tahoe architectural style from that era, it was turned into this fine bed-and-breakfast after a refurbishing in 1979. All bedrooms are decorated in mountain style and brim with extras such as fresh flowers, books, and down comforters. Each room has its own nook for relaxing with a book, and all have either a queen- or a king-size bed. There's also a large living room with a fireplace, and a full breakfast is served in the dining room. *236 Grove St., Box 8529, Tahoe City, CA 96145, tel. 530/583–1001 or 888/518–8898. 4 rooms, 1 suite, 1 cabin. Facilities: dining room. AE, MC, V. $100–$225.*

Richardson House

This Victorian-era house built in 1881 has mostly been maintained in its original style. It's a warm B&B, and despite its intimate size and friendly atmosphere, guests don't feel suffocated or imposed upon. Marvelous antiques decorate the rooms; there's also a parlor where guests can compare notes on the day's ski adventures. *10154 High St., at Spring St., 11 mi from resort, Box 2011, Truckee, CA 96160, tel. 530/587–5388 or 888/229–0365. 8 rooms, 6 with bath. Facilities: dining room. AE, D, MC, V. $100–$150, including full breakfast.*

River Ranch Lodge

This marvelous inn sits serenely on a fat curve in the scenic Truckee River, just 3 miles from the Squaw Resort Village. The rustic timbered structure built in the 1950s replaced the original inn built in 1888, which was a fashionable watering hole for train travelers. Updated in 1960, it housed Olympic dignitaries. The comfortable, woodsy, cozy rooms meticulously re-create an Early American pioneer motif, with antiques and hand-crafted period furnishings. There are no fireplaces or hot tubs in the guest quarters, but there's a sweet fireside room and a dramatic lounge and restaurant cantilevered over the rapids of the river. *Rte. 89 and Alpine Meadows Rd., Box 197, Tahoe City, CA 96145, tel.530/583–4264 or 800/535–9900 in CA, fax 530/583–7237. 19 rooms. Facilities: restaurant, lounge. AE, MC, V. $100–$150, including Continental breakfast.*

Sunnyside Resort

This pretty little lakeside mountain lodge is 3 miles south of Tahoe City, on the west shore of Lake Tahoe. The wood-and-rock structure is nestled amid tall pines. All rooms have a view of the lake and rustic, elegant decor, with locally crafted wooden furnishings and bold, textured country-style fabrics. Rooms come in several sizes; some have a fireplace and wet bar, and most can accommodate four people comfortably. Sunnyside is a quiet spot that's good for couples but a little too low-key for families. *1850 W. Lake Blvd., Box 5969, Tahoe City, CA 96145, tel. 530/583–7200 or 800/822–2754, fax 530/583–2551. 23 rooms. Facilities: restaurant, lounge. AE, MC, V. $110–$175.*

Inexpensive

Hostel at Squaw Valley

Bring your own sleeping bag if you stay at this standard old-fashioned dormitory-style hostel, with bunk-style single beds split into male-only and female-only units. It housed Olympic athletes in 1960. Bathrooms (segregated by gender) are shared, but the accommodations are clean and reasonably quiet, even though they're usually filled with singles. The biggest bonus here is the two-minute walk from the lifts. There is a community microwave and refrigerator. *1900 Squaw Valley Rd., Box 6655, Tahoe City, CA 96146, tel. 530/583–7771 or 800/544–4723. 100 beds. $24–$28 per person; cash only.*

Tahoe City Travelodge

On the north shore of Lake Tahoe in Tahoe City, this excellent motel is a cut above many others around the lake. Meticulously maintained, its rooms are in color-coordinated soft pastel tones, with brass fixtures and quilted bedspreads. All rooms are larger than average and have either double or king-size beds, large bathrooms with massage showers and hair dryers, and coffeemakers. There's also a marvelous lake-view deck with a hot tub and a sauna. A good family spot, it has rooms large enough for four and is fairly quiet. *455 N. Lake Blvd., Box 84, Tahoe City, CA 96145, tel. 530/583–3766 or 800/578–7878, fax 530/583–8045. 47 rooms. Facilities: hot tub, sauna. AE, D, DC, MC, V. $75–$96.*

Tahoma Lodge

A quiet little nest of mountain cabins, duplexes, and apartments about 15 miles from Squaw, this is an excellent choice for families or groups. The rustic cabins have wooden furnishings and touches like wainscoting, high-beamed ceilings, oak-panel trim, and a wood stove. With one or two double beds and a small but complete kitchen, the cabins are comfortable, clean, cozy, and romantic. The lodge is a three-minute walk from cross-country skiing trails. *7018 W. Lake Blvd., Box 72, Tahoma, CA 96142, tel. 530/525–7721. 11 units. Facilities: hot tub. MC, V. $60–$260.*

WHERE TO EAT

Restaurants and bars in Squaw are spread across the valley. There are select spots in Tahoe City, Truckee, Incline Village, and Squaw and at a host of small lakeside communities. If you are staying at the resort, several places are noteworthy, but after more than a few days you may want to explore a little farther afield.

On the Mountain

Alexander's

The red-and-white-checked tablecloths and cafélike awnings give a warm, charming ambience to this spot. Alexander's has casual dining, offering chili, burgers, goulash, and sandwiches for lunch. The more expansive evening menu includes pizzas and daily specials such as lemon catfish and chicken Parmesan. At 8,200 feet, the dining room has an awe-inspiring view of Lake Tahoe through the big windows—it's definitely worth the trip. *High Camp Bldg., top of cable car, tel. 530/583–2555. Reservations essential. AE, MC, V.*

Expensive

Christy-Hill

The stark, minimalist decor here enables you to appreciate the stunning view of the peaks across the lake, a good reason in itself to enjoy an early dinner and, if you can, secure a table by the large window. The room is dominated by the river-rock fireplace with wood trim that provides a foil for the whitewashed walls. The Northern California cuisine has Southwestern influences: baked Fanny Bay oysters are served with fresh salsa; a Southwestern chowder (containing clams, mussels, shrimp, and sometimes smoked salmon) has a spicy chili-based broth. Among the meat dishes are corn-fed beef tenderloin sautéed with mushrooms and roasted shallots or elk broiled with green peppers, roasted red bell peppers, and shiitake mushrooms. For dessert, try the crème brûlée. *115 Grove St., Tahoe City, tel. 530/583–8551. MC, V.*

Glissandi

A spectacularly spacious and formal dining room with soaring windows and elegant tuxedoed waitstaff makes this a place to go for a special evening. The Scandinavian decor includes sleek lines, buffed and polished blond wood, and expanses of granite. The contemporary French and Californian menu may include such appetizers as baby bay scallops with shiitake mushrooms and leeks and entrées like roast wild boar with fresh morels and celery root, breast of duck with chipotle sauce, and tenderloin of beef with onion confit and Roquefort cheese. It's creative cooking, beautifully presented in a sophis-

ticated atmosphere. *Resort at Squaw Creek, 400 Squaw Creek Rd., Olympic Valley, tel. 530/583–6621. AE, D, DC, MC, V.*

Graham's of Squaw Valley

This is a pleasant, semiformal dining room with sophisticated rustic decor based on light-color walls, subtle wood trim, formal table settings, and two fireplaces. The mostly Mediterranean menu changes often and offers traditional dishes from Spain, such as seafood paella with saffron rice; from France, cassoulet de Toulouse (white beans, duck confit, lamb and garlic sausages, and tomatoes); and from Italy, *farfalle alla Norma* (sautéed eggplant, olives, hot peppers, garlic, tomato, and fresh basil). Other entrées include sea bass wrapped in parchment paper. *Christy Inn Lodge, 1650 Squaw Valley Rd., Olympic Village, tel. 916/581–0454. MC, V.*

Wolfdale's

Owner-chef Douglas Dale has created a casually elegant atmosphere inside the oldest building in Tahoe City (built on the South Shore in 1889, then barged across the lake to its present site in 1901) with a cross-section of Japanese and American art, smart ceramic plates and bowls on crisp white linen, fresh flowers in hand-thrown vases, and black lacquer chopsticks. A unique appetizer is the tepee of grape leaves stuffed with dilled rice and smoked trout. Maritime entrées may include grilled swordfish with Thai tamarind lobster sauce, salmon with a glaze made from enoki mushrooms, or a fiery Thai stew with shrimp and scallops, snow peas, and shiitake mushrooms. For fowl, the choice may be roast quail with fennel sausage over kale and foie gras risotto. *640 N. Lake Blvd., Tahoe City, tel. 530/583–5700. Reservations essential. MC, V.*

Moderate

Cottonwood

High above the restored railroad town of Truckee is Hilltop, site of the first chairlift in North America and now site of the restaurant. The bar is decked with historic wooden skis, sleds, and skates, along with photos of Truckee's early ski days. In the dining area fine California cuisine is served in the simple, understated elegance of white tablecloths and crystal under high, open-truss ceilings. The menu offers fresh seafood, fowl, and vegetables, grilled and roasted with light sauces: braised free-range rabbit with andouille sausage, firecracker prawns in sweet chili sauce, or a mixed grill of seasonal vegetables with polenta and lime cilantro-butter. *Old Brockway Road, just off Rte. 267, ¼ mi south of downtown Truckee, tel. 530/587–5711. Reservations essential. AE, DC, MC, V.*

Montagna Ristorante

Northern Italian cuisine is the specialty at this restaurant in the Resort at Squaw Creek. The casual decor focuses on the large, open kitchen with its brick ovens and walls and includes beamed ceilings, white walls, and light classical music playing in the background. You can choose from among four varieties of brick-oven pizza (try the pesto and wild mushroom pie), unique pasta dishes such as linguine *di Gamberi* (shrimp and scallops with garlic, parsley, white wine sauce, and lemon butter), and rotisserie specialties including rosemary chicken and herb-marinated lamb loin with wild mushrooms. *400 Squaw Creek Rd., Olympic Valley, tel. 530/583–6300. AE, D, DC, MC, V.*

River Ranch Restaurant

This classic Tahoe resort lodge has two quiet and cozy dining rooms. One overlooks the Truckee River through a wide window, and the other has a large stone fireplace. Both have rustic log walls, sturdy pine tables and chairs, local art, and candlelit place settings. The menu is straightforward American, with a mix of seafood and grill specialties. The grill puts forth citrus-marinated chicken breast and a selection of corn-fed Kansas beef, including pepper steak with a delicious pepper-brandy sauce. Fish entrées include Idaho rainbow trout done with almonds and shiitake mushrooms, and game items include fresh elk loin. *Rte. 89 and Alpine Meadows Rd., Tahoe City, tel. 530/583–4264. AE, MC, V.*

Sunnyside Resort

The deck at Sunnyside is a Tahoe institution for breakfast, lunch, and dinner because of its location on an unusually sunny promontory on the west side of the lake. Inside is the nautically themed Chris Craft dining room. Nibble on deep-fried zucchini and then choose from daily fish, pasta, and steak specials, all served with fisherman's chowder and San Francisco sourdough bread. *1850 W. Lake Blvd., Tahoe City, tel. 530/583–7200. AE, MC, V.*

Inexpensive

Hacienda del Lago

You'll get first-rate Mexican grub with second-rate Mexican decor, but it's a great spot with excellent prices for large portions of burritos, enchiladas, tacos, fajitas, and other standards. There's also a wild happy hour (4–6) with marvelous multiflavored margaritas, drink specials, and free nachos and other Mexican munchies. *760 N. Lake Blvd., upstairs in Boatworks Mall, Tahoe City, tel. 916/583–0358. Reservations not accepted. MC, V.*

Lanza's

When you're ready for that Italian food fix, this is the place to visit. Classic country Italian style is presented—not too fancy, just well priced and well prepared. Pasta is plentiful, including manicotti, cannelloni, lasagna, and fettuccine. Veal comes Parmesan, *piccata*, and Milanese. Also try the calamari, and leave room for the homemade spumoni ice cream. *7739 N. Lake Blvd., next to Safeway, Kings Beach, tel. 916/546– 2434. Reservations not accepted. MC, V.*

Rosie's Café

An institution in the Tahoe area, Rosie's has a charming atmosphere (with bicycles, skis, and snowshoes providing much of the funky decor, as well as deer antlers serving as lamps), après-ski appeal, and good, old-fashioned American food. For entrées, which come with home-baked sourdough bread, soup or salad, and vegetables, you can have Southern-fried chicken with mashed potatoes and gravy, baby-back ribs, fish-and-chips, New York cut steak, stir-fry dishes, or a healthy choice of pastas. It's a cheerful, folksy place with live entertainment on Tuesday night. *571 N. Lake Blvd., Tahoe City, tel. 530/583– 8504. Reservations not accepted. AE, D, DC, MC, V.*

Sweet Potatoes Deli

This bright and lively pick-and-snack deli emporium is a good spot if you don't feel like having a full meal. Its large windows, sparkling white walls, and tile floors are softened by wooden shelves filled with books for browsing or buying. The excellent assortment of deli dishes includes gourmet sandwiches, homemade soups, chili, quiche, and baked goods, as well as pasta salads, cheeses, and meats. For a cup of coffee and some good conversation, there's also an espresso bar, liqueur coffees, yogurts, fresh fruits, and cheeses. You can eat at one of a dozen tables or take out. *400 Squaw Creek Rd., Resort at Squaw complex, base of Squaw Creek chairlift, Olympic Valley, tel. 916/583–6300, ext. 6935. AE, MC, V.*

Best Bets for Breakfast

Firesign

There's almost always a wait, but it's worth it. Pancakes, waffles, and lots of different baked goods are offered, as well as fancier dishes such as eggs Benedict and Cape Cod Benedict (the traditional egg dish served with spinach and smoked salmon). You can eye the dogsled in the rafters while you wait for your morning repast. *1785 W. Lake Blvd., Tahoe City, tel. 916/583– 0871. DC, MC, V.*

Rosie's Café

This is an all-day café, but breakfast is where it really shines, with a lineup of omelets, scrambled egg dishes, muesli, and espresso drinks. Try the *huevos rancheros* or the All-American: two eggs, two slices of bacon, two pancakes, and home fries. *571 N. Lake Blvd., Tahoe City, tel. 916/583–8504. AE, D, DC, MC, V.*

NIGHTLIFE AND ENTERTAINMENT

Après-Ski

Bar One

This classic après-ski bar has a roaring fire and live music and dancing. It's a moving and grooving place, popular with an older crowd that is beyond the hard-belly stage, but the dance floor still rocks. *Olympic House, base of mountain, tel. 530/583–1588. AE, MC, V.*

Plaza Bar

At this sports bar, skiers swap tall tales with colorful local characters while they soak up big-screen TV sports. The cheerful bar is decorated with sporting memorabilia from the 1960 Winter Olympics. You can choose from a tremendous variety of beers, as well as among a repertory of hot, sweet cocktails. *Base village, Squaw Mountain, tel.530/583–1588. AE, MC, V.*

Loud and Lively/Dancing

Crystal Bay Club

The classiest gambling place in Crystal Bay is also the center of most of the action. Locals claim it also has the best food deals of all the casinos. The real attractions are the gaming and the lounge acts. It's full-blown glitz and cash, some occasional headline acts, and in general, a place to have fun watching other people lose money. *Rte. 28, Crystal Bay, NV, tel. 775/831–0512. AE, D, DC, MC, V.*

Elevations

At this spot you can hear live bands nightly, ranging from rock to blues to reggae. The quality and tempo are high, inspiring patrons to dance up a storm. Despite all the action, Humpty's has a neighborhood pub atmosphere, with an affable crowd of twenty- and thirty-somethings. *877 N. Lake Blvd., Tahoe City, tel. 530/583–4867. MC, V.*

Naughty Dawg

At this classic saloon with a neosurf "arf-deco" decor, you'll find one of the best selections of specialty beers in the area. It's a funky place with daily special events and good finger food. Generally an under-30 crowd hangs out here. *255 N. Lake Blvd., Tahoe City, tel. 530/581–3294. AE, D, DC, MC, V.*

More Mellow

Bullwhacker's Pub

This sports bar has multiple TVs, billiards, shuffleboard, and live entertainment, such as an acoustic guitarist or blues bands, six nights a week. The Old West theme adds some coziness; the copper bar counter and light fixtures contrast with dark woodwork. Generally, a thirty-something-plus group makes up the nighttime clientele. *Resort at Squaw Creek, 400 Squaw Creek Rd., Olympic Valley, tel. 530/581–6617. AE, D, DC, MC, V.*

Few regions of America conjure up images of skiing as does Colorado, the Rocky Mountain State, which has traded in its mining heritage for one of outdoor recreation. In many ways it is the epicenter of the American ski experience.

Sliced north to south by the mountains of the Continental Divide, Colorado is a spectacular blend of high peaks, deep canyons, and vast, open plains so visually stunning that former U.S. president Teddy Roosevelt once remarked on looking at it: "The scenery bankrupts the English language." Dominating that scenery are the Rocky Mountains, three times as large in area as the Swiss Alps and home to 1,140 peaks over 10,000 feet, with 54 topping out at more than 14,000 feet.

This monumental barrier to east–west travel forces prevailing westerly winds from the Pacific to rise high up into the stratosphere and then release the moisture as the white gold now mined by more than 28 ski resorts across the state. These range in size and stature from the storied and world-renowned Aspen to the vastness of Vail to the quiet isolation of Steamboat. Regardless of size or stature, all of Colorado's ski resorts share the common bounty of frequent and intense snowfalls and the gateway city of Denver.

Closest to Denver is the Fraser Valley, a narrow slash of land cutting north from the Berthoud Pass (50 miles from Denver) and flanked on the east by the towering Continental Divide and to the west by the rugged Vasquez Ridge. In this valley lies Winter Park, a resort created by recreation-seeking Denverites and considered by many to be their own backyard ski area. Seventy-five miles west of Denver is Summit County, a four-resort (Copper Mountain, Keystone, Arapahoe Basin, and Breckenridge), four-town (Frisco, Silverthorne, Dillon, and Breckenridge) swath of the Arapaho National Forest, where the Ten Mile and Gore ranges clash in a marvelous display of 45 13,000-foot peaks. Just 20 miles farther west is the Vail Valley, a narrow aspen-draped mountain dip that cuts deep into the Gore Range and is home to America's largest single ski resort, Vail, and its neighbor, Beaver Creek.

In central Colorado is the Roaring Fork Valley, sandwiched between the Sawatch Range on the east and the Elk Mountains to the south and west, and Aspen, possibly America's best-known ski resort. This 50-mile-long valley is crowned by more than 500 peaks reaching higher than 12,000 feet, including Mt. Elbert, at 14,400 feet the Continental Divide's highest point.

Southwestern Colorado is home to two more resorts, Crested Butte, in the Elk Mountains, and Telluride, in the San Juan Mountains. Both have endured the boom-and-bust cycle of mining, and now the well-preserved Victorian towns are a comfortable counterpoint to the modern resorts on their outskirts. Finally, northwestern Colorado is where you'll find Steamboat (the resort and the town), in a wide river valley of ranch land and steaming thermal springs.

GETTING TO COLORADO RESORTS

By Plane
Denver International Airport (DIA; tel. 303/342–2000), about 25 miles east of downtown Denver, is served by **American** (tel. 800/433–7300), **America West** (tel. 800/235–9292), **Continental** (tel. 303/925–4350 or 800/525–0280), **Delta** (tel. 800/221– 1212), **Frontier** (tel. 800/432–1359), **Mesa** (tel. 800/637–2247), **Mexicana** (tel. 800/531–7921), **Midwest Express** (tel. 800/452–2022), **Northwest** (tel. 800/225–2525), **TWA** (tel. 800/221–2000), **United** and **United Express** (tel. 800/241–6522), and **US Airways** (tel. 800/428–4322).

Car Rental
Alamo (tel. 800/327–9633), **Avis** (tel. 800/331–2847), **Budget** (tel. 303/527–0700), **Dollar** (tel. 800/800–4000), **Enterprise** (tel. 800/720–7222), **Hertz** (tel. 800/654–3131), **National** (tel. 800/227–7368), **Payless** (tel. 303/342–9444), **Resort** (tel. 303/342–3444), and **Thrifty** (tel. 800/367–2277) have offices at Denver's airport.

By Bus
Greyhound Lines (tel. 303/293–6555 or 800/231–2222) has a station in downtown Denver and offers daily service to most Colorado resorts.

By Train
Amtrak's *California Zephyr* (tel. 800/872–7245) has daily service with sleeping accommodations into Denver from the West Coast and Chicago.

ASPEN MOUNTAIN

Box 1248
Aspen, CO 81612
Tel. 970/925–1220 or
800/525–6200
www.skiaspen.com

STATISTICALLY SPEAKING
Base elevation: 7,945 feet

Summit elevation: 11,212 feet

Vertical drop: 3,267 feet

Skiable terrain: 675 acres

Number of trails: 76

Longest run: 3 miles

Lifts and capacity: 1 gondola,
1 high-speed quad, 2 quads,
1 high-speed double, 3 doubles; 10,775 skiers per hour

Daily lift ticket: $62 (valid also
at Snowmass, Aspen Highlands, and Buttermilk)

Average annual snowfall: 300
inches

Number of skiing days
1997–98: 133

Snowmaking: 210 acres, 31%

Terrain mix: N 0%, I 35%,
E 65%

Snowboarding: no

Cross-country skiing: 80 kilometers of groomed cross-country terrain in Aspen and
Snowmass areas

Aspen sits in the Roaring Fork Valley, a wide, U-shape cut of land created by glacial activity that lies in the heart of central Colorado's 2-million-acre White River National Forest. The valley stretches for nearly 50 miles northwest from the town of Aspen to the community of Glenwood Springs, between the Sawatch Range to the east and the Elk Mountains on the south and west. These strapping glacier-topped mountains created more than 15 million years ago provide the melt that feeds the restless Roaring Fork River, which rushes northeast until it merges near Glenwood Springs with the mighty Colorado River. The valley's original inhabitants, the Ute Indians, were supplanted in the mid-1800s by prospectors and miners who came to reap the region's bounty of lead, zinc, copper, silver, and gold. By 1884 Aspen was a thriving frontier boomtown with more than 3,500 hardy souls; after the railroad was extended west over the Continental Divide, the once-obscure mining town flourished, and by 1892 it had become the third-largest city in the state, behind only Leadville and Ashcroft. Unfortunately, the mining mother lode that had financed the boom also ultimately created the bust when silver was demonetized in 1893 and prices hit rock bottom. Within just 30 days every mine in the area was forced to close.

For the next 40-odd years the once-splendid brick and sandstone buildings lay virtually dormant, and by the early 1920s the population reached its nadir of just 350. In 1937, however, the town was resuscitated when a small ski area and winter sports center opened on Aspen Mountain. Later, during World War II, the illustrious 10th Mountain Division—America's fighting skiers—trained here. Among those storied soldiers of the snow was Friedl Pfeifer, an Austrian-born, naturalized-American U.S. ski instructor who foresaw the skiing mecca that Aspen was to become. In partnership with Chicago industrialist Walter Paepcke, Pfeifer formed the Aspen Skiing Corporation and in 1947 opened the world's longest ski lift on Aspen Mountain.

The evolution from abandoned mining town to thriving ski resort had begun, and in 1950 the staging of the Fédération Internationale du Ski (FIS) World Alpine Championships thrust Aspen into the

USEFUL NUMBERS
Area code: 970

Children's services: Powder
Pandas at Buttermilk, tel.
970/920–0935; Aspen Skiing
Co. provides a list of screened
child-care providers, tel. 970/
925–1220. Aspen Sprouts
(2 to 5 years), tel. 970/920–
1055; Aspen Kids' Club
(8 weeks to 4 years), tel. 970/
925–3136.

Snow phone: tel. 970/925–
1221 or 888/277–3676

Aspen Valley police: tel. 970/
920–5400

Eagle County sheriff: tel. 970/
963–0375

Aspen Valley Hospital: tel.
970/925–1120

Aspen Central Reservations:
tel. 970/925–9000 or 800/
290–1325

Aspen Chamber Resort Association: tel. 970/925–1940

Aspen Visitor Center: tel. 970/
925–5656

Avalanche hot line: tel. 970/
920–1664

Road conditions: tel. 970/
920–5454

Highway conditions: tel. 970/
639–1234

Towing: Al's Towing and
Recovery, tel. 970/920–0428;
Tom's Mobile Assistance, tel.
970/923–6741

FIVE-STAR FAVORITES
Best run for vertical: North
Star

Best run overall: Spar Gulch

Best bar/nightclub: Ajax
Tavern

Best hotel: Hotel Jerome

Best restaurant: Piñons

skiing spotlight. Success begat expansion, and other ski areas opened, including Snowmass Resort (*see* Snowmass, *below*), 12 miles away, and the smaller Buttermilk and Aspen Highlands, 2 miles away. Although Aspen Mountain dominates the town with its rugged presence, Snowmass nestles comfortably into the outskirts.

To its credit, the big banana of American ski resorts has survived with its soul relatively intact and its position in the pantheon of big-time ski resorts mostly unshaken. That's not to say that Aspen has not felt pressure from challengers jockeying for its number-one position: the resorts of the '90s and the new millennium are definitely out to unseat the resort of the century. It won't be easy, though, for to call Aspen merely a ski resort is to call the *Queen Elizabeth II* merely a boat or the Grand Canyon just another hole in the ground. In addition to being a resort, Aspen is so many other things. It is a town rich in history that's laced with style and yet marvelously complete as a community. When you look beyond the soap-opera lifestyle of the glitterati and the media bombardment of the paparazzi, what you find is a diverse and exciting combination of frills and substance.

The entire town of Aspen—which can be explored on foot—is compacted into a square mile between the banks of the Roaring Fork River on one side and Castle Creek on the other. Within a four-block cobblestone pedestrian mall beats the heart of the community: shops, boutiques, restaurants, galleries, and bars housed in perfectly preserved historic buildings.

A car is not necessary here, not only because of Aspen's size but also because this mountain community has one of the most efficient—and free—public transportation systems anywhere. The system is supplemented, in turn, by numerous private shuttles that ferry people from the airport to hotels and from there to either Aspen Mountain or to the Rubey Park Transportation Center, where buses leave for Snowmass Village, Aspen Highlands, and Buttermilk.

The efficient transportation system makes it convenient to stay at a reasonably priced accommodation outside the pricey downtown hub yet still participate in downtown activities. It also makes it easy to socialize and lodge in town but ski the considerably larger and more varied terrain of Snowmass, just 20 minutes away by shuttle.

HOW TO GET THERE

By Plane

Denver International Airport is about 200 miles from Aspen (*see* Getting to Colorado Resorts, *above*). United Express, America West, and Northwest Jet Airlink have daily flights into Aspen's **Sardy Field Airport,** between Aspen and Snowmass. Five major airlines fly daily nonstop from 11 U.S. cities into **Eagle County Regional Airport** (*see* Vail, *below*), 70 miles north and east of Aspen. Daily direct van and limousine service to Aspen is available.
Colorado Mountain Express (tel. 970/949–4227 or 800/525–6353) runs trips from Denver and Vail. **High Mountain Taxi** (tel. 970/925–8294 or 800/528–8294) provides prepaid charter service to and from Denver International Airport for groups of up to seven people ($550).

By Car

Aspen is a four-hour, 200-mile drive from Denver. From DIA follow Peña Boulevard toward Denver for 12 miles to I–70. Take I–70 west for about 3½ hours to CO 82 in Glenwood Springs. Follow CO 82 south for about one hour, passing Snowmass Village and the airport. CO 82 will become Main Street in Aspen.

Aspen Airport is served by **Avis** (tel. 800/331–1212), **Budget** (tel. 800/527–0700), **Hertz** (tel. 800/654–3131), and **Thrifty** (tel. 800/367–2277). Other car-rental companies in Aspen include **Alamo** (tel.

800/327–9633) and **Rocky Mountain Rent-A-Car** (tel. 970/925–2880).

By Bus

Greyhound Lines (tel. 970/945–8501 or 800/231–2222) runs five trips daily from Denver to Glenwood Springs, 40 miles from Aspen. A round-trip ticket costs $51. **Aspen Limousine Service** (tel. 970/925–2400 or 800/222–2112) runs vans from the Glenwood Springs Station to Aspen for $40 round-trip.

By Train

Amtrak's *California Zephyr* (tel. 970/925–9563 in Glenwood Springs or 800/872–7245) makes weekly runs from Denver to Glenwood Springs, 40 miles from Aspen.

GETTING AROUND

High Mountain Taxi (tel. 970/925–8294) provides taxi service around Aspen. There is also free regular shuttle bus service around Aspen and between Aspen and Snowmass, leaving from Aspen's Rubey Park Transportation Center (tel. 970/925–8484).

THE SKIING

Two things initially surprise first-time visitors to Aspen Mountain: the first is its size, just 675 acres—less than one-quarter the acreage of nearby Snowmass; the second is the absence of any novice runs. Those curiosities aside, this is a magnificent, rippling mountain whose peaks thrust high above its namesake town, its steep chutes, mogul-rich pitches, and gladed ridges tucked in the folds of its granite apron.

What you see from the base area is only the tip of this multifaceted mountain, but the hidden treasures are relatively easy to discover. From the top you can reach any of the three main ridges that comprise the mountain's skiing network. To your left as you look down (the west) is Ruthie's Ridge, the site of most of the straight-ahead giant slalom cruising runs; from Ruthie's you can also reach the area known as the Dumps, a series of double-black-diamond gladed chutes. On the far west extreme of Ruthie's is Aztec, site of one of the toughest World Cup downhill courses in the world.

The middle ridge is actually a separate peak called Bell Mountain, and its three sides—Face, Ridge, and Back—offer a series of snow-packed mogul pitches and some outstanding tree skiing. The uppermost part of the mountain, on the eastern fringe, is Gentleman's Ridge, with both the easiest intermediate runs and the tough, mean, and unrelenting far-eastern pitches of Walsh's Gulch.

In between Gentleman's Ridge and Bell Mountain Ridge are Spar and Copper gulches, which funnel skier traffic to the gondola base. Spar has the steepest sides as it cuts a distinct V-shaped groove through the heart of the mountain, but it's also well groomed and begs to be skied fast. Copper is wider and gentler, with a ripple of moguls just smooth and round enough to provide exhilaration without acceleration.

Getting up the mountain is a snap, as the entire town serves as a base area. In the center of town is the Silver Queen gondola, a six-passenger bullet that shoots to the summit in just

15 minutes—how long you'll have to wait for this varies from 5 to 10 minutes, depending on time of year, traffic, and weather. Although this is the fastest way to be transported up the mountain, it's also the most crowded; during weekends and holidays savvy skiers head over to the slower but less busy Lift 1A, a few blocks west of the gondola. Lift 1A begins a two-lift ride that lets you off at either the lower mountain, Ruthie's Ridge and the Dumps, or at the summit runs. The three-leg journey all the way to the top (1A to Ruthie's Lift, then a short run down to the bottom of Ajax Express) takes about 25 minutes.

Aspen Mountain's simple layout and lift system make it easy to reach all sectors. There are no terminally tedious traverses, few flat spots, no endless cat tracks—just an honest, straightforward ski area best characterized by the 3-mile descent down 3,300 vertical feet from the summit to the base area at the bottom of the gondola.

Novices

There are no novice trails on Aspen Mountain. Even the most modest intermediate runs—of which there are precious few—are beyond the capability of beginners and even wannabe intermediates. Beginners and borderline intermediates should head either for Snowmass, with its vast variety of novice and intermediate runs, or better still to Buttermilk's superb novice terrain.

Intermediates

If you can't handle bumps or are unable to link together strong, precise turns on unforgiving terrain, you may be overestimating your ability to handle—and, more important, to enjoy—Aspen Mountain. For the steady, strong intermediate skier, however, Aspen Mountain has a tremendous mix of steep giant-slalom cruising and even steeper bump skiing.

The Silver Queen gondola is the fastest route to the summit, where most of the tamest intermediate runs are found. You can stick to the upper part of the mountain by riding Lift 3, the high-speed quad, which serves the runs to the left (looking down); or Lift 7, which gives access to the runs off Gents Ridge to the right. Keep in mind that this moderate terrain can be the most crowded part of the mountain. From the summit try 1&2 Leaf, a wide, well-groomed trail that's one of the easiest on the mountain. Next to that is Copper Cutoff, which is slightly steeper but still consistently maintained.

Another good, well-groomed cruiser is Dipsy Doodle, which cuts under Lift 3 and winds across to Bonnie's Restaurant. Stay to the right on the upper part of the run if you don't like bumps. Buckhorn is still another good cruiser, although it becomes heavily traveled and as a result develops icy and bare spots. Silver Bell and Silver Dip are a pair of smooth trails that feed you back to the bottom of Lift 3; after skiing on either you can try Blondies, a slightly steeper and shorter run that sometimes develops small moguls. A good combination for a mixture of some steep cruising, a little more wide-open bowl-type skiing, and a few bumps is Buckhorn to Ruthie's Road to North American.

When the crowds start to build on the upper mountain, head for Bell Mountain—the middle peak—which tends to be much less crowded than the runs served by the gondola. If you're heading over from the summit, take 1&2 Leaf, staying to the right of the gondola, then follow one of the traverses that go to either side of Bell. You can also get to Bell Mountain runs from the base area by taking Lift 4, skiing across Little Nell to the bottom of Lift 5, and then cruising down Deer Park.

If you want a little challenge, try the Face of Bell, which is not a single run but a broad area of glade skiing that holds the snow well. It occasionally develops a good crop of moguls that tend to be well rounded and fairly easy to pick through. You can spend several hours exploring the Face, taking different routes through the trees and riding Lifts 3 and 6 for shorter runs or Lift 5 for longer runs. Although the Face is considered an expert area, a strong intermediate can handle most of the terrain—and avoid the rest. It's a good place to head after you've warmed up on some of the more traditional blue runs.

Spar Gulch is a good warm-up run if you start the day on Bell, but as it's the main thoroughfare down the mountain, it gets crowded, especially in the afternoon. You can pick up the tempo on Spar by skiing up and down the Face.

Another good way to avoid the crowds is to start your day on Lift 1A, at the west end of town. This takes you halfway up the western ridge, Aztec, and from there you can ski down to Lift 8, which takes you to the top of the area known as Ruthie's. Ruthie's Run is a fantastic high-speed cruiser that forms part of the World

Cup downhill course. For the full measure of this run, take Ruthie's, which is fairly flat; veer left on Summer Road to the top of Aztec, which is steep but smooth; and then pick up Spring Pitch to Strawpile to 5th Avenue, heading back to the bottom of Lift 1A. Keep in mind that while Ruthie's side of the mountain is less crowded than other areas, it's best to ski it in the morning before the sun turns the snow heavy and the moguls develop.

Don't overlook the lower part of the mountain—to the west side—served by Lift 1A. Magnifico Cutoff/Lower Magnifico is a smooth, groomed cruiser; or try Strawpile, a wide giant-slalom cruiser with good pitch. You can add some zest to Strawpile by cutting right just below Ruthie's restaurant and hammering down the small, well-rounded moguls on Corkscrew.

Experts

In the morning before the snow gets junky, head up Lift 1A (at the west end of town), then shoot up Lift 8 to the area known as the Dumps (from the gondola you can reach the Dumps by skiing down Buckhorn to Ruthie's Run and staying left all the way over to the top of Lift 6). Immediately to the left of Lift 6 is Bear Paw Glade, a steep section with monster moguls and deep snow that will really wake up your knees. When you reach the end of Bear Paw, keep right to reach Lift 6 again. If you stay left, you'll shoot into Spar Gulch for a faster and longer run down to the bottom of Lift 5. Zaugg Dump, Perry's Prowl, and Last Dollar are other bump runs in the Dumps; all tend to have good snow,

fat but well-shaped moguls, and not much skier traffic. These trails are for those who can launch a turn anytime on any bump. All these short, steep bumpers are reached from International, which is a fairly tame, wide boulevard from which most experts cut away as soon as possible. However, if you stick it out past Last Dollar to Silver Queen, you'll be rewarded: this is an outrageous deep-powder power run that begins with a mogul field and then plunges down toward the Elevator Shaft, a precipitous pitch that's one of the steepest on the mountain. From the Elevator you can go down one of two steep, narrow, and mogul-packed runs: either cut right down Niagara over to Lift 5 or go left via Tower Ten Road to Franklin Dump.

In late morning take Lift 5 to the Face of Bell Mountain, where you can dance in the glades; or from the top of Lift 5, follow the Ridge of Bell to Shoulder for the longest ride on Bell Mountain. Just before Tower 19 cut left onto the Shoulder of Bell—a steeper, more heavily moguled run than the Face. The Ridge and the Shoulder usually have the best mogul runs on the mountain, and you'd better be prepared to handle the terrain because everyone in the gondola gets a "bump's-eye" view of your talent, especially when you're on the Ridge. Both the Shoulder and the Ridge feed back down to the bottom of Lift 5, but skier traffic can become heavy at lunchtime and at the end of the day, especially through the Grand Junction area. You can avoid the crowds by keeping right (looking down) through the trees.

If you have a hankering for super-steep and deep trails, head for the

Walsh's Gulch area, on the east side of the mountain. Be warned, though, that this is tough, ungroomed terrain, so don't overestimate your ability. Take the gondola to the summit and ski across 1&2 Leaf to North Star for a good, steep bump run. Take the same route to a trio of runs that drop like elevator shafts down toward the Roaring Fork River. These three runs were opened in 1985, along with a number of unnamed, unpatrolled, and officially unrecommended alternatives. Before that they were the private preserve of the daring. Sadly, during the 1970s three local skiers were killed as they attempted to take on the 500 vertical feet of the most sustained steeps and avalanche-prone runs on Aspen Mountain.

These days active patrolling and steady traffic reduce the avalanche danger, but they're still the sort of runs that can beat you to death with their relentless 35- to 40-degree pitch and primo moguls. The first run you'll encounter is Walsh's, where—unless there was a good dump the night before—the first 100 yards or so is too steep to hold a lot of snow. Going into Walsh's straight over the top can be disastrous, so if there isn't much snow, it's best to cut left by the trees for a few turns and head back to the main chute to Hyrup's. This run merges into Walsh's halfway down, then into Kristi. Both are as mean and unrelenting as Walsh's, with the same penalty for the adrenaline-challenged: whichever route you choose, there's only one way back to the Gent's Ridge chair, and that's via Lud's Lane—a terminally tedious flat (even a bit uphill) that requires a lot of momentum to overcome.

WHERE TO STAY

Accommodations in Aspen range from the laughably expensive to the moderately inexpensive, from ultraluxurious hotels and condos to small lodges, inns, and more modest hotels. Whether you plan to ski at Aspen Mountain or Snowmass (which has its own centralized village), your lodging decision for the most part will be based on price not location. The public transportation system for the mountains is excellent, and both resorts are accessible from almost anywhere in the Roaring Fork Valley. **Aspen Central Reservations** (tel. 800/262–7736) books accommodations. **Affordable Aspen** (tel. 800/243–9466) books reservations for inexpensive bed & breakfasts and smaller lodges throughout Aspen and the Roaring Fork Valley.

Expensive

Hotel Jerome

The Jerome is everything a great ski hotel should be: steeped in tradition, ideally situated between the town and the mountain, and luxurious to the point of decadence. It opened in sumptuous style in 1889 and has been the physical and social heart of Aspen ever since. Victorian grandeur oozes from a dazzling array of vintage furnishings, crystal chandeliers, intricate woodwork, and gold-laced floor tiling. All rooms are large, with high ceilings and such ultraluxurious touches as oversize beds, antique armoires and chests, and huge bathtubs. *330 E. Main St., 81611, tel. 970/920–1000 or 800/331–7213. 93 rooms, 16 suites. Facilities: 2 restaurants, bar, lounge, hot tubs, heated outdoor pool, health club, 24-hr desk* service, 24-hr room service, shuttle, ski valet, ski storage, ski shop, laundry. AE, DC, MC, V. $160–$1,300.

Little Nell Hotel

An Aspen institution, Little Nell scores high on the pampering scale. This hotel offers European elegance with its open, airy spaces, stone walls, soft earth tones, hanging tapestries, Belgian wool carpets, and large, over-stuffed down couches around the massive lobby fireplace. The luxurious rooms have a fireplace, one king-size or two queen-size beds with down comforters, a plush down couch and chair, and a large marble bathroom. Just 17 steps from the Silver Queen gondola, the Little Nell is technically the only ski-in/ski-out accommodation in Aspen. *675 E. Durant Ave., 81611, tel. 970/920–4600 or 888/ 343–6355, fax 970/920–4670. 77 rooms, 15 suites. Facilities: 2 restaurants, bar, lounge, hot tubs, heated outdoor pool, health club, spa facilities, 24-hr desk service, 24-hr room service, shuttle service, ski valet, ski storage, laundry. AE, D, DC, MC, V. $425–$4,000.*

The Residence

For exclusivity, luxury, and charm all in one tiny money-is-no-object package, this is the place. In the historic Aspen Block Building in the center of Aspen, the hotel contains just seven individually designed one- and two-bedroom apartments. The apartments have French and English antiques, Persian rugs, crystal chandeliers, and fireplaces. Each also has a fully equipped kitchen and dining room stocked with crystal, china, and silver. *305 S. Galena St., 81611, tel. 970/*

920–6532, fax 970/925–1125. 5 apartments. Facilities: concierge, health club and spa privileges. AE, DC, MC, V. $550–$2,250.

St. Regis Aspen

At the foot of Aspen Mountain, just a block and a half from the gondola and stretching across almost an entire block of downtown, this striking, massive château comes complete with turrets and pitched arches. Customized furnishings, original art, plush carpets, and polished stone and marble decorate the public spaces inside; details such as king-size beds, oversize bathrooms, and St. Regis mainstay items such as terry-cloth robes, down comforters, humidifiers, and deluxe toiletries make the guest rooms unforgettable. *315 E. Dean St., 81611, tel. 970/920–3434 or 800/ 241–3333, fax 970/920–7353. 231 rooms, 26 suites. Facilities: Restaurant, bar, lounge, hot tubs, outdoor pool, health club, ski shop, spa facilities, beauty salon, 24-hr desk service, 24-hr room service, ski valet, ski storage, laundry. AE, D, DC, MC, V. $339–$4,000.*

Sardy House

This 1892 Victorian treasure was one of the country's first homes to be built with indoor plumbing, central heating, and electricity. Guest rooms are elegantly decorated with cherry-wood furnishings, Laura Ashley comforters, custom-print wallpaper, oversize beds, and, in all but two rooms, whirlpool baths. Breakfast is served either in your room or in the exquisite dining room. *128 E. Main St., 81611, tel. 970/920–2525 or 800/321–3457, fax 970/920–4478. 14 rooms, 6 suites.*

Facilities: restaurant, bar, parlor, hot tub, heated outdoor pool, ski valet, ski storage. AE, DC, MC, V. $265–$750.

Moderate

Boomerang Lodge
This comfortable, functional property has a wide range of accommodations, from standard hotel rooms to smartly appointed studios and deluxe rooms to three-bedroom apartments. There's even a log cabin. The nicest lodgings are the deluxe units, decorated in earth tones with a Southwestern flair, each with a balcony, an enormous marble bath, a fireplace, and a wet bar. The staff is most hospitable. *500 W. Hopkins Ave., 81611, tel. 970/925–3416 or 800/992–8852, fax 970/925–3314. 34 rooms. Facilities: pool, hot tub, sauna, ski storage, daily maid service, laundry. AE, D, DC, MC, V. $119–$532, including Continental breakfast.*

The Gant
This condominium complex at the base of the mountain on 5 acres of prime downtown Aspen real estate is a great find for families or groups who want a little luxury, more than the standard amount of space, and proximity to the action without breaking the bank. The Gant is not cheap, but it's reasonable compared to other properties that provide the same services. The one- to four-bedroom units are comfortably and individually furnished by independent owners, and although decor varies wildly from rental to rental, amenities are consistent: each has a fireplace, a full kitchen, multiple bathrooms, and a balcony. When reserving a room, ask for one of the upper-floor units, as noise travels between lower-floor

rooms at night. *610 West End St., 81611, tel. 970/925–5000 or 800/345–1471, fax 970/925–6891. 141 units. Facilities: 2 outdoor pools, 3 Jacuzzis, 2 saunas, shuttle service, laundry. AE, D, DC, MC, V. $175–$835.*

Hotel Aspen
Considering its great location on Main Street, just a few minutes from the mall and the mountain, this hotel is a good find. The modern exterior is opened up with huge windows to take full advantage of the view; inside reveals a Southwestern influence. Most rooms have a balcony or terrace and are comfortable, if not luxurious. Four guest rooms have hot tubs. *110 W. Main St., 81611, tel. 970/925–3441 or 800/527–7369, fax 970/920–1379. 45 rooms. Facilities: heated outdoor pool, 2 hot tubs, 24-hr desk service, ski storage. AE, D, DC, MC, V. $99–$329, including Continental breakfast and après-ski buffet.*

Limelite Lodge
In the early '50s this Aspen institution was a nightclub, but in 1958 it was converted to an inn by its present owners. Today it is a good value, particularly because of its prime location, just two blocks from the mall and three blocks from Lift 1A on Aspen Mountain. The guest rooms are furnished with brass or cherry-wood beds and wooden furniture. All are accessible from the outside, motel style, which makes the lodge convenient for families. *228 E. Cooper St., 81611, tel. 970/925–3025 or 800/433–0832, fax 970/925–5120. 63 rooms. Facilities: lounge, 2 outdoor pools, sauna, 2 outdoor whirlpools, 24-*

hr desk service, ski storage, laundry. *AE, D, DC, MC, V. $79–$200, including Continental breakfast.*

Molly Gibson Lodge
Rooms in this funky, laid-back lodge six blocks from the mountain may have Jacuzzis, fireplaces, or both. There are also six two-bedroom suites with full kitchens. The lodge's romantic atmosphere is suitable for couples, though families can make good use of the suites. *101 W. Main St., 81611, tel. 970/925–3434 or 800/356–6559, fax 970/925–2582. 44 rooms, 6 suites. Facilities: bar, 2 outdoor Jacuzzis, outdoor pool, shuttle service, ski storage. AE, D, DC, MC, V. $89–$369, including Continental breakfast.*

Inexpensive

Mountain Chalet
Since 1954 the same couple has owned and operated this property, providing clean, comfortable, and affordable accommodations in the heart of Aspen. The two-bedroom units have simple decor, basic furnishings, and small bathrooms. The chalet's folksy, friendly atmosphere overcomes the absence of designer trappings. Two or three bunk rooms that sleep four in each are available, as well as four apartments with full kitchens that accommodate six. The chalet is a block from the Silver Queen gondola. *333 E. Durant Ave., 81611, tel. 970/925–7797 or 800/ 321–7813, fax 970/925–7811. 47 rooms, 4 units. Facilities: hot tub, outdoor pool, health club, spa facilities, ski storage, laundry, game room, parking garage. D, DC, MC, V. $80–$360, including full breakfast.*

WHERE TO EAT

As you might expect, there's no shortage of restaurants in Aspen. There's also no shortage of extravagance, which translates into an exorbitant dinner bill at the end of the evening. Fortunately, though, moderately and inexpensively priced eateries abound as well.

On the Mountain

Ruthie's
There are many fine restaurants in Aspen, but none offers Ruthie's exceptional view of the town. At the only on-mountain restaurant with table service, standard Italian fare is spruced up with daily specials; try the penne with fresh chopped tomatoes or the veal chop with roast potatoes. There's also cafeteria service; enjoy the wraparound dining deck when weather allows. *Top of Lift 1A, tel. 970/920–0728. AE, MC, V.*

Sundeck
Friends meet here for lunch because it's easy to reach regardless of which side of the mountain you're skiing on. The Sundeck's innovative cuisine includes an organic salad topped with blackened salmon, homemade chilis and soups, and select daily grill specials. On a chilly day, the Sundeck, with its fireplace, is a great place to warm up. *Top of Silver Queen gondola, tel. 970/920–6335. AE, MC, V.*

Expensive

Ajax Tavern
The brains behind two of Napa Valley's finest eateries have created this bright, pleasant restaurant in the Little Nell Hotel (*see* Where to Stay, *above*), with its mahogany paneling,

diamond-patterned floors, leather banquettes, open kitchen, and an eager, unpretentious waitstaff. Chef Tobias Lawry's creative, healthful dishes, such as pork tenderloin with apple butter risotto, prosciutto, and basil, take advantage of seasonal produce whenever possible. The wine list, showcasing Napa's best, is almost matched by the fine selection of microbrews. *685 E. Durant Ave., tel. 970/920–9333. Reservations essential. AE, D, DC, MC, V.*

Century Room

Everything about the Hotel Jerome (*see* Where to Stay, *above*) is exquisite, and dinner in the Century Room is no exception. With its high, vaulted ceilings, massive stone-and-marble fireplace, designer wall coverings, and comfortable wingback chairs, it is at once both impressive and intimate. The menu mixes familiar items with innovative twists: the lacquered ahi on stir-fried baby bok choy with a gingery, garlicky butter sauce; or salmon crusted with mustard and served with basmati rice and saffron caper sauce. Another excellent choice is the venison chops, served with parsnip pancakes, roasted winter vegetables, and huckleberry sauce. To finish off a fine meal, indulge in the chocolate-chunk crème brûlée with raspberry compote. *Hotel Jerome, 330 E. Main St., tel. 970/920–1000. Reservations essential. AE, DC, MC, V.*

L'Hostaria

This Northern Italian restaurant is the brainchild of Dante Medri. He and his wife, Cristina, brought over all the furniture and fixtures from Italy to create a sophisticated yet rustic look, with an open-beamed farmhouse ceiling, sleek blond-wood chairs, contemporary art, and a floor-to-ceiling glass wine cooler in the center of the room. The menu relies on simple, subtle flavors in specialties such as goat cheese flan on mixed greens, gnocchi with duck ragout, risotto with veal sauce, and grilled veal filet mignon wrapped in bacon with fava beans and sweet baby corn. *620 E. Hyman Ave., tel. 970/925–9022. AE, MC, V.*

Matsuhisa

Renowned in New York, Los Angeles, London, and Tokyo, Matsuhisa brings its nouveau-Japanese cuisine to Aspen. The result: raves from locals and visitors alike. Mirrors hung about the downstairs dining area give a deceptive impression of space. Among the specialties are lobster with wasabi pepper, king crab claw tempura, or baby abalone with a light garlic sauce. While heavy on seafood, the menu also includes chicken and beef dishes, salads, and a variety of sashimi selections. *303 E. Main St., tel. 970/544–6628. Reservations essential. AE, MC, V.*

Piñons

Piñons adheres to an understated image, with Southwestern ranch-style decor including leather-wrapped railings, a teal green ceiling, and upholstered walls. The American-style menu scores high on creativity: For an appetizer, try the lobster strudel or pan-seared Canadian scallops with roasted vegetables. As entrées go, the sesame-crusted ahi is sensuously superb, and the Parmesan-crusted loin of veal is sensational. Still, simplicity rules, especially with side dishes such as pecan wild rice or the roasted garlic mashers. *105 S. Mill St., tel. 970/920–2021. Reservations essential. AE, MC, V.*

Renaissance
This small, understated, but elegant French restaurant has clearly scaled the culinary peak. The entrance is unobtrusive, and its interior matches, with a subdued minimalist style that makes use of soft colors and lighting and combines rough granite and smooth pastel silks draped from the ceiling. Owner/master chef Charles Dale keeps the 50-seat operation intimate so that each dish can be prepared with personal touches and served with the occasional table-side chat. The menu is French modern—succulently light dishes that rely on fresh herbs, complex marinades, and international spices. Notable specialties include the hot date-marinated rack of lamb, seared foie gras with carmelized pears, and crisp chilean sea bass with artichokes and shiitake mushrooms. Upstairs, the R Bistro offers a taste of the kitchen's splendors at down-to-earth prices. *304 E. Hopkins Ave., tel. 970/925–2402. Reservations essential. AE, D, DC, MC, V.*

Syzygy
The tongue-twisting name of this restaurant means "the alignment of three or more heavenly bodies within the solar system to form a nearly straight line." Well, there's nothing straight about Syzygy's eclectic menu. The food is crisply flavored and sensuously textured, floating from French to Asian to Southwestern influences without skipping a beat. Among the unusual entrées are horseradish-scented salmon roulade with vegetables and couscous; pistachio veal schnitzel with red beet risotto; and grilled pheasant with roasted chestnuts, rice, and huckleberry sauce. *520 E. Hyman Ave., tel. 970/925–3700. Reservations essential. AE, D, DC, MC, V.*

Moderate

Cache Cache
Chef Mike Barry is a practitioner of cuisine minceur—no butter or cream is used in his preparations. But the sunny flavors of Provence explode on the palate thanks to the master's savvy use of garlic, tomato, eggplant, fennel, and rosemary. The lamb loin sandwiched between crisp potato galettes (pancakes) on a bed of spinach and ratatouille is sublime; salads and rotisserie items are sensational. *205 S. Mill St., tel. 970/925–3835. AE, MC, V.*

Campo de Fiori
Authentic Tuscan and Venetian cuisine served in a warm atmostphere is the draw here. Wall-climbing vines, hand-painted murals on the walls, and small, crowded tables bubbling with conversation conspire to give the restaurant the distinctive ambience of an Italian trattoria. In addition to fresh seasonal entrées and fresh handmade pasta dishes, the restaurant has a broad selection of lamb and beef, fresh fish, and a delightful marinated seafood antipasto. *205 S. Mill St., 970/920–7717. AE, MC, V. Reservations essential.*

Takah Sushi
This is the oldest and smallest of the three sushi restaurants in Aspen; if

you want to sit at the 16-seat sushi bar, you'll have to get here either very early or very late in the evening because it fills up nightly. The excellent Japanese fare offered in the 60-seat dining room includes Chilean sea bass, Chinese duck, Japanese teriyaki and tempura, and, of course, sushi. *420 E. Hyman Ave., tel. 970/925–8588. AE, D, DC, MC, V. Reservations essential.*

Inexpensive

Boogie's Diner
This cheerful spot filled with diner memorabilia and an outrageous waitstaff resounds with rock-and-roll faves from the '50s and '60s. The menu has true diner range—from vegetarian specialties to grilled cheese and half-pound burgers (including turkey). Other items are excellent milk shakes, a monster chef salad, meat loaf and mashed potatoes, and a hot turkey sandwich. *534 E. Cooper Ave., tel. 970/925–6610. AE, MC, V.*

Flying Dog Brew Pub and Grille
Cheap and cheery, Aspen's only brew pub has a good selection of outstanding beers that you can try one at a time or as a four-glass sampler. A substantial selection of pub grub is available, too, from ribs to sandwiches to burgers and other assorted finger foods. *424 E. Cooper Ave., tel. 970/925–7464. AE, MC, V.*

La Cocina
For good inexpensive eats, follow the locals, and they'll lead you to this small Mexican restaurant, which they've been frequenting for more than 20 years. Almost every night the house is packed full. If the wait is too long, you'll likely cop a complimentary salsa dip or margarita for your trouble. *308 E. Hopkins Ave., tel. 970/925–9714. No credit cards.*

Red Onion
This lively century-old saloon may have the best burgers in town, in addition to comfort food ranging from meat loaf to gigantic sandwiches, wings, ribs, and chicken. There's also a Mexican menu, with a lineup of tacos, burritos, and enchiladas. *420 E. Cooper St., tel. 970/925–9043. MC, V.*

Best Bets for Breakfast

Main Street Bakery & Café
Perfectly brewed coffee and hot breakfast buns and pastries are served at this café along with a full breakfast menu including eggs and homemade granola. During late season when the sun is out, head out back to the deck for the mountain views. As locals will attest, this is also a good spot for lunch and dinner. *201 E. Main St., tel. 970/925–6446. AE, D, MC, V.*

Poppycocks
Just the place for the healthy breakfast crowd, Poppycocks serves up a variety of whole-grain and fruit-topped pancakes, waffles, granola-oatmeal cereal, crepes, and omelets. But it's the fruit smoothies that attract the oohs and aahs of the locals who pack the place before heading off to the lifts, which are only a block from the tiny restaurant. *609 E. Cooper St., tel. 970/925–1245. MC, V.*

Wienerstube
The Wienerstube (literally, a large Vienese living room) has been a favorite breakfast and lunch spot for decades. Locals meet around the large *Stammtisch* (communal table)

on a daily basis, and you're welcome to pull up a chair and eavesdrop on the local gossip. Comfortably seated, you can enjoy fresh cappuccino and Viennese pastry, or partake of the very good American-style breakfast menu. *633 E. Hyman, tel. 970/925–3357.*

NIGHTLIFE AND ENTERTAINMENT
Après-Ski
Ajax Tavern
At the bottom of Aspen Mountain, adjacent to the gondola, it offers bigger-than-life views of the mountain scene and golden rays from the setting sun. By 4 PM it's standing room only. Of course, no one wants to sit when the live band starts to play. *Little Nell Hotel, 685 E. Durant Ave., tel. 970/920–9333. AE, D, DC, MC, V.*

The Tippler
There's another wild deck scene going on here, just a stone's throw from the Ajax. This one attracts 35- to 45-year-olds looking to party. Music, mayhem, and mid-life crises are all on one packed deck. *535 E. Dean St., west of gondola, tel. 970/925– 4977. AE, MC, V.*

Loud and Lively/Dancing
Double Diamond
Thirty-somethings who act like twenty-somethings come here for high-energy cruising and dancing to either live entertainment or a DJ. *450 S. Galena St., tel. 970/920–6905. AE, MC, V.*

J Bar
This is the unofficial site of Hunter Thompson's mayoral campaign and the place where hard-drinking philosophers gather to spread their wisdom. Locals used to take up permanent residence here, but now most have moved on, making way for tourists. *Hotel Jerome, 330 E. Main St., tel. 970/920–1000. AE, DC, MC, V.*

Woody Creek Tavern
A visit to Aspen isn't complete without the pilgrimage out of town to Woody's. By its own admission this bar "has no redeeming features." Maybe so, but Woody's is a great hangout, with a grungy atmosphere, assorted bar games, and notable visitors, such as Don Johnson and Hunter Thompson, who come because it's just like Aspen was 30 years ago. *0002 Woody Creek Plaza; 6 mi north of town on Rte. 82, make first right; tel. 970/923–4585. No credit cards.*

More Mellow
The Bar
The Bar offers live jazz and dancing nightly in a sophisticated but comfortable setting with a huge central fireplace and original Western artwork. *St. Regis, 315 E. Dean St., tel. 970/920–3300. AE, DC, MC, V.*

Italian Caviar
Kick back and relax in overstuffed chairs and couches in front of the requisite crackling fire. There's live piano music nightly. *535 E. Dean St., tel. 970/925–3151. AE, MC, V.*

BEAVER CREEK SKI RESORT

BEAVER CREEK
SKI RESORT

Box 915
Avon, CO 81620
Tel. 970/949–5750 or
800/525–2257
www.snow.com

STATISTICALLY SPEAKING

Base elevation: 7,400 feet

Summit elevation: 11,440 feet

Vertical drop: 4,040 feet

Skiable terrain: 1,625 acres

Number of trails: 146

Longest run: 3.5 miles (Piece O'Cake)

Lifts and capacity: 6 high-speed quads, 3 triples, 4 doubles, 1 surface lift; 24,739 skiers per hour

Daily lift ticket: $59

Average annual snowfall: 331 inches

Number of skiing days 1997–98: 134

Snowmaking: 550 acres, 34%

Terrain mix: N 34%, I 39%, E 27%

Snowboarding: yes

Nordic ski trails: 37 kilometers

Beaver Creek, sister resort to Vail, is 10 miles down the valley, built into a plateau just above the small town of Avon. This ultraluxurious enclave for those who like to be pampered is a distinct contrast to the vastness of Vail, but that's the way its creators (Vail Resorts Inc.) wanted it: a resort experience that swaddles you in luxury and self-indulgence with everything from Ralph Lauren furnishings to slope valets who help you in and out of your skis; it's a resort for guests who want to go that extra step in convenience and luxury.

Created by big money, designed with computers, and crafted by environmentalists, it is an elegant, self-contained pedestrian-oriented village where service is the guiding philosophy. It's quieter than Vail, more geared toward families with comfortable elegance in mind and the pocketbook with which to indulge their whims. Yet at the same time, you can still get a taste of Vail—a shuttle bus connects the two resorts. If you spend a week at Beaver Creek, you would be remiss in not spending at least a day sampling the outstanding bowls of Vail or indulging in the more uptown nightlife and dining that the larger resort provides. Likewise, many's the day when savvy Vail locals, noting the peak-period crowds in town, head for Beaver Creek, where you can always count on shorter lift lines. (Multiday lift tickets at both resorts are interchangeable and are also honored at Keystone and Breckenridge.)

The village, which sits in terraced layers on either side of a small, scenic, and secluded valley, has won numerous awards for its architecture and design, eschewing the Tyrol styling of Vail for a more contemporary modern American feel, with lots of granite walls, slate roofs, sturdy timbers, and natural colors. The main village square, right at the bottom of the Centennial Express chair, is two levels of cobblestone walkways linking large hotels and condos, small lodges, stores, restaurants and bars, and other assorted elements of a chic alpine village. The Market Square pedestrian plaza adds even more shops and restaurants, an ice-skating rink, and Beaver Creek's Vilar Center for the Arts (tel. 970/845–8497), which is home to numerous cultural events throughout the season, from ballet to blues to Broadway shows. The square also has three alpine skier escalators—the height of skier luxury. Above and below the village center are the rest of the accommodation clusters—condos, town houses, private villas—the exposed timber and stone architecture nestled among trees and the natural contours of the land, their decidedly upscale interior decor rich with museum-quality collectibles, designer fixtures, and luxury touches that range from heated towel racks to handmade Persian carpets.

You enter Beaver Creek through security gates on the outskirts of Avon, a mile down the road, and once inside, you feel like you're in a private club. Bellpersons, doorpersons, and just about any other persons who can lift, tote, carry, or generally do your bidding are at your disposal. There are more subtle touches such as full-time fire tenders who maintain outdoor fire pits in the village square, drivers of Suburbans who chauffeur you around, bartenders who remember your name and how you like your Manhattan, and hosts who serve cookies and hot beverages in the morning lift lines. This is a resort for those who want service and more service. It's also a secluded retreat that offers direct access to the slopes from more than 40% of the accommodations. In sum, Beaver Creek is a resort that is seldom crowded, where lift lines are rare, and where everything is done with the skier's comfort and convenience in mind.

HOW TO GET THERE

By Plane

Beaver Creek is about 2½ hours by car from **Denver International Airport.** Vail's **Eagle County Airport** is 25 miles west of Beaver Creek, and America West has daily direct flights from Phoenix. American has direct flights from Atlanta, Chicago, Dallas, Miami, Newark, New York's La Guardia Airport, and San Francisco. Continental has daily flights from Houston and one weekly from Newark; Delta flies daily from Atlanta; Northwest has nonstops from Detroit (daily) and Minneapolis (Sat.). United flies daily nonstops from Los Angeles, Chicago, and weekly from New York/La Guardia. United Express offers at least six daily connecting flights to Vail-Eagle County from DIA.

By Car

From Denver International Airport take I–70 west 110 miles to Beaver Creek. Take Exit 167 for Avon and Beaver Creek. A word of caution: I–70 is one of the most heavily patrolled stretches of highway in the country, and it's prone to dangerous ice and snow accumulation.

By Bus

From DIA, **Colorado Mountain Express** (tel. 970/949–4227 or 800/525–6353) offers regularly scheduled nonstop shuttle service. The cost is $56 per person; children 12 and under ride half-price. Reservations are suggested.

THE SKIING

The skiing at Beaver Creek is precisely laid out on a semicircular ridge and the double dome peaks of Grouse Mountain, with the new lower-elevation areas of Bachelor Gulch and Arrowhead, to the west of the main village, reserved strictly for novices and intermediates. To the east of the main village is the higher of the two peaks (11,440 feet), where there's a marvelous high-altitude novice area. Below that, off a saddle that yields a midmountain day area, is an entire face of blue runs, intersected by a snaking green run that brings novices safely down from the upper green runs.

Grouse Mountain's second peak (10,688 feet) is where the toughest runs are found, but again they are intersected by a long, snaking blue run. Farther still to the west, where the western ridge begins to drop in elevation, is a small below-tree-line intermediate bowl area and a section of mainstream blue runs, as well as one of the most innovative features anywhere: a park set aside strictly for cross-country skiers and snowshoers.

The well-designed layout includes an excellent lift system that starts with three lifts from the village. The Centennial Express goes to mid-mountain at the Spruce Saddle day area; from there you can take either the Birds of Prey Express lift to the novice area or ski down to the Grouse Mountain Express lift or the Westfall lift, both of which serve black and double-black-diamond runs. The Strawberry Park Express goes from the village up the west ridge, where the moderate blue runs are good early morning warm-ups. From the top of the Strawberry Park chair you can also ski down the Larkspur Bowl to the bottom of Grouse Mountain. This lift also serves McCoy Park, the cross-country and snowshoeing center. The Elkhorn lift takes you over to Bachelor Gulch and Arrowhead. It's easy to move from one area to another, even for skiers of different abilities. One of the features that designers and environmentalists have considered when awarding the resort laurels for slope and trail design is that the trails have been carved from the heavily treed flanks of the mountain, not gouged out in wide swaths. The narrower, more natural cut of the trails at Beaver Creek may be a product of modern design, but they are also retro—a return to the more interesting twists and turns of trails cut around trees, not through them. Such trails have been shunned by most new resorts in favor of sweeping boulevards that can cater to the hordes delivered by quad chairs.

This is a well-groomed mountain, with virtually all trails except those in the Birds of Prey and Larkspur Bowl areas manicured daily by a fleet of state-of-the-art snow cats, all part of the pampering process for the well-heeled guests and part of the reason Beaver Creek is regarded as an intermediate's resort—a place to cruise and look good (despite the steeps of Birds of Prey).

Novices

Most mountains are designed with beginner trails on the mid- and lower mountain areas, but Beaver Creek's layout encourages novices to head to the top on the Centennial Express lift to Spruce Saddle at mid-mountain and then take a quick scoot across to the Birds of Prey Express lift, which goes to the eastern summit. You can ski the runs under the lift—Sheephorn, Centennial, and Flat Tops—or head to the right side (looking down the mountain) of the ridge and try some turns on Red Buffalo, Booth Gardens, and Powell. This excellent novice area gets the early morning sun. Its well-laid-out trails provide steady pitch as well as terrain variety. Booth Gardens and Powell are wide smoothies, with a series of rolls and stands of trees; West Buffalo and Flat Tops are narrower and carve more turns as they snake left and right around the ridge lines.

The Drink of Water lift, which can be reached from the bottom of the above-mentioned trails by way of Cinch, will take you back up to the top. When skiing in this area, however, make sure you don't turn off downhill from the long, winding Cinch run because you'll find yourself in black-diamond territory. For a really long run, zigzag along Cinch to the bottom of Centennial lift. Cinch is a bit of a snaking traverse, but it gives you an easy way down to the village, and along the way you can check out some of the blue trails that run down the front face of the lower mountain. You can also go from Cinch to Dally, another long connector trail that takes you over to the Red Tail Camp day area (a good place for novices and intermediates to meet up with experts who have been skiing Birds of Prey), where you can either try some of the blue runs in the Larkspur Bowl area or carry on (by way of Dally) down to the base of the Strawberry Park Express and its moderate blue terrain on the west ridge.

Intermediates

Larkspur Bowl is a good place to start the day; you reach it either by taking the Centennial Express (to Spruce Saddle) and then skiing Red Tail to the Larkspur lift, which you ride up, or by taking the Strawberry Park Express to the top. From Larkspur Bowl you have a choice of some intermediate skiing down the middle—on Larkspur, Bluebell, or Paintbrush—or some steeper stuff down either side. Lupine and Loco (on the right side of the bowl) develop substantial moguls; and Yarrow, to the left, is seldom groomed and is best skied on a day following a fresh snowfall so you can make the most of the bowl's free-form shape and pitch before funneling down through the lower marked trails. This is a good intermediate area that gives strong intermediates a chance to step up to those steeper, although short, black pitches without committing to the Birds of Prey. Directly under the Strawberry Park Express are Pitchfork and Stacker, a pair of high-end blue runs with some tough steep sections. On the eastern side, take the Centennial and Birds of Prey Express lifts to the summit for excellent cruising, specifically down the Latigo, Gold Dust, and Gold Rush trails. Latigo is a wonderful twisting high-speed cruiser with some tight turns and hidden drops. Gold Dust tends to run to bumps down the right side before smoothing out through the lower Gold Rush section. The Centennial Trail, which begins at the summit as a green run, is a long top-to-bottom cruiser that turns blue shortly after its junction with Cinch. Another option from Centennial is Red Tail, which veers left under the Birds of Prey lift and feeds into the base of the Grouse Mountain Express. Ride the Grouse Mountain Express to the top and come down the steep but wide high-speed cruiser called Raven Ridge. If you're feeling particularly daring, consider trying Ptarmigan or the black-diamond section of Raven Ridge—both are short, steep chutes that will give you a little adrenaline rush.

Another option is to take the Elkhorn lift up and follow Maverick and Sawbuck to the base of the new Bachelor Gulch area. You have several blue options off this lift, or you can take the Primrose catwalk to the top of the Arrowbahn Express lift at Arrowhead. This is a prime intermediate skiing area, and the lower elevation means it can be up to 10 degrees warmer—a boon on cold days. Just remember to start heading back before 3:30 PM if you don't want to end up at the Arrowhead base area at the end of the day. There is no public transportation back from Bachelor Gulch.

Experts

The Birds of Prey area, accessible from either the Westfall chair or the Birds of Prey Express lift via Centennial Express, is your domain. From the summit, cut down the western flank on either Peregrine, Goshawk, or Golden Eagle. All three trails are designated as double black diamonds, and you can count on their being packed with moguls. Golden Eagle is the toughest of the three and also the hardest to find. Look for the starting point just to the left of the top of the Westfall lift. All three of these chutes will spit you out at the bottom of the Grouse Mountain Express, which you can ride to the top for a crack at some more steep stuff.

Screech Owl, to the left as you get off the lift, starts out steep and moguled but becomes intermediate about halfway down. Turn right off the lift for a choice of Bald Eagle, Falcon Peak, or Osprey. These are all double-black-diamond runs, and most of the time they're covered with massive moguls. If you get your fill of the tough stuff halfway down, bail out by taking Camp Robber Road under the chair and picking up the slightly tamer Ruffed Grouse. For a real challenge, head to the Royal Elk Glades, off Grouse Mountain. This is rugged, exposed off-piste terrain, so be sure you're up for it.

SNOWBOARDING

For snowboarders, Beaver Creek's tree-lined slopes are full of natural glades and gullies to play in. A snowboarder's trail map indicates where to go for the best rides, such as underneath the Centennial Express lift. About midway down the lift line, just to the left of Centennial trail, is Moonshine, site of the experts-only Tag Heuer half-pipe and terrain park. If you're not yet adept at half-pipe riding, you can perfect your moves in Upper Sheephorn Park, just under the Birds of Prey Express lift. It's a **novice-to-intermediate** terrain-park run that has hits, jumps, spines, and slides specifically designed to challenge snowboarders. For wide-open carving and cruising, **intermediate** and **expert** riders can head to Bachelor Gulch (from the base, take the Settler's Way lift; follow the Maverick trail to the Bachelor Gulch Express). Nearly every trail in this groomed intermediate area screams "Carve Me!" **Experts** can head to Grouse Mountain and the double-black expert trails Screech Owl, Bald Eagle, and the Royal Elk Glades. For powder stashes, take the Centennial Express to the Rose Bowl lift via the Stone Creek Meadows trail. Many of the runs in here—Ripsaw, Spider, and Cataract, hold onto the snow and are the best places to start the day after a fresh snow, as the grooming machines tend to stay away from this out-of-the-way expert area.

OTHER SNOW SPORTS

One of the most enjoyable and accessible diversions is **ice-skating** at the lovely Black Family Ice Rink, in the center of Beaver Creek Village. The rink is open from 10 AM to 9 PM, and skates may be rented at a kiosk on the rink's north end. For a pleasurable tour, stop by the Hyatt Regency, where horse-drawn **sleighs** whisk guests around the resort base. Take a break from alpine skiing and ease into the relaxed rhythm of **cross-country skiing** or **snowshoeing** at the Beaver Creek Cross Country Ski Center and Mc Coy Park (tel. 970/845–5313), a lift-accessed and groomed park area atop Beaver Creek Mountain.

WHERE TO STAY

The Beaver Creek Village area offers a plethora of ski-in/ski-out hotel and condo facilities, almost all within the moderate to high-end range. Among their amenities are two outstanding spas, those at the Hyatt Regency and at the Lodge at Cordillera. Nearby Avon (2½ miles down the road) is where you'll find most of the more modestly priced accommodations: If price rather than convenience is a factor, Avon is your best bet. Vail, with its 30,000 beds, is just 10 miles down the highway. A convenient $3 shuttle runs every 20–30 minutes from either Avon or Vail. All lodging can be booked through **Vail–Beaver Creek Central Reservations** (Box 7, Vail 81658, tel. 800/427–8308 or 970/845–5745).

Expensive

Hyatt Regency Beaver Creek
This grand full-service hotel is at the center of Beaver Creek. It has ski-in/ski-out access to the slopes and valet service that ensures your boots are warmed and your skis carried to the snow. Included in a standard hotel room with knotty-pine furnishings are

niceties such as bathrobes. Some suites—appropriately sized for larger groups—also have a fireplace and a kitchen. *Box 1595, Beaver Creek Resort, Avon 81620, tel. 970/949–1234 or 800/233–1234, fax 970/949–4164. 290 rooms, 5 suites, 26 units. Facilities: 3 restaurants, 2 bars, 8 hot tubs, outdoor pool, health club, spa, 24-hr desk service, shuttle, ski valet, ski storage, laundry, game room. AE, D, DC, MC, V. $215–$3,000.*

Lodge at Cordillera

A stunning château perched on 3,000 acres of pristine mountain wilderness above the Squaw Creek Valley, the lodge is just 20 minutes from Beaver Creek. The stone-and-stucco building, with its steep, sloping tile roof is styled in the tradition of the Spanish Pyrenees and includes one of the most exotic spa facilities in ski country. Inside are wood and wrought-iron furnishings and walls bedecked with original lithographs by Picasso, Miró, and Dali. The rooms are sumptuously comfortable, with polished wood, marble trim, and stunning views of the surrounding Gore and Sawatch mountain ranges. *Box 1110, Edwards 81632, tel. 970/926–2200 or 800/877–3529, fax 970/926–2486. 20 rooms, 3 suites, 5 lofts. Facilities: restaurant, bar, hot tub, indoor-outdoor pool, health club, spa, 24-hr desk service, cross-country skiing, ski storage, shuttle. AE, MC, V. $200–$850.*

The Pines

This small Beaver Creek winner combines posh digs with unpretentious atmosphere. The rooms are spacious, light, and airy, with blond-wood furnishings, pale pink ceilings, and fab-

rics in dusty rose, mint, and white. Each room has a TV/VCR (tapes are free), mini-refrigerator, and coffeemaker; several rooms have balconies overlooking the ski area and mountain range. The air of quiet pampering is furthered by little extras like a ski concierge who arranges complimentary guided mountain tours and a free wax for your skis. The Grouse Mountain Grill serves up superb new American cuisine in an unparalleled setting with huge windows and wrought-iron chandeliers. *Box 36, Avon 81620, tel. 970/845–7900 or 800/859–8242, fax 970/845–7809. 60 rooms, 12 units. Facilities: restaurant, bar, pool, hot tub, spa, exercise room, laundry service. AE, D, MC, V. $205–$1,995.*

St. James Place

This marvelously stylish condo, in the heart of Beaver Creek Village, offers a variety of large one-, two-, and three-bedroom units. Each is individually owned—many on a time-share basis—so furnishings and designs vary. Every unit is a complete living environment, complete with a gas fireplace and a deck. *Box 1593, Avon 81620, tel. 970/845–9300 or 800/626–7100, fax 970/845–0099. 54 units. Facilities: restaurant, bar, 3 hot tubs, sauna, steam room, indoor pool, health club, 24-hr desk service, ski storage, laundry. AE, MC, V. $350–$1,200.*

Moderate

The Centennial

The bright and modern lodge rooms and one- to three-bedroom apartments in this seven-story complex all have plush carpeting and floral-print-covered furnishings. The large lodge rooms can easily accommodate four. The larger apartments, which have full kitchens, fireplaces, and washers and dryers, offer good value for families and groups; the multilevel layout gives everyone a little more privacy. *Box 348, Avon 81620, tel. 970/845–7600 or 800/845–7060, fax 970/845–7677. 3 lodge rooms, 23 units. Facilities: lounge, hot tubs, outdoor pool, ski storage, laundry, ski-in/walk-out. AE, MC, V. $120–$1,195.*

The Charter

This resort offers accommodations ranging from a standard lodge room for two to four guests to five-bedroom units that can comfortably house 12. The condos are furnished with plenty of big comfortable couches and easy chairs and have large windows, fireplaces, and balconies. *120 Offerson Rd., Box 5310, Avon 81620, tel. 970/949–6660 or 800/525–6660, fax 970/949–4667. 65 lodge rooms, 115 units. Facilities: restaurant, bar, hot tubs, steam room, indoor and outdoor pools, health club, spa, 24-hr desk service, shuttle, ski valet, ski-in/walk-out, ski storage, laundry. AE, MC, V. $150–$1,650.*

Embassy Suites Beaver Creek Lodge

This all-suite hotel is only a few hundred yards from the lifts. The suites, with kitchenettes, gas fireplaces, large bedrooms, and living rooms with pull-out sofas, are large enough for a group of four. You'll also find robes, slippers, and bottled water in every room. The one- to three-bedroom condos are individually owned, with decorating schemes ranging from Bavarian style done in lots of blue and burgundy, with vaulted ceilings

and deep-mahogany wood trim, to Ralph Lauren style, with green-and-blue plaids and forest green carpeting. *26 Avondale La., Box 2578, Beaver Creek 81620, tel. 970/845–9800 or 800/362–2779, fax 970/845–8242. 71 suites, 6 units. Facilities: restaurant, bar, lounge, hot tub, steam room, indoor pool, outdoor pool, health club, 24-hr desk service, complimentary breakfast, ski valet, ski storage, laundry. AE, D, DC, MC, V. $200–$2,400.*

Inn At Beaver Creek

With a lift just 5 yards from its back entrance, this inn is a truly convenient ski-in/ski-out facility. It's a small, elegant lodge with a European feel. The public spaces are exquisite, with some handcrafted furnishings, plants, a stone fireplace, and a grand piano. The rooms are all large, bright, and decorated with Colonial-style furnishings and coordinated eiderdowns and pillows. *10 Elk Track La., Beaver Creek 81620, tel. 970/845–7800, fax 970/845–5279. 37 rooms, 8 suites. Facilities: bar, lounge, hot tub, sauna, steam room, outdoor pool, 24-hr desk service, shuttle, ski storage, laundry, 24-hr concierge, inter-village limousine. AE, MC, V. $210-1,300.*

Poste Montane

This is a small European-style lodge. Rooms are elegantly decorated in deep, rich colors and flowery wallpaper. The lodge rooms and deluxe rooms are large enough for four guests; the suites (two bedrooms, three baths) can easily accommodate six people. All deluxe rooms and suites have fireplaces. The lobby has dark wood paneling, forest green carpets, and comfy leather couches. In the afternoon there's a wine and cheese party in the lobby. *Box 5480, Avon 81620, tel. 970/845–7500 or 800/497–9238, fax 970/845–5012. 7 deluxe rooms, 4 studios, 13 suites. Facilities: restaurant, bar, pool, hot tub, sauna, steam room, shuttle, ski storage, ski shop, laundry. AE, MC, V. $195–$790, including full breakfast and après-ski buffet.*

Inexpensive

Christie Lodge
The Christie isn't much to look at with its prosaic gray-siding exterior, but this property is an affordable deal. It's in Avon (2½ miles down the road from the resort) and offers one- and three-bedroom suites housed in seven buildings connected by an atrium. Clean and comfortable, the suites are decorated in relaxing pastel colors and come complete with a kitchenette, a fireplace, a balcony, and mountain views. Families and foursomes tend to lodge here. *Box 1196, Avon 81620, tel. 970/949–7700 or 888/325–6343, fax 970/845–4535. 280 suites. Facilities: restaurant, bar, lounge, hot tubs, sauna, indoor pool, health club, 24-hr desk service, shuttle service, laundry, game room. AE, D, DC, MC, V. $99–$399.*

Lodge at Avon Center
On the bank of the Eagle River, tucked in a thicket of evergreens, stand these modestly priced one- to four-bedroom condos—an excellent deal for families. Each unit is individually owned and decorated and contains a full kitchen, a fireplace, and a balcony. *100 W. Beaver Creek Blvd., Box 964, Avon 81620, tel. 970/949–6202 or 800/441–4718, fax 970/949–*

7757. 40 rooms, 25 units. Facilities: restaurant, bar, ski storage, laundry, shuttle. AE, MC, V. $135–$525.

Seasons Lodge Arrowhead
About 2 miles from the entrance to Beaver Creek, you'll find this attractive, modern three-story stone building with a distinctive old-world porte cochere. The lodge rooms and one-, two-, and three-bedroom condo units are delightful blends of European alpine and Southwestern influences. The decor is a mix of exposed beams and dark wood furnishings, stone fireplaces, and brightly colored Navajo-style drapes and coverings. *Box 1370, Edwards 81632, tel. 970/926–8300 or 800/846–0233, fax 970/926–2390. 30 units. Facilities: hot tub, outdoor pool, lounge, ski-in/ski-out. AE, D, DC, MC, V. $65–$500.*

WHERE TO EAT
There is an ample number of restaurants at Beaver Creek, with some additional inexpensive eateries in nearby Avon—and of course Vail is just 20 minutes away, with its excellent variety in all price categories.

On the Mountain

McCoy's
Although the lunch fare here is traditional—soups, salads, and sandwiches—the breakfast menu is a notch above the competition's. The pancakes are excellent, and there's a good selection of other morning staples. *Base of Centennial Express lift, tel. 970/949–1234. AE, D, MC, V.*

Spruce Saddle
You have two choices for dining at this midmountain restaurant at the top of the Centennial lift. On the

lower level is a large, bright dining court with a good selection of American heritage cuisine: buffalo burgers, spicy duck pizza, wild beans, and chilies, along with a pasta station. The upper level houses Rafters, the fine-dining section. *Spruce Saddle, tel. 970/845– 5520. AE, D, MC, V. Rafters, tel. 970/845–5528. AE, D, MC, V.*

Expensive

Beano's Cabin

Everything about Beano's is fantastic: the name, the history, and the food. You begin your journey at the Rendezvous Cabin, at the top of the escalators at the south end of the plaza in One Beaver Creek. There a sled host meets you, checks you in, and whisks you off by sleigh. During your 2-mile ride, the sled host fills you in on some mountain history. Your destination is a midmountain Montana pine-log cabin, warmed inside by a crackling fire and live dinner music. Here, a six-course meal of homemade soup, freshly baked bread, salad, and a choice of entrée is served. Take your pick from salmon, roast duck, grilled venison, loin of lamb, or the special of the day, but save room for dessert—especially the crème brûlée. *1 Beaver Creek, tel. 970/949–9090. Reservations essential. AE, MC, V. No smoking.*

Mirabelle

Inside a restored century-old farmhouse just down the road from the Beaver Creek Resort, this excellent French restaurant is owned by the folks who brought the Left Bank (*see* Where to Eat *in* Vail, *below*) to Vail. The decor is particularly fetching, with a French-country-cottage style based on rough whitewashed walls

with exposed beams, bright floral-print curtains, and elegant color-coordinated table settings. The wide-ranging menu offers fish, fowl, and game, with especially good veal and breast of duck entrées. *55 Village Rd., tel. 970/949–7728. AE, D, MC, V.*

Patina

The Southwestern/Pacific Rim menu here offers something for just about everyone, from Southwestern Caesar salad to wood-fired pizzas to sizzling Thai snapper to duck with wild plum sauce and scallion pancakes. There are even tapas and sushi bars. Some specialties are light on calories. *Hyatt Regency Beaver Creek, tel. 970/845–2825. AE, D, DC, MC, V.*

Restaurant Picasso

Though this stylish French restaurant offers amazing views of Vail Valley from its 8,500-foot vantage point, the main attraction is an extraordinary collection of original Picasso lithographs. In addition to all the visual stimulation, Picasso's serves an impressive menu including roast lamb rack served with provençal vegetables. A lighter spa menu is also available. *Lodge at Cordillera, tel. 970/ 926–2200. AE, DC, MC, V.*

Splendido

This ultraposh restaurant is the height of decadence, with marble columns and statuary and custom-made Italian linens adorning the tables. Chef David Walford, who apprenticed at Northern California's Auberge du Soleil and Masa's, is a master of new American cuisine, borrowing merrily from several different traditions. He is equally adept at turning out grouper baked with Moroccan spices, couscous, and fennel as he is at preparing lobster and white-bean chili with potato tortillas or elk chop in black pepper and pinot noir sauce with parsnip and sweet potato pancakes and chanterelles. Pastry chef Matt Olehy excels both at standards like crème brûlée and at such imaginative offerings as caramel-pumpkin crostata (puff pastry) with eggnog ice cream. *17 Chateau La., Beaver Creek, tel. 970/845–8808. AE, DC, MC, V.*

Moderate

Fiesta's Café & Cantina
Authentic Mexican fare includes enchiladas, tacos, tostadas, and burritos in addition to daily specials such as chicken, beef, or shrimp fajitas or shrimp-filled chile relleños. The burrito *carne adovada* (pork marinated in hot red chilies) is a house specialty. *Edwards Plaza Bldg., 4 mi west of Beaver Creek, Edwards, tel. 970/926–2121. AE, D, DC, MC, V.*

Golden Eagle
The mixed menu offers selections of seafood, pasta, and game. Try the game pâté as an appetizer, and if you're eager for more game, order either the loin of elk or the medallions of venison. Another interesting combination is the lobster and eggplant bisque, followed by the excellent roast duckling with a port wine sauce. More mainstream items include grilled salmon with fusilli, Southwestern-style shrimp scampi served with roasted red peppers, and grilled rainbow trout with wild rice. *Village Hall, tel. 970/949–1940. AE, MC, V.*

TraMonti
This breezy trattoria in the Charter at Beaver Creek showcases the vibrant progressive cuisine of chef Curtis Cooper. You can choose from a variety of traditional and nouveau pasta entrées, everything from spaghetti puttanesca to lobster ravioi in a saffron cream sauce. Also on the menu are seafood specialties such as almond crusted sea bass and veal, chicken, and beef dishes. *120 Offerson Rd., Beaver Creek, tel. 970/949-5552. AE, DC, MC, V. Reservations essential.*

Inexpensive

Brass Parrot
There's no pretense here: It's good, basic pub grub in a sports bar atmosphere. You can chow down on chicken, prime rib, fish-and-chips, and spaghetti. *Avon Centre, tel. 970/949–7770. AE, D, MC, V.*

Cassidy's Hole in the Wall
If you're looking for *the* burger, you're in the right place: The Big-Bob one-pounder should sate you. Sandwiches, Mexican fare, and specialties such as chicken-fried steak and a 2-foot-long rack of ribs head the menu in this Western saloon that spans two floors. Looking for the action? Stay at ground zero. If you're partial to watching rather than participating, you'll want to be upstairs. *82 E. Beaver Creek Blvd., Avon, tel. 970/949– 9449. Reservations essential for 8 or more. AE, D, MC, V.*

China Garden
Here you can eat Mandarin and Szechuan dishes as well as traditional egg rolls, barbecued spare ribs, and wonton soup. The take-out service is fast, and the eat-in restaurant is a cut above most area Chinese restaurants. *Avon Centre, tel. 970/949– 4986. AE, D, DC, MC, V.*

The Gashouse

This classic local hangout, in a 50-year-old log cabin with trophy-covered walls, draws up-valley crowds who swear by the steaks, delicious ribs, and sautéed rock shrimp with chili-pesto pasta. Stop in for a brew and some heavenly jalapeño chips and watch how the Vail Valley kicks back. *Rte. 6, Edwards, tel. 970/926–3613. AE, DC, MC, V.*

Best Bets for Breakfast

Coffee Gallery

Come here for the best coffee in Beaver Creek, and you'll also get a good selection of muffins and pastries. *Beaver Creek Mall, tel. 970/949–1273. AE, MC, V.*

Terrace Restaurant

Favorite early morning eats include the omelets and the biscuits and gravy, especially on a cold day. If you want something lighter, try a cinnamon roll from the assortment of baked goods. *The Charter, tel. 970/949–6660. AE, MC, V.*

NIGHTLIFE AND ENTERTAINMENT

Although there are several good spots in Beaver Creek Village and in nearby Avon, the evening activities tend to be fairly subdued: hot-tub soaking and fireside lounging. Remember, however, that Vail, only 20 minutes away, has a much greater variety of entertainment (*see* Nightlife and Entertainment *in* Vail, *below*). If partying is on your mind, leave the car here and take the shuttle bus.

Après-Ski

Coyote Café

At this popular après-ski hangout the atmosphere is lively and fun—with impromptu dancing, entertainment, and happy-hour surprises. *Village Hall, tel. 970/949–5001. AE, D, MC, V.*

Crooked Hearth Tavern

For a subdued if not romantic après-ski atmosphere, head for the Tavern in the Hyatt Regency. The large lobby bar offers live piano music and a warm, blazing fire maintained by a full-time fire tender. Complimentary munchies and happy-hour specials are provided. *Hyatt Regency Beaver Creek, tel. 970/949–1234. AE, MC, V.*

Loud and Lively/Dancing

Dusty Boot Saloon

The scene at the bar is festive, with the emphasis on ale quaffing, mingling, and carousing. The après-ski crowd tends to be on the young side, but forty-somethings won't feel out of place either. *St. James Place, tel. 970/845–8930. AE, MC, V.*

Paddy's Sports Bar & Grill

Thirteen TV screens join five large-screen monitors and one superscreen here. Children can easily occupy themselves in the playroom and games arcade while adults watch the day's big game or sports videos. *40801 Rte. 6, at Rte. 24, tel. 970/949–6093. AE, D, MC, V.*

More Mellow

TraMonti

If you've boogied till you're beat or just want a pleasant piano-bar environment and a nightcap, this may be your prescription. *The Charter, tel. 970/949–5552. AE, MC, V.*

COPPER MOUNTAIN SKI RESORT

Box 3001
Copper Mountain, CO 80443
Tel. 970/968–2882 or
800/458–8386
www.ski-copper.com

STATISTICALLY SPEAKING

Base elevation: 9,712 feet

Summit elevation: 12,313 feet

Vertical drop: 2,601 feet

Skiable terrain: 2,433 acres

Number of trails: 118

Longest run: 2.8 miles

Lifts and capacity: 1 six-person high-speed, 4 high-speed quads, 5 triples, 6 doubles, 6 surface; 30,630 skiers per hour

Daily lift ticket: $50

Average annual snowfall: 280 inches

Number of skiing days 1997–98: 183

Snowmaking: 380 acres, 15.6%

Terrain mix: N 21%, I 25%, E 54% (advanced 36%, extreme 18%)

Snowboarding: yes

Cross-country skiing: 25 kilometers of set tracks and skating lanes in Arapaho National Forest

One of the leading resorts in Summit County—Colorado's prime skiing country—Copper Mountain shares the terrain of the wondrously scenic Ten Mile Range with Keystone, Breckenridge, and Arapahoe Basin. In spite of a mix-and-match condo village and a homogenized approach to the hotels and restaurants, this resort feels pleasant and offers an abundance of good skiing on trails that are among the best laid out in the country.

A merger with Intrawest—the company that developed the Blackcomb resort in British Columbia—is giving Copper a village worthy of this great ski mountain. Over the next 5 years, 1,000 residential units and commercial spaces will be built in the village at the bottom of the Colorado Super Bee lift, and improvements will be made on the mountain.

For the 1998–99 season, Copper unveiled a new 40,000-square-foot day lodge in the east river area and a rejuvenated village—a welcome facelift to the resort's dated 1970s architecture. Further enhancing the Copper experience is a new six-person "superchair," the only one of its kind in Colorado. Most skiers, however, will spend most of their non-skiing time in the Village Square—the resort's main hub, perched along the serpentine bank of Ten Mile Creek. The rather ordinary architecture here is slated for updating, but it is in any case eclipsed by the soaring peaks of the Ten Mile Range and the stunning scenery of the Arapaho National Forest.

The Village Square is a good focus for families with teens because most of the shops, restaurants, and other facilities are within strolling distance. Two high-speed quads converge just in front of the Copper Commons restaurant, providing fast access to midmountain and any of Copper's three distinct levels of terrain. The Village Square is also the hub of Copper's nightlife, so it tends to stay busy into the evening. Weigh both sides of this feature: there will be plenty of action, but it can also be noisier than the other clusters of accommodations.

To the west is the Union Creek base area, with standard condos and town houses, plus immediate access to the tremendous novice ski slopes on this part of the mountain. It's an ideal (and quieter) location. Though it's a bit of a hike from the Village

Children's services: day-care,
tel. 970/968–2882, ext. 6345;
instruction, tel. 970/968–
2882, ext. 6346

Snow phone: tel. 970/968–
2100; 800/789–7609

Summit County Sheriff's
Dept.: tel. 970/453–2232

Hospital: Colorado Mountain
Medical Center, tel. 970/968–
2330; Summit Medical Center
(Frisco), tel. 970/468–6936

Resort Association: tel. 970/
968–6477

Avalanche hot line: tel. 970/
668–0600

Road conditions: tel. 970/
453–1090

Towing: Paul's Towing, tel.
970/968–6311

FIVE-STAR FAVORITES

Best run for vertical: Andy's
Encore

Best run overall: Drainpipe to
Far East

Best bar/nightclub: O'Shea's

Best hotel: Club Med

Best restaurant: Rackets
Restaurant

Square, the Copper shuttle bus makes it an efficient alternative.

At the east end of the resort is the Super Bee lift base area, which tends to draw a younger, crash-and-burn crowd that wants fast access to Copper's steepest and bumpiest terrain and a place to party at the end of the day. The new day lodge is worth the extra effort required to travel to this nether region of the Copper complex.

HOW TO GET THERE

By Plane
Copper Mountain is 95 miles west of **Denver International Airport.**

By Car
Copper Mountain is 75 miles, or 1½–2 hours, west of Denver, off I–70 Exit 195.

By Bus
From the Denver airport, buses and vans leave every half hour for Copper Mountain. Call **Resort Express** (tel. 800/334–7433) for times. Round-trip fare from the airport is $88.

GETTING AROUND
A car can be useful in Summit County if you plan to do any exploring or ski more than one resort. However, the **Summit County Stage** (tel. 970/668-0999, no charge) is an efficient public-transit alternative. Buses leave Copper Mountain, Keystone, or Breckenridge at the top of the hour and meet at the Frisco Transfer Center on the half hour for connections to each resort. There are other stops along the route.

There's ample day parking at each of Copper's three base areas, although the only time you bother with a car at Copper is when you are heading to the nearby towns for a change of scenery.

THE SKIING
Just like the well-organized village complex at Copper, the skiing is neatly subdivided into three distinct areas. Copper Peak at 12,441 feet and adjacent Union Peak at 12,313 feet combine for 118 runs that are

primarily north-facing (which means they tend to hold onto their snow longer) and run west to east with increasing degrees of difficulty. Novices and never-evers tend to stick to the Union Creek area to the west; the center of the complex serves intermediates with a pair of high-speed quad chairs; and the toughest terrain is found on the eastern flank of Copper Peak, including the splendid bowl skiing found off the top of the Storm King surface lift.

The surface lift—a quirky throwback in lift technology—is necessary because high winds occasionally sweep the summit, but elsewhere the mountain is well served by a fleet of 22 chairlifts that cover the two peaks with the great efficiency that is typical of this resort. It's easy to get around Copper. The runs are well marked, cross-mountain lift transit is remarkably free from long catwalks or flats, and it's easy for groups to split up, chase their own level, yet still occasionally rendezvous with each other.

The hub of the mountain, and its busiest area, is where the American Flyer and the American Eagle quads converge, at the edge of the Village Square. It's always busy first thing in the morning, but the two quads nicely split the mountain: upper intermediates, experts, and thrill seekers head up the Eagle to the bowls and steeps of Copper Peak; more temperate intermediates choose the subtle cruisers and demibowl skiers access them from the Flyer. Novices have their own area, which can also be reached via the Flyer or from the less busy Union Creek base area.

Skiers heading for the first tracks in the bowl areas tend to avoid lineups by taking the Super Bee lift at the east end of the resort, but unless you are staying in that area, you'll have to take a shuttle bus.

Novices

Beginners will want to start off at the Union Creek area (to the left, looking down the mountain), where you won't get into trouble on the mix of blue and green runs. The base chair (K) serves a trio of gradual green runs, and for a little more gusto, the Timberline Express quad takes you farther up the mountain for more novice/intermediate runs. You can also take the American Flyer quad from the Village Square, but make sure you turn right when you get off the lift. This is a superb beginners' area that neither overwhelms nor bores the novice. And for an added bonus, lift tickets good in this area only are free in January and February for novice skiers or those who want to try snowboarding. High Point, which begins just below the steeper slopes of the upper Union Bowl, is a wonderful wide cruising run that cuts in smooth easy curves back and forth across this part of the mountain. It tends to be the busiest run in this area because it's the first trail you come to after turning right off the lift. However, you can also cut right (looking down) at a Y junction and take Coppertone, a slightly narrower, well-groomed run that incorporates a few more dips and rolls.

The H chair will take you to a pair of beautiful, wide, and winding green runs called Easy Feeling and Scooter. If you're skiing Scooter, cut left (looking down the mountain) toward the bottom of the run, to Hidden Vein; if you veer right, you'll end up at the base of the American Flyer lift. As you gain confidence, you can move over to the west side of the ridge (left, looking down) by taking the H chair to a connector trail called Minor Matter, then taking the Timberline Express quad to a point just below the tree line (you can also access this point from the American Flyer lift). From here take High Point, a moderately steep but wide and speed-controlled slope that connects to Scooter about halfway down, for a long, easy, but interesting novice cruiser.

From the top of the Timberline Express quad, turn left to Roundabout, a long, looping catwalk that will take you to the bottom of the L chair, which serves the shortest and tamest of Copper's terrain. Or cut right on Soliloquy when it merges with Roundabout, then scoot back over to the Timberline Express lift. If you want to ski with your buddies off the American Flyer lift, you can play on Coppertone and High Point, but be prepared for more traffic than you've encountered on the western runs.

Intermediates

Your fastest way up to mid-mountain is on either the American Flyer or American Eagle high-speed quad. The Flyer serves part of the green/blue terrain on the lower flanks of Union Peak but also gives access to the two chairs that serve the above-tree-line steeps of Union Bowl. It's steep up here, but there's a nice mix of wide-open bowl skiing and some spirited glade dancing. For steep—and occasionally deep—terrain, try Southern Star or Union Peak; for some fun with the firs, try Timberidge, a long multi-faceted run that combines pitch and trees in equal amounts.

For more variation, consider skiing Copper Peak, on the east side of the mountain. To reach it, take the American Eagle to mid-station and ski down to the New Excelerator Quad and ride it to the top. From here, you can access the challenging Collage and Andy's Encore—almost 2,000 vertical feet of some groomed terrain and some moguls. When you're ready to head back, take Copperopolis to Bouncer for a long and fast cruiser with good drop-offs, pitches, and turns.

Experts

There's no doubt about it—Copper Peak is your playground. Ride the American Eagle to the Excelerator, and the Excelerator to the Storm King poma, where you'll have your choice of the Hallelujah Ridge or Hallelujah Bowl, or the even steeper Spalding and Resolution bowls. This is above-tree-line skiing, with some excellent vertical and a good place to play in the powder. The steep chutes of the Spalding Bowl spit you out into the Spalding Glades for a high-speed giant-slalom run to the bottom of the Resolution lift. Pick your own chute down the bowl, do it all over again from the Resolution lift, and when the snow cruds up, head out of the bowls and go for a good high-speed top-to-bottom cruise on Andy's Encore. Just make sure you cut right on Ore Deal near the bottom, rather than left to the winding Skid Road, which is tediously tame and long.

From the A lift you can take Formidable for a fast, undulating steep or Far East for a good, steep mogul run. A great overall run is Drainpipe, a chute off the B lift, to Far East.

For a backcountry experience, you can ski Copper Bowl, an advanced-only area. From the top of the Storm King poma or R or S lifts, drop into this south-facing bowl—wide open at the top and tree-gladed lower down. For even more challenge, hike into the in-bounds Tucker Mountain extreme area.

SNOWBOARDING

A snowboard terrain park opened in early 1997, and a snowboard-specific trail map is available. For beginning snowboarders, Copper offers one of the best deals in the state: Access to the K and L lifts, serving over 50 acres of beginner terrain, is free in January and February. Copper has long appealed to serious shredders because it hosts the longest-running amateur snowboard race series in the country.

Beginners involved in lessons ride the K and L lifts on the resort's west side, which access the best terrain to learn your turns, with mellow, steady slopes that will prevent you from losing your momentum. Roundabout, a trail just to the left of the L lift, goes all the way to the base of Union Creek, paralleling the lift. A mellow, gentle trail with a steady pitch, it's the best place to start the day. After a few runs, you can branch off onto the Fairway and Prospector trails, both to the right of Roundabout. In January and February, beginners can get a free pass for these two lifts only.

Intermediates head directly for the American Eagle and American Flyer quad lifts, in front of the Village Square. For half-pipe riding, catch the Liberty Trail just below the American Flyer lift. There, you'll encounter a mellow, easy half-pipe designed just for fledgling pipe pilots. Cruisers should take the American Flyer lift, exiting left onto High Point trail to Loverly, a challenging green run with lots of rollers. Or try Bittersweet, a long, steady cruiser with plenty of steep sections and a few jumps on either side of the trail. Advanced intermediates can take the short trail from the American Eagle quad to the new Excelerator quad. From here, head left to Ptarmigan. In the trees between Ptarmigan and Hallelujah is a succession of log slides to play on.

Experts can check out the Olympic-size competition half-pipe on Carefree Trail. It's not lift-served, so you have to either hike or head down to the bottom of the G lift for a ride back to the top. For steep, off-piste boarding, take the American Eagle to Excelerator. A short traverse on the unmarked Easy Road, to your right, takes you to the Storm King surface lift. From the top, you can drop into either the steep Copper Bowl or the challenging Spalding Bowl—both offer chutes, cornices, and wide-open, ungroomed powder runs. For high-speed carving, head for the six-person Super Bee lift on the resort's east side. Just to the left of the lift you encounter Andy's Encore, a fast, groomed run that descends 2,300 vertical feet.

OTHER SNOW SPORTS

For family entertainment at the resort (Copper Welcome Center, 800/458–8386; or 970/968–2318, ext. 7885), try **snow tubing, ice skating, cross-country skiing, snowshoe-**

ing, snowmobiling, hot-air ballooning.

NEARBY

Copper is within 20 minutes of Breckenridge, Keystone (*see below*), and Arapahoe Basin Resorts. The free Summit County Stage (tel. 970/668–0999) links Copper with Breck and Keystone. Keystone operates a separate shuttle to A-Basin. Challenging **Arapahoe Basin** (tel. 970/468–0718) is a favorite of Colorado skiers. Something of a throwback to the wild, untamed early days of skiing, A-Basin offers an experience similar to that of Mad River Glen in Vermont or Alta in Utah. Those who like steeps will fall in love with A-Basin's Palivacinni, a series of rocky chutes, bumps, and tight tree runs that will challenge even the most able experts. **Breckenridge** (tel. 970/453–5000) is, based on skier visits, the second most popular resort in North America. It is also the epicenter of Summit County shopping, dining, and après ski. The oldest existing mining town on Colorado's western slope, Breckenridge has more than 100 stores and boutiques, as well as the county's widest variety of dining and drinking establishments. It's a family resort that offers a huge variety of terrain: everything from pool-table flats to some of the steepest in-bounds skiing in North America on Peak Eight.

WHERE TO STAY

For convenience, and in most cases good value, it makes sense to stay on the mountain. Virtually all the 900 on-mountain properties are owned and operated by the resort, which gives you convenient one-stop shopping through Copper Mountain Lodging Services (tel. 800/458–8386) but doesn't offer much in the way of variety. Most on-mountain hotels and condos run from moderate to expensive, while the best budget choices are found in nearby Frisco, Dillon, and Breckenridge. Nearly every unit is within walking distance of one of the lift areas; for those that are not, an excellent free shuttle system serves the entire Copper complex. Even if you stay in the surrounding towns, the Summit County shuttle-bus system is just as efficient and just as free. **Summit County Central Reservations** (Box 446, Dillon, CO 80435, tel. 970/468–6222 or 800/365–6365) covers the entire region and can find you anything from a humble bed-and-breakfast to a four-bedroom condo.

Expensive

Club Méditerranée
Copper Mountain's Club Med is the first and only North American operation of the famed French fun club. Ski or snowboard instruction with an international staff of instructors is included in the rate. The small but comfortable rooms are in neutral tones with Southwestern art. A preferred place to relax is the country-inn-style lobby on the first floor, with a big fireplace, comfortable armchairs, and floor-to-ceiling windows overlooking the slopes. The international buffet and disco are open to nonguests when the club isn't full— call ahead for availability. *50 Beeler Pl., Copper Mountain 80443, tel. 970/ 968–2161 or 800/258–2633, fax 970/ 968–2216. 236 rooms. Facilities: 2 restaurants, bar, disco, piano bar, 4 Jacuzzis, 2 saunas, twice-daily aerobics*

and stretch classes, maid service, ski storage, laundry, game room. *AE, MC, V. $1,000–$1,500 per person for 7 nights, including all meals, lift tickets, and instruction.*

Copper Mountain's Central Village

Most accommodations at Copper are predictably practical. The condo-based Central Village complex is the most convenient, within easy walking distance of the lifts, and the most favored by families. Units range in size from one to five bedrooms, with one, two- and three-bedroom pent-houses also available; most have a fireplace and a balcony. Most of the 14 buildings have saunas and laundry facilities, some have hot tubs and underground parking, and one has an outdoor pool. All include use of the Copper Mountain Racquet and Athletic Club. *Box 3001, 0209 Ten Mile Circle, Copper Mountain 80443, tel. 970/968–2882 or 800/458–8386, fax 970/968–6227. 600 units. Facilities: indoor hot tub (most), use of health club, sauna, 24-hr room service, 24-hr desk service, shuttle, maid service, ski storage, laundry (most). AE, D, DC, MC, V. $150–$1,125.*

Woods and Legends
Town Homes

These units are definitely the class of Copper. The two small subdivisions of town houses have some of the largest and most upscale properties at the resort. Units have either three or four bedrooms, with full kitchens, dining areas, patios, garages, and in some cases, private hot tubs. Suitable for a large family or for two or three couples, they are spacious, comfortable, and beautifully decorated, many in country florals. *Box 3001, Copper Mountain Resort, 0209 Ten Mile Circle, Copper Mountain 80443, tel. 970/968–2882 or 800/458–8386, fax 970/968–6227. 54 units. Facilities: use of Copper Mountain Health Club, 24-hr desk service, shuttle, maid service, ski storage, laundry. AE, D, DC, MC, V. $550–$1,688.*

Moderate

Galena Street Mountain Inn

This pink-stucco inn is in nearby Frisco, 6½ miles from Copper Mountain. The reproduction mission furniture is simple but stylish, with square lines softened by light-colored paint. Rooms have curved moldings, washed-oak window trim, and down comforters. *106 Galena St., Frisco 80443, tel. 970/668–3224 or 800/248–9138, fax 970/668–5291. 15 rooms. Facilities: hot tub, sauna, shuttle, ski storage. AE, D, DC, MC. $85–$165, including full breakfast.*

Holiday Inn

A major renovation, completed in 1998, has given this Holiday Inn more of a ski lodge atmosphere, with lots of natural wood furniture. The rooms accommodate groups of four, and the Frisco location is convenient, via a free shuttle or by an easy drive, to Keystone, Copper Mountain, and Breckenridge. Families may find it a bit noisy. *1129 N. Summit Blvd., Frisco 80443, tel. 970/668–5000 or 800/782–7669, fax 970/668–0718. 217 rooms. Facilities: restaurant, bar, indoor hot tub, indoor pool, exercise machines, sauna, 24-hr desk service, shuttle service, maid service, laundry, game room. AE, D, DC, MC, V. $135–$225.*

Lake Dillon Condotel

Its scenic location overlooking Lake Dillon gives this otherwise uninteresting stucco block building a touch of style. The one-, two-, and three-bedroom units are a good value. All come with a kitchenette, a fireplace, and a balcony, and each has an unobstructed view of the lake and the Ten Mile Range. *Box 308, 401 W. Lodgepole St., Dillon 80435, tel. 970/468–2409 or 800/323–7792, fax 970/468–0375. 27 units. Facilities: indoor hot tub, ski storage, laundry, game room. $90–$280.*

Ten Mile Creek Condominiums

In Frisco, this pleasant and comfortable condo complex is the most moderately priced in the area for the level of luxury it offers. Its two-, three-, and four-bedroom units are well maintained and well equipped, each with a full kitchen, a balcony, and a fireplace. *200 Granite St., Frisco 80443, tel. 970/668–3100 or 800/530–3070, fax 970/668–5273. 40 units. Facilities: indoor hot tub, indoor pool, sauna, laundry. AE, D, MC, V. $145–$235.*

Inexpensive

Continental Divide Lodge

This is a cute but not fancy Western-style lodge, comfortable and quiet without a lot of frills, just a half block from Frisco's Main Street. The lodge unit sleeps two to four, and the larger unit handles up to 10, with a small kitchen and fireplace. *Box 1919, 520 Galena St., Frisco 80443, tel. 970/668–0373. 2 units. Facilities: outdoor hot tub, ski storage, laundry. MC, V. $65–$450.*

Frisco Lodge B&B

Built in 1885, this is a classic period house, with relatively small rooms and a nice, comfortable feel. The rooms are rustic, some with a shared bath, but all are more than adequate for couples, and several can be connected to accommodate small families. There's a common living room with a fireplace. A full breakfast, featuring eggs, cereal, and pastry, is part of the price. *Box 1325, 321 Main St., Frisco 80443, tel. 970/668–0195 or 800/279–6000, fax 970/668–0149. 19 rooms, 9 with bath. Facilities: outdoor hot tub. AE, D, MC, V. $35–$125, including full breakfast.*

Sky Vue Motel

You'll find clean and comfortable rooms with sturdy bleached-oak furnishings, beige wallpaper with teal- and mauve-colored paintbrush strokes, and teal drapes and bedspreads. About half the rooms have small efficiency kitchens. *305 S. 2nd St., Frisco 80443, tel. 970/668–3311 or 800/672–3311. 26 rooms. Facilities: indoor hot tub, indoor pool, maid service, laundry. D, MC, V. $51–$114.*

WHERE TO EAT

On the Mountain

The Commons

This market-style cafeteria offers chili, burgers, and an expansive pasta, salad, and fruit bar, as well as pizza that's been voted the county's best. It tends to be the busiest spot on the mountain, but an efficient layout gets you in and out fast. On sunny days the outdoor patio is the perfect place to munch. *Copper Commons Bldg., base of American Eagle lift, Copper Mountain, tel. 970/968–2318, ext. 6574. AE, D, DC, MC, V.*

Solitude Station

The Solitude Station is a good place to go to avoid the really heavy lunchtime crowds, and it's a convenient rendezvous spot. The food is basic cafeteria fare, with your best bets—such as the hamburgers and chicken sandwiches—coming off the outdoor grill. *Solitude Station Bldg., top of American Eagle lift, Copper Mountain, tel. 970/968–2882, ext. 6522. AE, D, DC, MC, V.*

Expensive

Blue Spruce Inn

In a historic Rocky Mountain log cabin, the Blue Spruce serves Continental cuisine, including lamb chops sautéed in pesto and bread crumbs and served with a demiglace, veal scallopini with wild mushrooms, and trout sautéed with cracked peppercorn with Saga blue cheese in lemon-butter sauce. All are done with a deft touch, and the atmosphere is pure romance. *20 Main St., Frisco, tel. 970/668–5900. AE, D, MC, V.*

Dining in the Woods

Take a horse-drawn sleigh ride to a heated miners' tent in the woods, enjoy live performances of country and folk music, and settle in for a Western repast, including smoked trout appetizers, broiled flank steak or mesquite smoked chicken, and bread pudding for dessert. *Departures 5 PM– 8 PM from Copper Commons Bldg., Copper Mountain, tel. 970/968–2882, ext. 6320. Reservations essential. AE, D, DC, MC, V.*

Pesce Fresco

Pesce Fresco is the spot at Copper for hearty breakfasts, a surprisingly affordable sit-down lunch, après-ski hors d'oeuvres, dinner, and evening nightcaps. The dinner menu is mainly fish, with some solid if uninspired pastas. Among the highlights are pesto tortellini with broccoli, tomatoes, mushrooms, and cheese; grilled salmon; Rocky Mountain trout; and lasagna with roasted chicken. The understated decor, good service, and jazz entertainment make it a popular gathering place. *Mountain Plaza Bldg., Copper Mountain, tel. 970/968–2882, ext. 6505. AE, D, DC, MC, V.*

Poirrier's Cajun Cafe

No matter where you are staying, it's worth the drive to Breckenridge to eat here. The main attraction is Cajun cuisine that you can make as hot as you like. The entrée list relies heavily on catfish, fried, grilled, and blackened in a variety of dishes; but the crawfish delicacies, the Cajun sausage platter, and the gumbo are also excellent. On dark teal walls above wood wainscoting, the dining room mixes portraits of 19th-century figures with paintings of bayou scenes and Mardi Gras. *224 S. Main St., Breckenridge, tel. 970/453–1877. AE, D, DC, MC, V.*

Rackets

Rackets offers the best food in Copper, despite its health-club café atmosphere. Among the entrées on the Southwestern menu are lamb with roasted garlic and shiitake mushrooms; tortilla-encrusted salmon with red-chili sweet-and-sour sauce; and Taos chicken with black bean bacon sauce and avocado-zucchini salsa. A variety of healthy, hearty soups can be ordered à la carte, and there is an excellent, less expensive salad bar with fresh vegetables and pasta and vegetable salads. *Copper Mountain Athletic and Racquet Club, Copper Mountain, tel. 970/968–2882, ext. 6386. AE, D, DC, MC, V.*

Moderate

Barkley's Margaritaville

Prime rib, fajitas, and burritos are the staples. There's a children's menu and plenty of meal-size appetizers, which go for half price during the bar's happy hour, 3:30–6:30 PM. The bar and the dining room rub shoulders and are decked out with strings of chili peppers and Mexican hats. Together they bring in a good mix of locals and tourists. *620 S. Main St., Frisco, tel. 970/668–3694. AE, MC, V.*

Double Diamond Restaurant

Pizza, pasta, and ribs are the bill of fare here. The food is hearty and basic, and the atmosphere befits a ski area, with rustic log-cabin decor and ski videos on the big-screen TV. The slope-side deck is a gathering spot après-ski, with happy hour from 3 to 5 PM. *East Village's Foxpine Inn, 154 Wheeler Pl., Copper Mountain, tel. 970/968–2880. AE, D, MC, V.*

O'Shea's

This all-purpose restaurant sets the standard for hearty, family-style fare for all three meals. Its Village Square convenience makes it busy and a little rowdy every night. The menu emphasizes buffalo, with buffalo burgers, ribs, nachos—even a buffalo Caesar salad. Children under 12 eat free with their parents. *206 Ten Mile Circle, Copper Junction Bldg., Copper Mountain, tel. 970/968–2882, ext. 6504. AE, D, MC, V.*

Inexpensive

Blue Moon Baking Company

In addition to its excellent bagels, this stylish local deli in Silverthorne has some fine soups and pastas and a good selection of cold cuts and cheeses. Breakfast stars homemade granola, scones, muffins, and turnovers. The Blue Moon's take on casual café style includes dried flowers hanging side by side with watercolors painted by a local artist. You can eat in or take out, but just get there before closing, at 6 PM. *253 Summit, Summit Plaza Shopping Center, Silverthorne, tel. 970/468–1472. No credit cards.*

Claimjumper

The Claimjumper serves good, basic dinner fare, with various daily specials. The owner does his own hickory smoking out back, which gives a nice bite to the meat and fish items (try the smoked buffalo burgers). For lighter appetites the smoked trout is a good bet. Also available are Mexican and vegetarian dishes, pasta, and salads. Large windows and hanging plants brighten the dining area, which has counter seating and comfortable oak booths. *805 N. Summit, Frisco, tel. 970/668–3617. AE, D, MC, V.*

Frisco Bar & Grill

Burgers, ribs, and red meat are presented in myriad forms at prices that even locals can afford. Daily specials and appetizers are an even cheaper alternative, while Tex-Mex, pasta, and seafood round out the offerings. More bar than grill, the F.B.&G.—as it's known in the area—is a Frisco tradition. *Boardwalk Bldg., 720 Granite St., Frisco, tel. 970/668–5051. Reservations not accepted. AE, MC, V.*

Imperial Palace

This is a good spot to satisfy the urge for egg rolls, fried rice, wok-cooked vegetables, and sweet-and-sour anything. It's not adventurous Chinese cooking, but it's reliable, familiar, and tasty. Spicy Szechuan and Hunan dishes are also on the menu. *Village Square, Copper Mountain, tel. 970/ 968–6688. MC, V.*

Best Bet for Breakfast

Lizzie's Bagelry and Coffeehouse
At Lizzie's you can grab a cup of coffee and a bagel on the run as you head for the American Flyer lift. Or you can sit, enjoy a cappuccino, and chat with locals about the best places to ski. Fresh-baked bagels, espresso drinks, and fresh-squeezed juices make up the bill of fare. *Village Square West Bldg., Copper Mountain, tel. 970/968–2036. No credit cards.*

NIGHTLIFE AND ENTERTAINMENT

Après-Ski

B-Lift Pub
This pub in the East Village has a daily happy hour from 4 to 6 PM, attracting a boisterous younger crowd, including many locals. Cheap shots, dollar beers, and some good music keep things lively, along with a pool table and a large-screen TV. *Snowflake Bldg., base of B lift, 104 Wheeler Pl., Copper Mountain, tel. 970/968–2525. MC, V.*

Kokomo's Bar
Kokomo's really cooks, with live entertainment, drink specials, and a formula après-ski approach that's big on special events and audience participation. *Copper Commons Bldg., base of America Eagle lift, Copper Mountain, tel. 970/968–2318. AE, D, DC, MC, V.*

Loud and Lively/Dancing

Moose Jaw
This is definitely a locals' hangout. Pool tables beckon the unwary, and a plethora of old photographs, trophies, and newspaper articles makes the barn's wooden walls all but invisible. *208 Main St., Frisco, tel. 970/668–3931. D, MC, V.*

O'Shea's
At the bar the theme is sports, and the entertainment is nonstop. TV screens compete for attention in the background, while the large, fun, noisy crowd holds its own front and center. There's live music from 5:30 to 10 PM every Friday. *206 Ten Mile Circle, Copper Junction Bldg., Copper Mountain, tel. 970/968–2882, ext. 6504. AE, D, MC, V.*

More Mellow

The Pub
If you enjoy a taste other than that of the dry/light beers sweeping the nation's beer market, the Pub's selection of English ales, lagers, and bitters will appeal. There's also a good selection of single-malt and specialty Scotches, as well as cigars to savor. *Copper Commons Bldg., base of American Eagle lift, Copper Mountain, tel. 970/968–2318. AE, D, DC, MC, V.*

CRESTED BUTTE MOUNTAIN RESORT

Box A, 500 Gothic Rd.
Mt. Crested Butte, CO 81225
Tel. 970/349–2333
www.crestedbutteresort.com

STATISTICALLY SPEAKING

Base elevation: 9,375 feet

Summit elevation: 12,162 feet

Vertical drop: 3,062 feet

Skiable terrain: 1,160 acres

Number of trails: 85

Longest run: 2.6 miles

Lifts and capacity: 3 high-speed quads, 3 triples, 3 doubles, 5 surface (includes a "Magic Carpet" for kids); 17,440 skiers per hour

Daily lift ticket: $49

Average annual snowfall: 300 inches

Number of skiing days 1997–98: 152

Snowmaking: 300 acres; 21%

Terrain mix: N 13%, I 40%, E 47%

Snowboarding: yes

Crested Butte takes you back in time: not necessarily back to the mining era, when settlers were just staking their claims to this rugged and beautiful corner of the Elk Mountains, but back to the 1960s, when life seemed less pretentious. They march to the beat of a different drummer in Crested Butte: not the bell-bottomed, pony-tailed Woodstock beat that characterizes the expatriate hippies in Telluride, but a rhythm that's a little more square. A little more straight-on. A little more neighborly. Even the shuttle-bus driver bringing you from nearby Gunnison Airport will offer to make stops at the liquor and grocery stores if you want to stock up. And local residents say hello when passing you on the street.

Elk Avenue, a 1,000-yard stretch of immaculately preserved Victoriana, is the main thoroughfare and one of the largest National Historic Districts in the country. What were once the bordellos, saloons, feed stores, and public buildings of a coal-mining town are now the restaurants, bars, shops, and boutiques of a resort. But the basic character remains unchanged: The clapboard and log structures have been renovated but not altered, leaving an atmosphere that is still true grit, not true glitz. Folks chat, stop, and linger a while, creating an atmosphere as natural as the wilderness of the West Elks and the Ruby Range, which surround this 150-year-old Colorado community.

Three miles from town is a single, soaring broad-hipped butte crowned with a distinctive arrowhead of a peak that at 12,162 feet traps around 300 inches of snow annually and yields some of the best in-bounds expert terrain in the state, maybe even the country. This is Mt. Crested Butte, a marvelous modern extension of the town, with its comfortable—not flashy—condo village whose attitude is as friendly and unaffected as the town's. This is a resort that actually offers free skiing at the beginning and end of the season (usually November 20–December 19 and April 5–18). This town and resort have a symbiotic relationship that is as unique as any you'll find in American ski country; in few other places are the pleasures of the mountain and treasures of the town so closely interwoven.

Children's services: day-care, tel. 970/349–2259; instruction, tel. 970/346–2209

Snow phone: tel. 970/349–2323

Police: tel. 970/349–6516

Hospital: Hughston Sports Medicine Clinic, tel. 970/349–4370; Gunnison Valley Hospital, tel. 970/641–1456

Crested Butte Chamber of Commerce: tel. 970/349–6438

Crested Butte Mountain Resort Properties: tel. 970/349–4600

Road conditions: tel. 970/641-8008 or 303/639–1234

Towing: Crested Butte Auto Repair, tel. 970/349–5251; AAA Towing, tel. 970/641–2628

FIVE-STAR FAVORITES

Best run for vertical: Banana Funnel

Best run overall: Paradise Bowl to Treasury

Best bar/nightclub: Kochevar's Saloon

Best hotel: Crested Butte Marriot Resort

Best restaurant: Soupçon

HOW TO GET THERE

By Plane

Flights from major cities land at **Denver International Airport** (*see* Getting to Colorado Resorts, *above*), 250 miles away. **Gunnison Airport** (tel. 970/641–2304) is 30 miles from the resort and has daily United Express flights coming from Denver. American flies direct to Gunnison from Dallas/Fort Worth. American West has two daily flights from Phoenix, and Delta flies in daily from Atlanta.

By Car

Crested Butte is 230 miles from Denver. Take Route 285 south to Poncha Springs; head west on Route 50 to Gunnison; then take Route 135 north into Crested Butte.

By Bus

Greyhound Lines (tel. 800/231–2222) has regularly scheduled service from Denver, Colorado Springs, and Grand Junction into Gunnison.

GETTING AROUND

By Shuttle

A shuttle bus, **Mountain Express** (tel. 970/349–5616), travels every 15 minutes between town and resort, making it easy to stay slope-side. Service is complimentary. **Alpine Express** (tel. 970/641–5074 or 800/822–4844) provides service between the town and the resort, as well as from Gunnison Airport.

By Taxi

Crested Butte Town Taxi (tel. 970/349–5543) offers daily service around town and to nearby surrounding areas, from 8:30 AM to 2:30/3:00 AM.

THE SKIING

Just as the town of Crested Butte has eschewed the slinky status symbols that drive other remodeled ski towns, so, too, has the resort bucked the middle-of-the-road tendency that other liability-cautious resorts have adopted when it comes to the skiing. These days most ski areas don't promote extreme skiing for fear of lawsuits and even higher insurance premiums, but not Crested Butte.

The resort is unique because it hasn't tamed the radical stuff. I'm talking about the double-black-diamond dares of the Extreme Limits—gonzoid, out-of-bounds, take-your-life-in-your-own-hands terrain that few want and even fewer can handle. After all, this is where the U.S. Extreme Freeskiing and Snowboarding Championships are held annually.

A legacy from an earlier time, this resort's extreme side goes back to the days when test pilots and air jockeys came to "the Butte" to tempt fate, to carve and twist and spin in reckless and radical abandon. Though it has been mellowed some by increased common sense and modern ski patrolling, that attitude is still here.

Oh, don't misunderstand, this is an all-around ski mountain, with a well-balanced mix of terrain from novice to advanced. The lower flanks of this intimidating-looking spire of a mountain provide a mellow novice area, while the midsection is mostly heads-up intermediate skiing with some advanced options that give you a taste of the Butte's wild side without committing you to the resort's 500-plus acres in the Extreme Limits—some of the steepest, gnarliest, most untamed in-bounds skiing in America.

Fanatics and families alike can seek their own level, and whether you're experiencing the thrill of those first linked turns on a mile-long novice run, stoking your way down an ego-stroking intermediate boulevard, or driving your skis down a 50-degree pitch, you're still pushing your own limits as far as you dare.

As you look up the mountain, the shoulders to the left and right are for adrenaline junkies and other experts—tough, steep, untamed double-black-diamond territory. The middle section of the mountain is mostly intermediate, with groomed, steep high-speed cruisers and some good but less extreme black runs; beginners have a section with long, meandering trails of the lower part of the mountain all to themselves.

All lift traffic starts with the Keystone or Silver Queen high-speed quad lifts, which terminate at the village base area. The Queen shoots straight up to a point just below the summit, where you can take the High lift for the extreme chutes or come back down the middle of the mountain on intermediate trails. The Keystone lift from the village cuts left to a mid-mountain ridge and gives novices access to the majority of the green runs; intermediates can ski from it down the lower part of the North Face and ride the Paradise or Teocalli lifts.

Although the overall layout appears to favor experts (47% of the terrain), other levels can be comfortable here because of the number of transition runs that encourage a novice to tackle a modest blue run and intermediates to try a groomed black run.

Novices

Crested Butte's excellent novice terrain is well contained on the lower shoulder of the mountain, and there's little chance of inadvertent interaction with more advanced skiers. There are long, well-groomed green runs plus a smaller area of shorter runs for those first-ever turns. The Peachtree lift, which starts from the village center, serves those gentle slopes, and once you can turn your skis comfortably in either direction, you can head for the Keystone lift, which gives you a larger and slightly more challenging choice. If you go to the left as you get off the lift, pick up Houston, a mile-long extrawide boulevard that lets you carry your speed with security. Or take a sharp left onto Peanut, a gently undulating carpet where you can practice linking turns. From Peanut pick up Roller Coaster, which gives you a taste of some short, slightly steeper pitches; or Smith Hill, with its scattering of island glades.

Once you've gained confidence, head down to the Painter Boy and Gold Link lifts by taking Keystone to the top and coming down Houston. Here's a secluded mini–mountain network of blue/green runs that lets you open the envelope of experience a little wider. These are all groomed runs, with a slightly steeper pitch than you will have been used to, but their width and smooth cut makes them skiable for novices with basic ski control and a little ambition to improve. They are seldom crowded and contain no surprises like drop-offs, but you can get your first taste of smooth, well-rounded moguls on Cascade.

Intermediates

Like all levels at Crested Butte, intermediates have a chance to push their experience meter a notch higher if they take advantage of the full range of terrain. You can start the day by taking either the Keystone or Silver Queen lifts from the base village. If you take the Silver Queen, turn left off the lift and head for Keystone (the run), then Silver Queen Road; you can catch the early morning sun in the Paradise Bowl area. This wide-open bowl is a leg warmer that leads to the narrower intermediate runs of the lower Paradise.

From the Keystone lift, go right, into the network of blue runs that encompasses the lower two-thirds of the mountain's north face. Drop down Meander through some trees and a steep at the end for a little adrenaline booster, then cut right onto the wide, tree-surrounded boulevard known as Bushwacker to the bottom of the Teo-calli lift. Ride it to the top back to your original starting point.

Head right down Bushwacker again and take Paradise off to the right to Paradise lift, which takes you up to the wide and well-groomed Paradise Bowl area. Ski into the bowl and work your way down, staying right so you can pick up Canaan, a narrow (but not too narrow) and lightly trafficked twister that leads to Upper Treasury, a straight shot that pitches and dips through the trees to the bottom of the East River lift. From the top of this lift, on this lower hip of the mountain, there are a couple of steep cruisers such as Black Eagle and Lower Treasury, or if you feel you can handle a black run, try the show-me-what-you-can-do bumps on Resurrection under the chair.

When you're ready to try some more challenging trails off the already-visited Paradise lift, take the East River lift to the top and turn right to Daisy, which you'll stay on all the way to the Paradise lift. Ride Paradise to the top and turn right onto Ruby Road, a steep, wide powder field that narrows as it cuts over to the Silver Queen lift and turns into the superlong and steep International. This leg burner—often ungroomed—

takes you to the bottom of the Silver Queen lift. From the top of this lift, turn left onto Keystone for some well-rounded moguls. To avoid the slew of greens that lie below, take a sharp right onto lower Ruby Chief and cruise down to the bottom of Paradise lift. An alternative to this route is to take Silver Queen Road from the top of Silver Queen lift and move into the Paradise Bowl.

Experts

Do you want radical, untamed vertical chutes and eyeball-high moguls? To reach such challenges, ride the Silver Queen lift and go left on upper Keystone to the steep and bumpy Jokerville, Twister, and Crystal runs. When you're ready to move on, ski International or Silvanite down to the Silver Queen lift and take Keystone down a short stretch to the High lift to reach the Headwall, a vast, steep bowl dotted with glades that is ungroomed, untamed, and out of this world for those who can handle it. Ski down the Headwall to the North Face lift and take it to the top to reach the Extreme Limits, the steepest and largest lift-served terrain in North America. (A typical black-diamond slope at other American resorts averages between 27 and 33 degrees. By comparison, Crested Butte's extreme terrain averages 39 to 44 degrees.) Before tackling North Face, Spellbound Bowl, Phoenix Bowl, and Third Bowl—all high on the mountain's shoulders—remember that you're taking on the wilderness and all that goes with it: wide, steep couloirs, exposed rocks, heart-stopping cliffs, thick timber, and deep, ungroomed snow.

Another area for such extremism is the Banana Funnel, reached on the Silver Queen lift; turn left and then left again under the lift to explore the steep, narrow chutes of Upper Forest, Upper Peel, and Hot Rocks.

A good way to determine whether you're up to these extreme areas is to ski the Tower 11 chutes. To reach them, just ski down the right side of Paradise Bowl until you reach a marked gate in the boundary rope—then traverse a short distance to the edge of the chutes. They are steep, forested runs filled with deep snow that cross under the Paradise chair. If that feels comfortable, you can push your envelope by progressing your way across the North Face into steeper and more radical terrain.

You should note that the resort's staunch promotion of its extreme skiing does not suggest laxness toward irresponsible or reckless pursuit of the radical. If you are unsure, don't get in over your head. There are free guided tours of the Extreme Limits by the Crested Butte Resort guides twice daily, or you can arrange to join one of the extreme-skiing workshops that include lessons and guided tours.

SNOWBOARDING

Snowboarders can practice their skills here in a controlled environment or test their mettle on some of the most radical terrain in the country. A snowboarders-only terrain park on Smith Hill Run contains log slides, quarter pipes, and other obstacles. But what Crested Butte is really becoming known for is its adventure snowboarding: the steep, adventurous, no-holds-barred terrain in the Extreme Limits area. As testament to this reputation, the U.S. Extreme Snowboarding Championships have been held here four years in a row, and the ESPN X Games returned for its second season in 1999.

Beginning and novice snowboarders can spend days riding the lower slopes off the Keystone Express lift–and should. Beyond this vast expanse of easy, freeway-width slopes there is little else that truly qualifies as beginner terrain. Having mastered Roller Coaster, Poverty Gulch, Mineral Point, and Smith Hill, confident and adventurous beginners can progress to the intermediate Keystone trail just below the top of the Twister lift. If you can easily ride Keystone, you'll be ready for the numerous intermediate trails that cluster in the Paradise Bowl basin.

Intermediates can start the day on the Silver Queen Express lift. At the top, make your way down the narrow upper Keystone trail, taking a sharp right at Silver Queen Road, a cat track that leads to Paradise Bowl. Here the terrain is open, with easy mogul fields and lots of ravines, banks, and natural hits. If you like to ride walls, the Canaan trail at the midway point of the Paradise lift offers big-wave riding time. When Canaan gets icy and crowded, the Ruby Chief and Forest Queen trails, just a tad farther down the hill, offer an escape valve.

Crested Butte is ideal for **expert** snowboarders, but even the double-black-diamond slopes at most resorts won't prepare you for the cliff bands and 45-plus-degree slopes in Crested Butte's Extreme Limits. Before venturing out onto Headwall, the North Face, or Phoenix Bowl, test your abilities on Upper Peel, Forest, and Hot

Rocks, all just south of the Silver Queen quad. If you can't handle these trails with ease, forget about taking the High Lift to The Headwall. When you are ready for some really gnarly terrain, cross over from the Silver Queen lift to Paradise Bowl via Silver Queen Road. As you enter the bowl, look for a surface lift off to the right; this is the North Face poma, and it provides access to Crested Butte's treacherous back country. Mountain guides are available, and it's worthwhile to take a tour with one—a wrong turn in the Extreme Limits can lead you to the edge of a 50-foot cliff, with no way down but to walk out—or jump.

OTHER SNOW SPORTS
Crested Butte's No Limits Center (tel. 888/954–6487) offers a whole host of activities, some mild, others wild. Expert guides take participants through intensive programs in **ice climbing, winter mountaineering, rescue training,** and **avalanche survival.** Also available are less-demanding activities, such as **dog sledding** and **snowshoeing.**

NEARBY
A rustic wilderness retreat 12 miles north of Crested Butte just off the scenic Kebler Pass Road, **Irwin Lodge** (Box 457, Crested Butte, 81224, tel. 888/464–7946), accessible solely by snowmobile in winter, has 2,200 skiable acres, 2,100 feet of vertical, and a whopping 600 inches of snow per season. Activities include snowshoeing, cross-country skiing, guided snowmobile tours, and backcountry skiing on untracked bowls and trails. **Monarch Ski & Snow-**

board Area (1 Powder Pl., Monarch, 81227, tel. 719/539–3573 or 888/ 996–7669), roughly 30 miles east of Gunnison on Highway 50, is a 670-acre resort that skis like a much bigger mountain, with a good balance of terrain, from tame beginner slopes to challenging expert trails that rival anything at the better-known Colorado mountains. Located at the convergence of two winter weather systems, Monarch often has one of the highest snow accumulations in Colorado. Monarch also offers some of the least expensive Sno-Cat powder tours in the country.

WHERE TO STAY

The modern mountain village is made up of large resort hotels, shops, restaurants, and condos stacked on the hills around the base of the ski area. In the town of Crested Butte, small inns and B&Bs are part of the flavor of Colorado's largest National Historic District. A shuttle bus system links the two. Families and groups tend to stick to the on-mountain accommodation, while couples tend to feel more at home in the more personalized in-town lodgings. All accommodations can be booked through **Crested Butte Vacations,** tel. 800/544–8448.

Expensive

Crested Butte Club
The beautifully restored circa-1880 Croatian Miners' Hall in the town of Crested Butte is the epitome of Victorian elegance, enhanced by all the modern touches. The rooms are designer-decorated with period cherry furnishings, four-poster or canopy beds, fireplaces, and huge copper bath-

tubs. The lounge and piano bar are soothing oases of dark wood and brass trim. It's definitely a place for romantics. *512 2nd St., Crested Butte 81224, tel. 970/349–6655 or 800/815–2582. 6 rooms, 1 suite. Facilities: indoor lap pool, steam bath, hot tub, weight-lifting gym, aerobics room, climbing wall, massage, spa. MC, V. $150–$225, including Continental breakfast.*

Crested Butte Marriott Resort
This six-story, horseshoe-shape, off-white stucco building only 35 yards from the lifts is the only full-size, full-service ski-in/ski-out hotel on the mountain. The public areas are spacious, with deep carpets of maroon and dark green. Each of its standard rooms is large, with a sitting area with a sleeper couch and several comfortable chairs. The suites are twice as large. Both the rooms and the suites are finished in green and beige and come with a balcony, a mini refrigerator, and a whirlpool tub. Some of the king-size suites have a fireplace. *500 Gothic Rd., Mt. Crested Butte 81225, tel. 970/349–4060 or 800/544–8448, fax 970/349–4466. 210 rooms, 52 suites. Facilities: 2 restaurants, lounge, indoor pool, sauna, 3 hot tubs, exercise room, recreation room, laundry. AE, D, DC, MC, V. $59–$806.*

Crested Mountain Village
This modern-looking condo complex stands slope-side in the mountain village and comprises five different buildings—the Buttes, Crested Mountain, Crested Mountain North, the Penthouses, and Crested Butte Lodge. All but the lodge have units ranging from studios to three bedrooms, with fireplaces and balconies. The condos

are decorated with modern, comfortable, practical furnishings whose styles depend on the owner—anything from Southwestern with its requisite gentle earth tones to contemporary minimalist decor with lots of smooth surfaces and gray tones. *500 Gothic Rd., Mt. Crested Butte 81225, tel. 970/349–4718 or 800/950–2133, fax 970/349–2144. 22 rooms, 66 units. Facilities: indoor pool, hot tub, sauna, daily housekeeping. AE, D, MC, V. $54–$684.*

Gateway at Crested Butte
These ski-in/ski-out condos next to the Peach Tree lift are some of Crested Butte's nicest. The one- to three-bedroom units accommodate up to eight people. All have a full kitchen, fireplace, washer and dryer, and two balconies—most overlooking the slopes. A hot tub and sauna will soothe your muscles after a hard day on the steeps. If you don't mind being out of town a little—but want to be right in the middle of the ski action—this is the place to stay. *400 Gothic Rd., Mt. Crested Butte 81225, tel. 970/349–5705 or 800/451–5699. 17 units. Facilities: sauna, hot tub. AE, D, MC, V. $185–$510.*

Village Center Condominiums
These three condo buildings, about 50 feet from the lifts, are an excellent slope-side deal, with a combination of one-, two-, three-, and four-bedroom units. The decor is ultramodern, with high ceilings, white walls, and contemporary furnishings. The individual units are not overly large, but they are well laid out to maximize space. Each comes with a fireplace and a balcony. *Box 5200, Mt. Crested Butte 81225,* *tel. 970/349–2111 or 800/521–6593, fax 970/349–6370. 30 units. Facilities: outdoor hot tub, ski storage. D, MC, V. $130–$485.*

Moderate

Claim Jumper
This entire B&B is filled with a truly outrageous collection of memorabilia and antiques. Each of the rooms is themed to the hilt and could be a museum in its own right. One is a complete replica of a service station, gas pump and all; another is wall-to-wall Coca-Cola trinkets, including a soda machine; while yet another is bow-to-stern nautical gear. Rooms are equipped with a queen-size bed; suites have a queen and two twins, making them a good choice for families. Gourmet breakfast is included. *714 Whiterock Ave., Crested Butte 81224, tel. 970/349–6471. 5 rooms, 2 suites. Facilities: hot tub, sauna. MC, V. $89–$129, including full breakfast.*

Elk Mountain Lodge
The miners who originally stayed in this turn-of-the-century hotel in the town of Crested Butte certainly never enjoyed the kind of luxury it now offers. The elegant lobby with its chintz-covered furnishings and grand piano sets the tone, and the peerless good taste continues in the individually decorated rooms. Room occupancy is limited to two guests, but children can be accommodated in an adjoining room—there are three sets of these. *129 Gothic Ave., Box 148, Crested Butte 81224, tel. 970/349–7533 or 800/374–6521, fax 970/349–5114. 19 rooms. Facilities: bar, hot tub, library. AE, D, MC, V. $88–$118, including full breakfast.*

Nordic Inn

If you prefer slope-side small-inn accommodations, this family-owned Norwegian-style lodge about 300 yards from the lifts is a good choice. The decor in the rooms and suites is Scandinavian simplicity, with lots of wood and mountain antiques. The rooms are not huge; if you need a little extra space, pick one of the suites or one of the adjacent chalets. *14 Treasury Rd., Mt. Crested Butte 81225, tel. 970/349–5542, fax 970/349–6487. 24 rooms, 2 suites, 2 chalets. Facilities: hot tub, sundeck. AE, MC, V. $107–$315.*

Sheraton Crested Butte Resort

In the heart of the mountain village, this modern hotel has an opulent lobby of cabin logs and river stone, and a massive hearth; furnished with comfy, overstuffed furniture, it's the ideal place to curl up with a book or browse the morning paper. Amenities such as a restaurant with a lovely breakfast buffet, a deli, an exercise room, and a gift shop make this an excellent hotel for families. *6 Emmons Rd., Crested Butte 81225, tel.: 888/223–2469 or 970/349–8000, fax 970/349–2397. 143 rooms, 109 suites. Facilities: pool, hot tub. AE, D, MC, V. $81–$320.*

Inexpensive

Cristiana Guesthaus

This cozy Euro-style lodge in the town of Crested Butte combines B&B friendliness with the privacy of an inn. Some of the simple, homey, individually decorated rooms will handle up to four people. Smoking is not permitted. *621 Maroon Ave., Box 427, Crested Butte 81224, tel. 970/349–5326 or 800/824–7899, fax 970/349–1962. 21 rooms. Facilities: sauna, hot tub. AE, D, MC, V. $65–$87, including Continental breakfast.*

Last Resort

This delightfully unpretentious B&B in downtown Crested Butte has wood, stucco, and brick decor. The best room is the Miner's Cabin, the original cabin around which the rest of the house is built. All rooms and suites are equipped with skylights and balconies; the suites also have Jacuzzis. Despite the luxuries, the mood is rustic and homey, as reflected in dark woods, overstuffed furniture, and simple pastel colors. Breakfast is served in either the solarium or your room. *213 3rd St., Box 722, Crested Butte 81224, tel. 970/349–0445 or 800/349–0445. 4 rooms, 2 suites. Facilities: solarium, steam room, library. MC, V. $95–$105, including full breakfast.*

Manor Lodge

The European-style Manor Lodge, about 250 yards from the lifts, is an alternative to condo living on the mountain. The rooms are fairly large; some have a fireplace. The wood-and-brick decor creates a cozy mountain ambience. *650 Gothic Rd., Mt. Crested Butte 81225, tel. 970/349–5365 or 800/826–3210, fax 970/349–5360. 53 rooms, 4 suites. Facilities: restaurant, bar, hot tub, laundry, indoor ski storage. AE, MC, V. $73–$135, including Continental breakfast.*

WHERE TO EAT
Expensive
Le Bosquet

Owners Candace and Victor Shepard offer a French country menu and decor. This is an elegant place for couples seeking romantic ambience and fine dining. An award-winning wine list complements main entrées that include roast duckling in a port wine cherry sauce, hazelnut chicken, and roast Colorado rack of lamb. *6th and Bellevue/Majestic Plaza, Crested Butte. 970/349–5808. Reservations essential. AE, D, MC, V.*

Soupçon

Here you'll find innovative French cuisine in an atmosphere that is reminiscent of a small country inn in the heart of France. It's tiny and tucked away off the main street in a minuscule log cabin built at the turn of the century. The menu changes daily and is posted on a chalkboard; there are two seatings nightly. Some exceptional dishes that are always available are swordfish with béarnaise sauce and roast duckling with plum sauce. *Just off 2nd St. behind Forest Queen, 127A Elk Ave., Crested Butte, tel. 970/349–5448. Reservations essential. AE, MC, V.*

Timberline Restaurant

This restored miner's cabin characterized by clean lines and light woods offers intimate dining upstairs and something a bit more lively below. The menu is Continental, and the twists are pure Rocky Mountain. You'll rarely see the same menu twice. Entrées may include venison with wild mushrooms or pheasant braised with a ginger sauce. The crisp-skinned whitefish is deliciously different. *21 Elk Ave., Crested Butte, tel. 970/349–9831. Reservations essential. AE, MC, V.*

Moderate

The Bacchanale

This small house turned restaurant—complete with antique tables, stained-glass windows and light fixtures, and the good old red and green found in so many houses of Italian cuisine—has a lineup of northern Italian dishes that includes the requisite pasta choices but also excellent veal and seafood dishes. The seafood fra diavolo, a blend of shrimp and scallops in a tomato and jalapeño pepper sauce, certainly lives up to expectations. *208 Elk Ave., Crested Butte, tel. 970/349–5257. AE, D, MC, V.*

Idle Spur Brewery and Pub

Crested Butte's first microbrewery is a rollicking spot, with massive log beams and a huge stone fireplace—half bar and half restaurant—and serves the best steaks in town, all aged Colorado beef. The portions are huge and cooked precisely as ordered. There's also a choice of ribs and prime rib. *226 Elk Ave., Crested Butte, tel. 970/349–5026. AE, MC, V.*

The Slogar

This is another creation of Mac and Maura Bailey (who also own Soupçon, above). The skillet-fried chicken, the centerpiece of the meal, is served with all-you-can-eat helpings of delicious sweet-and-sour coleslaw, mashed potatoes, fresh-baked biscuits, and sweet corn. Ice cream tops off the meal. If you are totally antichicken, you can switch to steak, accompanied by the same dishes. It's in a great setting—a totally renovated 1882 Victorian restaurant. *517 2nd St., Mt. Crested Butte, tel. 970/349–5765. MC, V.*

Swiss Chalet

At this wood-trimmed, chalet-style mountain restaurant with dark green and red decor and low ceilings, you can sample cheese and meat fondues, plus raclette in two varieties—one with traditional Buendnerfleisch and another with beef tenderloin. There are also some good German specialties, such as schnitzel, smoked pork loin chops, and a particularly good dish of grilled venison medallions served with lingonberry sauce. *620 Gothic Rd., Mt. Crested Butte, tel. 970/ 349–5917. AE, MC, V.*

Woodstone Grille

Mount Crested Butte's finest dining in a relaxed, mountain atmosphere: With a blend of Italian cuisine and some American favorites, the menu includes stuffed lobster, olive crusted filet mignon, spectacular desserts, and an extensive wine list. *Sheraton Crested Butte Resort, 6 Emmons Rd., Mt. Crested Butte, tel. 970/349–8030. AE, D, MC, V.*

Inexpensive

Antler's Restaurant

Entrées here feature Bistro-style cuisine, including habanero mango grilled chicken, certified Black Angus beef, a wide selection of burgers, hearty salads and sammies, and an extensive list of tasty appetizers. The Antler deck is a great meeting spot for burgers and brats. The more than ample breakfast offering called the Silver Queen buffet, is a great place to fuel up before hitting the slopes. *Marriott Resort Hotel, Mt. Crested Butte, tel. 970/349–4042. AE, D, MC, V.*

Donita's Cantina

Among the attractions here are monster margaritas, great salsa served with a mountain of nacho chips, and fajitas in superlarge portions, sizzling and spicy. Olé! Watch out for long lines, however. *330 Elk Ave., Crested Butte, tel. 970/349–6674. Reservations not accepted. AE, D, MC, V.*

Karolina's Kitchen

The menu here is simple but extensive, with a series of daily blue plate specials ranging from meat loaf to fresh fish, plus other items, including enormous sandwiches, hamburgers, fish-and-chips, cajun chicken, kielbasa and sauerkraut, and beef bourguignonne. There's nothing if not variety here, and no entrée costs more than $10. *127 Elk Ave., Crested Butte, tel. 970/349–6756. MC, V.*

Wooden Nickel

This saloon-restaurant, where the decor is dark wood, the artwork portrays local scenes, and the back bar is 100 years old, offers a late-night menu and a happy hour from 3 to 6 daily. It serves fast food, done well, in a lively hive. The menu covers a wide range of tastes, including steaks, ribs, sandwiches, burgers, steamed clams, fresh fish, and lots of other staples. *222 Elk Ave., Mt. Crested Butte, tel. 970/349–6350. AE, D, DC, MC, V.*

Best Bets for Breakfast

Bakery at Mount Crested Butte

Here you can drink the best coffee on the mountain and enjoy an awesome lineup of muffins, breads, nut bars, cookies, and pastries, as well as the

Bierox, a veggie pocket. *Opposite bus center, Mountain Village, tel. 970/349–1419. No credit cards.*

Bakery Café
In the center of town, this café has a full range of baked goods including croissants with different fillings and bagels, breads, and breakfast pastries. Specialty coffees and fresh-squeezed orange juice are available. *302 Elk Ave., tel. 970/349–7280. MC, V.*

NIGHTLIFE AND ENTERTAINMENT
Après-Ski

Rafters
Right at the bottom of the lifts, Rafters is a natural after-ski watering hole. Count on its being crowded and noisy. It always has music. The beer is cheap, and the margaritas strong. *Gothic Bldg., Ski Village, tel. 970/349–2298. AE, D, MC, V.*

Loud and Lively/Dancing
Kochevar's Saloon
This saloon and gaming hall has been around for almost a century, and not a lot has changed. It's still the original log building that Butch Cassidy once vacated in a hurry, and the games are still the main theme—shuffleboard, pool, darts, and now, sports on TV. *127 Elk Ave., Crested Butte, tel. 970/349–6745. MC, V.*

More Mellow
Crested Butte Club Pub
Complete with its wood-and-brass decor (including a back bar from 1886) and log fire, this is just the spot to sip some suds or enjoy a late night-cap. It has comfortable wingback chairs, an easy pace, and a dart board. There are TVs for sporting events. *Crested Butte Club, 512 2nd St., Crested Butte, tel. 970/349–6655. D, MC, V.*

KEYSTONE RESORT

KEYSTONE RESORT

Box 38
Keystone, CO 80435
Tel. 970/496–2316 or
800/222–0188
www.vailresorts.com

STATISTICALLY SPEAKING

Base elevation: 9,300 feet

Summit elevation: 12,200 feet

Vertical drop: 2,900 feet

Skiable terrain: 1,860 acres

Number of trails: 116

Longest run: 3 miles

Lifts and capacity: 2 high-speed gondolas, 5 high-speed quads, 1 quad, 2 triple chair-lifts, 5 doubles, 5 surface; 27,873 skiers per hour

Daily lift ticket: $52

Average annual snowfall: 230 inches

Number of skiing days 1997–98: 210

Snowmaking: 859 acres; 46%

Terrain mix: N 51%, I 36%, E 13%

Snowboarding: yes

Among Summit County's four ski resorts, Keystone competes with Copper Mountain for size and variety of terrain. A merger of Keystone and Breckenridge with Vail Resorts (Vail and Beaver Creek) makes Keystone part of the world's largest ski company. For Keystone it also means an interchangeable lift ticket with the other three resorts as well as deep pockets to fund additional capital improvements.

Keystone has long been known for good, all-around skiing on three peaks and a well-run resort area, but overall it has lacked the spirit of Colorado ski areas that have grown up around established local communities, such as Breckenridge. Now, however, efforts are being made to change all this. Intrawest—the folks who developed the award-winning Blackcomb resort in Canada and recently bought Copper Mountain—began a $1 billion, 15-year village upgrade in 1995 to create a pedestrian village at the heart of Keystone. Already several new stone-and-timber ski-in/ski-out lodges, along with taverns, brew pubs, cafés, and upscale shops, have revitalized the River Run base area. Plans eventually call for a performing arts theater, an expanded cross-country center at the golf course, and bike paths and boardwalks linking the resort's several neighborhoods.

Even now, Keystone has much to recommend it: an enviable range of terrain spread over a vast ski-able area, an ample variety of accommodations, arguably the best grooming outside Utah's Deer Valley or nearby Beaver Creek, the largest night-skiing operation in the country, and a superb shuttle-bus system. It also draws more than a million skiers a year, everyone from executive family types with cash to spare to penny-wise day-trippers from Denver.

With the new development has come something heretofore unknown to Keystone: an active nightlife. The opening of Keystone's slopes to snowboarders in 1996 has brought a youthful energy to the resort, and several new après-ski spots keep both skiers and locals around after the slopes close. If you're in need of more action, head over to nearby Frisco, which has some good and funky nightspots. If you crave action on the slopes, the Outback area should satisfy all but the most manic.

Children's services: tel. 970/
496–4182

Snow phone: tel. 970/496–
4111

Police: Summit County sheriff's dept., tel. 970/668–8600

Medical center: Snake River
Health Services, tel. 970/496–
1440

Hospital: Summit Medical
Center, tel. 970/668–3300

Summit County Chamber of
Commerce: tel. 970/668–2051

Avalanche hot line: tel. 970/
668–0600

Taxi: Around Town Taxi, tel.
970/453–8294; Rainbow Taxi
tel. 970/453–7246

Road conditions: tel. 970/
453–1090

Towing: Paul's Towing, tel.
970/468–6936

FIVE-STAR FAVORITES

Best run for vertical: Ambush

Best run overall: Geronimo

Best bar/nightclub: Out of
Bounds

Best hotel: Ski Tip Lodge

Best restaurant: Keystone
Ranch

Most of the ski-in/ski-out accommodations are now at the River Run base area, where the Skyway gondola provides quick access to the summit and the more challenging runs on North Peak and Outback. The Mountain Village base area at the bottom of the Peru Express, on the west end of Keystone Mountain, also has slope-side condominiums.

Outside the ski area boundaries, about a mile down the highway toward Frisco, is the Keystone Village center, with the Keystone Lodge (the resort's flagship hotel), a restaurant and shopping arcade, and the largest outdoor skating rink in North America. This is a nice alternative to the River Run base area, but as it's not within walking distance of most area hotels, it tends to be a quiet spot, frequented mostly by guests of the Keystone Lodge. Shuttle buses connect guests from any of the resort's lodging properties with the lifts. If you value privacy, efficiency, and moderately upscale pampering, this is a terrific place to ski.

HOW TO GET THERE

By Plane
Denver International Airport (*see* Getting to Colorado Resorts, *above*) is 75 miles to the east.

Shuttle Service
Resort Express (tel. 970/468–7600) runs an hourly shuttle from Denver International Airport between 9 AM and 11 PM and to the airport between 6 AM and 8 PM. The trip costs $44 one-way and $88 round-trip.

By Car
From Denver International Airport take I–70 west to Exit 205 and go 6 miles north on U.S. 6 to the Keystone Resort. All major car-rental companies have offices at Denver International Airport (*see* Getting to Colorado Resorts, *above*).

By Bus
Greyhound Lines (tel. 800/231–2222) runs six trips daily from Denver to Silverthorne, 6 miles west of Keystone. The round-trip fare is $20.

By Train
See Getting to Colorado Resorts, *above*.

GETTING AROUND

Keystone is small enough so that you don't need a car. The **Keystone Shuttle** (tel. 970/496–4200) is a free regular bus service that stops at all points throughout Keystone and also connects the resort to the neighboring slopes at Breckenridge. Buses run between 7 AM and 2 AM. For Arapahoe Basin, take the **KAB Express** (tel. 970/496–4200). For the rest of Summit County, take the **Summit Stage** (tel. 970/668–0999).

THE SKIING

The skiing at Keystone actually runs over three mountain peaks: 11,640-foot Keystone Mountain, North Peak at 11,660 feet, and the Outback at 12,200 feet. You get to the backside peaks from the summit of Keystone Mountain, either by skiing down to the foot of North Peak or by riding the Outpost gondola from the top of Keystone Mountain to the top of North Peak.

The three peaks and four faces have a predictable mix of runs. Keystone Mountain bears the majority of the novice and intermediate slopes; North Peak caters to the upper intermediates and quasi-experts; and the Outback, where the runs are seldom groomed, serves up the most consistently challenging terrain, including 633 acres of above-timberline bowl skiing for aggressive intermediate and strong expert skiers.

Novices

Start your day at the Mountain House base area, where the Peru Express quad takes you to a nest of green trails on the front side of Keystone Mountain. The beginners' area and the children's bunny slopes are also adjacent to the Peru Express. It's best to keep to the right (looking down) of the quad on your way down, picking up runs like Silver Spoon, Gold Rush Alley, or Fredda's Way, all of which are smooth, groomed, and wide. Just make sure you stay right where all three of these runs converge at the base of the Ida Belle lift; from here you can take the long, winding Schoolmarm back to the Peru Express. When you're ready to ascend to the summit, take the Peru Express, ski down Silver Spoon, and ride the Saints John lift to the top. From there you can ski a scenic green wave across the mountain's shoulder before turning down Gold Rush Alley, for a taste of slightly steeper green, or Pack Saddle Bowl, for some wide-open slopes. If you feel you're up to some well-groomed blue runs, HooDoo, off the Peru Express, is a good start, or try Paymaster, via the Saints John lift with a short scoot down Schoolmarm.

For a change of scenery, ride the Outpost gondola from the Keystone summit to the North Peak summit, enjoy lunch at the Outpost Lodge, then take Fox Trot and Anticipation down to the Nordic Skiway, which will take you back to the Ruby lift, at the base of Keystone Mountain.

Intermediates

It really doesn't matter where you start, because eventually you are going to head to the backside of Keystone Mountain and then explore North Peak and the Outback. From the Mountain House base area take the Argentine double and then the Montezuma Express quad to the summit. From the River Run Plaza end of the resort, it's a straight shot on the River Run gondola. There's a series of tempting intermediate runs down the face of Keystone Mountain that you can use for warm-ups, but don't go below the base of the Montezuma quad because you'll run a speed-controlled green all the way back to the crowds at the bottom. For some good heads-up speed and groomed snow, your best choices here are the Flying Dutchman, Frenchman, and the Wild Irishman.

When you're ready to move on, head over the backside and take a good cruise down Mozart, a sprightly blue run and a good way to get to the bottom of North Peak. Here you can push the envelope a little bit with some steeper, bumpier runs such as Star Fire or Last Alamo. Want to move up another notch? Try the ungroomed bumps on Ambush or Powder Cap, or practice your turns-on-demand in the partially gladed runs of Geronimo and Cat Dancer.

To move over to the Outback, take Anticipation, on the backside of North Peak, all the way down to the base of the Outback Express quad. From its top you'll find just about anything in the intermediate spectrum: the extrasteep Oh Bob and Elk Run; heads-up glade skiing on Wolverine and Wildfire; and the wild, ungroomed bumps of Big Horn and Porcupine. Try them all, and when you're ready to go that one extra step, head over to the heavily wooded Black Forest section of the Outback for some of the deepest snow and thickest woods on the mountain.

When you are ready to leave the Outback, there is a long, flat ski-out back to the base of North Peak, so

carry a good head of speed as you pass the base of the Outback Express. Even so, you may end up walking, especially if you try it with a snowboard.

Experts

Head immediately for the Keystone Mountain summit on the River Run gondola at the River Run Plaza. From the top get warmed up on either Mineshaft or Diamond Back, two groomed, but wild, high-speed giant-slalom runs down the backside of Keystone Mountain. Grab the Santiago Express to the top of North Peak, and if the crowds are not too bad, try a run down Geronimo—steep, treed, and bumpy—or Cat Dancer—steeper and often bumpier—before heading back up on the Santiago lift. From here take a run down the intermediate Anticipation to the base of the Outback Express quad.

Your steepest and most challenging terrain on the Outback is a quartet of high-speed slashes through the woods—the Grizz, Badger, Bushwacker, and Timberwolf, where the snow is never groomed and turn-on-demand is your key to survival.

You can make turns through the trees all day here, but when it's time to leave, it can be a tedious glide on the endless Nordic Skiway to get back to the lift on Keystone Mountain. Leave early, before the track gets crowded, and spend the last few runs of the day on either North Peak or the front side of Keystone Mountain.

SNOWBOARDING

Snowboarders have long coveted the powder stashes and wide-open bowls on Keystone's Outback, but until 1996 the resort was one of the few hold-outs that banned boarders. Since then, snowboarder-friendly improvements include Area 51 (a 20-acre terrain garden) and multiple half-pipes in Packsaddle Bowl.

Besides opening its slopes to snowboarding, Keystone has invested in such improvements as terrain parks, half-pipes, trails, and maps to help riders find the most snowboard-friendly terrain. Area 51 in Packsaddle Bowl includes a 4- to 6-ft deep beginners' half-pipe and an Olympic-size experts' pipe. The terrain garden has hips, spines, gaps, and rails in a variety of sizes and configurations suitable for intermediate and expert riders. Area 51 is also lighted, allowing riders to huck big air until 9 PM. With an additional 17 trails, the area gives boarders the opporunity to ride for 12½ hours a day. New to Keystone is Upper Jackwhacker, a terrain park on its namesake trail. If you like to hunt powder in the trees, try any of the following sticklines: Wildwoods to Wolverine and Wildfire, or in between the Geronimo and Blackhawk trails.

NEARBY

When you're ready to turn things up a notch, your best bet is to head for nearby **Arapahoe Basin** (tel. 970/468-0718), where you will find some of the steepest, highest skiing in the state.

WHERE TO STAY

Keystone has some impressive lodges at the River Run base area, within walking distance of the River Run Gondola, as well as well-built condominiums in the Ski Tip Ranch neighborhood, a short shuttle bus ride from the slopes, and the slope-side Chateaux d'Mont units at the base of Keystone Mountain. Most properties are owned and operated by Keystone. These usually upscale accommodations are consistent in price and quality; units closest to the lifts tend to be the most expensive, while taking a shuttle ride if you stay at those farther away can save you considerable money. Most units have access to Keystone Fitness Center (pool, health club, and spa). **Keystone Central Reservations** (tel. 800/222-0188) handles the bookings for all their properties. To explore the options in nearby Frisco, Dillon, and Breckenridge, call **Summit County Central Reservations** (tel. 800/365-6365). In these communities you'll find smaller inns, lodges, motels, and bed-and-breakfasts, most within an easy walk of dining and nightlife options. Dillon is 6 miles from Keystone, Frisco is 12 miles, and Breckenridge 20 miles. A shuttle-bus network links all three communities with Keystone.

Expensive

Chateaux d'Mont
This is a classy ski-in/ski-out condo complex that has fine views overlooking the slopes. The suites—with two or three bedrooms—have tasteful furnishings ranging from French provincial to Colorado Southwest and are loaded with extras, including complimentary snacks and beverages, a pair of terry-cloth bathrobes, turndown service, complimentary Continental breakfast and après-ski hors d'oeuvres, and fresh flowers. A balcony or terrace, a fireplace, a hot tub, a washer and dryer, and a whirlpool bath are

part of every unit, and guests have access to Keystone Fitness Center. *Bldg. 21996, U.S. 6, Keystone 80435, tel. 970/496–2316 or 800/222–0188, fax 970/496–4343. 14 units. Facilities: 24-hr desk service, maid service, ski storage. $245–$1,175.*

Inn at Keystone

The seven-story towerlike redbrick structure, built in 1990, houses a modern full-service hotel with comfortable but not overly luxurious rooms and suites. Outdoor hot tubs overlook a spectacular view of Keystone Mountain, and guests have access to the health club at Keystone Lodge. All rooms are equipped with mini-refrigerators and coffeemakers, and two suites have hot tubs. Throughout the hotel a shiny, modern art deco theme prevails, with an emphasis on turquoise, pink, and black. *23044 U.S. 6, Keystone 80435, tel. 970/496–1334 or 800/222–0188, fax 970/496–4343. 86 rooms, 17 suites. Facilities: restaurant, bar, 3 outdoor hot tubs, 24-hr desk service, shuttle, maid service, ski storage. AE, D, DC, MC, V. $115–$338.*

Keystone Condominiums

You'll find all shapes and sizes of condo convenience at the scattered properties managed by Keystone, ranging from studios to five-bedroom houses. Most come with a kitchen, a fireplace, 24-hour switchboard service, daily housekeeping, and either a sauna, a Jacuzzi, or a pool. All have access to Keystone Fitness Center. Mountain Premium is the priciest group, with all its units slope-side, followed by Village, Resort II, and the earliest condos in Keystone, Resort I.

U.S. 6, Keystone 80435, tel. 970/496–2316 or 800/222–0188, fax 970/496–4343. 1,300 units. Facilities: restaurant, bar, hot tub, 24-hr desk service, shuttle, maid service, ski storage, laundry. AE, D, DC, MC, V. $105–$1,095, including Continental breakfast.

Keystone Lodge

This is a large, modern, sprawling hotel bordered by Keystone Lake on one side and U.S. 6 on the other. Midway along the length of the resort area, it's a five-minute shuttle bus ride from the lifts. The standard double rooms and suites are luxurious, though not overly large, and are decorated with Western motifs. Try for one with a balcony lakeside. *U.S. 6, Keystone 80435, tel. 970/468–2316 or 800/222–0188. 152 rooms. Facilities: restaurant, bar, hot tub, pool, 2 tennis courts, health club, spa, 24-hr desk service, shuttle, maid service, ski storage, laundry. AE, D, DC, MC, V. $150–$350.*

Moderate

Allaire Timbers Inn

Nestled in a wooded area at the south end of Main Street in the town of Breckenridge, this stone-and-timber log cabin inn has a great room anchored by a huge stone fireplace, as well as a reading loft and sunroom with a green slate floor and wicker furniture. The main deck and hot tub offer spectacular views of the Ten-Mile Range. *9511 S. Main St., Breckenridge 80424, tel. 970/453–7530 or 800/624–4904, fax 970/453–8699. 8 rooms, 2 suites. Facilities: outdoor hot tub, shuttle, maid service, ski storage. AE, D, MC, V. $130–$245, including full breakfast.*

Ski Tip Lodge

This painstakingly preserved 1860s stagecoach stop converted into an idyllic bed-and-breakfast has a variety of cozy rooms filled with antiques; uneven floors, bent beams, and a massive stone fireplace complement the period decor. Guests have access to Keystone Fitness Center. A buffet breakfast is included in the price, and the restaurant also serves a fine four-course dinner. *0764 Montezuma Rd., 1 mi off U.S. 6, Dillon 80435, tel. 970/496–4202 or 800/222–0188. 9 rooms, 7 with bath; 2 suites. Facilities: restaurant, bar, shuttle service, maid service, ski storage. AE, D, DC, MC, V. $120–$250, including full breakfast.*

Twilight Inn

The three-story log structure was built in 1987, but the owners based their design on neighboring historic buildings in downtown Frisco. The guest rooms are filled with antiques; no two rooms look alike, but all share a casual country feel. You can sleep in an antique mission-style sleigh bed, a Shaker-style four-poster, an iron-and-brass bed, or, most delightful of all, Aspen-log bunk beds. The common areas include a library, a TV room, and a living room in which a Continental breakfast is served each morning. *308 Main St., Frisco 80443, tel. 970/668–5009 or 800/262–1002. 12 rooms, 8 with bath. Facilities: indoor hot tub, steam room, maid service, ski storage, laundry. AE, D, MC, V. $90–$128, including Continental breakfast.*

Woods Inn

In 1994 a two-story log lodge was built right next to an authentic log cabin B&B in the heart of Frisco's historic district, about a block from Main Street. The B&B is comfortably rustic, with a variety of room choices from single to queen-size with bunk bed; there are two sitting rooms, a reading room, and spa facilities. The lodge has a flexible configuration of rooms and studios that can be opened up to produce large suites, complete with spacious living room areas. The brightly colored rooms in both buildings have lodgepole pine furniture. *205 S. 2nd Ave., Frisco 80443, tel. 970/668–3389 or 800/668–4448. 7 rooms share 2 baths (B&B); 12 rooms (hotel). Facilities: outdoor hot tub, ski storage. AE, D, MC, V. $45–$120, including full breakfast (in B&B only).*

Inexpensive

Dillon Super 8 Motel

This inexpensive standard motel is mostly frequented by college students; expect a lively and sometimes noisy atmosphere. Rooms are large and clean and have the basic amenities, some with two double beds, others with one queen-size bed. *808 Little Beaver Trail, Dillon 80435, tel. 970/468–8888 or 800/800–8000, fax 970/468–2086. 61 rooms. Facilities: 24-hr desk service, shuttle, maid service, ski storage. AE, D, DC, MC, V. $75–$115, including Continental breakfast.*

Luxury Inn

This affordable hotel in the middle of nearby Silverthorne has a log exterior. Rooms range in size from standard to king, most with multiple beds. Guests gravitate toward the hot-tub room, where a large window overlooks the mountains. *540 Silverthorne Ln., Silverthorne 80498, tel. 970/468–0800 or 800/742–1972, fax 970/267–0797.*

59 rooms. Facilities: indoor hot tub, 24-hr desk service, shuttle, maid service. AE, D, DC, MC, V. $50–$120, including Continental breakfast.

Snowshoe Motel

Groups may enjoy this funky, old-style ski motor lodge, although families may find it a little too noisy. Its tidy two-story gray cedar exterior has balconies looking onto the street. Some rooms have kitchenettes, and there is a two-room suite with a kitchen and a whirlpool tub. All rooms have a private entrance, and some connect. 521 Main St., Frisco 80443, tel. 970/668–3444 or 800/445–8658, fax 970/668–3883. 36 rooms, 1 suite. Facilities: indoor hot tub, sauna, 24-hr desk service, shuttle, maid service. AE, D, DC, MC, V. $38–$130.

WHERE TO EAT

In Keystone are some of the finest dining establishments in Summit County, while Breckenridge is an up-and-coming epicurean center. Keystone and the nearby towns of Silverthorne and Frisco also offer a good range of medium-price family eateries.

On the Mountain

The Outpost

This magnificent log-and-glass structure on the top of North Peak has views as lofty as the ceiling beams that support its roof. The upscale ski cafeteria serves pasta, meat, and poultry favorites. The deck barbecue is a favorite on warm days. (See also Alpenglow Stube and Fondue Chessel, below). Outpost Lodge, top of North Peak, Keystone, tel. 970/496–4386. AE, D, DC, MC, V.

Expensive

Alpenglow Stube

This is the finest on-mountain restaurant in Colorado. The decor is warmly elegant, with exposed wood beams, a stone fireplace, antler chandeliers, and floral upholstery. At night the gondola ride you take to get here is itself worth the price of a meal. Dinner is a six-course extravaganza composed of such Stube specialties as smoked saddle of rabbit in tricolor peppercorn sauce or rack of boar in Poire William sauce. At lunch plush slippers are provided when you remove your ski boots. Outpost Lodge, top of North Peak, Keystone, tel. 970/496–4386. Reservations essential. AE, D, DC, MC, V.

Great Northern Tavern

The exceptional dinner menu makes this upscale brew pub the place for a leisurely, intimate meal. A 35-ft mahogany bar and matching mahogany chairs and tables give the restaurant a feeling of casual elegance; a huge stone fireplace gives it warmth; and two huge brass brew kegs behind a glass wall give it authenticity. Chef Larry Johnson produces a creative nouveau American menu featuring wild game, such as venison with roasted-shallot juniper berry demi-glace, as well as such entrées as lamb and goat cheese meat loaf with garlic-mushroom sauce. For appetizers, try the rock shrimp cakes. River Run Village base, Keystone, 970/262–2202. Reservations essential. AE, D, DC, MC, V.

Keystone Ranch

A former working cattle-ranch house, this handsome 1930s log building is nestled in the trees at the Keystone Golf Course. Contrasting with the woody exterior, the dining room's Oriental rugs, antiques, and fine china create an elegantly rustic ambience. The outstanding six-course prix-fixe meal may include Muscovy duck over foie gras, veal medallions, and peppered trout. *Keystone Golf Course, Soda Ridge Rd., Keystone, tel. 970/ 496– 4386. Reservations essential. AE, D, DC, MC, V.*

Ski Tip Lodge

In this 1860s stagecoach station almost everything on the menu will melt in your mouth. The four-course prix-fixe dinner is American cuisine with a Colorado twist. The main course may be a hickory-smoked tenderloin, braised Ringneck pheasant, or red trout paupiettes with crab, shrimp, and spinach. The delicious homemade bread and soup offered in the first course are a meal in themselves. Quilts, antiques, and a stone fireplace make the lodge's Old West charm irresistible. *0764 Montezuma Rd., 1 mi off U.S. 6, Keystone, tel. 970/ 496–4202. AE, D, DC, MC, V.*

Moderate

Cafe Alpine

The eclectic menu at this cozy house offers Continental fare with Asian and Southwestern flair. Try the grilled yellowfin tuna with pink guava and mango sauce and green papaya slaw or the chili-rubbed Rocky Mountain chicken with pico de gallo, ravioli, and ancho posole broth. At the tapas bar (after 4) you can sample small plates of food from around the world. *106 E. Adams Ave., Breckenridge, tel. 970/453–8218. AE, D, DC, MC, V.*

Fondue Chessel

It's a worthwhile experience, complete with a great view, excellent fondues, and the requisite live Alpine music. The prix-fixe four-course traditional Swiss fondue meal, includes cheeses, salad, and chocolate fondue for dessert. A crusty French bread, apples, and crisp vegetables are provided for dipping in the fondue, a blend of Gruyère and Emmental Swiss cheeses accented with white wine. The raclette cheese comes with your choice of scallops, shrimp, chicken breast, veal sausage, or beef tenderloin. *Timber Ridge Room, Outpost Lodge, top of North Peak, Keystone, tel. 970/496–4386. Reservations essential. AE, D, DC, MC, V.*

Historic Mint

Built in 1862, this raucous eatery originally served as a bar and brothel. The old days are still evident in the bar's brass fittings and hand-carved wood, as well as in the antiques and vintage photographs covering the walls of the dining area. Red meat and fish are the specialty here; you cook your own on lava rocks sizzling at 1,100 degrees. A well-stocked salad bar complements your entrée. If you prefer to leave the cooking to the chef, there's a prime rib special. *347 Blue River Pkwy., Silverthorne, tel. 970/468–5247. MC, V.*

Ida Belle's Bar and Grill

In keeping with its previous incarnation as a gold mine, this restaurant has a dining room that is reached through the old mineshaft entrance and is supported by hardwood pillars and decorated with gold pans, picks, and photographs from mining days. The cuisine is mild but tasty Tex-Mex, with highlights such as chili and fajitas; the ribs and half-pound burgers are also good. For dessert, it has to be the Mal Brown sundae: a chocolate brownie with three scoops of vanilla ice cream, topped with hot fudge, whipped cream, nuts, and a cherry. *Lakeside Condominiums, next to skating pond, Keystone Village, tel. 970/496–4289. AE, D, DC, MC, V.*

Inexpensive

Gassy's Food & Spirits

This restaurant, named for miner Gassy Thompson, who lived in town in the late 1800s and was said to have made his living by swindling other miners, serves hearty American fare in generous portions. Pork barbecue is the specialty, with burgers and extra-large sandwiches vying for second place. Memorabilia from Colorado's mining days—picks, buckets, lamps, and drawings—keeps Gassy's spirit alive despite the now-honest dealings. *Mountain House, base of Keystone Mountain, Keystone Rd., Keystone Village, tel. 970/496–4130. AE, D, DC, MC, V.*

Kickapoo Tavern

This rustic bar and grill has Colorado microbrews on tap and big portions of home-style American food like chili and hearty sandwiches. The central location, outdoor patio, and TVs tuned to favorite sporting events keep the place hopping day and night. *Jackpine Lodge, River Run Plaza, Keystone, tel. 970/468–4601. AE, D, DC, MC, V.*

Best Bet for Breakfast

Razzberries at the Inn

Fill up on steak, eggs, hash browns, pancakes, and fruit at the all-you-can-eat breakfast bar overlooking the mountain before you head out to ski. *The Inn, 23044 U.S. 6, Keystone, tel. 970/496–1334. AE, D, DC, MC, V.*

NIGHTLIFE AND ENTERTAINMENT

Après-Ski

Out of Bounds

Overlooking Keystone Lake, this is a cross between a sports bar and a mountain lodge. There are 29 TVs in the bar, making it ideal for watching big sports events. Vintage ski equipment lines the walls of the log cabin-like, split-level interior. The restaurant prepares an extensive appetizer menu, sandwiches, burgers, and daily fish specials. *1254 Soda Springs Rd., tel. 970/496–4386. D, MC, V.*

Loud and Lively/Dancing

Breckenridge Brewery and Pub

The "Breck Brew Pub" has not only a great selection of homemade beers but also occasional top-quality live blues, Motown, and other R&B bands. This is a bar with all the right ingredients; just ask the locals. *600 S. Main St., Breckenridge, tel. 970/453–1550. D, MC, V.*

Salt Creek Saloon

For a boot-scootin' good time, head for this country-and-western bar in Breckenridge. Occasionally live bands perform, and line-dancing lessons are offered several nights a week. *110 E. Lincoln Ave., Breckenridge, tel. 970/453–4959. AE, D, DC, MC, V.*

Snake River Saloon

Live music with rockabilly leanings makes this a good spot to drink beer if you like a loud, music-driven environment. The crowd is generally under 30, but the occasional over-30 "senior" slips in. *23074 U.S. 6, 1 mi east of Keystone, tel. 970/468–2788. AE, DC, MC, V.*

More Mellow

Inxpot

After skiing or dinner sink into an overstuffed armchair in front of the fire, grab a book or a Hollywood script from the library shelves, play a board game, and enjoy espresso drinks, spirits, cheese and crackers, and desserts. *Black Bear Lodge, River Run Plaza, Keystone, tel. 970/496–4627. AE, D, DC, MC, V.*

Ski Tip Lodge

Sipping a brandy by the fireside at this old Western lodge filled with antiques is a good way to cap an evening. *0764 Montezuma Rd., 1 mi off Rte. 6, Dillon, tel. 970/496–4202. AE, D, DC, MC, V.*

SNOWMASS SKI RESORT

Box 1248
Aspen, CO 81612
Tel. 970/925–1220 or
800/525–6200
www.skiaspen.com

STATISTICALLY SPEAKING

Base elevation: 8,104 feet

Summit elevation: 12,510 feet

Vertical drop: 4,406 feet

Skiable terrain: 3,010 acres

Number of trails: 83

Longest run: 4½ miles

Lifts and capacity: 7 high-speed quads, 2 triples, 6 doubles, 5 surface lifts; 24,321 skiers per hour

Daily lift ticket: $62

Average annual snowfall: 300 inches

Number of skiing days 1997–98: 142

Snowmaking: 130 acres, 4%

Terrain mix: N 7%, I 55%, E 38%

Snowboarding: yes

Cross-country skiing: 48 miles of trails

This immense, self-contained resort is larger than the combined acreage of the other three areas (Aspen Highlands, Aspen Mountain, and Buttermilk) that make up the Aspen scene. Snowmass is large enough to be ranked among the five largest resorts in America, yet it's difficult to separate it from Aspen. Most people who visit Snowmass Resort spend at least some time in the town of Aspen, and visitors to Aspen—even those addicted to Aspen Mountain—would be remiss in not spending a day or two at Snowmass.

But make no mistake: One could visit Snowmass for a week and still not experience the entire gigantic extent of its six mountain sections. All levels of skiers can be challenged here and, although Snowmass is often marketed as a complete family destination because 55% of its terrain is designated intermediate, it encompasses enough curl-your-toes steeps to keep hard-core extremists happy.

At the base of this massive mountain is the Snowmass Village and shopping mall—the pedestrian epicenter of the resort—with a rapidly expanding selection of shops, restaurants, bars, hotels, and condominiums. The most appealing feature of the Snowmass complex is that virtually all of the accommodations are ski-in/ski-out, in pocket-size developments nestled on the mountain's lower flanks amid the cedars and aspens.

HOW TO GET THERE

By Car

Snowmass is 200 miles from Denver International Airport. Follow I–70 west for 3½ hours to Glenwood Springs. Follow Route 82 for 45 minutes to the Snowmass Village exit. Turn right on Brush Creek Road and follow signs to the village.

GETTING AROUND

Everything is within easy walking distance in Snowmass Village, and the **Snowmass–Aspen shuttle bus** (tel. 970/925–8484) runs constantly from 8 to 10 and 3 to 6. At other times it runs every 15 min-

Children's services: day-care, tel. 970/923–1220; nighttime baby-sitting, tel. 970/923–6080; instruction, tel. 970/923–0570 or 800/525–6200

Snow phone: tel. 970/925–1221 or 888/277-3676

Police: tel. 970/920–5400

Aspen Valley Hospital: tel. 970/925–1120

Snowmass central reservations: tel. 970/923–2000 or 800/598-2004

Resort association: tel. 970/923–2000

Road conditions: tel. 970/920–5454

Towing: Al's Towing, tel. 970/925–2265

FIVE-STAR FAVORITES
Best run for vertical: Baby Ruth

Best run overall: Hanging Valley Wall

Best bar/nightclub: Mountain Dragon

Best hotel: Silvertree Hotel

Best restaurant: La Boheme

utes. Shuttle buses take you just about anywhere in Snowmass.

THE SKIING

Snowmass is an elongated ridge of peaks and valleys that for the most part lack the knee-pounding precipitousness of the unforgiving Aspen Mountain—a vertical peak that ripples and folds into itself. That's not to say that Snowmass is all easy skiing, but it does have some of the longest, widest, most meticulously groomed intermediate slopes in Colorado. Despite its sprawling acreage it's remarkably easy to move around the mountain, picking your favorite runs from the six distinct sectors: Elk Camp, High Alpine/Alpine Springs, Big Burn, Sam's Knob, Two Creeks, and Campground. Except for the last two, all sections funnel into the base area.

On the east side on the lower face of the ridge is the new Two Creeks expansion, a series of mainly intermediate runs that meander through a massive stand of aspen before funneling down into a newly constructed base area. One of the more intriguing runs is Long Shot, which originates in the Elk Camp area above and descends 3,200 feet to the Two Creeks base. At the top side of the far eastern end of the Snowmass Ridge is Elk Camp, a mostly intermediate section that starts just above timberline and offers some of the easier intermediate runs on the mountain. Because of its exposure above timberline, it can also be one of the coldest parts of the mountain, so you'd best head for it on sunny days or days when the wind is light. To the west of that easy cruising section is the High Alpine area (also above timberline), with its tremendous variety of advanced and expert runs in the Hanging Valley Wall. Here you'll find steep, wide-open bowls and tree skiing in the slightly lower Hanging Valley Glades. When the light is flat or it's snowing, this is your best choice as long as you can manage the steeps; the lower portion turns into some easy-to-handle intermediate terrain.

The Big Burn and the wide-open intermediate and upper-intermediate boulevards, for which the resort is best known, crisscross the middle of Snowmass. On clear, sunny days this is generally the busiest part of the mountain, but on windy or snowy days visibility becomes a major problem, and you're better off heading to another area, such as Sam's Knob, which is about 1,200 feet lower and protected somewhat by the thick stands of trees. It's directly above the village, near the west end of the ridge, and has a collection of mostly advanced-intermediate runs, with a few long, winding beginner trails cutting a circuitous, gentle path down to the village. At the far west side is the Campground area, with some of the longest concentrated advanced-intermediate trails on the mountain. This area is usually one of the least crowded sections of Snowmass, and because of its lower elevation it tends to be the best choice on cold or windy days.

Each of the individual Snowmass areas is easily reached from the central base village. Early morning traffic tends to spread out quickly; the only notable traffic jam usually occurs at the Burlingame lift, which takes you up to the Sam's Knob lift. From the top of Sam's Knob you can ski down to the Big Burn lift or head down into the Campground area. To avoid this crush, you can go to the Alpine Springs or Naked Lady lifts (via the Wood Run chair from the lower village area) or take the Funnel chair up to the Elk Camp lift or Two Creeks area.

Novices

If you're an absolute beginner or extremely timid novice, the place to start out is Assay Hill, the easiest beginner slope at the resort, or Fanny Hill, a slightly longer but similarly easy green run. Both have their own lifts and are immediately above the village area, making the chairs easy to

reach from the mall. This setup is also fairly unintimidating, as more advanced skiers don't join you on the chairs—a first-time experience that's often more frightening than going down the mountain.

When you're ready to tackle something a little longer, take the Funnel lift along the east side of the mountain and try a long, easy cruise on the wide and flat Funnel Bypass. You can also ride the Burlingame lift up the middle of the mountain to the Sam's Knob chair, which you can take to the top of Sam's Knob. As you get off the lift, turn left and head for the wide-open Max Park for an introduction to skiing bowls. Take note: this green run is a little steeper than those previously mentioned, and it can also become quite crowded with more-advanced skiers heading for the Knob's intermediate trails or those heading down to the Big Burn lift.

To avoid the crowds, don't take the chair to the summit; instead, begin from the top of the Burlingame lift, where you can move easily over to Lunchline, a bit of a catwalk; to Scooper, which is slightly steeper than Lunchline but much less crowded; and to Dawdler, for a long, winding run back to the village.

Intermediates

When you're ready to move up to gentle intermediates, your best bet is to head for the Elk Camp area on the eastern side of the resort. The mostly blue runs in this area are wide and well groomed and provide an excellent place to work on turns and enjoy gentle cruising. The cut of the runs is graceful and gradual, and if you continue past the bottom of the Elk Camp lift you can enjoy a long top-to-bottom intermediate cruise of more than 2 miles on smooth Adam's Avenue. If the weather isn't suitable for the exposed Elk Camp, head for the top of Big Burn but keep in mind that the easiest runs from the top are those to the left (looking down); the runs get more difficult as you go to the right. The easiest way from the top is via Sneaky's (to the far left, looking down) or Mick's Gully, which, although it has a slight gully shape, doesn't have the steepness or walls usually found in similar gully runs. It has a steady, easy pitch, and like Sneaky's, brings you back to the green Max Park.

Experts

The best area for experts is the High Alpine; the fastest route is on the Wood Run and Alpine Springs chairs, then up the High Alpine double chair. If you feel like taking a long cruising run just to get the legs warmed up, turn right off the High Alpine chair and follow the narrow traverse (a little uphill pushing is required) that leads to Green Cabin. From the top, Green Cabin—which is usually groomed—drops to rolling, wide-open terrain, then narrows slightly as it cuts through the trees above Gwyn's High Alpine restaurant, then dips and rolls to the right before widening at a broad speed-control section. Make sure you turn right just below this and head back to the Alpine Springs chair; if you go left, it's a long, flat meander down to the village. On the next run head for Reiders, which starts out as a wide-open cruiser with the occasional tree patch, then turns bumpy. If you don't like the moguls, head to the side

in the trees, where there's usually good powder. Another good, but short, cruiser is Showcase, which runs directly under the High Alpine chair. It's fairly tame at the top, but be careful if you're carrying too much speed because the run drops off about midway down, when it becomes much steeper. The Edge—just to the right (looking down) of Showcase is another good combo run, with fast, groomed cruising up top, then a steeper mogul section—interspersed with clumps of trees—on the bottom half. All three of these runs take you to the bottom of the High Alpine chair, but if you drop any lower, you are in mostly blue territory back to the bottom of the Alice Springs lift. For a spectacular steep, turn left off the High Alpine chair to Baby Ruth. When you feel sufficiently warmed up, head for the Hanging Valley Wall. Turn left off the High Alpine chair for a short traverse; then you'll have to take your skis off for a five-minute hike up to a control gate. From here you can turn right to the Headwall or left to Roberto's. Most regulars take Headwall because it usually has better snow thanks to better exposure, is protected from the prevailing winds, and generally draws lighter traffic. Many people end up taking Roberto's because it has the most obvious entrance. Roberto's is narrower and cut between high rock faces; big bumps build up through the middle section. Below Roberto's and the Headwall, which converge in a fairly flat area, you have three choices. Stick to the left-hand boundary line and you'll enter the Union area, which is usually not crowded. It's a pretty, gladed route, not too steep, and generally has good powder. Staying with the main trail on the flats will take you to the Wall, which is wide open and has the most vertical drop of any run on the mountain but also tends to be the most crowded. Another option is to head for the Ladder, on the right side of the flats, which is a narrower run and because of its northeast exposure tends to have better snow.

Another area where you can get your adrenaline fix is the Big Burn, which is served by the Big Burn and Sheer Bliss chairs. To the left (looking down) it's mostly intermediate territory, but to the right is a good selection of black runs. For bumps try West Face or Free Fall, and for good speed cruising try the steady, even pitch of KT Gully.

SNOWBOARDING

For snowboarders, Snowmass has a comprehensive boarding program that is among the best in the country. A special terrain map points out the numerous snowboard-friendly trails and terrain parks while steering riders away from flat spots. Air junkies will want to visit Trenchtown, a new terrain part in Coney Glade area that has two lift-accessed half-pipes, video evaluation, piped-in music, and a yurt hangout complete with couches and snacks. There are also other snowboarding terrain features and amenities unknown to other resorts. Every lift, for example, has its own tool table for fine-tuning snowboard bindings.

Beginners would be advised to start at Buttermilk Mountain rather than learning to snowboard at Snowmass; fewer people and plenty of mellow beginner runs make the learning

process there smoother. That said, Snowmass also has excellent instructors and plenty of green-square trails. Most riding begins at Assay Hill, a mellow beginner run just below the main Snowmass Center. Having learned the basics, most beginners progress to the Fanny Hill lift and to the Burlingame and Coney Glade chairs, which access big, freeway-width runs ideal for learning to link turns.

Intermediates find Snowmass ideal, particularly if you like long, steady all-mountain cruisers. From Elk Camp, try Bull Run to Funnel to Fanny Hill. From High Alpine, take the black-diamond run Edge (a little steep and untamed, but manageable for strong intermediates) to the mellower Naked Lady, then follow that down to the Alpine Springs chair. From the Big Burn, take Mick's to Max Park to Lower Bonzai down to Fanny Hill. And from Sam's Knob, take a ride down Sunnyside to Ute Chute to Lunchline to Scooper and into Fanny Hill.

Experts may become addicted to Trenchtown, the new terrain park and half-pipe area in the Coney Glade area just below the Burlingame lift. However, it's worthwhile to do some backcountry roots riding in the Cirque, the massive bowl area in the Big Burn. It's a hike to get there, but The Cirque offers narrow chutes, bomb drops, and powder stashes that justify the extra effort. For dawn patrollers, the best place to find early-morning fresh powder is Sam's Knob, but hit it early—it gets trampled and tracked out by midday, when it's best to turn your attention to the trees in Sneaky's or over in the Big Burn.

OTHER SNOW SPORTS

For **snowshoeing,** stop at the equipment rental shop at the Two Creeks base (tel. 907/920–1220), where tours depart at 12:30 to 2:30 PM. To see the photogenic Maroon Bells mountains, stop in at the T-Lazy 7 Ranch (tel. 970/925–4614) to arrange a guided **snowmobile** jaunt or a trip on a **horse-drawn carriage.** Or, let the Siberian huskies at Krablooniks Kennels (tel. 970/923–4342) carry you on a **dogsled** through the backcountry surrounding Snowmass.

NEARBY

If you're an expert skier or simply want to escape the madding crowds at Snowmass and Aspen Mountain, check out **Aspen Highlands** (tel. 970/925–1220). A member of the Aspen Skiing Co. quartet, the Highlands offers a variety of black- and double-black-diamond bump runs and off-piste trails in a compact 530-acre ski area. There are also plenty of groomed cruisers, mainly on the front side, and a cluster of easy beginner trails near the base.

For first-time skiers and boarders, **Buttermilk Mountain** (tel. 970/925–9229 or 800/525–6200) offers one of the most acclaimed learn-to-ski programs in the business. But intermediates and even experts (particularly snowboarders) can profit from a morning of instruction at Aspen's primary learning center. Lately, snowboarders have begun hanging here due to the exceptionally well-groomed half-pipe and teaching terrain park, a fitting rival to the Trenchtown facility at Snowmass.

WHERE TO STAY

Virtually all the accommodations at Snowmass Village are condominiums, with most buildings dating from 1967, when the resort opened. Many have been renovated in recent years, but there remains a sameness about them. About 90% of the accommodations are ski-in/ski-out, so if slopeside convenience is your preference, it makes sense for you to stay at Snowmass. For one-stop booking, contact Snowmass Central Reservations (tel. 800/598–2004). *See also* Where to Stay *in Aspen, above.*

Expensive

The Crestwood

These condos are comfortable, practically furnished with couches and plenty of chairs, and well designed for families and small groups. The units range in size from spacious studios to one-, two-, and three-bedroom units, each with a fireplace. The decor is a pleasant mix of wood and stucco, with wheat-color furnishings and broadloom carpeting. *400 Wood Rd., Box 5460, Snowmass Village, 81615, tel. 970/923–2450 or 800/356–5949, fax 970/923–5018. 122 units. Facilities: heated outdoor pool, 2 Jacuzzis, sauna, exercise room, complimentary airport shuttle, laundry, ski storage. AE, D, DC, MC, V. $186–$1,005.*

Silvertree Hotel

The only full-service ski-in/ski-out hotel at Snowmass is definitely a class act. Although the rooms aren't especially large, they are comfortable and beautifully decorated with oak furniture. About half have balconies facing the surrounding mountains or the mall. For extra space, consider a suite, designed for four or more, with such luxurious appointments as extra-large bathrooms and mountain-facing balconies. There are also condos, from studio to five-bedroom in size, all with a kitchen, and some with a fireplace and a balcony. *100 Elbert La., Box 5009, Snowmass Village, 81615, tel. 970/923–3520 or 800/525–9402, fax 970/923–5192. 262 rooms, 15 suites, 200 units. Facilities: 4 restaurants, bar, lounge, 2 heated outdoor pools, 2 hot tubs, 2 saunas, health club, steam room, 24-hr desk service, shuttle, ski valet, ski shop, laundry, game room. AE, D, DC, MC, V. $145–$1,316.*

Snowmass Lodge & Club

This upscale lodge and villa complex is one of Snowmass's most complete facilities, with a selection of standard, premium, and deluxe rooms and one-, two-, and three-bedroom villas. Although it's not ski-in/ski-out, it is only about five minutes from the lifts by shuttle bus. The spacious, ultramodern lodge rooms include pine antiques and have a balcony overlooking the mountain or the golf course. The villas—better suited to families or small groups—are equally well appointed, with plush furniture and a fireplace. The lodge building is cozy, with a fireplace, plush couches, and hardwood floors. *0239 Snowmass Club Circle, Box G-2, 81615, tel. 970/923–5600 or 800/525–0710, fax 970/923–6944. 76 rooms, 54 villas. Facilities: restaurant, 2 snack bars, bar, health club, 3 outdoor pools (1 heated), 3 hot tubs (1 outdoor), saunas, steam room, 2 indoor tennis courts, weight room, aerobics gym, massage center, golf, cross-country center, 24-hr desk service, shuttle, ski concierge, ski storage, baby-sitting, laundry, dry cleaning. AE, D, DC, MC, V. $368–$848.*

Woodrun V Townhouses

These ultraluxurious town houses have a multilevel layout that provides lots of space, as well as some privacy. The complex is across Fanny Hill from the mall, so you can just click into your bindings and catch a lift up the mountain; in the evening you'll have only a five-minute walk to the Snowmass Mall. The units are exceptionally well furnished in a Southwestern motif and are remarkably complete, with luxury extras such as a hot tub, stone fireplace, private balcony, wet bar, multiple TVs, oversize master bathroom, and laundry facilities. Two-bedroom units have various bed configurations. *Wood Rd., Box 5550, 81615, tel. 970/923–4350 or 800/525–9402, fax 970/923–5494. 3 units. Access to facilities at Silvertree Hotel (see above). AE, D, DC, MC, V. $240–$1,316.*

Moderate

Laurelwood

These studio-size condos, two levels above the Village Mall and a 20-yard walk from the slope, have a sensible layout that makes them a cost-efficient option for four people. It's not often that you find condo convenience in pint-size packages, but Laurelwood has put them together nicely without the added cost of multibed-room units. These are well-designed quarters with high ceilings, lots of light to give the illusion of space, and little extras such as a full kitchen, a fireplace, and a balcony with a view of the mountain or the valley. *Snowmass Resort, Box 5600, 81615, tel. 970/923–3110 or 800/356–7893, fax 970/923–5314. 52 units. Facilities: outdoor pool, hot tub, sauna, daily maid service, ski storage, laundry. AE, MC, V. $120–$375.*

Stonebridge Inn

The boxy, industrial exterior does little to reveal Stonebridge's true character: This mountain inn is an excellent hotel option in a village gone condo crazy. The inn's rooms and suites are not loaded with frills, but they're roomy and comfortable: The functional, homey decor has an alpine flavor. Rooms are equipped with a coffeemaker and a mini-refrigerator. *300 Carriage Way, Box 5008, 81615, tel. 970/923–2420 or 800/ 922–7242, fax 970/923–5889. 90 rooms, 5 suites. Facilities: restaurant, bar, lounge, heated outdoor pool, outdoor hot tub, sauna, 24-hr desk service, room service, complimentary airport shuttle, ski storage, laundry. AE, D, MC, V. $70–$260, including Continental breakfast.*

Top of the Village

These good-sized two-, three-, and four-bedroom condos are tucked into the side of the hill just above the Village Mall. The trade-off for ski-in/ski-out convenience is the 450-yard trek up from the village. The condos appeal mostly to families who want to be close to the slopes yet far enough away from the commotion in the mall. The units are family-friendly— not designer decorated—and each has a fireplace and a private balcony. *855 Carriage Way, Box 5629, 81615, tel. 970/923–3673 or 800/525–4200, fax*

970/923–4420. 86 units. Facilities: heated outdoor pool, Jacuzzi, exercise room, sauna, daily maid service, ski lockers, shuttle. No credit cards. $220– $825.

Wildwood Lodge

If you prefer hotel accommodations to condos, this hotel on the Snowmass Village Shopping Plaza, 400 yards from the slopes, is a good choice because of the friendly staff. The contemporary, comfortable decor evokes a rustic Western-lodge feeling, and rooms have practical extras such as mini-refrigerators and coffeemakers. Many have a balcony overlooking the mountain. *40 Elbert La., Box 5037, 81615, tel. 970/923–3550 or 800/ 525–9402, fax 970/923–4844. 150 rooms. Facilities: restaurant, bar, hot tub, heated outdoor pool, sauna, health club, 24-hr desk service, shuttle, ski valet, ski storage, laundry. AE, D, DC, MC, V. $59-$269, including Continental breakfast.*

Inexpensive
Pokolodi Lodge

This friendly, no-frills motel-style lodge in the center of the Village Mall provides all of the basics at a basic price. Comfortable, clean rooms can accommodate four close friends or a small family. Units are furnished with a coffeemaker, mini-refrigerator, and TV. Newspapers are provided daily. *25 Daly La., Box 5640, 81615, tel. 970/ 923–4310 or 800/666–4556, fax 970/ 923–2819. 50 rooms. Facilities: outdoor hot tub, heated outdoor pool, 24-hr desk service, shuttle, ski storage, laundry. D, MC, V. $89–$198, including Continental breakfast.*

Snowmass Inn

This is one of the original properties at Snowmass and so commands a prime location in the middle of the Village Mall, a short stroll from the slopes. Guest rooms are spacious and comfortable, although slightly outdated and beginning to show signs of wear. Each unit has a queen-size bed and a queen-size sofa bed, plus basic creature comforts such as a refrigerator and coffeemaker. *67 Daly La., Box 5640, 81615, tel. 970/923–4202, fax 970/923–2819. 39 rooms. Facilities: outdoor pool, Jacuzzi, sauna, 24-hr desk service, shuttle, ski storage, laundry. MC, V. $85-$170.*

Tamarack Townhouses

There are only three buildings with six units each in two- or four-bedroom layouts in this small but well-designed complex of town houses. All units have multiple bathrooms and fireplaces. Each is decorated according to the owner's taste. Tamarack is just a few minutes' walk from the main Snowmass Village area and an even shorter distance from Lift 18. *135 Carriage Way, Box 5550, 81615, tel. 970/923–2420 or 800/525–9402. 18 units. Facilities: outdoor pool, Jacuzzi, sauna, ski storage. AE, D, DC, MC, V. $150–$837.*

The Willows

This is another comfortable but not deluxe group of town houses a short walk from the village mall. The four dark-wood structures are built like steps up the side of the hill. Available in studio and two-bedroom sizes, units are individually owned and decorated. Some have undergone a recent face-lift, but others are a bit dated. In general, all are well maintained and well equipped, with a fireplace, a laundry room, and a full-size kitchen. *Village Mall, Box 5550, 81615, tel. 970/923–4350 or 800/332–7619. 280 units. AE, D, DC, MC, V. $70–$446.*

WHERE TO EAT

You have the option of taking the 20-minute drive or shuttle bus to Aspen (*see* Where to Eat *in* Aspen, *above*), but don't overlook the expanding selection of restaurants in Snowmass.

On the Mountain

Gwyn's High Alpine Restaurant

Both cafeteria-style and full-service breakfast and lunch are offered here. If you go the cafeteria route, choose from a menu of veggie burgers and other sandwiches, fajitas, salads, and excellent soups. In the sit-down area you can order entrées such as grilled salmon and a variety of pastas. To be sure of a seat, make reservations for 11:30 AM; seating at other times is first-come, first-served. *Center of mountain, top of Alpine Springs and Naked Lady lifts, tel. 970/923–5188. AE, MC, V.*

Ullrhof

The most popular restaurant on the mountain has long lines, but the cafeteria setup moves things along. In addition to burgers, soups, stews, chili, and sandwiches, some healthier salads have been added to the menu. On sunny days the deck sees a lot of action. *Snowmass Mountain, base of Big Burn lift, tel. 970/923–5143. Reservations not accepted. AE, MC, V.*

Expensive

Cowboys Restaurant & Bar
Don't let the rustic ranch-house decor and Western memorabilia fool you. This is a fine-dining spot with a lineup of Southwestern-style entrées that lean heavily toward fresh game. Consider the Rocky Mountain trout with chipotle mashed potatos or the rack of Colorado Lamb with ratatouille. Also commanding high praise are the prime Colorado beef and the Cajun catfish soup. After dinner the cowboy atmosphere continues with live country-and-western entertainment and dancing. *78 Elbert La., Silvertree Complex, tel. 970/923–5249. AE, MC, V.*

Krabloonik
Owner Dan MacEachen has a penchant for dogsled racing, and Krabloonik (Eskimo for "big eyebrows," the name of Dan's first lead dog) helps subsidize his expensive hobby. The restaurant is in a rustic log cabin where a woodstove provides the only heat and light comes via propane lanterns. The menu is primarily game, and although some domestic meat and poultry dishes are available for the timid, you'll do best if you stay on the wilder side. Elk loin, mesquite-grilled caribou, wild boar, and roasted breast of pheasant lead the list of favorites. No matter what you choose as an entrée, order wild-mushroom soup as an appetizer. *4250 Divide Rd., tel. 970/923–3953. Reserve 2 wks in advance for dogsled ride. MC, V.*

La Boheme
Snowmass's flagship restaurant consists of two rooms separated by a large bar; the understated decor emphasizes calm pastel tones, modern beech furnishings, plenty of windows, and impressionist paintings. Nightly live music sets the tone for haute French cuisine hallmarked by subtle spices and fresh herbs. Try roast pheasant with raspberry poivrade (peppercorn sauce with peppers and port); other favorites are striped bass baked in parchment and a mixed grill of red deer and caribou. When you make your reservation, ask for a table next to the large window that overlooks the village. *315 Gateway Bldg., upper level of mall, tel. 970/923–6804. AE, DC, MC, V.*

Moderate

Brothers' Grille
Chef Dave Brillhart, who oversees the kitchen of this American grill, proudly boasts his usual first-place position in the Snowmass Village Chili Shoot-Out, and his white-bean chicken chili also hits the spot on a cold day. Other selections are blackened prime rib sandwich and a variety of burgers, salads, and pastas. *100 Fall La., Silvertree Hotel, tel. 970/923– 8285. AE, D, DC, MC, V.*

Il Poggio
This slick Italian eatery opts for marble-and-granite minimalism. Excellent pasta dishes are served, including capellini with shrimp and prosciutto, ravioli with herbed ricotta, and fettuccine with wild mushrooms and sun-dried tomatoes. Specialty pizzas come with an eclectic variety of toppings. *54 Elbert La., Snowmass Mall, tel. 970/923–4292. MC, V.*

La Piñata
For Mexican or traditional Southwestern fare, this restaurant, with its

casual, convivial atmosphere and pleasant, subdued decor (light brick and wood walls offset by brightly colored wall hangings) is a good choice. The menu includes such oddities as ahi fajitas marinated in orange tarragon and served with melon salsa, smoked seafood enchiladas, and grilled pork crown glazed with Southwestern cranberry chutney. *65 Daly La., lower level of mall, tel. 970/923–2153. Reservations essential for 6 or more. AE, MC, V.*

Sage Restaurant
The bistro food served here ranges from appetizers and pizzas to salads and sandwiches. Among the favorites are grilled pork tenderloin with smoked-Gouda scalloped potatoes and grilled trout with crab relish and pesto vegetable noodles. A four-course prix-fixe meal is offered nightly—reserve ahead. Decor is comfortably casual, with sandstone-color brick complemented by blond-wood trim and Southwestern art and wall hangings. *Snowmass Lodge & Club, 0239 Snowmass Circle, 81615, tel. 970/923–0923. AE, D, DC, MC, V.*

StoneBridge Restaurant
In the StoneBridge Inn, just a stone's throw from the mall, kick back to live bluegrass music on Saturday evenings around the stone fireplace in the bar. The upstairs dining room, done in rustic Southwestern decor with log chairs, has views from every vantage point. The menu offers something for everyone, from chicken potpie to pepper-crusted elk medallions to ruby red Rocky Mountain trout. *300 Carriage Way, tel. 970/923–2420. AE, D, DC, MC, V.*

Wildcat Cafe
This cheerful, lively spot has a bright atmosphere complemented by stylish, modern furnishings, colorful table settings, and plenty of windows with views over the mountain. Worthwhile dishes here include eggs Benedict, grilled salmon, steak, and Far East chicken. There's also a children's menu. Outdoor seating is available. *Snowmass Center, tel. 970/923– 5990. MC, V.*

Inexpensive
Snowmass Pizza
For a fast, cheap, good pie—the best on the mountain—stop here. You can also get basic fast foods such as tacos, soups, chili, hot dogs, and heroes. Make your choice at the walk-up window, then grab a picnic table outside—or call for delivery. *35 Village Sq., Snowmass Mall, tel. 970/923– 5711. Reservations not accepted. No credit cards.*

The Stewpot
There's a lot more than stew on the menu here, but stick to the namesake dish—a hearty bowl served with homemade bread. Beef and chicken are the standard ingredients, but there's also a stew of the day that sometimes includes other meats. Daily soup specials—tomato cheddar, chicken vegetable barley—and a selection of sandwiches are also offered. The two-story restaurant has a casual atmosphere enlivened by windows overlooking the mall and by the photography of local artists that hangs on the walls. *62 Snowmass Village Mall, tel. 970/923–2263. Reservations essential for 6 or more. MC, V.*

Best Bet for Breakfast

Paradise Bakery

Stop here on your way to the slopes for a great selection of fresh-baked breads, muffins, cinnamon rolls, stuffed croissants, and yogurt. Paradise also has the best coffee on the mountain: Try the cappuccino, espresso, or latte. *100 Elbert La., Silvertree Plaza, tel. 970/ 923–4712. No credit cards.*

NIGHTLIFE AND ENTERTAINMENT

Snowmass is a quiet spot after dark. The après-ski scene cooks for a while, but when it cools down, Aspen is the place for action.

Après-Ski

Cirque Cafe

This place rocks with nonstop dancing and happy-hour prices. From the deck to the cavernous bar (with live music), the Cirque is always packed, usually with an under-30 crowd. *105 Village Sq., Timbermill Bldg., tel. 970/ 923–8686. AE, D, DC, MC, V.*

The Conservatory

Live music and impromptu dancing draw the thirty-something crowd in this otherwise family-oriented resort. The scene at the Conservatory isn't as crazy as in other major après-ski spots, so you can feel comfortable without feeling old. *100 Elbert La., Silvertree Hotel, tel. 970/923–3520. AE, D, DC, MC, V.*

Loud and Lively/Dancing

Cowboy's

In this down-home place you can stomp and hop to the hottest C&W sounds, performed live. The dance floor really heats up with timid two-steppers and wild whirlers wearing Stetson hats and boots. *78 Elbert La., Silvertree Plaza, tel. 970/923–5249. AE, MC, V.*

The Tower

Magicians-cum-bartenders bring sorcery to this cheerful spot. Local and imported talent performs comedy routines regularly for an audience filled with people of all ages. *45 Village Sq., Snowmass Village Mall, tel. 970/923– 4650. AE, DC, MC, V.*

More Mellow

La Boheme

The live jazz in this low-key spot attracts couples and parents who have just tucked the kids into bed. *315 Gateway Bldg., upper level of mall, tel. 970/923–6804. AE, DC, MC, V.*

Mountain Dragon

This usually quiet spot is the hangout of choice for many of the resort's ski instructors. Sometimes there's live entertainment, but the place is most often filled with small talk. *22 Elbert La., Village Mall, tel. 970/923–3576. AE, MC, V.*

STEAMBOAT SKI RESORT

2305 Mt. Werner Circle
Steamboat Springs, CO 80487
Tel. 970/879–6111 or
800/922–2722
www.steamboat-ski.com

STATISTICALLY SPEAKING
Base elevation: 6,900 feet

Summit elevation: 10,568 feet

Vertical drop: 3,668 feet

Skiable terrain: 2,939 acres

Number of trails: 140

Longest run: 3 miles

Lifts and capacity: 1 gondola, 4 express quads, 1 quad, 6 triples, 6 doubles, 1 ski-school chair, 4 surface lifts; capacity 32,158 skiers per hour

Daily lift ticket: $52

Average annual snowfall: 335 inches

Number of skiing days 1997–98: 141

Snowmaking: 438 acres; 15%

Terrain mix: N 13%, I 56%, E 31%

Cross-country skiing: 30 kilometers

Snowboarding: yes

In the northwest corner of Colorado, where the Continental Divide veers east, merging with Rabbit Ears Pass, there's the Yampa River Valley. Here, ruggedly timbered slopes of the Park Range, to the east, and the Elkhead Range, to the north, yield to the scattered sagebrush and grassy meadows of the largest river valley in this part of the state.

Once a summer hunting ground for the wandering Ute tribe, the region is blessed with hundreds of thermal hot springs. Among the towns that established themselves around these waters was Steamboat Springs, a ranching community on the banks of the Yampa River. Besides the ranchers from Utah, Texas, and Wyoming who raised cattle and horses, there were Norwegian immigrants who brought with them their masonry and ski-jumping skills and were ultimately responsible for the onset of the ski industry in this part of the state. These Scandinavians blazed ski trails as a means of delivering the mail and built ski jumps to entertain themselves in their spare time, much as they had done at home. In particular, a young Norwegian, Carl Howelsen, already a champion jumper in his home country when he arrived in Steamboat in 1912, dazzled everyone with his jumping exploits and went on to introduce local residents to ski jumping and cross-country racing. In 1914 he established the Winter Carnival and the first jumping competitions. Skiing continued to be a big part of the community through the next five decades, as numerous national championships were staged and skiing became part of the curriculum in local schools. Between 1950 and the mid-1960s, 74 Steamboat skiers competed in Junior National teams, and 11 made the National and Olympic teams. Since the early days Steamboat has produced 52 Olympic athletes.

In 1962 the resort that was to become Steamboat's centerpiece was opened on nearby Storm Mountain by a group of local businesspeople led by Jim Temple, son of an early ranching family. The mountain was renamed Mt. Werner in 1964 in honor of Wallace "Buddy" Werner, who began skiing in Steamboat at age two and during the '50s and '60s led America's Olympic challenge to European skiers. Buddy was killed in an avalanche in Switzerland that same year,

USEFUL NUMBERS
Area code: 970

Children's services: day-care, tel. 970/879–6111, ext. 218

Snow phone: tel. 970/879–7300

Police: tel. 970/879–1144

Routt County Search and Rescue: tel. 970/879–1090

Medical center: Routt Memorial Hospital, tel. 970/879–1322

Resort association: tel. 970/879–0880

Steamboat Central Reservations: tel. 800/525–2628

Road conditions: tel. 970/879–1260

Towing: A-Towing, tel. 970/879–1951

FIVE-STAR FAVORITES
Best run for vertical: Dropout

Best run overall: Shadows

Best bar/nightclub: The Inferno

Best hotel: Torian Plum

Best restaurant: La Montana

but his legacy can be seen everywhere at today's Steamboat resort.

When you think of modern-day Steamboat, two images come to mind: One is a leather-faced cowboy in chaps and a Stetson hat astride a horse galloping in knee-deep snow, and the other is light champagne-color powder star-bursting in a delicate spray against a cobalt blue sky as skiers cut first tracks in the morning sun. Both images are authentic, which is one reason for Steamboat's enduring popularity as both a ski destination and a resort town.

Steamboat Springs has retained some of its treasures from the Old West, including its cow-town facade and locals who are proud to be descendants of some of the original ranchers who settled here. The streets, lined with hotels, restaurants, and shops, are extra-wide, a legacy from the days when ranchers pushed thousands of head of cattle through town en route to the rail yards on the Wyoming border.

Although one complements the other in a comfortable way that is only matched by, say, Crested Butte or Telluride, the resort and the town are self-contained entities, and you can be comfortable staying in either place. In town, small hotels, lodges, and inns offer a moderately priced alternative to the posh resort, with its cluster of classy condos and stylish hotels. Perhaps the primary difference between staying in town and lodging in the ski village is that life is so convenient at the latter. If you stay there, expect instant access to the lifts; a built-in village plaza with shops, restaurants, and watering holes; and generally larger, more luxurious accommodations. Also expect resort accommodations to be significantly more expensive. The resort tends to be a bit quieter at night than town, a trait that families with children or couples looking for a private, romantic getaway find appealing. A new resort hotel, the Grand Summit Hotel and Conference Center, offers a full-service lodging experience not unlike that of the classic resort inns of the Northeastern mountains.

In town, you will find European-style lodgings—typically small, owner-operated inns with fewer than 75 rooms. You'll have to shuttle to and from the mountain, but the regular service can whisk you back and forth in about 10 minutes. The town offers varied architecture and a slightly rambunctious nightlife. Lincoln Avenue is the strip to stroll: a mile-long stretch of restaurants, bars, boutiques, and other diversions housed in a mix of Victorian, cowboy-funk, and ski-town chic buildings.

There's an earthy realism to the town, even as it succumbs to the demands of tourists; real ranchers still stroll the town's sidewalks, and there's an earnest friendliness between cowboys and skiers that goes right to the heart of Steamboat's origins.

HOW TO GET THERE

By Plane

There are connecting flights from **Denver International Airport** (tel. 303/342–2000; *see* Getting to Colorado Resorts, *above*) into **Steamboat Springs Airport** (5 miles from the resort) and to the **Yampa Valley Regional Airport** in Hayden, 22 miles from the resort, which also receives several carriers' direct flights from major U.S. cities.

By Shuttle

Alpine Taxi/Limo (tel. 970/879–2800 or 800/343–7433; $57 one-way) has four daily shuttle trips from Denver International Airport to Steamboat. From either Yampa Valley Regional Airport or Steamboat Springs Airport, the following shuttle services are available: **Alpine Taxi/Limo** (tel. 970/879–2800) and **Steamboat Taxi** (tel. 970/879–3335). **Steamboat Central Reservations** (tel. 800/922–2722) can help make car-rental reservations and other ground transportation arrangements.

By Car

Steamboat Springs is 157 miles, or a three-hour drive, northwest of Denver. From Denver International Airport, take Peña Boulevard for 15 miles to I–70W. Once you're through the Eisenhower Tunnel, take the Silverthorne exit onto Route 9 north to Kremmling, then take U.S. 40 west over Rabbit Ears Pass and on to Steamboat Springs. Travelers are advised to carry chains or other traction devices, which are often required on Rabbit Ears Pass.

For car rentals from Denver International Airport, *see* Getting to Colorado Resorts, *above*. Car-rental companies available at Yampa Valley Regional Airport and Steamboat Springs Airport are Avis and Hertz.

By Bus

Greyhound Lines (tel. 800/231–2222) offers bus service from Denver twice daily.

GETTING AROUND

A car is not necessary at Steamboat because the town and the resort are only 3 miles apart, and most major properties provide a free shuttle between the resort and the town. There's also a free town shuttle. Even if you miss the shuttle bus, there are a number of taxi services that will do the run for about $10. The **Steamboat Springs Transit shuttle** (tel. 970/879–5585) is your best way, though; it's fast (about 10 minutes from resort to town), convenient (roughly every 20 minutes with stops along the route), and free. If you need a cab, call **Alpine Taxi** (tel. 970/879–2800 or 800/343–7433).

THE SKIING

The four peaks that make up Steamboat Resort provide a big, broad-faced mountain ridge that sucks in the ultralight snow dropped from storms as they race across the desert lands to the west. When the powder lies deep and untouched, the forested flanks of the four peaks provide nature's most demanding slalom course. For sheer lump-in-your-throat thrills there's nothing quite like dancing through thigh-deep powder in a grove of aspens.

For the most part, though, Steamboat's 2,939 acres are a near-perfect cruising playground for intermediates and upper intermediates. Of course, there's considerable novice terrain, and the experts will find their share of thrills, but for the majority of skiers this is the place to let loose, try some ego cruising, then back off into your comfort zone. The lack of congestion is a nice feature here. You won't find too many people skiing in your way; Steamboat doesn't draw a huge day-skier crowd, and the relatively small number of destination skiers seldom makes a dent in the resort's uphill capacity, so lineups are rare except for the early morning traffic on the Silver Bullet gondola, which you can avoid by taking the Christie lifts to the Thunderhead/Arrowhead combo and then the Burgess Creek chair, which will give you access to the Sundown Express and the summit of Sunshine Peak.

The skiing on Mt. Werner's four peaks is well divided into abilities, so everyone can ski at his/her own level but won't get hopelessly separated from the gang. The key here is the Thunderhead Peak area, a midmountain rendezvous accessible to skiers of all abilities. It's an excellent place for lunch, with its three restaurants, and lifts and trails from all parts of the resort converge here. Below Thunderhead are mostly novice and easy intermediate trails, and above that (on Mt. Werner, Storm Peak, and Sunshine Peak) are mostly intermediate and expert trails.

Storm Peak, at 10,372 feet, is where most of the upper-intermediate and advanced skiers go for steep powder fields and densely packed glades. From this point you can also ski down the backside into the Morningside Park area, which is a mix of intermediate and moderately expert slopes, and more important, gives you access to the top of Mt. Werner and its black-diamond runs, which are a mix of steep glades, couloirs, and narrow chutes.

Sunshine Peak, at 10,385 feet, is mostly intermediate cruising with a good variety of short, steep pitches and slightly more open glades, and long, smooth, wide-open cruisers. At the very bottom of the resort is the Christie Peak area, with its collection of novice slopes served by the Christie chairs.

Intermediates and up should consider skiing the mountain the way the locals do, by following the sun. Start at the Morningside Park area in the early morning, tackle Mt. Werner closer to noon (and stop for lunch at the Four Points Hut midway down Storm Peak), and then in the afternoon move over to the aptly named One O'Clock, Two O'Clock, and Three O'Clock runs on Sunshine Peak.

Novices

For absolute beginners or even second-timers, there are four lifts serving the gentlest terrain on the mountain. These start just to the left of the gondola base and take you up increasing distances, which you can opt for as you gain confidence. The shortest, the Preview, is a free lift so beginners can get their taste of terror before buying a pass. The South Face, Headwall, and Pony lifts let you work your way down a smooth, wide, slow-skiing zone until you're ready to move on to more challenging runs. When you want to ski some longer distances, head for the Christie II and III lifts and play around on some lengthier, winding trails called Boulevard, Giggle Gulch, and Yoo Hoo. Your next step up would be on the Silver Bullet gondola to Thunderhead Peak, the point on the mountain from which you can reach all other peaks.

Thunderhead is a good spot for lunch and a convenient place for novices to meet up with their more advanced skiing friends. You can do a little safe exploring from Thunderhead: turn left off the gondola and take Why Not to So What, a green/blue combo that will test but not terrify you. To the right off the gondola, there's Spur Run, which will take you down to the chairs that serve Sunshine Peak. Head up here if you feel like moving things up a notch and trying a long blue cruising run such as Tomahawk.

Intermediates

Although more than 50% of Steamboat's runs are designated intermediate, a good steady blue skier will quickly graduate to some of the mountain's black runs. It's the snow that will test your mettle with its dry, light consistency, which helps put a bite in your edge, a spring in your step, and a brake on the vertical. From the base area take the Silver Bullet gondola to Thunderhead, then ski down Huffman to the Sundown Express lift, which will take you to the top of Sunshine Peak. Head right as you get off the chair for some sweet cruising runs that wind around the trees. If you stay high on the ridge and take Tomahawk, you'll be able to pick from a half dozen short but steep straight shots through the trees and shoot down to either Flintlock or Quick Draw. Either of these will bring you out to the bottom of the Sunshine chair, which you can take back up to the Sunshine Peak; here you'll find a mixture of good blue cruising runs to the right and steeper, more direct blacks to the left. For nonstop giant-slalom cruising in the Sunshine Peak area, try a few runs on High Noon, Flintlock, or Quickdraw.

By riding the Storm Peak Express, you get a chance to ski the Upper Storm Peak snowfields—steep, wide bowl-like areas that are sprinkled with stands of aspens and firs. It's up-tempo intermediate skiing best done after a fresh overnight snowfall. Below the snowfields are a trio of serious, narrow, mogul-studded black runs—Twister, Nelson's Run, and Hurricane—that you may want to avoid. Instead, opt for Sunset or Rainbow, running under the Burgess Creek chair and down to the bottom of the Storm Peak Express.

Experts

If you think you have the right stuff, then there's some stuff here to keep you honest. The trails may not be as tough and unrelenting as some you'll find at Crested Butte or Jackson Hole, but when the snows run deep and the moguls grow steep, all but the most manic group of renegade extreme skiers will find that edge on the wild side. Ride Silver Bullet gondola, and then take a quick warm-up scoot down Rudi's Run to Ego to catch the Storm Peak Express. The Storm Peak snowfield is high-speed yahoo cruising around the trees, especially after a good snow; when coupled with one of the three drop-off trails—Nelson's Run, Twister, or Hurricane—either one will send your excitement meter into the red zone.

For a dance in the steep and snow-packed glades that are among the finest in Colorado, slide to the right as you get off Storm Peak Express down to the heavily treed flank of Sunshine Peak. Pine, fir, and aspen are more densely packed here than a Manhattan parking lot. Although there are only three or four officially designated runs, your particular route down may be more a result of survival tactics than topography. Closet and Shadows are the steepest and densest trails; there are also some steep chutes, which are called Three O'Clock, Two O'Clock, and One O'Clock. In between Two and Three is Twilight, a run that the truly deranged use as their own treed slalom run. This is not a place for the tree-timid.

The upper reaches of Mt. Werner are where you'll find the steepest, snowiest, and in some cases, the best glade runs on the mountain. To access the top of Werner, take the runs down Morningside, reached from the top of either the Sundown, Storm Peak, or Bar-UE lifts, then come back up the Morningside lift to Mt. Werner's summit. Try Chutes 1, 2, 3, or the Ridge, and Crow Track—which will shunt and bump you down to the wider Flying Z snowfield with its tree clusters, then down into the high-speed Dropout. This route follows the northern perimeter of the resort, and traffic is usually light. If you do find a lot of skiers on the Storm Express, stop at the bottom of the Flying Z, where it meets the Bar UE chair, and take it back up to the top.

SNOWBOARDING

Home to Olympic half-pipe bronze medalist Shannon Dunn, Steamboat offers an excellent environment for nurturing boarders. It lacks the super-steep terrain of Crested Butte or the deep moguls of Telluride, but Steamboat has incomparable powder. Snowboarders have access to the entire mountain and to all lifts. Two terrain parks are designed to accommodate everyone from small shredders to experts. Kids can rip it up at the Bee Hive, located on Giggle Gulch, which is accessible from both the Christie III and Christie II lifts. Older riders can check out the Dude Ranch, a half-pipe and terrain park just below the Bashor lift. There's also a terrain park on the lower part of Storm Peak, just above Thunderhead.

Steamboat's **beginner** trails are scattered about the mountain; a wrong turn onto a black trail can quickly get a beginner in above his or her head. To avoid that, start off riding the chairs clustered around the base area. These access mellow, easy terrain with just enough slope to keep fledgling boarders on their feet. Once you've gained your riding legs, catch the Southface lift, veer skiers' right to the Christie Base, and ride either of the two chairlifts. From here, you can access the Yoo Hoo trail, a long, sweeping run that deposits you in the Rough Rider basin, or try Giggle Gulch or Swinger. Avoid the long, flat run called Right of Way, a road used by intermediate and advanced riders to get back to the base. Icy conditions and zero slope make this a tough run for beginners to handle. **Intermediate** riders can head right up on the Silver Bullet Gondola; veer right and you'll board down into the Priest Creek drainage. Take the Sunshine Express to the top of Sunshine Peak, where a treasure trove of intermediate runs is well suited to snowboarding. Among the best are High Noon and One O'Clock, both of which offer opportunities for glade runs through branchless stands of Aspen trees. **Experts** can warm up on runs like Oops, Ted's Ridge, and Vertigo on the lower mountain, just off the Silver Bullet. But inevitably, you'll find yourself drawn to Storm Peak and the challenging runs on Mt. Werner. Though not known for extreme terrain, Steamboat has several treacherous glade runs and chutes; virtually all of them are accessed along the knifelike edge of Mt. Werner. From the Gondola, take Vagabond trail, veering right onto Surprise. Head for the Storm Peak Express lift, which deposits you atop its namesake mountain. From here, it's a short, walking traverse to the double-black-diamond chutes 1, 2, and 3. Once you've mastered these, you can venture farther down the ridge to Christmas Tree bowl. All runs on Mt. Werner funnel down into the Big Meadow, an intermediate trail that winds down to the Bar U lift.

OTHER SNOW SPORTS

One call to Steamboat Central Reservations (tel. 970/879-0740 or 800/922-2722) and you can book any number of adventures in the region. One of the most unusual is the Bridgestone **Winter Driving** School, which teaches drivers how to handle snowy and icy conditions. Numerous guest ranches offer **horseback riding,** cookouts, and **sleigh rides.** Cross-country skiers can explore 30 km of tracked trails at the **Ski Touring** Center (tel. 970/879–8180), or explore many more miles of marked trails on Rabbit Ears Pass. **Ballooning** is a favorite activity, and there are no fewer than three different companies to choose from: Aerosports Ltd. (tel. 970/879–7433), Balloons Over Steamboat (tel. 970/879–3298), or Pegasus Balloon Tours (tel. 970/879–9191). Or, spend some time in the backcountry **dogsledding** with Steamboat Dog Sled Express (tel. 970/879–4662).

NEARBY

Tiny **Howelson Hill** (tel. 970/879–8499 or 800/525–2628), smack-dab in the middle of town, isn't a bad place to start your Steamboat ski vacation—or your Olympic career. Just 25 acres and less than 440 ft in vertical rise, Howelson has nonetheless been the starting point for the careers of more Olympians than any other ski area in America. Half of the terrain here is designated expert, 25% intermediate, and 25% beginner. On the Pony Land lift, beginners and kids ride free. On lunch hour, many locals take advantage of a "nooner" ticket, which lets them ski from 11 to 1 for just $2.

WHERE TO STAY

Most of the accommodations at the resort are condos, with precious few smaller hotels or lodges, especially if you want to stay on the mountain. The old town of Steamboat is only a 10-minute shuttle bus ride away, and it has a good selection of moderately priced traditional ski-country–style accommodations. Although condos are run by different condo companies, all lodgings (even those in town) can be booked through **Steamboat Central Reservations** (Box 774728, Steamboat Springs 80477, tel. 970/ 879–0740 or 800/922–2722).

Expensive

Bear Claw Condominiums
These slope-side brick-and-wood condos with red-iron balconies and great views of the mountain are ski-in/ski-out accommodations. The units range in size from studios to four bedrooms, each decorated in earth tones, with woodwork and the occasional Western collectible. Studios are relatively spacious, and the four-bedroom unit (with a loft) is so huge that 10 people could stay here without tripping over each other. Each unit has a balcony, a fireplace, a full kitchen with high-tech appliances, and a TV/VCR. *2420 Ski Trail La., Steamboat Springs 80487, tel. 970/879–6100 or 800/232–7252, fax 970/879–8396. 67 units. Facilities: pool, sauna, health spa, game room, laundry, housekeeping. AE, D, MC, V. $295–$1,365.*

Dulany Condominiums
Brick fireplaces, light-wood cabinetry, polished tiles, and Tiffany-style lamps give these two- and three-bedroom wood-and-stucco condos a warmer touch than any other accommodation in Steamboat. All units have complete kitchen facilities with upscale appliances, a washer-dryer, and a balcony. Although there's lots of space in all the units, the curl-up-in-front-of-the-fire ambience is not sacrificed. Best of all, the condos are just 50 yards from the gondola. *Steamboat Resorts, Box 2995, Steamboat Springs 80477, tel. 970/879–6007 or 800/525–5502, fax 970/879–2353. 25 units. Facilities: outdoor hot tub. AE, MC, V. $225–$975.*

Sheraton Steamboat Hotel and Conference Center
Now equipped with a 23-unit luxury condo tower, retail shopping space, and a remodeled entry, lobby, and restaurant, the Sheraton is ready to go head-to-head with some of the better resort hotels in Vail and Aspen. Best of all, it's also ski-in/ski-out, just steps from the gondola in Ski Time Square. There are standard hotel rooms plus some larger suites, as well as some moderately priced apartment units in an adjacent building. The major conference facilities attract large groups. *2200 Village Inn Ct., Box 774808, Steamboat Springs 80477, tel. 970/879–2220 or 800/848–8878, fax 970/879–7686. 270 rooms, 3 suites, 35 units. Facilities: 2 restaurants, 1 lounge, game room, gift shops, heated outdoor pool, health club, 4 hot tubs, sauna, laundry. AE, D, DC, MC, V. $105–$1,500.*

Waterford Townhomes

Each of these rustically designed dark brown wooden town houses has timber-beamed ceilings, a massive stone fireplace, a separate dining area that seats 10, and a kitchen large enough to whip up a meal for every trail hand in the valley. All the units are large, with three or four bedrooms, and are suitable for families or groups who like their creature comforts and plenty of room. Other touches include a washer-dryer, a private hot tub, and a sauna. The gondola is just 400 yards away. *Steamboat Resorts, Box 2015, 2025 Walton Creek Rd., Steamboat Springs 80477, tel. 970/879–7000 or 800/525–5502, fax 970/879–7263. 28 units. Facilities: heated outdoor pool. AE, MC, V. $195–$750.*

Moderate

Ptarmigan Inn

Steamboat should have a few more places like the Ptarmigan, a small tan-stucco European-style lodge with ski-in/ski-out access to the lifts. The emphasis at this Best Western property is on hotel-style service without sacrificing personalized pampering. The spacious, comfortable rooms come with queen- or king-size beds; most have a balcony and a refrigerator. This is a friendly and intimate spot that's good for couples and families. *2304 Après Ski Way, Box 773240, Steamboat Springs 80477, tel. 970/879–1730 or 800/538–7519, fax 970/879–6044. 77 rooms. Facilities: restaurant, lounge, heated outdoor pool, hot tub, sauna. AE, D, DC, MC, V. $99–$269.*

Ranch at Steamboat

These two-, three-, and four-bedroom town houses are 1½ miles from the slopes (a complimentary shuttle gets you there), and for that minor inconvenience you get one of the best deals in full-size accommodations found at the resort. The ranch-style timber-and-stone town houses are deluxe if not designer and perfect for families who want to be in a quiet location. Each unit is spacious, with a balcony overlooking the mountains and a private bathroom for each bedroom. There's a full-size kitchen plus an electric barbecue on the balcony, a fireplace, and a washer-dryer. *1 Ranch Rd., Steamboat Springs, 80487, tel. 970/879–3000 or 800/525–2002, fax 970/879–5409. 88 units. Facilities: heated outdoor pool, 2 hot tubs, sauna, housekeeping. AE, MC, V. $115–$695.*

Torian Plum

The Torian Plum is opposite the gondola, with easy ski-in/ski-out access, and the full-size lobby and 24-hour service make it feel more like a hotel than a condo complex. The units range in size from one to three bedrooms, and all come with well-equipped kitchens. They are well decorated and, more importantly, well maintained—with modern furnishings, imaginative decorations, and pine trim and cabinetry. Each unit also has a fireplace, a whirlpool bath, a balcony, a washer-dryer, a TV, and a VCR. *1855 Ski Time Square Dr., Steamboat Springs 80487, tel. 970/897–8811 or 800/228–2458, fax 970/879–5381. 47 units. Facilities: outdoor pool, sauna, ski storage, daily housekeeping, laundry, underground parking, concierge. AE, MC, V. $205–$1,185.*

Trappeur's Crossing

This ranch-style wooden condo complex with cathedral windows has well-designed units that can accommodate the extra bodies who sometimes tag along with groups or families. The one-bedroom unit (750 square feet), for instance, has one queen-size bed in the main bedroom, a second in a small den, a third in a small loft, and a full-size sofa bed in the living room. The larger units are similarly laid out, with up to four bedrooms that can easily sleep 10. There are full kitchen facilities, a fireplace, a balcony, and a TV/VCR in all units. The only drawback here is the five- to seven-minute two-block walk to the gondola. *1855 Ski Time Square Dr., Steamboat Springs 80487, tel. 970/ 879–8811 or 800/228–2458, fax 970/ 879–5381. 34 units. Facilities: indoor-outdoor pool, 2 hot tubs, sauna, laundry. AE, MC, V. $150–$885.*

Inexpensive

Harbor Hotel

One of the oldest hotels in Steamboat, the cream-color stucco-and-brick Harbor is bedecked with English antique furnishings, dark woods, and stonework. In addition to the original section, there's a newer annex, as well as condos. All offer Euro-lodge ambience. Whether you choose a room, a suite, or a condo, these are among the best deals in town. *703 Lincoln Ave., Box 774109, Steamboat Springs 80477, tel. 970/879–1522 or 800/ 543–8888, fax 970/879–1737. 86 rooms, 3 suites, 24 units. Facilities: Jacuzzi, sauna, steam room. AE, D, DC, MC, V. $50–$350.*

Inn at Steamboat

This pale-yellow-and-blue inn, larger than average, is a delightful spot that retains a cozy, home-style feeling. The large rooms are decorated in earth tones, and most have a great view of either the ski mountain or the surrounding Yampa Valley. The great stone fireplace in the lobby warms comfortable couches. *3070 Columbine Dr., Box 775084, Steamboat Springs 80477, tel. 970/879–2600 or 800/ 872–2601. 32 rooms. Facilities: heated outdoor pool, bar. AE, D, MC, V. $59– $189, including Continental breakfast.*

Rabbit Ears Motel

As motels go, this dark-wood structure with a flat roof is clean, comfortable, and affordable, in addition to being in the center of old Steamboat and just across the road from the community-run hot springs. Some rooms are oversize, and most have two double or queen-size beds. There are also suites with lovely riverfront views. Rabbit Ears is a friendly, family-run operation with such in-room extras as coffeemakers, refrigerators, and microwaves. *201 Lincoln Ave., Box 573, Steamboat Springs 80477, tel. 970/879–1150 or 800/828–7702, fax 970/870–0483. 32 rooms, 33 suites. AE, D, DC, MC, V. $65–$160, including Continental breakfast.*

Steamboat Bed and Breakfast

This is a pretty little tin-roofed colonial-style house set in the middle of Steamboat Springs' historic section. Its rooms are all individually decorated and have private baths. There is also a TV with VCR in the conservatory room. Coffee and tea are served throughout the day. *442 Pine St.,*

Steamboat Springs 80477, tel. and fax 970/879–5724. 7 rooms. Facilities: Jacuzzi. AE, D, MC, V. $105–$125, including full breakfast.

WHERE TO EAT

Combined, the resort area and the town of Steamboat have a large and varied selection of restaurants, cafés, and bars, and as there are only 3 miles between mountain and town, it's easy to try many no matter where you are staying.

On the Mountain

Hazie's
Delicious sit-down lunch fare is served in an elegant, uncrowded two-level dining room at the top of the Silver Bullet Gondola overlooking a spectacular view of the mountain. Expect a great lineup of light-bite soups and salads, such as the grilled salmon Caesar or the clam and shrimp chowder plus a selection of monstrous sandwiches and assorted entrées, including sautéed crab cakes. *Top of Silver Bullet gondola, tel. 970/879–6111, ext. 218. Reservations essential. D, MC, V.*

Ragnars
The look is Norwegian, with cream-color and flowered walls and antique ski photos. You get big portions of Scandinavian specialties among other fare. Try the *fiske suppe* (fish soup) for starters and for an entrée, the Tout-Paris: lobster, shrimp, and scallops with chanterelles, mushrooms, and white asparagus served in a flaky pastry shell. *Rendezvous Saddle, halfway down High Noon run, tel. 970/879–6111, ext. 218. Reservations essential. D, DC, MC, V.*

Expensive

Hazie's
Named for Hazie Werner, wife of local skiing legend Buddy Werner, this beautiful mountaintop restaurant offers a view that takes in the entire Yampa Valley with its twinkling lights and endless skies. The menu is Continental, the atmosphere is romantic but comfortable, and the mood is mountain high. There is a four-course daily special ($60, includes Gondola ride); other entrées are a mix of fish, such as the John Dory Filet Meunière, and meat—chateaubriand with béarnaise sauce and rack of Colorado lamb. *Top of Silver Bullet gondola, tel. 970/879–6111, ext. 465. Reservations essential. AE, D, DC, MC, V.*

L'apogée
This is an intimate, candlelighted French restaurant filled with wildlife art and stained glass. Chef Richard Billingham changes the menu often to keep things interesting and fresh and to be able to use seasonal ingredients. The focus is on game such as medallions of Texas Nilgai antelope and seafood such as fresh jumbo scallops wrapped in smoked bacon, yellowfin tuna *poki* rolled in spinach leaves, and fresh mahimahi. Regardless of what specials come out of the kitchen, you can count on fine dining, great service, and the choice of one of the largest wine cellars in town. *911 Lincoln Ave., tel. 970/879– 1919. Reservations essential. AE, MC, V.*

Mattie Silks
Mattie Silks made a reputation for herself as one of Denver's most colorful turn-of-the-century madams, and her namesake restaurant is keeping

her name and style alive some seven decades after she passed from the scene. The ornate interior, with velvet curtains and decorative lamps, is perfectly matched to the fine dining found here. It's a Continental menu with some interesting variations and some traditional dishes. For your entrée consider the tournedos Gorgonzola (grilled medallions of beef tenderloin with Gorgonzola cheese crust) or the Jamaican jerk chicken marinated in island spices. *1890 Mt. Werner Rd., tel. 970/879–2441. Reservations essential. AE, D, MC, V.*

Moderate

Antares Restaurant

In a restored 1908 livery stable with stone-and-wood decor, this upscale bistro has a menu that can best be described as eclectic international. It offers an exotic array of dishes with a Pacific Rim influence and flavored with fresh herbs. The sesame-crusted ahi tuna salad with field greens, the chicken with broccoli and straw mushrooms, or the Thai chili sautéed prawns are all excellent choices. For a light dessert try the fresh blueberries sautéed in Frangelico or the peach bread pudding. *57½ 8th St., tel. 970/879–9939. Reservations essential. AE, MC, V.*

Coral Grill

This warm and woodsy restaurant offers spectacular views of the mountain. Fresh seafood is flown in daily, and the menu changes according to what's available. Oysters on ice or oysters Rockefeller are good starters. Some reliable favorite entrées include panfried Rocky Mountain trout, Cajun-style broiled red snapper, and baked salmon. There's also a hearty selection of meat and poultry dishes, including veal, beef, chicken, duckling, and a mixed grill. *Sundance Plaza, Anglers Dr., halfway between town and resort, tel. 970/879–6858. Reservations essential. AE, MC, V.*

La Montana

This restaurant's Southwestern style is enhanced with local artworks and the owner's photography. The sizzling-good fajitas are the house specialty, and there are six versions from which to choose (including elk). Another popular special is the blend of elk, lamb, and chorizo sausages, braided and then grilled over a mesquite fire. Other noteworthy entrées include elk loin with pecans and bourbon cream sauce; red chili pasta; and jumbo shrimp stuffed with crabmeat, Monterey jack cheese, and pico de gallo (a hot salsa mix), and then wrapped in bacon and smothered in Hollandaise sauce. For the more timid there are the standard Tex-Mex favorites such as burritos, enchiladas, and tacos. *Après Ski Way at 25 Village Dr., tel. 970/879–5800. Reservations essential. AE, D, MC, V.*

Ore House at the Pine Grove

In a 100-year-old barn, this rustic restaurant, decorated with ranch memorabilia and Western art, is an institution in Steamboat. Not-to-miss appetizers include coyote shrimp with Cajun spices and mesquite teriyaki steak bits. Although the focus is on meat such as prime rib—which comes in three cuts, from 8 to 16 ounces, plus a blackened version done with roasted garlic sauce—don't overlook the fresh fish, which is flown in daily and can include swordfish, mahimahi, or salmon. Game is big on the menu, too, including buffalo steak in a peppercorn sauce or elk loin in a lingonberry sauce. *1465 Pine Grove Rd., Pine Grove Ctr., tel. 970/879–1190. AE, D, MC, V.*

Riggio's Fine Italian Food
The tone here is set with ceiling fans and a handcrafted wooden bar. Besides excellent pasta dishes, including manicotti, lasagna, and several spaghetti variations, veal, chicken, and seafood are creatively prepared and served. The veal piccata is delightfully light, and the saltimbocca is a full-flavored scallopini smothered in eggplant, prosciutto, cheese, and Bardolino sauce. Vegetarians can enjoy the stir-fry Italiano, with vegetables sautéed in olive oil and tossed with pasta al pesto. *1151 Lincoln Ave., tel. 970/879–9010. Reservations essential. D, DC, MC, V.*

Inexpensive

The Inferno
In Gondola Square, the Inferno is both a red-hot nightclub and a smokin' place for teens and young adults who want to wrap their hands around an all-American burger or a pizza. Try the spicy Dante's Delight pizza or opt for the mellower California Pie loaded with artichokes, mushrooms, broccoli, and onions. This is not the place for a quiet, relaxed meal, but if you seek standard American comfort food, you'll find it here. *Gondola Square, at base of Mt. Werner, tel. 970/879–5111. AE, MC, V.*

Old Town Pub
The building that this restaurant occupies has been a hotel, a hospital,

and a post office, but its latest tenant is probably the most popular. You'll find good family dining here, with three-course menus that run the gamut from shrimp scampi to prime rib to linguine puttanesca. There's a good selection of steaks and a terrific Sunday brunch that includes eggs Benedict and French toast made with croissants. *600 Lincoln Ave., tel. 970/ 879–2101. AE, D, MC, V.*

Steamboat Smokehouse
It's kind of like a deli, kind of like a barbecue pit—and kind of wacky here. The rustic rock walls sport mounted animal heads, and the floor is a sea of peanut shells. There's a mother lode of hickory-smoked meats from which to choose, in a sandwich or as an entrée. Sides such as fries, smokehouse rice, and Mr. B's smoked beans are necessary accoutrements. *Thiesen Mall, 912 Lincoln Ave., tel. 970/879–5570. AE, MC, V.*

Best Bets for Breakfast

In Season Bakery–Deli Café
In this small brick-walled café, you'll find a great selection of coffees to enjoy, with classical music in the background and an awesome array of fresh-baked breakfast goodies, not to mention the divine eggs Benedict. *131 11th St., tel. 970/879–1840. MC, V.*

Mazzola's
If you can't start the day without a hearty breakfast, Mazzola's offers a breakfast buffet that will stretch your ski pants–but not your wallet. In addition to eggs, hash browns, bacon, and other standard buffet fare, you'll find seasonal fruits, waffles, cereals, and yogurt. The regular menu includes breakfast burritos, huevos rancheros,

and the unusual breakfast calzone, an Italian turnover stuffed with scrambled eggs and melted cheese. *917 Lincoln Ave., tel. 970/879–2405. AE, D, DC, MC, V.*

Winona's
With an in-house bakery that creates fabulous cinnamon rolls, as well as fresh scones and muffins, Winona's is a great place to start the day. An ample breakfast menu that includes nine varieties of omelets, two styles of eggs Benedict, several choices of pancakes (including the yummy granola-raisin stack made with Winona's own granola), makes this a local favorite. *617 Lincoln Ave., tel. 970/879–2483. MC, V.*

NIGHTLIFE AND ENTERTAINMENT
Après-Ski
Slopeside Grill
This place is so close to the slopes you can practically ski in the front door. Inside it's fun, with a four-sided bar, lots of locals, and a sports bar atmosphere. Happy hour starts late (9 PM) and features $2 pints and $5 pizzas. When the weather's right, there's also seating on the outdoor patio. *Torian Plum Plaza, tel. 970/879–2916. AE, D, MC, V.*

Loud and Lively/Dancing
Heavenly Daze Brewery
Steamboat's own log-cabin-style microbrewery gets up a good head of steam with daily specials and a half-dozen local brews. The three floors are filled with action from après-ski until midnight, with some folks grabbing dinner in between. Check out the pool tables on the third floor.

1860 Ski Time Square Dr., tel. 970/ 879–8080. AE, MC, V.

Inferno Restaurant & Bar
The decor here is urban industrial with a hint of neon disco and two old-style tin-topped bars. It's definitely the hippest place on the mountain, with live rock music nightly, a large and well-used dance floor, and an assortment of bar games and TVs. *Base of mountain in Gondola Sq., tel. 970/879–5111. AE, D, MC, V.*

Tugboat Grill & Pub
This is one of the oldest spots on the mountain and attracts a mixed crowd, from families in the early evening to more aggressive partyers once the live entertainment and dancing kicks in. The music ranges from funky to plain old C&W, and depending on the act there's occasionally a cover charge. *Pine Grove Ctr., Mt. Werner Dr., Ski Time Sq., tel. 970/879–7070. AE, D, MC, V.*

More Mellow
Antares Restaurant
This is a pleasant late-evening spot, with wood-paneled walls, brass fittings, and bar or table seating. Live jazz is on tap each Sunday, blues music on Wednesdays; the cozy atmosphere is unique in Steamboat. *57½ 8th St., tel. 970/879–9939. AE, MC, V.*

Harwig's Bar
A soothingly mellow bistro with warm, rustic decor and comfortable furniture, Harwig's has light music that's just right for conversation. *911 Lincoln Ave., tel. 970/879–1980. AE, MC, V.*

TELLURIDE SKI RESORT

TELLURIDE SKI RESORT

565 Mountain Village Blvd.
Box 11155
Telluride, CO 81435
Tel. 970/728–6900
www.telski.com

STATISTICALLY SPEAKING

Base elevation: 8,760 feet
(Town of Telluride); 9,540
(Mountain Village)

Summit elevation: 12,247 feet

Vertical drop: 3,522 feet

Skiable terrain: 1,050 acres

Number of trails: 66

Longest run: 2.85 mi

Lifts and capacity: 1 gondola,
2 high-speed quads, 2 triples,
5 doubles, 1 poma, 1 Magic
Carpet; 12,076 skiers per hour

Daily lift ticket: $53

Average annual snowfall: 325
inches

Number of skiing days
1997–98: 138

Snowmaking: 155 acres; 15%

Terrain mix: N 21%, I 47%,
E 32%

Snowboarding: yes; all runs
and terrain park

Cross-country skiing: 30 kilometers (10 kilometers
groomed) of Nordic trails

At the headwaters of the San Miguel River, deep in the San Juan Mountains, is Telluride—a town and ski resort just far enough off the beaten path to serve as a hideout for fan-weary Hollywood types. In fact, this high-mountain hideaway has gained considerable cachet in recent years, as the counterculture crowd that gravitated here during the '60s and '70s ceded a slice of this spectacular mountain valley to such high rollers as Oprah Winfrey, Ralph Lauren, and Tom Cruise.

Historically, the town has endured the boom and bust cycle so common to small isolated communities dependent on capricious gold and silver prices. During the boom, things were fine, of course: Grand Victorian-style hotels were built, an opera house opened, and the population swelled from 100 to 5,000 or more. Come the bust, in the 1930s, the tiny town clung to life, much as it clings to two historical footnotes—the exploits of an extroverted bank robber and an introverted lawyer. A baby-face Butch Cassidy chose Telluride for the debut of his legendary bank-robbing career, and L. L. Nunn created the first practical application of AC electricity when he ran 8 miles of transmission line into the valley, making the small mountain town the most brightly illuminated community in the world.

Telluride is still struggling, but these days the fight is to reconcile the values of the community with the growth of Mountain Village, 6 miles down the road. Some vocal locals decry the arrival of the glitz-and-spritzer ski set as the first step down the path to the Aspenization of their wholesome, whole-wheat, nonconformist, ecopacifist community.

Fortunately, the fundamental character of the town remains unchanged. It began life as an 80-acre tent city in 1878, grew into a thriving mining town at the turn of the century, and finally became a high-alpine recreation retreat during the 1960s and '70s. Organized skiing didn't appear until 1973, when Joseph T. Zoline, a businessman from California, decided that snow was a commodity that could be mined as surely as the ore and minerals that had sustained the town for more than a century. He envisioned a $100-million megaresort that would rival the best in the United States. Now that vision is becoming reality, especially

USEFUL NUMBERS
Area code: 970

Children's services: rentals and instruction, tel. 970/728-7545

Snow phone: tel. 970/728-7425

Police: tel. 970/728-3081

Medical center: tel. 970/728-3848

Telluride Central Reservations/Guest Services: tel. 970/728-4431 or 888/605-2573

Telluride Resort Accomodations: tel. 970/728-6621 or 800/538-7754

Telluride Ski & Snowboard School: 970-728-7533 or 800/801-4832

Telluride Chamber of Commerce: tel. 970/728-3041

Road conditions: tel. 970/249-9363

Towing: Towman, tel. 970/728-4114

FIVE-STAR FAVORITES
Best run for vertical: Bushwacker, off Lift 9

Best run overall: Kant-Mak-M to Spiral Stairs to Lower Plunge

Best bar: New Sheridan Bar

Best hotel: The Peaks Resort & Spa

Best restaurant: La Marmotte

since a gondola linking the town and the Mountain Village was completed in the summer of 1996.

Although it has generally been conceded by even the most diehard locals that the gondola is an acceptable eco-friendly addition to the community, most are still on the alert for more offensive lifestyle intrusions. In sharp contrast to the century-old mining town, with its original brick and wooden buildings and street-loads of character and characters, is the ultramodern Telluride Ski Area, which, according to some, is spreading too quickly across the mountain.

The collection of condos on Telluride Mountain, known as Mountain Village, appears haphazard, with nondescript architecture and an atmosphere that's a far cry from the feeling of the old town. Nonetheless, it is perfect for families who enjoy the solitude and comfort of self-contained condo living plus easy access to the novice areas.

There are plenty of alternative accommodations plus some good-spirited nightlife in and around town. The gondola now connects the two parts of Telluride to give visitors easy access to both the town and the resort, and as Mountain Village continues to grow and as the town continues to adjust to growth, this man-made umbilical cord should help link even more intimately the two aspects of Telluride.

HOW TO GET THERE

By Plane
Denver International Airport (DIA), more than 300 miles (a day's drive) away, is the closest international airport (*see* Getting to Colorado Resorts, *above*). **Telluride Regional Airport** (tel. 970/728-4868) is 5 miles from the resort. America West has several flights daily from Phoenix, and Continental and United have daily flights from Denver. **Montrose Airport** (tel. 970/249-3203) is 67 miles from Telluride; Continental and United fly here daily from Denver; America West has daily service from Phoenix. Continental runs a direct flight daily from Houston and offers Saturday service from Newark and Cleveland. **Grand Junction Airport** (tel. 970/244-9100), 127 miles north of Telluride, has daily service from Denver on United Express and from Salt

Lake City on Delta Sky West. **Gunnison Airport** (tel. 970/641–2304), 125 miles northeast of Telluride, has service from Dallas/Fort Worth on American, Saturday service from Houston on Continental, and thrice-weekly flights from Atlanta on Delta.

By Shuttle
Telluride Transit (tel. 970/728–6000 or 800/800–6228) and **Telluride Shuttle & Taxi** (tel. 970/728-6667 or 888/212-8294) run pre-scheduled shuttle service from the Telluride Regional ($7), Montrose ($28), Gunnison ($40), Durango ($40), and Grand Junction ($40). All prices are per person one-way with a four-person minimum.

By Car
Telluride Airport is an easy 5-mile drive down Route 145 into town. It's a different story if you're coming from DIA: The 330-mile journey goes through some tough but beautiful mountain areas. Allow at least a full day in each direction. From DIA follow I–70 west 200 miles to the Clifton exit; follow Route 141 south for 5 miles to Route 50; turn left and follow Route 50 south to Montrose, where it becomes Route 550; continue 27 miles south and turn right at Ridgway onto Route 62W; follow it for 30 miles to Route 145S, which after 18 miles brings you to Telluride. **Hertz, Budget,** and **Dollar** operate out of the Montrose and Telluride regional airports. **Avis** and **Hertz** have offices in Gunnison. (*See* Car Rental *in* Getting to Colorado Resorts, *above.*)

By Bus
Telluride Transit (tel. 970/728–6000) offers prearranged service from Montrose and Gunnison airports and also stops in Grand Junction.

By Train
Amtrak's (tel. 800/872–7245) daily *California Zephyr* service from the West Coast and Chicago stops in Denver and Grand Junction (120 miles north of Telluride).

GETTING AROUND
A car in Telluride is unnecessary and, frankly, unwelcome. Narrow, icy streets and limited street parking make getting around town difficult. Telluride is small, and almost everything is within a short walking distance anyway. Three local **taxi** services, Mountain Limo (tel. 970/728–9606), Skip's Taxi (tel. 970/728-6667), and Telluride Transit (tel. 970/728–6000), provide transportation in town and between town and resort. But you'll probably do what the locals do, and ride the **gondola,** which takes just 12 minutes from town to Mountain Village. The view is spectacular, day or night, and best of all, it's free.

THE SKIING
Telluride's reputation has preceded its emergence as an all-around destination resort, and although much of the beast has been cut, trimmed, and groomed out of the vertiginous, avalanche-prone slopes, most people still regard it as one of Colorado's toughest ski areas. Although you'll still find some of the toe-curling, radical in-your-face runs that first attracted the on-the-fringe crowd in the '60s and '70s, the boomers of the '90s have sent their message. Wise to marketing ways, the resort has

responded with winch-cat grooming and trail-widening plus the development of one of the best beginner areas and ski schools anywhere. Another nice feature is the mountain's layout: It is broken into three distinct areas. The front face of the mountain, almost immediately above the old town, is where the hotshots and wanna-be experts gather for regular shots of adrenaline. Mid-area on the mountain is directly above the ski village, and that's where most of the intermediate terrain is found. To the north is a marvelous novice area with meticulous grooming and some of the longest green runs in the state.

Novices
Telluride has set aside a mountain just for you, and it has a quad chairlift to take you up to some of the finest beginner runs around. They are long, meandering trails, alternately gentle and slightly pitched, that cascade easily from the 10,000-foot summit. From Lift 10 you can go left or right. If you choose to go left, take the blue Sundance to Double Cabin. Next time up, come off the chair to the right and follow Double Cabin the whole way to the base. For something slightly steeper but just as wide, pick up Bridges or Galloping Goose. The best part of this designated novice area is that all the runs head back to the Mountain Village, which means skiers at this level can easily meet up with friends skiing the more advanced runs at lunchtime or at the end of the day. When you've built up your confidence, head over to the gondola or lifts 2 and 4 for green-blue combinations such as Boomerang or the slightly more challenging Peek-a-Boo.

From either of these runs you can ski directly back to the base of Lift 4 or take the Village Bypass cutoff to the bottom of Lift 10. If you're keen to explore without getting into trouble, try Telluride Trail, a long, easy green run that winds its way into town from the top of Lift 7. When you reach the bottom of the run, take Lift 7 to the top and pick up Boomerang, which will lead you to the village area.

Intermediates
Although Telluride's reputation is based on its ferocious expert terrain, surprisingly almost 50% of its runs are intermediate. That percentage has increased slightly over the past couple of years as the resort has taken to some serious grooming, causing a number of black runs to be downgraded to blue intermediates. There's a good mix of intermediate and upper-intermediate runs in the Gorrono Basin area, which is served by Lifts 2, 3, 4, and 5. The steeper stuff tends to be found off the top of Lift 6, while the longer runs are found off the top of Lift 9, which is good if you're starting your day from the town side of the mountain—where you can catch the early sun. From the top of Lift 9 try the moderately steep combination of Upper See Forever, Upper Lookout, and Lower Lookout, a stiff intermediate challenge that starts off steep through a gladed area, narrows slightly while maintaining good pitch, then widens as it curves to the bottom of Lift 9 (take this back to the top rather than continuing down to the base of Lift 8). Your other choice on this side of the mountain is the tame version of the Plunge, the famed black-diamond drop that helps give

Telluride its expert reputation. The groomed-down intermediate version is actually marked double blue, which tells you that it's just a little tougher than your average blue run. It's steep, narrow, and when groomed, a high-speed joyride for upper intermediates and experts. The Gorrono Basin is your next-best bet; you can reach the crossover trail to the left of Upper See Forever about a third of the way down from the top. There are about a dozen runs in this area, including Lower See Forever, Misty Maiden, and Peek-a-Boo for cruising or Hermit for some solid bumps. Although they are medium-length runs, they sustain good pitch; if they offered a longer, more sustained challenge, they might be considered black runs. Grooming has mellowed them, and it can be fun tripping up Lift 4 and ripping down the pitch of Humboldt Draw, Pick and Gad, or Peek-a-Boo. It's heads-up skiing, and there's enough variety to keep you coming back for more. When you are ready to move up a notch, the black-diamond runs off the top of Lift 6 (reached from the top of Lift 9) are a good intermediate challenge because they are steeper but also well groomed. Silver Glade, Zulu Queen, and Chongos are supersteep and supergroomed runs perfect for pushing the intermediate envelope.

Experts

Although winch-cat grooming has taken the edge off some of Telluride's supersteep expert terrain, the core runs that gave it its fearsome reputation remain intact, and double-black-diamond addicts will love the combination of steep, unrelenting terrain and power-packed bump runs.

The Plunge—Telluride's signature run—and Spiral Stairs (both reached by Lifts 8 and 9 from the town side) are two of the most intense sustained mogul runs anywhere; from Lift 11 you can challenge some sublimely steep, powder-stuffed chutes like Electra and Dynamo. Most of the expert terrain is best reached from the town side; if you are starting from the resort village, it's a three- or four-lift ride that you should take into account when setting a time for meeting friends. If you don't want to plunge into the Plunge, try one of the good alternatives from the top of Lift 9. Bushwacker, Kant-Mak-M, and Mammoth are narrow, steep, unpredictable, twisting slashes with lots of drop-offs, tight turns, and patches of bumps. They are among the longest expert runs on the mountain, but you can start off with a little more pacing by turning right off Lift 9 and heading for the expert terrain on Gold Hill Ridge. Two lifts serve this area, where there are a dozen shorter (but no less steep) runs. The runs become steeper the farther along the ridge you go until you reach the Gold Hill summit, at 12,247 feet, and the insanely steep Little Rose beckons you. All the runs off this ridge are an exquisite mix of snow-filled chutes, eyes-over-your-ski-tips steepness, and tricky little glades. When you feel like stretching your runs out a little, you can always head back to the town side of the ridge and play on high-speed cruisers such as Power Line and East Drain.

SNOWBOARDING

Snowboarders have access to the entire mountain and to all lifts. The Surge Air Garden Terrain Park and half-pipe are located underneath lifts 3 and 5, and two satellite parks can be found off lifts 6 and 10.

Novice riders can check out Double Cabin, a long and winding double green with rounded walls that give you the feeling of riding big, rolling ocean waves. From the Big Billie's base area, take the Sunshine Express lift. Pick up Double Cabin by heading to the right, then stay to the right just below Enchanted Forest. After a few runs, take the alternate trails Galloping Goose, San Joaquin, and Bridges for variety. **Intermediate** riders can start at the Sunshine Express lift, ducking into the woods of Enchanted Forest for some easy glade riding. Another possibility is to catch Chair Four at the Mountain Village base area, heading right down Lower See Forever and past the Surge Air Garden Terrain Park, a favorite hangout for experts that's also a good place for intermediates to practice low-flying airs. The area that surrounds the park is packed with intermediate trails ideal for hard-booted euro-carvers and freestylers alike. **Experts** tend to ride on the town side of the mountain, where double-black-diamond slopes predominate. Often in shadow, these slopes can get quite icy late in the afternoon. Among the best runs is West Drain, a snaky natural pipeline in the woods just below Log Pile. From the Telluride Station base, take Chair 8. At the top, transfer to Chair 9. Descend on Upper See Forever, watching for the Log Pile trail on the right. This steep, treacherous glade run will funnel down to West Drain, which also can be accessed a little farther down Upper See Forever.

OTHER SNOW SPORTS

Snowshoeing, ice-skating, horse back rides, sleigh rides, snowmobile tours, and more are available through Telluride's concierge service (tel. 800/525–2717). But the must-do activity is the free-falling ride over Telluride resort with legendary local pilot **Glider Bob.** Ask the concierge service for details.

NEARBY

Purgatory Resort (tel. 800/861–5216) is Telluride's nearest resort neighbor, but it's still a 100-mile, 2-hour drive. The ski area is low-key and anti-glitzy, and its lift pass prices ($43) are reasonable for the excellent services offered. Seventeen miles north of Durango on U.S. 550, Purgatory has snowcat skiing service in addition to 690 acres of groomed and gladed trails.

WHERE TO STAY

If you stay in the town of Telluride you can enjoy its Victorian character, the chance to interact with the locals, and the convenience of walking to the restaurants and nightspots—in short, to be in the center of the action. Families, on the other hand, may place a higher premium on being away from the hubbub and closer to the beginner and intermediate terrain at the ski village. Many of the newer, more luxurious accommodations are centered around the ski village, whereas in-town lodgings are of the small-hotel, lodge, and B&B variety. This is not to say they are without luxury, but these more intimate places are geared to smaller groups, couples, and those for whom a curfew is not a problem. The gondola back up to Mountain Village shuts down at midnight. If you prefer ski-in/ski-out convenience, Mountain Village is your best choice, although most in-town accommodations are within a short walk of town lifts and the gondola.

The majority of accommodations in Telluride are run by several different management companies. The **Telluride Visitors Center** (700 W. Colorado Ave., Box 653, Telluride 81435, tel. 970/728–6265 or 888/783–0257, fax 970/728–6475) represents all Telluride accommodations.

Expensive

Aspen Ridge

For large family groups or two or three couples, these town houses are just right. All units are three-bedroom, three-bathroom monsters loaded with such niceties as a fireplace, a sauna, a hot tub or jetted bathtub, a steam shower, and a garage. The kitchen is appliance-packed with anything that plugs into a wall socket, and the overall decor is refined mountain elegance with modern, stylish furnishings, local artwork, and subdued colors such as dusty rose and sandstone. Four units sit right on a ski run: book early if you want ski-in/ski-out convenience. You can board the gondola just across the street from the front entrance. *100 Aspen Ridge Dr., Box 11165, Telluride Mountain Village 81435, tel. 970/728–4217 or 888/707–2767, fax 970/728–6557. 13 units. Facilities: ski storage, laundry. MC, V. $600–$700.*

Hotel Columbia

The Columbia may be small in size, but it's big in style and stature, with a sumptuous elegance that is matched by few places in town. The spacious rooms and suites are decorated in rich tones and superbly appointed with a down comforter, overstuffed chairs, a fireplace, a luxurious bathroom (with steam shower, bathrobes, and a six-foot claw-foot tub), original art, fresh flowers, and a balcony with a superb view of the surrounding mountains and the San Miguel River. The hotel is just a couple of hundred feet from the gondola and two blocks from downtown. *300 W. San Juan Ave., Box 800, 81435, tel. 970/728–0660 or 800/201–9505, fax 970/728–9249. 19 rooms, 2 suites. Facilities: restaurant, lounge, library, rooftop hot tub, desk service (7 AM–midnight), daily maid service, ski storage, laundry. AE, MC, V. $160–$455.*

Ice House

No alpine import, this lodge, and particularly its condo units, are decorated in modern Southwestern style. Antique Navajo rugs on the raw-plaster walls, clay lighting fixtures, and a dark-maroon-and-green color scheme set the tone. The odd-shaped building has a wooden exterior and a sky-lighted mezzanine on the third floor that can be viewed from a fourth-floor balcony. Service is unobtrusive but attentive, and there is the sense of quiet intimacy you would expect to find in a small inn. The hotel is a block from the gondola, two blocks from downtown. Rooms are appropriately sized for couples, and small families can manage in the suites. The condos can sleep eight and are equipped with a full kitchen, a balcony, and a dining area. *310 S. Fir St., Box 2909, 81435, tel. 970/728–6300 or 800/544–3436, fax 970/728–6358. 20 rooms, 22 suites, 13* units. *Facilities: bar, lounge, Jacuzzi, outdoor pool, steam room, 24-hr desk service, ski storage, ski valet, laundry. AE, D, DC, MC, V. $175–535, including full breakfast.*

Peaks Resort & Spa

At this château in the mountains you'll find oversize rooms and every conceivable service, including a spa considered to be one of the ten best in North America. The spa facilities are heavenly: indoor and outdoor swimming pools, saunas, steam rooms, Jacuzzis, weight rooms, aerobics classes, massages, and more. The Peaks, in the Mountain Village just a short schuss from the slopes, is the place to stay if money is no object and convenience is up there on your list of priorities. The rooms and suites are sumptuously furnished with plush couches and chairs and elegantly styled with rich draperies, area rugs, and wall coverings, all reflecting a Southwestern motif. They're loaded with touches such as terry robes and extralarge bathrooms with marble vanities. There's also a spectacular view from all rooms. *136 Country Club Rd., Box 2702, Telluride Mountain Village 81435, tel. 970/728–6800 or 800/789–2220, fax 970/728–6175. 149 rooms, 28 suites. Facilities: 2 restaurants, bar, spa, 24-hr desk service, ski storage, ski valet, shuttle to Telluride Airport, laundry. AE, DC, MC, V. $355–$1,550.*

Moderate

Alpine Inn B&B

If you enjoy the friendliness and homespun ambience of a B&B, this reincarnation of an original 1903 Telluride hotel will suit you fine. All but two of the rooms—each larger than the average B&B unit—have private baths, and all are beautifully decorated and furnished with period antiques and handmade quilts. The suite has a fireplace, a terrace, and a whirlpool. If you're interested in mingling with other guests, the glass solarium, where a full breakfast is served, is a good meeting place, as is the hot tub. Otherwise, this lodging allows for privacy, as rooms are comfortable enough to hide away in. The location, about two blocks from the Oak Street lift and gondola, is convenient. *440 W. Colorado Ave., Box 2398, 81435, tel. 970/728–6282 or 800/707–3344, fax 970/728–3424. 7 rooms, 1 suite. Facilities: hot tub, ski storage. MC, V. $120–$500.*

Pennington's Mountain Village Inn

This alpine inn, on the 12th fairway of a golf course halfway between Telluride and the ski village, is marvelously isolated. Under the many-peaked roof are sumptuously decorated rooms with cathedral ceilings and French-country decor. Guest rooms and the slightly larger suites, which have a separate sitting area, are outfitted with a king- or queen-size bed, a deck offering panoramic views of Sunshine Mountain and Mt. Wilson, and a small fridge packed with snacks and juices. Full breakfast is served to guests in their rooms or in the dining area. A daily happy hour is convened in the lounge. *100 Pennington Ct., Box 2428, 81435, tel. 970/728–5337 or 800/543–1437, fax 970/728–5338. 9 rooms, 3 suites. Facilities: lounge, library, billiards, Jacuzzi, steam room, ski storage, laundry. AE, D, MC, V. $140–$300, including full breakfast.*

Riverside Condominiums

This is a good condo deal, in downtown Telluride on the bank of the San Miguel River, just two blocks from the Oak Street lift and gondola. One-, two, and three-bedroom units are available; the absence of four-bedroom megagroup units may account for Riverside's quiet atmosphere. At five blocks from the main drag, it's a little removed from the action but close enough to essential stores and services, making it a good choice for families. The units are well equipped with a kitchen, a fireplace, a washer-dryer, and a balcony. The only drawback for those with youngsters may be the absence of a pool, but adults appreciate the hot tub on the deck overlooking the mountains. *460 S. Pine St., Box 100, 81435, tel. 970/ 728–6621 or 800/538–7754, fax 970/ 728–6160. 25 units. Facilities: 2 hot tubs, ski storage, laundry. AE, D, MC, V. $190–$425.*

San Sophia B&B

This distinguished, comfortable, luxurious mountain inn is among the finest in Colorado. Snuggled up against its namesake mountains, the property is ideally located, one block from the Oak Street lift and gondola, in Old Telluride. Inside the turreted building are 16 distinctive rooms, each washed in pastels and named for a local mine. Furnishings include Victorian antiques and brass beds with handmade quilts. The bathrooms have double oval-shape tubs, terry robes, and a monster basket of toiletries. For an extramemorable experience try the upper-turret room, with its 360° view. Families with children should call ahead for restrictions. *330*

W. Pacific Ave., Box 1825, 81435, tel. 970/728–3001 or 800/537–4781, fax 970/728–6228. 16 rooms. Facilities: library, observatory, Jacuzzi, ski storage, laundry service. AE, MC, V. $180– $295, including full breakfast and après-ski snacks.

Inexpensive

Bear Creek B&B

Contemporary design and decor lend an all-American feel to this downtown inn, a change of pace from all the historic B&Bs in the area. Rooms are large, with natural-wood furnishings, brightly colored upholstery, and pastel wall coverings. The living room has a friendly fireplace, and on the roof is a deck with a jetted spa and a panoramic view. *21 E. Colorado Ave., Box 2369, 81435, tel. 970/728–6681 or 800/338–7064. 10 rooms. Facilities: sauna, steam room, ski storage, MC, V. $117–$237, including full breakfast and après-ski snacks.*

New Sheridan Hotel

Here's another of Telluride's small inns that gets high marks for its authentic style, reasonable prices, and good location—in the heart of downtown Telluride, just a block from the gondola. Built in 1892, it has recently been totally renovated. Rooms vary from small (with shared bathrooms) to suites with sitting areas. All are impeccably furnished with antiques and period pieces such as canopy beds and antique armoires and are decorated in soft tones of rose, beige, and off-white. It's a friendly spot, with socializing revolving around the breakfast table, the après-ski munchies in the library, and the two rooftop hot tubs. A half block away are six newer condos that sleep six. *231 W. Colorado Ave., Box 231, 81435, tel. 970/728–4351, fax 970/ 728–5024 or 800/200–1891. 10 rooms, 2 with bath, 8 suites, 6 units. Facilities: hot tub, fitness room. AE, D, DC, MC, V. $90–$225.*

Oak Street Inn
This clean, comfortable place is the cheapest accommodation in town and attracts a hard-partying crowd of budget skiers who would rather spend money in the saloon than on a room. No-frills guest rooms have double beds or bunks and can sleep as many as six. It's the sort of no-fuss, conveniently located place—only three blocks from the Oak Street lift—of which all ski resorts should have more. *134 N. Oak St., 81435, tel. 970/728–3383. 24 rooms, 2 with bath. Facilities: TV lounge, sauna. AE, D, MC, V. $42–$72; $14 each additional person.*

Telluride Lodge
These are deceptively luxurious condos, with the rather plain exterior concealing spacious, well-decorated, and well-equipped units that can sleep up to 10. The units range in size from studio to three bedrooms, with the latter spread over three floors. All come with a full kitchen, a fireplace, a TV, and distinctive decorating touches. The lodge is just 200 feet from the Coonskin lift and about a five-minute walk from downtown. *747 W. Pacific Ave., Box 127, 81435, tel. 970/728–4446 or 800/662–8747, fax 970/728–5228. 45 units. Facilities: hot tubs, steam room, ski lockers, laundry. AE, MC, V. $165–$590.*

WHERE TO EAT
On the Mountain
Giuseppe's
On a clear day 11,890 feet up (via Lift 9), you'll be able to see all the way to Utah. It gets crowded here at peak hours on sunny days. The menu includes Italian fare such as pizza and pasta and an excellent black bean, potato, and cheese stir-fry. *Top of Lift 9, tel. 970/728–7503. No credit cards.*

Gorrono Ranch Restaurant
Ranch-style dining and ranch-style portions are two sure bets at this restaurant in an original homestead at midmountain. A daily barbecue with burgers, chicken, and steaks is offered, as well as fresh lobster. *Misty Maiden run under Lift 4, tel. 970/728–7566. D, MC, V.*

Expensive

Campagna
If you want authentic Tuscan cuisine, there is no other place in Telluride to have such a meal. The cozy dining room of this Victorian house has great ambience. The decor is warm, and the antique tables, oak floor, and old photos of Italy promote the illusion of eating in an Italian home. Hallmark dishes include delicate pastas in unusually light sauces, as well as braised or grilled meats and fish. Try the New Zealand rack of lamb with rosemary and garlic or the whole roasted snapper stuffed with fennel. *435 W. Pacific Ave., tel. 970/728–6190. Reservations essential. MC, V.*

La Marmotte
This restaurant, French to the core, rates as the best overall in town. Walk through the door of what was once an

icehouse, and the brick walls, lace curtains, and fresh flowers greet you like a kiss on both cheeks. The menu is a mix of traditional and nouvelle French haute cuisine, with a range of entrées that include duck-leg confit and sautéed pink duck breast in a white bean and roasted garlic sauce, grilled veal chop with five-grain rice and tomato-coriander sauce, rack of venison, Colorado lamb, and Atlantic salmon. *150 W. San Juan St., tel. 970/ 728–6232. Reservations essential. AE, D, MC, V.*

221 South Oak Street

Owners Hope Anderson and Joan Sullivan opened this upscale bistro serving regional American cuisine in 1992, choosing as their location a historic home nestled in the trees. The cozy yet elegant decor includes a cushy earth-tone couch at the entrance and gilt-framed paintings on the walls. Oak Street's eclectic fare includes a tasting menu that changes daily in response to the availability of fresh ingredients. Chef Robert Scherner's favorite menu staples include seared tuna with warm spinach salad and shrimp dumplings; smoked salmon with pickled baby beets and a mustard vinaigrette; and goat cheese strudel wrapped in phyllo. *221 South Oak St., tel. 970/728–9507. Reservations essential. AE, MC, V.*

Moderate

Bistro Nouveau

This hip, happening American bistro has stylish decor, with whitewashed walls splashed with color, sleek modern furnishings, and exposed wood. The menu is as loose as the atmosphere, with a range of dishes including lamb, fish, and pasta presented in Colorado ranchlands style. There are also low-fat, spa-style dishes like herb-crusted chicken with roasted vegetable hash and grilled shrimp flavored with soy, sesame, and ginger. *115 W. Colorado Ave., tel. 970/728–1915. AE, MC, V.*

Excelsior Cafe

This delightfully intimate restaurant is spread over two floors of a magnificently restored Victorian house. The Italian menu includes a fantastic Caesar salad, deli meats and imported cheeses, a delicious thin-crust pizza, and more traditional pasta and veal entrées. The Excelsior is a good spot for a couple of romantics looking for a quiet, quaint place to break bread. *200 W. Colorado Ave., tel. 970/728– 4250. AE, MC, V.*

Leimgruber's Bierstube

Pronounce the name correctly (lime-groob-ers) and you won't sound like a tourist. It's a warm, friendly place with log walls, handcrafted furnishings, and lots of antiques. German specialties such as schnitzel (Wiener or Jäger), sauerbraten, smoked pork, and bratwurst are all prepared in classic style. There's also an excellent selection of wines and German beers. *573 W. Pacific Ave., tel. 970/728– 4663. AE, MC, V.*

Limeleaf at Swede-Finn Hall

Swedish and Finnish miners were some of the earliest settlers in Telluride. The Swede-Finn Hall, a legacy of mining days, has also served as a church, a basketball court, and a storage shed. Today it's a cheerful restaurant with a bistro menu. The owners have tried to preserve the building's original 1890s look, with wood floors, 12-foot ceilings, a large stage at one end for occasional music, and walls adorned with yellowing antique photographs of the early gold-rush days of Telluride. There's even an old-fashioned billiards hall in the basement and a bar that serves beer from five Colorado microbreweries. On the menu you'll find such local delights as Rocky Mountain trout, quail, venison, and a variety of European dishes, including vegetarian shepherd's pie, bouillabaisse, and Athenian chicken pasta. *472 W. Pacific Ave., tel. 970/728–2085. Reservations essential. MC, V.*

Powder House

An American-bistro atmosphere combines with Rocky Mountain cuisine to make Powder House a casual, satisfying place for a meal. Roast duckling, elk tenderloin, buffalo sausage, fresh fettuccine, sautéed shrimp, scallops, crab, and roasted chicken head the list of entrées, but don't overlook the large lineup of appetizers, including a smoked-game platter and fried calamari. The food is dynamite—and, incidentally, the building in which Powder House resides was once used as an explosives storage shed. *226 W. Colorado Ave., tel. 970/728–3622. AE, MC, V.*

Inexpensive

Floradora

A Telluride institution, this great little restaurant has been around since 1978, when the current owners began as dishwasher and waitress. The straightforward menu, well-prepared family-style meals, and casual friendly attitude make it a local favorite. The

menu is varied but not fancy, with prime cuts of beef, Southwestern specialties (like chicken fajitas), and great burgers. *103 W. Colorado Ave., tel. 970/728–3888. AE, D, MC, V.*

Roma Café and Bar

During the 1890s the Roma was a lounge, and today the downstairs is still dominated by the marvelous original Brunswick bar with its 12-foot French mirrors. The decor is early American saloon, with lots of wood, brass, and mirrors; and the menu is resoundingly Italian, with a good selection of fresh, homemade pasta dishes, including penne, lasagna, ravioli, and daily spaghetti specials. *133 E. Colorado Ave., tel. 970/728–3669. MC, V.*

South Park Café

This classic American diner, part deli, part pizzeria, part pasta palace, is the place to get almost any comfort food you crave. The thin-crust New York-style pizzas, with dozens of exotic toppings, are a rave. Farther down the menu, you'll find everything from Philly Cheese sandwiches to Tandoori chicken, a variety of pasta dishes, and salads—from traditional Caesar to the exotic Oriental chicken. *300 W. Colorado Ave., tel. 970/728–6108. MC, V.*

T-Ride Country Club

If you enjoy nothing more than the aroma of a sizzling backyard barbecue, you'll love the T-Ride Country Club. A large selection of meat, fowl, and fish is done to perfection, and there's also a large salad bar. If you have to wait, there are 11 TVs and 14 beers on tap. T-Ride is a loud, raucously happy place with huge windows that overlook the street. *333 W.*

Colorado Ave., tel. 970/728–6344. AE, D, MC, V.

Best Bets for Breakfast
Sofio's Mexican Café
The best breakfasts in town are found here, including light, fluffy omelets, French waffles, pancakes, seafood Benedict, and Mexican specialties such as huevos rancheros (eggs with salsa). Fresh-squeezed juices and tasty, strong coffee will get you going in the morning. *110 E. Colorado Ave., tel. 970/728–4882. AE, MC, V.*

Steaming Bean
Get your java jolt here—you won't find better coffee in town—and try the soups, muffins, and pastries. A good selection of gentle wake-up blends plus an eye-opening espresso and designer flavors are available. *221 W. Colorado Ave., tel. 970/728–0793. MC, V.*

NIGHTLIFE AND ENTERTAINMENT
Après-Ski
Leimgruber's Bierstube
This is definitely the place to be for après-ski. But get here early because it fills up fast with locals and in-the-know visitors. There are personalized beer mugs hanging over the bar, a half dozen German beers on tap, and the ever-present challenge of the Boot, a monster beer glass that only the bold dare order. It's a friendly spot that eventually turns into the more refined dining room mentioned above. *573 W. Pacific Ave., tel. 970/728–4663. AE, MC, V.*

Loud and Lively/Dancing
Fly Me to the Moon Saloon
If you want to shake some ache out of your legs, try the legendary spring-loaded dance floor here. The saloon hosts the hottest live bands in town most nights and packs in the crowds—especially the very hip under-30 set. *132 E. Colorado Ave., tel. 970/728–6666. No credit cards.*

Last Dollar Saloon
This main street bar is also known as the Buck by locals, and has the best artificial gas fireplace around. Beyond that, it's a cheerful place, with wooden floors, brick walls, tin ceilings, and windows overlooking the street scene. There is also a hearty selection of some 40 beers, a multitude on tap, plus some good music. *100 E. Colorado Ave., no phone. No credit cards.*

New Sheridan Bar
This big, Western-style saloon in the revamped oldest hotel in town practically guarantees a good time. It's rough and ready, with wooden floors, walls loaded with antiques (or maybe just junk), and a huge bar. Tradition allows for local cowboy Roudy Roudebush to occasionally ride his horse right into the bar. Beer is the beverage of choice, and the bartenders keep it flowing as the crowd keeps on growing. Now and then there's live entertainment. *New Sheridan Hotel, 231 W. Colorado Ave., tel. 970/728–3911. MC, V.*

More Mellow
Eagles Bar
The first thing you notice about this stylish, modern bar is the collection of eagles carved from solid pieces of wood. This is a hip establishment done in soothing Southwestern colors and dominated by a large square bar adjacent to a stylish dining area. Numerous microbrews on tap provide

the liquid refreshment, and the duck-stuffed spring rolls are the upscale bar munchies that match the trendy scene. *100 W. Colorado Ave., tel. 970/728–0886. AE, D, DC, MC, V.*

Powder House
This is a great place for your last stop of the night, where you can meet friends and enjoy the cozy atmosphere as you sip on a nightcap or indulge in a delicious dessert. This well-established Telluride institution has a pleasant feel and a soothing ambience. *226 W. Colorado Ave., tel. 970/728–3622. AE, MC, V.*

VAIL SKI RESORT

Vail Resorts Inc.
Box 7
Vail, CO 81658
Tel. 970/845–5725 or
800/525–2257
www.vailresorts.com

STATISTICALLY SPEAKING

Base elevation: 8,120 feet

Summit elevation: 11,450 feet

Vertical drop: 3,330 feet

Skiable terrain: 4,644 acres

Number of trails: 174

Longest run: 4.5 miles

Lifts and capacity: 1 gondola, 1 enclosed high-speed quad, 9 high-speed quads, 1 fixed-grip quad, 3 triples, 5 doubles, 22 surface lifts; 46,161 skiers per hour

Daily lift ticket: $59

Average annual snowfall: 341 inches

Number of skiing days 1997–98: 163

Snowmaking: 347 acres, 7.5%

Terrain mix: N 28%, I 32%, E 40%

Snowboarding: yes

Cross-country skiing: Golden Peak and Vail Golf Course

Vast in scale and scope, 4,644-acre Vail draws more skiers than any other winter resort in the nation. Known worldwide for its unstinting customer service and amenities, Vail is also an awe-inspiring place to ski. From its miles of groomed cruisers to its untamed back bowls, Vail has it all. Though known for its country club clientele, Vail strives to accommodate everyone. Here, a person's castle can be a 10-bedroom designer house on a hill, a modest motel room in the shadow of a gas station, or anything in between. It's still possible for the ultra-moneyed set to short-circuit a platinum credit card in one week of unabashed luxury here. But there are ways and means for almost any self-respecting skier, regardless of income, to experience Vail.

The four mountain centers (Golden Peak, Vail Village, Lionshead, Cascade Village) that make up Vail's base area are strung along I-70. An efficient and free shuttle bus service between them makes getting around reasonably easy. Each center focuses on pedestrian-only malls with modern Tyrolean/American architecture.

Vail's rapid growth in the 1990s wasn't without controversy. In 1998, eco-activists torched five on-mountain buildings (including the elegant Two Elks Lodge, a favorite spot for lunch) and four ski lifts as a protest against Vail's planned 885-acre expansion into National Forest land said to be prime habitat for a species of lynx. Since the incident, Vail Associates has increased security at Vail, Beaver Creek, and its Summit County resorts, Breckenridge and Keystone.

HOW TO GET THERE

By Plane

Denver International Airport (DIA), 120 miles and two hours' drive away, is the closest international facility (*see* Getting to Colorado Resorts, *above*). United Express offers six daily connecting flights to **Vail–Eagle County Airport** (33 miles from the resort, 30 minutes by car). Five major airlines provide nonstop service into Vail–Eagle County: America West has daily flights from Phoenix; Ameri-

Area code: 970

Children's services: day-care, tel. 970/479–3285; instruction, tel. 970/476–3239 or 970/476–3229

Snow phone: tel. 970/476–4888

Police: tel. 970/479–2200

Vail Valley Medical: tel. 970/476–2452

Vail Valley Tourism and Convention Bureau: tel. 800/824–5737

Road conditions: tel. 970/479–2226

Towing: Vail Amoco Service, tel. 970/476–1810

FIVE-STAR FAVORITES

Best run for vertical: Prima Cornice

Best run overall: Riva Ridge

Best bar/nightclub: Club Chelsea

Best hotel: Sonnenalp Resort

Best restaurant: Game Creek Club

can serves Dallas, Chicago, Miami, Newark, New York/La Guardia, and San Francisco. Continental serves Houston (daily) and Newark (Saturday only); Northwest serves Minneapolis (daily) and Detroit (Saturday only); and United flies from New York, Chicago, and Los Angeles, as well as from Denver. From DIA, **Colorado Mountain Express** (tel. 970/949–4227 or 800/525–6353; $56 per person; reserve ahead) offers regularly scheduled nonstop shuttle service.

By Car

Vail is 100 miles west of Denver, and for the most part it's an easy, scenic drive. From DIA follow I–70 west for two hours to the resort. There are three exits for Vail: Exit 180 into East Vail, Exit 176 for Vail Village, and Exit 173 for West Vail. If you're uncertain about the location of your accommodations, take the Vail Village exit. A word of caution about driving on I–70: Radar traps are more common here than on any other stretch of highway in ski country. On Sundays, expect heavy traffic and delays owing to the number of skiers returning to Denver.

GETTING AROUND

No matter where you stay in Vail, you're never far from the action, be it superb skiing or lively nightlife and schmoozing. Because the efficient **Town of Vail** bus system (tel. 970/328–8143) travels everywhere from the Golden Peak area all the way over to Beaver Creek, you won't need a car here. **Vail Valley Taxi** (tel. 970/476–8294) provides transportation in town and between town and resort.

THE SKIING

Vail Mountain is a rippling behemoth that stretches for nearly 7 miles above the Gore Valley, giving skiers 4,644 acres of terrain, 3,330 feet of vertical, and a network of 31 lifts. It's unprepossessing, without the craggy peaks and deep valleys of other Colorado mountains. In fact, so benign is the view from the valley that the original developers bypassed it many times in search of more dominant peaks. Just prior to opening day, December 15, 1962, in a *New York Times* article, historian Marshall Sprague described it as "a placid, oblong pile, nicely clad in aspen, spruce, and lodgepole pine." But it's what you don't see from the valley that makes Vail special. The front face, or north slope, provides immense variety of length and pitch; and the south-facing bowls offer some of the purest, wildest open-terrain skiing on the continent. The 11,450-foot summit is just below timberline, so the north face is protected from wind; yet the elevation helps produce an annual snowfall of more than 340 inches.

There are 174 marked trails, the longest of which runs 4½ miles down the face, but the 3,734 acres of back-bowl skiing—all of which are left ungroomed, providing the entire spectrum of snow conditions, from fresh powder to breakable crust—yield a virtually limitless number of routes down the mountain. You could ski Vail for a year and not discover all its virtues, but fortunately visitors vacationing for a week or so can benefit from the most extensive modern lift network in the country. The scope and immensity of the terrain may be staggering at first, but 10 detachable quad chairs are strategically situated to provide access to individual faces and bowls on the mountain.

Vail's size makes it the most egalitarian American ski resort, a place with something for every level of skier. With some searching, one can find the throat-gurgling steepness of Jackson Hole, Taos, or Snowbird, the primitive powder of Alta, the elite image of Deer Valley (at nearby sister resort, Beaver Creek), and the remoteness of Big Sky. In its tremendous mass, Vail manages to provide as much or as little challenge as needed.

Novices

There are several well-defined novice areas at Vail. It's important to pay careful attention to trail markers because a wrong turn can lead to a serious misadventure. Never presume that because the base area is in sight, you can't get into trouble: There are some heady black-diamond runs leading into Vail Village. First-time skiers should begin at the Gopher Hill lift, in the Golden Peak area, on the far-eastern side of the resort. It serves a wide, well-groomed beginner run that allows you no opportunity to get in over your head. Once you've found your ski legs, take a ride on the Riva Bahn Express lift to the midway point at Fort Whipper Snapper and try the long cruising run called Mule Skinner. Green runs are accessible from every lift on the front side of the mountain. When in doubt, you can follow many long, winding catwalks that will ease you down to ground zero. If you're starting from Vail Village, the Vista Bahn lift to Mid-Vail will give you access to Lion's Way or Gitalong Road. Lion's Way will take you to the Avanti Express, and Gitalong winds back to the Vista Bahn or Avanti lifts. These are all well-groomed runs protected from the wind by trees, so all maintain a good, firm base. With a little luck you'll catch some sun on these runs by early afternoon.

From the top of Avanti take Over Easy down to where the Mountaintop Express and Wildwood Express lifts meet. The Mountaintop Express will take you to the summit, where you can choose Ramshorn to the west or Swingsville to the east. From Wildwood Express head down Eagle's Nest Ridge and turn right just before the

Avanti lift to the Meadows. This beautifully groomed wide-open trail bypasses several black runs, depositing you at the Mountaintop Express–Wildwood Express intersection.

If you start your day from the Lionshead Center and ride the newly updated gondola, take Cub's Way (a well-protected run with groomed snow that zigzags all the way down to Avanti Express lift) to stay out of harm's way or follow Owl's Roost (a wide run with packed, groomed snow that leads you through the trees) down to Ledges and then to Cub's Way. Pay special attention at this junction because this is where Ledges turns expert.

The Eagle's Nest Practice Park, with five trails served by five lifts, is also ideal terrain on which to start out. The snow here is typically better than that at the base, and there's a wide variety of terrain.

Intermediates

Arguably no other resort in America offers as much variety for intermediates as Vail. Starting from Vail Village, take the Vista Bahn Express up to Mid-Vail, then the Mountaintop Express to the summit. From here you have a choice of Cappuccino, a fast, well-groomed cruising glade run; Expresso, which is slightly steeper and prone to substantial mogul development; or Whistle Pig, the steepest of the three, where the moguls tend to be the biggest.

If bumps are not your thing, head for Christmas, to the right (looking down) of Swingsville. It's a good, fast giant-slalom run that cuts through the trees and remains mostly mogul-free. Another challenging choice is the designated-black Riva Ridge, perhaps the best overall intermediate-to-advanced run on the mountain. Regardless of its color, a strong intermediate should be able to handle it. If you want a real challenge, follow Riva Ridge to Tourist Trap—an extremely steep section just below Mid-Vail. Your other option, however, is to bail out on Compromise, then rejoin Riva Ridge all the way to the bottom.

If you take the Wildwood Express lift from Mid-Vail, take Race Track or Hunky Dory (both to the left as you get off the lift). Both are excellent wide-open, bowl-like runs that you can cruise down without getting into any trouble. From Mid-Vail you can travel east on the Gitalong Road catwalk to the Trans Montane catwalk and head up the Northwoods Express lift or go west along Lion's Way to the Avanti Express.

At the top of the Northwoods lift turn left onto the Timberline catwalk; you'll pass a couple of steep black-diamond runs—First Step and North Star—that a strong intermediate could handle. Serious moguls grow on the top sections, but the rest is manageable. If you stay on Timberline past the black runs, you'll see Northwoods, a wide-open cruiser with a series of rolls, and Snag Park, a slightly steeper run that eventually merges with Northwoods. Another choice, especially on fresh-powder days, is Gandy Dancer, which can be reached by going right from the Northwoods Express lift, skiing Swingsville Ridge for a short time, and picking up Gandy Dancer on your right under the Northwoods Express lift. Although this is a black run, most strong intermediates can handle it because it is usually well groomed and virtually mogul-free.

The Avanti Express lift gives you access to Avanti, a blue-black cruiser that drops and pitches with consistency and is usually well groomed; and Picaroon, another intermediate-expert combination with some extremely steep pitches. Berries is a good choice, although it does get fairly difficult toward the bottom half. If you don't want to try the black portion, cut left on Ledges and pick up Lodge Pole or Columbine.

There is another excellent set of intermediate runs to the right (getting off the lift) of the Game Creek Express, at the west end of the mountain in the Game Creek Bowl. Except for the occasional mogul-shaving operation, the Woods and Baccarat are rarely groomed but are prime intermediate runs. Showboat, immediately under the lift, has a split personality: The right side offers fairly smooth, straightforward cruising, but the left side builds up with moguls. You can take Chair 7 (Game Creek Express) to the top and ski Eagle's Nest Ridge to the Eagle's Nest area. From here Simba, Bwana, Safari, and Born Free, four fairly steady cruising runs, take you back to the Lionshead gondola.

For the most part, the back bowls of Vail are a cut above the intermediate rating, although the right conditions, plenty of snow, and a little work—and a workout—will get you down in one piece, even if you do a lot of traversing. If you want to give the bowls a try but don't want to damage your health or ego, start from the temporary One Elk Lodge (on the eastern back side of the mountain)

and tackle the designated-blue West and East Poppyfields (wide-open bowls with a little pitch but lots of room to maneuver). These runs will put you at the bottom of the Orient Express lift. Come off to your left, follow the short catwalk, and ski West and East Poppyfields for the second time.

Experts

Vail's back bowls beckon many expert skiers, especially after a good overnight snowfall. Go early, when the morning sun has begun to soften the snow, before the powder gets too chopped up; by midday the snow turns heavy and wet. To reach the back bowls and avoid crowded lift lines, go to the Riva Bahn Express lift, at the east end of the resort. Connect with the Highline lift and ski down to Sourdough to reach the West Wall (surface) lift. Take the West Wall and—voilà—you'll be at the top of the China Bowl.

If you start early to beat the crowds, the journey from Golden Peak lift to the China Bowl can take less than 40 minutes. It's time well invested because this is where you'll spend most of the morning, enjoying the sublime skiing in this massive bowl area and riding the relatively uncrowded Orient Express quad. Try Shangri-La, which takes you through the trees, or attempt the extreme steeps of Dragon's Teeth, Genghis Khan, and Emperor's Choice. Another option from the Orient Express lift is to skirt the top of the ridge toward the Siberia Bowl, where Red Square, Gorky Park, Rasputin's Revenge, and Orient Express offer steep, ungroomed terrain.

Serious expert skiers can head farther east to the Inner and Outer Mongolia bowls. This is the wildest area at Vail—not in the radical sense, but because the terrain is so vast—and it should never be skied alone. Be especially cautious when the light is flat or visibility low, because it's easy to become disoriented here. At times the snow can turn cruddy, but the experience of being able to point your skis and not have boundaries is priceless. Keep in mind that the route back to the Orient Express lift is by way of the long Silk Road catwalk, so try to carry some speed as you reach the bottom of the bowl. This is primitive skiing at its best, with a wild variety of snow surfaces that can include deep soft stuff, chopped-up crud, sun-kissed crust, and wind-packed powder, all accented by the sheer steepness and isolation.

During late morning head west toward the Sundown Bowl and take a run down Forever, which has one of the longest sustained verticals on the back side. The runs in this vast bowl have the southernmost exposure and are therefore warmest.

Around lunchtime you can take the Wildwood Express lift to the relatively uncrowded Wildwood Smokehouse on the north-facing front side of the mountain. From Wildwood ski east along the Minturn Mile to the Skipper, then pick up Look Ma. Ride the Mountaintop Express lift and get ready for Prima, Prima Cornice, and Pronto—three mogul-studded brutes that are as steep as anything you will ever ski. Prima Cornice, for instance, slants as much as 43%.

SNOWBOARDING

Vail has gone out of its way to welcome snowboarders, re-grading flat spots and creating boarder-friendly snowboard zones with terrain garden features, half-pipes, and other amenities. A lighted terrain park with two half-pipes for day and night riding and the UnVailed Park for expert boarders, with a 300-foot technical half-pipe, both opened in 1996. A special trail map for snowboarders indicates log slides, handrails, and other features on the mountain. Of course, the ultimate terrain for skiers or snowboarders is the back bowls on a powder day.

Most of the better **beginner** areas are concentrated on the western side of the resort; start the morning on the Eagle Bahn gondola at the Lionshead base, and you can practically be assured of finding a full day of excellent snowboarding terrain. From the top, take Cub's Way, an easy, winding slope that crosses the Born Free trail before leading down to Minnie's Lift. Take Minnie's to the top, and you'll discover Practice Parkway, a loopy, mild run that swirls back down to the base of Minnie's or connects to Ledges and back down to lower Cub's Way. If you stay on this trail, you can meander your way down to Vail Village on Getalong Road, an easy snowcat pathway through the trees. If you begin the day from Vail Village, take the Vista Bahn Express to Mid-Vail, where you can pick up the Mountain Top Express. Follow the Timberline catwalk down to the Sourdough lift–and a cluster of easy runs with names like Boomer, Tin Pants, and Flap Jack.

One problem beginners face at Vail is getting back to where they began; if you find yourself at the wrong base area at the end of the day, it's sometimes best to simply catch the free shuttle rather than work through an exhausting maze of lifts and trails.

Intermediates should stay on the front side of Vail and avoid the temptation of the back bowls—unless the snow is fresh. A deep layer of powder will soften the moguls sufficiently for upper-intermediates to tackle the wide-open spaces of China Bowl. But once the snow gets choppy (usually by midday after a fresh snow), it's best to retire to the easier, groomed trails on the front side. That said, intermediate riders can start from any of the base areas and find easy access to excellent boarding terrain. Among the better runs are Born Free, Simba, and Bwana, just off the Pride Express lift. All are long, with prominent hits and catwalks suitable for launching small airs—just be sure the jump area is clear. Intermediates can head to Mule Skinner Park, a moderate entry-level terrain park. Another on-mountain snowboard mecca is the Golden Peak Halfpipe and Park, a huge terrain garden and double-barreled half-pipe.

Experts head directly for the back bowls; depending on which base you depart from, you can work your way to mid-Vail and the Mountain Top Express lift. If bowl skiing isn't your thing, drop down the Timberline catwalk to Snag Park, and gather up some fresh powder in the pine trees. Below Snag Park is Hairbag Alley, an expert's pathway that winds through a tight valley bottom before depositing you at the base of the Highline

lift. From this lift, you can explore the steep and steady bump runs called Blue Ox, Roger's, and Highline; often, running the path under the lift will take you through piles of fresh powder. Pride Park, under the Pride Express (Chair 26) is Vail's traditional expert's terrain park.

OTHER SNOW SPORTS

Adventure Ridge (tel. 970/476–9090) is an on-mountain activities site offering **snowmobile** tours, **ice-skating, laser tag, snowshoeing, ski-bike** tours, and a popular **tubing** hill. One of the niftiest kids' attractions are **mini-snowmobiles** that they can pilot around a closed course.

NEARBY

Vail is just one ridge away from Summit County and its many resorts—Copper, Keystone, Arapahoe Basin, and Breckenridge. Although it would take you a season to ski all the trails of Vail, you may wish to vary the routine and visit the Summit resorts. Copper is closest, but your Vail Resorts lift pass is valid at both Keystone and Breckenridge.

WHERE TO STAY

Which of the resort's four village areas you stay in will be determined by how much money you want to spend, whether you want to be in the center of the action, and with whom you'll be traveling. The Golden Peak area, at the far-east end of Vail Resort, is suitable for families and those looking for a quiet atmosphere. Most of the accommodations are in the upper moderate price range because you pay a premium for access to the

Golden Peak lifts. These two lifts serve the beginners' area and connect with the upper lifts and more difficult terrain.

The action is in Vail Village, at the center of the resort. You'll pay top dollar for most of the accommodations, which are European-style lodges. The emphasis is on design, service, and poshness. This village is the nightlife hub, and bars, bistros, and boogie spots line Bridge Street, a 150-yard stretch of entertainment. Most of the lodges, inns, and elegant condos in Vail Village are within walking distance of the high-speed Vista Bahn lift, which takes you to midmountain in nine minutes.

Lionshead, the third village and westernmost base area, is more condo than Tyrolean in its styling, but it offers the greatest variety of accommodations in terms of size and price. This village, too, has its own nightlife, but it leans toward sports bars rather than piano bars, and the crowd tends to be younger and more spirited. Lionshead, however, offers the easiest access to the Adventure Ridge Activities Center, and therefore can be a good strategic locale for families with young children.

Farther west is Cascade Village, the least developed of Vail's four village areas. It's served by the Cascade Village lift, which you must take to reach the main lift network at the Lionshead center. You can also take the Vail shuttle bus into Lionshead or Vail Village. At the end of the day, guests of the Cascade Club can ski back to Cascade on the green Cascade Way Trail.

For a less expensive option, move away from the resort proper and bunk down in one of the smaller, inexpensive motels and small lodges across the highway.

Vail has an astonishing number of condominiums, ranging from practical studios to sumptuous four- and five-bedroom units. When comparing prices, don't let the per-night rate mislead you: do your math and divide the space by the number of occupants paying the freight. You can make your own arrangements by calling direct, or you can book virtually anything through **Vail Resorts Central Reservations** (tel. 800/404–3535). The Vail Valley Tourism and Convention Bureau (tel. 800/824–5737) may also be of assistance.

Expensive

Christiania at Vail
Bavarian styling makes this a Vail classic: Individually designed rooms and suites have wood-beam ceilings, rustic hand-carved furnishings, and fluffy eiderdown comforters. Public spaces are as cozy as the guest quarters and include an elegant but unpretentious lobby decorated with stone, wood, and stucco. In addition to the hotel's beauty, the location is superb—only 100 yards from the Vista Bahn lift. There are also 50 condos, most of which have kitchen facilities, a fireplace, and a Jacuzzi and/or steam bath. *356 E. Hanson Ranch Rd., 81657, tel. 970/476– 5641 or 800/530–3999, fax 970/476–0470. 22 rooms, 50 units. Facilities: bar, heated outdoor pool, sauna, daily maid service, ski storage, ski valet. AE, MC, V. $160–$1,250, including Continental breakfast.*

Lodge at Vail
This wonderful place—one of three hotels around which most of Vail Vil-

lage was built in 1962—is at once elegant and informal. Styled after the famous Lodge at Sun Valley, the Lodge at Vail brings the same European elegance to Colorado. A new wing includes 18 luxury guest rooms and suites that complement the smaller, but comfortably appointed, rooms of the main hotel. Suites have fireplaces, kitchens, and balconies that overlook the mountains and village. Rates, which vary according to the view outside your window, include a buffet breakfast that is one of the best morning meals in Vail. *174 E. Gore Creek Dr., 81657, tel. 970/476–5011 or 800/331–5634, fax 970/476–7425. 63 rooms, 40 units. Facilities: 2 restaurants, bar, outdoor lap pool, Jacuzzi, exercise room, sauna, 24-hr desk service, shuttle service, ski storage, ski valet, laundry. AE, DC, MC, V. $350–$2,225.*

Manor Vail
Young families enjoy the convenience of these condos close to the lifts and children's center. The lodge rooms and studio, one-, and two-bedroom units are designed for comfort. Each is privately owned, and you may walk into Southwestern, early American, or colonial decor. There's a wood-burning fireplace and a private balcony in all units (except the lodge rooms). *595 E. Vail Valley Dr., 81657, tel. 970/476–5000 or 800/950–8245, fax 970/476–4982. 143 rooms, 83 units. Facilities: restaurant, bar, 2 outdoor pools, 2 Jacuzzis, sauna, 24-hr desk service, shuttle, daily maid service, ski storage, ski valet, laundry. AE, D, DC, MC, V. $185–$1,900.*

Sonnenalp Resort
This family-owned-and-operated business is actually two separate lodges, both within Vail Village and minutes from the Vista Bahn lift. Austria Haus and Bavaria Haus are the quintessence of European style, with wood trim and detailing and comfortable well-decorated rooms. Units range from simple hotel rooms to two-bedroom units with a fireplace and a balcony. *20 Vail Rd., 81657, tel. 970/476–5656 or 800/654–8312, fax 970/476–1639. 59 rooms, 91 units. Facilities: 3 restaurants, 3 bars, 4 Jacuzzis, heated outdoor pool, 2 indoor pools, 2 spas, 6 saunas, exercise room, 24-hr desk service, shuttle, ski storage, laundry, game room. D, DC, MC, V. $260–$1,660.*

Vail Cascade Hotel & Club
Although it looks like a château on the outside, this giant hotel in Cascade Village eschews traditional Tyrolean decor in favor of a more American, Ralph Lauren lodge style inside. Its luxurious guest quarters incorporate dark woods, deep jewel tones, balconies, and expansive views. The condo units have one to three bedrooms and a kitchen. *1300 Westhaven Dr., 81657, tel. 970/476–7111 or 800/453–7133, fax 970/479–7025. 289 rooms, 50 units. Facilities: 3 restaurants, bar, outdoor pool, beauty salon, 2 outdoor hot tubs, sauna, steam room, health club, cinema, 24-hr desk service, shuttle, ski storage, ski valet, laundry service, meeting rooms. AE, D, DC, MC, V. $219–$1,300.*

Moderate
Gasthof Gramshammer
At this small, personal, A-frame lodge in the heart of Vail Village each room

is different in size and decor, but all have traditional Austrian carved-wood furnishings and accents, bright floral-print curtains and upholstery, folk art, and artifacts, as well as balconies. *231 E. Gore Creek Dr., 81657, tel. 970/476– 5626 or 800/610–7374, fax 970/476–8816. 27 rooms, 5 apartment suites. Facilities: 2 restaurants, bar, ski storage, ski shop. AE, MC, V. $138–$610, including Continental breakfast.*

Simba Run
The large two-bedroom ivory, brown, and burgundy units at this modern condo complex about a mile and a half from the Lionshead gondola are filled with soft pillowy sofas and chairs, handsome drapes, and well-crafted accents. Each condo has a splendid view of the valley. *1100 N. Frontage Rd., 81657, tel. 970/476–0344 or 800/746–2278, fax 970/476–0888. 70 units. Facilities: indoor pool, Jacuzzi, saunas, steam rooms, exercise room, shuttle, laundry, game room. No credit cards. $165–$495.*

Sitzmark Lodge
For the money, this small, owner-operated European-style property is outstanding. It's in the center of the action, allowing you to walk to a variety of restaurants, shops, and bars, and you are one block from the slopes. All rooms have a balcony that overlooks Gore Creek or the mountain, as well as a refrigerator. The decor is European modern: bright upholstery and sleekly designed furnishings of blond wood. *183 Gore Creek Dr., 81657, tel. 970/476–5001, fax 970/476–8702. 35 rooms. Facilities: restaurant-bar, outdoor whirlpool,* sauna, outdoor pool, ski storage, laundry. D, MC, V. $165–$495, including Continental breakfast and après-ski refreshments.

Vail Village Inn
The family-run inn's buildings are arranged around a quad, with three sides bordered by accommodations and a fourth by retail stores and restaurants. Bavarian-style architectural details are everywhere, from ceiling panels to room furnishings. Guest quarters range from basic to luxurious (a four-bedroom condo with a private elevator) and are priced accordingly. *100 E. Meadow Dr., 81657, tel. 970/476–5622 or 800/445–4014, fax 970/476–4661. 72 rooms, 15 units. Facilities: restaurant, bar, lounge, heated outdoor pool, sauna, Jacuzzi, 24-hr desk service, shuttle, ski storage, laundry. AE, DC, MC, V. $95–$1,500.*

The Willows
The traditional European-style exterior of this four-story lodge gives way to a Rocky Mountain–modern interior with plenty of wood and stone. The location, minutes from the Vista Bahn lift, makes this an exceptionally attractive deal. Condos have a good-size kitchen and fireplace. *74 Willow Rd., 81657, tel. 970/476–2233 or 888/945-5697, fax 970/476–5714. 4 rooms, 42 units. Facilities: whirlpool, steam room, ski storage, laundry. AE, MC, V. $69–$1,400, including Continental breakfast and après-ski refreshments.*

Inexpensive
Black Bear Inn
Inside this honey-bronze log building on the banks of Gore Creek is a cozy

great room with a gas stove. The cabin rooms have a sitting area either by the bay window overlooking the mountain or with a sleep sofa flanked by carved trunks. Down comforters cover handcrafted queen-size or twin beds, and local artists' watercolors decorate the log walls. You won't find a TV or radio in your room. *2405 Elliott Rd., West Vail 81657, tel. 970/476–1304, fax 970/476–0433. 12 rooms. Facilities: ski storage, laundry, TV in common room. MC, V. $115–$195, including full breakfast and après-ski snacks.*

Christie Lodge

This pleasant condominium hotel with one- and three-bedroom suites is certainly a bargain if you're willing to forgo the convenience of slope-side accommodations. The units are modern and cozy, with mini-kitchens, fireplaces, and balconies. The airy, bright hotel lobby has overstuffed couches and lots of hanging plants, indoor trees, and flowers. In Avon, the lodge is convenient to both Vail and Beaver Creek; shuttles connect with both resorts. *Box 1196, Avon 81620, tel. 970/949–7700 or 888/325–6343. 280 units. Facilities: 2 pools, 3 Jacuzzis, sauna, fitness room, shuttle. AE, D, MC, V. $99–$399.*

Minturn Inn

This 1915 three-story home is older than the town of Vail itself. The three owners, all originally from New England, have painstakingly restored it into a charming inn with 10 theme rooms. The Angler, for example, has carved wooden fish and fly-fishing paraphernalia, while the 10th Mountain Division sports skis and snow-

shoes on the walls. The beds are handmade of logs, with quilt coverings. Most rooms have views of the red cliffs unique to the area and the river; some have Jacuzzis and steam showers. The only drawback is that you'll need a car to reach the ski slopes—Minturn lacks public transportation. *442 N. Main St., Box 186, Minturn 81645, tel. 970/827–9647 or 800/646–8876, fax 970/827–5590. 10 rooms, 8 with bath. Facilities: sauna. AE, D, MC, V. $79–$229, including full breakfast and après-ski snacks.*

Roost Lodge

This property should be high on any bargain hunter's list because it's one of the best deals in Vail. The rooms are very functional, with a variety of bed arrangements. The lobby invites guests to lounge and swap stories by the fire. The lodge is one block from the town bus stop. *1783 N. Frontage Rd., West Vail 81657, tel. 970/476–5451 or 800/873–3065, fax 970/476–9158. 70 rooms, 2 suites. Facilities: indoor pool, outdoor Jacuzzi, sauna, shuttle, ski storage. AE, D, DC, MC, V. $62–$350, including Continental breakfast and après-ski snacks.*

Tivoli Lodge

This family-run traditional Bavarian-style lodge sprang up in the heart of Vail during the village's early years. Guest rooms are bright and spacious, decorated with stucco, floral fabrics, and dusty rose carpeting and furnished with light-oak furniture and small refrigerators. The room rate is determined by the view: If you can live without seeing the peaks from your window, you can save dollars.

Most units have more than one bed and can comfortably sleep three or four people, which is one reason the Tivoli is popular with families. There is a bus stop across the street. *386 Hanson Ranch Rd., 81657, tel. 970/ 476–5615 or 800/451–4756, fax 970/ 476–6601. 50 rooms. Facilities: bar, lounge, heated outdoor pool, 2 outdoor Jacuzzis, sauna, ski storage, laundry. AE, D, DC, MC, V. $125–$249, including Continental breakfast.*

WHERE TO EAT

Aside from Aspen, Vail has the largest number of dining options of any U.S. ski resort, running the gamut from fancy to frugal. Restaurants located all over the mountain offer numerous lunch and après-ski options, from pizza to haute cuisine.

On the Mountain

Wine Stube

This full-service restaurant at Eagle's Nest serves Continental cuisine and game, including fresh venison salad and buffalo stew. There's also an espresso bar and, of course, a good selection of wines. *Top of Eagle Bahn lift, tel. 970/479–2034. Reservations required. AE, D, MC, V.*

Expensive

Game Creek Club

Vail's exclusive on-mountain lunch club is open for dinner as well. A heated gondola whisks you up Lionshead to Eagle's Nest. From here you catch an open snowcat (covered in inclement weather) for the short ride to the Bavarian-style lodge. Be prepared to linger over a five-course prix-fixe meal. Entrées are Continental with an Asian flair—dishes like seared

ahi served sushi style with cucumbers and sesame vinaigrette or a more traditional beef tenderloin with blue cheese crust served with lyonnaise potatoes and green peppercorn sauce. *600 Lionshead Circle, tel. 970/479– 4275. Reservations essential. AE, D, DC, MC, V.*

La Tour

The two carpeted dining rooms, decorated with French paintings and pictures of the owners' friends, draw families as well as the business crowd. Try the roast rack of Colorado lamb, whole Maine lobster, or chestnut-crusted venison loin. *122 E. Meadow Dr., tel. 970/476–4403. Reservations essential. AE, MC, V.*

Montauk Seafood Grill

Alaskan bass, Florida grouper, Maine lobster, swordfish, halibut, mahimahi, and crab are here for the picking in this nautically decorated restaurant. Pair your seafood choice with one of the three daily sauces served. There's also a raw bar with a variety of oysters, clams, and other shellfish. If you don't like fish, you can also get steak or pasta. For dessert try the signature Sand Pie. *549 Lionshead Circle (in mall), tel. 970/476- -2601. AE, MC, V.*

Tyrolean Inn

The antlers and other hunting trophies adorning the walls should clue you in to the specialty of this Bavarian-style inn: game, much of it raised on owner Pepi Langegger's ranch. The menu includes elk, caribou, buffalo, wild boar, salmon, duck, pheasant, and trout, among others. Try the sautéed elk medallions forestière or the Tyrolean game grill, or play it safe with the Wiener schnitzel or the pan-seared filet mignon. *400 E. Meadow Dr., tel. 970/476–2204. Reservations essential. AE, MC, V.*

Moderate

Blu's

You have to love a restaurant that offers dishes such as Kick Ass California Chicken Relleño (a whole poblano pepper packed with jack cheese and wrapped in a chicken breast) and Gypsy Schnitzel (scallops of pork tenderloin, green peppers, onion, mushrooms, in a marsala sauce). The rest of the menu is similarly diverse, with a little of everything from fish to fowl, including pasta and seared tuna. Blu's is a lively spot, more bistro than restaurant, and enjoys a great location in the heart of Vail Village. *193 E. Gore Creek, tel. 970/476–3113. AE, DC, MC, V.*

Fiesta's!

The Marquez sisters, Debbie and Susan, use family recipes brought to Colorado by their great-grandparents to create Fiesta's award-winning authentic southwestern cuisine. Among the menu favorites are shrimp *carnitas* (marinated shrimp served on a platter with warm handmade tortillas) and blue corn enchiladas, served Santa Fe–style with an egg on top. Also try the handmade corn tamales stuffed with pork and smothered in a classic New Mexican chile sauce. Fiesta's is a warm, brightly decorated place with lots of New Mexican folk art and paintings. *57 Edwards Access Rd., Edwards Plaza, 4 mi west of Beaver Creek, tel. 970/926–2121. Reservations essential. AE, D, DC, MC, V.*

Kaltenberg Castle Brewhouse

Licensed by His Royal Highness Prince Luitpold of Bavaria, this Bavarian-style brewhouse is a new addition to the Lionshead base area at Vail. A massive building decorated with dark beams and sturdy European furnishings—including the requisite suits of armor and Prince Luitpold's coat of arms—the restaurant is a lively après-ski gathering spot as well as a delightful place to sample traditional Bavarian cuisine such as *Rindsgoulasch mit Semmelknoedel* (beef goulash with sour cream and bread pudding) or Wiener Schnitzel with potato salad. The beers (all brewed in conformity with Germany's beer purity laws, originated by Luitpold's ancestors) will satisfy serious beer drinkers. Prost! *Base of Eagle Bahn Gondola, tel. 970/479–1050. AE, MC, V.*

Michael's American Bistro

This very sleek, stylish boîte overlooks the atrium of the Gateway Mall, but the space is dramatic: fancifully carved wood columns, lacquered black tables, and striking photographs and art. The hip atmosphere is further accentuated by the cool jazz and the slinky waitstaff garbed entirely in black. You could make a meal of the openers alone: wild mushroom pizza with carmelized red onions, Parma prosciutto, seared Tuna sashimi, and more. Entrées include veal scallopini, tofu with rice noodles, and elk tenderloin. The extensive wine list has several bargains under $25. *12 S. Frontage Rd., tel. 970/476– 5353. AE, D, DC, MC, V.*

Ore House

Known for its steaks, the Ore House also offers all sorts of other meaty specials, such as beef kebabs and prime rib, as well as chicken, seafood, and vegetarian entrées. Start things off right with an order of popcorn shrimp and finish with the key lime pie. Decor is true to the Western mining theme, with mining carts converted into tables and Western art and stock certificates hanging on the walls. *232 Bridge St., tel. 970/476–5100. Reservations essential for 8 or more. AE, DC, MC, V.*

Up the Creek

This casual restaurant 5 yards from Gore Creek is decorated with soft-pastel–colored walls, whimsical watercolors, and small, intimate table settings suited to groups of two or four. The menu is heavy on fish: panfried trout, sesame crusted tuna, seafood jambalaya, and seafood fetuccine. If you're interested in something from the field rather than the stream, try the rack of lamb or the Limousin-beef tenderloin from the local JJ Ranch. *223 Gore Creek Dr., tel. 970/476–8141. AE, D, DC, MC, V.*

Inexpensive

Bully Ranch

This saloon is pure Western—complete with wooden floor, beamed ceiling, large bar, and cowboy memorabilia on the walls. Menu selections range from build-your-own barbecue platters of chicken, ribs, and kielbasa to Southwestern lasagna (tortillas layered with three cheeses, roasted peppers, and chorizo in a spicy green-chili sauce). *Sonnenalp Resort, 20 Vail Rd., tel. 970/476–5656. D, DC, MC, V.*

Clancy's Windy City Irish Pub

Clancy's is a self-styled Chicago diner with a menu of hearty entrées as well as finger-food favorites such as chicken fingers, onion rings, and chicken wings. Locals frequent Clancy's for its high activity level and low prices, and the many TV screens appeal to fans of "da Bulls and da Bears." *1300 Westhaven Dr., tel. 970/476–3886. AE, D, MC, V.*

Hubcap Brew Pub

Vail's original brew pub is the locals' favorite hangout for intense cheek-to-jowl ambience, an excellent selection of beer (ale and amber, wheat, and golden stout), and off-the-wall munchies. The rotisserie chicken, steamed mussels, meat loaf, and chicken potpie are big hits. *143 E. Meadow Dr., tel. 970/476– 5757. AE, MC, V.*

The Saloon

Skiers in the know do the "Minturn Mile" at the end of the day, bushwhacking out the bottom of Game Creek Bowl and ending up a few steps from this venerable gathering place. (Warning: this is not ski-area-maintained terrain, and there is no transportation back. Of course, you can always drive here.) The reward is margaritas made with real lime juice, serve-yourself chips and homemade salsa, specialties like chili relleños and the steak and quail plate, and a bar that's always packed with locals. *146 N. Main St., Minturn, tel. 970/827–5954. Reservations not accepted. AE, MC, V.*

Best Bets for Breakfast

Daily Grind

This is a great place to catch a cappuccino or other specialty coffee or a quick conversation with locals heading out to find the untracked powder. There's a selection of baked goodies and deli sandwiches. *288 Bridge St., tel. 970/476–5856. MC, V.*

DJ McCadam's Diner

If you're heading up the mountain on the gondola at Lionshead, DJ's is the place to fuel up with a hearty breakfast. The French toast is the toast of the town, and breakfast blintzes get glowing reviews. Omelets and other egg dishes are available, too. *616 W. Lionshead Circle, Concert Hall Plaza, Lionshead Mall, tel. 970/476–2336. No credit cards.*

NIGHTLIFE AND ENTERTAINMENT

Après-Ski

Red Lion

This is the après-ski gathering spot, just down the hill from the gondola. The deck is wildly popular, and later on there is mellow live entertainment. Try the heaping mound of nachos as an appetizer. *304 Bridge St., tel. 970/476–7676. AE, D, MC, V.*

Loud and Lively/Dancing

Garfinkel's

Garfinkel's is a ski-school hangout, predictably popular with the younger set—especially snowboarders. *536 W. Lionshead Mall, tel. 970/476–3789. AE, MC, V.*

Garton's

You can find everything from rock to reggae, from Cajun to country in this big barnlike structure. *Crossroads Shopping Center, tel. 970/476–0607. AE, MC, V.*

More Mellow

Club Chelsea

Club Chelsea has it all: a quiet piano bar that feels like a speakeasy, a raucous disco, and a room for cigar smoking complete with leopard-skin couches around the fire. *304 Bridge St., tel. 970/476–5600. AE, D, DC, MC, V.*

Pepi's Bar

Relax to live music in this piano bar with one of your favorite people. *Gasthof Gramshammer, 231 E. Gore Creek Dr., tel. 970/476–5626. AE, DC, MC, V.*

WINTER PARK RESORT

Box 36
Winter Park, CO 80482
Tel. 970/726–5514
www.skiwinterpark.com

STATISTICALLY SPEAKING

Base elevation: 9,000 feet

Summit elevation: 12,060 feet

Vertical drop: 3,060 feet

Skiable terrain: 2,886 acres

Number of trails: 134

Longest run: 5.1 miles

Lifts and capacity: 7 high-speed quads, 8 doubles, 5 triples; 34,910 skiers per hour

Daily lift ticket: $50

Average annual snowfall: 370 inches

Number of skiing days 1997–98: 172

Snowmaking: 294 acres, 20%

Terrain mix: N 9%, I 22%, E 69%

Snowboarding: yes

Owned by the City of Denver and a favorite weekend destination for Denverites, Winter Park is true to its slogan: "Colorado's Favorite Resort." Although it doesn't attract the glitterati that flock to Aspen or the CEO-type crowd that migrates to Vail, it's a reliable all-around resort, with excellent skiing, a good choice of reasonably priced accommodations, and one of the country's finest ski programs for people with disabilities. What Winter Park lacks, however, is a ski-town image that can be captured in a visual vignette. The town itself—2 miles from the resort and its three mountains—is spread out along 2 miles of Route 40 in a series of prosaic, interconnected shopping plazas. First-time visitors could easily drive past the resort— barely visible from the highway—and not realize it. That Winter Park's physical style is unmemorable is not a problem for day skiers from Denver, as most of them seldom venture beyond the slopes before heading back to the bright lights of the city. For destination skiers scanning brochures, however, the resort seems disjointed and unglamorous.

This, however, will change with the construction of a new base village, whose first phase is scheduled to be finished in January 2000. The new village will be anchored by a grand hotel reminiscent of the eastern resort lodges that flourished in the early half of the 20th century. Two new buildings will include 220 condominium units, with shopping and restaurants.

For now, the resort is physically nondescript but not without personality. Here the locals shuffle rather than bustle, the train still brings skiers into Winter Park, and hat-wearing cowboys from nearby ranches mingle with nose-ring-studded snowboarders from the suburbs of Denver.

There are a few things that could be improved. The parking at the resort is chaotic, and the alternative, shuttle-bus service, could be better—although its fleet of cramped school buses does get the job done. There is only one on-slope condo complex, and even that property stretches the definition a bit, as it is somewhat of a hike to the slopes. Again, the new base should alleviate some of these shortcomings. And really, these are minor inconveniences when you consider that this is one of the most reasonably priced, unpretentious resorts in the country. There

Children's services: day-care, tel. 970/726–1551

Snow phone: tel. 970/726–7669

Police: tel. 970/725–3343

U.S. Forest Service: tel. 970/887–3331

Winter Park Security: tel. 970/726–1500

Hospital: 7 Mile Medical Clinic, tel. 970/726–8066

Winter Park/Fraser Valley Chamber of Commerce: tel. 970/726–4118

Road conditions: tel. 970/725–3334

Towing: All Season's Towing, tel. 970/726–5527; DJ Towing (AAA), tel. 970/887–9414; Hilly's Hooker Service, tel. 970/726–5841

FIVE-STAR FAVORITES
Best run for vertical: Derailer

Best run overall: Cranmer

Best bar/nightclub: Winter Park Pub

Best hotel: Vintage

Best restaurant: The Divide Grill

are no $1,000-a-night hotel rooms here, but there is an assortment of modestly priced accommodations that make a weeklong family ski vacation as affordable as a weekend at many other areas. It's not just a family affair, either. Singles and groups can enjoy the same relatively inexpensive benefits, and although nightlife options are not endless, there's more than enough variety to satisfy all but the most torrid party animals.

HOW TO GET THERE

By Plane
Denver International Airport (*see* Getting to Colorado Resorts, *above*) is 85 miles southeast of Winter Park.

By Car
From the airport take I–70 west for about 60 miles to Exit 232 (U.S. 40) and continue north for 25 miles over the Berthoud Pass and into Winter Park.

By Bus
Greyhound Lines (tel. 800/231–2222) provides daily service to and from Denver.

By Train
The **Ski Train** (tel. 303/296–4754) leaves Denver's Union Station weekends at 7:15 AM and departs from Winter Park at 4:15 PM, arriving in Denver at 6:15 PM. **Amtrak**'s *California Zephyr* (tel. 800/453–2525) serves Winter Park daily from Los Angeles, San Francisco, Seattle, and Chicago. The train has sleeping accommodations.

By Shuttle
The **Home James** (tel. 970/726–5060 or 800/451–4844) shuttle service has regularly scheduled round-trip service between Denver and Winter Park. The one-way rate is $37 per person, round-trip $74. Reservations are advised. Private charter service to the airport and to other ski resorts through Home James is also available.

THE SKIING

For many years the skiing at Winter Park was considered terminally tame: it was thought of as a great place for families and groups of modest intermediates but one that lacked the steep, challenging runs found in other Rocky Mountain resorts. This misleading reputation had developed in part because the resort emphasizes its enormous innovative teaching programs rather than Mary Jane's vertigo-inducing steeps and back-breaking bumps; these Volkswagen-size bumps are considered to be among the most challenging in North America. For expert extreme skiers with a backcountry bent, there is the Vasquez Cirque, a new 550-acre expansion with pitches up to 55°. Contrary to popular perception, Winter Park offers a complete ski experience that rivals that of any other resort in the Rockies.

The terrain is divided into five neatly defined areas, which allows skiers to pick their niche without getting in over their heads or becoming bored. Winter Park is an excellent area for novices and fledgling intermediates; Vasquez Ridge turns things up a notch with solid intermediate trails; Mary Jane pulls no punches with some of the steepest, heaviest mogul runs in Colorado; and the Parsenn Bowl gives intermediates 200 acres of above-tree-line bowl skiing without the prohibitive challenges of expert bowls. To reach the steep in-bounds bowl skiing of the Vasquez Cirque requires a bit of hiking—by intention. According to the resort, the extra effort helps weed out the curious but underskilled skiers who aren't ready for these unabashedly expert environs.

There are two main base areas: the village at the bottom of Winter Park mountain and the Mary Jane base area. Both have parking, but slots fill quickly with the day-skier traffic from Denver, so it's better to avail yourself of the shuttle bus that runs between most accommodations and the two base areas. Although this setup allows novices and intermediates to explore their own limits without interfering with each other, it makes meeting up at the end of the day a bit difficult, especially for beginners, who might have trouble finding a safe route to Mary Jane. Intermediates and experts can more readily scoot back from Mary Jane to Winter Park. Consider this when making arrangements to meet, and put the onus on better skiers to make the trek. (The other option is for novices to hop on the free shuttle bus that connects the two base areas.)

Moving from mountain to mountain is fairly easy, with very few flat sections except for the extremely long runoff from the Vasquez Ridge area (the Big Valley). To avoid this as you head from Vasquez to Winter Park, take Buckaroo, a medium-pitch, groomed blue run that will take you to the bottom of the Olympia chair, which goes to the top of Winter Park. From the top of Vasquez Ridge you can also take the green Gunbarrel Run (turn left off the Pioneer Express) over to the High Lonesome Express, which goes to the top of Mary Jane, where novices will find a half dozen green runs and intermediates and experts can access the steeper blue and black runs of the Parsenn Bowl area. From the top of Mary Jane you can make your way back to the Winter Park base area by skiing down Whistle Stop to Allan Phipps or Cranmer Cutoff, which is also green.

Advanced and intermediate skiers can avoid the novice area by taking Cranmer (blue) or one of a half dozen blue/black runs.

Novices

Nearly half the trails at Winter Park mountain are green, and most are easy to reach from the far right (facing the mountain) of the base area. The Gemini Express lift takes you about a third of the way up the mountain to Discovery Park, a 30-acre enclosed learn-to-ski area. Here you can practice on the gentle, rolling, well-groomed terrain of Porcupine, Bobcat, and Marmot Flats. When you are ready to leave this area, Parkway will ease you back down to the bottom of the Gemini lift, or you can scoot to the left looking down the mountain and feed to the bottom of Marmot Flats, where three lifts converge. Any of these chairs will take you higher up the mountain to the gently undulating, meticulously groomed Allan Phipps or March Hare trails. The Cranmer Cutoff intersects both and carries you back down to Parkway and Larry Sale. If you aren't ready for such long runs, either stay on Allan Phipps all the way to the bottom (where the three lifts meet) or hop the Discovery lift, which serves a shorter green run called Bill Wilson's Way.

Aggressive novices may want to take the Zephyr Express lift from the Winter Park base to the summit at Winter Park and then follow an easy catwalk to the High Lonesome Express lift, which climbs to the top of Mary Jane. What's nice about Mary Jane is its modest beginner area at the base, which lets first-timers stay on the same mountain as their more advanced friends. From the summit there are a half dozen green runs that wind down through the trees to the bottom of High Lonesome. Switchyard is a wide boulevard that follows the ski-area boundary (on the left, looking down); it includes some interesting dips and rolls and also tends to be busy. Hobo Alley and Whistle Stop (to the right, looking down) are much narrower trails that cut through the trees and tend to be less exposed if it's windy. You can either continue to the bottom of Winter Park on March Hare or Allan Phipps or ride the lift back to the higher elevation.

Intermediates

If you start from the Winter Park base area, take the Zephyr Express lift to the summit and turn right off the lift for the steady pitch and groomed terrain of the Hughes, Bradley's Bash, or Cranmer runs. Upper and Lower Hughes and Bradley's Bash are most consistently groomed and more suited to cruising, and Cranmer is groomed on one side and left ungroomed on the other, making it an excellent run on which to practice a few mogul turns with an easy escape route. In general the runs on the left or backside of Mary Jane are mid- to upper intermediate, and the middle and right-side runs are considerably steeper and bumpier. Take the Summit Express lift to the Mary Jane summit, from which you can reach more than a dozen intermediate runs on the backside of Mary Jane or on the Parsenn Bowl farther up. The Parsenn Bowl beckons from the top of Mary Jane, but watch the weather. If it's clear, head down to the Timberline lift and play in the bowl with its wide, swooping, treeless terrain. On bad-weather days when visibility is low or the light is flat, it's best to stick to the below-treeline runs. If you've never experienced the freedom of a wide-open bowl, skiing the Parsenn is a perfect introduction because it's not toe-curling steep yet is precipitous enough to let you carry the speed to handle deep snow. Although it's mostly ungroomed, it is usually well mannered enough not to inhibit first-time powder hounds; the more than 200 acres offer lots of space for wide, sweeping turns and no areas where you can get into trouble. A few new gladed runs allow for some challenging but not too threatening tree skiing.

Vasquez Ridge, at the far west end of the resort, is another great intermediate playground. From Mary Jane take Lonesome Whistle to Wagon Train, which will take you to the bottom of the Pioneer Express lift; if you're coming from Winter Park, take Jabberwocky to Wagon Train for some quality cruising on groomed terrain. The majority of runs on Vasquez Ridge are solid high-speed cruisers with good pitch and roll. Stagecoach, Sundance, and Quickdraw are good choices for steady pitch and groomed snow, but all eventually feed into Big Valley, a tediously long ski-out that winds back to the bottom of the lift. To avoid the hassle, pick up Buckaroo from Sundance about halfway down.

Once you're comfortable, move up a notch: Gambler and Aces and Eights are two short, steep mogul runs that are worth a try. Toward the end of the day make sure you take Gunbarrel from the top of the Pioneer Express, as it will take you back to the High Lonesome Express lift and to runs leading to Winter Park.

Experts

The Mary Jane section of the resort has gained a reputation for some of the steepest, most sustained mogul runs in the West. From the Winter Park base area the Zephyr Express is your fastest way to the top: plunge into things with a sharp turn to the left to access a mean bump chute called Outhouse, which takes you back down to the Mary Jane base. The Summit Express lift gives you a fast trip to the top and a number of solidly advanced bump or glade runs. For steep glades try Sluice Box or Pine Cliff, and for bumps take either Gandy Dancer or Drunken Frenchman.

The truly hard-core have a good selection of mostly ungroomed, wildly steep runs down the right side of Mary Jane. Try the precipitous quartet Hole-in-the-Wall, Awe Chute, Baldy's Chute, or Jeff's Chute to really drive your knees into your chest. These runs are among the steepest on the mountain and accessible only through control gates, but they'll give any steep-freak a good ride, especially after a good dump, when they become choked with snow and stay that way long after other runs have been skied off. At the bottom of these chutes, look for the cut through the trees, which will take you to Cannonball and the lower half of Long Haul—two steep bump runs with fantastic lines, thanks to the high-caliber skiers who inhabit them. And don't ignore the Winter Park side: Mulligans, Retta's, and Engledive offer some steep thrills.

For the terminally adventurous, there's the new Vasquez Cirque, a 252-acre playground of plunging chutes, powder meadows, and challenging glades. Not for the faint-hearted, this expert haven is rivaled only by Crested Butte's extreme limits—and is even more difficult to access. To reach this pristine terrain, take the Timberline lift to the top of Parsenn Bowl; it's then a 20- to 30-minute hike to the Vasquez Cirque on a well-trodden, signed pathway. The Cirque spills into a drainage to the north of Vasquez ridge; a long trail takes you to the Big Valley run and the base of the Pioneer Express lift.

SNOWBOARDING

Snowboarders have three different terrain parks from which to choose. Two terrain parks on the Winter Park side have rail slides, quarter pipes, and a series of jumps; the new half-pipe on Jabberwocky is open to snowboarders only. On the Mary Jane side, Stone Grove is a favorite for boarders who like to ride the glades.

Beginners should get their start at Discovery Park, a 30-acre learn-to-ski and snowboard area with a gentle slope, gladed adventure trails, and rolling terrain with banked turns. Access is on the Gemini Express lift. As you advance, try more challenging terrain just off the Olympia Express lift. Cranmer Cutoff winds around the resort and is a good place to learn the basics of bank riding.

Intermediates can check the runs in the Parsenn Bowl, one of the few off-piste sites that are manageable for less-than-expert boarders. Access is aboard the Timberline Chair

lift, down-valley from the Summit Express quad.

Experts can have a blast on most of the black-diamond terrain on the Mary Jane side, although the moguls will eventually take a toll. Try staying to the sides of runs like Trestle, Cannonball, Long Haul, and Short Haul. Powder hounds can pop into the trees along any of these runs to find fresh stashes. Eventually, experts will make the long hike into the Vasquez Cirque; be forewarned, however, that this terrain is only for those with years of experience and the ability to handle heavy steeps, rock bands, cornices, and narrow chutes.

Special events for snowboarders throughout the season include a SuperCarve clinic to help skiers make the transition to snowboarding, the Bump Jamboree (a unique mogul competition), and a freestyle snowboarding camp.

OTHER SNOW SPORTS

Snowshoe Tours depart at 1 PM daily from the information desk in the Winter Park Base Area (tel. 970/726–5514), where you can also check on a plethora of activities including guided **snowmobile** tours to the top of the Continental Divide, **sleigh rides, dog sled** trips, **tubing** hills, **ice skating,** and **cross-country skiing.**

NEARBY

Silver Creek Resort (tel. 970/887–3384 or 888/283–7458) is a modest and uncrowded area in the Fraser Valley about 15 miles north of Winter Park. Offering night skiing and snowbiking, Silver Creek is a quiet hideaway from the crowds that flock to Winter Park on weekends.

WHERE TO STAY

The town of Winter Park and the Fraser Valley have some of the best-value accommodations in Colorado. The emphasis is on practical condo units, with small mountain inns and a number of standard motels also available. There are a dozen or so bed-and-breakfasts. Most accommodations are on either side of U.S. 40 between the resort and the town of Fraser, about 4 miles down the valley from the slopes. Slope-side accommodations are limited to one condo complex, but a shuttle bus system connects virtually every place to the mountain. All accommodations can be booked through **Winter Park Central Reservations** (tel. 970/726–5587 or 800/729–5183).

Expensive

Crestview Place

This condo complex in the middle of the town of Winter Park, 2 miles from the slopes, is a good choice if you want to be within walking distance of the stores, restaurants, and nightlife. The units are large, with high ceilings, multiple bathrooms, and full kitchens. All have a unified design scheme of mauve, lavender, and teal. Unfortunately, the building and the individual units are starting to show signs of wear. Still, they can be comfortable and convenient for large groups, families, and even groups of families. Amenities are spartan, with laundry rooms on alternating floors and two hot tubs. The Winter Park shuttle bus stops at the front door. *78737 U.S. 40, Box 3095, Winter Park 80482, tel.*

970/726–9421 or 800/228–1025. 19 units. Facilities: 2 indoor hot tubs, shuttle, maid service, ski storage, laundry. AE, D, MC, V. $92–$576.

Gasthaus Eichler

This traditional stone, stucco, and wood Bavarian-style mountain lodge is a warm, woodsy, homey place in the middle of town. Guest rooms have whirlpool tubs and are individually decorated with such nice touches as lace curtains, down comforters, and complimentary toiletries. There's a pleasant fireside lounge and a German restaurant (*see* Where to Eat, *below*). Its five-course dinner and lavish breakfast are included in the cost of a room. *78786 U.S. 40, Box 430, Winter Park 80482, tel. 970/726–5133 or 800/543–3899, fax 970/726–5175. 15 rooms. Facilities: restaurant, bar, lounge, shuttle, maid service, ski storage. AE, MC, V. $108–169, including breakfast and dinner.*

Iron Horse Resort Retreat

If the convenience of ski-in/ski-out accommodation is your preference, the Iron Horse is your only choice— that is, until the new Zephyr Mountain Lodge is completed, sometime after New Year's Day 2000. The Iron Horse is a condo complex at the Mary Jane end of the resort. It has rooms, studios, and suites and is a good spot for families and large groups looking for extra space and the convenience of hotel-type service and amenities. The condos are well appointed, with a fireplace and full kitchen facilities. The smaller lodge rooms are good for couples. *257 Winter Park Dr., Box 1286, Winter Park 80482, tel. 970/726–8851 or 800/621–8190, fax 970/*

726–2321. 133 units. Facilities: restaurant, lounge, 4 outdoor hot tubs, indoor-outdoor pool, health club, steam room, 24-hr desk service, maid service, ski shop, ski storage, laundry, game room. AE, DC, MC, V. $139–$599.

Vintage Hotel

This is the only traditional full-service hotel in Winter Park, and its rooms and suites are among the resort's most luxurious. Smaller studio and one-bedroom units have a kitchenette and a fireplace; larger penthouse suites give you more space to spread out in front of the fire and full-size kitchens for preparing meals. The hotel is temptingly close to the slopes (although it is not ski-in/ski-out), with a spectacular view from the rooms facing the mountain. Reproduction Victorian furniture and wallpaper adorn the guest rooms and the comfortable library, where easy chairs and sofas surround the fireplace. The hotel's isolation makes it more suitable for couples than for those looking to socialize in town. *100 Winter Park Dr., Box 1369, Winter Park 80482, tel. 970/726–8801 or 800/ 472–7017, fax 970/726–9250. 112 rooms, 6 suites. Facilities: restaurant, bar, deli, outdoor hot tub, outdoor pool, exercise room, sauna, 24-hr desk service, shuttle, maid service, ski shop, ski storage, laundry, game room. AE, D, DC, MC, V. $160–$545.*

Moderate

Anna Leah

You'll feel like you're staying at a good friend's house at this B&B, thanks to the congenial owner, Patricia Handel, who will accommodate almost any request. The inn is just past the town

of Fraser, about 5 miles from the ski area. With balconies overlooking the national forest and the Continental Divide, it has a wonderfully serene feel. *1001 County Rd. 8, Fraser 80442, tel. 970/726–4414 or 800/237–9913. 5 rooms. Facilities: maid service, ski storage. V. $100–$170, including full breakfast.*

Beaver Village Condos

These accommodations are deluxe for the money and range in size from studio to three bedrooms, all with a kitchen and a fireplace. The decor suggests upscale Southwestern, with Native American patterns meeting pastel greens and blues. The one-bedroom units are good for couples or for two or three friends who aren't fussy about privacy. Families and groups, especially those who want to be slightly removed from the main-street action of Winter Park, may like the larger units. *50 Village Dr., Box 349, Winter Park 80482, tel. 970/726– 8813 or 800/824–8438. 130 units. Facilities: 3 indoor hot tubs, indoor pool, sauna, shuttle, ski storage, laundry. AE, D, MC, V. $110–$460.*

Grand Victorian

This luxury B&B is a three-story neo-Victorian in downtown Winter Park. Amenities include robes, slippers, and potpourri sachets in the rooms and an afternoon happy hour featuring Colorado wines and beers. The huge gourmet breakfast may include potato pancakes, quiches, or delectable macadamia nut waffles. *78542 Fraser Valley Parkway, just off U.S. 40, Winter Park 80482, tel. 970/ 726–5881 or 800/204–1170. 10 rooms. Facilities: whirlpool baths,* *shuttle, maid service, ski storage, meeting room. AE, D, DC, MC, V. $65–$175, including full breakfast.*

High Country Haus Condominiums
These large, well-maintained units are great for families, within walking distance of town, and spaced around a recreation complex complete with hot tubs, a heated pool, a sauna, and a game room. Units are spread among 24 buildings surrounding the recreation complex and range in size from one to three bedrooms. Each has a full-size kitchen, a fireplace, multiple bathrooms, and extra sleeping space for unexpected guests. *78415 U.S. 40, Box 3095, Winter Park 80482, tel. 970/726–9421 or 800/228–1025, fax 970/726–8004. 145 units. Facilities: 4 indoor hot tubs, indoor pool, sauna, shuttle, ski storage, laundry, game room. AE, D, MC, V. $86–$538.*

Inexpensive

Sundowner Motel
At this motel in downtown Winter Park, the larger-than-average rooms have one queen-size or two double beds and a good-sized bathroom. Two guests will be more than comfortable, four a comfortable squeeze in the regular rooms. Some larger rooms sleep six. Rooms have a refrigerator, a microwave, and a coffeemaker, and there's an outdoor hot tub in a gazebo. *78869 U.S. 40, Box 221, Winter Park 80482, tel. 970/726–9451 or 800/521–8279. 22 rooms. AE, D, MC, V. $54–$106.*

Super 8 Motel
Okay, so what if it is a national chain? Affordability, convenience, and antiseptic new hotel rooms make this no-surprises hotel perfect for people who are just looking for a place to sleep. It's centrally located with easy access to downtown shops, restaurants, and nightlife. Amenities include a hot tub, Continental breakfast, and cable television. *78655 U.S. 40, Box 35, Winter Park 80482, tel. 970/726–8088. 60 rooms. $69–$148, including Continental breakfast.*

Viking Lodge
In the middle of Winter Park, this is a good bet if you want easy access to dinner and nightlife. The units come in a variety of sizes, from small economy rooms to deluxe suites. Walls are wood paneled, floors are carpeted, and the furniture is virtually damage-proof—not fancy, but not fragile either. *U.S. 40 and Vasquez Rd., Box 89, Winter Park 80482, tel. 970/726–8885 or 800/421–4013. 22 rooms, 3 units. Facilities: indoor hot tub, sauna, shuttle, maid service, ski shop, ski storage, game room. AE, D, MC, V. $55–$275, including Continental breakfast.*

Woodspur Lodge
This classic log-cabin lodge is on the edge of the Arapaho National Forest, about 1½ miles from town. The small rooms are more rustic than posh, with furnishings handmade from local lodgepole pines, and the emphasis is on mingling in the common areas. Breakfast, dinner, and après-ski hors d'oeuvres are included in the room rate and are served in a dining area with a giant fireplace and a soaring roof. Many rooms have adjoining access. *111 Van Anderson Dr., Box 249, Winter Park 80482, tel. 970/726–8417 or 800/626–6562, fax 970/726–8553. 32 rooms. Facilities: private bar (guests only), 2 outdoor hot tubs,*

sauna, shuttle, maid service, ski storage, laundry, game room. D, MC, V. $146–$156, including full breakfast and dinner.

WHERE TO EAT

On the Mountain

Club Car

At the base of Mary Jane, the Club Car is a sit-down restaurant and bar that's the perfect place for lounging with a beverage and a sandwich on a warm spring afternoon. The menu includes deli sandwiches, soups, salads, and burgers. Don't miss the "Nutty Blonde" dessert, a warm bed of white chocolate and macadamia nuts beneath vanilla ice cream. *Mary Jane Base, Winter Park, tel. 970/726–8105. AE, D, MC, V.*

Lodge at Sunspot

This striking log-and-glass structure on the summit of Winter Park Mountain has two excellent places to eat. The Sunspot dining room (*see below*) is an upscale sit-down restaurant with a diverse lunch menu that includes everything from soups and sandwiches to full meals. The Provisioner is a serve-yourself deli-marketplace with fresh baked goods, soups, salads, bratwurst, fast food, and a panoramic view. Both restaurants get busy between noon and 2, so be prepared to wait. *Top of Zephyr Express lift, Winter Park, tel. 970/726–8155. AE, D, DC, MC, V.*

Sundance Cafe

This is a good choice on busy days because it's in what is generally the least crowded area of the resort. The best dishes are the beef stew or chili in a bread bowl. *Top of Pioneer Express, Winter Park, tel. 800/453–2525. No credit cards.*

Expensive

Divide Grill

This is a romantic, subdued place with lovely views of its namesake, the Continental Divide. The grill is airy, well lighted, and decorated in burgundies, greens, and traditional brass trim. Menu favorites include elk medallions, aged steaks, seafood, and an eclectic assortment of pasta dishes. *Cooper Creek Sq., Suite 305, Cooper Way, Winter Park, tel. 970/726–4900. AE, DC, MC, V.*

Gasthaus Eichler

Winter Park's most romantic dining spot has quaint Bavarian decor, antler chandeliers, and Strauss playing softly in the background. Veal is the specialty here, done in a variety of ways, including veal Parmesan, veal dumplings, and a sublime veal schnitzel. Meats are cooked with a Black Forest twist, as are such traditional German staples as sauerkraut, bratwurst, and goulash. The dining room, of white stucco and natural wood, overlooks woods and a mountain stream. *78786 U.S. 40, Winter Park, tel. 970/726–5133. AE, MC, V.*

Sunspot Dining Room

The Lodge at Sunspot is a magnificent log-and-stone complex at the top of the Zephyr lift. Rough-hewn log beams and furniture are accented with Southwestern rugs hung on the walls. You should visit for lunch to enjoy the view, but be sure to return by gondola for an evening meal, followed by a horse-drawn sleigh ride. The prix-fixe menu offers game and fish paired with interesting side dishes such as wild rice from Minnesota and Idaho red potatoes roasted in olive oil and herbs. The restaurant is open for dinner on Thursday, Friday, and Saturday only, so plan accordingly. *Top of Zephyr Express lift, Winter Park, tel. 970/726–1446. Reservations essential. AE, D, DC, MC, V.*

Winston's at the Vintage

This classy but casual restaurant and pub was built around a massive 19th-century English bar, transported from what was reportedly Winston Churchill's favorite watering hole in London. Wood wainscoting and a collection of paintings depicting Churchill complete the mood. The menu is a bit of Britain and a bit of everything else, with a deservedly renowned flagship beef Wellington (carved at the table) and a good selection of meat, fish, and pasta dishes. The tri-color cheese tortellini marinara is exceptional. *Vintage Hotel, 100 Winter Park Dr., Winter Park, tel. 970/726–8801. Reservations essential on weekends. AE, D, DC, MC, V.*

Moderate

Deno's Mountain Bistro

Deno's truly does it all: it doesn't look like much from the outside, but it serves huge lunches, is positively jammed with people for après-ski, and has a great dinner menu with some of the largest portions you'll ever confront. The food is American bistro, with a little of everything from angel-hair pomodoro (in tomato sauce) with rock shrimp to grilled Rocky Mountain trout and the best burgers in town. The downstairs is a more refined dining area, with tablecloths and candlelight, a dark-wood

bar, and skiing pictures on the walls. *78911 U.S. 40, Winter Park, tel. 970/726–5332. AE, D, DC, MC, V.*

Fontenot's Cajun Cafe

The only spot in town for Cajun has become known for its fresh fish. Favorites include the catch of the day, blackened and served with a raspberry butter sauce, blackened catfish, crawfish étouffée, and of course, gumbo and jambalaya. For lunches try the po'boy sandwiches (a small is enough for all but the mightiest of appetites); the blackened snapper po'boy is a local favorite. The atmosphere at this shopping-center restaurant is just a step up from coffee shop, but the food is authentic and the service friendly. *78521 U.S. 40, Winter Park, tel. 970/726–4021. D, MC, V.*

Last Waltz

This homey place is the seventh of owner-chef Nancy Waltz's restaurants. The huge menu jumps from bagels and lox to burritos without missing a beat. The south-of-the-border dishes are best: zesty *calientitas* (fried jalapeños filled with cream cheese and served with a devilish salsa) and black bean tostadas are especially noteworthy. *78336 U.S. 40, Winter Park, tel. 970/726–4877. Reservations not accepted. AE, D, DC, MC, V.*

Inexpensive

Crooked Creek Saloon

An interesting selection of meal-size sandwiches—a chicken breast, grilled cheese, and grilled vegetables, for example—and a daily fish special are among the inexpensive, filling choices here. Steak, ribs, pasta, and chicken complete the menu. An extension of the Grand County Historical Society, the saloon is filled with photographs documenting the settling of Fraser and Winter Park. *401 Zerex (U.S. 40), 2 mi from Winter Park, Fraser, tel. 970/726–9250. MC, V.*

Hernando's Pizza Pub

Here the specialties are pizzas and pastas, with a respectable selection to eat in or take out. Try the Roma pizza, with a layer of olive oil, fresh basil, and minced garlic covered with Roma tomatoes and the toppings of your choice. The most popular pasta is the vegetarian lasagna (a meat version is also available). Long wooden tables and benches, along with a crackling fireplace and a busy bar area, create a rustic, casual atmosphere. *78199 U.S. 40, Winter Park, tel. 970/726–5409. AE, MC, V.*

Rudi's Deli

The only true deli-style eatery in Winter Park, Rudi's has such deli delights as soups, chili, stews, and some excellent home-baked bread to eat in or take home. Try the holiday-on-a-bun (turkey, cream cheese and cranberry sauce). *Park Plaza Center, Winter Park, tel. 970/726–8955. No credit cards.*

Smokin' Mo's

For Texas- and Oklahoma-style barbecue, Smokin' Mo's is a welcome addition to the Winter Park culinary scene. Meats are smoked with hickory imported from Osage County, Oklahoma, and there are plenty of side orders from which to choose. The rough-hewn log walls are festooned with rusty farm tools, and on each table there's a generous roll of paper towels for cleaning up after the ribs. *Cooper Creek Square, Winter Park, tel. 970/726– 4600. AE, DC, MC, V.*

Best Bets for Breakfast

Carver's Bakery Café

Carver's is a delightfully bright and breezy breakfast spot with lots of natural light to get the sleep out of your eyes. There's an ample selection of baked goods—muffins, croissants, and pastries—plus excellent omelets with a variety of fillings. *93 Cooper Creek Way, behind Cooper Creek Square, Winter Park, tel. 970/726–8202. AE, D, MC, V.*

Moffat Bagel Station

For one of the better bagels this side of New York, plus coffee that will jump-start you, stop here. It's also a good place to hang out and learn about the best backcountry snowshoeing, cross-country skiing, and more. There are fresh muffins and scones for those who eschew bagels. *U.S. 40, Winter Park, tel. 970/726–5530. No credit cards.*

NIGHTLIFE AND ENTERTAINMENT
Après-Ski

Derailer Bar

In the West Portal Station at the Winter Park base area, the Derailer packs them in early with après-ski prices, live entertainment, and great pizza by the pan. Near the site of the historic Moffat Tunnel, opened in 1926, the bar has a railroad theme: a mural on railroad history covers one wall. Several TVs turn the place into a sports bar during games, and the view of the slopes provides close-up live action. The crowd is mostly young. *West Portal Station, Winter Park, tel. 970/726–5514, ext. 1957. AE, D, V.*

The Slope

Hot bands and a happy hour from 2 to 7 ensure nonstop action at the bar that's been voted the number-one après-ski bar by the *Rocky Mountain News*. If you're more inclined to play than to dance, there's a giant game room. The action, an easy quarter mile from the Winter Park base area, continues well into the night. *1161 Winter Park Dr., Winter Park, tel. 970/ 726–5727. MC, V.*

Loud and Lively/Dancing

Deno's Mountain Bistro
Upstairs the atmosphere is high-octane and happening, with occasional live music and a good mixture of locals and visitors watching sports on the pub's 11 TV sets (*see* Where to Eat, *above*).

Rome on the Range
Dance downstairs, shoot pool upstairs, or just pull up a cowhide-covered stool to the bar. Line-dancing lessons are offered once a week. *78941 Hwy. 40, Winter Park, tel. 970/ 726– 1111. AE, V.*

Slade's Underground
Geared to the younger set, this place has the Fraser Valley's highest concentration of tattoos and body piercings.

Slade's rocks late in the evening with local bands. In the middle of Winter Park, it's downstairs from Rudi's Deli (*see above*). *78727 Hwy. 40, Winter Park, tel. 970/726–7144. AE, MC, V.*

Winter Park Pub
Owner Mike Shanahan is an avid Packers fan—go figure. A locals' favorite, this bar has excellent pub food such as Chicago-style pizza, nacho platters, and a wide selection of microbrews. Theme nights—the Disco Inferno, "Flip Night" (toss a quarter for drink prices), and Mystery Beer Night—keep patrons entertained. *78260 Hwy. 40, Winter Park, tel. 970/726–4929. AE, MC, V.*

More Mellow

The Rails
A large fireplace dominates this laid-back spot where relaxing in comfy chairs and couches is the name of the game. The decor is modern, and train prints line the walls. Things liven up every other Wednesday, when comedy troupes perform. *Iron Horse Resort, 275 Winter Park Dr., Winter Park, tel. 970/726–8851. AE, DC, MC, V.*

There is a certain irony that the state of Idaho, with its spectacular wilderness fashioned by geologic activities that created mountains as high as 12,662 feet should be best known to outsiders for the lowly potato. For beyond that ubiquitous tuber are some 83,000 square miles of recreational wilderness that includes more than 2,000 lakes, 200 mountain peaks above the 12,000-foot mark, America's deepest gorge (Hell's Canyon), petrified lava fields, and dense forests that cover 40% of the state.

Wedged between Wyoming and Montana to the east and Oregon and Washington to the west, Idaho is bisected by the northernmost range of the Rocky Mountains before they continue across the Canadian border. Snuggled in among these towering peaks and reaping the benefits of moisture-laden storms from the West Coast are 15 ski resorts, including the state's best-known natural commodity after the potato—Sun Valley.

Discovered by Austrian count Felix Schaffgotsch, who remarked that "among the many attractive spots I have visited [during a six-week tour through the mountains of California, Wyoming, Utah, and Colorado], this combines more delightful features than any place I have seen in the U.S., Switzerland, or Austria for a winter sports resort." Built by a millionaire railroad tycoon and visited by movie stars, royalty, presidents, and literary luminaries, Sun Valley is arguably the most storied and enduring of all U.S. ski resorts.

The physical attributes of Idaho's Northern Rockies are not overshadowed by the glitterati that give the resort its luster. The sharp peaks provide a craggy crown for skiing's royal resort, and the perfectly shaped Bald Mountain is the skiing jewel in this regal setting. The low-lying Wood River valley is a verdant, wildlife-rich counterpoint to the jagged peaks, with its ranches and small communities providing an amiable mix of longtime residents and seasonal escapees from urban life.

SUN VALLEY
SKI RESORT

Sun Valley, Idaho 83353
Tel. 208/622–4111 or
800/786–8259
www.sunvalley.com

STATISTICALLY SPEAKING

Base elevation: 5,750 feet

Summit elevation: 9,150 feet

Vertical drop: 3,400 feet

Skiable terrain: 2,054 acres

Number of trails: 78

Longest run: 3 miles

Lifts and capacity: 7 high-speed quads, 5 triples, 5 doubles, 1 surface lift; 28,180 skiers per hour

Daily lift ticket: $54

Average annual snowfall: 200 inches

Number of skiing days 1997–98: 144

Snowmaking: 630 acres, 31%

Terrain mix: N 36%, I 42%, E 22%

Snowboarding: yes

When railroad tycoon Averell Harriman made Sun Valley America's first destination resort in 1936, the place sparkled with glamour like fresh powder in the moonlight. Gary Cooper, Darryl Zanuck, Judy Garland, Clark Gable, and Bing Crosby led the charge from Hollywood, and later ice queen Sonja Henie and Marilyn Monroe followed in their footsteps. The Sun Valley of the '40s and '50s was a mecca for moguls, a hangout for celebs, and the seasonal home of Ernest Hemingway, who wrote parts of *For Whom the Bell Tolls* in his room at the Sun Valley Lodge. Hundreds of visits by presidents and royalty, millionaires and movie stars, entertainers and athletes have given Sun Valley a unique star-studded aura, a halo of fame now tinged by nostalgia.

For the glory days did not last indefinitely. In the late '60s Aspen and Vail began siphoning away the chic and sleek, and for more than a decade Sun Valley lapsed into a development coma while other major resorts were indulging in a building orgy. The resort didn't so much lose its luster as get dusted by the winds of change gusting through the modern destination resort industry. In short, cash had replaced cachet as the defining quality of a ski resort, and Sun Valley was slow to jump on the bandwagon. This was probably a blessing in the long run. The resort weathered its decline with considerable dignity, keeping its original style intact; and when the modernization spending spree did get underway at the start of the '90s, Sun Valley was ready to embrace it without being swallowed up by it. A mountainwide lift rejuvenation gave Sun Valley the second-largest number of detachable quads in America, after Vail, and one of the biggest automated snowmaking systems in the world. The glamour that Harriman created blended easily with the new, expanded accommodations. By 1995 Sun Valley was once again regarded as one of the country's preeminent ski resorts.

Nestled toward the upper end of the Wood River valley and surrounded by the Pioneer, Boulder, and Smoky mountain ranges, Sun Valley is actually a fairly diversified area made up of several distinct parts. The original Sun Valley is a self-contained community centered around the Sun Valley Lodge, a complex consisting of a conference center, condos, town

Area code: 208

Children's services: day-care, Sun Valley Resort, tel. 208/ 622–2288; instruction, tel. 208/622–2248

Snow phone: tel. 208/622– 2095 or 800/635–4150

Police: Ketchum, tel. 208/ 726–7833; Sun Valley, tel. 208/622–5345

Hospital: Wood River Medical Center, Sun Valley, tel. 208/ 622–3333; Wood River Medical Center, Hailey, tel. 208/ 788–2222

Chamber of Commerce: tel. 208/726–3423 or 800/634– 3347

Road conditions: tel. 888/ 432–7623

Towing: AAA, tel. 208/726– 3955; Dick York Auto, tel. 208/726–4583

FIVE-STAR FAVORITES

Best run for vertical: Inhibition

Best run overall: Limelight

Best bar/nightclub: Whiskey Jacques'

Best hotel: Sun Valley Lodge

Best restaurant: Ketchum Grill

houses, and assorted shops. One mile away, linked by a walking path/bike trail and the free KART shuttle bus, is the older community of Ketchum, the former sheep-shipping and mining town that retains a character evocative of 60 years ago when it was the end of a spur line for Harriman's Union Pacific Railroad. Today Ketchum is charming, it still has a permanent population of only about 3,800, and although SUVs are now more common than pickup trucks, it retains a funky, rustic appearance, with older wood-sided and log homes scattered among the newer brick buildings and plazas. It's the heart of the Sun Valley area's nighttime action, with a comfortable mix of restaurants, bars, galleries, and coffee shops. The newest development in the area is Elkhorn Village, about 1½ miles from Ketchum and a mile from the Sun Valley Resort. It's a hillside cluster of large private houses and condominium buildings, with the Elkhorn Resort at its center. It, too, is linked to Ketchum, Sun Valley Resort, and the two ski mountains by the KART shuttle system.

Two mountains? That's right. Although the dominant 9,150-foot Bald Mountain (known as Baldy) is the main mountain at Sun Valley, there's also Dollar Mountain, Sun Valley's original ski hill and the site of the world's first chairlift. At 6,638 feet, it's a tiny knob of a mountain by today's ski resort standards, but it's the hill of choice for never-evers, novices, kids, and half-pipe-loving snowboarders. Both mountains are linked to the three main accommodation centers by the KART shuttle, with Dollar just a minute's ride from Sun Valley and Elkhorn and about five minutes from Ketchum. The big one, Baldy, is about a five-minute shuttle ride from Sun Valley and Elkhorn, and only a minute from Ketchum. The shuttle bus is definitely the way to go because parking is limited almost everywhere, especially at the Warm Springs base area (there is more parking at the River Run base area).

Sun Valley perennially ranks at or near the top of North American ski areas for its rich diversity of off-hill activities. Indeed, even those unfortunate souls who don't alpine ski or snowboard can enjoy a wonderful wintertime vacation at this one-of-a-kind resort. Savvy cross-country skiers know that Sun Valley is the Rocky Mountain West's premier Nordic skiing getaway; the greater Wood River valley boasts more than 150 kilometers of exquisitely groomed trails for both the skating and classic techniques. Pups are even permitted to accompany their skiing best friends on some trails. Backcountry telemarkers and snowboarders head to the powder-covered slopes surrounding Galena Summit (on Route 75 northwest of town). Dogsled rides, ice skating, and snowshoeing are among the other popular winter-recreation pursuits, while indoor options include gallery-hopping and catching a screening of *Sun Valley Serenade,* the 1941 Hollywood movie starring Sonja Henie, John Payne, and Milton Berle. The classic flick shows daily at the Sun Valley Opera House, in the Sun Valley Resort complex.

This remarkable mix of the old and the new works well, giving Sun Valley a unique blend of historical tradition and contemporary development, rough, woodsy texture, and high style. It also continues to attract the rich and famous; celebs such as Brooke Shields, Clint Eastwood, and Bruce Willis are among the many who have houses in Sun Valley.

HOW TO GET THERE

By Plane

Friedman Memorial Airport (tel. 208/788–4956), in Hailey, is served by SkyWest Airlines/Delta (tel. 800/453–9417) with connections through Salt Lake City and Horizon Airlines/Alaska (tel. 800/547–9308) from Seattle.

By Car

From Boise (160 miles away), take I–84 south to Mountain Home, then Route 20 east to Route 75N to Hailey, Ketchum, and Sun Valley. From Salt Lake City, Utah (292 miles away), follow I–15 north to Tremonton, Utah, then I–84 west to Twin Falls, and then take Route 75 north to Hailey, Ketchum, and Sun Valley.

All major car-rental companies are represented at Salt Lake City Airport, and the following are available at Boise Airport: **Avis** (tel. 208/383–3350); **Budget** (tel. 208/383–3090); **Hertz** (tel. 208/383–3100); **National** (tel. 208/383–3210); **U Save** (tel. 208/322–2751). Cars from Avis, Budget, and Hertz may be dropped off at Friedman Memorial Airport, and U Save rentals can be dropped off at the Sun Valley Resort.

By Bus

Sun Valley Express (tel. 800/634-6539) and **Sun Valley Stages** (tel. 800/821–9064) meet flights daily at the Boise Airport, taking guests directly to the Sun Valley Resort.

GETTING AROUND

Sun Valley Resort, Elkhorn Village, Ketchum, and the base areas at both mountains are all connected by the scheduled **KART bus service** (tel. 208/726–7140), which runs from 7:30 AM to midnight. It's a good idea to use it because parking is limited at the base areas of Baldy and in and around Ketchum. Pick up a schedule when you arrive and keep it with you. Taxi service is also available from **A-1 Taxi** (tel. 208/726–9351).

THE SKIING

The skiing at Sun Valley takes place on two mountains, the relatively modest Dollar Mountain, with its gentle novice terrain, and Bald Mountain (known as Baldy), a perfectly pitched, broad-shouldered beast that many consider the finest single ski mountain in America. The reason for this is consistency. Unlike those at so many other ski areas, the runs on Baldy streak from top to bottom with near-perfect fall-line precision, no flat spots, no run-outs, no bailouts, just a steep, straight-up peak that lets you kick into your first turn from the get-go and never lets up for 3,400 vertical feet. It's straight-shot skiing, with mile-long runs leading to a clutch of intermediate and expert bowls; the thickly timbered lower slopes cut through with well-groomed and extra-wide cruising trails. Also, the infinite variety on three faces lets you follow the sun throughout the day.

Novices

The place for you is Dollar Mountain. With four lifts carrying you up to several different elevations (the highest at 6,638 feet), Dollar gives you variety and some challenge but not too much. Lessons are always in progress, and you will notice that all ages are enrolled. Lessons, by the way, are an especially rewarding experience here, for Sun Valley has one of the best ski schools in the country; you'll advance faster and gain more control than you will by trying to master technique solo.

To ski Dollar, start by going up Poverty Flats, taking the Quarter Dollar lift. If you find yourself skating, then you have passed the test and are ready to progress to Half Dollar. This lift gives you access to four runs (Hidden Valley, Graduation, Half Dollar Bowl, and Cabin Practice Slope), where you can make some turns and get comfortable before taking Dollar lift to the top. All the runs are extremely well groomed, so you don't have to worry about moguls, powder, or ice.

When you have conquered Dollar Mountain, go over to Elkhorn by taking Dollar lift to the top and skiing off to your left onto the cat track that leads past Sepp's Bowl and Sheep-herder to the Elkhorn area. You can then take Joint Venture to the base of the Elkhorn lift, which gives you access to two green runs, Elkhorn Bowl and Joint Venture, as well as some intermediate trails. From the top you can ski back down on another cat track to the base of Dollar and to wide, gentle Sepp's Bowl.

Intermediates

The place for you is Bald Mountain; start at the River Run base to catch the morning sun. Take the combined nine-minute ride on River Run and Lookout Express and go off to your right to ski Upper College to Lower College, cutting back to the right at the bottom to catch Lookout Express again, or to the left to sample lively blue runs like Graduate, Janss Pass, and Can-Can, all served by the Frenchman's lift. This area also offers some outstanding glade skiing. To follow the sun, take Challenger or Lookout Express to the top again, ski down Ridge to Blue Grouse or Cutoff, and then pick up Roundhouse Lane to Gun Tower Lane to catch the Seattle Ridge lift on the south side of the mountain.

On Seattle Ridge you'll catch the sun from early morning to midafternoon as you ski the designated slow-skiing runs of Gretchen's Gold, Southern Comfort, Christin's Silver, Byron's Park, Seattle Ridge, or Broadway. Don't be fooled by the novice designation of these runs: they are challenging. Remember, the pitch at Sun Valley is probably more than you are used to. When you're ready to step it up a little, head for the intermediate bowls reached from the top of Baldy. Mayday, Lefty, Farout, and Sigi's all have good, sustained pitch, and they start out wide open at the top, gradually tapering down to narrower tree-surrounded sections. The Mayday lift is the most direct access to the summit—a seven-minute ride that will put you in bowl heaven. If you find these bowls a little too steep, you can head for the Christmas bowl area, which starts at the top of the Christmas lift. These are moderately pitched bowls that give you a good feel for skiing the wide-open spaces without pushing your fear meter into the red zone. When you feel like returning to groomed terrain, all the bowls in this area feed back to the confluence of the Exhibition, Christmas, and Cold Springs lifts, which give you access to groomed cruisers.

From the top of the Christmas lift, you can start to move over to the Warm Springs side of the mountain by taking the Warm Springs Face, an invigorating, groomed, and wide cruiser that lets you carry speed with confidence yet provides enough surprise to keep you heads-up. Here, you have the choice of returning to the Warm Springs base area or heading for the Flying Squirrel lift, where you'll find some good intermediate bump runs.

Experts

From the River Run base area, ride the River Run and Lookout Express chairs up, turn right (looking up), and take Limelight, a wonderfully wide and pure fall-line cruiser that will get your legs warmed up. Run this a few times before the crowds start to build up, then ski under the chair on Upper River Run, where you'll usually find some good medium-size moguls, especially down the left-hand side of the run. Avoid going right down to the River Run base area; instead pick up the Exhibition chair where the Lookout Express, Sunnyside, and Exhibition chairs all converge. From here you can ski down Lower Christmas Bowl to Inhibition for a super-steep vertical. Ride the Cold Springs chair back up to the top of Exhibition chair. Underneath the Exhibition chair is Exhibition, another steep mogul run; it's short but gnarly, with large moguls. Beat yourself up on that for a little while, then take the Lookout Express and head for the bowls. You can try a few blue bowl runs from the top of the Lookout Express quad chair, or you can take the triple Lookout chair across the top of the bowls and over to the summit of Baldy. From here you have a choice of three of Sun Valley's meanest bowls—Little Easter (steep); Easter (steeper); and Lookout (steepest). If you want the max in steepness, stick close to the right-hand side (looking down) and ski Lookout, then ride Mayday chair back to the summit. This is just a seven-minute ride, and it's your best and least crowded access to the bowl area.

Although there are only eight named bowls, this is actually a wide and wild area, with wind-sculpted chutes, ridges, and gullies, wide-open swaths of steepness, and some tantalizing glade areas midway down the Lookout Bowl.

SNOWBOARDING

Although snowboarders are allowed everywhere on Bald Mountain except Christin's Silver and Southern Comfort, under the Seattle Ridge chair, there are no special grooming features specifically for them. But the mountain's steady pitch, efficient lift system, consistently terrific snow conditions, and lack of long catwalks make it very snowboard-friendly. The only special on-slope provision for snowboaders is on Dollar Mountain, which has a new 350-foot halfpipe on the Hidden Valley Run. The Sun Valley Ski and Snowboarding School at Dollar can quickly transform just about any neophyte into a nimble rider.

WHERE TO STAY

Accommodations in Sun Valley cluster in three main areas—Sun Valley Resort, Elkhorn Village, and downtown Ketchum. All are connected by the KART shuttle service and are no more than a 10-minute ride from the ski area. The resort is a self-contained village center, and along with Elkhorn Village, generally has the most expensive and upscale accommodations. Ketchum has more of a price mix, but it also has some properties in the expensive range. If you are price-conscious or prefer to be within walking distance of the town's nightlife, Ketchum is your best choice.

Expensive

Idaho Country Inn

This magnificent 9,000-square-ft mountain house, standing on a knoll halfway between Ketchum and Sun Valley, is a peeled-log and river-rock dwelling that is practically a museum of the area's natural heritage. The large, individually designed and themed rooms, all with views of the mountains and each reflecting a slice of Idaho life, are decorated with willow canopied beds, wagon-wheel headboards, handmade armoires, log and pine chairs, and wildlife art. There's a library with an excellent collection of natural history books about the area, a living room where afternoon appetizers are served next to a massive rock-faced fireplace, and an adjacent dining room where you get a full Idaho breakfast. *134 Latigo La., Box 659, Sun Valley 83353, tel. 208/ 727–4000 or 800/635–4444, fax 208/ 725–0193. 11 rooms. Facilities: outdoor hot tub, library. AE, MC, V. $132– $175, including full breakfast and après-ski snacks.*

Knob Hill Inn

This large, sprawling, ultradeluxe European-style Relais & Chateaux lodge, 2 miles from the River Run base area, is wonderfully soothing for romantics. From its sloping roof and carved balconies to its brick walkways and courtyard, the inn displays the clean lines of modern mountain chalet design. Inside it continues the theme with softly rounded doorways and windows, brick and stucco walls, light-color wood trim, Tibetan rugs, cedar beams, and tiled floors of slate and marble. The rooms and suites are all spacious and have balconies; the decor is modern, with soft pastel tones of jade and peach, original art on the walls, and large marble-tile bathrooms with oversize tubs and separate showers. *960 N. Main St., Box 800, Ketchum 83340, tel. 208/726–8010 or 800/526–8010, fax 208/726–2712. 20 rooms, 4 suites. Facilities: restaurant, café-bakery, indoor lap pool, indoor-outdoor hot tub, exercise area, sauna. AE, MC, V. $185–$375.*

Pennay's at River Run

You can ski from your door to the magnificent River Run Plaza, with its luxury restaurants and high-speed quad; you're also within easy walking distance of downtown Ketchum's shops, bars, and movie theaters. Pennay's borders the Big Wood River, and its fully equipped, beautifully furnished one- and two-bedroom apartments all have large kitchens, wood fireplaces, and a bath for each bedroom. The furnishings are modern in style and muted in tone, and the huge outdoor Jacuzzi hot pool is a must after a day on the slopes. *Box 1298, Sun Valley 83353, tel. 208/726–9086 or 800/736–7503, fax 208/726-4541. 19 units. MC, V. $175–$350.*

Sun Valley Resort

At the Sun Valley Resort you have a choice of three distinct accommodation types: the lodge, the inn, and the surrounding condominiums and cottages. They are all part of a 4,200-acre wooded estate village that wraps around a small lake just a mile from Ketchum. Every manner of recreation and service lies within the confines of this classy resort.

The Sun Valley **Lodge** may be the most famous resort lodge in America, and the very famous have cavorted here, as the photos lining the walls and hallways attest. The concrete exterior is stained and textured to look like a wooden mountain lodge. Its rooms have a country-floral motif, with Laura Ashley drapes, Oriental rugs, and handsome French provincial furniture in rich, dark woods. As comfortable as the rooms are, the real ambience of the lodge can only be savored in the common areas: the high-ceilinged sunroom with a grand piano, the glass-enclosed circular pool, the Duchin Bar with its leather couches, the dining room with its crystal chandeliers and polished dance floor, and the outdoor rink shimmering with a thousand tiny lights.

The **Inn** was built in 1937 to handle the overflow from the instantly popular Lodge, and aside from its Tyrolean styling, it offers the same rustic Western grandeur as the Lodge and the same luxury in its guest rooms.

The log, stone, and board-and-batten **cottages** were the houses of the original founders of the resort, which have been totally renovated and decorated in the same style as the Lodge and Inn. They all have at least two bedrooms, a marble bathroom, and a brick fireplace. The **condos,** scattered in tree-shrouded clusters around the fringe of the property, are more modern in furnishings, with warm earth tones and pastel hues and fireplaces.

Guests at the resort have access to all facilities; a shuttle bus makes scheduled runs around the property as well as to Dollar Mountain (less than two minutes away) and Bald

Mountain (about 10 minutes away). *1 Sun Valley Rd., Sun Valley 83353, tel. 208/622-4111 or 800/786–8259, fax 208/622–2030. 148 lodge rooms, 113 inn rooms, 200 condominium units, 6 cottages. Facilities: 7 restaurants, lounge, 2 outdoor pools, exercise room, game room, bowling alley, ice rink, sauna, massage room. AE, D, DC, MC, V. $99–$1,000.*

Moderate

Best Western Kentwood Lodge
You can't beat the location of this lodge in the center of Ketchum. The playful Western decor includes custom-made log furniture, steel cowboy-cutout fire screens, and Indian rugs on the walls. There's a large glassed-in pool and Jacuzzi off the lobby and a café serving breakfast and lunch. The rooms all have either a king- or two queen-size beds, a microwave and refrigerator, and either a fireplace or a balcony; some also have a full kitchen, sleeper sofa, and a Jacuzzi. The best part is the amiable owners. *180 S. Main St., Ketchum 83340, tel. 208/726–4114 or 800/805–1001, fax 208/726–2417. 57 rooms. Facilities: café, indoor pool, hot tub, weight room, coin laundry, meeting rooms. AE, D, DC, MC, V. $79–$149.*

Best Western Tyrolean Lodge
This classic Austrian-style lodge sits close to the lift at the River Run base area and within walking distance of downtown Ketchum. The style is European both inside and out. Each spacious and tastefully appointed room has oversized beds with down comforters. Other amenities include a great room with a large stone fireplace and a Continental champagne breakfast. *Box 202, Sun Valley 83353, tel. 208/726–5336 or 800/333–7912, fax 208/726–2081. 56 rooms. Facilities: sauna, indoor and outdoor hot tubs, exercise room, laundry, game room. AE, D, DC, MC, V. $80–$150.*

Elkhorn Resort
The centerpiece of the Elkhorn Village area combines a full-service four-story stucco hotel with a cluster of upscale condominium units set around the central village plaza area. The owners renovated the hotel in 1998, and it reflects the rich mining legacy of Idaho. A beautiful, hand-cut river-rock fireplace focuses the main lobby. Hotel rooms vary in size from standard to spacious two-bedroom suites, all decorated in earth tones with modern furnishings. The larger suites have fireplaces, full kitchens, and whirlpool tubs. The adjacent condominiums range from studio to four-bedroom and have similar modern decor, although individual owners have added their personal touches. The KART bus makes regular stops to shuttle you to the mountain or to Ketchum, or you can catch the Elkhorn lift to the top of Dollar Mountain. *1 Elkhorn Rd., Sun Valley 83354, tel. 208/622–4511 or 800/355–4676, fax 208/622–7524. 125 rooms, 7 suites, 75 condominium units. Facilities: 2 restaurants, lounge, child-care services, bakery-coffee shop, indoor and outdoor hot tubs, sauna, exercise room, ice-skating, post office, general store, meeting rooms. AE, D, DC, MC, V. $84–$325.*

Premier Resorts Sun Valley
This property management company handles the bulk of the condominium

and house rentals in the area. It represents properties ranging from one-bedroom condos to luxurious private homes throughout the valley, from serene Elkhorn and the town of Ketchum to units alongside the cross-country ski trails in Sun Valley and slope-side at Warm Springs. Amenities, which vary by property, can include a fully equipped kitchen and a fireplace, a hot tub, a sauna, and laundry facilities. *Box 659, Sun Valley 83353, tel. 208/727–4000 or 800/635–4444, fax 208/725–0193. 350 units, 235 houses. AE, D, MC, V. $65–$6,000.*

Tamarack Lodge
The Tamarack, in downtown Ketchum, has spacious guest rooms with mildly Austrian decor. Room layouts range from a standard hotel room to a king-size suite with a separate bedroom and a living room. All rooms have a microwave, a refrigerator, a hair dryer, and a coffeemaker. The larger units come with a wet bar and some rooms have a wood-burning fireplace. *Box 2000, Sun Valley 83353, tel. 208/726–3344 or 800/521–5379, fax 208/727–4040. 21 rooms, 5 suites. Facilities: indoor pool, outdoor hot tub. AE, D, DC, MC, V. $92–$134.*

Inexpensive

Bald Mountain Lodge
This 1920s log-cabin motel in the center of Ketchum covers the basics well, with small but comfortable rooms and slightly larger family units with a small sitting area and modest kitchen facilities. The decor is of the knotty-pine rec-room period, with carpeted floors and a mix of single, double, and queen-size beds. *151 S. Main St.,*

Box 2000, Sun Valley 83353, tel. 208/726–9963 or 800/892–7407, fax 208/726–1854. 7 rooms, 23 kitchen units. AE, D, DC, MC, V. $45–$100.

Christiania Lodge
The location of this U-shape gray-wood motel in the middle of Ketchum is hard to beat, and so is the price of the large, clean rooms with two queen-size or double beds (10 suites also have a king-size bed), foldaway kitchenettes, and entrances overlooking a central courtyard. The slightly larger king suites have fireplaces and more ample kitchens. The KART shuttle bus stops right outside the door. *Box 2196, 651 Sun Valley Rd., Ketchum 83340, tel. 208/726–3351 or 800/535–3241, fax 208/726–3055. 28 rooms, 10 suites. Facilities: outdoor hot tub. AE, D, DC, MC, V. $64–$94.*

Ketchum Korral Motor Lodge
This cozy little complex tucked away on a side street two blocks from the center of town offers log cabins and one large motel-type building with an additional nine rooms. The log cabins, built in a grove of trees in the '30s, were a preferred hangout of Hemingway. They are rustic, with wood-burning stone fireplaces, rough barn-board walls, and full kitchens. One large cabin has two queen-size beds, one queen-size sleeper sofa, and one twin bed. The smaller units come with one queen-size bed and a queen-size sofa bed. The motel rooms are slightly more contemporary in decor and furnishings. *310 S. Main St., Box 2241, Ketchum 83340, tel. 208/726–3510 or 800/657–2657, fax 208/726–5287. 9 rooms, 8 cabins. Facilities: outdoor hot tub. AE, D, MC, V. $45–$125.*

Ski View Lodge

These gingerbread-style log cabins with brightly painted window and door frames are right out of the '40s, and it's just the sort of place you might find if you were stumbling around in the woods. In fact, they are just a few blocks from downtown Ketchum and a good choice if you're looking for basic rustic accommodations on the cheap side. Each unit has a full kitchen, two double beds, and a comfortable, woodsy ambience. And the best part is that your pet is welcome. *409 South Main St., Box 2254, Ketchum 83340, tel. 208/726–3441. 8 units. MC, V. $40–$70.*

WHERE TO EAT

There's a tremendous variety of dining options in Sun Valley, Elkhorn Village, and downtown Ketchum, ranging from high-end gourmet to specialty cuisine and Western staples.

On the Mountain

River Run Lodge

This two-story timber-and-rock masterpiece has turned River Run into the main base area at Sun Valley. Besides fine food, you can get ski and snowboard demos and rentals, lockers, and lift tickets here. Plush carpets, leather chairs, marble tabletops, and towering fresh-flower arrangements give it the feel of a four-star hotel rather than a ski area base lodge. The food is as elegant as the setting, starring brick-oven pizzas, fresh roasts, made-to-order wok specialties, and the crèpe of the day. A jazz trio or pianist plays après-ski. *River Run base area, Sun Valley, tel. 208/622–4111. AE, MC, V.*

Seattle Ridge Lodge

When it comes to style, this on-mountain restaurant rivals America's best, and it is without a doubt the champion in the quality of the food. The massive cathedral-size log cabin exudes so much luxury and elegance that you almost feel you should take your ski boots off on entering. Polished pine beams, marble floors, Oriental rugs, leather chairs and couches, magnificent chandeliers, and Ralph Lauren antiques set the tone. You can lunch in the dining room in front of a central three-sided fireplace or wander outside to the glass-enclosed cobblestone patio. The full menu includes everything from giant baked Idaho potatoes with a choice of more than 20 toppings to perfectly cooked roast beef carved by the chef from a massive haunch. *Top of Seattle Ridge chairlift, Sun Valley, tel. 208/622–4111. AE, MC, V.*

Expensive

Chandler's

This cozy, intimate house in downtown Ketchum has several small dining rooms. The menu emphasizes American cuisine using fresh Idaho ingredients, with specialties such as elk loin in a red wine reduction with caramelized shallots or grilled fresh salmon on garlic potato purée and sautéed spinach with basil and sun-dried tomato sauce. The best deal is the prix-fixe American dinner menu, which includes a soup or salad, a choice of six entrées, and dessert. *200 S. Main St., Ketchum, tel. 208/726–1776. Reservations essential. AE, D, MC, V.*

Evergreen Bistro

This eclectic, upscale bistro is a slice of Montparnasse in the mountains.

The seven dining rooms make up a kind of Franco-American collectibles museum, with Moulin Rouge posters; reproduction Renaissance paintings and tapestries; a mix of pine and French provincial chairs, corner cupboards, and pedestal tables; steamer trunks; and a massive copper bistro bar in the main foyer. The menu is a mélange of French, Asian, and Southwestern influences. The Provençal-style bouillabaisse is exceptional, with a generous mix of shellfish in a fennel, garlic, and saffron broth. There's also grilled Idaho trout served Cajun style; New York–cut steak served with watercress, Stilton butter, and Belgian endive; and something called Vegetable Chaos, a medley of seasonal vegetables with a stuffed chili-and-mushroom bundle. Preferred tables are next to the fire or in an alcove in the Fireplace Room. *171 1st Ave., Ketchum, tel. 208/726–3888. Reservations essential. AE, MC, V.*

Lodge Dining Room
The elegance of this oval-shaped dining room with high-back leather chairs and immaculate crystal and linen place settings evokes memories of the rich and famous who have dined and danced here. This is one of the last bastions of such a crowd; the softly lighted polished dance floor still lures many. The menu is primarily Continental, with some local specialties such as Rocky Mountain trout or Idaho beef. The entrées change daily, but may include pan-seared elk medallions and ahi with citrus-fruit compote. *Sun Valley Lodge, 2nd floor, Sun Valley, tel. 208/622–2150. Reservations essential. AE, D, DC, MC, V.*

Trail Creek Cabin
This is a meat-and-potatoes experience that includes a romantic sleigh ride to a rustic 1938 log-and-rock cabin. It might look rough, but notables like Hemingway, Gary Cooper, and Ava Gardner used to come here for New Year's Eve dinner. The horse-drawn sleigh ride leaves from the Sun Valley Inn and takes about a half hour. The atmosphere is casual and bustling, with table-side entertainment. The specialty of the house is the barbecued ribs, but there's also a good selection of grilled steak, chicken, duck, trout, and lamb. *Sun Valley Resort, Sun Valley, tel. 208/ 622–2135. Reservations essential. AE, D, DC, MC, V.*

Moderate
China Pepper
This hip, modern Thai restaurant in a colonnaded building just off Main Street has been voted by locals as Ketchum's best restaurant for several years running. It's an airy, wide-open space with stone-tile floors, large tropical trees, chrome-and-glass tables, and large abstract canvases on the walls. The menu is Thai and Chinese—hot and spicy but light. Entrées range from Thai shrimp (tiger prawns poached and served with coconut-peanut sauce on a bed of spinach) or Thai-style barbecued duck (char-broiled and smothered in a spicy orange barbecue sauce) to crisp pork (flash-fried strips of pork tossed with bell peppers, water chestnuts, and bamboo shoots in a hoisin sauce). There's also a sushi bar. *511 Leadville St., Ketchum, tel. 208/726–0959. AE, MC, V.*

Ketchum Grill

Built in 1885, this Ketchum classic served as home to the town's first postmaster. With wooden floors, period brass lighting fixtures, and a gallery of photo stills of classic cowboy movies starring the likes of Roy Rogers, Tom Mix, and Gene Autry, it has a casual, cheerful atmosphere. You'll find great entrées such as grilled homemade fennel sausages, braised rabbit with pancetta and fresh herbs, or warm spinach salad with bacon and grilled chicken breast. The pizzas are unique; among available toppings are rock shrimp, pesto, pine nuts, and fontina cheese. *520 East Ave. N., Ketchum, tel. 208/726–4660. AE, MC, V.*

Pioneer Saloon

This is the place to go when you have a craving for extra-large portions of red meat. It's small—just 30 tables or so—but it attracts a loud and lively crowd that spills over from the bar up front. The barn-board walls are decked with fishing and hunting collectibles and period firearms. The prime rib comes in four sizes; the largest, called the full cut, weighs in at about 32 ounces, while the thick, red, and juicy steaks are either sirloin, rib eye, or New York–cut, a monster at 14 ounces. Ribs are also available occasionally. *308 N. Main St., Ketchum, tel. 208/726–3149. Reservations not accepted. AE, MC, V.*

Sawtooth Club

It's not because I sat next to Michael Keaton or bumped into Clint Eastwood as I was leaving that I have such a fondness for this place. Rather, it's because this is a first-rate restaurant with a great casual bistro ambience, a cheerful, lively feel, and a creative, high-quality menu. The main-floor bar (voted the best in town) focuses on a large see-through fireplace surrounded by comfy couches and offers a café menu. The restaurant above is appointed with antique wooden tables, accented by burgundy and blue linen napkins. The ambitious menu, termed "Idaho Style Fine Dining"— meaning excellent food *and* respectably large portions—encompasses items such as grilled T-bone, Idaho pork tenderloin, and marinated, wood-grilled breast of duck in warm blackberry port sauce. Another favorite is the mesquite-grilled Idaho rainbow trout. *231 Main St., Ketchum, tel. 208/726–5233. AE, MC, V.*

Inexpensive

Bob Dog Pizza

Bob Dog is top dog for pizza with 16 designer varieties, plus a list of more than 40 ingredients such as pine nuts, snow peas, smoked oysters, fresh cilantro, caramelized red onions, and smoked chicken from which you can create your own. Cheese choices include gouda, feta, brie, and asiago. The crusts are crisp and thin with an herb flavoring, and there are three salads to choose from. The trade is mostly take-out and delivery, but limited seating is available. *Lower Giacobbi Square, 451 4th Street E., Ketchum, tel. 208/726–2358. MC, V.*

Desperados

This is a good spot for fresh, healthy Mexican dishes, with some novel variations on the most popular themes. The white walls are decorated with bright posters, paintings, and signs.

Try the fish taco, filled with lightly breaded cod, or the *carne asada* burrito—charbroiled steak, guacamole, cheese, and tomatoes, rolled in a soft flour tortilla. There's also an excellent selection of house salsas, including a blindingly hot jalapeño and carrot version. *211 4th St., Ketchum, tel. 208/726–3068. AE, D, MC, V.*

Konditorei

The Konditorei, which has been a Sun Valley institution since the early 1960s, is renowned for its fine freshly baked goods. The menu offers a variety of light meals, salads, and sandwiches. The place has a cozy, informal European ambience, with exposed brick walls decorated with Austrian antiques and artifacts, a warming fire burning in the copper-faced fireplace, and light classical music playing in the background. Try the Idaho smoked trout salad, the quiche of the day, or a daily soup special served with hot homemade bread. Be sure to save room for the pastry or something from the big selection of Continental cakes and tarts. *Sun Valley Resort, Sun Valley, tel. 208/622–2235. AE, D, DC, MC, V.*

Smoky Mountain Pizza and Pasta

This is a classic Italian eatery with wood-slat chairs, pine walls, and red-and-white-checked tablecloths. The food is strictly mainstream—homemade pasta (try the spicy chicken linguine) or pizza—and the atmosphere is warm and homey. *200 Sun Valley Rd., Ketchum, tel. 208/622–5625. D, MC, V.*

Best Bets for Breakfast

Java on Fourth

This is a good spot for a cup of joe to go in various designer flavors or just strong and fresh *café ordinaire*. There's also a daily lineup of fresh-baked muffins, scones, and cookies along with the standard breakfast and lunch specials, which change daily. *191 4th St., Ketchum, tel. 208/726–2882; 310 N. Main, Hailey, tel. 208/788–2444. No credit cards.*

Kneadery

For a traditional home-style breakfast in a rustic atmosphere with fireplaces and wooden floors, get here early or endure the wait. It's well worth it. The egg dishes come with a mound of hash browns, sliced tomatoes, and a muffin of your choice. For a special treat, try the Idaho smoked trout and eggs. Waffles, pancakes, and various homemade breads round out the hearty, belly-filling menu. *260 Leadville Ave., Ketchum, tel. 208/726–9462. AE, MC, V.*

NIGHTLIFE AND ENTERTAINMENT
Après-Ski

Apples

A bustling hangout for locals and visitors alike, it has good, thumping music, happy-hour munchies, the cheapest beer in town, and an outside patio. *215 Picabo St., Sun Valley, tel. 208/726–7067. No credit cards.*

Bald Base Club

Better known as the BBC, this is definitely the hottest après-ski spot in town—it's *the* place to be seen. It hums with live bands and loud crowds and lots of impromptu dancing. *Opposite Warm Springs base area, 106 Picabo St., Ketchum, tel. 208/726–3838. AE, MC, V.*

Loud and Lively/Dancing

Boiler Room

In the village at Sun Valley, this popular watering hole is home to one of the best après-ski entertainers in the country. Mike Murphy, the "Funny Guy," plays nonstop for 2 hours (5:30 to 7:30 PM) Monday through Friday. Get here early—he sells out fast. *Sun Valley Resort, Sun Valley, tel. 208/ 622–2148. AE, D, MC, V.*

Pioneer Saloon

Its rough barn-board walls are decked with dozens of trophy heads of buffalo, moose, elk, bighorn sheep, and other animals, plus a collection of antique hunting rifles. Wrought iron, hardwood floors, and a long oak bar give it the classic American saloon atmosphere: It's the genuine article, the locals' favorite watering hole, and attracts visitors of all ages. *308 N. Main St., Ketchum, tel. 208/726– 3149. AE, MC, V.*

Whiskey Jacques'

This is the only place in town that has live music almost nightly. Things start hopping at 4 PM, with a happy hour weeknights. There are also big-screen TVs and a good munchie menu of burgers, hand-tossed pizzas, and calzone. *271 Main St., Ketchum, tel. 208/ 726–5297. MC, V.*

More Mellow

Duchin Lounge

Ah, to savor a quiet cocktail at the Duchin is to savor the elegance of the original Sun Valley. Leather couches, dark-wood wainscoting, rich brocade upholstery, and a long mahogany bar with a dozen seats give it a clubby Ivy League feel. There are also a live light-jazz trio (après-ski and evenings) and a small dance floor. *Sun Valley Resort, Sun Valley, tel. 208/622–2145. AE, D, DC, MC, V.*

Lobby Lounge

The Elkhorn's quiet lobby bar has a rich, woody ambience, lots of comfortable chairs, and live entertainment. *1 Elkhorn Rd., Sun Valley, tel. 208/622–4511, ext. 1044. AE, D, DC, MC, V.*

T he state of Maine is a land of striking contrasts. Between its 3,478-mile-long eastern shoreline of rocky coves and white-sand beaches and the mountains on the west side of the state, Maine enjoys some of the richest geographic diversity in the northeastern United States. At 33,000-plus square miles, it is larger than all of the other New England states combined, and it is dotted with some 6,000 lakes, 32,000 miles of rivers and streams, and 17 million acres of dense forest. It yields a cornucopia of wildlife from moose to puffins, and a population of just over 1 million leaves its natural wonders wide open for year-round recreation, including skiing.

The mountains that contain the state's ski resorts are an extension of the Appalachians called the White Mountains and are on the western edge of Maine, at the New Hampshire border. With some peaks topping the 4,000-foot mark, they receive steady, plentiful snowfalls, thanks to the drift of moist Atlantic air pushed inland from the coast, and with their heavily forested flanks and rugged outcroppings they remind many people of the craggy scenery of the Pacific Northwest.

This section of the state is also known as the Western Lakes and Mountains Region. Its forests are speckled with thousands of lakes and rivers strung like pearls across 200 miles of wilderness, from the Sebago Lakes, just outside Portland, to the Rangeley Lakes, near the Canadian border.

There are about a dozen ski resorts throughout the state, but the only true destination areas are two: Sunday River, near Bethel, and Sugarloaf/USA, at the north end of Carrabassett Valley. Sugarloaf, which occupies a striking peak that is distinctive for its above-tree-line summit, has long been the main resort in the state, but more recently Sunday River has emerged as one of the fastest-growing, largest resorts in the Northeast.

GETTING TO MAINE RESORTS

By Plane

Portland International Airport is served by Business Express (tel. 800/345–3400), Continental (tel. 800/525–0280), Delta (tel. 800/221–1212), United (tel. 800/241–6522), and US Airways (tel. 800/428–4322), with connections from other major centers. **Bangor International Airport** is served by Business Express (tel. 800/345–3400), Continental (tel. 800/525–0280), Comair (tel. 800/221–1212), Northwest (tel. 800/225–2525), and US Airways Express (tel. 800 428–4322). Boston's **Logan International Airport** is served by all major carriers.

Car Rental

Portland's airport has car-rental service from **Avis** (tel. 800/331–1212), **Budget** (tel. 800/527–0700), **Hertz** (tel. 800/654–3131), and **National** (tel. 800/328–4567). Bangor Airport has **Avis, Budget, National,** and **Hertz.**

By Bus

Vermont Transit (tel. 800/231–2222) has scheduled service into either Portland or Bangor.

By Train

Amtrak (tel. 800/872–7245) has regularly scheduled service into Boston.

SUGARLOAF/USA

SUGARLOAF/USA

R.R. 1, Box 5000
Carrabassett Valley, ME 04947
Tel. 207/237-2000 or
800/843-5623
www.sugarloaf.com

STATISTICALLY SPEAKING
Base elevation: 1,400 feet

Summit elevation: 4,237 feet

Vertical drop: 2,820 feet

Skiable terrain: 530 acres

Number of trails: 126

Longest run: 3 miles

Lifts and capacity: 2 high-speed quads, 2 high-capacity quads, 1 triple, 8 doubles; 21,805 skiers per hour

Daily lift ticket: $47 weekdays; $49 weekends and holidays

Average annual snowfall: 240 inches

Number of skiing days 1997–1998: 180

Snowmaking: 490 acres, 92%

Terrain mix: N 24%, I 48%, E 28%

Snowboarding: Half-pipe, 2 playgrounds

The locals call it Ohmygosh Corner, and it's easy to see why. Sugarloaf/USA is way up there in Maine (50% of the clientele is from the state). After driving hours, perhaps even seeing a moose, you suddenly see it around a bend of Route 27—the 'Loaf. On a clear day it is a triangular jewel, white-capped and waiting with both above-tree-line skiing in the Snowfields and scores of challenges snaking down from its cap. The resort also has a policy of allowing boundary to boundary skiing on all of its 1,400 acres, opening up a world of glades and trees for enterprising (and expert) skiers and boarders.

In the Carrabassett Valley near the town of Kingfield, Sugarloaf retains the wildness of its Maine logging heritage. You can see it as you look at the rugged Bigelow Mountain range from the summit of Sugarloaf, second-highest peak in Maine. (In fact, this mountain range contains the highest concentration of 4,000-foot mountains in the Pine Tree State.) That wilderness logging heritage shows up, too, on the historic Appalachian Trail, which travels up and over these high mountains. You can hear it in Sugarloaf's trail names—Skidder, Tote Road, Moose Alley. This is one big mountain that presents challenges for all.

The resort has more than 900 condominiums, rooms with mountain views, 21 restaurants, and a village center with a grocery, shops, and lots of après-ski activities. Sugarloaf also turns part of its base lodge into a concert hall, attracting big-name rockers and country crooners during the ski season.

At night streetlights show a path up to the base lodge. A stream rushes by. Bridges are perfect places for a quiet chat or more. The ski-in/ski-out aspect of Sugarloaf lets you put on your boots at the foot of your bed if you want to. Two lifts run up and down above the accommodations, giving skiers a bird's-eye view of it all.

HOW TO GET THERE

By Plane

Portland International Airport is 2½ hours from Sugarloaf, and **Bangor International Airport** is about two hours away. Boston's **Logan Interna-**

Children's services: day-care, instruction, tel. 207/237–2000

Snow phone: tel. 207/237–6808

Franklin County Police: tel. 207/778–9891; nonemergencies, tel. 207/237–2300

Medical Center: Carrabassett Valley Clinic, Sugarloaf, tel. 207/237–2051

Hospital: Franklin County Hospital, tel. 207/778–6031

Chamber of Commerce: tel. 207/235–2100 or 800/843–2732

Road conditions: tel. 207/871–7740

Towing: Sugarloaf Auto Work, tel. 207/237–2071

FIVE-STAR FAVORITES
Best run for vertical: Gondola Line

Best run overall: Tote Road

Best bar/nightclub: Widowmaker Lounge

Best hotel: Grand Summit Resort Hotel

Best restaurant: One Stanley Avenue

tional Airport is four hours from Sugarloaf. (*See* Getting to Maine Resorts, *above.*)

By Car

From the south take the Maine Turnpike from Portland to Auburn, Exit 12, and follow Route 4 north through Farmington. Then pick up Route 27 north to Kingfield and follow the road to the resort. From the west, including Montreal and elsewhere in Quebec, head east on Route 10 to the U.S. border. From northern Maine take I–95 south to Newport, then take Route 2 west to Skowhegan. Pick up Route 201 north to Route 148, then west through Madison to Route 201A, and north to North Anson. Then take Route 16 west to Kingfield and Route 27 north to Sugarloaf.

Portland and Bangor International airports are served by major car-rental firms (*see* Getting to Maine Resorts, *above*).

GETTING AROUND

Sugarloaf is self-contained; once you get here, you won't need the car. Free **Carrabasset Valley shuttle buses** (tel. 207/235–2645) make their way four times every hour around the 'Loaf. Depending on the season and where you are staying, the front desk can also radio one in for you. However, if you are staying in nearby Kingfield or the even smaller village of Stratton, a car is essential because there is no shuttle service linking either community to the mountain.

THE SKIING

Like most ski resorts, Sugarloaf is influenced by its location and topography. The summit is above tree line and exposed to the elements; it can get downright cold and windy here. Because it's so far north, nearly hugging the Canadian border, the snow can come early and stay late here, making spring skiing a pleasure. But because the mountain is so big, it offers something for everyone. Experts can find their steeps and bumps, intermediates have cruisers to explore, and beginners can experience wide, mellow slopes of white.

Sugarloaf used to have a reputation for crowds, but the recent additions of two high-speed quads have changed that perception. There is a secret to Sugarloaf—it is called West Mountain. Underutilized, this is where to park to avoid the rush. The West Mountain double lift goes to Bullwinkle's, a mountain lodge with hot food—a good place to sneak into for an early or late snack or lunch. Beginners can warm up on Horseshoe to the West Mountain Trail, under the lift. Intermediates and experts can head down the Bucksaw Crosscut to Tote Road to the base and the rest of the 'Loaf.

Novices

Never-ever skiers start on the gentle, wide Birches Slope, between Sugarloaf Inn and the base lodge. Once you've progressed past beginner, you owe it to yourself to continue down Snowbrook Trail to the rest of the accommodations. There's a tunnel, and kids (both young and old) just love to ski through it.

The Skidway lift, a short double chair, gives green-circle skiers access to the Landing. From here the Double Chair East is your ticket to Boardwalk (nice and wide, but everyone is there) and Lower Winter's Way, narrower but fun. The first blue run you may want to try can be reached from the Whiffletree quad: Buckboard. Remember, there are always West Mountain and Lower Tote Road, too.

Intermediates

Go to the King Pine Bowl and stay there. Don't be fooled by the single black diamonds. Strong intermediates can revel on the wide, steep, well-groomed pitches of Haulbeck (half bumped up) and Rip Saw. Blue-square Ramdown and Boomauger are pleasures. Take the Whiffletree quad, ski down Tohaul, and ride the King Pine quad.

The addition of a high-speed quad at the base of the mountain has helped alleviate some of the lift lines. It also gives quick access to popular cruisers such as King's Landing and more challenging Hayburner and Upper Double Bitter. Also, Tote Road, which from the summit to the base is 3 miles long, is filled with ear-to-ear-grinning turns.

Later in the day, when the base quad gets busy, move over to the central corridor of the mountain. Take Spillway East for Lower Narrow Gauge, and Competition Hill, which are black-diamond zippers for advanced intermediates and experts. Get to Competition Hill early to avoid the Carrabasset Valley Academy racers. From the top of Spillway West, the Spillway Crosscut goes east to King Pine Bowl. Test your nerves by looking down. Choker is the place for first bumps. Don't forget Timberline quad, which goes to the top of the mountain. From it take the Timberline trail, an easy cruiser, which offers great views of the Crocker Mountains.

Experts

The summit beckons. The Snowfields are the only lift-served above-tree-line skiing in the East. Timberline will get you there. The supersteeps are here in the form of double-black diamonds. White Nitro (groomed), Bubble Cuffer (narrow and bumpy), and Powder Keg will teach you respect.

During seasons of abundant natural snow, experts can reach what's known as the backside, where there's no snowmaking. Hike up past the radio antenna and schuss down chutes, through trees, and over rocks. It's for experts only. Good bump runs are Skidder and those under the gondola line when they don't groom it.

The glades, scattered throughout the ski area, tantalize the adventuresome skier. They're not marked, so ask for assistance from instructors or ski patrolers. Max Headroom, between the Gondola Line and Upper Winter's Way, will test your nerve. Rookie River, just off the Lombard Crosscut, follows a frozen river.

SNOWBOARDING

Sugarloaf has one of the largest half-pipes in the country. It was redesigned and made more difficult in 1998 for competitions. Of Sugarloaf's two terrain parks, double-diamond Stomping Grounds, on the Peavy Crosscut, with 8 acres of tabletops, spines, rolls, and jumps designed by a boardercross racer, is for expert riders only. The Quarantine Zone, near the Whiffletree high-speed quad, is a tamer version of Stomping Grounds. **Beginner** boarders should head to Whiffletree quad for the Whiffletree and Buckboard trails. The Bucksaw lift takes boarders to several mellow trails, including Windrow and Horseshoe. Confident beginning boarders should check out Broccoli Garden glade at the top of the Whiffletree quad. **Intermediate** boarders can head to King Pine bowl. Haul Back and Ramdown will challenge you. The Swedish Fiddle Glade, just off King's Landing, introduces boarders to riding in the woods. Tote Road is a good cruiser for boarders. For **advanced** sliders, the snowfields present the greatest challenge on the mountain. In King Pine bowl, check out Misery Whip, narrow as a pencil, and Ripsaw, a winding, rolling trail

that ends with a headwall. Traveling around the mountain is easy, but keep up your speed on the cross-cuts, especially Spillway.

OTHER SNOW SPORTS

The resort features a 101-kilometer network of cross-country trails, guided snowshoeing treks, toboggan runs, and an ice-skating rink at its outdoor center (tel. 207/237–2000).

NEARBY

For a change of pace, try **Saddleback** (Box 490, Rangeley, 04970, tel. 207/864–5671). It's quieter, with varied terrain and wonderful views of the Rangeley Lake region and the White Mountains.

WHERE TO STAY

Accommodations at Sugarloaf are concentrated in three distinct areas. In and around the resort are some of the most architecturally pleasing, well-built, and stylish condos found at any eastern resort. Fourteen miles south on Route 27 is the pleasant little town of Kingfield, with a collection of smaller inns, motels, and B&Bs, while 7 miles north on Route 27 is the even smaller village of Stratton, where most of the inexpensive options are found. In general, you pay a premium for staying at the mountain, so if price is a consideration, the drive in either direction is worth the effort.

Expensive

Bigelows

These four-, five-, and six-bedroom units are five minutes from the Whiffletree quad. They are among the most spacious and luxurious units on the mountain. Each comes with a full kitchen, a fireplace, and a minimum of two baths.

The Commons
This property contains a selection of three-, four-, and five-bedroom triplex units, each with two or three full bathrooms, a completely equipped full-size kitchen, living and dining areas, a fireplace, and a deck. All have access to the slopes from the Snubber chair midstation.

Gondola Village
This is a four-story apartment building with a combination of standard hotel-size rooms with two queen-size beds and larger two-bedroom units with two bathrooms and a full kitchen. There are also one-bedroom and one-bedroom-with-loft units available. It's just behind the Whiffle-tree lift.

Grand Summit Resort Hotel
This six-story polychrome-brick hotel is the flagship of the resort. The building dominates the mountainside area with its gabled roof and stylish alpine look. Inside, the rooms have wood trim, pastel tones and accents, solid furnishings, and large windows. If you have a choice, go for the slope-side up-mountain views. Most rooms are well equipped with a queen-size bed, a sleeper sofa, a microwave, a wet bar, and a mini-refrigerator. *R.R. 1, Box 2299, Carrabassett Valley, 04947, tel. 207/237–2222 or 800/ 527–9879, fax 207/237–2874. 119 rooms. Facilities: restaurant, lounge, sauna, steam room, 2 indoor hot tubs, private ski locker room, library. AE, D, DC, MC, V. $100–$270.*

Inn on Winters Hill
This hilltop mansion overlooking the quaint community of Kingfield is a great alternative to staying at Sugarloaf. The turn-of-the-century Georgian Revival house has large rooms in the main building as well as in the attached carriage barn. The rooms are individually styled, with soft tones, period antiques, and vibrant quilts and curtains, plus grand furnishings such as bird's-eye maple beds, armoires, chests, and side tables. The entire establishment, including the magnificent wood-paneled, antique-laden lobby-lounge area and restaurant, has a warm and hospitable ambience. *R.R. 1, Box 1272, Kingfield, 04947, tel. 207/265–5421 or 800/ 233–9687, fax 207/265–5424. 4 rooms in main house, 16 rooms in carriage barn. Facilities: dining room, lounge, indoor hot tub and pool, recreation room, cross-country skiing, snowmobile rentals, dogsled rides. AE, MC, V. $76–$135.*

Snowbrook Village
By the Snubber chair, these one- and two-bedroom units (also available with loft) are furnished in a no-frills but comfortable manner. There is a full kitchen in all units, and some come with a fireplace.

Sugarloaf Condominiums
The hundreds of tastefully designed condos here are sited out of view of the access road, so you don't even realize the extent of the clusters until you drive to the north and east of the slopes. The condos east of the access road are served by the Snubber chairlift. Most units are similar in style, size, and furnishings. The only excep-

tions to this more-than-acceptable standard are the slightly more upscale units at the Village on the Green. All of the following rooms, condos, town houses, and duplexes are privately owned and managed by several different rental agencies. The foremost among these is the **Sugarloaf Mountain Corporation**; by renting through it you gain free access to the Sugarloaf Sports and Fitness Center on Mountainside Road in the midst of the condos. The center's facilities include an indoor pool, indoor and outdoor hot tubs, a sauna, a steam room, a Jacuzzi, and a 25-station fitness room. Adult ski lessons are also included in the price. *Sugarloaf Mountain Corp., R.R. 1, Box 5000, Carrabasset Valley 04947, tel. 207/237–2000 or 800/843–5623, fax 207/237–3052. 912 units. MC, V. $125–$1,226.*

If the sports center is not important to you or you don't mind paying $10 per day to use it, the alternate rental group, **Mountain Valley Property,** can provide up to 30% savings for the same units. *Mountain Valley Property, Box 281, Carrabassett Valley 04947, tel. 207/235–2560 or 800/435–7162, fax 207/235–2584. 100 units. AE, D, MC, V. $95–$453.*

Village on the Green
These duplexes are among the nicest units on the mountain. Their luxurious furnishings and stylish decor complement a spectacular view of the mountain from just off West Mountain Road. They come with either three or four bedrooms, two or three bathrooms, a full kitchen with high-quality appliances, a fireplace, and an attached garage.

Moderate

Herbert Hotel
This handsome three-story restored Beaux Arts–style building, constructed in 1918, is in historic downtown Kingfield. The rooms are furnished with antiques, some of which are the hotel's originals, and bright-colored quilts, area rugs, and drapes. All rooms come with private baths equipped with whirlpool tubs, and there's a variety of bed options, including double, twins, queen, and king. The lobby is a comfortable hangout, with a roaring fireplace, stuffed moose heads, and several laid-back dogs. *Main St., Kingfield, 04947, tel. 207/265–2000 or 800/843–4372, fax 207/265–4594. 33 rooms. Facilities: dining room, bar, hot tub, sauna. AE, D, DC, MC, V. $49–$164, including Continental breakfast.*

Spillover Motel
This modern two-story gray-wash motel is on the outskirts of Stratton some 10 minutes north of the mountain. Each unit has two double beds and enough space so four won't feel overly crowded. Rooms are tastefully decorated with no-nonsense furnishings and pleasing earth-tone colors. *Rte. 27, Box 427, Stratton, 04982, tel. 207/246–6571. 20 units. AE, MC, V. $62–$74, including Continental breakfast.*

Sugarloaf Inn
This inn was the first structure, built in 1960, to house skiers overnight on the mountain. Well located behind the Sawduster chair, it is just far enough away from the noise of the village. The rooms are not overly large, but guests have privileges at

the Sugarloaf Sports and Fitness Center. Also in the hotel is a large, comfortable lounge dominated by a giant brick fireplace and the slope-view Season's Restaurant. *Sugarloaf Mountain Corp., R.R. 1, Box 5000, Carrabassett Valley, 04947, tel. 207/237–2000 or 800/843–5623, fax 207/237–2000. 42 rooms. Facilities: restaurant, lounge. AE, MC, V. $120–$188.*

Three Stanley Avenue

This early 19th-century farmhouse is today a bed-and-breakfast run by the same folks who own one of the area's best restaurants—One Stanley Avenue—right next door. The rooms are cozy, comfortable, and decorated in a country Victorian motif, with period furnishings and collectibles, floral print curtains, and bright-colored handmade quilts. There are no TVs or telephones in the rooms. *Box 169, Kingfield, 04947, tel. 207/265–5541. 6 rooms, 3 with bath. Facilities: restaurant, lounge. AE, MC, V. $35–$60, including full breakfast.*

Inexpensive

Putts Place

Jim and Elaine Poitras are your hosts at this small but charming B&B, about 10 minutes from the mountain in nearby Stratton. The four rooms, all on the second floor, are cozy and snug, with plump featherbeds, colorful quilts, and handmade crafts and antiques. Rooms have either a double bed or two or three twins. Breakfast, which varies daily, consists of such homemade goodies as pumpkin-raisin or walnut bread, orange-flavor cream cheese, and French toast. After dinner there's a comfortable fireplace lounge, where you'll find assorted games and Elaine's ever-present jigsaw puzzle, which needs your contribution for its completion. *Rte. 27, 8 Main St., Stratton 04982, tel. 207/246–4181. 4 rooms. MC, V. $50, including full breakfast.*

Stratton Motel

This modest small motel has basic rooms, with two double beds and cable TV. There is also a condo that sleeps eight, with a full kitchen, a full bath, a living room, and a small dining room. *Main St., Rte. 27, Box 284, Stratton, 04982, tel. 207/246–4171. 5 rooms, 1 condo. Facilities: cross-country skiing, snowmobiling. AE, D, MC, V. $40–$95.*

Widow's Walk

This rambling Victorian bed-and-breakfast is on the National Register of Historic Places. Living up to its name, the hotel has a widow's walk and a three-story tower. Each room is artfully decorated with simple furnishings and bright bed covers and curtains. The comfortable living room has a fireplace and lots of plush, comfy chairs. Breakfast and a hearty dinner are served family style. *171 Main St., Box 150, Stratton, 04982, tel. 207/246–6901 or 800/943–6995. 6 rooms share 3 baths. Facilities: dining room, ski storage room, recreation room. MC, V. $48, including full breakfast; $5 per person additional for dinner.*

WHERE TO EAT

The resort and the nearby Kingfield and Stratton villages offer a small but varied assortment of restaurants. Overall, this is a fairly quiet night scene, with a lot of condo cooking and stay-at-home entertainment.

Expensive

Double Diamond

Before you head into the dining room, check out the spacious bar replete with antique sports equipment including sleighs, toboggans, golf clubs, and hockey gear. It's in contrast to the sumptuous, candlelighted, and carpeted dining room, where the menu offers honey-bourbon salmon filet, lamb brochettes, and fresh Maine haddock. *Mountain Village, Sugarloaf, tel. 207/237–2222. Reservations essential. D, MC, V.*

Herbert Hotel

This distinctive hotel has a cozy, comfortable dining room. To re-create a Gilded Era setting, the hotel installed two reproductions of 1910 Hunter ceiling fans with solid brass grape cluster cases and French crystal shades. The menu includes venison with a mushroom madeira sauce, haddock Olympia, and black bean cakes with cajun salsa. End the meal with bananas Foster or chocolate mocha mousse. *Main St., Kingfield 04947, tel. 207/265–2000 or 800/843–4372. AE, D, DC, MC, V.*

Julia's at the Inn on Winters Hill

This delightfully formal dining room is part of the Georgian Revival mansion that is now an inn. There are two dining rooms here, the Pink and Green rooms, both small and intimate. The Pink Room has a massive brick fireplace with a mirrored cherry-wood mantel and cherry and birch flooring. A set of wood-and-glass pocket doors separate it from the Green Room, which has the same exceptional woodwork and trim. The menu is a mix of Continental and con-temporary New England: beef tenderloin in a mushroom madeira sauce, blueberry-apple duck breast, and veal chambord. For dessert try Dessert Julia, a raspberry and Grand Marnier compote over homemade ice cream. *Inn on Winters Hill, Winters Hill Rd., Kingfield, tel. 207/265–5421. Reservations only. AE, D, MC, V.*

One Stanley Avenue

Set in a picturesque Victorian house, One Stanley Avenue offers what chef and owner Dan Davis calls classic Maine cuisine. The menu includes Maine mussels with dill dressing; roast duck with rhubarb, red wine, cinnamon, and lemon glaze; chicken with fiddlehead ferns and hemlock needles, and roasted rabbit smothered in raspberry sauce with sage butter. For dessert, try the blueberry and raspberry cream. *1 Stanley Ave., Kingfield, tel. 207/265–5541. Reservations essential. AE, MC, V. Closed Mon.*

Shucks

Check out the bar first at this restaurant because you won't find a more appealing view of adjacent Bigelow Range than through the full-size windows in the wide-open lounge. Then head for the private and more sedate dining room with its stylish wine-color and dark-wood ambience. Oysters are the order of the day, in every style, flavor, and fashion you can imagine. Go for the rack of lamb encrusted in baked rosemary and served with garlic-mashed potatoes. *Mountain Village West, Sugarloaf, tel. 207/237–2040. AE, MC, V.*

Moderate

Gepetto's

At this casual and lively spot, a large, U-shape bar separates the dining area from the lounge, and warm, woodsy decor welcomes you. The menu is large and varied, offering classic American favorites served in hearty portions. There are spare ribs, pork tenderloin, and teriyaki sirloin on the meat side of the menu; on the seafood side are fresh lobster and several other nightly fish specials; in addition, there are pastas and pizza. *Mountain Village West, Sugarloaf, tel. 207/237–2192. AE, MC, V.*

Hug's

This intimate Italian restaurant has simple country-cottage decor, with candlelight and historic photographs of Sugarloaf over the years on the walls. The menu reflects a careful home-cooked approach that goes with the familial ambience. For an appetizer try the artichoke hearts with fresh basil and romano. Pasta specialties include fettuccine with pink Alfredo sauce, agnolotti (rolled half-moon-shaped pasta filled with Romano cheese, pesto, and pink Alfredo sauce), and wild mushroom ravioli in walnut pesto or Alfredo sauce. Nightly veal specials include those cooked marsala, francese, and piccata styles. *Rte. 27, 1 mi from access road, Carrabassett Valley, tel. 207/237–2392. D, MC, V.*

Longfellow's

In a classic 1860s post-and-beam building on Main Street in Kingfield and filled with antiques of that era, this is a rustic and comfortable dining spot with a large and varied menu.

There's a heavy emphasis on chicken, with such choices as chicken Florentine or Cajun chicken (with sautéed onions and hot red peppers). There's an equally large list of fish entrées, including a three-cheese haddock, baked stuffed scallops, and a shrimp stir-fry. Pasta is not overlooked either, with a half dozen choices including linguine Parmesan and lasagna. *Main St., Kingfield, tel. 207/265–4394. AE, MC, V.*

Porter House

This restaurant in a restored 1908 farmhouse is well worth the 12-mile trip from the resort. The feel here is rustic, with wood stoves, hardwood floors, and a collection of antique postcards. But the food is modern–and terrific–with a menu that includes roast duckling, filet mignon, haddock, and, of course, porterhouse steaks. A plus is the outstanding wine list. *Route 27, Eustis, tel. 207/246–7932. MC, V.*

Season's

In the Sugarloaf Inn, this restaurant has a casual, family-friendly feel. Menu favorites are lobster, crab cakes, salmon, roast duck, and a great kid's menu. Check out the views of the mountain from the Greenhouse. *Sugarloaf Mountain Corp., R.R. 1, Box 5000, Carrabassett Valley, 04947, tel. 207/237–2000 or 800/843–5623. AE, D, V.*

Inexpensive

Bag and Kettle

A convenient position in the middle of the village makes this pub-restaurant a popular spot, but it's also a good dinner choice because of its prices and standard family faves from chicken to "bag burgers" (that is, take-out) to wood-fired brick-oven pizza. The restaurant also brews its own beer. The busy, bustling atmosphere is cheerful and friendly, and how many places offer a chance to read antique sheet music (which decorates the walls) while awaiting your meal? *Mountain Village, Sugarloaf, tel. 207/237–2451. AE, D, MC, V.*

Nostalgia Tavern
Busy and lively, this place is popular with locals for its hearty portions and thrifty prices. With an adjacent bar, including pool tables and video games, it's a tad on the noisy side as well. You go here for the family dining favorites, which include daily specials such as baked haddock, monster portions of grilled steak or chicken, and a peerless 16-ounce prime rib. *Rte. 27, Kingfield, tel. 207/265–2559. D, MC, V.*

White Wolf Inn Café
Good, standard Maine fare is served up here at reasonable prices, drawing a strong local clientele. A live white wolf (her name is Luna) greets diners, and a collection of wasps' nests (no longer active) decorates the wall. There's always a fish special and usually a game dish or two on the evolving menu, plus all the traditional standards from steak to pasta. It's a funky spot with a lot of character. *Main St., Stratton, tel. 207/246–2922. D, MC, V.*

Best Bets for Breakfast
Mainely Yours
At this classic diner, standard breakfast fare in hearty portions for a good price includes two eggs, bacon, home fries, and toast. On the healthier side

are a fresh fruit bowl and some great homemade breads (try the pumpkin) and muffins. *9 Main St., Stratton, tel. 207/246–2999. MC.*

Narrow Gauge Food Court
For a slope-side grab-and-go breakfast, this cafeteria is a good choice. The coffee is strong and varied, and there's a good lineup of muffins, sweet breads, and bagels. *Main base lodge, Sugarloaf, tel. 207/237–2000. MC, V.*

NIGHTLIFE AND ENTERTAINMENT
Après-Ski
Widowmaker Lounge
This is the hottest après-ski spot on the mountain, with a giant U-shaped bar, live entertainment, lots of promotional themes and giveaways, and a spirited crowd that thrives on the action. There are pool tables and a deck. *Main base lodge, Sugarloaf, tel. 207/237–2000. MC, V.*

Loud and Lively/Dancing
Judson's
This is a locals' bar where visiting skiers are also quite welcome. The old-fashioned decor includes skis and boots hanging on the walls and displays of bar mugs dating from the '20s. There are also TVs for sports fans and games for the action-oriented. *Rte. 27, Carrabassett Valley, tel. 207/235–2641. AE, MC, V.*

Shucks
A great view of the Bigelow Range makes this a must for an early end of the day; when the sun goes down, the appeal is in the multiple TVs that dominate this sports bar. *Mountain Village West, Sugarloaf, tel. 207/237–2040. AE, D, V.*

More Mellow

Bag and Kettle

This mellow tavern offers live entertainment on Monday night, usually in the form of local blues bands. The full bar features the restaurant's own microbrewed beer as well as a wide selection of beers from other local microbreweries. *Mountain Village, Sugarloaf, tel. 207/237–2451. AE, D, MC, V.*

Sugarloaf Brewing Company

This pub offers good microbrewed beer in a casual atmosphere. Be sure to try the delicious pale ale. There's live entertainment on Wednesday nights and good pub-style food. *R.R., Box 2268, Access Road, Carrabassett Valley, 04947, tel. 207/237-2211. MC, V.*

SUNDAY RIVER
SKI RESORT

Box 450
Bethel, ME 04217
Tel. 207/824-3000
www.sundayriver.com

STATISTICALLY SPEAKING

Base elevation: 800 feet

Summit elevation: 3,140 feet

Vertical drop: 2,340 feet

Skiable terrain: 654 acres

Number of trails: 126

Longest run: 3 miles

Lifts and capacity: 4 high-speed quads, 5 fixed quads, 4 triples, 2 doubles; 28,000 skiers per hour

Daily lift ticket: $47 weekdays, $49 weekends

Average annual snowfall: 155 inches

Number of skiing days 1997–1998: 184

Snowmaking: 491 acres, 91%

Terrain mix: N 25%, I 35%, E 40%

Snowboarding: 2 half-pipes, snowboard park, 3 playgrounds

Good snow and short lift lines—this simple formula has made Sunday River, a self-contained destination ski resort outside Bethel, Maine, a major force in eastern skiing. Moreover, there doesn't seem to be a year when Sunday River doesn't offer a major improvement.

In 1995–96, the resort added its eighth peak of skiing, Oz, which includes more than 40 acres of gladed terrain. The Jordan Grand Resort and Conference Center, which opened in 1998–99, and a planned base lodge for 1999–2000, will be the cornerstones of a new alpine village at Sunday River.

All this development is well thought out. Whenever the resort adds a new lift, it cuts new, wide trails. It has also added a train station, shopping, a movie theater, and more, to the town of Bethel.

Commercial skiing at Sunday River started in 1958 on Barker Mountain; it was then a local area with about 70 acres of skiing. Innovation, progressive thinking, and good fortune contributed to its success, and since it was purchased by Les Otten in 1980, Sunday River has had a streak of record ski seasons and expanded to more than 654 acres. It now encompasses eight peaks, three base lodges, one mountain lodge, 18 chairlifts, two slope-side hotels, a conference center, slope-side condominiums, a ski dorm, and town houses.

The resort has no main center of shopping, restaurants, and glitz. The three existing base lodges—Barker, White Cap, and South Ridge—provide all that skiers need. South is the hub, with guest services, the ski school, food, and rental shops. Barker has ticket sales, pay phones, more guest services, a lounge, and a ski shop, while White Cap has tickets, rentals, a cafeteria, and a pub.

That good snow mentioned earlier comes from one of the most powerful snowmaking systems in the country. More than 1,300 snow guns blanket the slopes, meaning snow comes early and stays late. It stays so late, in fact, that every May 1 is a free ski day at the mountain.

Children's services: day-care, tel. 207/824–3000; instruction, tel. 207/824–3000

Snow phone: tel. 207/824–5200

Medical center: Bethel Area Health Center, tel. 207/824–2193

Hospital: Stephens Memorial Hospital, tel. 207/743–5933

Police: tel. 207/743–8934

Chamber of Commerce: tel. 207/824–2282

Road conditions: tel. 207/774–8866

Towing: Autotech, tel. 207/824–3363; Gaudreau's Repair, tel. 207/824–2807

FIVE-STAR FAVORITES

Best run for vertical: White Heat

Best run overall: Shockwave

Best bar/nightclub: Suds Pub

Best hotel: Bethel Inn and Country Club

Best restaurant: Briar Lea

HOW TO GET THERE

By Plane

Portland International Airport (tel. 207/774–7301) is 75 minutes from the resort by car, and Boston's **Logan International Airport** is three hours away by car. (*See* Getting to Maine Resorts, *above.*)

By Car

From Boston take I–95 north to the Maine Turnpike; from Portland follow the turnpike north to Exit 11, Gray. Follow Route 26 north to the exit for Bethel and Sunday River. Sunday River Ski Resort is 6 miles north of Bethel, Maine, off U.S. Route 2E, in the town of Newry.

GETTING AROUND

A free shuttle, the **Trolley** (tel. 207/824–3000), makes the rounds through the resort every 20 minutes. **Bethel Express** (tel. 207/824–4646) provides taxi service.

THE SKIING

With eight peaks from which to choose (White Cap, Locke, Barker, Spruce, North, Aurora, Oz, and Jordan Bowl), this is a cruiser's delight. A relative newcomer to eastern skiing, Sunday River has had the luxury of carefully considering the way it cuts new trails. The result: many are wide, between 100 and 200 feet across, providing more space for skiers who don't like to be too close to the woods. Yet there are also classic steep and winding trails and challenging glades for experts, zingers for intermediates, and slow, gentle slopes for fledgling snow lovers.

Each peak has its own lift and trail network of at least four major runs, totaling 18 lifts and 126 trails. More advanced skiers can start from the less-congested Barker and White Cap lodges. Most families and beginners head to the South Ridge Lodge. At the South Ridge Learning Center, beginners learn to ride the lifts and glide down the hill. Sunday River believes so strongly in its learn-to-ski program that if it doesn't work for you, you get your money back. To avoid crowded slopes, which can be a problem at Sunday River, head to Aurora, Oz, or Jordan peaks.

Novices

The learning area at South Ridge is served by three lifts—the South Ridge Express detachable quad, the Fall Line double, and the South Ridge triple. Once up, beginners can choose from about a dozen ways down on such trails as Broadway, Double Dipper, and Easy Street.

You can then take the South Ridge Express to Lower Lazy River and catch the Sunday River Express lift to the top of Barker Mountain for a mellow time winding around the mountain on Three Mile Trail. Spruce Peak also offers a beginner run: the Spruce Peak triple takes you up to the playful Sirius, Aludra, and Light's Out combo. North Peak offers a pair of delights: Dreammaker itself eases down to the South Ridge base area, or you can take it to Ridge Run for a 1¼-mile run that will help you find muscles you didn't know you had. The rolling Lollapalooza, a 1½ mile run, winds along the outskirts of Jordan Bowl.

Often overlooked on White Cap is the green cruiser Moonstruck, off the White Cap quad. From the White Cap you can also take a good first blue run on Starlight.

Intermediates

A good, strong intermediate can attack every peak here. The Sunday River Express detachable quad, at the base of Barker Mountain, will be your focus. Get there at 8:30, avoid it at noon, and come back after 1:30. Barker Mountain is a blue-square delight, with the winding Lazy River and Ecstasy and the slightly steeper Sunday Punch. For some fun take Ecstasy to steep, slanting Cascades, on Locke Mountain. Off Cascades is a little-known but great trail—very consistent in pitch with nice rolls and turns—called Wildfire, in the Lower White Cap area. Although it says black diamond, Right Stuff, on Barker, is one of the easier of the difficult runs, which most strong intermediate skiers can handle.

Two premiere blue runs are the wide-cruising Risky Business and the long, wide American Express, on Spruce Peak, accessible from the Spruce Peak triple. North Peak, reached from the North Peak Express Quad, has several good intermediate runs: 3-D has bumps and a fairly steep upper section, while Grand Rapids is gentle. In Jordan Bowl, Rogue Angel and Excaliber are the longest blues on the mountain. Don't forget Aurora's Northern Lights—a scenic trail with continually changing pitches and rolls.

Experts

It's called the longest and steepest in the East and it's on White Cap: it is White Heat, a double black diamond with the White Heat quad overhead, making the embarrassment potential high if you don't know your stuff. The right side is groomed, and a strong advanced skier can make his or her way down. This is also a place to bail out, but be careful—it gets skied off toward the end of the day. The left side has huge bumps—experts only. Also on White Cap, Obsession is a more playful expert trail with curves and sweeps. Another White Cap special is Shockwave, a double-black that twists and widens out to a sudden drop. White Cap is also home to a pair of glades for experts—Chutzpah and Hard Ball.

Steep pitches mark a trio of trails at Barker Mountain—Right Stuff, Top Gun, and Agony—which you reach on the Sunday River Express detachable quad. For a challenge try Vortex, on Aurora. It's cut for southpaws, so right-handed skiers should make sure they know their stuff. Locke Mountain's T-2 was an old racing trail and goes right down the face of the hill. Between Barker and Spruce are some new glades known collectively as Last Tango.

On Oz, check out Emerald City and Flying Monkey, narrow trails dotted by trees. For a greater challenge, try the steep and woodsy Celestial on Aurora. And the truly expert skier should consider Spruce Cliffs, off Risky Business, a trail that's open only after big snowstorms: It's elemental skiing—a steep descent through trees and over rocks.

SNOWBOARDING

Sunday River has integrated snowboarding into the resort through an artful mix of playgrounds and terrain parks with its network of trails and glades. The snowboarding parks, halfpipes, minipipe, and playgrounds give boarders of all skill levels a variety of hips, ramps, spines, and tabletops to catch air from and refine their acrobatic moves. The Park, on the Starlight Trail off the White Cap quad, is for experienced riders. Who-ville, on the Express Lane in South Ridge, has smaller elements and is a good place to practice your tricks. The terrain playgrounds are off Spruce Peak Triple. Smackerels and Phat are both on the Risky Business trail. In 1998 a boardercross course opened for both skiers and boarders on Rocking Chair.

The resort's main half-pipe, off the Tempest, was recently lengthened to 450 feet. It is lit at night Wednesday through Sunday. A smaller pipe for novices is on South Ridge at the corner of Easy Street and Broadway. Both pipes are maintained with a state-of-the-art pipe dragon. Spruce Cliffs, open after a good dump of snow, is for only the most expert riders. Maintain your speed as you move from one mountain to the next, especially on Kanas and Roadrunner.

OTHER SNOW SPORTS

Other sports activities include **snowshoeing** trails, nighttime **tubing** and half-pipe snowboarding, and **ice-skating.** The Sunday River **Cross-Country** center on the Access Road offers 60 kilometers of trails for skiers of all levels.

NEARBY

The smaller **Mt. Abram** (Box 120, Locke Mills, 04255, tel. 207/875–5003) has night skiing.

WHERE TO STAY

Sunday River is fortunate. Although the rapid growth of the ski area has produced its share of condominium sprawl, it has been tempered by the presence of Bethel, Maine, just 7 miles from the resort. Despite its classic picture-postcard collection of quaint and tasteful Colonial architecture, Bethel is also a sturdy working town. It's here you'll find the real accommodation gems, plus a good selection of after-dark options. There are classic Colonial resort hotels, historic lodges, small inns, bed-and-breakfasts, and a variety of interesting independently owned hotels and motels within the town and its environs and along the highway between the town and the resort.

Most of the on-mountain accommodations are condos of indistinguishable appeal and among the higher-priced in the area, though the resort has added two slope-side, full-service hotels to the mix. If slope-side convenience is your choice (particularly for larger groups or families who want kitchen facilities), the prices vary according to ski-in/ski-out access and the newer units' frills, such as pools and hot tubs. You can make most arrangements through **Sunday River Central Reservations** (tel. 800/543–2854).

Expensive

Bethel Inn and Country Club

The Inn, the social high-water mark of the town, is smack in the middle of historic Bethel. Opened in 1913, it is a perfect rendering of the elegant Colonial, a white-and-yellow three-story mansion—clapboard, columns, and all. The traditional inn has been augmented by a small, stylish collection of new town houses, but the 200-acre property has softened the modern intrusion. The rooms in the inn come in three sizes, including suites, all tastefully done with country florals and calico prints, handmade quilts, and antique furnishings; some rooms and suites also have fireplaces. Standard rooms are quite small, but each has its cozy elegance. The condos are all two-bedroom layouts, complete with a full kitchen, a fireplace, and a washer-dryer. Furnishings are mostly well-crafted Colonial reproductions. *The Common, Bethel 04217, tel. 207/824–2175 or 800/654–0125,*

fax 207/824–2233. 57 rooms, 40 units. Facilities: dining room, pub, outdoor pool, hot tub, sauna, library. AE, D, DC, MC, V. $65–$180 per person, including full breakfast and dinner (in rooms).

Holidae House

Designed and built more than 100 years ago by a local lumber baron as his showcase, this Victorian house was the first in town to be electrified. Most of the first floor is common space, with a living room and a family room heated with a wood-burning stove; both rooms are furnished with antiques, Oriental rugs, and lace curtains. Wood abounds—flooring, wainscoting, staircases—and the rooms are filled with an astonishing collection of period antiques and well-crafted reproductions. The larger-than-average rooms come with queen-size beds and private baths. *Main St., Bethel 04217, tel. 207/824–3400 or 800/ 442–5826. 9 rooms. Facilities: breakfast room, whirlpools. AE, MC, V. $45– $150, including Continental breakfast.*

Jordan Grand Resort Hotel

The hotel is Sunday River's effort to spice up the lodging choices at the mountain. This upscale, full-service facility adjacent to the Lollapalooza trail has standard hotel rooms, suites, and penthouses that sleep 12. Most units have full kitchens. *Monkey Brook Road, Box 450, Bethel, 04217, tel. 207/824–5000 or 800/543–2854. 195 units. Facilities: 2 restaurants, heated outdoor pool, health club, game room, child care. AE, MC, V. $117– $840.*

Sunday River Condos

At Sunday River the eight buildings of

slope-side wood-stained condos are virtually indistinguishable in their barrackslike uniformity. Though aesthetically unappealing, they nonetheless provide good value for families and groups, are functional and comfortable, and eliminate the drive to and from the slopes each morning. Several of the buildings have their own built-in water-sport facilities, others have shared access, and most have ski-in/ski-out lift or slope access. The studio, one-, two-, and three-bedroom condos are all well maintained, clean, well equipped (with a kitchen), and functional in design and decor. If you have a choice when booking, note that condos on the South Ridge side have access to the novice trails, while those on the Whitecap side access only the intermediate and advanced trails. *Sunday River Ski Resort, Box 450, Bethel, 04217, tel. 207/824–3000 or 800/543–2754, fax 207/824–2111. 402 units. Facilities: restaurant, 3 outdoor pools, 2 indoor pools, 7 saunas, 6 hot tubs, laundry facilities. AE, D, DC, MC, V. $110–$400.*

Telemark Inn

Ten miles outside Bethel lies the secluded Telemark Inn, a gloriously restored Adirondack-style lodge nestled at the foot of Caribou Mountain. Inside it's a remarkable example of what money and fine carpenters and cabinetmakers could achieve at the turn of the century. The inn is filled with wood-paneled walls, Norway pine plank floors, and a trove of handcrafted furnishings carefully restored by owner Steve Crone. The rooms, filled with antiques and paintings, sleep four on beds piled high with handmade quilts. Dining is fam-

ily style at the 7-foot-diameter cherrywood dining table, and further relaxing is possible in the wood-fired sauna, on the natural skating rink, or swaddled in blankets on a sleigh pulled by Morgan draft horses. The Telemark offers 22 kilometers of groomed cross-country skiing trails. Its only drawback for serious alpine skiers might be the 15-mile drive to the resort, but for families or groups who want both alpine and cross-country skiing, it's a wonderful compromise. *R.F.D. 2, Box 800, Bethel 04217, tel. 207/836–2703. 6 rooms. Facilities: dining room, hot tub, ice-skating, dogsledding, skijoring. AE, MC, V. $110 per person, including full breakfast and dinner.*

The Victoria

This restored 19th-century house has 15 units, including four two-bedroom suites and a two-bedroom town house. It was owned by a Bethel cattle baron who used to drive his herds to Boston. The inn, decorated in Victorian style, is listed on Maine's Register of Historic Places. *32 Main St., Bethel, 04217, tel. 207/824–8060, or 888/774–1235. 15 units. Facilities: dining room. MC, V. $95–$350, including full breakfast.*

Moderate

L'Auberge Country Inn

This century-old building that was a barn, a theater, and a carriage house seems best suited to its present incarnation—as an intimate and elegant country inn. The rooms are large and light-filled, done in pastel tones with coordinated wall coverings and pine, beech, and birch antique furnishings. Guests can relax in the lobby common space, where there's a fireplace, a baby grand Steinway, and lots of reading material. *Mill Hill Rd., Box 21, Bethel, 04217, tel. 207/824–2774 or 800/760–2774. 5 rooms, 2 suites. Facilities: dining room. AE, D, MC, V. $75–$125.*

Norseman Inn and Motel
Just 5 miles from the ski area, the Norseman is a pleasantly comfortable and remarkably restored 200-year-old farmhouse and 100-year-old barn. The tasteful conversion from working farm to skier accommodations resulted in the creation in the old farmhouse of 10 B&B rooms (no TVs, some with shared baths) outfitted with antiques, while the barn has 22 more modern rooms, with private bath, queen-size beds, and cable TV. The rooms are bright and decorated in fresh, soft colors. There's also lots of comfortable common space, including a rug-strewn woody lobby with a fireplace, a piano, and a large-screen TV, where wine and cheese are served après-ski. *Rte. 2, 134 Mayville Rd., Bethel, 04217, tel. 207/824–2002. 32 rooms. Facilities: cross-country skiing. MC, V. $58–$98.*

Snow Cap Inn
They could do with a few more places like the Snow Cap Inn up at the mountain. It's a warm, rustic traditional ski lodge: nothing fancy, but aesthetically pleasing and a good alternative to the condo ghettos. This is a substantial log building with a large, woody lobby centered on a hand-carved tree trunk and a massive stone fireplace. The rooms are clean and comfortably decorated; each has two queen-size beds. The inn is a

good spot for couples rather than families, and it tends to draw a good number of forty-somethings. *Sunday River Rd., Box 450 R, Bethel 04217, tel. 207/824–7669 or 800/543–2754, fax 207/824–2111. 32 rooms. Facilities: games room, outdoor hot tub, Jacuzzi. AE, D, MC, V. $64–$69 per person, including Continental breakfast.*

Sudbury Inn
This all-purpose hospitality emporium is probably the best-known spot in town—thanks to the efforts of owners Cheri and Fuzzy Thurston and its location in the middle of Bethel. Built at the turn of the century when the railroad hit town, it's a stylish Victorian mansion with rooms and suites (and a carriage house with rooms), as well as an excellent restaurant and Sud's Pub, the hottest nightspot in town. The interior is a genuine study in Victoriana. The lobby is awash in chintz and floral wall coverings, Oriental rugs, velvet wingback chairs, original art, and fresh flowers; the rooms are filled with the antiques and fussy knickknacks of the period. It's a lively, friendly, well-run place with appeal for both families and couples. *151 Lower Main St., Bethel 04217, tel. 207/824–2174 or 800/395–7837, fax 207/824–2329. 17 rooms, 5 suites. Facilities: restaurant, pub. AE, MC, V. $95–$160, including full breakfast.*

Inexpensive
Chapman Inn
On the edge of the Bethel Common is one of the town's oldest buildings, with an odd collection of rooms, bunk beds, and efficiency apartments. The main house, with white-wood clap-

board and black shutters, built around 1865, has decent-size rooms that are clean, comfortable, and furnished with period and custom pieces. Next door, the former barn has sleeping space for 21 in three sets of bunk beds, dormitory style. Guests share two floors plus a common area with a game room, a TV, cooking facilities, and saunas. Also available in an adjacent building are suites in a one-, two-, or three-bedroom layout. *1 Mill Hill Rd., Box 206, Bethel 04217, tel. 207/824–2657 or 877/359–1498. 9 rooms, 5 with bath, 1 suite, 1 dorm. Facilities: 2 saunas. AE, D, MC, V. $25–$53 per person, including full breakfast.*

Douglass Place

The little gray-haired lady with a twinkle in her eye is exactly the type of proprietor you would expect to find at this homey traditional-style B&B. Barbara Douglass started the business in 1982. The cozy confines of this green-trimmed white Colonial- and Victorian-style house, built in the early 1800s, seem unchanged since the Douglass offspring occupied what are now the four guest rooms. The neat-as-a-pin house is filled with family antiques, memories, and memorabilia, and each room has little touches like handmade quilts, unique pieces of furniture, and colorful throw rugs. The rooms range in size from small, with single or twin beds, to larger, with one queen-size bed and a sofa; all are bright and cheery. Downstairs are a dining room, an indoor Jacuzzi, a pool table, a Ping-Pong table, and a piano where the occasional sing-along will break out. This quiet spot is about 4 miles from the resort. *162*

Mayville Rd., Bethel, 04217, tel. 207/824–2229. 4 rooms share 2 baths. AE. $60, including Continental breakfast.

Inn at Rostay

At this comfortable motel 4 miles from the resort both hot breakfasts and family-style dinners are served. Most rooms have a queen and a double or two double beds. There's also an efficiency in the main building. *186 Mayville Road, Bethel, 04217, tel. 207/824-3111 or 888-754-0072. 18 rooms. AE, D, MC, V. $40–$95, plus $5 per person for breakfast.*

Snow Cap Lodge and Ski Dorm

This excellent modern dormitory facility, simple and with a stained-wood exterior, has 200 bunk beds in rooms that sleep eight. The good-size rooms come with two separate bathroom facilities. Technically they are sex segregated, but four cozy couples can request their own mixed unit. The best room in the building is the more private Bus Drivers room, which has just one double bed. Common space is bright and clean, with three TVs, Ping-Pong tables, and laundry facilities. It stands about 500 yards from the South Ridge base lodge. Call well in advance, as groups love this place. *Sunday River Ski Area, Box 450, Bethel, 04217, tel. 207/824–2187 ext. 225 or 800/543–2754, fax 207/824–2111. 200 beds. Facilities: games room, laundry. AE, D, MC, V. $35 per person.*

WHERE TO EAT

There are numerous dining spots at the resort that will prove to be filling and adequate if you don't feel like taking the drive into Bethel, but the town itself has a much greater variety of restaurants, and it's well worth the effort to check them out.

Expensive

Bethel Inn Restaurant

This enormous formal dining room has a comfortable country feeling to it even though it's filled with elegant trappings such as brass chandeliers, a large fireplace, white linen tablecloths, fresh flowers, tabletop candles, and hand-painted plates. In the center a pianist plays soft classical music while you dine. The menu combines New England favorites—broiled lobster and broiled fresh swordfish—with Continental dishes such as scampi Milanaise (jumbo shrimp sautéed in garlic, chives, and white wine) and roast duckling glazed with a sweet and sour sauce. Other exceptional entrées include a 16-ounce portion of prime rib, broiled haddock with lemon-pepper seasoning, and Cajun-style broiled swordfish. *Bethel Inn, Broad St., the Common, Bethel, tel. 207/824–2175 or 800/654–0125. Reservations essential. AE, D, DC, MC, V.*

Briar Lea Restaurant

This restaurant reflects its New England heritage, but with bistro influences. Inside the 150-year-old restored Georgian house are antiques, exposed beams and columns, and wood floors. The eclectic menu includes everything from traditional lobster to pork loin medallions with peppered apples and onions, to sea scallops with a pine nut pesto sauce to chicken *au secours* (with prosciutto, garlic, and scallions in a red wine and cream sauce). For dessert, try the house specialty, a four-layer chocolate bourbon cake. *150 Mayville Rd., Bethel, tel. 207/824–4717. AE, MC, V.*

Sudbury Inn Restaurant

Just down the road from the Bethel Inn is the smaller but livelier Sudbury Inn, with its three-room restaurant. In true country-inn style, it comes with table linens, crystal and silver place settings, a crackling fireplace, and intimate table arrangements. The menu is a mixture of New England specialties, Continental favorites, and lighter bites such as stir-fries and even pizza. Try the roasted Maine lobster Sudbury, a shelled lobster roasted and served on a bed of fettuccine with cream sauce or an excellent scallopini of veal done with fresh spinach, sautéed shrimp, and béarnaise sauce. For dessert try any of the supremely decadent homemade desserts. *151 Lower Main St., Bethel, tel. 207/824–2174 or 800/395–7837. Reservations essential. AE, D, MC, V.*

The Victoria

Set in an 1895-era grand home, this establishment has three separate dining rooms—one with handpainted scenes of Venice and Rome. The restaurant is intimate yet casual with a menu that includes rack of lamb, seafood Alfredo, tenderloin *au poivre,* and raspberry roast duck. For dessert, treat yourself to the chocolate crème brulée. *32 Main St., Bethel, tel. 207/824–8060 or 888/774–1235. MC, V. Reservations essential. MC, V.*

Moderate

Madison

The Madison is some 14 miles east of the ski area, but it's worth the drive for some fine food and a delightful atmosphere. The dining room is built of modern mortise-and-tenon beams with intricate exposed trusses supporting the roof. The high end of the dining room is all glass and provides a serene view of the river and the snow-dappled trees, and the entire space is a trophy room documenting the owner's successful hunting ventures. The Madison is definitely noted for its meat—try the prime rib with all the trimmings or the rack of lamb baked with fresh rosemary and Dijon mustard. *Rte. 2, Rumford, tel. 207/364–7973 or 800/258–6234. Reservations essential. AE, D, DC, MC, V.*

Moose's Tale at the Sunday River Brewing Company

At the intersection of Route 2 and the Sunday River Access Road stands a shrine to brew pubs, with stainless steel tanks displayed behind a glass wall and back-reflected by mirrors. The huge bilevel space has interior trusses, no shortage of windows, a large moose head over the fieldstone fireplace, and a lively bistro atmosphere that spills over from the bar into the dining area. It's definitely casual, and so is the menu, with a sterling lineup of hearty fare that runs the gamut from straightforward bar and finger food, such as wings, burgers, and interesting sandwich combos, to entrées that include sirloin steak rubbed in hot Texas spices, seafood strudel, honey and grain mustard glazed salmon, and chicken marsala, plus pasta and the catch of the day. It's a cheerful spot, perfect for families. *1 Sunday River Rd., Bethel, tel. 207/824–4253. MC, V.*

Walsh and Hill Trading Company Restaurant

This Western lobster house, as legend would have us believe, was the cre-ation of J. P. Walsh, a Montana cattle-man, and Lillian Hill, a teacher from the woods of Maine. Evidently, as the menu explains, their torrid affair got them thrown out of Montana, where Lillian had gone to teach in a territory school. With her cowboy in tow, she returned to Maine, where they took up lobstering and cattle raising. Apoc-ryphal or not, the story gives a raison d'être to this steak and seafood empo-rium with its brass fixtures, dark wood, and gold-and-green decor. The menu offers a variety of steak cuts plus a large selection of seafood including fresh Maine lobster and grilled marinated shrimp. It's a cheer-ful, casual place and one of the few restaurants with a two-sided fireplace. *Fall Line Condominium Bldg., Sunday River Rd., Bethel, tel. 207/824–5067, ext. 396. Reservations essential. AE, D, DC, MC, V.*

Inexpensive

Bottle and Bag

This all-purpose restaurant and take-out deli is on Route 2 about halfway between the mountain and Bethel. The exterior is red barn-board siding, while inside is basic wood paneling with pine and oak fixtures. You can stop for pasta dishes or sandwich-and-soup combos, or pick up beer, wine, cold cuts, bread, and cheese to take home. This place opens at 5:30 for breakfast, and it's worth a stop just for their red flannel hash (cooked in beet juice). *Rte. 2, Bethel, tel. 207/824–3673. D, DC, MC, V.*

Breau's Pizza & Subs

You can't miss this pizza/ice cream parlor as you drive down Route 2 because the neon sign advertising the daily special will blind you. The pizzas come with a thick or thin crust and a wide variety of toppings; if you're really hungry, try the five-meat pizza: ground beef, pepperoni, ham, barbecued chicken, and salami, topped with two different cheeses. *Rte. 2 , Bethel, tel. 207/824–3192. D, MC, V.*

Sud's Pub
This is the best low-budget eatery in town because of its lively atmosphere and friendly, woody, pubby decor. The menu is huge, with a selection of bar and finger foods ranging from calamari to nachos to peel-and-eat shrimp, plus a good lineup of interesting soups and salads such as lobster gazpacho, shrimp and tomato salad, and tortellini and chicken salad. It also has huge hamburger and sandwich plates plus the best pizza in town. There's also a great selection of microbrewed beer. *Sudbury Inn, Lower Main St., Bethel, tel. 207/824–6558. AE, D, MC, V.*

Best Bet for Breakfast
Bethel Inn and Country Club
If you like to start your day with an elegant and refined breakfast, head here. There's white linen and crystal service in a serene environment with the full range of breakfast options, including standard egg dishes, fresh fruit, waffles, pancakes, and a great selection of fresh pastries and sweet breads. *The Common, Bethel, tel. 207/ 824–2175 or 800/654–0125. AE, D, MC, V.*

NIGHTLIFE AND ENTERTAINMENT
Après-Ski
Foggy Goggle Pub
The restaurant has good pub food and live entertainment, including acoustic and comedy acts. *South Ridge base lodge, Sunday River Rd., Newry, tel. 207/824–3000. AE, MC, V.*

Loud and Lively/Dancing
Bumps! Pub
This is Sunday River's nightclub, where rock and country bands perform during ski season. It also has good pub food, including pizza, nachos, and potato skins. *White Cap base lodge, Sunday River Road, Newry, tel. 207/824–5269. AE, MC, V.*

Sud's Pub
In this cheerful pub there's live entertainment nightly, including acoustic groups and rock bands. *Sudbury Inn, Lower Main St., Bethel, tel. 207/824– 6558. AE, D, MC, V.*

Sunday River Brewing Company
On weekends you can dance to live band music on the small dance floor. *1 Sunday River Rd., Bethel, tel. 207/ 824–4253. AE, MC, V.*

T he sweeping ranchland, the broad river-washed valleys, the thick, rich forests, and the string of crowning mountain ranges of Montana all have one thing in common: lack of people. As one of the least-populated states in the United States, Montana is a vast, expansive tableau of natural attributes made all the more dramatic by the absence of a smothering population. Wildlife is still the master of this domain—deer, elk, moose, bears, eagles, and buffalo all comfortably thrive on millions of acres of protected wilderness, including the ecosystem of the greater Yellowstone Park area. The state is sliced by an extension of the Canadian Rockies from north to south. More than 50 mountain ranges form this rugged wall, with the tallest peaks topping 12,000 feet.

This is also, along with Wyoming, the classic cowboy state, with the touch and easy independence of the American cowboy manifesting itself in the pure and empty wilderness of a state that some call "the last best place." The images reinforce this. Ranches outnumber shopping malls, horses are more common than four-wheel-drive vehicles, Stetsons are more functional than decorative, and cows outnumber people 4 to 1. You make your mark here with substance not sizzle; and the stoicism inherent in individualism is tempered by an effusive enjoyment of the state's most precious resource—the land.

The modern counterpoint to all this is the state's ski resorts. Isolated peaks that hum with modernity, they are beacons of commerce that rely on the resources of nature to attract skiers who prefer the northern lights dancing in the night sky to the light show of a trendy nightspot. The largest of these resorts is Big Sky, in the southwest corner of the state adjacent to the 3-million-acre Spanish Peaks Wilderness area. Big Sky's long-standing appeal lies in its unhurried pace and uncrowded skiing, but it also has taken bold steps in development. A single-span tram lift to the top of 11,166-foot Lone Mountain, opened in 1995, gives Big Sky one of the greatest vertical drops in the United States—4,180 feet.

BIG SKY RESORT

Box 160001
1 Lone Mountain Trail
Big Sky, MT 59716
Tel. 406/995–5000 or
800/548–4486
www.bigskyresort.com

STATISTICALLY SPEAKING

Base elevation: 6,970 feet

Summit elevation: 11,166 feet

Vertical drop: 4,180 feet

Skiable terrain: 3,500 acres

Number of trails: 78

Longest run: 6 miles

Lifts and capacity: 1 tram,
1 gondola, 1 quad, 3 high-
speed quads, 3 doubles,
3 triples, 4 surface; 18,000
skiers per hour

Daily lift ticket: $48

Average annual snowfall: 400
inches

Number of skiing days
1997–98: 150

Snowmaking: 400 acres, 11%

Terrain mix: N 10%, I 47%,
E 43%

Snowboarding: yes

It's hard to compare Big Sky with any of the other 29 resorts in this book. It is indeed unique—as unique as the state of Montana itself. Big Sky is an unaffected major-league resort perched at the base of Lone Mountain, a perfect pyramid of a peak halfway between Bozeman and Yellowstone National Park—in the middle of nowhere.

Of course, that's part of its uniqueness. Surrounded by 10,000 acres of spectacular wilderness acquired in the early '70s by the late NBC newscaster Chet Huntley and his partners, Big Sky is a wide-open and gloriously scenic resort where spotting a golden eagle in flight is more exciting than catching a fleeting glimpse of a celebrity. Notwithstanding the 170,000-acre spread owned by Ted Turner and Jane Fonda over in the next valley, there's considerably more wildlife than star life at Big Sky. Buffalo still roam in the wild valleys, elk and moose slide easily through the woods, and ranches are more common than alpine chalets.

You roll up to Big Sky through a broad plateau gently rising from the Gallatin Canyon that slices through the Madison Range of the Rocky Mountains. Immediately to the north is the Spanish Peaks Wilderness Area; just to the south lies the western border of Yellowstone National Park. Combined, these two vast areas surround the resort of Big Sky with more than 3 million acres of pristine wilderness dramatically accented with a parade of peaks that top the 11,000-foot mark.

This riveting tableau of mountains and sky reduces the resort to a speck in the distance, and when you arrive, you see that the mountain village stands in harmonious balance with the surrounding wilderness, rolling ranch lands, and rugged forested foothills. It's an American classic, with clean lines and simple designs, free of both the Swiss and Austrian kitsch and the fake cowboy facades that crop up in so many other Western resorts. There's no need to import a back-to-nature wilderness theme either, for Big Sky is surrounded by the real thing.

The mountainside development, though prosaic in patches, is reasonably well laid out, its sturdy stone-and-beam buildings tucked into knolls, perched on the edge of streams, or surrounded by trees. The

FIVE-STAR FAVORITES
Best run for vertical: Little Rock Tongue

Best run overall: Elk Park Ridge

Best bar/nightclub: Half Moon Saloon

Best hotel: Buck's T-4

Best restaurant: Rocco's

heart of the Mountain Village is the combination of Huntley Lodge, Yellowstone Conference Center, and Shoshone condominiums, all adjacent to the Mountain Mall complex, an open, double-deck structure with elaborate ironwork that gives it a galleria feeling. It's the center of activity during the day, and after dark the numerous restaurants and bars— including those in the adjacent Huntley Lodge—are about the only nightlife happening at the ski-base area of Big Sky.

Spread out around this are the various condominium complexes. Although the first wave of condos built in the '70s look a bit dated and blandly uniform now, the new ones, such as Arrowhead and Shoshone, are striking stone-and-wood structures that should set the standard for future building.

The Mountain Village offers a total of about 2,100 beds, most within walking distance of the Village Mall and the base-area lifts. Six miles away at the bottom of Big Sky Road is Meadow Village, a subdivision with private homes, condominium buildings, restaurants, and shops. It's much more spread out than the Mountain Village, so you really need a car to get around, but the accommodations here are also considerably less expensive. There is another patchwork collection of small hotels and motels north of Meadow Village and down the Gallatin Canyon, and you'll also find some more nightlife options here. Unlike Steamboat or Crested Butte, Big Sky has no quaint restored Victorian town to focus it: there's just the Mountain Village, the lower Meadow Village, and the scattering of hotels and restaurants down the Gallatin Canyon. This is a quiet resort, more a place where you come to get away from it all than to end up in the middle of it all (though it does have some entertaining diversions and knock-'em-down bars). This is not a resort that attracts an uptown crowd with attitude. It's a resort for those who want a low-key wilderness experience and who like the pace and price of a mountainside village that has not become smothered in glitz. And if you want to take a day off from skiing, there are plenty of other snow-related activities available. Snowshoeing, dogsledding, sleigh riding, horseback riding, snowmobiling, and snow-coach tours of Yellowstone National Park are worthy diversions.

HOW TO GET THERE

By Plane
Gallatin Field, in Bozeman, Montana, 45 miles north of Big Sky, is the nearest airport. **Delta** and **Skywest** (tel. 406/388–4021 or 800/221–1212), **Northwest** (tel. 406/388–4202 or 800/225–2525) and **Horizon** (tel. 406/388–1733 or 800/547–9308) have daily scheduled flights from Salt Lake City, Minneapolis/St. Paul, and Seattle, respectively.

Shuttle Service
4 × 4 Stage (tel. 406/388–6404 or 800/517–8243) has a shuttle bus meeting all flights into Bozeman; the one-hour drive to Big Sky costs $36.50 round-trip. **Mountain Taxi** (tel. 406/995–4895) runs cabs between the airport and the resort for about $130 round-trip for four people and equipment.

By Car
From Bozeman take Route 191 south 45 miles to the turnoff to Big Sky. The resort is 45 miles north of West Yellowstone on Route 191.

The following major car-rental companies have outlets at Gallatin Field, in Bozeman: **Avis** (tel. 406/388–6414), **Budget** (tel. 406/388–4091), **Hertz** (tel. 406/388–6939), and **National** (tel. 406/388–6694). **Thrifty, Enterprise,** and **Dollar** also have outlets close to the airport.

By Bus
The nearest **Greyhound** (tel. 406/587–3110 or 800/231–2222) bus station is in Bozeman.

By Helicopter
Helicopter landing areas are available in the Mountain Village (upper) and Meadow Village (lower) areas of the resort. You must obtain prior permission if you want to do any helicopter skiing on Lone Mountain.

GETTING AROUND
A car is definitely an asset at Big Sky because it allows you the flexibility and freedom to move back and forth from the mountain to the valley and the surrounding environs. If, however, you plan to bunk down in the village and make only the occasional foray down to the valley (5 miles), you can use the free **Snow Express** (tel. 406/995–5000) shuttle bus, which runs in several loops (around the village, the meadow, and the valley) and includes stops at individual accommodations, restaurants, resorts, and nightspots. The service runs from 7 AM (9 AM if the overnight temperature goes below –20°) to 11 PM, so even if you have a car, it's a good alternative if you plan to sip a few suds. If you miss the last bus or are feeling flush, taxi service is available (see How to Get There, above).

THE SKIING
The skiing at Big Sky takes place on two peaks. To the left of the base area is Andesite Mountain, an 8,800-foot three-sided peak of mostly intermediate terrain; to the right is Lone Mountain, the 11,166-foot Fuji-like cone that has both some of the toughest and some of the easiest runs at the resort. Whichever mountain you choose, you won't lack for long, wide-open cruising. That's the hallmark of Big Sky, and the abundance of these

runs has given the area a reputation as strictly an intermediate mountain. In fact, there's plenty of steep and rugged skiing in the above–tree-line bowls off the Lone Peak triple chair, and the immense amount of terrain served by the new Lone Peak tram is a playground for experts only. The Challenger chair serves some gulp-and-go double-black pitches as well as some outrageous glade skiing. For even more challenge, check out the ultrasteep wide-open bowl of the South Wall area and the ridge of the Pinnacles area, which has some of the steepest terrain on the mountain. Still, intermediates are the core group at Big Sky, and the runs are groomed to reflect that sit-back-and-let-them-run comfort zone. You can't get much closer to intermediate heaven than on the middle section of the massive upper bowl, served by the Lone Peak Triple. This is a wondrous expanse of intermediate bowl skiing with a combination of marked runs and seek-a-way-down options.

The major lifts, including the gondola, all originate from the Mountain Village, so it's easy to move back and forth between the two mountains to meet up with friends as well as follow the sun as it moves from Lone Mountain to Andesite Mountain. With short lift lines and fast lifts, it's easy to rack up impressive vertical. You may be cruising, but you'll also be working.

Novices

If you are a never-ever or raw novice, you'll need to start on your own lift, the Explorer, a double chair that serves the green runs on the lower part of Lone Mountain. It's just a short shuffle from the Mountain Mall area and away from the more heavily trafficked gondola loading areas. White's Wing is a good place to start. Turn right off the chair, and you'll find this deliciously wide, smooth carpet curving naturally back down to the bottom of the lift. There are no cutoffs and no surprises.

Warm up on that for a few runs and then turn left off the chair and head for Mr. K., a slightly narrower, teensy bit steeper run with the occasional roll and swell. Your third choice off this lift is Lone Wolf, directly under the chair, a relatively straight shot that will let you experiment with some speed. When you are ready for a longer run, take Gondola 1 to the top. Lower Morning Star and Mr. K are the only green runs down from this point. Turn right off the chair and follow the sign for the upper part of Mr. K. It starts out a little narrower and slightly steeper than the lower runs, but with some steady snow plow turns you should be able to work your way through this and then spread out a little about a third of the way down.

If you are heading back to the gondola and want to try some blue terrain, cut right on Marmot Meadows, which starts out green, then turns blue for a short stretch as it leads back to the base.

The other exclusively green area at the resort is the series of long runs on the south face of Andesite Mountain. To get to them, take the Ramcharger quad and then ski down toward the top of the Southern Comfort triple chair. Three runs snake down this flank with a moderate pitch that incorporates some interesting rolls and modest drop-offs. Deep South and Sacajawea are the narrowest, curving gracefully through the trees, while El Dorado runs wider and steeper right under the chair.

From here you can also take a stab at some blue runs when you are ready. Ponderosa, to the right off the Southern Comfort triple, is a medium-grade intermediate, steeper than you might be used to, but wide, groomed, and smooth, with a long green runoff section near the bottom. Keep in mind that if you want to return to the main base area from the top of Andesite, you'll be on moderately intermediate terrain all the way. Africa is the most direct, but it is narrow and steep. Hangmans is not quite as steep, and it's definitely wider. The easiest route back is on Pacifier, a wide, gentle trail that meets up with Africa close to the bottom, past most of its pitch.

Intermediates

This is really your mountain. Almost 50% of the runs are marked blue, and if you enjoy wide-open giant slalom–style cruising on well-groomed slopes, Big Sky is ideal. Start the day either by riding Gondola 1 and then skiing down Crazy Horse or by riding the Swift Current Express chair (twice as fast as the gondola) and skiing Lobo Meadows. Both are well-pitched warm-up runs with some good pace and lots of rolls; true, you'll hit some moguls if you ski down the left side of Lobo, but overall these are a good taste of the resort's renowned cruising runs.

Calamity Jane, reached from either gondola, is another good blue challenge, a little steeper, with some mellow bumps to warm the legs and a steep optional cutoff called Huntley Hollow. If you want to try the bowls,

it's best to get up there around mid-morning on a sunny day. The Lone Peak triple, down and to the right of the gondolas, takes you up to about 1,000 feet below the 11,166-foot summit, and from up there a vast expanse of steep intermediate bowl skiing lies before you. The two marked trails, Never Sweat and Upper Morning Star, are the easiest ways down the bowl because they tend to be well traveled, but once you gain some confidence, experiment a little. Slide across the bowl, pick fresh snow, or tackle a steep pitch: this is free-form bowl skiing, and the routes down are limited only by your imagination.

After lunch the sun moves over to Andesite Mountain, and you can rack up some impressive mileage by riding the Ramcharger quad and skiing the long, blue cruisers on that face. Hangmans is a good place to start (see Novices, above). By turning left off the chair, you can head down upper Silverknife, a long cruiser to the bottom that offers several options, such as the steep mogul pitches of south and north Ambush or the lightly gladed Meadows area. You can also split to the right at the intersection with Elk Park Ridge about halfway down and head for the Elk Park Meadows, a wide expanse of ungroomed glades that takes you to the bottom of the Thunder Wolf quad.

If you still have spring in your legs and want to try a few black runs, there are a half dozen short, steep shots on either side of the chair. Broken Arrow and Mad Wolf, never groomed, are great leg-burning, endless mogul runs. Crazy Raven and Snakepit are shorter but steeper. You can also continue with wide-open cruising from the top of the Thunder Wolf chair by heading down Big Horn, a long, looping boulevard, or by heading back over to the blue runs served by the Ramcharger chair.

Experts

The trail map identifies 43% of Big Sky's 3,500 acres as expert terrain, so you won't lack for excitement. Although there are a number of challenging bump runs and steep pitches on Andesite Mountain and on the lower half of Lone Mountain, the real action is at the top of the 11,166-foot Lone Peak Tram. Riding the tram to Lone Peak is itself breathtaking. Once at the top, skiers who aren't up for double-black-diamond terrain can ride the tram down to the midway point. Experts can choose from the terrain offered by the south face and slopes above the bowl, including the Big Couloir, a steep, narrow chute directly under the tram. This is serious stuff: you are required to ski with a partner, have an avalanche transceiver and shovel, and sign in with the ski patrol. If you are an adventurous intermediate and don't want to ride the tram back down, a breathtaking run down the moderately pitched and wide-open Liberty Bowl on the south side of Lone Peak should boost your ego.

For less hair-raising but still keep-on-your-toes skiing, stick to the bowl on either side of the Lone Peak triple. To the left of this lift is the South Wall, an ultrasteep, craggy expanse that combines vertical thrill with heads-up skiing. To the far right of the Lone Peak chair is the Challenger chair, an experts-only lift that rises to a sharp ridge in the midst of double-black territory. Immediately under the lift are Little Rock Tongue and Big Rock Tongue, two tough couloirs that are brutally steep and gloriously wild, with narrow chutes, scattered glades, deep snow, and cliffs. On the far side of the same ridge is the Nashville Bowl, a natural north-facing snow trap where the mode is full-bore powder blasting in the open areas and in the patches of glades.

At the top of the Challenger lift is a rope tow up to the craggy area known as the Pinnacles (note that the tow, used by the ski patrol to reach areas for avalanche blasting, is not always open). Here you'll find some steep, narrow, and tree-stuffed chutes; or if that's not good enough, you can hike (for about 15 minutes) farther up the ridge to the A–Z Chutes, a collection of radical pitches—narrow and rocky—that attract the resort's extreme-skier brigade. If this sounds tempting, try to take a local skier along for company.

SNOWBOARDING

Big Sky is a snowboarder's paradise, catering to every rider from experienced freestylers and free riders to first-timers. If it's your first time on a board, the Explorer lift offers great beginning terrain: wide, uncrowded trails with gentle pitches. Try Lone Wolf or White's Wing until you get the hang of it, and then you should be ready to take the Swiftcurrent chair farther up the mountain. Big Sky's state-of-the-art terrain park has a half-pipe, hits, banked turns, and kickers. The pipe itself is 400 feet long and 50 feet wide, with 12-foot walls, as well as its own inter-park rope tow and a stereo system. To get to the half-pipe, take the Ramcharger chair from the base and head left to the North Ambush run. The Lone Peak triple chair and tram, the Challenger chair, and the Shedhorn lift all offer steeps, glades, airs, and wide-open bowls for the experienced rider. Going to the top of Lone Peak and cruising down the powder-filled Liberty Bowl is a local favorite. Some of the best tree riding can be found in Kurt's Glades and Moonlight by the Challenger lift. If you feel daring enough to drop a few cliffs on a powder day, Challenger's Big and Little Rock Tongue, Moonlight, and the bowl under the Lone Peak triple offer endless possibilities for big air.

NEARBY

Bridger Bowl (15795 Bridger Canyon Rd., Bozeman, tel. 406/586–1518 or 800/223–9609), 16 miles north of Bozeman, offers skiers and snowboarders a chance to ride a medium-size, local mountain that receives 350 inches of snow every year. Bridger has a variety of terrain to suit every level of skier and is known for its short lift lines, good snow, and friendly atmosphere.

WHERE TO STAY

Most skiers at Big Sky stay in condos in one of three distinct areas. The units at the Mountain Village tend to be the newest and the most expensive, while the lower Meadow Village, 15 minutes from the slopes, offers more moderate (in price and decor) units. There is a range of smaller and/or more unusual accommodations down the Gallatin Canyon, between the entrance to the resort

and a point about 7 miles down the highway. When you're weighing the options, keep in mind that a regular shuttle bus links the lower Meadow Village and environs to the mountain. Almost all condos are individually owned, which has two effects on the accommodation available: first, only a portion of units at a complex may be for rent at any given time, and second, interior design in adjoining units can vary from art deco to rustic Southwestern to drab and dreary. When completed in the summer of 2000, the 10-story Summit Hotel Condominium will dramatically change the Mountain Village. The ski-in, ski-out, full-service hotel will offer 98 condominiums with one-, two-, and three-bedroom suites and have the capability of locking off to 222 hotel rooms. It will also have underground parking, two levels of shopping and dining, and eight two-story luxury penthouses. Two companies manage most of the condominium properties: Golden Eagle Property Management (Box 160008, Big Sky 59716, tel. 406/995–4800 or 800/548–4488) handles the majority of the properties in the Meadow Village area, while Triple Creek Realty & Management (Box 160219, Big Sky 59716, tel. 406/995–4848 or 800/548–4632) deals with the Mountain Village properties.

Expensive

Arrowhead
These freestanding chalets at the bottom of the Silver Knife Run are all three-level luxury dwellings, each with three or four bedrooms, on a pleasant, tree-surrounded hillside.

The pastel-and-wheat-colored Southwestern furnishings are not quite as elegant or distinctive as those in the Beaverhead condominiums (see below), but you do get lots of space: large bedrooms, including a master bedroom with a king-size bed and Jacuzzi, and more than ample living and dining areas. The kitchen is both big and well equipped, and the living room has a stone fireplace. Guests can use the health spa facilities at the Huntley Lodge *(see below)*. *1 Lone Mountain Trail, Box 160001, Big Sky 59716, tel. 406/995–5000 or 800/ 548–4486, fax 406/995–5001. 23 units. AE, D, DC, MC, V. $393–$578.*

Beaverhead

These large, luxurious two- to four-bedroom units in a private little town house–style enclave are among the nicest on the mountain, with the added bonus of ski-in/ski-out access on the White's Wing beginner run. They all have vaulted cedar-lined ceilings, large floor-to-ceiling stone fireplaces, and a split-level living room/dining room area. You can really spread out in the full-size kitchen and breakfast nook. Guests have access to the Huntley Lodge facilities. *1 Lone Mountain Trail, Box 160001, Big Sky 59716, tel. 406/995– 5000 or 800/548–4486, fax 406/995– 5001. 48 units. Facilities: washer-dryer, private garage. AE, D, DC, MC, V. $362–$859.*

Lone Mountain Ranch

This marvelously preserved 1915 working ranch is a self-contained cross-country skiing resort with a 65-kilometer trail network. It's linked by a regular shuttle to Big Sky, 5 miles away. The log cabins, nestled in the pines on either side of a brook, accommodate from 2 to 10 people amid polished wood, bright Native American fabrics, antiques, and eiderdown. All that's lacking are telephones, TVs, and radios. In the Ridgetop Lodge, each of the six guest rooms has a king-size and a single bed and is decorated in traditional lodgepole-pine furniture and handmade quilts. The restaurant *(see Where to Eat, below)* serves outstanding food. A seven-night minimum stay is requested. The package includes all meals plus a sleigh-ride dinner, cross-country or two days of downhill skiing, and evening programs. *Lone Mountain Access Rd., Box 160069, Big Sky 59716, tel. 406/995–4644 or 800/514–4644, fax 406/995–4670. 24 cabins, 6 rooms. Facilities: restaurant, bar, 2 outdoor hot tubs, rental shop, massage service. D, MC, V. $1,250–$1,600 (per 7-day week, MAP).*

Shoshone Condominiums

These condos, connected to the Huntley Lodge, are in a great ski-in/ski-out location. The units, with one bedroom or one bedroom with loft, are smart, upscale, and well designed, with first-class furnishings and a pleasant sand-and-wheat-color decor that includes lots of wood trim, textured wall coverings, Berber carpeting, and natural finishes. Spacious common areas have deep couches and a gas fireplace, and the kitchens are full-size. Guests have use of the Shoshone Health Center (heated outdoor pool, saunas, hot tubs, and exercise gym). *1 Lone Mountain Trail, Box 160001, Big Sky 59716, tel. 406/995–5000 or 800/548–4486,* fax 406/995–5001. 94 units. AE, D, DC, MC, V. $264–$554.

Snowcrest

Regarded as the finest slope-side lodging in the Mountain Village, the Snowcrest Lodge has elegantly furnished units that offer privacy in the heart of the action and accommodate up to 10 people each. The two- and three-bedroom upscale lofts have three baths, full kitchens with separate living and dining areas, stone fireplaces, laundry equipment, and private balconies with outdoor hot tubs. The interiors are artistic with vaulted ceilings, tile floors, leather furniture, and wood accents. The magnificent stone-and-wood building, directly at the base of the ski area, also houses skier services, the rental shop, the ski school, cafés, and shops downstairs. *1 Lone Mountain Trail, Box 160001, Big Sky 59716, tel. 406/ 995–5000 or 800/548–4486, fax 406/ 995–5001. 4 units. AE, D, DC, MC, V. $568–$938.*

Moderate

Big Horn Condominiums

These duplex condos have ski-in/ski-out access on their own poma lift to the Silver Knife trail. The units all have three bedrooms, so they are perfect for large groups. They are bright, with contemporary furnishings and muted tones—not upscale-designer fancy but more than comfortable, with a large central stone fireplace, a full kitchen, a dining room, and three bathrooms. *1 Lone Mountain Trail, Box 160001, Big Sky 59716, tel. 406/995–5000 or 800/ 548–4486, fax 406/995–5001. 48 units. Facilities: washer-dryer, private garage. AE, D, DC, MC, V. $378–$556.*

Buck's T-4

Despite the Best Western sign over the front entrance, Buck's is an authentic Big Sky institution, with big rooms, two restaurants, and a lounge. Originally built as a lodge for local hunters, it has expanded into a sprawling hospitality complex. The three-story main building is finished in light-brown log siding with a dark-brown trim. A wooded hill rises directly behind the hotel, and to one side there's an equestrian center where horses graze on open pastures. Room decor runs to rich colors, country floral bedcovers, and solid, well-made furnishings. *U.S. 191, 1½ mi south of Big Sky entrance, Box 160279, Big Sky 59716, tel. 406/ 995–4111 or 800/822–4484, fax 406/ 995–2191. 72 rooms, 2 suites. Facilities: 2 restaurants, bar, 2 outdoor hot tubs. AE, D, DC, MC, V. $91–$328, including daily lift tickets.*

Huntley Lodge

This is the only full-service hotel at the resort, and it's right in the heart of the Mountain Village, with ski-in/ski-out access to the slopes and direct connection to the Shoshone condominium complex and the Yellowstone Conference Center. The large multi-story building has a stone-and-wood lobby with big-game trophies, elk-antler chandeliers, and numerous fireplaces and sitting areas. The rooms are freshly decorated in peach and wheat tones, with Colonial reproductions and a small wet bar/fridge; the larger rooms have sleeping lofts and accommodate up to six. *1 Lone Mountain Trail, Box 160001, Big Sky 59716, tel. 406/995–5000 or 800/548–4486, fax 406/995–5001. 204 rooms. Facilities: restaurant, bar, pool, 2 outdoor* *hot tubs, exercise room, sauna. AE, D, DC, MC, V. $160–$262.*

Saddle Ridge Townhomes
These cozy, elegant condos provide isolation from Mountain Village combined with ski-in, ski-out convenience. In the Moonlight Basin on the north side of the resort at the base of the Iron Horse lift, the three-story units are bright, open, and nicely furnished in a classic Montana style. The two- and three-bedroom lofts have 2 baths, full kitchens, dining rooms, stone fireplaces, laundry facilities, and private outdoor hot tubs and can accommodate up to 10 people. The view from Saddle Ridge is breathtaking: Lone Peak to the west and the Spanish Peaks to the north. It's useful to have your own wheels here, although the Snow Express makes regular stops. *1 Lone Mountain Trail, Box 160001, Big Sky 59716, tel. 406/995–5000 or 800/ 548–4486, fax 406/995–5001. 85 units. AE, D, DC, MC, V. $301–$556.*

Sky Crest Condominiums
The Sky Crest is a good on-mountain complex with large units. The extra-large three-bedroom with loft accommodates 14. The interior decor is fairly utilitarian, with durable and sensible furnishings in dirtproof earth and wheat tones, but stone and wood accents contribute a little mountain character. You get a large kitchen and dining room, a fireplace, a sun room, a Jacuzzi, and a bathroom for each bedroom. The mountain is just a half mile away. *1 Lone Mountain Trail, Box 160001, Big Sky 59716, tel. 406/995– 5000 or 800/548–4486, fax 406/995– 5001. 35 units. Facilities: laundry, shuttle, underground parking. AE, D, DC, MC, V. $306–$521.*

Corral Motel
Five miles south of Big Sky, you'll run across the Corral, a straight-up roadside motel with straightforward motel rooms that are among the cheapest in the area. Each room has two or three queen-size beds and not much else except cleanliness and comfort. If you crave TV, duck into the adjoining restaurant and bar. The shuttle bus to Big Sky stops outside three times a day from either direction. *42895 Gallatin Rd., U.S. 191, Gallatin Gateway 59730, tel. 406/995–4249. 8 rooms. Facilities: restaurant, bar, hot tub. AE, D, MC, V. $45–$70.*

Golden Eagle Lodge
The heart shapes carved in the railings that surround this quaint Bavarian-style three-story wood-and-stucco lodge are pretty much the extent of the frills here. It's great for groups on a budget; dormitory-style rooms sleep up to eight in a variety of bedding arrangements. You won't find much in the way of extras, but it's a good, clean, and comfortable economy lodging with a bright, cheery interior of blue-painted and stained-wood trim. This is a quiet and well-run spot suitable for families. There are also standard double rooms without phones. *Little Coyote Rd., Box 160008, Meadow Village, Big Sky 59716, tel. 406/995–4800 or 800/548–4488, fax 406/995–2447. 6 rooms, 9 dormitories. D, MC, V. $45 double room; $65 dormitory (up to 4 people), $8 each additional person.*

Hidden Village
This "village" of isolated condo town house–style buildings is indeed hid-

den in 40 wooded acres on the side of a hill, with stunning views of the Spanish Peaks Wilderness Area to the north and Lone Mountain to the west. The individual condos can have very different interiors; although many of the units are extremely modern and trendy, a good number do suffer from a drab decor of dark wood and institutional fabrics. But this is more than compensated by the excellent size, price, and location of all the accommodations. The units, ranging from two to five bedrooms, are among the largest of the Meadow Village rental properties. They have full-size kitchens, separate dining and living rooms, and striking rough-stone fireplaces. *Off Andesite Rd., Box 160008, 6 mi from slopes, Big Sky 59716, tel. 406/995–4800 or 800/548–4488, fax 406/995–2447. 140 units. Facilities: outdoor hot tub. D, MC, V. $140–$500.*

Silverbow

This neat gathering of condos is built in the classic Meadow Village style: rustic chalets with cedar siding and sloping cedar-shake roofs. Try for one of the units with more modern furnishings, but even if you end up in one with tacky circa-'60s decor, you'll appreciate the value of these large, versatile one- to three-bedroom condos next to a golf course 6 miles from the slopes. The smallest unit sleeps four with space to spare, and the largest will handle eight. Each unit has a fireplace and a full kitchen. *Black Otter Rd., Box 160008, Big Sky 59716, tel. 406/995–4800 or 800/548–4488, fax 406/995–2447. 30 units. Facilities: sauna, whirlpool. D, MC, V. $110–$240.*

WHERE TO EAT

Mountain Village dining at Big Sky is pretty limited and mostly mainstream. It is, however, convenient if you don't feel like driving or hopping the shuttle bus into the valley area, where there is considerably more variety as well as some entertaining nightlife options.

Expensive

Buck's T-4 Restaurant

Busy, bustling, casual, and friendly, Buck's serves up first-rate meals with an emphasis on wild game dishes in two dining rooms with wooden booths, stucco walls, and wagon-wheel chandeliers. The New Zealand red deer, sautéed in port wine, shallots, thyme, and butter sauce and garnished with artichoke hearts, is outstanding. Other winners include fillet of panfried rainbow trout topped with pecans and wild boar sautéed and served on a bed of sweet vermouth cream sauce with huckleberries. For dessert, try either the Russian cream with fresh raspberries or the apple dumpling with homemade cinnamon ice cream. *U.S. 191, 1½ mi south of Big Sky entrance, Big Sky, tel. 406/995–4111 or 800/822–4484. AE, D, DC, MC, V.*

Café Edelweiss

"An Irishman from Miami in Montana cooking German food," is how John Kelly, the owner of this tiny Tirol look-alike, sums up his place in the Big Sky culinary scene. The restaurant's interior is a monument to wooden curlicues, with storybook characters and endless scrollwork carved into every post, beam, and panel. The Continental menu emphasizes traditional Austrian dishes (schnitzels, excellent bratwurst and knockwurst sausages, and Schweine-braten, a pork roast with homemade sauerkraut), and the quiet, low-key ambience attracts a steady crowd of couples and other romantics. *Meadow Village, U.S. 191, Big Sky, tel. 406/995–4665. AE, D, MC, V.*

First Place
A wall of windows overlooks the Gallatin Valley, and massive fieldstones and square-cut ceiling beams harmonize with the subdued lighting and soft apricot tones of the table settings. The house specialty is pheasant with port sauce and mushrooms, or try the rack of lamb, charbroiled with rosemary and garlic. The small, snug wood-walled lounge, decorated with hunting trophies, is a nice place for an aperitif or nightcap by the fire. *Meadow Village, Big Sky, tel. 406/995–4244. AE, D, MC, V.*

Lone Mountain Guest Ranch Dining Room
In the massive log building at the center of the ranch property, it's a bright, amber-hued room with 30-foot vaulted ceilings, massive beam work, a large stone fireplace, three elk antler chandeliers, a collection of Native American artifacts, and tables glowing with linen and crystal. The menu has an unmistakable Western theme, with entrées such as Montana bison medallions done with rosemary, garlic, and lingonberry and Montana trout baked with spinach and brie and served in lemon-butter sauce. A changing selection of vegetarian dishes includes a vegetable strudel (fresh country vegetables baked in pastry and served with baked polenta and Gorgonzola). *Lone Mountain*

Ranch, Big Sky, tel. 406/995–2782. Reservations essential. D, MC, V.

Moderate

All Goods
At this pleasantly casual restaurant, the ambience is mountain rustic and the menu straightforward Montana barbecue. A selection of old photos of the early days at Big Sky Resort adds a certain color to the dull, clean, modern decor. The baby-back ribs, hickory smoked and charbroiled with an excellent sauce, are a good example of what the place does best. The bar serves more than 40 beers, including a multitude of local microbrews. *West Fork Plaza, Meadow Village, Big Sky, tel. 406/995–2750. AE, D, DC, MC, V.*

Dante's Inferno
This is a large, barnlike structure with posts, pillars, beams, and a curious mix of decorations, including trophy heads and a pair of model World War I–vintage biplanes. The food is authentic Italian, with the buffalo mozzarella and pancetta imported from Italy. There are five different pastas nightly; pizzas and calzones are made with a cornmeal crust; and focaccia sandwiches come with pasta chips. Meals can be served family style for larger groups. The wine list contains affordable selections from Italy and California. An après-ski happy hour from 3 to 6 features live entertainment and drink specials. *Mountain Mall, Big Sky, tel. 406/995–3999. AE, MC, V.*

Rocco's
This large barn of a restaurant with Wedgwood blue walls and a big stone fireplace at the center can't decide

whether to specialize in Italian or Mexican cuisine—so it does both superbly. The homemade salsa, in three styles, is as distinctive as the rich marinara sauce used in the pasta dishes. The Mexican side of the menu has the favorites—enchiladas, burritos, and fajitas, plus excellent chili rellenos. Italian fare is represented by a variety of pasta dishes including lasagna and by mainstay items such as chicken parmigiana, veal marsala, and scampi. *Golden Eagle Lodge, Meadow Village, Big Sky, tel. 406/925–4200. AE, D, MC, V.*

Twin Panda

The bright and cheerful Twin Panda serves old favorites—chow mein and egg rolls, with a few Szechuan dishes thrown in—and the clientele consists mostly of families or groups of young people. *Arrowhead Mall, 3rd floor, Mountain Village, Big Sky, tel. 406/995–2425. AE, MC, V.*

Inexpensive

Buck's Grill

If Mom and Dad prefer the dining room at the other end of Buck's T-4 complex (*see* Expensive, *above*), this is a good place for the kids to come to feast on deep-pan pizza, hero sandwiches, charbroiled burgers, or a first-rate homemade chili. The decor is kid-proof, with green tiles on the floor, solid wood tables, and inexpensive Western prints on the walls. *Buck's T-4, U.S. 191, 1½ mi south of Big Sky entrance, Big Sky, tel. 406/995–4811. AE, D, DC, MC, V.*

The Corral

Have you ever had a buffalo burger? If not, you should seriously consider sinking your teeth into one at this kitschy, funky, friendly locals' hangout. The fainter of heart can stick with the sandwiches, regular burgers, and daily specials such as fresh seafood and a delicious Italian marinated beef kebab. The atmosphere is as much of a draw as the food: the log walls are awash in collectibles and there's an old wood stove, a jukebox, gambling machines, and four TVs. *42895 Gallatin Rd., U.S. 191, 5 mi south of Big Sky entrance, Gallatin Gateway, tel. 406/995–4249. AE, D, MC, V.*

Mountain Top Pizza

Good, hearty pizza is the bill of fare here—choose from traditional varieties as well as specialty toppings like black bean salsa. Skiing and snowboarding photos and old skis dot the walls. *Mountain Mall, Big Sky, tel. 406/995–4646. AE, MC, V.*

Scissorbills Bar and Grill

This lively, youthful little place serves basic burgers, sandwiches, soup, salads, and chili in a brass- and fern-filled space. *Arrowhead Mall, upstairs, Big Sky, tel. 406/995–4933. MC, V.*

Best Bets for Breakfast

The Corral

Here you can get trucker-size portions of everything from pancakes, classic Western steak and eggs, and scrumptious hash browns to egg dishes in every form, including standout deep omelets. *42895 Gallatin Rd., U.S. 191, 5 mi south of Big Sky entrance, Gallatin Gateway, tel. 406/995–4249. AE, D, MC, V.*

Huntley Lodge Dining Room

Up in the Mountain Village, the Huntley Lodge dining room serves an excellent two-part buffet breakfast. On one side there are hot dishes—eggs, crepes, French toast—and on the other side a fruit, cereal, yogurt, and muffin selection. *Huntley Lodge, 1 Lone Mountain Trail, Big Sky, tel. 406/995–5783 or 800/548–4486. AE, D, MC, V.*

NIGHTLIFE AND ENTERTAINMENT

Nightlife action is spread out between the Mountain Village and the surrounding valley. Most immediate après-ski action is in the village and is followed by early evening trips to the valley's more eclectic bars.

Après-Ski

Saloon

The Saloon at Lone Mountain Ranch is relatively mellow. A long copper bar with log stools is perfect for lounging, or you can settle in front of the copper corner fireplace. Occasionally a solo guitarist entertains. *Lone Mountain Ranch, Big Sky, tel. 406/995–4644. D, MC, V.*

Loud and Lively/Dancing

Half Moon Saloon

This big barn of a saloon has wide-plank hardwood floors, a long bar, three pool tables, shuffleboard, and multiple TVs. If you don't like what's showing on the screen, you can always watch moose and elk out the back door. This is a cheerful, friendly place where locals hold court, but visitors also feel welcome. *45130 Gallatin Rd., Gallatin Gateway, tel. 406/995–4533. MC, V.*

Lolo's Saloon

This loud, lively bar is downstairs from Mountain Top Pizza. The nightly rock and jazz attract mainly an under-30 crowd. There's live entertainment on weekends beginning at 9 PM and a good-size dance floor. *Mountain Mall, Big Sky, tel. 406/995–3455. MC, V.*

Rocco's

This hybrid bar/restaurant occasionally turns into an all-out dancing nightclub when the owner, Larry, decides to perform with his group, the Piranha Brothers—a raunchy rock-and-roll group that can shake the rafters of the large barnlike structure. *Golden Eagle Lodge, Meadow Village, Big Sky, tel. 406/995–4200. AE, D, MC, V.*

Scissorbills Bar and Grill

Scissorbills attracts a younger crowd. It's a classic fern-bar atmosphere: bright, lots of brass and wood, plus good, loud recorded music. *Arrowhead Mall, Big Sky Mountain Village, Big Sky, tel. 406/995–4933. MC, V.*

More Mellow

Buck's Lounge

There has been a bar here continuously since 1945, and the wooden floor and walls still have the original planks. It's small and comfortable, with light country-and-western music playing in the background and some gambling machines in a small alcove. *Buck's T-4, U.S. 191, 1½ mi south of Big Sky entrance, Big Sky, tel. 406/995–4111. AE, D, DC, MC, V.*

Chet's

Chet's mellows out with a solo guitarist or duet on one side and live poker on the other. *Huntley Lodge, 1 Lone Mountain Trail, Big Sky, tel. 406/995–5784. AE, MC, V.*

S kiing in New Hampshire often gets short shrift in the realm of Eastern skiing, mostly because the more storied resorts of Vermont, and to a lesser extent Maine, attract the most publicity and the biggest crowds.

Such anonymity mirrors the character of this unique slice of New England, a state whose license plates sport the phrase LIVE FREE OR DIE. For generations this quiet independence has forged a character as tough as the granite peaks that form some of the most dramatic mountain landscapes in the eastern United States.

The White Mountains' Presidential Range—a wall of high peaks and outcrops that cuts a dazzling northeast–southwest swath through the state—includes more than 40 peaks that top the 4,000-foot mark, among them Mt. Washington, at 6,288 feet, the highest mountain in New England.

Almost a dozen ski resorts within the 730,000 square miles of White Mountain National Forest stake their claim in New Hampshire's beautiful wilderness. Some, such as Wildcat and Cannon mountains, have achieved cult status for their steep, straight-ahead narrow trails; another, Tuckerman's Ravine on Mt. Washington, offers the last stand against conformity with its absence of lifts and its 2-mile hike to its steep snowfields. For the most part, however, these remain secret places, known best by locals and only slowly being discovered by visitors from out of state.

Curiously, although the world may not be beating a path to New Hampshire resorts, the World Cup is, and in its wake more and more people are discovering Waterville Valley, the state's largest and most modern resort. This self-contained community doesn't have the steepest or toughest runs in New Hampshire (nearby Loon Mountain can arguably stake that claim) but has hosted more World Cup races than any other resort in the country except Vail.

WATERVILLE VALLEY SKI RESORT

WATERVILLE VALLEY SKI RESORT

Waterville Valley, New Hampshire 03215
Tel. 603/236–8311 or
800/468–2553
www.waterville.com

STATISTICALLY SPEAKING

Base elevation: 1,984 feet

Summit elevation: 4,004 feet

Vertical drop: 2,020 feet

Skiable terrain: 255 acres

Number of trails: 52

Longest run: 3 miles

Lifts and capacity: 2 high-speed detachable quads, 2 triples, 3 doubles, 1 T-bar, 1 J-bar, 1 platter, 1 handle tow; 14,626 skiers per hour

Daily lift ticket: $40 weekdays; $46 weekends

Average annual snowfall: 136 inches

Number of skiing days 1997–1998: 144

Snowmaking: 255 acres, 100%

Terrain mix: N 36%, I 44%, E 20%

Snowboarding: yes

This tidy resort and town offers parking lot–to-mountaintop coddling, which amounts to a ski experience that's both sanitized and ultimately satisfying.

When former U.S. ski team star Tom Corcoran—the resort's founder—first cut these trails in the '60s, most New England resorts had narrow, twisting trails. Today almost every resort worth its boomer business has moved to wider, highly groomed boulevards similar to those Corcoran created for Waterville Valley. The broad, well-groomed trails of Mt. Tecumseh and the neatly maintained condos of the adjacent village were created with families in mind. And with weekly packages costing less than $400 (including lift tickets) it's affordable for groups and couples to pack up and get away, too.

Although the main village is about a mile from the slopes, the efficient shuttle makes the commute painless and a car unnecessary. At first the village—the focus of Waterville Valley's less-than-torrid nightlife—seems sterile, with a two-level collection of small specialty stores, restaurants, and bars. But the normally taciturn New Hampshire locals become positively garrulous when dealing with visitors from out of state. The character of the village will come, but it already has the characters to compensate.

It has the depth as well. Without ever leaving the village, you can ice-skate, swim, sled, cross-country ski, play indoor tennis, snowshoe, work out in a health club, or lounge in a hot tub. In the world of all-inclusive vacations, Waterville is making an impact.

HOW TO GET THERE

By Plane

Boston's **Logan International Airport** is served by most major carriers, with connections from many major cities. United and Delta Business Express fly direct from Pittsburgh, PA, and Plattsburgh, NY, into **Manchester Airport,** about 70 miles from the resort. Continental, Delta, and US Airways also fly into Manchester from Boston with connections from other major cities.

By Car

From Boston it's 130 miles and about 2½ hours to the resort. Take I–93 north to Exit 28, then follow Route

Children's services: day-care, instruction, tel. 603/236–8311, ext. 3136.

Snow phone: tel. 603/236–4144

Police: tel. 911 or 603/236–8809

Medical center and ambulance: tel. 603/524–1545

Waterville Valley Chamber of Commerce: tel. 800/237–2307

Road conditions: 603/485–3806

Towing: Mobil station, tel. 603/236–8604

FIVE-STAR FAVORITES

Best run for vertical: Gema

Best run overall: Upper Bobby/Lower Bobby

Best bar/nightclub: Legends 1291

Best hotel: Golden Eagle Lodge

Best restaurant: Valley Inn

49 11 miles east to Waterville Valley. From New York, 325 miles away, it's about six hours; take I–95 to I–91 to I–84 to the Massachusetts Turnpike; then pick up I–290 to I–495 to Route 3N to I–93 north to Exit 28. From Manchester, 70 miles away, about 1½ hours, take I–293 to I–93 north to Exit 28. All major rental agencies are represented at both airports.

By Bus

Concord Trailways (tel. 603/536–4430) has daily scheduled trips from Logan Airport to Plymouth ($26 one-way), 25 minutes from the resort. From there you can take a $23 cab ride or arrange with your hotel for a shuttle pickup.

GETTING AROUND

Park the car at your accommodation and leave it. Even if you're among the first arrivals of the day at Waterville Valley, it's still a fair hike to the lifts from the parking lots. Shuttle service is efficient, and Waterville Valley and environs are best explored on foot anyway.

By Shuttle

The **Waterville Valley shuttle bus** (tel. 603/236–8311) runs between the village and the mountain and in and around the village area at 10-minute intervals daily 7:30–4:30 from December through March.

By Taxi

It's unlikely you'll need a cab in Waterville Valley, but if that occasion arises, there are two services: **Fred Gall's Town Taxi** (tel. 603/536–4649) and **McGill and Sons Taxi Service** (tel. 603/536–2435).

THE SKIING

The Waterville Valley ski area focuses on the 4,000-foot Mt. Tecumseh, one of the state's most majestic skiable mountains. All the resort's skiing programs center around the base of the mountain, making it easy to find your companions or get around.
Mt. Tecumseh offers a good mix of mostly wide, well-groomed giant-slalom cruising runs. What you won't find here is buckle-your-knees, in-your-face skiing. Overall, the skiing rates as solid intermediate, with

the White Peak quad followed by the Valley Run triple providing the speed to get you up and down as fast and often as your legs can handle.

Waterville Valley's lifts open at 8 (9 on nonholiday weekdays), so really ambitious skiers can get an earlier-than-usual start. The locals' tried-and-true strategy is to hit the slopes for first tracks and call it a day at about 11 AM, when the crowds arrive.

Novices

Lower Meadows, a gentle slope at the bottom of the mountain, tucked behind the rental shop and away from the main drag, allows beginners to find their edge comfortably. Lower Meadows' three ultrawide, smooth trails leading from its double chairlift are a good place to get started. There is little variety among these three, however, so eventually you'll want to spread your wings and try Valley Run, which, although designated blue, is suitable for novices with the basics under their belts. You can take Valley Run double chair about three-quarters of the way up or grab the Valley Run triple chair if you want to go higher up the mountain. The new Quadzilla quad can whisk you up to the top of Valley Run. From any of these points you'll be able to enjoy one of the nicest lower-intermediate trails in New England. In addition to its flawlessly groomed terrain, Valley Run tends to be warmer than other runs because it's protected from the wind and basks in the morning sun. When skiing Mt. Tecumseh, if you're at all nervous, stay on the trails to the right side (looking down the mountain) because they're straightforward and predictable; for a bit more challenge and some dips and rolls, ski the left side.

Intermediates

If you're a reasonably strong intermediate skier, there are probably only a few testy little bump runs on the mountain that may be out of your domain. The rest of Waterville Valley's runs are pure intermediate cruisers, and by linking several you can enjoy some excellent top-to-bottom skiing. Start by taking the High Country express quad and the Valley Run double to the summit, then go to the left (looking down the mountain) to the rolling Tree Line Trail to White Caps, just below the High Country double. Although White Caps periodically offers a few bumps, overall it allows you to maintain good speed to the point just above the top of the World Cup triple chair. From there you can either continue straight down the chute on steeper, bumpier terrain designated black or cut left to the more forgiving Sel's Choice. Although Sel's is also marked black, it is actually a first-rate upper-level intermediate cruiser that skis like a good giant slalom course, with several pitch variances and banked turns. If you enjoy Sel's Choice, you can reach it directly by riding the World Cup triple chair and staying in this area for a while. By not taking the High Country quad and the High Country double to the summit, you escape some of the crowds.

Another high-speed cruiser is Express (to the far right, looking down the mountain), reached from the High Country express quad to Oblivion and then to Upper Valley. This is especially good early in the day, when you can catch the morning sun. Also try Tree Line to Upper Bobby's to Psyched to Exhibition—a series of runs that streaks straight down the face of the mountain but tends to be well traveled and prone to icy patches.

To really steer clear of the crowds, you can take the Northside double lift—the least busy lift on the mountain—to Waterville Valley's northern flank. From there you can ski Tippecanoe and Tyler Too, a pair of standard, wide-open Waterville Valley cruisers; or Tangent and Periphery, a pair of narrower though slightly more tedious blue trails.

Experts

Let's be frank: If you're looking for true challenge, you'll find Waterville Valley lacking, especially on the north face of the mountain, where Sel's Choice is your only choice. But while you're there, start by taking a few warm-up runs on this first-rate giant slalom cruiser. Then head over to the Sunnyside triple chair, which serves Ciao, Gema, and True Grit—three short, steep mogul runs. The latter is the toughest and bumpiest on the mountain. The bumps are biggest on the left side of the trail, but when they get too big and too hard, the right side is the better alternative. Gema, which runs parallel, has about the same pitch as True Grit, but it's skied less, hence the moguls are smaller. Ciao is wider than the other two and a little less bumpy. Bobby's Run is the other expert trail to head for, especially after a decent snowfall. It can be reached from either the Sunnyside triple chair or the High Country quad. Bobby's

seems to be the favorite of patrollers, who frequently close it off when the snow is sparse (there's no snowmaking here), prompting some local wags to suggest that they are keeping it for themselves. But when there's a foot of fresh powder, it's a great cruiser with good pitch, few bumps (because it's skied so little), and a nice sweeping curve that takes you to the bottom of the chair.

SNOWBOARDING

Waterville built one of the first snowboard parks in the East and hosts major national events. The gentle boarder learning area gives new riders a safe spot to learn to feel the edges and turn the board before heading up to the more challenging stuff. For that, go to the Boneyard snowboard park on Exhibition, where huge tabletops, style hits, handrails, and other goodies will keep you flying. A powerful snowmaking system points exclusively at the half-pipe on Upper Valley Run, providing the soft, deep snow so good for carving. A good trail for boarders is Oblivion, which has ledges and powder stashes.

OTHER SNOW SPORTS

Waterville's **Cross Country** Skiing Center (tel. 603/236–4144) offers 20 kilometers of groomed trails, as well as seemingly endless options for backcountry skiers. There's also a **skating** rink, nighttime Sno-Cat rides, and family events.

NEARBY

Waterville is a hub of New Hampshire skiing, surrounded by resorts that each offer their own unique personality. Steep, rough and wild, **Cannon**

Mountain (Rte. 93, Franconia, tel. 603/271–2006) offers a true taste of old New England skiing, with winding trails, great off-piste, and yes, slow lifts are what skiers love about the place. A sister resort of Waterville, **Loon Mountain Resort** (Lincoln, tel. 603/745–8111), just up the road, offers wider, more groomed-out skiing as well as a comfortable gondola that makes cold days easier to take.

WHERE TO STAY

The accommodations at Waterville Valley are low-key—about 80% of the 6,500 beds are in nests of condos, town houses, and private chalets built into the hillside between the village and the resort. There are also a few hotels, inns, lodges, and B&Bs for those who want to eschew the take-care-of-yourself approach of condo living. None of these are flashy pamper palaces, just solid, unpretentious living spaces, strong on quality and value. Virtually all accommodations are within 1½ miles of the mountain or within walking distance of the town square, and many of the more distant ones are served by the shuttle, which goes to the slopes. Accommodations in town can be booked through **Waterville Valley Central Reservations** (tel. 800/468–2553). If you're looking for cheaper, motel-style accommodations, you may have to commute from the nearby towns of Plymouth or Campton.

Expensive

Resort Condominium Rental

This organization rents some of the largest condo and town house units in the valley, ranging in size from one to four bedrooms and most within walking distance of the town square. The exteriors are stained in different colors, and on the inside the units are generally bright and well furnished in a mountain-modern style that includes white walls and a lot of wood. All come equipped with full kitchens including dishwasher and microwave, plus a woodstove or fireplace and usually a washer-dryer. *Valley Rd., Box 379, Waterville Valley, 03215, tel. 603/236–4101 or 800/ 556–6522, fax 603/236–4890. 50 units. Facilities: sports center, shuttle service, ski storage, game room. AE, D, DC, MC, V. $189–$369.*

Town Square Resort

Once the bargain basement of accommodations at Waterville, the Town Square condos are newly renovated and sparkling. The good news is that while the renovations are pristine, they're not so extravagant that the roomy units are overpriced. Each unit has three bedrooms on a two- or three-floor layout. The comfortably furnished common areas include a large kitchen, a dining area, and two bathrooms.They're in the middle of all the action too, and shuttle-hooked to the ski slope. *Village Rd., Waterville Valley, 03215, tel. 603/236–4071 or 800/468–2553. 33 units. Facilities: sports center, shuttle service, maid service, ski storage, laundry, game room. AE, DC, MC, V. $379.*

Village Condominium

These one- and two-story clapboard condos have from one to five bedrooms and are fully equipped, with a kitchen, a fireplace, a living/dining room, and laundry facilities, making them popular with families and groups. Some have access to the sports center; ask when booking. *Rte. 49, Waterville Valley 03215, tel. 603/236–8301 or 800/468–2553, fax 603/236–3363. 25 units. Facilities: sauna, maid service, shuttle, ski storage, laundry, game room. D, MC, V. $290–$600.*

Windsor Hill Condominiums

These one-, two-, and three-bedroom redwood-clapboard condos and town houses are among the closest to the slopes. Each has a kitchen or kitchenette, a fireplace, and laundry facilities. The decor is standard modern, with functional, not fancy, furnishings. *Jennings Peak Rd., Box 440, Waterville Valley 03215, tel. 603/236–8321 or 800/343–1286. 132 units. Facilities: ski storage, laundry. MC, V. $140–$355.*

Moderate

Black Bear Lodge

Known as a condo hotel, this rambling six-story clapboard lodge is dominated by families drawn to the large, functional, comfortable suites that can easily sleep six people. Each unit has one or two bedrooms, a large living area with a Murphy bed, a kitchen, and a dining area. The suites are well maintained, and the furnishings are unremarkable but definitely childproof. *Village Rd., Box 357, Waterville Valley, 03215, tel. 603/236–4501 or 800/349–2327, fax 603/236–4114, ext 232. 98 suites. Facilities: whirlpool, sauna, steam room, laundry, indoor-outdoor heated pool, maid service, ski storage, 24-hr desk service, shuttle, game room. AE, D, DC, MC, V. $199–$269.*

Golden Eagle Lodge

The peaked roofs and corner turrets of this large hotel next to the village square proudly announce that it was built in the grand style of earlier New Hampshire resorts. The one- and two-bedroom suites can easily handle six people. Each has a separate living and dining area, a complete kitchen, and one or two full bathrooms. The furnishings are above average, with big couches, comfy chairs, and modern appliances. In the morning there is complimentary coffee in the impressive wood-and-stone lobby. *Snowbrook Rd., Box 495, Waterville Valley 03215, tel. 603/236–4551 or 800/910–4499, fax 603/263–4947. 139 suites. Facilities: lounge, indoor pool, whirlpool, sauna, 24-hr desk service, shuttle service, maid service, laundry, game room. AE, D, DC, MC, V. $279–$319.*

Snowy Owl Inn

Small enough to be charming yet large enough to provide all the amenities, this inn just off the village square has a crisp, rustic cleanliness. There is a soaring atrium lobby, amber-hued wood finishings, antiques, and massive fieldstone fireplaces. The Snowy Owl draws equal numbers of families (thanks to its unique bunk-bed rooms) and couples searching for a little low-key privacy. *Village Rd., Box 379, Waterville Valley 03215, tel. 603/236–8383 or 800/766–9969, fax 603/236–4890. 83 rooms. Facilities: indoor pool, whirlpool, shuttle, 24-hr desk service, maid service, ski storage, game room. AE, D, DC, MC, V. $65–$230, including Continental breakfast and après-ski refreshments.*

Valley Inn

A wood exterior gives this attractive alternative to a hotel an innlike feeling. The rooms range from standard (with two full-size beds) to larger, more luxurious suites. The extra-large two-story apartment suites have more of a designer's touch. *Tecumseh Rd., Box 1, Waterville Valley 03215, tel. 603/236–8336 or 800/343–0969, fax 603/236–4294. 47 rooms, 5 suites. Facilities: restaurant, bar, lounge, heated indoor-outdoor pool, whirlpool, sauna, shuttle, 24-hr desk service, maid service, ski storage. AE, D, DC, MC, V. $75–$275.*

Inexpensive

Best Western White Mountains

This motel on the edge of Campton, 15 minutes south of Waterville Valley, has a chalet-style exterior, but the room decor is pure modern American, with basic pine furnishings and one king-size or two double beds. *Rte. 3, Exit 27 off I–93, R.R. 1, Box 355, Plymouth, 03264, tel. 603/536–3520 or 800/370–8666, fax 603/536–8114. 101 rooms. Facilities: indoor pool, Jacuzzi, sauna, steam room, 24-hr desk service, laundry, game room. AE, D, DC, MC, V. $49–$125.*

Susse Chalet Hotel

In Plymouth, 20 minutes south of Waterville Valley, you'll find this two-story chain hotel with a misty-mauve-and-beige concrete exterior. There's nothing flashy about the comfortable wallpapered rooms. The color scheme is off-white, and furnishings are light wood. *Rte. 3, R.F.D. 1, Box 4, Plymouth, 03264, tel. 603/536–2330 or 800/524–2538, fax 603/536–2686. 38 rooms. Facilities: outdoor pool, 24-hr desk service, laundry. AE, D, DC, MC, V. $50–$90, including Continental breakfast.*

WHERE TO EAT

The selection of food in Waterville Valley, with a couple of notable exceptions, is limited, with the emphasis on traditional dishes prepared in traditional ways.

On the Mountain

Schwendi Hutte

Just below the summit of the mountain, on a plateau where the High Country double chairlift begins, this restaurant has a cafeteria and table service with white cloths and real cutlery. Start with Daphne's lobster bisque and then choose between German sausages and sauerkraut, large sandwiches with dips, salads, and side dishes such as sweet and sour braised red cabbage. *Top of mountain, tel. 603/236–8330, ext. 3144. AE, D, DC, MC, V.*

Sunnyside Up Lodge

To find the lodge, keep tight to the left side of the upper valley run and turn uphill just past the bottom of the Sunnyside triple chair, about a third of the way down the mountain. This striking log structure has a standard repertory of good, wholesome lunchtime fare, from burgers and sandwiches to soups, chili, stew, and salads served cafeteria style. It tends to be less crowded than other places on the mountain because it's so easy to miss. *Beside Valley Run, tel. 603/236–8311, ext. 3292. No credit cards.*

Expensive

Valley Inn

For a somewhat formal (and candlelit) dining experience, visit the Valley Inn, where the menu includes seafood, beef, pork, chicken, and pasta. Popular dishes are steak Horatio (twin tournedos of beef sautéed with wild mushrooms and smothered in a port, cognac, and heavy cream sauce) and duckling with maple sauce and cranberry-pecan fritter. Service is fairly slow, so relax and enjoy the ambience. *Tecumseh Rd., Waterville Valley, tel. 603/236–8336. AE, D, DC, MC, V.*

William Tell
It's worth a 7-mile drive west to find this small country restaurant with stucco and wood-beam construction, two small dining rooms that are quiet and romantic, and taped classical music in the front room. If you like traditional Bavarian, Austrian, and Swiss dishes such as schnitzel, fondue, and fresh venison, you'll get your fill here. Try the pepper steak. *Rte. 49, Thornton, tel. 603/726–3618. AE, MC, V.*

Moderate

Chile Peppers
Antique barbed wire and Southwestern prints hang on the walls of this eatery, where Tex-Mex staples are featured. Chile Peppers caters to skiers with its hearty selection of fajitas, tacos, and enchiladas. The food here may not be authentic Mexican, but it's well priced and filling. A margarita tops off everything nicely. If you prefer Tex to Mex, there's a lineup of standards such as ribs, steak, seafood, and chicken. *Town Square, Waterville Valley, tel. 603/236–4646. AE, DC, MC, V.*

Common Man Restaurant and Bar
Antique lanterns, a fireplace, and a woodstove help create a rustic atmosphere at this seafood restaurant that offers an abundance of fresh fish. The shellfish stew is a must, with shrimp, scallops, mussels, and king crabs in a spicy tomato broth served over linguine. *Town Square, Waterville Valley, tel. 603/236–8885. Reservations not accepted. AE, D, MC, V.*

Inexpensive

Jugtown Deli
You can stock up here for a do-it-yourself dinner back at the condo or sit down at the tables. A good selection of deli food—cold cuts, fancy breads and buns, cheeses, and other snacks—is available. *Town Square, Waterville Valley, tel. 603/236–8662. AE, MC, V.*

Old Waterville Valley Pizza Company
Pizza in this town-square eatery is pretty good, with a medium-thick crust and a selection of toppings. They also have pastas, salads, hot and cold subs, soups, and hamburgers. *Town Square, Waterville Valley, tel. 603/236–4173. No credit cards.*

Best Bet for Breakfast

Coffee Emporium
If you like to take your time and smell the coffee, then this is where you'll find the best selection in town. The bright dining room is filled with coffee paraphernalia and cookbooks. Full breakfast is also served, including Belgian waffles, egg dishes, and a large selection of breakfast pastries and muffins. *Town Square, Waterville Valley, tel. 603/236–4021. No credit cards.*

NIGHTLIFE AND ENTERTAINMENT
Après-Ski

World Cup Bar & Grill
The A-frame loft bar is always packed for après-ski, when there's often live

entertainment and sports action on the big-screen TV. World Cup flags hang on the walls, and a large picture window lets in the sunset. *Upstairs at Waterville Valley base lodge, tel. 603/236–8311, ext. 3142. AE, D, DC, MC, V.*

Loud and Lively/Dancing

Common Man Restaurant and Bar
The rustic atmosphere makes it easy to curl up in front of the fireplace with a few bar munchies; or if you've got energy to spare, you can dance to a live band on weekends. *Town Square, Waterville Valley, tel. 603/236–8885. AE, D, MC, V.*

Legends 1291

A DJ delivering delirium and a crowd as high-octane as it gets in Waterville Valley make this the best place to shake it loose on the dance floor. You may find guitar music, a live band, or a DJ, depending on what night you're here. *Town Square, Waterville Valley, tel. 603/236–4678. AE, MC, V.*

Many aspects of New Mexico surprise and enchant visitors—1,000-year-old Pueblo villages, sweeping desert vistas, a lively artistic and creative community—but the biggest surprise of all is the skiing. For here in the land of adobe dwellings, tumbling sagebrush, and ocher-colored buttes, are the Sangre de Cristo Mountains, sun-kissed peaks that soar high above the desert floor reaping the benefits of climatic clashes between the dry air of the lowlands and the moist air traveling from the west.

There are just four ski resorts in these mountains, and of these the best known and largest is Taos Ski Valley, the southernmost resort in the United States and one that has gained a worldwide reputation for its steep, challenging slopes, consistent snowfall, and extraordinarily sunny days.

Taos is a magical, mystical place, a physical and spiritual Shangri-la surrounded by the stunning peaks of the Sangre de Cristo Mountains, bathed in pure desert air, and steeped in history and culture. Native Americans have inhabited the Taos pueblo for 1,000 years, creating an intricate multitiered adobe structure that stands today as the world's oldest apartment building. The centuries have brought little change to Taos—the pueblo is still without electricity or running water—although large-scale tourism has introduced a commercial element.

The Taos pueblo stands near the town of Taos, a community of traditional adobe buildings surrounding cobblestone courtyards, plazas, and quiet side streets. This old, compact town is also home to one of the largest concentrations of art galleries and Native American crafts shops found anywhere in America. It has long been the adopted home of assorted writers, artists, and musicians, all drawn by its serene isolation and the mystique of its ancient culture. The stark Southwestern canvases of Georgia O'Keeffe, who lived in New Mexico for decades, are world famous. D. H. Lawrence was also a devotee.

TAOS SKI VALLEY

TAOS SKI VALLEY

Box 90
Taos Ski Valley, NM 87525
Tel. 505/776–2291
www.taosweb.com/skitaos

STATISTICALLY SPEAKING

Base elevation: 9,207 feet

Summit elevation: 11,819 feet

Vertical drop: 2,612 feet

Skiable terrain: 1,094 acres

Number of trails: 72

Longest run: 5¼ miles

Lifts and capacity: 4 quads, 1 triple, 5 doubles, 1 surface; 15,500 skiers per hour

Daily lift ticket: $42

Average annual snowfall: 302 inches

Number of skiing days 1997–98: 143

Snowmaking: 96% of beginner and intermediate slopes only

Terrain mix: N 24%, I 25%, E 51%

Snowboarding: no

Taos Ski Valley is 18 miles from the town of Taos and 2,000 feet higher, at the fringe of the Carson National Forest, where the sage and piñon of the desert give way to the tall pines of the mountains. To get here, you drive through flat desert scrubland bathed in the surreal Southwestern light and up a slash of a valley called the Rio Grande Gorge. The resort is the offspring of the late Ernie Blake, a native of Switzerland, who scratched and clawed to make his dream of a European-style alpine village and ski mountain into a reality. Everything about Taos Ski Valley reflects the vision and single-minded determination of this extraordinary man.

The mountain village itself is a tiny, pedestrian-oriented enclave of a dozen small lodges and a modest number of condominiums nestled on either side of the Rio Hondo Creek, all connected by a network of walkways and bridges and all within easy walking distance of the base area lifts. It could easily have been transported lock, stock, and chalet from the mountains of Europe, and you are just as likely to hear French and German spoken as you are Spanish and English. Many of the early entrepreneurs came here from the classic resort centers in Europe and brought with them the concept of packaged ski weeks including lessons, meals, lift tickets, and accommodations for an all-inclusive single price. Most of the original hotels and lodges at the mountain still offer this arrangement, and it is not a bad way to take your first week at Taos (although there are other alternatives). The lessons are excellent (two hours each morning), it's a good way to get to know the mountain, the food packages are generous, and the price at an average of about $1,300–$1,500 per person per week is a good deal.

Besides, the togetherness approach produces a spirited camaraderie that compensates for the decided lack of nightlife at the mountain village. If you are staying in the village, a car is not required, but if you stay in town, it's a must. A car is useful in either case because there is so much else to see and do in the area.

Anytime is the right time to visit Taos, but Christmas is particularly magical. The Pueblo tribe make

Children's services: day-care, tel. 505/776–2291, ext. 1332

Snow phone: tel. 505/776–2916

State police: tel. 505/758–8878; town police, tel. 505/758–2216; sheriff, tel. 505/758–3361

Medical center: Mogul Medical, tel. 505/776–8421

Hospital: Holy Cross Hospital, tel. 505/758–8883

Taos County Chamber of Commerce: tel. 505/758–3873 or 800/732–8267

Resort services: tel. 505/776–2233 or 800/776–1111

Taos Ski Valley Lost and Found: tel. 505/776–2291, ext. 1411

Road conditions: tel. 505/841–9256

Towing: Towing Unlimited, tel. 505/758–3793

FIVE-STAR FAVORITES
Best run for vertical: Walkyries Chute

Best run overall: Powderhorn

Best bar/nightclub: Sagebrush Inn

Best hotel: St. Bernard

Best restaurant: Lamberts of Taos

bonfires of piñon wood, masked dancers stage traditional torchlighted parades, and the town glows softly from the thousands of *farolitas* (lights made from candles inside sand-filled paper bags).

The high mountain hamlet contrasts strikingly with the centuries-old desert community; the towering peaks of the Sangre de Christo Mountains, including Mt. Wheeler, New Mexico's highest peak, at 13,161 feet, yield to the flat sun-scorched earth of the New Mexican plateau. It is this quality of majesty and mystery that draws you back to Taos.

HOW TO GET THERE

By Plane

Albuquerque International Airport (tel. 505/842–4366), 135 miles south of Taos, is the major airport closest to the resort. It is served with regularly scheduled flights by America West (tel. 800/235–9292), American (tel. 800/433–7300), Continental (tel. 800/525–0280), Delta (tel. 800/221–1212), Mesa Air (tel. 800/637–2247), Northwest (tel. 800/225–2525), Southwest (tel. 800/435–9792), TWA (tel. 800/221–2000), and United (tel. 800/241–6522).

By Car

From the Albuquerque airport, take I-25 to Santa Fe, pick up Route 84 heading north to Espanola, and then follow Route 68 into Taos. This is a marvelously picturesque drive on snow-free roads, and a stop in Santa Fe is a perfect halfway break.

At the Albuquerque airport the following car rentals are available: **Advantage** (tel. 800/777–5500), **Alamo** (tel. 800/327–9633), **All American** (tel. 800/242–7743), **Budget** (tel. 800/527–0700), **Dollar** (tel. 800/421–6868), **Enterprise** (tel. 800/325–8007), **Hertz** (tel. 800/654–3131), **National** (tel. 800/328–4567), **Payless** (tel. 800/541–1566), and **Thrifty** (tel. 800/367–2277).

By Bus

Frequent daily and weekly shuttle buses operate between the Albuquerque airport and Taos and Taos Ski Resort. Check with either of the following for rates and schedules: **The Pride of Taos** (tel. 505/

758–8340 or 800/273–8340) or **Faust's Transportation** (tel. 505/758–3410).

By Train
Amtrak (tel. 800/872–7245) provides service into Lamy or Raton (90 miles east of Taos on Route 64).

GETTING AROUND
A car is useful in Taos because of the distance between the resort and the town and the myriad side trips you can take; also, the shuttle service (**Faust's Transportation,** tel. 505/758–3410, $10 round-trip) between the slopes and the nightlife of Taos is infrequent—just three runs each way daily. Faust's also operates a taxi service (tel. 505/758–7359) between the ski valley and town; it costs $35 one-way for the first two passengers.

THE SKIING
If there is one ski resort in America or, perhaps, in the entire world that can truly be said to bear the personal stamp of one man, it is Taos Ski Valley. It's impossible to ski this marvelous sun-drenched, north-facing mountain without constant reminders of its creator, Ernie Blake. In the 1950s Ernie sought a mountain that would provide challenge, and when he spotted this isolated peak while flying over the area, he knew he had found his mountain. From then until his death in 1989, he worked tirelessly to realize his vision of the perfect American ski resort.

Ernie's legacy is evident in little touches, like the witty sign at the bottom of the fiercely steep and mogul-studded Al's Run that reads: "Don't panic. You're looking at only 1/30th

of Taos Ski Valley. We have many easy runs, too!" Although there's truth in that statement, it's also equally true that Taos is a mountain of supreme challenge, where 51% of the runs are black diamond and 19 of those 36 runs are double black diamond. Ernie personally named the toughest runs—after Greek gods, Mexican revolutionaries, and German generals who died in their attempts to assassinate Adolf Hitler.

Ernie knew what he wanted in a ski resort, and the broad-shouldered north-facing mountain ridge has it all. Its high altitude and southerly latitude provide a perfect combination of sun and snow—desert-dried snow that Blake described as "fluffy as egg whites and dependable as a Swiss watch." Ernie believed that challenge was essential to the total skiing experience, and he made sure that challenge was built in by personally supervising the cutting of every trail in the early years, insisting on runs that others claimed were too steep to be skied. He resolutely resisted running a lift to the summit of the mountain, 12,481-foot Kachina Peak, where some of the steepest and most outrageous skiing is found. "Americans are too lazy," he said. "The hike is good for them."

And hike they do, for up to an hour to reach the Kachina Peak with its free-fall chutes or for 15 to 20 minutes to the Highline and West Basin ridges. Those areas are the true taste of Taos, but even visiting experts should tackle them only in the company of a guide—or at least a knowledgeable local. Challenge may be the keynote of Taos, but there's plenty of variety here, too. The part of the mountain served by lifts is surprisingly compact and easy to move around on. No matter what your ski level, you can follow the sun across its breadth.

Novices

Despite Taos's fearsome reputation, a good range of green runs is sprinkled around the mountain—in fact, there's a green run down from the top of all the lifts. Start off in the company of the ski school. If you want to go it alone, your best bet is to start by taking the Lift 1 to the top and following White Feather, a long, perfectly groomed run that cruises in and around the trees all the way down. With your legs warmed up, take Lift 1 again, but this time follow White Feather to the base of Lift 6, and at the top go off to the left to hook up with Honeysuckle. With black runs all around you, Honeysuckle is your sanctuary. You'll find the occasional steep pitch, but overall this is a mellow cruise that alternately widens and narrows before snaking back to the bottom of Lift 7. You can also make a sharp left turn at the top of Lower Totemoff, a consistently wide pitch that tends to be less busy than Honeysuckle. This is good because it's also slightly steeper as it shoots down to Lift 7. Take this lift, follow Honeysuckle again, but instead of turning left at the bottom, cut right down Winkleried, a fairly flat runoff that takes you over to the base of the Kachina lift. If you go left off the Kachina lift, you'll find Easy Trip, a tight, winding run through the trees that connects up with Japanese Flag,

which in turn leads you back to Honeysuckle.

If you want to head back to village center, pick up Rubezahl at the base of the Kachina lift. You can ride this extremely mellow and scenic trail for nearly 2 miles, letting your skis run here because there are several flat spots. Keep moving at a steady pace, especially as you come within sight of the village. You can play with this circuit for several days, exploring some of the short cutoff runs that link this green route. When you are ready to try something a little more challenging, head for Porcupine, to the right off Lift 1. This is a well-groomed, wide, and friendly blue run, with enough rolls and pitches to give you some challenge and some easier sections where you can take a breather before pressing on. You can also get to Porcupine on Lift 5, but it operates only when the mountain is busy. At the bottom of Porcupine you can connect with White Feather again and follow this long, flat lower section back to the village center.

Intermediates

Although only 25% of the runs at Taos are blue, you won't lack for challenge or variety. Start your day by heading up Lift 1 from the village, and ski down White Feather until you reach Powderhorn, a good medium-grade blue run that has a variety of rolls and dips to warm your legs. It's always groomed and wide enough to get some good, wide giant-slalom turns working. Near the bottom cut a hard left onto Whitefeather and follow it to the bottom of Lift 8. This lift will take you up to Lower Stauffenberg, a steeper, not always groomed roller-coaster run with a good sustained pitch; it connects up with Don't Tell, then Willy Tell back to the bottom of Lift 8.

Take this back up again and turn left onto Mucho Gusto, a short, fairly steep pitch that carries you to the bottom of Lifts 2 and 6. From the top of either you can turn left and follow Bambi, a moderate blue run that's wide and groomed and fairly easy cruising. Just make sure you don't drop over onto Zagava, a nasty black pitch that starts just above the top of Lift 5. Instead, turn left onto Upper Powderhorn, a gentle speed-controlled pitch that goes back to Lifts 2 and 6. From the top of either you can head down Honeysuckle until you connect with Baby Bear, which will take you to the bottom of the Kachina chair. You can also cut off Honeysuckle onto either Upper Totemoff, with its medium-size moguls on the upper part, or Lone Star, a steep but bump-free pitch. Both will take you to the bottom of Lift 7; or if you turn right onto Winkleried, you can get over to the Kachina chair.

The top of Kachina puts you on Shalako, one of the best blue runs on that mountain. It starts out as a mini-bowl, a steep and wide extension of the seriously steep chutes off the top of the Kachina Ridge, and then narrows slightly as it dips and rolls through some trees before linking up to Baby Bear; here it mellows out as it heads down to Winkleried and back to the base of the chair. You can skip Baby Bear by cutting left onto Papa Bear for a short taste of some decent-size bumps. Keep in mind that to return to the village from this part of the mountain, you have to either take

the long run out Rubezahl or head back up Kachina and follow Shalako to Japanese Flag to Honeysuckle (both green runs) to the base of Lift 7, and from its top take the short Seventh Heaven lift, which deposits you at the top of Bambi. Check your watch and make sure you have time to do this.

Experts
You may as well plunge right in and tackle the precipitous and demanding Al's Run by taking Lift 1. This is a tough, bumpy first-run challenge that will get the legs pumping. You can avoid some of the bumps by staying to the left (looking down), but don't expect much reprieve. Another, less bumpy alternative from the top of Lift 1 is the combination of Rhoda's, Inferno, and Snakedance, three connected runs that are just as steep as Al's Run but not as heavily moguled. Next head for Lift 2 or 6, and as you get off, turn right and take the High Traverse into the steep bowl runs of the West Basin Ridge. Stauffenberg is the most popular choice from here, although as a result it also tends to be the busiest. Less crowded alternatives are Reforma, Blitz, and West Blitz, which are steep and wide and provide some high-speed giant-slalom cruising. Narrower pitches with straight-shot verticals for speed junkies are Spitfire, Oster, and Fabian. You can take an extended hike—about 15 minutes—to the West Basin Ridge, where you'll find the wide-open bowl terrain of St. Bernard, Thunderbird, Hondo, and Wonder Bowl. These are real snow traps and, because of the effort required to reach them, are seldom, if ever, busy. The only downside

is the need to take the blue Lower Stauffenberg (which connects to Don't Tell and Willy Tell) down to the bottom of Lift 8; take it to the top and then ski down another blue run (Mucho Gusto) to the bottom of Lift 6 to get back up to the High Traverse. From there you can stay in the West Ridge Basin or turn left off the lift and head for the gladed runs of the Walkyries Bowl. Walkyries Chute, Sir Arnold Lunn, and Lorelei Trees are all steep and deep snow runs with tightly packed thickets of trees and sudden and unpredictable drop-offs.

When you are ready for Taos's ultimate test, it's time to head for Kachina Peak. You ride Lift 6 to the beginning of a 60- to 75-minute hike up to the Highline Ridge, and for obvious reasons this route is not for the faint of heart or weak of legs. Never, under any circumstances, attempt to tackle this alone; all skiers are required to check into the patrol shack before starting out. It's a strenuous hike, but the effort will be rewarded by the runs that give Taos its fearsome reputation. Everything from the Highline Ridge is ultrasteep, double-black-diamond stuff, and if the patrollers have any suspicion that you can't handle this, they'll send you back down. You can have another, less demanding steep bowl experience in the Hunziker Bowl, which is a five-minute hike to the right (looking down) of Lift 4. The Hunziker Bowl looks innocent enough when you start out on its mellow, concave upper part, but it quickly turns ultrasteep and narrow, forcing you into quick, short, precise turns. If you really want to experience the full measure of the Taos mystique, try to hook up with a local or an area guide and always keep a trail map in your pocket.

OTHER SNOW SPORTS

You can extend your Taos snow experience with a bounce down the new **tubing** hill or an idyllic spin on the **ice-skating** rink in the base village. Or you can rent **snowshoes** from any of the on-mountain ski shops and trek into the 13,000-ft peaks and high alpine lakes in the Kit Carson National Forest. Check with the Forest Service for avalanche conditions.

NEARBY

Angel Fire Resort (Box drawer B, Angel Fire, NM 87710. tel. 505/377–6401 or 800/633–7463), a medium-size family mountain 28 miles east of Taos, has a challenging variety of snowboarding terrain plus a terrain park at the top of the mountain. **Red River Ski Area** (Box 900, Red River, NM 87558, tel. 505/754–2382), 35 miles southwest of Taos, is a family and beginner ski mountain that has "the lowest, slowest and unscariest" lift in the Southern Rockies. **Ski Rio** (Box 159, Costilla, NM 87524. tel. 505/758–7707 or 800/227–5746), 48 miles northeast of Taos, has night snowboarding and one of the only half-pipes in the region.

WHERE TO STAY

Eighteen miles separate the town of Taos from the mountain village; where you choose to stay depends on your priorities. Mountainside accommodations tend to be slightly more expensive but obviously more convenient. It's also fairly quiet in the evenings, with a limited number of dining spots. This is not necessarily a problem, as many lodges offer package deals with meals included. The town of Taos is wonderfully rich in history, culture, dining, and entertainment options, and if you want to take full advantage of them, your best bet is to choose a hotel in town. There are also numerous accommodations on Ski Valley Road, but at any of them a car is essential.

Reservations and other arrangements can be booked through the **Taos Valley Resort Association** (Box 85, Taos 87525, tel. 505/776–2233 or 800/776–1111). There's also the **Taos Bed & Breakfast Association** (Box 2772, Taos 87571, tel. 505/758–4747 or 800/876–7857), which can book you into any of the numerous B&Bs in the area.

Expensive

Chalet Montesano
Unlike most accommodations at the Taos mountain village, this secluded and stylish retreat is tucked away in the woods, a short walk from the ski village. It's a large Swiss alpine–style chalet with studios, a one-bedroom, and suites. The decor in all units is mountain elegance, with rich honey-colored and pine-paneled walls. There's a marvelous light-filled, cedar-lined spa with an indoor lap pool and a Jacuzzi, plus exercise equipment. Four of the suites have fireplaces. Serene and romantic, this place does not accommodate children under 14. *Box 77, Taos Ski Valley 87525, tel. 505/776–8226 or 800/723–9104, fax 505/776–8760. 7 units. Facilities: health spa, Jacuzzi, indoor lap pool. AE, D, MC, V. $130–$276.*

St. Bernard Condominiums
These excellent modern condominiums are among the most upscale at the resort. The two-bedroom, two-bathroom units sleep six people. The decor is modern Southwestern, with soft pastel tones, well-crafted furniture, and lots of colorful accents. Each unit comes with a fully equipped kitchen and a fireplace. They usually rent by the week, though exceptions are sometimes made. *Box 676, Taos Ski Valley 87525, tel. 505/776–8506 or 888/306–4135. 12 units. Facilities: hot tub. AE, MC, V. $975–$1,320 per week, including dinner nightly at St. Bernard Hotel (see below), 6 days' skiing, and lessons.*

St. Bernard Hotel
When you stay at the St. Bernard, you don't just get a room, you get an experience: a symphony of lodging, dining, ski lessons, entertainment, and skiing orchestrated by Jean Mayer, owner of the lodge, technical director of the Taos Ski School, and one of the pioneers of Taos Ski Valley. The rustic log-and-cedar lodge is a marvelous European-style hostelry with cozy accommodations. The lodge, just steps from the lifts, comprises three buildings. The rooms are actually quite small but not lacking for anything (except TV, telephone, and fireplace) with their quaintness enhanced by white wood-trimmed walls, handmade wooden furniture, bright quilts, and tapestries. Meals at the St. Bernard are equally satisfying, with a seven-course dinner that changes daily but leans heavily toward Continental dishes rich with sauces or toward more traditional local accents. *Box 88, Taos Ski Valley*

87525, tel. 505/776–2251. 28 rooms. Facilities: restaurant, lounge, indoor hot tub, workout room, massage, ski shop. No credit cards. $1,190–$1,490 per person, including 3 meals daily, 6 days' skiing, and lessons.

Salsa del Salto
About halfway between the mountain village and the town of Taos, this elegant bed-and-breakfast is a stunning hacienda, designed and built out of native adobe by architect Antoine Predock as his private residence. The interior is anchored by an enormous two-story four-sided stone fireplace, and each of the individually designed rooms has a spectacular view of the surrounding mountains. Bedroom decor extends the New Mexican theme with soft pastel shades of turquoise and peach accented by vivid artwork and striking Navajo-print eiderdowns and sheets, splashy area rugs, and handmade furniture in bleached and painted woods. Box 1468, El Prado 87529, tel. 505/776–2422 or 800/530–3097. 10 rooms, 1 suite. Facilities: library, outdoor pool and hot tub, tennis court. MC, V. $95–$160, including full breakfast and après-ski snacks.

Taos Inn
This marvelous genuine adobe inn is both the physical and cultural heart of Taos. The lobby—with its soaring vigas (projecting wooden roof beams), polished wood floors, arched walls, wrought-iron fixtures, and central fountain (once the town well)—is a local institution. The rooms, like the lobby, are decorated with local art and pottery and filled with handmade furniture and bright rugs, bed covers,

and tapestries. Twenty-two of the rooms have a wood-burning kiva fireplace. Be sure to eat at the restaurant, Doc Martin's. 125 Paseo del Pueblo Norte, Taos 87571, tel. 505/758–2233 or 800/826–7466, fax 505/758–5776. 36 rooms. Facilities: restaurant, bar, pool, indoor Jacuzzi. AE, DC, MC, V. $60–$225.

Moderate

Austing Haus
The Austing Haus is the creation of Paul Austing, the energetic owner, who started in 1982 with just four rooms and now commands an empire that includes the main A-frame-style motel building, the nearby Columbine Lodge, a riverfront building, and several private homes that he oversees for absentee owners. He built the lodge, just a mile from the mountain, from scratch, using mortise and tenon joinery and not a single nail. The rooms at the main lodge and the Columbine are all large and comfortable, with stucco walls, exposed beams, wood trim, and Colonial-style furnishings; many have fireplaces. The private houses have three bedrooms. Box 8, Taos Ski Valley 87525, tel. 505/776–2649 or 800/748–2932, fax 505/776–2649. 45 rooms, 3 houses. Facilities: indoor hot tub, meeting rooms. AE, D, DC, MC, V. $120–$165, including Continental breakfast.

Inn at Snakedance
Previously known as the Hondo Lodge, this was the first accommodation at Taos, originally built as a hunting lodge before the resort opened and now smack in the middle of the mountain village just 10 yards from the quad lift. It's a magnificent structure

made of massive pine timbers cut during a copper-mining operation in the 1890s; the renovation added stucco and brick and a gabled roof true to its hunting-lodge heritage. Inside, it's all exposed beams and stone floors, with a large stone fireplace dominating the lobby area. The rooms are decorated in contemporary mountain style and range in size from standard to deluxe fireplace rooms. Two adjoining units can handle seven persons. *Box 89, Taos Ski Valley 87525, tel. 505/776–2277 or 800/322–9815, fax 505/776–1410. 58 rooms, 2 suites. Facilities: restaurant, lounge, library, health spa with indoor hot tub, sauna, exercise room, massage. AE, MC, V. $195–$215, including full breakfast.*

Kandahar Condominiums
The Kandahar overlooks the mountain village from the edge of Strawberry Hill, a beginners' run that gives you ski-in/ski-out access to the lifts. The building itself is an unremarkable elongated chalet-style structure, but the studios and one- and two-bedroom units are comfortable and spacious, if a little dated in decor. The style is Southwestern rec room, with white walls, dark-wood trim, and earth- or wheat-toned carpets and couches. All the units come with a separate living room, a full kitchen, a fireplace, and two bathrooms. These are good value for slope-side accommodations. *Box 72, Taos Ski Valley 87525, tel. 505/776–2226 or 800/756–2226, fax 505/776–2481. 16 units. Facilities: indoor hot tub, steam room, laundry. MC, V. $250–$400.*

Taos Mountain Lodge
This adobe-style lodge nestles amid the pines and aspens about a mile from the mountain village. The suites are decorated in contemporary Southwestern style, with handmade furnishings, bright handwoven rugs, original art, and polished wood trim. Two standard loft suites have a main-floor bedroom with a queen-size bed and a spacious loft bedroom, as well as a living room and a small kitchenette; eight larger, deluxe loft suites add a full kitchen and a fireplace. The inviting central lobby has a saltillo tile floor, a viga ceiling, and a large stone fireplace. *Box 698, Taos Ski Valley 87525, tel. 505/776–2229 or 800/530–8098, fax 505/776–8791. 10 units. Facilities: indoor and outdoor hot tubs. AE, D, MC, V. $90–$275.*

Inexpensive
El Pueblo Lodge
One of the best bargains in the area, ideal for families, groups, and even budget-minded couples, El Pueblo Lodge is well located, just a few minutes' walk from the Taos Plaza. A complex of six traditional adobe-style buildings surrounds a landscaped courtyard. The rooms and condos are all spacious, clean, and well decorated with traditional Southwestern furnishings, exposed beams, latilla (shaved strips of wood) ceilings, and colorful area rugs. The standard rooms come with two double beds, the efficiency units have a kiva fireplace and a kitchenette, and the condos have either one, two, or three bedrooms, each with a private bath, a full kitchen, a separate living room with a large stone fireplace, and a dining area. *412 Paseo del Pueblo*

Norte, Box 92, Taos 87571, tel. 505/ 758–8700 or 800/433–9612, fax 505/ 758–7321. 45 rooms, 3 units. Facilities: heated outdoor pool, hot tub, laundry. AE, D, MC, V. $68–$235, including Continental breakfast.

Fechin Inn

The 73-year-old Fechin House, built by Russian artist and Taos resident Nicolai Fechin, with its intricate wood carvings and warm adobe charm, is the inspiration behind the new Fechin Inn. Hidden directly behind the Fechin House—which is now an art museum—this large hotel has an enormous atrium with dark wood detail, tile floors, rustic furniture, and roaring fireplaces. The rooms, standard hotel layout, are spacious with Southwestern accents, reproductions of Fechin's work, gas fireplaces, and large bathrooms. Only two blocks from the Taos plaza, the inn has all the amenities of a high-end hotel, including full massages and an exercise room. 227 Paseo del Pueblo Norte, Taos 87571, tel. 505/751–1000 or 800/811–2933, fax 505/751–7338. 81 rooms, 14 suites. Facilities: outdoor hot tub, fitness room, massage. AE, D, MC, V. $109–$488, including Continental breakfast.

Old Taos Guest House

This 150-year-old hacienda of traditional adobe construction is nestled in a secluded grove of trees on a 7½-acre rise just 2 miles from the Taos Plaza. It has been converted into a quiet and cozy bed-and-breakfast with rooms and suites around a picturesque stone courtyard. Each room is decorated in Southwestern style, with vigas and beams, red oak floors, and handmade wooden furnishings all accented with bright Navajo rugs and bedcovers. All rooms and suites have outside entrances on the courtyard. 1028 Witt Rd., Box 6552, Taos, 87571, tel. 505/ 758–5448 or 800/758–5448. 9 rooms, 2 suites. Facilities: outdoor hot tub. MC, V. $70–$125, including Continental breakfast.

Sagebrush Inn

This 1929-vintage pueblo mission-style inn 3 miles from downtown Taos was originally an upscale stopover for well-heeled guests from the East Coast, and the painter Georgia O'Keeffe actually lived here for a while during the 1940s. Today it's a lively hotel, a striking example of classic Southwest architecture, with graceful portals, intimate patios, adobe construction, and a near-priceless collection of rugs, pottery, antiques, and paintings. All the rooms and suites have hand-carved furniture, terra-cotta-tiled bathrooms, Navajo-style rugs and bedcovers, pottery lamps, vigas, and tin light fixtures. S. Santa Fe Rd., Box 557, Taos 87571, tel. 505/758–2254 or 800/ 428–3626, fax 505/758–5077. 48 rooms, 52 suites. Facilities: 2 restaurants, lounge, 2 indoor hot tubs. AE, D, DC, MC, V. $60–$140.

WHERE TO EAT

Because many of the on-mountain lodges offer only all-inclusive meal packages, the mountain village does not have a lot of dining options. However, Taos has an extensive variety, ranging from small local diners to upscale restaurants. There's also much emphasis on traditional Southwestern cuisine, with spicy chili, salsa, and cilantro the most common taste enhancers.

On the Mountain

Phoenix Restaurant

If you want beer or wine with your food, this is the place. It has a number of daily specials, plus sandwiches and burgers cooked on the outdoor barbecue. *Base of Lift 4, tel. 505/776–2291. No credit cards.*

Whistlestop

This basic on-mountain eatery offers a fairly standard lineup of pizzas, sandwiches, soups, and chilis. *Base of Lift 6, tel. 505/776–2291. No credit cards.*

Expensive

Doc Martin's

This is the historic home of Doc Martin, Taos's first doctor, who bought this house (now part of the Taos Inn) in the 1890s. Today it is one of Taos's best restaurants, under the able supervision of chef Patrick Lambert, who trained at Napa's Mustard Grill, among other places. His blending of Asian ingredients with Southwestern flavors, using locally grown organic produce, results in such signature dishes as herb-crusted rack of lamb with roasted shallot souflée or wild salmon with red-curry coconut milk. The best deal is a $16.95 prix-fixe meal, with a choice of five entrées, offered Sunday through Thursday. The restaurant's extensive wine list has won numerous awards. *Taos Inn, 125 Paseo del Pueblo Norte, tel. 505/758–1977. AE, DC, MC, V. Reservations essential.*

Lambert's of Taos

This is the class act in Taos—a refined, clean-lined restaurant with white-on-white decor, soft lighting, marble-top tables, blond hardwood floors, and crystal and linen place settings. The main dining room is the largest, with tables for about 40, but you can also dine in one of three smaller rooms. The menu of contemporary American grill cuisine changes weekly according to the chef's whim. Entrées might include broiled halibut and asparagus stew served on linguine, pepper-crusted lamb served with a garlic pasta, grilled pheasant with port wine sauce and squash soufflé, or grilled pork tenderloin with chipotle sauce and warm potato salad. *309 Paseo del Pueblo Sur, Taos, tel. 505/758–1009. Reservations essential. AE, D, DC, MC, V.*

Trading Post

The first thing that greets you at the entrance of the Trading Post is the restaurant's signature sizzling grill, heavy with the aromas of the day's specials and surrounded by frenetic chef activity. Menu items include rib eye steak seared in lemon parsley oil, lamb chops with a light tomato mint salsa, and a hearty-portioned crisp garlic pork chop. The decor is contemporary Southwestern, with a low-lit warm ambience. *4179 Hwy 68, Taos, tel. 505/758–5089. D, DC, MC, V.*

Villa Fontana

Carlo Gislimberti, the co-owner and chef of this intimate and formal Italian restaurant housed in a traditional adobe building, has won high praise for his innovative Northern Italian cooking. Carlo is also a preeminent mycophagist (mushroom epicure), and his wild mushroom soup is to die for. The many daily specials include osso buco (succulent veal shanks braised in wine and herbs). Among his fish dishes are whole Dover sole and grilled salmon. *Rte. 522, 5 mi north of Taos, tel. 505/758–5800. AE, D, DC, MC, V.*

Moderate

The Bavarian

Isolated from the main village at the base of the Kachina lift is a Bavarian paradise. Its golden timbers draped with lace and sheepskin emanate coziness, as do the Austrian music and the waitstaff's traditional Bavarian dress. The fare is hearty Bavarian at its best: panfried pork chops, grilled venison medallions, and Bavarian spaetzle with onions, sausage, bacon, and garlic. Don't miss a large stein of one of the excellent imported beers. *Base of Kachina lift (No. 4), Taos Ski Valley, tel. 505/751–6661. AE, MC, V.*

Glass Dining Room

The atrium-style room is festooned with plants, paintings, and antiques and built with the same nail-free craftsmanship for which the Austing Haus is renowned. It's a bright, cheery room; if you prefer a little intimacy, ask for a table in the raised alcove near the fireplace. The menu offers a little of everything—medallions of beef bordelaise and traditional steaks; scampi, orange roughy, and sea kabobs; and a selection of chicken and pasta dishes. For dessert, the homemade apple strudel is outstanding. *Austing Haus, Taos Ski Valley, tel. 505/776–2649. DC, MC, V.*

Inn at Snakedance Dining Room

The dining room here is large and formal without being too fussy—a vaulted ceiling with exposed beams, wide windows, hand-plastered walls decorated with old black-and-white photographs of the region and local artwork, and a large stone fireplace. The menu offers traditional Southwestern fare such as organic chicken chipotle with barbecue sauce or prawns sautéed in white wine and basil served over spinach noodles with a grilled red pepper sauce, as well as broiled New York strip steak with grilled roasted green chili butter. *Inn at Snakedance, Taos Ski Valley, tel. 505/776–2277. MC, V.*

Stakeout Grill and Bar

The Stakeout, about 8 miles south of town, has a spectacular setting high atop Outlaw Hill with a 360-degree panorama of the surrounding countryside. The restaurant, in an old adobe building, has Wild West artifacts and collectibles that add to its rustic and casual atmosphere. Steaks are a mainstay, big and charbroiled. Seafood options include grilled salmon, Alaskan king crab legs, and baked rainbow trout, and there are veal scallopini sautéed with marsala wine and artichokes and chicken roll wrapped in goat cheese and sun-dried tomatoes. *Rte. 68, Outlaw Hill, 4 mi south of Ranchos de Taos, Taos, tel. 505/758–2042. AE, D, DC, MC, V.*

Inexpensive

Bravo

Bravo is Taos's neighborhood gathering place. Resident artists and architects mingle in this brightly lit gourmet deli and restaurant over wine or salmon bisque. Community tables encourage the exchange, but cozy two-person spots also make room for intimacy in the cacophonous atmosphere. The food is divine, ranging from hearty crusty-bread sandwiches to designer pastas. The wine selection is immense, filling the back walls of the restaurant. *1353-A Paseo del Pueblo Sur, Taos, tel. 505/758–8100. AE, MC, V.*

El Pueblo Café
This is a classic diner with a lunch counter, lots of cheap chrome, fake wood tables, and a delightful greasy-spoon atmosphere. The menu has two sides—standard comfort food, such as fried chicken, pork chops, burgers, sandwiches, and breakfast all day, and traditional Mexican dishes including fajitas, red or green chili relleños, burritos, tacos, and enchiladas. Fast, friendly, and virtually unknown by visitors, it has the best Mexican grub in town. *625 Paseo del Pueblo Norte, Rte. 522, Taos, tel. 505/758–2053. D, DC, MC, V.*

Outback
This is a wonderful, rough place, with wooden floors and walls and a noisy, steamy atmosphere. The restaurant, warmed by a giant antique woodstove, is redolent with the aromas emanating from the large open kitchen. It's not fancy and can get awfully crowded, but it serves the best pizza in town—thick crusted with more than a dozen choices of toppings. There's also an excellent selection of salads served with fresh-baked pita bread, daily soup specials, pastas, and calzone. *Paseo del Pueblo Norte, Rte. 522, Taos, tel. 505/758–3112. MC, V.*

Tim's Stray Dog Cantina
This is a loud and lively spot on the mountain much favored by a young local crowd for its good, inexpensive northern New Mexican dishes. In addition to enchiladas, burritos, tacos, and tortillas, there is an excellent chili relleño, as well as cilantro chicken, panfried trout, and tequila shrimp. Tim's, though, is best known for its green chilis; amateurs beware—these are real sizzlers. *Taos Ski Valley mountain village, tel. 505/776–2894. AE, MC, V.*

Best Bets for Breakfast
Casa Fresen Bakery
In the heart of Arroyo Seco, a small village on the Ski Valley Road up to the mountain, this is a good place to stop for fresh-baked breads, muffins, pastries, and cakes. It also has the best coffee in the area. *482 State Rd., Rte. 150, Arroyo Seco, tel. 505/776–2969. MC, V.*

Michael's Kitchen
Enter Michael's kitchen any day of the week, any time of the day, and you can expect a crowd. But this doesn't mean your breakfast will be delayed, it only shows the popularity of this New Mexican-style bakery and diner. Don't let the pastries displayed in glass cases distract you from Michael's famous breakfast burrito, smothered in red or green chili. Breakfast is served all day. *304 Paseo del Pueblo Norte, Taos, tel. 505/758–4178. AE, D, MC, V.*

NIGHTLIFE AND ENTERTAINMENT
If you come to Taos for the nightlife and entertainment, you're sure to be disappointed, especially up in the mountain village, where the action is severely limited after the après-ski period. The town of Taos is a little

livelier, but it still doesn't have the action-oriented bar and nightclub scene found at some other resorts.

Après-Ski
Martini Tree
In the main base lodge building, this busy, hustling spot has live entertainment, high-decibel conversations, dancing, and a large sundeck. It tends to attract a younger crowd. *Taos Ski Valley Mountain Village, tel. 505/776–2291. AE, MC, V.*

Rathskeller
When the sun is shining, the Cheeseburgers in Paradise Sun Deck is the place to hang out, but when the weather turns foul, step inside to this woody bar filled with antiques, atmosphere, dancing, and live entertainment—reggae, rock, jazz, and blues. *Hotel St. Bernard, Taos Ski Valley, tel. 505/776–2251. No credit cards.*

Loud and Lively/Dancing
Eske's Brew Pub
This is something a little different for Taos—a British-style pub. Eske's presents a sterling lineup of well-crafted brews, including a novel and delicious green chili variety. It's a friendly, comfortable place in a 70-year-old flat-roofed adobe building renovated by members of the Taos ski patrol. Live entertainment—jazz or folk—happens at least four nights a week, and you can graze on an eclectic mixture of pub grub. *106 Desgeorges La., near Taos Plaza, Taos, tel. 505/758–1517. MC, V.*

Sagebrush Inn
Live country-and-western entertainment is the ticket here, and the place really jumps even though it's 2 miles outside town. The lounge actually spills out into the lobby, giving it a free-form kind of atmosphere, and a steady stream of dancers roams the dance floor. It's definitely one of the livelier spots in town. *1508 Paseo del Pueblo Sur, Taos, tel. 505/758–2254. AE, D, DC, MC, V.*

More Mellow
Adobe Bar
One of the best places to relax, have a slow cocktail, and watch live music, the bar is nestled between the Inn's lobby and the dining room. When you're settled in front of the band—ranging from mariachi to jazz—all peripheral activity disappears. *In Taos Inn, 125 Paseo del Pueblo Norte, Taos, tel. 505/758–2233. AE, MC, V.*

No state in the United States can count as many individual ski resorts as New York. From the Catskills in the southern part of the state to the rugged Adirondacks in the north, some 70 individual ski areas range in size from tiny two-lift mom-and-pop local areas to the storied Olympic region of Lake Placid with towering Whiteface Mountain.

Although the well-rounded mountains of the lesser ranges provide 99% of the state's resorts, it is the mighty Adirondacks that provide the best skiing. In the northeast corner of the state, within a day's drive of more than 35 million people, they encompass an area slightly larger than the state of Connecticut and run north nearly to the Canadian border. In all, this rugged range has 42 peaks that top the 4,000-foot mark, including Mt. Marcy, at 5,344 feet, with its Lake Tear of the Clouds, the northern source of the Hudson River. Their general elevation is higher than that of any range east of the Rockies. The 6-million-acre Adirondack Park—2.6 million acres of which are under the jurisdiction of the New York State Forest Preserve and must remain "forever wild"—is spectacular not only for its peaks but also for its vast tracts of dense forest, its countless lakes and gushing trout streams, and its impressive gorges and waterfalls.

The marvelous resort town of Lake Placid has been shaped by the surrounding Adirondack wilderness, the money of the rich, and the sweat of Olympic athletes. It is a town full of memories of a gilded age: beginning about a century ago, millionaires built their luxury retreats here and on surrounding lakes as refuges from the cities and their powerful businesses. Their sprawling "camps" still dot the shorelines here, their luster somewhat dimmed but their style still a fond memory. If ever a town was inextricably linked with the five rings of the Winter Games, it is this tiny mountain village. In the 1932 and 1980 Olympics the athletes created images and memories of snow and ice that are at least as enduring as the camps of the rich and reclusive.

WHITEFACE MOUNTAIN SKI CENTER

Wilmington, New York
Tel. 518/946–2223
www.orda.org/
whiteface.shtml
Olympic Regional Development Authority
Olympic Center
Lake Placid, New York 12946
Tel. 518/523–1655 or
800/462–6236

STATISTICALLY SPEAKING

Base elevation: 1,200 feet

Summit elevation: 4,867 feet

Vertical drop: 3,216 feet

Skiable terrain: 174 acres

Number of trails: 67

Longest run: 3 miles

Lifts and capacity: 1 quad, 2 triples, 6 doubles, 1 handle tow; 11,470 skiers per hour

Lift ticket: $39 weekdays, $39 weekends

Average annual snowfall: 168 inches

Number of skiing days 1997–98: 143

Snowmaking: 165 acres, 95%

Terrain mix: N 32%, I 34%, E 34%

Snowboarding: yes

Cross-country skiing: 31 miles (Mt. Van Hoevenberg)

Lake Placid, no longer a playground of the rich and storied, is now an egalitarian winter-sports center with a plethora of medium-price accommodations. Families and groups of college students with varied interests and conservative budgets take advantage of the diverse options available within close range. Evidence of Olympic influence is everywhere, from the unsurpassed—in eastern North America, at least—Olympic winter-sports facilities to the extensive services in town. You could easily spend a couple of days in Lake Placid and stay entertained even if you never hit the Olympic slopes on Whiteface Mountain. Shops, restaurants, bars, cafés, and hotels line Main Street, and within a 5-mile drive there's virtually unlimited winter-sports excitement. Ride the Olympic bobsled or luge runs; ski the meticulous trails of the Mt. Van Hoevenberg Olympic Cross-Country Center; take a spin around the 400-meter Olympic speed-skating oval; or simply stand in the Olympic arena and recall the improbable victory of an overachieving U.S. team against the heavily favored Russians in the 1980 Olympic hockey tournament. Quite simply, Lake Placid offered a great diversity of winter resort possibilities for nearly 20 years—long before other ski areas began adding off-slope and after-hours events and activities. As a result, the Olympic Region consistently scores at or near the top of ski-magazine surveys for total resort experience year in and year out. The town itself is actually on Mirror Lake, separated from Lake Placid by a narrow isthmus. It is quite compact, with action-packed Main Street running the length of Mirror Lake. The majority of the stores, restaurants, bars, and accommodations are strung between the Olympic speed-skating oval at one end of town and the venerable Mirror Lake Inn at the other. The south end of Saranac Avenue (heading west away from the lake) is lined with numerous motels and restaurants, but for most visitors Main Street is the main track.

The Olympic Regional Development Authority (ORDA) manages the facilities left over from the Olympics and develops innovative programs to ensure maximum usage. The area would benefit from an efficient shuttle system, which would reduce backed-up traffic between town and the mountain

Children's services: instruction, tel. 518/946–2223

Snow phone: tel. 800/462–6236

Police: tel. 518/523–3306

Medical center: tel. 518/523–3311

Lake Placid Visitors Bureau: tel. 518/523–2445 or 800/447–5224

Whiteface Mountain Regional Visitors Bureau: tel. 518/946–2255

Road conditions: tel. 800/847–8929

Towing: Central Garage, tel. 518/523–3378

FIVE-STAR FAVORITES

Best run for vertical: Cloudspin

Best run overall: Cloudspin to Broadway to Lower Boreen

Best bar/nightclub: The Cottage

Best hotel: Mirror Lake Inn

Best restaurant: Nicola's Over Main

and help Lake Placid match the developments taking place at other ski areas.

HOW TO GET THERE

By Plane

Albany International Airport (tel. 518/242–2200), is the closest international airport to Lake Placid/Whiteface, which is a 2½-hour drive away. Many major airlines serve Albany, among them American Airlines (tel. 800/433–7300), Continental and Continental Express (tel. 800/525–0280), Delta (tel. 800/221–1212), Delta Express (tel. 800/325–5205), Northwest (tel. 800/225–2525), United (tel. 800/241–6522), and US Airways (tel. 800/428–4322). The **Lake Placid Airport** (tel. 518/523–2473), a mile south of the village on Route 73, serves chartered aircraft. The **Adirondack Airport** (tel. 518/891–4600) is northwest of Saranac Lake, 16 miles from Lake Placid on Route 186, just off Route 86. USAir Express (tel. 518/891–2290) flies here from Newark, Albany, and Boston.

By Car

From the metropolitan New York City area and northern New Jersey, take the New York State Thruway (I–87) north to Exit 24 (Albany) then the Northway (I–87) to Exit 30. Follow Route 9 north 2 miles to Route 73 and continue 28 miles west to Lake Placid.

From Buffalo, Rochester, Syracuse, and points west, take I–90 (the west section of the New York State Thruway) east to Exit 36 (Syracuse) and pick up I–81N to Watertown. At Route 3 go east to Saranac Lake, then take Route 86 east to Lake Placid.

From Boston, Springfield, and Hartford, take I–90 west (here it's the Massachusetts Turnpike) to Albany, then I–787 north to Cohoes. Connect with Route 7W and then take I–87 north. Follow I–87 to Exit 30 and pick up Route 9N for 2 miles to Route 73. Continue for 28 miles west to Lake Placid.

Avis (Adirondack Airport, Cascade Rd., tel. 518/523–1498 or 800/331–1212) and **Hertz** (69 Saranac Ave., tel. 518/523–3158 or 800/654–3131) have offices in Lake Placid.

By Bus

Adirondack Trailways (tel. 800/225–6815) has regularly scheduled service from Albany and New York City and its suburbs.

By Train

Amtrak (tel. 800/872–7245) has a line from New York City with a stop in Westport, New York (40 minutes from Lake Placid). Shuttle bus service to Lake Placid is available through **Lake Placid Sightseeing Tours** (tel. 518/523–4431) and **Adirondack Trailways** (*see above*).

GETTING AROUND

A car is indispensable in Lake Placid, both because of the absence of an efficient shuttle bus system and because it's 9 miles from the town to the mountain, which is in the hamlet of Wilmington. At Whiteface there's parking by the mountain and a free pickup and drop-off service to take you from your car to the base lodge and back if you don't get a parking space close enough to walk.

Lake Placid Sightseeing (tel. 518/523–4431) has scheduled runs between the major hotels in the village and the mountain for $5 per person (one-way or round-trip). Call for times. The downtown area is small enough to walk everywhere, but if you want to take a taxi, try **Jan's Taxi** (tel. 518/523–1891).

THE SKIING

Whiteface Mountain is not the highest peak in the Adirondacks, but its Olympian reputation overshadows others in the region. Whiteface sits alone, 9 miles by road from Lake Placid, exposed on all sides and occasionally buffeted by cold winds from Canada or shrouded in low clouds produced by warm and cold fronts clashing in the sky above.

Because it's in the Adirondack Forest Preserve, the mountain is not excessively built up. You won't have to navigate condos or souvenir shops on these slopes—the trails, the lifts, a base lodge, a midstation lodge, and other skiers are all you'll see besides what's here naturally.

The mountain has taken its share of knocks from skiers who complain about the frigid weather, the windswept slopes, and the relatively antiquated lift network that runs to the summit of Whiteface and its shoulder peak of Little Whiteface. There's truth in all three complaints: Whiteface can be brutally cold and windy, and despite the nearly 100% snowmaking, many of the exposed runs on the upper mountain can be rock-hard and icy. But almost every ski mountain in the East can be battered by the hand of winter, and on a good skiing day Whiteface's 3,216 vertical feet (the greatest of any mountain in the East) can be as good as it gets.

More annoying than the capriciousness of winter weather, however, is the tediously slow collection of old, fixed-grip chairlifts that pale in comparison to the fast, modern, detachable quads that most resorts now provide. In 1997 Whiteface replaced the rickety Summit triple with a fixed-grip quad, but its top terminal is so small that the chair is run at 3/4 speed to allow people to clear the area. As a result, it takes more than 20 minutes to ride the two chairs to the summit. Whiteface could use an upgrade.

Another anomaly of this Olympic mountain is that it has more to offer experts and beginners than true intermediates. Experts will relish the steep challenge of the upper mountain, and novices won't get into any trouble from midmountain on down, but intermediates will find themselves caught between the two areas. They must either put up with reasonably tame cruising or push themselves into tackling some of the black trails on Little Whiteface.

Those problems aside, Whiteface can be an exhilarating experience, a true northeastern in-your-face clash with nature. It's certainly one of the most challenging mountains east of the Rockies. Its temperament is moderated by the top-to-bottom snowmaking that is just one of the region's Olympic legacies.

Novices

Beginners at Whiteface have their own secluded sections to the left and right of the main base area. Neverevers should start at the Bunny Hutch lift (to your right, as you look up the mountain) and try the Bronze, Silver, or Gold runs—a trio of smooth, wide, gentle trails that meander down the slope. Main Street, Runner Up, and Medalist, on the same side, also give a good, smooth ride. To the far left of the base area is the Bear lift, which serves a trio of wider, softly falling novice runs called Wolf, Bear, and Deer.

When you're ready for something a little longer, take the Valley triple chair to midmountain, turn right off the lift and enjoy the long way down

on Easy Way to Upper Boreen. From here take Ladies Bridge to Boreen, then link up with Bronze, Silver, or Gold to the bottom. This series of trails starts out a bit steep at Easy Way but quickly turns to gentle slopes.

Intermediates

Steady intermediates may be a little frustrated when skiing Whiteface because their share of the terrain is considerably less than that at more modern resorts. For instance, there are only two blue trails that come down from the summit, Paron's Run and the Follies, so if you want to enjoy upper-elevation skiing, you may have to push your limits by taking on some of the steeper black runs. Start by riding the Valley triple lift and the Summit quad lift to Paron's Run, a mile-long reasonably wide giant-slalom cruiser that winds its way down to the shoulder of Little Whiteface. Here it connects with the shorter, steeper pitches of Lower Northway, Excelsior, and Lower Cloudspin. All three take you back to the base of the summit quad, where you can catch a ride back to the summit without getting caught up in the lower mountain traffic. If you find the upper part of Paron's Run a little too steep, the Follies lets you skirt the advanced intermediate section off the summit and reconnects with Paron's Run a little farther down the mountain.

In the notch just below Little Whiteface, Paron's runs into Excelsior, a relentlessly twisting intermediate run with tight turns and drop-offs— take it to the bottom of the Summit quad, or cut left early and ski Connector to Lower Cloudspin. You can stretch out your summit run by getting on Broadway, just below the Summit quad lift, then connecting with River Run and then Danny's Bridge and Boreen for a long cruise to the valley. The only problem with this route is that you are forced to take the generally busy Valley triple lift back up to midmountain, then the Summit quad lift back to the top. You won't get into any real trouble on any of these blue runs: all are good, wide cruisers with the occasional drop-off and slightly steeper pitch, and they have the most consistent grooming on the mountain.

Your other option for a little more steepness and challenge or to warm up for the black runs is to ride the Little Whiteface lift from the top of the Mid-Station Shuttle lift or to ski down Upper Valley from the top of Valley triple and take a crack at Parkway and Thruway, a pair of short black-to-blue high-speed cruisers that were the courses for the 1980 Olympic giant slalom events. For a bit more challenge, try Mountain Run or the moguls on Wilderness, both black trails reached by the same lift.

On good snow days, strong intermediates can enjoy the steep, occasionally bumpy Essex and McKenzie runs, also accessible from the top of Little Whiteface. Although they're designated black, they're manageable. When you're ready to push the thrill meter up a notch, take the Summit quad to the top of Whiteface and take a run down either Upper Cloudspin or Skyward, the men's and women's Olympic downhill course. They may be steep and twisting, but they're generally bump-free.

Experts

Head straight for the summit and get your legs warmed up on either Skyward—the women's Olympic downhill—or Cloudspin, the men's Olympic downhill. Both are high-speed giant-slalom runs with plenty of pitch, numerous turns, drop-offs, and even the occasional bumpy section. Unless you're heading over to Little Whiteface double chair, don't drop below the base of the Summit quad lift: the run-out to the lower base area is a tame blue cruise. Though the runs from the summit have the most sustained vertical, it's off the Little Whiteface double that you'll find the highest concentration of expert trails: Wilderness is where the bumps grow largest, especially on the left side, where World Cup and Olympic-qualifier bump competitions are held; Upper Parkway and Upper Thruway—the Olympic giant-slalom courses—give you as much pitch without the bumps; or you can opt for the high-speed, generally well-groomed Upper McKenzie or the short, super-narrow and never-groomed Empire.

Experts with good timing are in for a treat at Whiteface: in 1998, mountain management began allowing skiers onto the open rock slides to the right of the Summit quad (looking up). For years "the Slides" were the province of poachers and backcountry skiers; now, with significant snow cover and favorable weather, ski patrol will allow experts to hike from the top of the Summit quad out onto the steep open face of the mountain's upper cirque. The runs are long and, in places, unskiable (a waterfall is circumvented by a newly cut trail through the woods around to its base). Slide Out, a narrow traverse through the woods from the bottom of the Slides, connects with Lower Skyward for the return to the base of the Summit quad. (Insider's tip: the Slides open up so much new terrain—almost 100 acres—that management does not add the acreage to the area's total for fear that, when closed, the Slides would drag down the percentage of Whiteface's open terrain.)

SNOWBOARDING

A 450-foot half-pipe was developed in 1999; located on Bear, a gentle beginner run to the left of the base area, the pipe benefits from its proximity to the Bear double chair, meaning riders can hoof back uphill along the rim of the pipe or opt for an easy lift ride. Whiteface uses a Bombardier HPG (half-pipe grinder) to fine-tune the pipe. Farther up the hill and on Danny's Bridge, boarders can look for an element-packed terrain park equipped with hips, quarters, triple and diamond jumps, and kickers of various sizes. When it's time to hit the mountain, snowboarders of at least intermediate ability should take the Little Whiteface double chair to the top of Little Whiteface and head for Excelsior. Its dozen-plus turns and plentiful drops offer ample opportunity for carving and improvising. Riders on narrower alpine boards and stiff boots tend to congregate on Mountain Run and then try to out-carve each other, especially in the morning when it's been freshly groomed. There's a critical but appreciative audience overhead, so don't blow it! Boarders who want to push the envelope should head for the summit and hike to the Slides (*see* Experts in The Skiing, *above*).

NEARBY

If you're in the mood to explore other slopes not spangled in Olympic regalia and hype, look into two areas not far away. **Big Tupper Ski Area** (Country Club Road, off Rte 30, Tupper Lake, tel. 518/359-7902 or 800/824-4754), 33 miles west of Lake Placid, has lots of good intermediate trails. Another intermediate haven, **Gore Mountain** (Peaceful Valley Rd., off Rte 28, North Creek, tel. 518/251-2411), about 80 miles south of Lake Placid, is operated by ORDA, so a multiday Whiteface pass is valid here as well.

WHERE TO STAY

One of the more practical legacies of the 1980 Olympics is the ample supply of medium-price accommodations that were built to handle the crowds. Around every corner downtown and immediately off the main thoroughfares, small motel and cabin developments with vacancy signs push their way to the road. Many of the nicer places are less visible. Accommodations can also be found in the surrounding area, including Saranac Lake, about 8 miles west on Highway 86, and all lodgings can be booked through the **Lake Placid Visitors' Bureau** (tel. 518/523-2445).

Expensive

Lake Placid Lodge
Built in 1882, this vestige of the age of Great Camps is on the shore of Lake Placid, about 4 miles west of the village. Its rooms combine rustic opu-

lence with modern comforts. All are woody and warm, with twig and birch-bark furnishings, antiques, Oriental rugs, fireplaces, and a great view of the lake. The location is pure romance. *Whiteface Inn Rd., Box 550, Lake Placid, 12946, tel. 518/523–2573, fax 518/523–1124. 17 rooms, 17 cabins. Facilities: restaurant, pub, lounge, library, game room, maid service, ski storage, cross-country skiing. AE, MC, V. $300–$700.*

Lake Placid Resort Holiday Inn

This plain blockhouse-style structure, built in 1969, occupies a high point overlooking the Olympic Arena and contains an unexpected variety of large, modern, brightly decorated rooms, suites, chalets, and condos. Extensive on-site amenities make this place suitable for families. *1 Olympic Dr., Lake Placid, 12946, tel. 518/523–2556 or 800/874–1980, fax 518/523–9410. 192 rooms, 13 suites, 2 chalets, 3 units. Facilities: 2 restaurants, bar, lounge, hot tub, indoor pool, fitness room, 24-hr desk service, maid service, ski storage, laundry, game room. AE, D, DC, MC, V. $109–$325.*

Mirror Lake Inn

This resort hotel on a terraced rise at the south end of Mirror Lake is a complex of five buildings anchored by the early 1920s main lodge, which was destroyed by fire in 1988 and carefully restored to neo-Colonial splendor, complete with white exterior, large windows, and high pillars. Inside, the grand style continues, with walnut floors, mahogany wall trim, and comfortable lounge areas full of plush furnishings and antique fix-

tures. Even the smallest rooms are large enough to be comfortable, with marble and mahogany bathrooms, pastel rugs and wall coverings, and plenty of wood trim. *5 Mirror Lake Dr., Lake Placid, 12946, tel. 518/523–2544, fax 518/523–2871. 110 rooms, 18 suites. Facilities: 2 restaurants, 2 bars, sauna, Jacuzzi, indoor pool, health club, massage, full-service salon, library, 24-hr desk service, maid service, ski storage, skating rink, fitness activities. AE, D, DC, MC, V. $125–$325.*

The Point

About 30 miles west of Lake Placid, this exclusive lodge was once the home of multimillionaire William Rockefeller. It is a picture of rustic elegance—set in a rugged woodland on Upper Saranac Lake—with a magnificent log main lodge plus four outbuildings with guest quarters that are spectacularly decorated in deep wine tones and much wood. Each has a massive stone fireplace, Oriental carpets, original art, and Adirondack furnishings and antiques. Dinner is served family style in the 30-foot-by-50-foot Great Hall, and the formal attire (black tie two nights a week) is a fitting salute to haute cuisine. If the snow is good, you can cross-country ski nearby, and when the lake freezes over, it's ideal for ice-skating. *HCR 1, Box 65, Saranac Lake 12983, tel. 518/891–5674 or 800/255–3530, fax 518/891–1152. 11 rooms. Facilities: bar, pub, maid service, ski storage, snowshoeing, ice-skating, ice fishing, cross-country skiing. AE, MC, V. $900–$1600, including all meals and activities.*

Moderate

Hungry Trout Motor Inn

This motel on 10 acres in Wilmington—about a half mile from the ski area and the closest full-service accommodations to Whiteface Mountain—is tucked away in the trees overlooking the Flume Falls section of the Ausable River. Each of the cozy, practical rooms has two double beds, a TV, and a coffeemaker. The two-room suites are a good choice for families or groups who want to be on the quieter side of Lake Placid. *Rte. 86, Wilmington, 12997, tel. 518/946–2217 or 800/766–9137, fax 518/946–7418. 20 rooms, 2 suites. Facilities: 2 restaurants, bar. AE, D, DC, MC, V. $59–$139.*

Interlaken Inn

You won't have to look hard to find this fully restored 1906 Victorian inn in a stand of trees overlooking Mirror Lake. The Interlaken is three stories high, and its clapboard exterior is painted a gay Colonial blue with cream trim. The rooms range in size from small and cozy to large and spacious, but each has a private bath and is a trove of antiques and reproductions, with four-poster, canopy, brass, and other period beds plus touches like bird's-eye-maple dressers, Lincoln rockers, and handmade quilts. *15 Interlaken Ave., Lake Placid, 12946, tel. 518/523–3180 or 800/428–4369. 11 rooms. Facilities: restaurant, bar, lounge, ski storage, maid service. AE, MC, V. $140–$210, including all meals.*

Stagecoach Inn

Built in 1833 as a stopover for coaches, this is the oldest hotel—and probably the oldest building—in Lake Placid. It still presents a striking portrait of the 19th century, with its wraparound front porch, Georgia pine wainscoting, antique furniture, lace curtains, and fireplaces. There are only nine rooms, each individually furnished with a brass-and-iron bed, a handmade quilt, Native American art, and antiques. Two of the larger rooms have fireplaces. *370 Old Military Rd., Lake Placid 12946, tel. 518/523–9474. 9 rooms. Facilities: maid service. MC, V. $60–$85.*

Wildwood on the Lake

On Lake Placid's Paradox Bay a ten-minute walk from Main Street, Wildwood offers a wide array of cottages and kitchenette units, in addition to lakeside and lakeview rooms, that are great for families and large groups. Some rooms and cottages have jet tubs, kitchens, fireplaces, and views of Whiteface Mountain. *388 Saranac Ave., Lake Placid 12946, tel. 518/523–2624, fax 518/523–3248. 28 rooms, 3 efficiencies, 2 cottages. Facilities: TV, VCR, Jacuzzis, sauna, whirlpool, maid service, ski storage. AE, DC, MC, V. $48–$165.*

Inexpensive

Adirondack Inn

This two-story stone-frame building opposite the Olympic Arena has straightforward hotel-type accommodations and is favored by ski groups and families. Rooms are comfortable, with two double beds and a bathroom, and the decor is cheerful, with floral print spreads, a table for two, and sliding glass doors that open onto a balcony. *217 Main St., Lake Placid 12946, tel. 518/523–2424 or 800/*

556–2424, fax 518/523–2425. 49 rooms. Facilities: 2 restaurants, bar, lounge, indoor pool, sauna, Jacuzzi, exercise facilities, 24-hr desk service, maid service, ski storage, game room. AE, MC, V. $60–$130.

Mt. Van Hoevenberg Bed & Breakfast

This pleasant natural-wood farmhouse—with just three rooms in the main building plus eight small cabins on the 5-acre property—is next to the Mt. Van Hoevenberg Olympic recreation facility. The rooms are basic, with either a double bed, two twins, or one double and bunks. Cabins are different sizes, with beds for as many as six, but all have complete kitchen facilities. Rte. 73, HCR 1 Box 37, Lake Placid 12946, tel. 518/523–9572. 3 rooms share 2 baths, 8 cabins. Facilities: ski-waxing room, sauna. AE, MC, V. $60–$150, including full breakfast (in rooms).

Town & Country Motor Inn

A clean, simple, centrally located motel-type lodge, it has a variety of modern rooms in sizes that can accommodate from two to six people. You get full value for your money here. 65–67 Saranac Ave., Lake Placid 12946, tel. 518/523–9268 or 800/283–4678, fax 518/523–8058. 24 rooms, 1 suite, 1 cottage. Facilities: maid service. AE, D, MC, V. $95–$120, including full breakfast.

WHERE TO EAT

Although there is no shortage of places to eat, Lake Placid is basically a meat-and-potatoes town, and there's little in the way of creative cuisine. Steaks and other standard meat dishes top most menus, but with a little effort it's possible to uncover a smattering of more adventurous offerings. You'll find the majority of eateries on and around Main Street, with a select few off the main drag.

Expensive

Averil Conwell Dining Room

This elegant but casual restaurant at the Mirror Lake Inn has a mahogany-trimmed fireplace, candlelight, a floral-print burgundy carpet, mahogany accents, murals and paintings by Lake Placid artist Averil Courtney Conwell, and best of all, a superb view of Mirror Lake. The menu is Continental, with regional touches like home-smoked items and the liberal use of real Adirondack maple syrup. There are excellent meat and fish entrées, such as succulent tournedos of beef and pan-seared salmon fillet. For dessert indulge in sinful banana bread pudding with a warm caramel sauce. 5 Mirror Lake Dr., Lake Placid, tel. 518/523–2544. Reservations essential. AE, D, MC, V.

Charcoal Pit Restaurant

A pleasant roadhouse atmosphere, simple wooden decor, and white tablecloths make this a good family spot. Although it's primarily a steak emporium—with the main attraction cooked to order over a real charcoal fire—it does have plenty of alternatives, such as Greek shrimp served with an olive-and-feta sauce, veal marsala, or veal Angela (with broccoli). 130 Saranac Ave., Rte. 86, Lake Placid, tel. 518/523–3050. AE, D, DC, MC, V. Closed Tues.–Wed. in Jan.

Hungry Trout

Antique fishing equipment and mounted trout decorate the walls of this secluded eatery next to the west branch of the fecund Ausable River. The mainstay of the menu is trout—rainbow trout, specifically—personally selected by owner Jerry Botcher, an aficionado of fly-fishing. The restaurant serves trout four ways: baked with lemon butter, blackened with Cajun spices, with a shallot and Grand Marnier butter sauce, and Rocky Mountain style, in a crisp seasoned crust. The menu includes other fish dishes, game, and daily specials, plus several varieties of steak. You also get a great view of Whiteface Mountain. *Rte. 86, Wilmington, tel. 518/946–2217. Reservations essential. AE, D, DC, MC, V.*

Lake Placid Lodge

If you have any questions about Adirondack style, look around in this elegant dining room for answers—every detail, down to the birch-bark bread baskets, has been carefully considered. The Adirondack-American offerings here are creative. The roast Maine lobster in a port wine and paprika jus is delicious, and every dish tastes even better than it looks. The burnt apricot cheesecake is surprisingly light. Look for seasonal menu changes. *Whiteface Inn Rd., Lake Placid, tel. 518/523–2700. Reservations essential. AE, MC, V.*

Moderate

Artist's Cafe

This is not a big place—only 45 seats—but it combines a view of Mirror Lake and barn-board decor heavy on wood and stone with well-pre-

pared food and friendly service. There's a wide variety of steaks, seafood, salads, and microbrewed beers. Try an all-time favorite: a pound of steamed fresh shrimp. The place is always busy, but if you have to wait, you can hang out in the cozy bar. *1 Main St., Lake Placid, tel. 518/523–9493. Reservations not accepted. AE, D, DC, MC, V.*

Great Adirondack Steak & Seafood

Here a display of Adirondack antiques and other collectibles (old skis, fishing poles, model trains, and so on) fills the walls. The emphasis is on large portions of popular standards, including monster T-bone steaks, prime rib, lobster, and shrimp. Six types of beers are brewed on the premises. *34 Main St., Lake Placid, tel. 518/523–1629. Reservations not accepted. AE, D, DC, MC, V.*

Nicola's Over Main

In just a few years, Mike and Nia Nicola have transformed a one-time auto parts store into probably the hippest eatery in Lake Placid. The food is Mediterranean to the hilt; the decor is modern, with a long, prominent bar near the entrance. There's a good wine list and great salads and appetizers (try the bruschetta with three spreads). The open kitchen offers up a half dozen can't-miss options of grilled chicken, veal, and seafood; the daily seafood specials, like grilled sea bass or shark, are always right-on. You can also choose from a dozen handmade wood-fired pizzas. (Tip: if it's busy, eat at the bar.) *2 Marcy Rd., Lake Placid, tel. 518/523–4430. Reservations essential. AE, MC, V.*

Thirsty Moose

The stylish ambience of this restaurant belies its casual nature. There's a cozy bar just off the dining area with a separate menu; booths and tables in the dining room surround a central fireplace. Favorites include shrimp tequila, rock shrimp served in a tangy cream sauce, and steak au poivre, a hearty sirloin smothered in a peppercorn and brandy cream sauce. In late 1999 look for a newly expanded wild-game menu. *215 Main St., Lake Placid, tel. 518/523–3222. AE, MC, V.*

Inexpensive

Black Bear Restaurant

A lively, casual spot with rough-hewn log beams, birch paneling, and a small bar up front, this is the perfect place to concoct a dinner of appetizers: pick your way through chicken fingers, potato skins, Cajun fries, crab cakes, deep-fried mozzarella, nachos, and wings. Portions are huge, but if you insist on having an entrée, there is an enormous selection of burgers plus a little of everything from the four basic fast-food groups—steak, chicken, seafood, and pasta. *157 Main St., Lake Placid, tel. 518/523–9886. Reservations not accepted. AE, D, DC, MC, V.*

Cottage Cafe

Warm and cozy, with a large stand-up bar and a fire in the hearth, the Cottage has a great après-ski feel. The menu consists of designer sandwiches with fillings such as artichoke hearts, provolone, tomatoes, and onions with cayenne mayonnaise. Salad options include feta, taco, and spinach, and there's also an excellent daily quiche, homemade soup, and delicacies like

baked brie and peel-your-own shrimp. *Mirror Lake Inn, 5 Mirror Lake Dr., Lake Placid, tel. 518/523–9845. Reservations not accepted. AE, D, MC, V.*

Downtown Diner and Bakery

This is a diner in the classic tradition, with a long counter, faux Tiffany lamps, and blue-checked tablecloths. The lunch menu's mainstays are good soups and burgers and staples like grilled cheese, chef's salad, and hot roast beef or turkey sandwiches, plus a daily special. *330 Main St., Lake Placid, tel. 518/523–1429. No credit cards. No dinner.*

Mr. Mike's Pizza and Italian Kitchen

Newly renovated and expanded, this big, airy Italian eatery delivers on all the staples: Mediterranean and Caesar salads, chicken and eggplant parmigiana, calzones and sandwiches, and pasta favorites like Alfredo and primavera. The pizza—try the chèvre or margherita—is some of the best in town. *332 Main St., Lake Placid, tel. 518/523–9770. Reservations suggested. AE, V.*

Best Bets for Breakfast

Aroma Round Coffee House

This unmistakable café—a lovely round post-and-beam structure just off Main Street—serves a small but thorough selection of hearty daystarters like grilled vegetable hash with poached eggs, French toast with berries and pure maple syrup, or fruit medley with ginger honey and chopped nuts. There's a wide array of baked breakfast goodies and gourmet coffees. There's live music in the evening on occasion. (A caveat: when the "Wait Around"—as some locals call it—gets busy, service can be slow.) *18 Saranac Ave., Lake Placid, tel. 518/523–3818. MC, V.*

NIGHTLIFE AND ENTERTAINMENT
Après-Ski

Cloudspin Lounge
You'll find this place in the main ski lodge at Whiteface. From about 3 PM to 5:30 PM it's packed, and the young singles crowd feasts on drinks and music daily, with a DJ on the weekends. *Rte. 86, Wilmington, tel. 518/ 946–2223. No credit cards.*

Dancing Bears Lounge
Cheap drinks and the best complimentary munchies in town draw a huge crowd to this bar in the Hilton. It's big, with a crackling fireplace and pictures of bears everywhere. There's also a dance floor, and live music that starts at 9 PM and goes till 1 AM on weekends. *Lake Placid Hilton, 1 Mirror Lake Dr., tel. 518/523–4411. AE, D, DC, MC, V.*

Loud and Lively/Dancing

R. F. McDougall's Saloon
This wonderfully warm, woody neighborhood pub has oak floors, spruce and cherry trim, and authentic prints and paintings from the Adirondacks. The twin centerpieces are the 17-foot handcrafted solid-cherry Victorian bar

and the massive stone fireplace. There's live music on occasion. *Hungry Trout Restaurant, Rte. 86, Wilmington, tel. 518/946–2217. No credit cards.*

Roomers Nightclub
At this below–Main Street nightspot, several pool tables, a handful of video games, TVs large and small, and a snaking, well-stocked bar surround the real reason everybody's here: the dance floor. The clothes are tight, the music can get cheesy, the DJ is relentless, and everyone seems to end up here late at night. *137 Main St., tel. 518/523–3611. No credit cards.*

More Mellow

Lake Placid Pub & Brewery
This two-tiered watering hole—down is the dark and smoky pub, upstairs the smoke-free hardwood-floored microbrewery—serves pub favorites from burgers to chicken burritos, as well as Ubu Ale and an assortment of other brews concocted on-site. The pool table is always in use, the clientele is retro-casual ski bum; skiers congregate here religiously on Tuesdays, when it's two-for-one, and on weekends. *14 Shore Dr., tel. 518/523– 3813. MC, V.*

Nowhere else in the world of skiing is there a place as unique as Utah, with more than a dozen ski resorts within an hour's drive of a major metropolitan area. That's Salt Lake City, the delightful urban center started by the Mormons in the 19th century and today a hub of high-tech activity as dozens of modern industries relocate here to take advantage of a favorable tax base and an equally favorable climate.

Beyond its business appeal, Salt Lake City deserves special mention because it would be a mistake to ski any of the Utah resorts described here and not savor the city. The city center is rich in attractions and dining, with a surprising diversity of restaurants, nightspots, and hotels, and its neat grid layout is a breeze to get around in by bus, by car, or on foot.

Ultimately, though, all roads lead to Temple Square—metaphorically, if not physically—and this Mormon showcase, with its Tabernacle Choir, museum, and Genealogy Center, is Utah's most famous attraction. If you travel here during the Christmas period, the appeal is even greater, with millions of lights decorating the square and carolers in full Christmas song.

To the west is the Great Salt Lake Desert, which wrings dry the moist air moving eastward from the Pacific coast and blesses the resorts that lie in the heart of the towering Wasatch Range just east of the city with prodigious amounts of some of the driest and lightest snow found anywhere. It's here that such resorts as the ultramodern Snowbird, the bustling Park City, the tony Deer Valley, and anachronistic Alta coexist and share the snowy bounty. All four are within a 40-minute drive of Salt Lake City, and shuttle buses connect them to one another. Each offers its own kind of mountain charm; if you come to ski one, you should take a day to ski one of the others.

These resorts are so close to Salt Lake that staying in the city is an alternative to slope-side accommodations, and if you're flying in from a distant point it means being able to ski the afternoon you arrive.

GETTING TO UTAH RESORTS

By Plane

The closest major facility, **Salt Lake City International Airport** (SLC; tel. 801/575–2400), is served by the following airlines, all of which make connections from most major cities: American Airlines (tel. 800/433–7300), America West (tel. 800/235 9292), Continental Airlines (tel. 800/525–0280), Delta Airlines (tel. 800/221–1212), Frontier Airlines (tel. 800/432–1359), Northwest (tel. 800/225–2525), Southwest Airlines (tel. 800/435–9792), Skywest (tel. 800/453–9417), TWA (tel. 800/221–2000), and United Airlines (tel. 800/241–6522).

Car Rental

The following car rental firms have desks at Salt Lake City International Airport: **Alamo** (tel. 800/327–9633), **Avis** (tel. 800/331–1212), **Budget** (tel. 800/527–0700), **Dollar** (tel. 800/800–4000), **Hertz** (tel. 800/654–3131), **National** (tel. 800/328–4567), and **Payless** (tel. 800/729–5377).

By Train

Amtrak's *Zephyr Express* (tel. 800/872–7245) serves Salt Lake City's downtown Rio Grande rail station (tel. 801/531–0188) daily from Chicago and Emeryville (near Oakland), California.

By Bus

The **Greyhound Lines** (tel. 801/355–9579 or 800/231–2222) terminal is on South Temple in downtown Salt Lake City and has regularly scheduled service from all major cities.

GETTING AROUND

UTA City Transit (tel. 801/287–4636) runs regularly scheduled bus service to the ski areas for $9 round-trip from various locations in the city. **Lewis Brothers Stages** (tel. 801/649–2256 or 800/826–5844) makes regular stops at most downtown hotels for a fare of $20 round-trip to and from the ski areas.

ALTA SKI RESORT

ALTA SKI RESORT

Box 8007
Alta, UT 84092
Tel. 801/359-1078
Fax 801/799-2340
www.altaskiarea.com

STATISTICALLY SPEAKING

Base elevation: 8,530 feet

Summit elevation: 10,550 feet

Vertical drop: 2,020 feet

Skiable terrain: 2,200 acres

Number of trails: 39 marked runs

Longest run: 3½ miles

Lifts and capacity: 2 triples, 6 doubles, 4 surface;

10,770 skiers per hour

Daily lift ticket: $31

Average annual snowfall: 500 inches

Number of skiing days 1997-98: 146

Snowmaking: 50 acres, 2%

Terrain mix: N 25%, I 40%, E 35%

Snowboarding: no

Alta is an old-fashioned, unpretentious resort that has resisted change and is proud of it. Unlike almost every other ski destination in the country, this one has eschewed the mania for high-speed quad chairs and trams, thus limiting the number of skiers on the mountain at any one time. Lift-ticket prices are about half those at most other resorts, so locals can still afford to ski here. Most important to ski purists, the management grooms terrain for all skiing abilities, allowing the mountain to retain its rustic beauty instead of becoming a sanitized highway of glossy white runs. This is why some people stay loyal to Alta and its simple beauty while others choose to go elsewhere.

At first glance there doesn't seem to be much to Alta, tucked away at the end of Little Cottonwood Canyon. The former mining town reached its zenith in 1883, when it had a population of 8,000 and nearly 200 buildings including a courthouse, a jail, and 26 saloons. In those days it was a raucous, rollicking town that recorded an average of one murder a day. But when the silver ran out it took with it the town's fortunes.

It wasn't until the 1930s that Alta emerged as a ski destination, when the first chairlift was constructed and the Alta Lodge opened for business. Skiing became the lifeblood of the new Alta and remains its most important industry. You may feel here as though you've stepped back in time, for Alta's base area is only a long, narrow wedge of modest development sandwiched between the high walls of the canyon. Within the canyon are five ski lodges, a handful of small businesses, and the ski area itself. It's one of the few privately owned ski resorts in the country. The decidedly more modern Snowbird lies less than a mile away, just over the ridge.

Alta has two base areas: the Albion day lodge, which serves the novice, intermediate, and expert terrain at the eastern edge of 11,000-foot Mt. Baldy; and the Goldminer's Daughter day lodge, which serves intermediate and expert terrain on the western edge. In between are Alta's accommodations, linked to each other by a unique rope tow. With a giant vertical bull wheel at each end, this tow moves skiers from one end of the resort to the other, passing

Children's services: day-care, tel. 801/742–3042; instruction, tel. 801/742–2600

Snow phone: tel. 801/572–3939

Police: tel. 801/572–1211

Ski Finder: tel. 801/943–6244; for pager, 801/533–1377

Medical Center: Snowbird Ski Resort, tel. 801/742–2222

Hospital: Alta View Hospital, Sandy, tel. 801/576–2600

Resort Association: tel. 801/942–0404

Road conditions: tel. 801/742–3333

Towing: AAA, tel. 801/364–5610

FIVE-STAR FAVORITES
Best run for vertical: Alf's High Rustler

Best run overall: Mambo

Best bar/nightclub: Alta Peruvian Bar

Best hotel: Alta Lodge

Best restaurant: Shallow Shaft

the shorter, more conventional uphill rope tows that carry skiers to the lodges built into the canyon's northern sides. This unorthodox means of transportation perfectly reflects Alta's charming personality—so simple, yet so efficient.

That's all there is to Alta: no mountain malls, no condo villages, no true epicenter, and little in the way of nightlife. It's just a resort with lots of character and lots of characters who like things more or less the way they have been for more than half a century.

HOW TO GET THERE

Shuttle Service

Several shuttle vans make the run between the Salt Lake City Airport and Alta/Snowbird. **Canyon Transport** (tel. 801/255–1841 or 800/255–1841) is the largest service, with regularly scheduled runs on the hour between Alta and the airport. The charge is $20 per person, one-way, from the airport or downtown SLC. **Lewis Brothers Stages** (tel. 801/649–2256 or 800/826–5844) has daily scheduled motorcoach service to Alta and all other SLC ski areas. The fare is $20 round-trip from downtown hotels.

By Car

From the airport just west of Salt Lake City follow I-80 east to I-215 south (also known as the Belt Route) to Route 210, and follow signs to Little Cottonwood Canyon. From the SLC downtown area take I-15 south to I-215 to Route 210, then follow signs to Little Cottonwood Canyon. The drive from the airport is about 25 miles, or 45 minutes, depending on weather conditions. Little Cottonwood Canyon is a high avalanche area, and driving is often tricky—or prohibited—due to a fall or the threat of one. Call 801/964–6000 for road conditions.

By Bus

The **Utah Transit Authority** (UTA, tel. 801/287–4636) serves Little Cottonwood Canyon from downtown SLC, making stops in the city center and at various locations throughout the valley. The fare is $4.50 one-way from downtown to the Canyon area, while a shuttle between Alta and Snowbird is free. *See also* Snowbird, *below.*

GETTING AROUND

A car is definitely not necessary at Alta. The entire length of the resort community can be walked in 10 minutes, and efficient **UTA** shuttle-bus service (tel. 801/287–4636) runs between Alta and Snowbird (1 mile away), with stops at each lodge in both resorts. The buses, which are free, run daily, every 15 minutes 9–5. **Canyon Transportation** (tel. 800/255–1841) runs a shuttle daily 5 PM– 11 PM between Alta and Snowbird, with stops at the lodges. Dial 7433 from any lodge in Snowbird or Alta for a pickup; the fare is $3 for a one-way ride. **Yellow Cab** (tel. 801/521–2100) is a third alternative if you want to travel outside the resort area.

THE SKIING

Like the resort itself, the skiing at Alta is quirky. Mt. Baldy is a broad, sloping giant that ripples and unfolds across Alta's front facade, providing a series of crests and valleys that have to be explored rather than just skied. At the western end of the Alta ridge the mountain reaches its maximum height of 11,068 feet, its wide face concealing steep pitches, chutes, and gullies that harbor challenging, mostly ungroomed runs.

The Alta trail map lists only 39 runs, but hundreds of routes lead down the mountain. You'll have to work to find them by taking the many traverses and cat tracks that link the sectors until you find your favorite way down. The owners of the resort haven't homogenized the base area with neatly organized condo satellites, nor have they cannibalized the mountain with wide boulevards or an indulgent, highfalutin lift system. Only eight lifts serve the 2,200 acres of skiable terrain, and like the features of the mountain itself, they effectively separate the green and blue terrain from the black.

The Albion, Sunnyside, and Cecret lifts serve the novice and easier intermediate trails, and primarily intermediates and experts ride the other five chairs. The system works well, providing all levels with distinct territory to explore, and limited parking guarantees the area will not be overrun. Alta caters to skiers without pampering them.

Although its vertical drop is 1,000 feet less than the 3,100 feet of neighboring Snowbird, Alta's terrain is highly challenging. The front face of Peruvian Ridge is uncompromisingly steep, with chutes, gullies, and heavily wooded areas; the western face yields a series of wide, steep bowls filled with the famous Utah powder; and the northern flank has exceptional tree skiing. To get the best of Alta, you must be willing to explore off the beaten track and take some remarkably long but ultimately satisfying traverses.

Of course, one of the primary ingredients in Alta's success is the snow. Alta receives an average of 500 inches a year. For the most part, it's the dry, desert-brushed powder that the state is justifiably famous for, and the resort— displaying the same policy of restraint that it applies to development—doesn't let its grooming machines run amok. Although there are plenty of groomed trails, there are lots of untouched runs for die-hard powder skiers.

Novices

Stick to the east side (to the left looking up) of the mountain, known as the Albion Basin, where the Sunnyside, Albion, and Cecret lifts are located. Practice linking your turns on Crooked Mile or Sunnyside, two deliciously long runs that wind down the meadowy terrain on Peruvian Ridge's lower flanks. On a snowy day when the trail is groomed, you'll be able to pick up speed and practice big, swooping giant slalom turns here. When you want a change of scenery, take another ride up the Sunnyside or Albion lifts, but stay to your left to get to the Cecret chairlift. Eventually Sweet and Easy connects to Sunnyside for another long cruise down to the base area.

Once you've gained some confidence on those long green runs, ride Sunnyside or Albion to the Supreme lift via Cecret lift. At the top of the chair take Big Dipper, a moderate blue run that will give you a taste of the trees to whet your appetite for the glade skiing that will come with experience. Don't worry, though, the trees aren't so tight that you need panic; they're just tight enough to challenge you. Next try Rock and Roll, another long, winding blue run with enough moderately steep pitches to make you work your edges, plus some broad sweeping stretches around islands of trees. These runs are mostly groomed, although you can find some loose powder off to the sides, especially if you skirt the trees. These marvelous intermediate blue trails are some of the mellowest cruisers in Utah: they're tame enough not to terrify but spicy enough to put some thrill into your skiing.

Intermediates

First thing in the morning ride the Wildcat lift to the top and follow the narrow cat track to the left to the top of Aggie's Alley, a long, wide, groomed leg-warmer with pitches and rolls and enough steepness to make things interesting. Run it top-to-bottom a couple of times before heading over to the base of the Germania lift, which gives you access to the higher elevations of the West Rustler face. Here two excellent blue runs give you the choice of solid steeps with some bumps (Mambo) or a long, wide bowl area (Ballroom); both connect to Main Street, a long, usually groomed run back to the base of the Germania lift. From the top take the traverse over the Germania Pass to Devil's Elbow, a beautifully long run that starts out steep in the trees, mellows slightly as it widens into meadows, goes through a series of rolls, then becomes a full-bore cruiser all the way to the bottom of the Sugarloaf and Cecret lifts. From the top of the Cecret lift, ski down to the Supreme lift, where you'll find some of the best tree skiing on the mountain. Get yourself in the mood to dance with the pines by taking either Challenger or Big Dipper, both of which have good glade sections and wide-open terrain. These two runs connect with the longer, well-groomed Rock and Roll, which takes you back to the bottom of the Supreme lift. At this point you can pick up the pace. The area served by the Supreme lift is a vast series of treed bowls with few marked trails but many routes down. Although this area, called Piney Glade and White Squaw, is considered black diamond, you can selectively pick your way through the trees, gullies, bowls, and chutes for an adventure as varied as it is gratifying.

Experts

This mountain begs to be explored beyond the 18 trails designated black diamond, because for every marked trail there are dozens of unmarked alternatives. If you're really keen to discover Alta's wild side, hook up with a local who's been up and down the mountain a zillion times and knows where to find the hidden treasures. (The bar at the Alta Peruvian Lodge is a good place to shop for local knowledge.) For your introduction to the mountain, however, ride the Wildcat lift to the top of the front face and take Warmup, a top-to-bottom, mostly groomed screamer that starts wide just above the tree line then narrows as it follows the fall line almost immediately under the Wildcat lift. From the top again take Peruvian Ridge, another ultrasteep run that skirts the eastern ridge then cuts into the middle, where you have a choice of the steeper Rock Gully, the even steeper Wildcat Face, or the untamed wilderness of the Wildcat area. Next take the Germania lift to Alf's High Rustler for a fast vertical run that starts off a cliff and shoots through some trees onto a wide hump slope. When you've had enough of the front face, take the Germania lift again to explore the unmarked bowl and backcountry skiing designated as Glory Hole, Yellow Trail, East Greeley, and Greeley Bowl. This is where you'll find the deepest, purest snow, and it's where you can experience free-form, break-the-rules skiing at its best. It's the best way to ski Alta: where the snow lies untouched, jump in with both feet. Follow your instincts or those of skiers who look like they know where to go, but don't assume you've found the ultimate run, because eventually you'll discover one that's just a little sweeter.

WHERE TO STAY

Because there are only five lodges in the base area, accommodations at Alta are straightforward. All properties connect with the rope tow that moves skiers across the resort, so all accommodations are considered ski-in/ski-out. All operate on the Modified American Plan (MAP), so your daily or weekly rate includes meals. Some properties don't take credit cards, but they do accept personal checks. An alternative to Alta's on-mountain lodges is nearby Snowbird (*see* Snowbird, *below*), just a mile down Little Cottonwood Canyon, or Salt Lake City, about a 45-minute drive away. If you're more interested in staying at a resort town, Park City (*see below*), about one hour from Alta, is another possibility.

Expensive

Alta Lodge

This Swiss-style log building has been expanded several times since it was first built as a lodge in 1939. From the roadside entrance you descend three flights of stairs (the entrance is a little below the level of the road because the lodge is built into the side of a hill; attendants take your luggage) to the main lobby, with its warm, rustic decor, where you'll get a truer sense of the coziness the lodge offers. Old-fashioned comfortable chairs, books, magazines, and parlor games are scattered about the common areas, and guests mingle as though at a family reunion. Rooms have different sizes and configurations, but some corner rooms have a private balcony and a fireplace. None of the Alta Lodge rooms is large, but all are comfortable and well furnished. *Little Cottonwood Canyon Rd., Alta 84092, tel. 801/742–3500 or 800/707–2582, fax 801/742–3504. 57 rooms, 48 with bath, 4 dorms. Facilities: TV room, lounge, 2 indoor hot tubs, 2 saunas. No credit cards. $108–$324 per person.*

Alta Peruvian Lodge

You'll first enter the plant-filled lobby, where a large stone fireplace dominates a room filled with handcrafted blond-wood furniture, books, and hotel guests relaxing after an intense day on the slopes. A picture window overlooks the outdoor swimming pool and hot tub, with the mountain in the background. This is the quintessential unpretentious classic ski lodge where après-ski means hot chocolate, apple cider, and brownies set out on tables around the room. The family-style dining room and the bar upstairs are equally cozy, but the rooms can be tiny, and more than half have shared bathrooms down the hall. Room styles vary from dorms to two-bedroom suites. The dorms have 24 bunks for men and four for women. At times the Peruvian seems a bit disheveled, as though there had been a big pajama party here the night before, but this is part of its simplicity and charm. *Little Cottonwood Canyon Rd., Box 8017, Alta 84092, tel. 801/742–3000 or 800/453–8488, fax 801/742–3007. 80 rooms, 4 dorms. Facilities: heated out-*
door pool, outdoor hot tub, sauna, bar, laundry, ski shop, gift shop, game room. $142–$250 per person, including 3 meals and lift ticket. AE, D, MC, V.*

Goldminer's Daughter

Although its quarry-rock walls and large atrium front give it a slightly grand appearance, Goldminer's is more of a motel than the other properties in the canyon. The narrow hallways in rough-cut wood and the low lighting make this place feel as though it's underground. Rooms are either large or small, the former equipped with a king-size or two double beds and a full bathroom, the latter with one double bed and a shower (no bath). All are done in Southwestern color schemes of beige, pink, and turquoise. Guest quarters are clean and comfortable, albeit cheerless. *Little Cottonwood Canyon, Box 8055, Alta 84092, tel. 801/742–2300 or 800/453–4573. 81 rooms, 4 suites, 2 dorms. Facilities: bar-lounge, 2 saunas, exercise room, indoor hot tub, laundry, game room, ski shop. $91–$100 per person. MC, V.*

Rustler Lodge

The fanciest lodge in Alta most resembles a traditional full-service hotel. The interior is decidedly upscale, with dark wood paneling, burgundy chairs and couches, handsome wooden backgammon tables, and a grand piano dominating a small sitting room off the main lobby. Rooms range in size and configuration from dorms to deluxe suites, the latter the largest and poshest, with a king-size bed and two pullout sofas. Sitting areas have comfortable armchairs, a coffee table, a wet bar, and a balcony. All but three units have a private bathroom. Guest quarters are handsomely decorated with dark woods, white brick walls, and richly colorful coverings and drapes. *Little Cottonwood Canyon, Box 8030, Alta 84092, tel. 801/742–2200 or 888/532 2582, fax 801/742–3832. 85 rooms, 4 dorms. Facilities: restaurant, bar-lounge, outdoor pool, indoor hot tub, 2 saunas, ski shop, laundry facilities, game room. No credit cards. $100–$650, double occupancy ($100 dorm), including breakfast and dinner.*

Moderate

Snowpine Lodge

Built in 1938 as a hostel for area workers, this is the oldest lodge in Little Cottonwood Canyon, the smallest, and possibly the friendliest. The original hand-carved granite walls and wide-plank wooden floors have been exposed, giving Snowpine the feel of a cozy cottage. There are just 16 rooms and two dorms (the women's sleeps five, the men's sleeps 12). None of the rooms is large, but all are spotless and tastefully appointed with coordinated rugs and bedcovers. *Little Cottonwood Canyon, Box 8062, Alta 84092, tel. 801/742–2000. 16 rooms, 8 with bath, 2 dorms. Facilities: outdoor hot tub, sauna. MC, V. $88–$139 per person, including breakfast and dinner.*

WHERE TO EAT

All of Alta's lodges operate on the Modified American Plan, and only one independent restaurant, the Shallow Shaft, supplements the dining rooms in the lodges and the on-mountain eateries. Nearby Snowbird (*see* Snowbird, *below*) and Salt Lake City (about 20 miles away) offer countless alternatives. Space can be a problem at some lodge dining rooms—especially in high season—but all accommodate outside guests when they have room. Call for reservations. Credit cards may not be accepted in all places.

On the Mountain

Alf's Restaurant

This on-mountain eatery serves the requisite stick-to-the-ribs, belly-warming skier's lunches: good stews and chili, hearty sandwiches, and grilled burgers. The large stucco building lacks charm, but the huge windows with great views down the mountain offer some compensation. *Bottom of Cecret and Sugarloaf lifts (access on Sunnyside or Sweet and Easy), tel. 801/742–2424. MC, V.*

Collin's Grill

Laid-back Alta puts on its best at this mid-mountain restaurant where you dine on china accompanied by crystal and silverware. The blond-wood-paneled walls retrace Alta's history through pictures of the past, and there also are videotapes of Alta's renowned skiing. Among the entrées is an oven-roasted quarter-chicken, or you may want to go with the chef's choice: salmon fillet. There are also hearty lasagnas, daily blue-plate specials, and specialty sandwiches such as the Collin's buffalo burger or the portabello mushroom sandwich. From your table you can watch skiers making the High Traverse in search of powder on West Rustler. *Bottom of Germania lift (access via Aggies Alley from Top of Wildcat or Collins lift, or Mambo, Main Street, and Ballroom from top of Germania lift), tel. 801/799 2297. MC, V.*

Moderate

Alta Lodge Dining Room

When space permits, you can get a reservation at this simple, wood-paneled room decorated with Middle Eastern weavings and paintings. Each table has fresh flowers, candles, and sweet floral-print napkins. Seating is family style. The menu changes daily and usually offers a choice of three entrées (perhaps steak or grilled tuna smothered in a delicious salsa), and there's always a choice of soup or salad, homemade bread, and a dessert, such as apple pie with homemade ice cream. *Alta Lodge, tel. 801/742–3500. Reservations essential. No credit cards.*

Rustler Lodge Dining Room

This baroque dining spot surrounds you with dark wood and deep-colored accents and is warmed by a huge round fireplace. The menu changes daily, and the emphasis is on regional American fare: well-prepared steaks and wild game. The pepper steak is especially good, as is the rack of lamb with gratin potatoes or the basil fettuccine with fresh seafood. *Rustler Lodge, tel. 801/742–2200. Reservations essential. AE, MC, V.*

Shallow Shaft

This is the only non-lodge-affiliated restaurant in Alta, and it's definitely worth a visit, if only to get you out of whatever lodge you've been eating and sleeping in for a week. The small interior is cozy and decorated in funky Southwestern style with a sandy color scheme and walls adorned with 19th-century mining tools found on the mountain. The menu is also Southwestern, with adventurous specials including lamb chops grilled and served in ancho-chili sauce and pork medallions braised in apple cider. The restaurant makes its own ice cream daily. *Alta Rd., tel. 801/742–2177. Reservations essential on weekends. AE, D, MC, V.*

Inexpensive

Goldminer's Daughter Cafeteria

This cafeteria is open only during the daytime—primarily for the skiing crowd. The offerings are decidedly American, with burgers, soups, and chili leading the way. The casual spot draws a young crowd. *Goldminer's Daughter Cafeteria, Level 2, tel. 801/742–2300. No credit cards.*

Best Bets for Breakfast

Alta Lodge or Rustler Lodge

Both serve an ample breakfast buffet with made-to-order dishes such as omelets, eggs any style, and pancakes, as well as a selection of cold cereals and breads. *Alta Lodge, tel. 801/742–3500; Rustler Lodge, tel. 801/742–2200. No credit cards.*

NIGHTLIFE AND ENTERTAINMENT

Nightlife at Alta is limited. Four of the five lodges have a bar or lounge, all open to outside guests who have a club card, per Utah's oddball liquor regulations. This pseudomembership allows you to drink unfettered and is in some cases transferable. Credit cards are not accepted at hotel lounges.

Alta Peruvian Bar

Mostly a locals' hangout, this is a good place to head if you want to pick up tips on powder stashes or other insider information. Walls adorned with hunting trophies and a large fireplace surrounded by well-worn couches suit the casual atmosphere. *Tel. 801/742–3000.*

Goldminer's Daughter Lounge
The liveliest of Alta's beer bars, this spot attracts a young crowd. The large, rough-hewn sports bar has lots of wood and lots of hustle (at least on an Alta scale). There's a Tex-Mex menu, recorded music, games, and a large-screen TV. *Tel. 801/742–2300.*

Rustler Club
You'll feel like you're in a British pub at the Rustler, with its long, highly polished oak bar, lounge chairs, large fireplace, and Tudor-style stucco-and-wood decor. It's mostly mellow, a place where people stop to sip a nightcap around the fire or play a game of darts. *Tel. 801/742–2200.*

Sitzmark Club
You'll find this small, dark bar upstairs at the Alta Lodge. It has a rustic, woodsy feeling, and the walls are decorated with period photographs from the early days of the resort. The small bar is in one corner, but the fireplace is the focus around which friends curl up to chat. *Tel. 801/742–3500.*

DEER VALLEY SKI RESORT

Box 1525
Park City, UT 84060
Tel. 435/649–1000 or
800/424-3337
Fax 435/645–6939
www.deervalley.com

STATISTICALLY SPEAKING

Base elevation: 7,200 feet

Summit elevation: 9,570 feet

Vertical drop: 3,000 feet

Skiable terrain: 1,750 acres

Number of trails: 84

Longest run: 2 miles

Lifts and capacity: 6 quads,
9 triples, 2 doubles;
1 gondola; 34,800 skiers per
hour

Daily lift ticket: $57

Average annual snowfall: 300
inches

Number of skiing days
1997–98: 128

Snowmaking: 475 acres, 29%

Terrain mix: N 15%, I 50%,
E 35%

Snowboarding: no

Deer Valley is just 1 mile from historic Main Street in the bustling former mining town of Park City. Deer Valley, however, a patrician preserve for the few, is soothingly serene. You can stay in Park City and ski at Deer Valley, or you can reside in the upscale pamper palaces of the latter and still ski the more expansive and varied terrain of the former. A free, efficient, and regularly scheduled shuttle service lets you easily explore both worlds.

Deer Valley's intimacy, service, and style are unmatched in the country. That's the way Edgar Stern, the multimillionaire entrepreneur and founder of Deer Valley, wanted it when he carved America's most civilized resort out of 2,000 acres of Wasatch wilderness. Unlike most western resorts, which are built on land leased from the U.S. Forest Service, Deer Valley is actually owned by Stern and his partner, Roger Penske of Indy 500 fame. Stern envisioned this as a blue-chip enclave for blue bloods and Fortune 500 captains, a resort built and run like a luxury hotel with as much attention lavished on the atmosphere, comfort, food, and service as on the skiing. His success is evident everywhere, from the cheerful attendants in dark green uniforms to the discreet architectural development of chalets and condominiums amid the aspens and firs to the ultimate luxury of them all—uncrowded and flawlessly groomed slopes, kept that way by the strict limit placed on the number of skiers and by the most meticulous grooming program found anywhere. Every night one-third to one-half of the mountain is groomed, and the rest is left in its natural state to challenge even the best of skiers.

Deer Valley has another unique feature. Because it is all built on private land, the lavish, upscale condominiums and private residences are up on the mountain, not in the valley below; vacation retreats dot the knolls and valleys, the ridges, and the forested slopes of Bald Eagle Mountain.

The resort itself encompasses four main mountains and two base areas. The lower Snow Park Lodge base area is what at most resorts would be called the day lodge, but it is, in fact, a magnificent cedar-and-sandstone complex that houses several restaurants, upscale boutiques, and shops. The main

Area code: 435

Children's services: day-care, tel. 435/649–1000, ext.

6612; instruction, tel. 435/645–6648

Snow phone: tel. 435/649–2000

Police: tel. 435/645–5050

Medical center: Park City Care, tel. 435/649–7640

Resort-office services: tel. 435/534–1779 or 800/754–8824

Road conditions: tel. 800/492–2400

Towing: tel. 435/645–7775

FIVE-STAR FAVORITES

Best run for vertical: Ruins of Pompeii

Best run overall: Birdseye

Best bar/nightclub: Troll Hallen Lounge

Best hotel: Stein Eriksen Lodge

Best restaurant: Glitretind

Deer Valley lodging check-in center is conveniently nearby on the approach to Snow Park Lodge. A mile up Bald Eagle Mountain, linked by road and two chairlifts, is the decadently isolated Silver Lake Village, a self-contained mountain community consisting of a small shopping concourse and a nest of upscale accommodations such as the Stein Eriksen Lodge, a grand hotel created by the Norwegian former Olympic slalom champion, and the Goldener Hirsch, a smaller but no less elegant replica of the original in Salzburg, Austria. Silver Lake provides access to Deer Valley's three other major peaks—9,400-foot Bald Mountain, 9,100-foot Flagstaff Mountain, and 9,570-foot Empire Canyon.

Accommodations are clustered in and around Snowpark and Silver Lake Village, most within a short distance of the lifts, and a shuttle service links the two areas around the clock. Luxury and attention to detail are the name of the game throughout the resort.

HOW TO GET THERE

Shuttle Services

The following companies provide regularly scheduled and prebooked shuttle service between the Salt Lake City airport and Deer Valley: **All Resort Express** (tel. 435/649–3999 or 800/457– 9457), **Canyon Transport** (tel. 801/255–1841 or 800/255–1841), and **Lewis Brothers Stages** (tel. 435/649–2256 or 800/826–5844). Fares range between $17 and $22 per person each way. A free, regularly scheduled bus service runs between Deer Valley and nearby Park City, with many stops along the 1-mile route.

By Car

Deer Valley is 35 miles east of downtown Salt Lake City and 1 mile south of downtown Park City. From Salt Lake City take I–80 east to the Park City exit, Route 224, which eventually turns into Park Avenue. Turn left at Deer Valley Drive and continue 1 mile to the Deer Valley lodging center. It's about a 40-minute drive. For car-rental information, *see* Getting to Utah Resorts, *above.*

GETTING AROUND

A car is not necessary or particularly practical at Deer Valley. The two village areas and most of the individual accommodations are served by the **Deer Valley Shuttle service.** A shuttle-on-demand service is also available through the concierge or bell desk at most hotels. To visit nearby Park City, your best bet is to take the free scheduled **Park City shuttle bus** service, especially in light of the lack of parking in Park City. The Park City shuttle bus also serves the Deer Valley resort. **Park City Transportation** (tel. 435/ 649–8567) also runs a taxi service around Deer Valley and between Deer Valley and Park City.

THE SKIING

The skiing at Deer Valley takes place on four distinct mountains—Bald Eagle Mountain, which has primarily novice and intermediate runs; Flagstaff Mountain, which is almost exclusively intermediate except for the double-diamond steeps of the Ontario Bowl; Bald Mountain, which is split evenly between intermediate and expert terrain, including the Mayflower and Perseverance bowls; and Empire Canyon, which offers a wide variety of skiing, from gladed intermediate terrain and powder-choked bowls to steep, vertigo-inducing chutes and tree runs. In 1998–99 skiing was introduced on Little Baldy Peak, a 7,950-foot knob just east of Bald Mountain that offers eight runs for beginners and intermediates. The 600 acres of gladed terrain on Bald and Flagstaff mountains are enough to sate any appetite for tree skiing.

Ordinarily, you might think it difficult to move around in a ski area with four sets of slopes, but the lift layout at Deer Valley is as well planned as all other aspects of the resort. From the Snow Park lodge at the base of Bald Eagle Mountain, two lifts—the high-speed, detachable quad Carpenter and the Clipper—take you up to the Silver Lake Village. From there you can ski Bald Eagle Mountain or fan out and ride the Quincy, Red Cloud, or Northside lifts up Flagstaff Mountain or take the Sterling or Wasatch lifts up to the summit of Bald Mountain. Empire Canyon is reached by cruising the Bandana trail down Flagstaff Mountain to the Empire Express lift. Little Baldy Peak, which is served by the Deer Crest quad and the Jordanelle Express gondola, is reached on Bald Eagle Mountain's Little Stick run. There are no flats or endless traverses, and almost always no congestion on the lifts.

Most of Deer Valley's runs face north or northeast, and most follow the fall line with remarkable precision, running among and around the trees, which for the most part have been left intact. With the arrival for the 1998–99 season of a lift into Empire Canyon, the gulp-and-go verticals of the Daly Chutes and Daly Bowl areas were opened to expert skiers. If you enjoy well-groomed runs with consistent pitch or dipsy-doodling your way through glades, explore the other three mountains. Deer Valley is a resort that makes novices feel like intermediates, intermediates feel like experts, and experts—well, if you're that much of an expert, you might be better off at nearby Park City. But before you dismiss Deer Valley, check out the special experts-only trail map that not only highlights the named black-diamond trails but also suggests off-piste routes down the mountains.

Novices

Your best place to start is Bald Eagle Mountain. From the Snow Park Lodge base area the Carpenter Express lift will take you to the top of Bald Eagle Mountain and Success, a wide, precisely groomed run that follows the fall line back to Carpenter Express. If this run seems too challenging, then stay on Wide West, a protected pure beginners' area that is served by the Burns and Snowflake chairlifts. Once you're warmed up, head back up Success and experiment with some of the short, slightly steeper cutoffs that link with it. Little Bell, to the right just down from the top of Success, is still green but involves some gentle rolls; Little Kate, to your right near the bottom, gives you a taste of some trees; and if you want to try a cutoff that's blue just to see if you can handle the pitch, cut right onto White Owl about halfway down.

When you're ready to move on, ride Clipper to Silver Lake Village, turn left, and take McHenry. The trail map designates it as a blue run, but it is actually as mellow as the green runs you have skied to this point. At the bottom of McHenry, ride the Wasatch lift and get off to your right. Ski down Sunset to Sunset West, making sure you stay to your left so that you eventually pick up Ontario. This whole section is a gently rolling run that alternately widens and narrows, giving you a chance to work on your turns and let your skis run back down

to the base of the Red Cloud and Quincy lifts that serve Flagstaff Mountain, as well as the Viking chair that caters to a small beginner's area.

By now you should be ready to try some blue runs. Take the Homestake lift to the top of Success, then stay to your left and catch either Last Chance or Dew Drop, a pair of wide, winding blue runs that have some steepness but also enough rolls and dips so that you can control your speed. Both eventually end up back on Success, where you can take a breather.

Intermediates

Bald Mountain, Flagstaff Mountain, and the new Deer Crest area on the resort's eastern flank are your best choices. To reach Bald Mountain and Flagstaff Mountain from the Snow Park Lodge area, take either the Carpenter Express, a high-speed quad, or Clipper, a slower triple, to Silver Lake Village. While Clipper drops you right across from the Sterling lift, from Carpenter Express you must make a short run down Homestake to reach Sterling. This lift will take you to the top of Bald Mountain, where you should start with a run on Birdseye, a long, winding cruiser that is usually groomed and perfect for high-speed giant slalom turns and ends up back at the bottom of the Sterling chair. Next up should be Nabob, a slightly narrower and somewhat steeper run that combines a series of rolls and pure fall-line pitch.

This will take you back to the bottom of the Wasatch chair. From the top of Wasatch head down Keno, a straight-shot blast that lets you rack up lots of high-speed vertical without worrying about bumps. Ride Wasatch up again and head down Tycoon, which starts out steep and extrawide, narrows somewhat, then widens out for a long, smooth cruise down to the bottom of the Sultan lift.

From the top of the Sultan, turn left and head over to the Perseverance Bowl. This is marked as a black-diamond, but if your legs are warm and your confidence buoyed, you should be able to handle it. The upper part is hardly ever groomed, so it does get bumpy, but because the skier traffic is always light at Deer Valley, the moguls remain smooth and well rounded—perfect for working on your bump technique. If you want to avoid the worst of them, keep to the far right on Perseverance and follow its arcing course around the shoulder of the mountain until it cuts back into the trees. It narrows somewhat as it approaches an intersection. To the right is Stein's Way, a steep pitch down to the bottom of the Mayflower chair (which serves mostly black and double-black runs); if you stay to the left, you'll end up back at the bottom of the Sultan chair. Stein's is an especially good area to ski on Deer Valley's frequent powder days.

To reach Flagstaff Mountain, take the Carpenter Express and follow Homestake past the Sterling lift to the Quincy and Red Cloud lifts. From the top of Quincy there's a collection of smooth, well-groomed cruisers that you can warm up on. Blue Bell, Sidewinder, and Lost Boulder all funnel you down to the Northside lift, which you need to ride to reach Empire Canyon. Like Quincy and Red Cloud, the Northside Express is surrounded by cruisers with some gladed runs tossed in. Even a beginner can

play here, as the Bandana run to the right of Northside is a wide, gentle cruiser that has ample room to work on turns.

You can reach Deer Crest, which has mostly intermediate terrain, from the top of Bald Eagle Mountain by following Big Stick to Little Stick and then Deer Hollow to the Deer Crest quad. From the top of the lift, the Jordanelle run offers a long, winding path down to the Jordanelle Express gondola on the resort's eastern edge. All the way down, the Jordanelle Reservoir is directly in front of you. Shorter options from the top of Deer Crest include Weasel and Kid's Delight, two blues that lead you back to the quad. The two expert-rated runs here, Flyer and Jack's Way, are ungroomed but easily handled by advanced intermediates.

Experts

Experts at Deer Valley have their own trail map, partly because the resort is trying to overcome its reputation for lacking challenging terrain and partly because there are some exquisite nuggets of advanced off-piste terrain that should be explored. Make sure you get a copy of the map—and use it.

Bald Mountain is where the majority of marked black and double-black runs are found. In fact, there are only two black runs on Bald Eagle Mountain—Know You Don't and Lucky Bill—which are hard-core, mogul-mashing ways back down to the Snow Park lodge. Flagstaff Mountain has only one marked black run, Square Deal, a short, wicked staircase of big bumps. But Flagstaff does give you access to the supersteep double-black glade skiing of the Ontario Bowl or the more heavily timbered sections known as DT's Trees and the Gumby Glade. Both these areas are free-form expanses of open faces, gullies, and tree islands—definitely the place to ski during or after a storm, when the snow is deep, ungroomed, and undisturbed.

Next you can tackle the black runs of Bald Mountain. Off the Sultan chair, Ruins of Pompeii offers a steep vertical drop that will grab your attention and help you understand why Deer Valley will host the 2002 Olympic slalom, mogul, and aerial events. For big-bump hounds, your two best bets are Rattler, under the Wasatch chair, or Narrow Gauge, under the Mayflower chair, where the bumps grow largest. The Mayflower Chutes—accessed through gates off the Mayflower Bowl—are a series of supersteep, narrow, rock-lined chutes that offer the kind of gulp-and-go challenge that Deer Valley is seldom given credit for. In fact, challenge abounds on the entire Mayflower Bowl: too steep to groom, the area has a good mix of steep, set-your-edges cruisers, glades, and bumps.

Another heads-up area is the Free Thinker Glade—reached from Stein's Way—or the Black Forest—reached from the top of Perseverance Bowl—where you'll find some of the heaviest and tightest timber on the mountain. If you yearn for excitement beyond warp-speed cruising on empty, pool-table-smooth, fall-line crank-and-go runs, the key at Deer Valley is to explore a little. Scour the glades for untouched snow, play slalom in the heavy timber, shoot the chutes—especially after a big dump—and use the fast and empty chairs to chalk up vertical.

Empire Canyon provides a new dimension for Deer Valley. Its east-facing flanks offer steep chutes, tight glades, and powder-rich bowls. Facing downhill from the top of the Empire Express, your immediate choices are Buckeye, Conviction, and Empire Bowl, double-blue and black-diamond pitches that offer treeless skiing that gives way to glades and bump runs winding back to the bottom of the lift. To reach Daly Bowl, a somewhat short but steep pitch, turn left off the lift and work your way down Solace to the edge of Anchor Trees. A narrow trail leads through the top of this thick glade to the bowl and Daly Chutes beyond. While a cornice grows along the top of the bowl, you can usually sneak around the northern edge of it and avoid a leap into the bowl. The Daly Chutes, double-black diamond shafts erosion cut into a rocky cliffside, should appease anyone hungry for supersteep runs.

WHERE TO STAY

Most of the lodging at Deer Valley is run by property management firms; it consists primarily of deluxe condominiums and luxury hotel suites in and around the two village areas of Snow Park and Silver Lake. Ultra-expensive and expensive are really the only two categories. Nearby Park City is the best bet if you're looking for more moderate prices or a more varied selection of small hotels, inns, and B&Bs. The following are some of the most impressive accommodations at Deer Valley; all rooms have concierge and daily maid service unless otherwise noted. If the facility is ski-in/ski-out, it is noted; all others are served by the Deer Valley shuttle service. Most accommodations at the resort, as well as much of the less expensive lodging throughout Park City and select lodging in Salt Lake City, can be booked through Deer Valley Lodging (tel. 435/649–4040 or 800/453–3833).

Expensive

Daystar

The three-bedroom town house units of Daystar are as elegant and sumptuous as they are spacious, with 2,000 square feet spread over three floors. The decor includes high beamed ceilings, brass and polished-wood trim, tiled entranceways, wood plank floors, handmade pine and bent-twig furniture, dark, richly colored fabrics, and large atrium-style windows. All bedrooms have their own bathrooms, and the kitchens are, as you might expect, full size and fully equipped. It's a third of a mile from the Snow Park base area. *Deer Valley Lodging, Box 3000, Park City 84060, tel. 435/649–4040 or 800/453–3833, fax 435/645–8419. 18 units. AE, D, MC, V. $425–$695.*

Fawngrove

Divided among six stone-and-clapboard structures with deep slanting roof lines, these units run smaller than most other Deer Valley condos, but they are just as luxurious in decor and furnishings. The two- to four-bedroom units have stone and beam work, large fireplaces, deep plush couches and chairs in subtle pastels and floral earth tones, large windows, and tiled entrance foyers; some even have private spa facilities. All bedrooms have private bathrooms. The fully equipped kitchen is a marvel of space-compacting efficiency; and the dining area, though small by Deer Valley standards, is certainly comfortable enough for six diners. In the same league design-, style-, and pricewise are the Courchevel, Queen Esther, and Stonebridge condo clusters. All these, like Fawngrove, are within a half mile of the Snowpark base lodge. *Deer Valley Lodging, Box 3000, Park City 84060, tel. 435/649–4040 or 800/453–3833, fax 435/645–8419. 60 units. AE, D, MC, V. $325–$890.*

Goldener Hirsch

This is a full-service hotel in a small, Austrian-style chalet. It exudes a marvelous Old World atmosphere that envelops you the moment you enter through the massive wrought-iron and glass doors and set foot on the fieldstone floor of the stucco-walled lobby. Rooms here run the gamut from regular-size hotel rooms to a large penthouse suite with separate living room and bedroom. Regardless of size, all rooms have clean white lines, soft pastel color schemes accented with printed wall coverings, handmade down comforters, and individual Austrian furnishings that range from hand-painted four-poster beds to hand-carved armoires and chests. This splendid hotel re-creates the quiet elegance of its namesake in Salzburg, Austria—no small feat in the Utah Rockies. It stands about 300 yards from the lifts at Silver Lake Village. *7570 Royal St. E, Box 859, Deer Valley, Park City 84060, tel. 435/649–7770 or 800/252–3373, fax 435/649–7901. 18 rooms with bath, 2 suites. Facilities: restaurant, lounge, indoor* and outdoor hot tubs, sauna, exercise room. AE, MC, V. $200–$850, including Continental breakfast.

Lodges at Deer Valley
Opened for the 1998–99 season, this condominium hotel is just a quarter mile from the Snow Park base area. You can find hotel rooms, suites, and condominiums here with all the comforts of home. The rustic interiors exhibit a Southwestern flair with wrought-iron lamps and rugged log walls. There's also a ski shop and ski storage on the premises and a common-area hot tub and an outdoor pool scheduled to open in 1999. *Deer Valley Lodging, Box 3000, Park City 84060, tel. 435/649–4040 or 800/453–3833, fax 435/645–8419. 87 units. AE, D, MC, V. $175–$750.*

Mont Cervin
These condos are split between two handsome fieldstone and gray-clapboard buildings in the Silver Lake Village area, just steps from the lifts. The classic and sturdy construction continues inside, with solid wood doors, solid oak and beech cabinetry, giant stone fireplaces, and contemporary furnishings. Opulence is the keynote throughout: each bedroom has its own bath; the monster master suites have a large bathroom with a Jacuzzi and access to the balcony hot tub. *Deer Valley Lodging, Box 3000, Park City 84060, tel. 435/649–4040 or 800/453–3833, fax 435/645–8419. 20 units. AE, D, MC, V. $700–$1,515.*

Pinnacle
If you're into deluxe to the max, choose the Pinnacle town houses. Set into the hillside about a half mile from the Snow Park Village base lodge, these three- and four-bedroom town houses are among the largest at the resort. With their striking blond wood and black-roofed exteriors, the units contrast sharply with the subtler style of surrounding buildings. Inside each unit the spacious living area rises three floors to an arched ceiling that towers over the massive central copper-faced fireplace trimmed with marble. The overall decor is rich with colorful ceramic tiles, handmade wooden furniture, antiques, wall tapestries, and Native American art. Off every bedroom is an en suite bathroom with a walk-in shower and tub. *Deer Valley Lodging, Box 3000, Park City 84060, tel. 435/649–4040 or 800/453–3833, fax 435/645–8419. 84 units. AE, D, MC, V. $625–$1,195.*

Powder Run
The Powder Run condos occupy three towering fieldstone and amber wood buildings 150 yards from Snow Park Lodge. The units, with either two or three bedrooms, have textured and hand-painted walls, floor-to-ceiling windows, plush couches and chairs, and myriad objets d'art. You get comfortable space and lots of luxury: a bathroom with a whirlpool tub connected to every bedroom, a huge stone fireplace in the immense living area, and a full-size kitchen equipped with every conceivable appliance. *Deer Valley Lodging, Box 3000, Park City 84060, tel. 435/649–4040 or 800/453–3833, fax 435/645–8419. 36 units. AE, D, MC, V. $495–$995.*

Stein Eriksen Lodge
Without a doubt, this is the flagship property at Deer Valley. It combines grandeur with intimacy, service, and

the convenience of a ski-in/ski-out location just 50 yards from the lifts. The lodge sits high on the hill at Silver Lake Village, its amber log-and-stone construction blending in perfectly with the surrounding pines and aspens. Inside, the hunter green and wine red carpeting and furniture, floral-print fabrics, polished-wood beams, paneled walls, and numerous floor-to-ceiling stone fireplaces create an atmosphere of rustic Norwegian elegance. All the guest rooms are lavishly decorated with imported fabrics, heavy brushed-pine furnishings, hand-painted tiles, colorful down comforters, and accessories in brass, copper, and wood. *7700 Stein Way, Box 3177, Park City 84060, tel. 435/ 649–3700 or 800/453–1302, fax 435/ 649–5825. 81 rooms, 51 suites. Facilities: 2 restaurants, lounge, heated outdoor pool, hot tub, sauna, exercise room. AE, D, DC, MC, V. $475–$2,150.*

Sterlingwood

These three- and four-bedroom town houses have a choice ski-in/ski-out location up the mountain in the Silver Lake Village area. The living area on the main floor has a high wood-lined ceiling with soft-toned sandstone walls decked with vivid art and wall hangings, lots of polished blond wood trim, the requisite floor-to-ceiling fieldstone fireplace, a glossy tiled entrance foyer, and thick plush carpeting. The large master bedroom, sprawling over the third floor, comes with its own fireplace and a large bathroom with a steam shower and a whirlpool tub. The remaining bedrooms are slightly smaller and simpler. Other amenities include a full-size kitchen, a dining area with seating for at least eight, a large outdoor deck with a hot tub, and a private garage for each unit. *Deer Valley Lodging, Box 3000, Park City 84060, tel. 435/649–4040 or 800/453–3833, fax 435/645–8419. 18 units. A, D, MC, V. $640–$1,465.*

Trail's End Lodge

New for 1998–99, this ski-in/ski-out condominium property stands next to Snow Park Lodge. The multi-bedroom units have floor-to-ceiling stone fireplaces. All units bear a Southwestern motif. The three-bedroom penthouse comes complete with an office equipped with data ports. There are also a heated soaking pool and meeting and convention facilities. *Deer Valley Lodging, Box 3000, Park City 84060, tel. 435/649–4040 or 800/ 453–3833, fax 435/645–8419. 15 units. AE, D, MC, V. $495–$1,440.*

WHERE TO EAT

The quality of food served in and around the resort is just what you'd expect from this opulent enclave. The dining is as important to the resort as its grooming. The resort's two day-lodge restaurants and other on-mountain locations and the remaining privately owned restaurants offer a uniformly excellent dining experience that lives up to its award-winning reputation.

For the most part, dress is casually elegant (many men don jackets, but they are not required). Keep in mind also that Park City, just a mile away, is a more varied, lively, and less expensive alternative.

On the Mountain

Silver Lake Lodge Restaurant

This magnificent, almost baronial six-room (each with a fireplace) lodge is in the middle of Silver Lake Village. Built of logs and stone, it has the opulence of a fine hotel, with tile floors and brass fittings (even the faucets in the bathroom). The lunch buffet presents a legion of daily specials, thick hearty soups, main courses like New York strip steak, fluffy omelets, stew, carved roasts of beef, turkey, or pork, grilled salmon, and designer pizzas. The salad bar is a grazing ground of greens, vegetables, pastas, and fruits both common and exotic. It's open for breakfast and lunch. *Silver Lake Village, tel. 435/649–1000. AE, D, DC, MC, V.*

Snow Park Lodge Restaurant

This dining room is identical in style and menu to the Silver Lake Lodge. *Snow Park Lodge, tel. 435/649–1000. AE, D, DC, MC, V.*

Expensive

Glitretind

The Glitretind is posh without being ostentatious, gracious without being overbearing, exemplary in service, and impeccable in decor, with softly colored textured walls, handsome wood trim, cranberry tablecloths, crystal glasses, hand-painted china, and fresh-cut flowers. It is, in a word, exquisite. The entrées include pepper-crusted beef tenderloin with cabernet wine sauce and basil mashed potatoes; seared Chilean sea bass with crab dumplings in an orange ginger sauce; and Berber spiced ahi tuna with lemon cashew rice cake and a cucumber sesame salad. *Stein Eriksen Lodge, Silver Lake Village, tel. 435/649–3700. AE, D, DC, MC, V.*

Goldener Hirsch Restaurant

The restaurant at the Goldener Hirsch is friendly and comfortable and unmistakably Austrian in style: the furniture was hand-carved in Austria, the waitstaff floats about in dirndls, and the tables are set with crisp white cloths. The menu consists of European standards such as Wiener schnitzel, as well as North American favorites such as rack of Utah lamb, served with spring vegetables; certified Angus beef; free-range chicken breast with sun-dried cherry stuffing; and a selection of wild game including New Zealand venison. *Goldener Hirsch, Silver Lake Village, tel. 435/649–7770. AE, MC, V.*

Olive Barrel Food Company

The Olive Barrel is a delightful spot with an Italian country-inn ambience of white stucco and brick walls decked with antiques and paintings, heavy wooden tables and chairs, wood-plank floors, a large brick wood-fired oven, and classical music in the background. The Italian soups and salads are excellent, and entrées include *agnello rosemarino della toscana* (roast lamb with chianti-and-rosemary sauce); cherry- and aspen-wood-smoked salmon with pesto; and osso buco *con risotto ala milanese* (seared veal shank simmered in red wine and herb sauce with rice). *Silver Lake Village, tel. 435/647–7777. Reservations essential. AE, MC, V.*

Valhalla

A new addition in 1998 to the Stein Eriksen Lodge, Valhalla offers intimate dining. There's room for just 35 guests; candles and soft classical music set a romantic mood. Crystal, silverware, and Italian linens add elegance. Appetizers range from house-smoked Arctic char and Napoleon of duck confit to foie gras. The unusual entrées include seared elk loin with roasted garlic and yam gallette; pan-roasted buffalo tenderloin with seared foie gras; and Casco Bay cod, grilled cod atop a lobster and shrimp fricassee. *Stein Eriksen Lodge, Silver Lake Village, tel. 435/649 3700. AE, D, DC, MC, V.*

Moderate

McHenry's

Casual in style (a rarity in swanky Deer Valley) but also chic, McHenry's bustles with an upbeat bistro atmosphere. It's a large restaurant with an open kitchen, lots of pine paneling, terra-cotta tile floors, and big overhead beams. The menu offers lighter fare including grilled turkey quesadilla, grilled chicken sandwich with eggplant, vegetarian burgers, or entrées such as grilled Atlantic salmon; roasted pepper, artichoke heart and shiitake mushroom pizza; or certified Angus rib eye steaks. *Silver Lake Lodge, tel. 435/645-6724. AE, D, DC, MC, V.*

Seafood Buffet

Plan to eat here at least once during your stay at Deer Valley. It's the talk of the mountain for its extensive selection of fresh seafood from both coasts (the choices vary nightly and seasonally) and its loose, casual atmosphere. The hot and cold choices from the buffet table include oysters on the half shell, crab legs, and fresh Chilean sea bass; table service brings the beverages. *Snow Park Lodge, tel. 435/645-6632. Reservations essential. AE, D, DC, MC, V.*

Inexpensive

Stewpot

This is a good spot for some fast and inexpensive noshing on a variety of homemade stews and soups. Two types of stew are served every day: the old-fashioned beef stew and another based on chicken, lamb, or pork. The menu also has all the predictables—burgers, salads, baked potatoes—plus a selection of home-baked breads. *1375 Deer Valley Plaza, tel. 435/645-7839. AE, D, MC, V.*

Best Bets for Breakfast

Silver Lake Lodge and Snow Park Lodge

Both serve a sumptuous buffet breakfast with custom-made items such as omelets, eggs Benedict, waffles with fresh fruit, and eggs any style. There's also an extraordinary fruit, yogurt, and natural cereal table, with grains and goodness from around the world. *Silver Lake Lodge, Snow Park Lodge, tel. 435/649-1000. AE, D, DC, MC, V.*

NIGHTLIFE AND ENTERTAINMENT

When the sun goes down and the lights go on, Deer Valley visitors and residents tend to turn inward toward the fireplace and the dining room table. There is no night scene to speak of at the resort, but if you want action, Park City is the place to head to (*see* Park City, *below*). At the resort there are two places to gather for après-ski, and many guests choose to dine early and linger over liqueurs in the resort's sumptuous restaurants.

Après-Ski

Snow Park Lounge

The Lounge is a lively emporium with musical entertainment, radical ski videos, contests, and a young crowd; it stays open until about 6 PM. The handsome hewn-wood and stone bar area is warmed by a giant central fireplace. *Snow Park Lodge, tel. 435/649-1000. AE, D, DC, MC, V.*

More Mellow

Troll Hallen Lounge

This is a marvelously serene scene, with live piano music setting the tone amid soft blond wood and polished brass decor. A fire crackles in the large stone fireplace; hors d'oeuvres and appetizers are served by a gracious and attentive staff. It's warm, slightly clubby, and a great people-watching spot. The lounge stays open for evening cocktails or a nightcap until midnight. *Stein Eriksen Lodge, Silver Lake Village, tel. 435/649-3700. AE, DC, MC, V.*

PARK CITY MOUNTAIN RESORT

Box 39
Park City, UT 84060
Tel. 435/649–8111
800/222–7275
Fax 435/647–5374
www.parkcitymountain.com

STATISTICALLY SPEAKING

Base elevation: 6,900 feet

Summit elevation: 10,026 feet

Vertical drop: 3,100 feet

Skiable terrain: 3,000 acres

Number of trails: 97

Longest run: 3½ miles

Lifts and capacity: 4 6-person chairs, 1 quad, 5 triples, 4 doubles; 27,200 skiers per hour

Daily lift ticket: $53

Average annual snowfall: 350 inches

Number of skiing days 1997–98: 173

Snowmaking: 47%

Terrain mix: N 16%, I 45%, E 39%

Snowboarding: yes

In the 1870s the town of Park City was the site of the largest silver-mining camp in the country. In those halcyon days its population swelled to nearly 10,000 fortune seekers, and its Main Street was a veritable sinners' den of bars, bordellos, and gambling houses. During the ensuing period of silver fever, hundreds of mines were opened, thousands of miles of tunnels were dug, $400 million worth of silver ore was mined, and 23 men became millionaires, including George Hearst, founder of the Hearst mining and newspaper empire.

The silver and the miners are long gone, but their legacy remains in the form of a busy, colorful resort town that combines the images of the past with the amenities of the present. In straitlaced Utah, Park City is still considered a veritable sin city. Most of the original buildings on Main Street have been so carefully preserved and restored that the entire district is now listed on the National Register of Historic Places. Most buildings house restaurants, bars, shops, galleries, museums, and hotels. Fanning out from this slice of history is modern Park City, a subdivision of contemporary hotels and condominiums spilling across the sage meadows, lining the high ridges, and filling the tiny canyon in and around the ski resort. Some skiers prefer this to Alta or Snowbird because it has more après-ski and evening opportunities as well as somewhere to go on a day off the slopes. Park City, the resort and the town, cozy up to each other; indeed they even overlap, with the lower slopes of the resort descending to the edge of town. In fact, one lift—the Town triple—begins its journey up the mountain from the foot of Park Avenue, in the heart of town.

This natural merging of community and resort makes it easy to commute between the mountain and the town on the free transit system that shuttles skiers from more than 75 in-town stops to the slopes as well as to the adjacent resort of Deer Valley, just 3 miles away. If you find even the five-minute shuttle inconvenient, there's also a well-developed village at the resort base, with lodging, bars, restaurants, and shops. For total convenience, many condo units provide ski-in/ski-out access.

Park City may no longer be the bawdy, rollicking town of its youth, but in its reincarnation as a ski resort it is spirited and zesty, with plenty of daytime and nighttime attractions to satisfy visitors.

HOW TO GET THERE

Shuttle Service

Several shuttle bus companies link the resort and the Salt Lake City airport and points in between. **Canyon Transport** (tel. 801/255–1841 or 800/255–1841), **Park City Transportation** (tel. 435/649–8567 or 800/637–3803), and **Lewis Brothers Stages** (tel. 801/359–8677 or 800/826–5844) all have scheduled shuttle service from the airport or downtown Salt Lake City. Rates range from $16 one-way in a motor coach to $125 one-way in a four-passenger limousine. All three have service desks at the Salt Lake City airport.

By Car

Park City is about 35 miles east of the Salt Lake City airport. From the airport take I–80 east to the Park City exit, Route 224, which turns into Park Avenue, and follow signs to Park City.

GETTING AROUND

As the shuttle bus system in Park City (Park City Transportation, tel. 435/615–5350) is efficient and free, a car isn't absolutely necessary unless you want to visit neighboring ski resorts or towns. Buses run throughout Park City between 8 AM and 11 PM, making regular stops about every 15 minutes at more than 75 locations in and around the town and resort. The shuttle serves Deer Valley as well. There are also taxicab companies in the Park City area, including **Ace Cab Co.** (tel. 435/649–8294) and **Park City Taxi** (tel. 435/649–8515). Rates vary based on distance, and they'll go anywhere you're willing to pay for.

THE SKIING

Park City offers about 3,000 acres of skiable terrain. It's known mostly as an intermediate's cruising resort, but it also has more than 650 acres of upper-elevation bowl skiing that includes some serious, supersteep stuff. The area is a crescent-shape ridge that runs north to south, and from the base elevation of just under 7,000 feet it's impossible to see the various faces and bowls off the top of Jupiter Peak, 3,100 feet above.

One of the unique aspects of the area is its terrain, which faces virtually every direction, making it easy to follow the sun around the mountain. The Pioneer, Crescent, and Ski Team ridge areas (served by the Payday, Ski Team, Three Kings, and First Time lifts) get the early morning rays, as does the intermediate and expert terrain sandwiched between Pinyon Ridge and the western flank of Pioneer Ridge (served by the six-passenger Bonanza, triple-seat Pioneer, and six-passenger McConkey's lifts); the Prospector area, on the west side of Crescent Ridge (served by King Con, the six-passenger, high-speed detachable Silverlode, and the Motherlode lifts), is the place to head midmorning; and by early afternoon the Jupiter Bowl is sunnyside up. This is also a neatly divided mountain, with distinct areas for all levels. Experts love the high bowls served by the Jupiter and McConkey's lifts, intermediates are usually happiest on the west face of Crescent Ridge, and novices can stick to the east side of Crescent Ridge.

Another of Park City's fine features is the lift layout, which quickly gets you to the top of the mountain. The old, poky gondola has been replaced by the six-passenger Payday lift that not only serves the front of the mountain but also leads you to the Bonanza lift, another six-seater, which runs to the Summit House Restaurant. From the top of Bonanza you can head down to the Pioneer lift via Mid-Mountain (green), connect with the six-passenger McConkey's lift that drops you at the top of McConkey's Bowl, or ski down Claimjumper (green) or Assessment (blue) to the Silverlode chair. If you want to avoid the base lodge area entirely, you can grab a shuttle bus to the Town lift, then take the Bonanza lift to the Summit House. Trails of all levels are accessible from these alternate lifts.

Park City has opened its entire area to snowboarders. There are also rental facilities and lessons available. There are no plans to create snowboards-only terrain, although a half-pipe can be found halfway down the Payday run.

Novices
Unlike some ski resorts, Park City offers novice skiers trails from the top of the mountain. These are easily reached via the Payday and Bonanza lifts. Homerun, 3½ miles of wide and ultraeasy (green) trail, runs from the top of the Bonanza lift all the way to the base of the Payday lift. Even intermediates can enjoy this long run in the early morning sun. If you're feeling apprehensive about the length of the run, First Time and Three Kings lifts also serve the three easiest and shortest novice runs, Three Kings, First Time, and Pick and Shovel. Once you've warmed up sufficiently and want to pick up the pace, start down Homerun and then cut left down Claimjumper as it veers toward the Prospector area. You're still in the green here, but it's a bit steeper and leads to the bottom of the Silverlode lift, from which you can explore some of the easier blue runs. Hidden Splen-

dor, for instance, is a beautiful wide-open, bowl-like run that is a bit steep but is always well groomed and should present no problems. Mel's Alley is a little narrower but has about the same pitch and is also always groomed. Both runs are reached directly from the top of the Silverlode lift, but if you want to eliminate the steeper upper part of the Prospector runs, you can follow Claimjumper and cut left onto either Powder Keg or Assessment, both of which are shorter and narrower but give you a chance to work on your turns before making the commitment to the longer runs. Both lead back toward lower Claimjumper (so you'll get some relief from the pitch) and will feed you back to the bottom of the Silverlode lift.

If you're feeling comfortable on those runs and are looking for a little more blue action, head to the King Con lift along Broadway, at the bottom of the Silverlode lift. King Con serves all blue runs, but at least half of them are always groomed and mogul-free, and you can't really get into any trouble if you have basic turns under control.

Intermediates

Whether you're starting from town on the Town triple or from the resort center on the Payday lift, the Payday trail should be your first choice for a stirring warm-up cruise. From the top of the Town triple lift there's about 500 yards of gentle green before you hit Payday (the Payday lift deposits you right at the top of the run), which starts out fairly narrow and then widens into a groomed, well-pitched autobahn cruiser that curves around

the eastern edge of the mountain and brings you back to the resort center. Once you're warmed up, head over to the Eagle lift, which will take you to the eastern tip of Crescent Ridge, accessing the heaviest concentration of blue runs on the mountain. The first run to take should be the wide, groomed Temptation, a cruiser that hooks left to lead you to the bottom of the King Con quad. This lift takes you to the summit of the ridge in less than six minutes, and in an hour or so (depending on the lift lines) you can explore each of these excellent intermediate trails: Sitka, Shamus, and Liberty have the steepest pitch and are the narrowest, while Courchevel, Chance, and High Card are wider and a little less steep, although they're usually left ungroomed. All these runs are fairly short, but they don't lack variety and have enough pitches, rolls, and drop-offs to keep things interesting; a moderate intermediate could easily spend an entire day in this area without getting bored. When you're ready to fly, take the King Con run to the bottom of the Silverlode lift. From the top of the lift the blue runs get steeper but are still well groomed, with one or two occasionally allowed to grow some decent-size bumps. Start on Parley's Park, which begins fairly wide, allowing you to adjust to the increased pitch. About halfway down you get to choose between Prospector, a steep expert run, and the lower section of Parley's Park, which, if you stay right all the way down, will take you back to the bottom of the Silverlode lift. The next run you should opt for is Hidden Splendor, a glorious wide run through the meadows and one that is sometimes left with ungroomed snow after a storm. If you stay right on this, it will take you to the bottom portion of Claimjumper, a temperate green; if you want to skip Claimjumper, stay left and pick up Mel's Alley, a narrow gully that cuts through the trees and back down to the bottom of the Silverlode six-passenger lift. For a long, groomed, steep cruise, veer left about halfway down Parley's Park onto Sunnyside, which takes you to the Motherlode triple chair.

You can also follow Parley's Park for about 500 yards and then swing left on to Single Jack, which makes a straight shot to the bottom of the Thaynes lift. Or, not far from the top of Single Jack you can veer right onto Lower Single Jack, a steep, but short, bump run that returns you to the Motherlode lift. From the top of Motherlode you can head a bit to the right and onto Double Jack, a steep expert bump run that takes you to the Thaynes lift. From the top of Thaynes, you can use the Thaynes or Hoist expert runs to return to the bottom of the lift or head right onto either Jupiter Access or Keystone, a pair of sedate trails that wind through the woods. You can use these to either reach the expert terrain served by the Jupiter chair or connect with Thaynes Canyon, which leads back to the Thaynes, Motherlode, and King Con chairs. If you're not ready for Jupiter, work out on the medium-size moguls that cover Double Jack, Thaynes, or the Hoist.

Experts
After a quick ride up Payday, warm up with a bump run down Widowmaker or Nail Driver and work your way down to the Ski Team lift. Once back at the top, get in some early morning steeps and bumps on Silver King, which has megamoguls and apart from the bowls is among the steepest runs on the mountain. After any kinks have disappeared, take the Payday and Bonanza lifts back to the Summit House and try a few runs down either the Hoist or Thaynes, both of which are steep, narrow, and bumpy and will take you down to the bottom of the Thaynes lift.

When you've had your fill of bumps, head for Blue Slip Bowl, a short, wide, and steep expanse of ungroomed snow from which you'll be able to judge if you're ready for more bowl action. If you're comfortable on this bowl, you must choose between the McConkey's six-passenger lift and the Jupiter lift, which serve the steepest and most demanding terrain on the mountain. If you head up the Jupiter lift, the wide-open faces far to your left are good tests, or if you're confident, drop into a radical collection of narrow chutes and gullies that plunge like elevator shafts through the densely packed evergreens. Try Silver Cliff, Six Bells, or Indicator for a real taste of gulp-and-go vertical, and keep in mind that trees are only your friends if you don't slam in to them. If you feel you aren't ready for these, try the wider, more open Fortune Teller or Shadow Ridge, both of which run directly under the lift. To the north of the Jupiter lift is Portuguese Gap, another staggeringly steep run through the trees, or you can opt to traverse over to Scotts Bowl, which is still ultrasteep but devoid of glades.

For another supersteep, head over to the east face of Jupiter Peak from Jupiter chair (requires about a 15-minute hike up the Pioneer Ridge), where you'll find the Puma Bowl. Another option is the McConkey's lift, which takes you to the top of McConkey's Bowl. Looking down from the top, you can enter the steep, powder-rich bowl on your right that feeds down into glades, or turn left and jump into the trees that are cut by the Sunrise and Buckeye trails. Thicker glades lie just south of the lift, while a short, lung-testing hike north along Pinyon Ridge leads up to Puma Bowl and its steep faces. Try to snag a local for a tour of this area.

SNOWBOARDING

The entire resort is open to snow-boarders, but if you crave air you'll head for the half-pipe on the Payday run. A lighting system enables night riding in the half-pipe, which also is furnished with a yurt where you can sit, warm up, and grab something to drink. As the snow piles up, the resort also builds terrain parks in various areas; these may have start ramps, small tabletops, flat spines, quarter pipes, and spine obstacles. If you prefer to cruise on your snowboard, the finely groomed and wide-open Sitka, Eureka, and Monitor runs served by the King Con lift, as well as the Sunnyside and Carbide Cut runs accessed from the Motherlode chair shouldn't be ignored. If you revel in powder, take the Jupiter lift to the caches on West Face and Scott's Bowl or McConkey's lift to the bowl of the same name.

OTHER SNOW SPORTS

Just north of Park City the **Utah Winter Sports Park** (3000 W. Bear Hollow Dr., tel. 435/658–4200), built in anticipation of the 2002 Winter Games, rises out of Bear Hollow. The park will stage the Games' ski jumping, bobsled, luge, and skeleton events, but you can already try your hand at ski jumping, bobsled, and luge here (reserve ahead).

NEARBY

Between the Park City Mountain Resort and the Winter Sports Park is **the Canyons** (4000 The Canyons Drive, tel. 435/649–5400), a quickly evolving four-season ski resort that, when fully built, will offer nearly 7,000 skiable acres of terrain, a village at its base, and hundreds of hotel rooms and condos.

WHERE TO STAY

Of all the resorts in Utah, Park City has the most varied accommodations. You can stay slope-side in hotels or condo units or choose from in-town historic bed-and-breakfasts, small European-style hotels, contemporary resort lodges, and condominiums. In the surrounding region are the ultra-deluxe hotels and condominiums of nearby Deer Valley (*see* Deer Valley, *above*) and the more mainstream hotels and motels in Salt Lake City, 35 miles away. Accommodations and/or packages can be booked through **Deer Valley Lodging** (tel. 800/453 3833), **Park City Mountain Reservations** (tel. 800/222–7275), **Park City Reservations** (tel. 800/ 453 5789), or **Premier Resorts** (tel. 800/545–7669).

Expensive

All Seasons

These stylish, modern two- and three-bedroom condominiums are among the most upscale in Park City. The decor and furnishings are ultradeluxe, with hardwood floors, Berber carpeting, Laura Ashley–style wallpaper, flagstone fireplaces, and contemporary artwork. Each comes with an equally modern full kitchen with ceramic counters and state-of-the-art appliances. Each bedroom has an en suite bathroom; all units have a sleeper sofa. Master suites include double-wide jetted tubs. Deluxe touches include comfortable, well-made Colonial-style chairs and couches and private decks. Next to the eighth green of the Park City Golf Course, it has a spectacular view of the mountain. *Park City Golf Course, 1485 Empire Ave., Park City, 84060, tel. 435/649–5500 or 800/331–8652, fax 435/649–6647. 16 units. Facilities: heated outdoor pool, laundry facilities. AE, D, MC, V. $290–$650.*

Lodge at Mountain Village

Three buildings at the base of the Park City lifts make up this large wood-and-stone complex with gabled roofs that blend nicely with the environment. There's easy access among the three buildings, and all units are spacious, even the studios. The huge four-bedroom units spread over two levels and can sleep up to 12 people in privacy and comfort. The interior decor is modern, with natural-color Berber carpeting, tile accents, stucco walls, and floor-to-ceiling windows and cathedral ceilings in the larger suites. This should be your first choice if you are looking for ski-in/ski-out

convenience, hotel service, and practical condo amenities. *Base of Payday lift, resort center, Box 3449, Park City, 84060, tel. 435/649–0800 or 800/824–5331, fax 435/649–1464. 140 units. Facilities: indoor-outdoor pool, sauna, steam room, indoor-outdoor whirlpool. AE, D, DC, MC, V. $180–$1,095.*

Silver King Hotel

Epitomizing the very best of modern mountain architecture, this ultra-stylish condo hotel has soaring windows, exposed beams, and an atrium lobby. Guests can choose from four unit sizes: studio, one-bedroom, two-bedroom, and larger penthouse suite. The decor in each is also modern but softened by handmade pine furnishings, peaceful colors, and little touches such as woven area rugs. Guests congregate in the expansive lobby, where a modern tile fireplace warms large sectional sofas. The hotel is just steps from the lifts. *1485 Empire Ave., Box 2818, Park City, 84060, tel. 435/649–5500 or 800/331–8652, fax 435/649–6647. 62 units. Facilities: indoor-outdoor pool, sauna, whirlpool. AE, D, MC, V. $105–$660.*

Washington School Inn

Few schools are like this inn, a marvelous example of turn-of-the-century architecture, with huge windows and a distinctive bell tower. It was home to thousands of students during its heyday, but in the mid-1930s it closed and then fell into disrepair. It was reincarnated as an elegant country inn in the 1980s. The interior is spacious and designer-perfect, with high, vaulted ceilings, cherry-wood wainscoting, and a stunning center staircase leading to the bell tower. The large rooms and suites are elegant, with country-style wall coverings, handwoven area rugs, tile-and-stone flooring, and four-poster canopy beds. There's a large hand-carved lobby fireplace, twig furniture, flagstone flooring in the spa area, and a comfortable sitting area with wingback armchairs. The inn is in town on the upper road, about a half mile from the ski area. No children under 8. *543 Park Ave., Box 536, Park City, 84060, tel. 435/649–3800 or 800/824–1672, fax 435/649–3802. 12 rooms, 3 suites. Facilities: sauna, exercise equipment, indoor hot tub, lounge. AE, D, DC, MC, V. $195–$379, including full breakfast and après-ski refreshments.*

Moderate

Shadow Ridge Resort Hotel

Guests are drawn to the Shadow Ridge for its comfortable ambience. The decor includes dark-wood trim and furnishings accented by white walls and heavy tapestrylike drapes and upholstery. It also has a remarkable selection of rooms, ranging from a standard twin to a spacious two-bedroom condominium suite with a full kitchen. All rooms come with a private balcony. Best of all, the hotel is just 100 yards from the Park City lifts, in front of the resort center. *50 Shadow Ridge Dr., Box 1820, Park City, 84060, tel. 435/655–3315 or 800/443–1045, fax 435/649–5951. 150 units. Facilities: heated outdoor pool, whirlpool, sauna, fitness center, lounge, billiard room, laundry facilities. AE, D, DC, MC, V. $200–$285.*

Silver Queen

Here's a classic, historic Park City structure right on Main Street in the heart of town. The wedge-shape building is solid brick, with intricate detailing, curved window tops, and a wraparound balcony that overhangs the sidewalk on two sides. Inside, the decor is period, with Colonial-style wall coverings, archways, wainscoting, latticework, and thick, richly colored carpeting. The units, available with either one or two bedrooms, are individually designed and decorated with pine antiques, brass beds, wicker accessories, dark-wood trim, tile and brick accents, and large, comfortable chairs and couches. Modern amenities include a full kitchen, a jetted tub, a fireplace, and a washer/dryer. There's a delightful European feel here in both the ambience and the service, and if you enjoy luxury in a historic setting, it's a good choice. *632 Main St., Box 2391, Park City, 84060, tel. 435/649–5986 or 800/447–6423, fax 435/649–3572. 12 units. Facilities: ski lockers. D, MC, V. $175–$395.*

Snowed Inn

Although it's been around only since 1987, this charming Victorian-style country inn is perfectly suited for the turn-of-the-century atmosphere of the original Park City. High ceilings and large windows, distinctive antique furnishings such as pine hutches, brass beds, colorful wall coverings, and goose-down comforters give rooms an old-fashioned feel. A sumptuous parlor with a towering mahogany-pillared fireplace encourages mingling. There is one family suite with a wood-burning fireplace. The inn's award-winning Juniper restaurant serves delightful American cuisine in a cozy setting. Horse-drawn sleigh rides are available afternoons and evenings. The inn is on the highway between The Canyons and Park City. *3770 N. Rte. 224, Park City, 84060, tel. 435/649–5713 or 800/ 545–7669, fax 435/645–7672. 10 rooms. Facilities: outdoor hot tub. AE, D, MC, V. $225–$315, including Continental breakfast.*

The Yarrow
Looking as though it's been transplanted from Colonial Williamsburg, this distinctive complex has a neat brick facade, wood-trimmed peaked windows, and an ersatz clock tower. Inside, the rooms and suites come in a variety of configurations, including studios, standard and deluxe rooms, and suites. In general, rooms are large enough to accommodate four, but if you need extra space, there are also a number of one- and two-bedroom condo units with enough beds to sleep six, along with a full kitchen, a fireplace, and living and dining areas. The Yarrow is just a short walk from town and from the ski lifts. *1800 Park Ave., Box 1840, Park City, 84060, tel. 435/649–7000 or 800/927 7694, fax 435/645–7007. 181 rooms. Facilities: restaurant, pub, heated outdoor pool, spa, exercise room, hot tub. AE, D, DC, MC, V. $249–$519.*

Inexpensive
Edelweiss Haus
This simple, unpretentious condo hotel is at the resort, just 1½ blocks from the lifts. The units range from standard hotel rooms to one- and two-bedroom condos, but all quarters are clean and comfortable. The larger condos have kitchen facilities. *1482 Empire Rd., Box 495, Park City, 84060, tel. 435/649–9342 or 800/ 245 6417, fax 435/649–4049. 30 rooms. Facilities: heated outdoor pool, outdoor Jacuzzi, sauna. AE, D, MC, V. $95–$360.*

Inn at Prospector Square
This sprawling inn, just minutes from Park City's Main Street and only a five-minute shuttle bus ride from the resort, is actually six buildings centered around the Prospector Square Athletic Club. It offers a mix of standard hotel rooms, studios with and without lofts, and one-, two-, and three-bedroom condominiums. Most units are utilitarian with basic child- and group-proof decor, but all are comfortable and well equipped. All condos have a full kitchen and a gas fireplace. Membership in the Athletic Club, which has all sorts of exercise facilities, including an indoor pool, runs $12 a day. *2200 Sidewinder Dr., Box 1698, Park City, 84060, tel. 435/ 649–7100 or 800/453–3812, fax 435/ 649–8377. 204 units. Facilities: 2 indoor hot tubs. AE, D, DC, MC, V. $142–$400.*

Old Miner's Lodge
Built in 1889 as a miners' boardinghouse, this lodge retains much of its original style, beginning with its exceptional length and grand position atop a hill high above town. In 1983 the lodge was renovated, with most of the original fittings, woodwork, and furnishings painstakingly restored. No two rooms are alike, but all are similar in the warmth and authenticity of furnishings, including such touches as claw-foot tubs, four-poster beds, wil-

low chairs and headboards, and handmade pine furniture. All suites have small fridges, and all rooms come with terry-cloth robes and down comforters, but there are no TVs. *615 Woodside Ave., Park City, 84060, tel. 435/645–8068 or 800/648–8068, fax 435/645–7420. 9 rooms, 3 suites. Facilities: outdoor hot tub. AE, D, MC, V. $100–$230, including full breakfast.*

Snow Flower
This four-building wooden complex, wedged into the side of a hill, is not the most stylish design in town. But it does have a ski-in/ski-out location and an impressive collection of rooms and suites, the largest of which is a five-bedroom monster with space for at least a dozen close friends. Each unit is individually owned, so decor and furnishings vary considerably. All come with kitchens (of varying sizes), fireplaces, and sensible furnishings. Guests are provided voice mailboxes. *400 Silver King Dr., Box 957, Park City, 84060, tel. 435/649–6400 or 800/852–3101, fax 435/649–6049. 142 units. Facilities: 2 heated outdoor pools, laundry, ski storage. AE, MC, V. $120–$950.*

WHERE TO EAT
Unlike neighboring Alta or Snowbird, Park City has a bustling and varied dining and nightlife scene. There are dozens of interesting spots, mostly along Main Street, ranging from the predictable to the avant-garde, with a lot of good old-fashioned Western ambience thrown in. To enjoy Park City's rollicking nightclub and bar scene, you'll have to abide by the club membership rule, which applies to all of Utah.

On the Mountain
Mid-Mountain Lodge
Although it's nearly a mile from its original site, this late-1800s lodge stands as the oldest mine building in Utah. Its three separate dining areas all have exceptional food. There's an excellent choice of daily specials—veggie lasagna, seafood casserole, and clam chowder—plus standards such as chili, sandwiches, burgers, and soups. *On Mid-Mountain run in Pioneer lift area, tel. 435/649–3044. MC, V.*

Summit House
The fairly standard selection of burgers, soups, salads, chili, and stews here gives you plenty to choose from. The crowds are smaller here than at Mid-Mountain. Diners can also sit on the outdoor deck and enjoy the spectacular 100-mile view. *Top of Bonanza lift, tel. 435/647– 5223. AE, D, MC, V.*

Expensive
Chimayo
Southwestern cuisine is the name of the game at this lively restaurant. Its decor includes soft-brown stone walls, huge wooden ceiling trusses, terracotta tiles, dramatic lighting, and a hint of mesquite in the air. For starters try the toasted corn chowder. Follow that with the Farmer's Market salad, with marinated cactus and adobo vinaigrette. For entrées there's an equally off-the-wall selection of such things as crab-stuffed grouper steamed in a banana leaf and served with avocado slaw or the seared elk burrito with blackened tomato sauce and Mexican oregano. For dessert try the grilled banana sundae. *368 Main St., tel. 435/649–6222. AE, D, MC, V.*

Gamekeeper's Grill

Housed in a historic, two-story brick building with copper highlights, this restaurant has a menu that reflects its name. You'll find pan-seared elk medallions, smoked buffalo ravioli, and wild-game chili competing for your attention against grilled salmon, Utah red trout, and herb-crusted rack of lamb with red chili jelly. The large portions leave little room for dessert. *508 Main St., tel. 435/647–0327. AE, MC, V.*

Riverhorse Café

The two large, upper-level warehouse rooms that make up this café resemble an ultramodern big-city supper club, with exposed beams, polished hardwood floors, black-and-white furnishings, and walls adorned with huge portraits of such well-known Native Americans as Sitting Bull and Geronimo. House specialties are seared ahi tuna in a puff pastry tart with eggplant and citrus sauce and charred rack of Utah lamb in a cabernet demi-glace with goat cheese ravioli, roasted garlic, fresh herbs, and mashed potatoes. *540 Main St., tel. 435/649–3536. Reservations essential. AE, MC, V.*

Moderate

Baja Cantina

For Mexican favorites, the Baja, at the base of the lifts in the resort center, is a good choice. It's a bright, busy greenhouse-style building with lots of tile and stucco and hand-painted bird-of-paradise art on the walls from floor to ceiling. The menu offers virtually anything you can think of from south of the border. Without exception, this is the best Mexican food in Park City.

1284 Empire Ave., resort center, tel. 435/649–2252. AE, D, DC, MC, V.

Claimjumper

The Claimjumper is a bustling place in the heart of the historic Old Town, with Americana decor including hardwood floors, brick walls, a large stone fireplace, hunter green curtains, and a menu printed on an empty wine bottle. The mainstay here is steak, ranging from an 8-ounce cut to a slab the size of your plate. It's all aged beef, cooked precisely as requested. There are variations on the steak theme, including prime rib, baby-back ribs, buffalo steaks, and monster burgers, plus a few nonbeef choices. *573 Main St., tel. 435/649–8051. AE, D, DC, MC, V.*

Grappa

In Park City's historic old town district, this restaurant specializes in ambience and northern Italian dishes. Heavy floor tiles, bricks, and timbers lend a rustic, warm, farmhouse feel, and tables on the wraparound balcony overlook those on the first floor. The menus, which change seasonally, offer appetizers such as homemade duck prosciutto with a summer-pear and balsamic-vinegar salad, and calamari fritti served with basil aioli and fresh marinara. Innovative entrées include crisp, pan-fried game hen with spinach tortellini and roasted garlic velouté, as well as pancetta-wrapped chicken fricassee filled with spinach-and-mushroom risotto and served with summer squash and greens. *151 Main St., tel. 435/645–0636. AE, D, MC, V.*

350 Main Seafood & Oyster Co.

This strikingly stylized art deco emporium has black-lacquer tables, pearl-color walls, maple-wood flooring, and a copper-tinted ceiling. The menu runs from cornmeal-crusted sea bass, peppered ahi tuna, and lobster ravioli to filet mignon, herb-marinated chicken breast, and a grilled vegetable platter. If you're not very hungry but just want to nibble, there's also a selection of fried catfish, barbecued shrimp, and an oyster bar that includes mussels, clams, and peel-and-eat shrimp. *350 Main St., tel. 435/649–3140. AE, D, DC, MC, V.*

Inexpensive

Burgie's

What you'll find at this lively place are beef, lamb, turkey, buffalo, and vegetarian burgers with all sorts of combos, low prices, and a cheerful, diner-style atmosphere. An interesting side dish is the mound of crisp, batter-dipped fried onion rings served with a mildly hot sauce. *570 Main St., tel. 435/649–0011. AE, MC, V.*

Main Street Delicatessen

This deli is a good spot for a fast sandwich, eat in or take it out. It's pleasantly furnished with pine chairs and tables and offers a good selection of deli meats and innovative designer sandwich combinations on a variety of breads. *525 Main St., tel. 435/649–1110. MC, V.*

Main Street Pizza & Noodle

This bright, modern pasta emporium with floor-to-ceiling windows makes California-style pizza as well as pastas and filling alternatives such as calzone and stromboli (pizza dough rolled over and filled with such items as Asian-style chicken, pepperoni, veggies, and cheese), soups, and sal-ads. *530 Main St., tel. 435/645–8878. AE, D, DC, MC, V.*

Mt. Air Café

Bring your appetite to this old-fashioned country diner serving comfort foods such as ground sirloin, liver and onions, roasted chicken, fish-and-chips, country-fried steak, and a variety of daily specials. Sit at the lunch counter or grab a booth. The café also serves breakfast all day. *Rtes. 248 and 224E, tel. 435/649–9868. AE, MC, V.*

Best Bets for Breakfast

Eating Establishment

Known as the Double E by locals, this is a good spot for hearty skillet breakfasts, including omelets, flapjacks, waffles, and ham and eggs. *317 Main St., tel. 435/649–8284; plaza level at resort center near Payday lift, tel. 435/649–7289. AE, D, MC, V.*

Morning Ray Café & Bakery

This café-style restaurant has a good selection of pastries, muffins, cereals, and specialty breads for the Continental crowd. Serious eaters can also hunker down to omelets, pancakes, and quiches, some prepared with organic ingredients. *268 Main St., tel. 435/649– 5686. AE, MC, V.*

NIGHTLIFE AND ENTERTAINMENT

Après-Ski

Baja Cantina

A must on the après-ski list, this restaurant has a crowded bar with happy-hour munchies, schmoozing, and the best margaritas in town. *1284 Empire Ave., resort center, tel. 435/649–2252. AE, D, DC, MC, V.*

Loud and Lively/Dancing

Alamo Saloon
A classic old-style saloon where you'll find the locals hanging out, this part–dance club, part–sports bar is raucous but not dangerous. The usually young crowd comes for the live rock music, billiards, pinball, darts, and lots of TVs. *447 Main St., tel. 435/649–2380. AE, D, MC, V.*

Lakota
Park City's only restaurant-cum-bar features live entertainment and a state-of-the-art audiovisual system that adds to the upbeat mood and convivial atmosphere. *751 Main St., in the Caledonian, tel. 435/658–3400. AE, MC, V.*

O'Shuck's
This 20-something sports bar in the heart of the historic district is the kind of place where you toss the peanut shells on the floor and forget about them. Ski memorabilia clings to the brick walls. *427 Main St., tel. 435/645–3999. MC, V.*

More Mellow

Mileti's
This popular locals' hangout is colored in soft pinks and greens with lots of mahogany fixtures and giant mirrors. It's the place for conversation and socializing. *412 Main St., tel. 435/649–8211. D, DC, MC, V.*

SNOWBIRD SUMMER AND SKI RESORT

SNOWBIRD SUMMER AND SKI RESORT

Snowbird, UT 84092
Tel. 801/742–2222 or
800/453–3000
Fax 801/933 2298
www.snowbird.com

STATISTICALLY SPEAKING

Base elevation: 7,760 feet

Summit elevation: 11,000 feet

Vertical drop: 3,240 feet

Skiable terrain: 2,500 acres

Number of trails: 66

Longest run: 2.5 miles

Lifts and capacity: 1 tram,
1 quad, 7 doubles; 11,000
skiers per hour

Daily lift ticket: $39, chairs;
$49, tram

Average annual snowfall: 500
inches

Number of skiing days
1997–98: 205

Snowmaking: 25 acres

Terrain mix: N 25%, I 35%,
E 40%

Snowboarding: yes

This is not a resort that relies on frills to make its point or to carve its place on the ski map. It's a resort for people who love to ski. In fact, there's a decided absence of frills at the minimalist base village area tucked near the end of Little Cottonwood Canyon just 20 miles from downtown Salt Lake City. The towering 10-story Cliff Lodge dominates the resort, and nearby are three slightly smaller condominium buildings, for a total on-mountain bed base of about 1,000. A hundred yards from this wall of granite is the base area plaza, which contains the three-story atrium-style Snowbird Center. Here you'll find a small selection of shops, including a deli-market, several sports stores, a liquor store, a pharmacy, a clinic, a post office, various resort-services offices, a base-area cafeteria, a nightclub, and three restaurants. A shuttle bus regularly circles the entire complex, but you can also cover the area on foot in under 30 minutes. That's it. Day one you can discover it all, and by day three if you yearn for more diversions, you'll be thinking about heading into Salt Lake City.

Above all this soars the 11,000-foot Hidden Peak, in a massively rugged part of the Wasatch Range. This, along with the legendary featherweight Utah powder, which averages more than 500 inches a year, is the main reason skiers come to Snowbird.

Powder. It defines Snowbird as much as the soaring granite peaks and the forests of Engelmann spruce, lodgepole pine, and Douglas fir. You come to Snowbird for the steep and deep—and no other reason. And that's the way builder Dick Bass envisioned his little slice of Cottonwood Canyon. Bass, an entrepreneurial adventurer—his other claim to fame is his ascent of the highest peaks on each of the seven continents—wanted a no-nonsense, purpose-built resort, and his sleek, steep, modernistic Snowbird fits the bill. The country's fastest tram takes eight minutes to get you to the top of 3,000 vertical feet of top-to-bottom skiing, and when the combination of snow-stuffed bowls, chutes, couloirs, and cirques have taken their toll, the village is right there.

Outside, the resort is a resilient buttress against the howling wind and snowstorms that sweep the canyon; inside, it's a comfortable, contemporary labyrinth of convenience. Like the mountain, this is a

USEFUL NUMBERS
Area code: 801

Children's services: day-care, tel. 801/933–2256; instruction, tel. 801/742–2222, 4164

Snow phone: tel. 801/933–2100

Police: Salt Lake City, tel. 801/799–3000

Medical center: tel. 801/742–2222, ext. 4195

Resort office services: tel. 801/742–2222, ext. 4005

Salt Lake Convention and Visitors Bureau: tel. 801/521–2822

Road conditions: tel. 801/742–2222

Towing: AAA, tel. 801/364–5610; Alta New Texaco, tel. 801/572–6010

FIVE-STAR FAVORITES

Best run for vertical: Great Scott

Best run overall: Chips

Best bar/nightclub: Tram Club

Best hotel: Cliff Lodge

Best restaurant: The Aerie

stern, stoic, and well-laid-out village. Towers of concrete and glass engulf the canyon timber, buildings are linked by paved stone pathways, and the only bright lights are a million miles straight up, studding the coal black sky with a lonely luminescence.

HOW TO GET THERE

Shuttle Services

From Salt Lake City International Airport, **Canyon Transport** (tel. 801/255–1841 or 800/255–1841) runs regularly scheduled service. No advance booking is necessary. The cost is approximately $20 per person one-way. **UTA City Transit** (UTA; tel. 801/287–4636) runs a ski bus every 15 minutes from the city center to Snowbird. One-way fare is $4.50.

By Car

Snowbird is 20 miles, about a 30-minute drive, from the heart of Salt Lake City, up Little Cottonwood Canyon. Follow I–80 east to I–215 south, then take Exit 6 and follow signs to Little Cottonwood Canyon. For car-rental information, *see* Getting to Utah Resorts, *above*.

GETTING AROUND

A free **ski shuttle bus** runs between Gad Valley and Snowbird Center from 8 to 5. In the evening this shuttle runs every 30 minutes until 11, and will drop you at any accommodation. There's also free regularly scheduled service between Snowbird and Alta (about a mile away), with stops at various locations. **Canyon Transport** (*see* Shuttle Services, *above*) offers service to downtown Salt Lake City. **Yellow Cab** (tel. 801/521–2100 or 800/826–4746) provides taxi service in the area.

THE SKIING

To get the lay of the land at Snowbird, know that the 125-passenger Snowbird tram is the line that divides the mountain neatly in half. Directly underneath the tram are some of the best straight-shot black-diamond plunges in the country; to the left (looking up) is the blue-black cruising and bowl skiing of the Peruvian Gulch area; and to the right, the Little Cloud Bowl area with its steep black-diamond cruising.

Below the Little Cloud Bowl, where the timberline starts, is the Gad Valley area, with a half dozen intermediate runs, and below that the minimal novice area. A long traverse called the Bass Highway links the Gad Valley with the tram side of the mountain. There's also a high-country traverse from the top of either the tram or the Little Cloud lift that is the highest ride on the Gad Valley side.

The skiing at Snowbird is tough. Many of the blue runs here would be rated black elsewhere. Experts and strong intermediates can ski from the tram and the Little Cloud lift, but less sturdy intermediates and novices are best advised to stick to the Wilbere, Gad, and Mid Gad lifts.

If you head over to the enormous bowl that holds Peruvian Gulch on its eastern edge and the Peruvian Cirque on the western lip from the Little Cloud lift, it's a fairly hard uphill slog that takes about five minutes. Coming from the top of the tram, there's a short uphill climb, then a tricky cat track to get over to the Little Cloud Bowl.

If you're a strong skier and want first crack at the early powder, head for the tram right away. If you are less dedicated, the sun warms the Gad Valley area in the morning and then moves to the Little Cloud Bowl by midday. It's a good way to warm up slowly and get comfortable before moving over to the Peruvian Gulch side of the mountain in the afternoon.

Overall, it's easy to get around at Snowbird, but if you feel intimidated by the unknown possibilities, the resort's free mountain-host tour service is an excellent way to become familiar with the layout. Skiers meet at prearranged times, are sorted into ability groups, and then are led on a mountain tour.

Another thing to remember at Snowbird is the two-level ticket system: An all-inclusive ticket is $49, and a chairlift-only ticket is $39. If the tram terrain is beyond your ability, there's no point in paying the full fare. The entire mountain is open for snowboarding.

Novices

If you have never skied before and are considering a visit to Snowbird—don't bother. This is not the place to take up the sport, notwithstanding the first-rate Snowbird ski school. Never-evers will be restricted to two short teaching runs—Chickadee and Chickadee Loop, served by their own chair—which are curiously also the main footpath for anybody walking from Cliff Lodge to Snowbird Center. It's a layout flaw that not only puts hazards in the way of beginning skiers, but also saddles Cliff guests with a tricky and slippery walk. Even experienced novices with a few days of skiing under their boots will find the green terrain extremely limited. There are just a half dozen novice slopes on the Gad Valley side of the mountain. If you fit that category and you're already here, the best way to start the day is to take the Mid-Gad lift up to the Mid-Gad station. From there you have only one choice: Big Emma, a green run that weaves easily through a wooded area before spilling out on to a wider, well-groomed section that takes you back down to the bottom of Gad Valley. About midway down Big Emma, you can detour onto West Second South and West Second South On-Ramp, both fairly short and flat in sections.

If you feel you are ready to step up to some modest blue runs, your best bet is to take the Gadzoom lift, which runs parallel to the Mid-Gad lift but takes you slightly higher up, to the bottom of the Little Cloud lift. From there you can try Lunch Run (turn right as you get off the lift), a fairly steep but well-groomed extension of Big Emma. A bit farther on the right is Bassackwards, a longer, slightly more challenging blue run that winds around the middle of the Gad Valley. Here you'll find a moderately difficult section of trees, then a wider, groomed stretch that feeds into Lower Bassackwards. This is a nice rolling cruiser—with a few steep pitches—that feeds back to the Gadzoom and Mid-Gad lifts. From this run you can also take the Wilbere Cutoff—cut right as you cross under the two chairs—to the bottom of the Wilbere lift. The Wilbere will take you to the top of Wilbere Ridge (make sure you turn right off the chair), a short run that will give you a taste of some steep pitches plus some interesting rolls and dips.

Intermediates

Unless you are a strong intermediate skier, your best bet is to start out on the Gad Valley side of the mountain, which enjoys the early morning sun. Take the Gadzoom lift and warm up on Lunch Run, a good, wide cruiser. As it crosses under the lift, pick up Bassackwards and enjoy some good pitches and rolls on your way down to the bottom of the Gad 2 lift. From the top of this lift, head for Bananas. On the upper part it's fairly steep and lightly treed, but once it curves under the Gad 2 lift, it widens out and is usually groomed, so you can carry good speed back down to the bottom of the Gad 2. Ride to the top of this lift again, turn left, and either take Election for some well-spaced bumps or head straight off the lift to the upper part of Bassackwards, which is steep and usually groomed. If you like a good, long cruising run without bumps or ungroomed stretches, stay on Bassackwards all the way back down to the bottom of the Gadzoom lift.

At the point where this run crosses under the chair, you can also cut hard right and take Wilbere Cutoff down to the bottom of the Wilbere lift. This section can get a little bumpy, but it's short, and you can stay on the right side to avoid the biggest moguls. A short ride on the Wilbere chair takes you to the top of Wilbere Ridge, another well-groomed cruiser through some stands of trees.

More aggressive intermediates looking to step up should consider heading back up the Gadzoom lift to the Little Cloud lift. Signs here indicate that you are heading for black-diamond territory, but anyone with a strong parallel turn can ski this terrain. It's wide open—almost bowl-like—and throws some nice dips and rolls at you, especially on the upper part. This is pick-your-own-route skiing, but you'll want to stick to the area marked Regulator Johnson (on your right going down) and definitely avoid the Gad Chutes, which drop off to your right about halfway down. These are double-black monsters, steep, ungroomed, and with lots of trees.

If you feel comfortable on Regulator Johnson, get back on the Little Cloud lift, turn right when you get off, and take the Road to Provo. This can be a tricky little traverse, so stay in control. You soon arrive at a pair of black bowl runs called Shireen and Mark Malu Fork. Again, a strong intermediate should be able to handle either one because they are wide enough to allow long, sweeping, speed-checking turns.

The Peruvian Gulch side of Snowbird doesn't offer much for the intermediate. Chips is the only blue run here (the only blue run off the tram), and though it's almost 3 miles long, it's a bit of a cat track along the top section before it widens out into a broad meadow that is usually groomed. At the lower end of the meadow, you'll begin a long, circuitous run back to the bottom of the tram. Watch the signs carefully because at numerous points the trail intersects with some black runs that you may not want to tackle.

Experts

There's no doubt that this is the mountain for you. It's even possible to rack up more vertical here than you'd get in a day of helicopter skiing. So cut loose and have fun. The tram, your fastest and most direct way to the top, is an eight-minute ride that unleashes almost 3,000 feet of vertical. Some locals play "beat the tram"—shooting down to the bottom fast enough to catch the same car back up to the top. The most direct and challenging route is Silver Fox, a vertiginous wall that shows little mercy to those not totally in control of their skis. From the top of the tram,

you can also turn right and head over to the Little Cloud Bowl area or turn left and take High Baldy over to the West Baldy area. If there has been fresh snow overnight, expect a crowd in both areas.

If you prefer a mellower start to your day, you might consider following the sun. Start on the Gad Valley side by taking the Gadzoom lift to the top and then enjoy some short, steep blacks that snap the knees awake. By midmorning head for the Little Cloud lift and pick up the pace on the steep, wide-open bowl. Little Cloud skirts along the top of the bowl for a twisting and spirited ride back down to the bottom of the Little Cloud lift; Regulator Johnson charts a steeper, more direct route down to the same spot. You'll catch the sun here and beat the traffic that arrives later in the day.

By early afternoon take the traverse over to the Peruvian Gulch side of the mountain, then follow the Cirque Traverse until you find a tantalizing way down. Great Scott and Upper Cirque are extreme steeps, more chutes than anything else and quite often require a leap of faith off a cornice. Farther along the traverse is the Peruvian Cirque, a more traditional and slightly less precipitous bowl. All three routes take you to the corner of the Cirque, where you can drop over the top of the ridge and tackle two double-black-diamond bump runs—Dalton's Draw and Mach Schnell—that combine steepness with monster moguls.

Remember, this is where you can really maximize the Snowbird vertical, running the full length of Hidden Peak on everything from narrow, steep chutes to sweeping, banked giant slalom cuts to knees-to-your-chest moguls. By mid-afternoon head over to the Peruvian Gulch area on the High Baldy Traverse. Here you can go a little more free-form in the steep openness of this vast bowl. Primrose Path is unrelenting and made for high speed, High Baldy lets you carve larger slalom turns, and everything in between is strictly pick-your-own-route down.

If you can't find enough powder on the front of the mountain, then head south past the top tram terminal into Mineral Basin, where you'll find 400 acres of treeless bowl skiing. Not as steep as Peruvian Gulch, Mineral Basin offers the same deep powder and a bit more elbow room. Accessed via Snowcat until spring 1999, the basin was scheduled to have a lift installed in time for the 1999–2000 season.

SNOWBOARDING

The same deep powder stashes that delight skiers have an equal pull on snowboarders. Boarders in search of the deep and steep need look no further than Peruvian Gulch, a wide expanse accessed by a lung-testing hike from the tram that is riddled with chutes and gullies that run deep with powder days after storms have given way to blue sky. The Peruvian Cirque area that falls beneath the tram is another favorite for boarders who enjoy carving long, sweeping turns. Two molded half-pipes were planned at press time (spring 1999) for Big Emma, which is accessed by the Mid-Gad lift. One is designed for competition snowboarders, the other for beginners. But beyond those, the granitic mountains that embrace

Snowbird offer many natural half-pipes in the form of U-shaped gullies and draws. You can find one on the fringe of the Black Forest run where Election comes together with Bassackwards. Another lies near the junction of Chip's Run and Whodunit, and still another waits about halfway down Chip's Run at its intersection with the upper half of Blackjack. Look for the many other natural terrain features, or talk a local into showing you where they are.

NEARBY

In Big Cottonwood Canyon to the north of Alta and Snowbird lies **Solitude** (tel. 801/534–1400), a smaller resort that lives up to its name. Crowds don't exist here, and the back bowls of Honeycomb Canyon pack enough powder and vertical to sate any expert, while the cruisers on the front of the mountain appease speed freaks.

WHERE TO STAY

Because lodging at Snowbird is limited to a single hotel, three condominium buildings, and a small number of privately owned and rented condo units, you might want to consider staying in nearby Salt Lake City, with its ample lineup of traditional chain hotels, bed-and-breakfasts, and numerous inexpensive motels. It's an easy 40-minute commute to the resort and gives you access to other activities besides skiing. The Alta resort, only a mile away, offers yet another range of alternatives (*see* Where to Stay *in* Alta, *above*). A free shuttle-bus service connects the two resorts. All rooms at the resort can be booked through **Snow-**

bird Central Reservations (tel. 800/453–3000).

Expensive

Canyon Services Condo Rentals

About a quarter mile from Snowbird, on the bypass road to the Alta resort, is a small cluster of private homes, town houses, and condominium buildings, known as the Village at Sugar Plum, Sugar Plum Townhouses, Superior Point, the Meadows at Sugarplum, and the View. A very limited number are available for rental; the upscale units range from two to five bedrooms. If you want space, exclusivity, and privacy, it's worth investigating the available options here. *Canyon Services, Box 920025, Snowbird 84092, tel. 801/943–1842 or 800/562–2888, fax 801/943–4161. 37 units. A, MC, V. $200–$1,400.*

Cliff Lodge

This massive concrete-and-glass structure is the only truly full-service hotel at the resort. It is something of an impersonal monster, with its unfinished concrete walls (deliberately left that way to harmonize with the nearby mountain) and its confusing labyrinth of shops, restaurants, and facilities. The accommodations come in three basic configurations: the standard hotel room, the slightly larger suites, and the two-bedroom suites, which are actually a combination of the first two. Overall, furnishings and decor are fairly ordinary, with beige and earth tones predominating, but they are spacious and meticulously maintained. On the roof, you'll find a 25-meter outdoor swimming pool. The lodge's location provides ski-in/ski-out access to the tram. There are also limited dormitory-style accommodations. *Box 929000, Snowbird 84092, tel. 801/742–2222 or 800/453–3000, fax 801/742–3204. 460 rooms, 47 suites. Facilities: 4 restaurants, 2 outdoor pools, health club, spa, ski rental, baby-sitting. AE, D, DC, MC, V. $219–$959.*

Moderate

Iron Blosam

This time-share building has only a limited number of units available at any given time. The room configurations are similar to those at both the Lodge and the Inn at Snowbird (*see below*); the decor of each unit varies slightly according to the individual owner's taste. *Box 929000, Snowbird 84092, tel. 801/742–2222 or 800/453–3000, fax 801/742–2211. 159 units. Facilities: restaurant, outdoor heated pool, whirlpool, exercise room. AE, D, DC, MC, V. $119–$729.*

Lodge at Snowbird and Inn at Snowbird

The lodge and the inn, two identical condo buildings next door to the Cliff Lodge, are remarkable only for their ordinariness. They both have the same unfinished concrete construction as the Cliff and a dour, gray decor that starts in the hallways and extends into the rooms, which are decorated in a kind of Mormon minimalism. Room layouts range from studios to studio lofts to one-bedrooms with loft. Not fancy but less expensive than the Cliff, the lodges are about a five-minute walk from the lifts, and both are on the Snowbird Village shuttle bus loop. *Box 929000, Snowbird 84092, tel. 801/742–2222 or 800/453–3000, fax 801/742–3311 for* lodge or 801/742–2211 for inn. 145 units in lodge, 42 units in inn. Facilities: restaurant, bar, heated outdoor pool, whirlpool spa. AE, D, DC, MC, V. $119–$729.

WHERE TO EAT

The resort has a small variety of interesting dining spots ranging from a steakhouse to fine dining on the roof of the Cliff Lodge; Salt Lake City is an alternative; so are the nearby hotel dining rooms of Alta (see Alta, above). Keep in mind that all purchases can be charged back to your room while you stay in Snowbird.

On the Mountain

Mid-Gad Restaurant

In Gad Valley at the top of the Gad lift, this is the only on-mountain cafeteria at Snowbird, and it serves the standard ski resort fare, including soups, stews, chili, sandwiches, burgers, pizza, and other snack-type lunches. Tel. 801/742–2222, ext. 4837. AE, D, DC, MC, V.

Expensive

The Aerie

This is Snowbird's most formal and most intimate dining room. The modern decor emphasizes glass, mountain views, polished black surfaces, and soft lighting, and a cocktail pianist adds a swanky, sophisticated touch. The menu is loosely Continental, with local specialties such as grilled free-range chicken with winter vegetable pastina, aged New York strip with cognac peppercorn sauce, and Long Island duck pasta with figs, red chard, leeks, and orecchiette. Cliff Lodge, 10th floor, Snowbird, tel. 801/742–2222, ext. 5500. AE, D, DC, MC, V.

La Caille

Ten miles from the resort, near the bottom of Little Cottonwood Canyon, this stunning replica of a grand 17th-century French château is well worth the trip. You enter through wrought-iron gates and proceed along a cobblestone driveway. Inside, arched ceilings, carved-wood garlands, a winding staircase, and 17th-century antiques establish a regal Gallic tone. You can feast on entrées such as chateaubriand served with béarnaise sauce and brittle pommes frites or fresh Norwegian silver salmon baked in parchment and served with a medley of fresh vegetables. 9565 Wasatch Blvd., Little Cottonwood Canyon, tel. 801/942–1751. AE, D, DC, MC, V.

Steak Pit

This is the oldest restaurant at Snowbird—an institution among regulars and popular with families. The dining room is casual and pleasant, with cedar tongue-and-groove walls, lots of plants, and wooden booths around the perimeter. The steak lineup, impressive in size but a bit uneven in quality, runs the gamut from filet mignon to top sirloin—with two sizes in each cut—plus combo plates such as steak and lobster. At this hearty-eater heaven, everything comes in large portions, including the all-you-can-eat salad. Snowbird Center, Level 1, tel. 801/742–2222, ext. 4060. AE, D, DC, MC, V.

Moderate

Keyhole Junction

This restaurant has rough-hewn wood trim, Southwestern art, small table groupings, and a huge stone fireplace. The fare is standard Southwestern, with specialties such as zesty *moles* (Mexican sauce made with chilis, garlic, and bitter chocolate) atop lamb, rabbit, and chicken, wild mushroom enchiladas, grilled Southwestern salmon, and a variety of fajitas. *Cliff Lodge, Level A, Snowbird, tel. 801/742–2222, ext. 5100. AE, D, DC, MC, V.*

Lodge Club Bistro
The glass atrium front wall at this intimate spot curls partway across the ceiling, adding a dramatic touch to the modern, minimalist decor of chrome furnishings, earth-tone walls, gray accents, modern art, white tablecloths, and subdued lighting. The menu includes a variety of light entrées, such as fresh Utah trout sautéed with lemon and toasted almonds, as well as heartier fare like seared tenderloin of elk in blackberry sage sauce and roasted eggplant and basil lasagna. *Lodge at Snowbird, tel. 801/742–2222, ext. 3042. AE, D, DC, MC, V.*

Wildflower Ristorante
If you've a passion for Italian cooking, this bright, warm, and welcoming restaurant in the Iron Blosam is the perfect choice. You can order pastas such as fresh pan-toasted gnocchi or lobster over pappardelle, and entrées such as seared peppered salmon fillet and herb-rubbed grilled porterhouse. *Iron Blosam, Level 3, Snowbird, tel. 801/742–2222, ext. 1042. AE, D, DC, MC, V.*

Inexpensive

Pier 49 San Francisco Pizza
For a fast-food fix or an early dinner on the cheap (it's open until 6 PM), this is a good bet. Sourdough-crust pizza comes with a good selection of exotic toppings, available by the slice or pie. You can eat in or take out. *Snowbird Center, Level 2, tel. 801/742–2222, ext. 4076. AE, D, DC, MC, V.*

Best Bets for Breakfast

The Atrium
The Atrium is a bright, cheery breakfast spot that offers an excellent buffet breakfast of muffins, pastries, hot and cold cereals, eggs in all styles, bacon, and custom-made omelets. *Cliff Lodge, Level B, tel. 801/742–2222, ext. 5300. AE, D, DC, MC, V.*

Espress Stations
If you're itching to get on the slopes but need to eat breakfast first, this establishment is quick and easy. Pastries, muffins, gourmet coffees, and, of course, espresso, are the staples here. *Cliff Lodge, Level C; top and bottom of tram; outside Snowbird Center, Level 3; tel. 801/742–2222, ext. 5700. AE, D, DC, MC, V.*

NIGHTLIFE AND ENTERTAINMENT
The best after-dark entertainment at Snowbird is gazing at the star-studded night sky, looking for wildlife as you ramble around the base area, or relaxing in the hot tub or pool. Snowbird after dark is, in a word, quiet. If you absolutely have to mingle, here is the lineup of choices.

Après-Ski

The Atrium
People come here for the après-ski munchies (of the nachos and buffalo wings variety), hot and cold beverages, and a mellow kind of atmosphere. You can sometimes catch some folksy live entertainment. *Cliff Lodge, Level B, tel. 801/742–2222, ext. 5300. AE, D, DC, MC, V.*

knocks against Vermont skiing) should not deter even spoiled, warm-weather western skiers from sampling Vermont skiing.

GETTING TO VERMONT RESORTS

By Plane
Boston's **Logan International Airport** is served by most major carriers, including American Airlines (tel. 800/433–7300), Continental (tel. 800/525–0280), Delta (tel. 800/221–1212), TWA (tel. 800/221–2000), and United (tel. 800/241–6522). **Bradley International Airport,** in Hartford, Connecticut, is served by all major airlines. **Albany Airport,** Albany, New York, has service by American, Delta, and United. Other choices are the airports in **Burlington,** Vermont, and **Lebanon,** New Hampshire, which are served by commuter airlines from Boston and Albany.

Most major car-rental firms have desks at both the Boston and Burlington airports, including **Avis** (tel. 800/331–1212), **Budget** (tel. 800/527–0700), **Hertz** (tel. 800/654–3131), **National** (tel. 800/328–4567), and **Payless** (tel. 800/237–2804).

KILLINGTON SKI RESORT

Killington Rd.
Killington, VT 05751
Tel. 802/422–3333
www.killington.com

STATISTICALLY SPEAKING

Base elevation: 1,045 feet

Summit elevation: 4,241 feet

Vertical drop: 3,150 feet

Skiable terrain: 1.200 acres

Number of trails: 205

Longest run: 10.2 miles

Lifts and capacity: 2 gondolas, 12 quads, 6 triples, 5 doubles, 4 surface lifts; 36,327 skiers per hour

Daily lift ticket: $52

Average annual snowfall: 252 inches

Number of skiing days: 1997–1998: 242

Snowmaking: 552 acres; 65%

Terrain mix: N 49%, I 20%, E 31%

Snowboarding: yes

When you think Killington, you think big. It's the biggest area in Vermont, in the East, and by acreage and number of trails, among the biggest in the country. When Killington opened on December 13, 1958, it had four lifts and seven trails on one mountain. Today Killington has skiing on seven mountains and nine separate skiing areas connected by 95 miles of alpine trails and served by 33 lifts. The lifts include the longest chairlift in the United States and a 2½-mile heated high-speed gondola, christened the Skyeship. The 10.2-mile Juggernaut is the longest alpine ski trail in the United States. Killington also has a staggering 14 on-mountain places to eat. The resort's Ground Zero fun center, opened in 1997, offers snowtubing, skating, nighttime gondola rides, and even a luge run.

Killington operates from mid-October through late May or early June, the longest ski season in the East for more than 35 consecutive years. The lengthy season is made possible by one of the most extensive snowmaking systems in the world, covering 44 miles of trail. The area's snowmaking is matched only by its snow grooming—its 26 vehicles groom more than 135,000 miles of trails each season, roughly equivalent to 5½ times around the world.

Among Killington's trails, the meandering Juggernaut passes through three townships. At the other extreme, on Outer Limits, a half mile of bumps the size of vans cascades down a 43% gradient that from the top looks like an egg carton stood nearly on end. There is one gently sloping hill, Snow Slope, reserved strictly for beginners, with its own lift system and base lodge. Broad trails, narrow trails, vastly popular trails, and virtually unknown trails are scattered over the seven peaks.

People love Killington Road because it houses skiing institutions—the Wobbly Barn and Pickle Barrel dance halls, Casey's Caboose and Mother Shapiro's restaurants, plus ski shops and clothing shops and just about every other commercial venture associated with snow. It's hated for much the same reason: too glitzy, too commercial, and too citified for a ski area in the middle of Vermont.

Actually, love and hate describe the way many skiers feel about Killington in general. You'll never

Children's services: day-care, instruction, tel. 802/773–1330

Snow phone: tel. 802/422–3261

Police: tel. 802/773–9101

Hospital: Rutland Regional Medical Center, tel. 802/775–7111

Resort office services: tel. 802/422–3333, ext. 6228

Killington-Pico Area Association: tel. 802/773–4181

Road conditions: tel. 800/429–7623

Taxi: Killington Travel Service, tel. 800/372–2007

Towing: Habro, tel. 802/422–3434; Buxton's Sunoco, tel. 802/773–9747

FIVE-STAR FAVORITES
Best run for vertical: Devil's Fiddle

Best run overall: Chute

Best bar/nightclub: Wobbly Barn

Best hotel: Cortina Inn

Best restaurant: Hemingway's

hear more grumbling from more people, which makes you eventually ask why they keep coming back year after year after year. The answer is: like Everest, it's there. It's loud, brash, commercial, fast-paced, over-adrenalized, too big, and impossible to ignore. It is the standard by which other areas in the eastern United States reluctantly measure themselves.

HOW TO GET THERE
By Car
Boston is 156 miles from Killington; the drive should take less than three hours. Take I–93 north to I–89, just south of Concord, New Hampshire. Follow that north to U.S. 4 at Rutland and take it to Killington Road. From Hartford (166 miles away) follow I–91 north to Exit 6 onto VT 103, north of Bellows Falls, Vermont; follow VT 103 to VT 100; take VT 100 north to U.S. 4 and follow that west to Killington. From Albany (110 miles away) take I–87 north to NY 149 and follow it east to U.S. 4; take that east to Killington. From Burlington (84 miles away) take U.S. 7 south to Rutland and U.S. 4 east to Killington. From Lebanon (39 miles away) take I–89 to U.S. 4 west to Killington. From New York (250 miles away) take the New York Thruway to Exit 24 in Albany and then follow the Albany instructions above.

By Bus
Vermont Transit Company (122 Merchants Row, Rutland, tel. 802/773–2774) offers daily service from Rutland to Killington with connections from most major centers.

By Train
Amtrak (tel. 800/872–7245) has scheduled service into Boston from most major centers, and connections are available to Rutland.

GETTING AROUND
Even though a free shuttle bus service, **the Bus** (tel. 802/773–3244), runs up and down Killington Road and between the resort and nearby Rutland, a car is really your best option. It gives you much more flexibility and a chance to explore the surrounding area

or dine at some of the outlying restaurants. If you head out for a night of imbibing, a designated driver is a good idea because the police do patrol the road regularly, even setting up a spot check at the entrance to U.S. 4.

THE SKIING

The big ski resort at the end of a 5-mile access road off U.S. 4 is not the only Killington. The resort begins 6 miles east of Killington Road, where U.S. 4 meets Route 100 as it wanders up from the south. That's the Sunrise area, formerly called Northeast Passage. The advantage of Sunrise (elevation 2,456 feet) is that crowds are few, parking spaces many, and the sun finds it and warms it first. The disadvantage is that the lift, the Northeast Passage triple, takes 17 minutes to carry you from the base station to the top. The skiing at Sunrise is a mixture of beginners' slopes, wide intermediate terrain, and a couple of steep and bumpy expert trails. The slopes are light on snowmaking and elevation.

One mile west of Sunrise along U.S. 4 is the next Killington entrance, the Skyeship base station.The trip up on the heated gondola takes just 12½ minutes. The eight-passenger Skyeship reaches only to Skye Peak (elevation 3,800 feet), which has two faces—one steep, the other moderately gentle.

Right beside the Skyeship entrance is a winding road that offers a third access to Killington, this one to the ` Bear Mountain Base Lodge. Although Bear Mountain (elevation 3,295 feet) is far from the largest of Killington's mountains, it is by far the most cele-brated, with some of the steepest terrain in the area and the mogul slope (some would say cliff) Outer Limits, which has lighted more smiles and ruined more knees than any other in the country. Mogul maniacs are drawn to its steep face like moths to a flame, drawing an audience on warm late-winter days at the Bear Mountain Base Lodge.

The next entrance off U.S. 4, on the other side of Skye Peak, is Killington Road, which takes you to the Killington base area, the center of the resort. Most of the trails down 4,241-foot Killington Peak's face are expert.

West of Killington Peak and reached from the main base area is Snowdon Mountain (elevation 3,592 feet), a good place for beginners and intermediates, though it has a few advanced trails thrown in. It's served by a triple and a quad chairlift, as well as a Poma lift, mainly for use by racers.

Rams Head Mountain, also reached from Killington Road, is the resort's westernmost peak. It stands 3,610 feet and is served by the Rams Head double chair, a leisurely lift that takes 14 minutes from bottom to top. Its trails are, with two exceptions, all beginner and intermediate. Ram's Head is the focus of family action at Killington, housing one of the best-organized skiing centers for kids in the nation. There's even a cocktail lounge where parents can wait for their children.

Across Killington Road from Rams Head Mountain lies the hill Killington devotes exclusively to learning, Snowshed. With three short chairlifts, including a high-speed quad and a Poma for the upper slopes, Snowshed is an ideal place for beginners to get the feel of skiing a bigger mountain without heading out to parts unknown quite yet. Snowshed offers a perfect spot for learning, and a place skiers don't have to leave all day if they don't want to.

On busy weekends and holidays, you should seriously consider skipping Killington Road completely and driving to Bear Mountain, the Skyeship station, or Sunrise. There are tickets, rentals, and food at all of them. The one thing that's unavailable at the three is lessons, which start at the Snowshed and Killington Peak base lodges, or, for children, Rams Head. But you can take a lift to lessons (be sure to allow enough time—the trail map indicates the number of minutes each lift takes), and you'll avoid snarled parking lots, long waits for tickets, and cold lift lines at the main bases.

Killington's extralong season means that early in the ski year, in October and November, you should expect to ski with too many young men with too much testosterone who go faster than they should—they haven't seen snow in a few months. You have two choices: put your baseball cap on backward and join them or wait until December to start your skiing/boarding season.

Late in the season—May and even early June—Killington has the only lift-served skiing in the East. The snow is soft, the sun is high, the mosquitoes are after you, and those same young men you met in October are still here. Only now they've mellowed out after a winter on snow and are much better company.

Should you get lost (which can happen even after reading this chapter, taking a tour, studying the trail map, and carrying a compass) and find yourself at the end of the day at one base area while your car is at another, Killington will shuttle you back to your car for a very small fee.

Novices
Every one of Killington's seven peaks can be skied from the top by beginners. Yes, surprisingly this megaresort with the fearsome reputation is entirely accessible to wedge-turning, steep-hating, snowplowing, speed-fearing novices. In fact, the very best way to get your bearings is to spend your first morning on a guided tour of the mountains. This is also the best deal. The tour—which leaves the Snowshed area at 10 on most days (check the schedule at the skier information desk)—is free, and it's conducted entirely on beginner terrain. To take it, wait under the MEET THE MOUNTAINS TOUR sign in front of Snowshed Base Lodge.

When you graduate from Snowshed, the natural progression is up to Snowdon and Rams Head. Novices on Rams Head will have the most luck on the gentle Caper, which leads to the base of the Snowdon chair, just below Killington's most vexing bottleneck. Be careful at the intersection of Mouse Trap, Mouse Run, Chute, and Racer's Edge—it's often a tangle of falling skiers and blasting snow guns. On busy days avoid it altogether.

The greatest indulgence for beginners, however, starts on Killington Peak. Here, at the top of the resort, is where the novice trail Juggernaut begins its 10-mile ramble. Most people assume they can do it in a half hour, but Killington advises leaving up to two hours to get through this meandering, level, sometimes uphill trail that ends at the Skyeship base station.

The gentler side of Skye is accessible from the Skye Peak quad; if you're a confident learner, you should try your legs on Pipe Dream, 4-Mile Trail, and Wanderer. When you find yourself at the top of Bear Mountain, remember every peak at Killington has an easy way down, and Bear Mountain is no exception. Shagback leads novices back to Snowshed, and Falls Brook Trail heads slowly down to the Bear Mountain Base Lodge.

Just above the Sunrise Village area across from the base of Bear Mountain, you can pick up the amiable Juggernaut Too, which works its slow way down to the Sunrise Base Lodge. The less-used Sun Dog has a gradual pitch and no surprise steeps as it winds down this hill. These trails are at relatively low elevation and all do not have snowmaking, so check their snow conditions before you start down.

Intermediates

Many of Killington's most challenging trails start gently, and then after you've committed yourself, drop like an elevator shaft. But they are marked: if the sign says double diamond, you can safely assume it means just that.

Try starting on the least-known intermediate trail, Swirl, on Rams Head. This perfectly named trail twists, turns, and swirls down the mountain, and if you get there early enough in the morning, you'll find yourself cutting clean tracks through unmarked snow. The long Chute

underneath the Snowdon quad is a good, steep cruiser.

For high-mountain intermediate skiing, the Glades triple, on Killington, is relatively uncrowded in the morning, and the trails from it are often piled deep with natural powder. Incidentally, the Glades has a lot of nonglade skiing; try Rime, just below the triple chair. You can make a short eastward swing from the top on 4-Mile Trail to Skye Peak and take a long cruise on it down to the Skyeship base station.

Experts

For a little-used run, try Catwalk, on Killington Peak. To get there, you have to de-ski at the top of the lift and hike a few yards on a path through snowy woods on the way to the peak. When you come to the start of Catwalk, before pushing off, look down. If your stomach stays below your throat, if there's been a recent and heavy snowfall, and if you can link tight turns on a steep and narrow trail, by all means ski it. If, on the other hand, at least one of these criteria is not met, continue walking to the peak and enjoy one of the finest views in New England.

Choosing to skip Catwalk is by no means bailing out—some tough double-black-diamond expert trails like Downdraft and the broad (200 feet across) but steep (up to 54% gradient) Double Dipper start here, too. Killington's tree skiing is on the double-black Big Dipper Glade, served by the Canyon quad, which tends to be less crowded.

Ski these for a while, or branch off to the east on Great Eastern to link up with the expert trails on Skye Peak.

On its more difficult face, Skye Lark, Skye Hawk, and Superstar will give you a shot of adrenaline as they drop precipitously toward the base of the Superstar detachable quad. Or head down the gentler side of the mountain on Skyeburst or Dream-Maker to the infamous Bear Mountain.

On Bear Mountain, besides the double-diamond egg carton that is Outer Limits, there's the steep, long, and devilishly difficult Devil's Fiddle. As the top half of the Fiddle is without snowmaking, ski it only after a snowfall. Each of these double-diamond trails has its own lift; when the crowds are up, head for the Fiddle, which gets much less traffic.

Sunrise, Snowdon, and Rams Head also have some strong stuff for strong skiers. Though short, Thunderball and the Judge, on Sunrise, can be white-knuckle runs when the bumps are up. On Rams Head, Upper Header and Lower Vagabond are both fairly steep and can be full of moguls.

Advanced skiers can arrange tailored tours on tougher terrain. Ask at the Snowshed Ski School desk for information about hiring a mountain guide.

SNOWBOARDING
Killington offers boarders their own shredder-friendly trail map that points out not only where trails and pipes are, but where boarders might hit annoying flats—and that's just the tip of the iceberg. Killington maintains two snowboard parks, three half-pipes, a whopping six alpine parks, and a boardercross course. The K-Pipe, just above the Killington base lodge, is among the best pipes in the country. The resort's connecting trails

slope slightly to help boarders move along with less effort. Beginners can take advantage of special boarding programs for adults, for women, and for young children that move boarders gradually up from simpler terrain parks to the gnarliest of pipes.

OTHER SNOW SPORTS
Killington's nonskiing action center, **Ground Zero** (base of K2 Gondola, tel. 802/422–6200), offers tubing, ice-skating, nighttime gondola rides, and other special events.

NEARBY
For a more personal, less crowded, more relaxed Vermont ski experience, you can take a day trip to a resort nearby. Family-friendly in every way, **Okemo Mountain Resort** (tel. 802/228–4041) has well-groomed trails, easy mountain access, and cruisers that make an intermediate skier feel like god(dess) of the mountain. **Ascutney Mountain Resort** (tel.802/484–7711 or 800/243–0011) attracts families with low lift-ticket and lesson prices and trails arranged to meet at the base.

WHERE TO STAY
This is condo country. There are more than three dozen complexes on Killington Road, which is the place to be for nightlife, and several more clusters on U.S. 4 toward nearby Rutland. The quality of individual units varies considerably; some are starting to show signs of wear and tear. A dozen properties are managed by Killington Resort—book those directly through the central reservations office (tel. 800/621–6867, fax 802/747–4419). There are also several note-

worthy private lodges, inns, and large hotels within a few miles of the slopes, and Rutland, 15 miles away, has many chain motels.

Expensive

Cortina Inn

This rambling two-story stucco building with brick and wood facades and canopied terraces is a refreshing change in this condo-crazed area. The large, bright, high-ceilinged lobby, which connects the two main buildings, is filled with comfortable chairs and couches, Persian rugs, and local art (for sale, of course). Spacious rooms have handcrafted furnishings, queen-size four-poster beds, and colorful quilts; 12 have fireplaces. Kids are welcome—family suites have bunk beds—but overall this place is better for couples. You can even take a spin on the skating pond or a moonlight sleigh ride. *HCR 34, Box 33, Killington 05751, tel. 802/773–3333 or 800/451–6108, fax 802/775-6948. 97 rooms. Facilities: 2 restaurants, bar, hot tub, indoor pool, spa, sauna, exercise room, skating pond, library, shuttle, game room, ski storage, 24-hr desk service. AE, D, DC, MC, V. $129–$244, including full breakfast.*

Fall Line Condominiums

The tan clapboard town house–style buildings are terraced on a hill above the access road and connected by cobblestone walkways, so the complex feels like a community. Wooden furnishings and comfortable couches, centered around a large brick fireplace, make the individual units cozy as well. Though the living area is small by condo standards, the bedrooms are extralarge, with high vaulted ceilings and large windows. There's a full kitchen in each unit, as well as a washer-dryer and a whirlpool. *Killington Resort Villages, Box 2460, Killington 05751, tel. 802/422–3101 or 800/343–0762, fax 802/422–6788. 40 units. Facilities: indoor pool, Jacuzzi, sauna, exercise room, game room, ski shuttle. AE, D, DC, MC, V. $125–$515.*

Highridge Condominiums

The units in this well-maintained complex, at the highest point of land in the main base area, have dark-stained wood and peaked roofs. Tastefully decorated, with especially large living areas that have high cedar-paneled ceilings and comfortable furnishings, they are bright and functional. Each unit has oak trim and a marble or slate fireplace. Light pours in through the windows, which also offer good views. The kitchens are compact but complete, and there's a good-size dining area. Every unit has a washer-dryer and an extralarge bathroom with a whirlpool and sauna. *Killington Resort Villages, Box 2460, Killington 05751, tel. 802/422–3101 or 800/343–0762, fax 802/422–6788. 100 units. Facilities: indoor pool, health club, exercise room, sauna, outdoor hot tub, game room, ski shuttle. AE, D, MC, V. $125–$715.*

Inn of the Six Mountains

This attractive hotel has an Adirondack look, with stained wood shingles, a rippled gable roof, natural stonework, and finished wood beams. A floor-to-ceiling fireplace is the lobby centerpiece. The rooms have pleasant, modern mountain-inn decor—wood trim, handmade armoires, a small desk, overstuffed chairs, and tasteful art. *R.R. 1, Box 2900, Killington Rd., Killington 05751, tel. 802/422–4302 or 800/228–4676, fax 802/422–4321. 99 rooms, 4 suites. Facilities: restaurant, bar, indoor lap pool, sauna, whirlpool, game room, shuttle, ski storage. AE, D, DC, MC, V. $89–$269, including full breakfast.*

Woods at Killington
This is a self-contained complex of individually owned contemporary town houses and condos with gray wood siding and cedar shingled roofs. Although decor varies, most units are well appointed with quality furnishings, including queen-size beds and artistic touches. They are remarkably complete—with a fireplace, a washer-dryer, a Jacuzzi, and a full kitchen. *R.R. 1, Killington Rd., Box 2210, Killington 05751, tel. 802/422–3244, fax 802/422–3320. 57 units. Facilities: restaurant, lounge, indoor pool, sauna, steam room, spa, laundry, aerobics, yoga, ski shuttle. AE, MC, V. $615–$942 for 2 nights.*

Moderate

Glazebrook Townhouse Resort
For the roominess of a town house at a reasonable price, these cedar-shake, blond-stained units are a good bet. The two- and three-bedroom units can comfortably sleep six and eight, respectively, and all have large living areas and a wide brick fireplace. They come loaded with a fully equipped kitchen, a sauna, a whirlpool, a washer-dryer, and a private deck. A minimum two-night stay is required. *Box 505, Killington Rd., Killington 05751, tel. 802/422–4425, fax 802/422–2221. 27 units. Facilities: 2*

restaurants, bar, sauna, ski shuttle. AE, MC, V. $642–$846 for first 2 days; $198–$264 per day thereafter.

Killington Village Inn
This red-clapboard barn-style inn has a genuine New England alpine feel, complete with knotty pine paneling, a huge fieldstone fireplace, and a cozy bar. The guest rooms are comfortable but spartan; the public spaces are more inviting. *Box 153, Killington Rd., Killington 05751, tel. 802/422–3301 or 800/451–4105, fax 802/422–3971. 20 rooms. Facilities: restaurant, indoor hot tub, game room, lounge. AE, D, DC, MC, V. $35–$58 per person, $14 each additional person, MAP.*

Red Rob Inn
This classic hillside New England inn is relaxed, pleasant, and unpretentious. Its facade is cedar, glass, and limestone, and the rooms are comfortable and bright, done in a white and woodsy minimalist style. Most come with a queen-size bed and a balcony or deck. *Box 2865, Killington Rd., Killington 05751, tel. 802/422–3303 or 800/451–4105. 33 rooms. Facilities: restaurant, lounge, indoor pool, outdoor hot tub, sauna, game room. AE, D, DC, MC, V. $78–$129, including full breakfast.*

Summit Lodge
You can't help noticing the dark rough-cut timber and cedar shingles of this hotel from the access road. Venture inside, and St. Bernards Henry and Heidi welcome you. Inside are exposed beams, stucco walls, and a trove of antiques from Calvin Coolidge's Plymouth, Vermont, home. Rooms are not fancy or especially large, but they are clean and woodsy, with antiques and

handmade furniture, and they have great views. *Killington Rd., Box 119, Killington 05751, tel. 802/422–3535 or 800/635–6343, fax 802/422–3536. 45 rooms, 8 family suites, 2 suites. Facilities: restaurant, lounge, outdoor pool, Jacuzzi, sauna, massage, racquetball, laundry, game room, library, ski storage. AE, DC, MC, V. $45–$70 per person.*

Whiffle Tree Condominiums
These stained-pine condos with peaked wood-shake roofs are starting to show signs of age. They are, however, one of the few places in the area to which you can ski back at the end of the day. The roomy units range from one to four bedrooms and have contemporary decor and most creature comforts, including a full kitchen and laundry facilities. *Killington Resort Villages, Box 2460, Killington Rd., Killington 05751, tel. 802/422–3101 or 800/343–0762, fax 802/422–6788. 72 units. Facilities: ski shuttle. AE, D, DC, MC, V. $105–$519.*

Inexpensive

Butternut on the Mountain
You'll find tasteful contemporary rooms at this country inn. The exterior is New England contemporary clapboard in an ivory tone with deep mauve trim. The rooms are not large, but they are comfortable, and the library doubles as a cozy fireside lounge. *Box 306, Killington Rd., Killington 05751, tel. 802/422–2000 or 800/524–7654, fax 802/422–3937. 18 rooms. Facilities: restaurant, indoor pool, whirlpool, game room, laundry, ski-tuning room, library. AE, D, MC, V. $80–$110.*

Comfort Inn Killington Centre
This upscale Comfort Inn has a mountain chalet look. The standard rooms

have two double beds; larger studio suites have a minikitchen, a dining area, and a whirlpool. *Box 493, Killington Rd., Killington 05751, tel. 802/422–4222 or 800/257–8664, fax 802/422–4226. 60 rooms, 20 suites. AE, D, DC, MC, V. $62–$206, including Continental breakfast.*

Little Buckhorn
This small chalet-style bed-and-breakfast is comfortable but spare. The top-floor rooms are wood-paneled and have high beamed ceilings. There are a quiet den area for reading or playing chess and an efficiency kitchen for making snacks. *Box 2318, Killington Rd., Box 2318, Killington 05751, tel. 802/422–3314 or 800/827–3314. 9 rooms. Facilities: indoor hot tub, sauna, ski locker. AE, MC, V. $32–$50, including full breakfast.*

Mountain Sports Inn
A traditional natural-cedar Austrian-style chalet, this inn provides clean, basic accommodations just 3 miles from the slopes. The rooms have light-oak furniture with rose and lavender accents. *R.R. 1, Box 2215, Killington Rd., Killington 05751, tel. 802/422–3315, fax 802/422–3315. 25 rooms. Facilities: ski-tuning room, exercise room. AE, D, MC, V. $44–$140, including full breakfast.*

WHERE TO EAT
You don't have to drive far to find restaurants in the Killington area. There are more than two dozen clustered on the access road between U.S. 4 and the resort, and many of the hotels and lodges offer a MAP arrangement for guests. There is, however, a distinct lack of diversity—steak, seafood, and pasta emporiums seem to

dominate Killington along with all other New England ski areas, and with just a few exceptions, most fall in the inexpensive to moderate range.

On the Mountain

Max's Place Restaurant

The modern stucco alpine-style building with brown decks is just off the Sun Dog and Juggernaut Too trails. A wide expanse of glass with views of the mountain, an oak-and-brass bar, and wooden tables covered with white cloths set the tone for the menu of burgers, soups, and salads in the daytime, and Black Angus steak, veal, and salmon at dinnertime. *Off Sun Dog Trail, Sunrise Village, tel. 802/422–8666. Closed Tues. and Wed. AE, MC, V.*

Summit Café

Atop Killington Peak, this lunch place combines spectacular views with designer sandwiches, soups, and salads. The fireplace completes the comfortable ambience. *Peak Lodge, Killington, tel. 802/422–3333. No credit cards.*

Expensive

Choices

Chef Claude specializes in gourmet meals served here or prepared and packaged for you to take back to your lodging. Orders should be called in one hour prior to pick-up. Choices may include herb-seasoned free-range roast chicken, Grecian rubbed roast leg of lamb, and pork roast marinated in apple cider. The intimate interior is contemporary, done in mauve and gray with high-back chairs, candles, and fresh-cut flowers. *Glazebrook Center, Killington Rd., Killington, tel. 802/422–4030. Reservations essential. AE, MC, V.*

Hemingway's

This is one of the landmark dining establishments in eastern ski country. The atmosphere is set once you enter the front door of this modest 1860s farmhouse. Richly stained and polished panels encircle a high wainscoted bar and room divider, and the sitting room has a fine Bukhara rug in front of a blazing fieldstone fireplace. All around are splendid sculptures and objets d'art. The large formal dining room has clean pastel tones, high-vaulted ceilings, and elaborate chandeliers; in the cozier brick-walled garden room, wrought-iron tables and chairs stand near a warming fireplace; and the intimate wine cellar has just a half dozen tables and the original stone walls and low ceiling. Popular entrées besides the house specialty, game birds, include Napoleon of beef tenderloin with Roquefort pastry and risotto with Maine lobster, shrimp, and grilled asparagus. The four-course vegetarian menu changes nightly. *Rte. 4, Killington, tel. 802/422–3886. Reservations essential. AE, DC, MC, V.*

Moderate

Casey's Caboose

Casey Jones's caboose has been replicated here as a restaurant, along with a 35-ton turn-of-the-century railroad snowplow car. It's a cheerful dining spot with lots of nooks and crannies—the best places to eat are up in or under the caboose observation compartment (two tables for two) or in the raised observation deck atop the old snowplow car (table for six). Casey's has a mainstream menu: if you're really hungry, go for the locomotive cut, 16 ounces of signature prime rib; if you can't handle that, the caboose cut is 4 ounces smaller. There are live Maine lobsters in tanks as well as a selection of steaks, ribs, pastas, seafood, and some outstanding buffalo wings. Do check out the $9 special each evening. *Killington Rd., Killington, tel. 802/422–3795. AE, D, MC, V.*

Charity's

The centerpiece of this cathedral-shape barn-board building is the exquisite 1887 cherry-wood bar with handrail and pillars of Italian marble, moved here in 1971 from its original installation in Davis, West Virginia. In the dining room is a huge fieldstone fireplace, and above the numerous booths are lead-glass lamps and other antiques, giving the whole place a 19th-century saloon atmosphere. The menu offers steaks, fresh pasta dishes, a smattering of seafood choices, and even some Mexican favorites like fajitas. *Killington Rd., Killington, tel. 802/422–3800. AE, DC, MC, V.*

Grist Mill

Picturesquely situated on the edge of Summit Pond, this post-and-beam rendering of an early grist mill is complete with a waterwheel and a wraparound deck. Lively and cheerful, it is decorated in earth tones and has a gigantic fieldstone fireplace, a wood stove, antiques, a large moose head, and a busy dance floor. The hearty New England fare includes steak, seafood, poultry (such as berry-glazed chicken breast stuffed with artichoke hearts and cheese), pasta, and some excellent soup-and-salad combos. *Killington Rd., Killington, tel. 802/422–3970. AE, D, MC, V.*

Mother Shapiro's Restaurant

In this looney place, decor is as important as the food; the interior has a Victorian decor overflowing with antiques, marble-top tables, beveled mirrors, and old church pews. The menu ranges from pot roast to pasta, from blooming onions to smoked mussels, from large portions of chicken to spaghetti. There's lots of seafood as well. The midnight breakfast menu is available weekends only. *Killington Rd., Killington, tel. 802/422–9933. AE, D, DC, MC, V.*

Mrs. Brady's Restaurant

This low-key, contemporary dining room has a warm, intimate feeling. In addition to burgers, prime rib sandwiches, and chicken parmigiana on a poppy seed roll, there is also a large salad bar, a full dinner menu with steak cuts, and a daily pasta special (such as fettuccine Alfredo with scallops), as well as baked stuffed lobster. The Fireside Bar Lounge is a nice post-ski stop. *Butternut on the Mountain, Killington Rd., Killington, tel. 802/422–2020. AE, D, DC, MC, V.*

Six Mountain Grill

This casual American dining spot has a natural wainscoting interior with big picture windows overlooking the Vermont mountains. The two levels are eclectically decorated with flowered wall coverings. Entrées include black Angus steak, Vermont baby-back ribs with pure Vermont maple syrup, and sun-dried tomato and basil ravioli. *Inn of the Six Mountains, Killington Rd., Killington, tel. 802/422–4302. AE, D, DC, MC, V.*

Wobbly Barn Steakhouse

This cavernous barn with its red-wood interior doesn't actually wobble, but the ceiling and floors of the restaurant do shake from the nightclub on the floor above. Meat here comes in all forms, either barbecued or mesquite-broiled. The cuts tend to be large and are cooked precisely to your specs. There is a smattering of seafood and chicken dishes, not to mention a bountiful soup, salad, and bread bar. Children are warmly welcomed. *Killington Rd., Killington, tel. 802/422–3392. AE, DC, MC, V.*

Zola's Grill
There's no shortage of oaky detail here, from the elaborate wood trim to the Windsor chairs. The menu features contemporary American food and changes regularly; for entrées, there is New England scrod with diced tomatoes and prosciutto or leg of lamb stuffed with goat cheese and served with a roasted garlic sauce. *Cortina Inn, Rte. 4, 3 mi west of Killington, tel. 802/773–3331. Reservations essential. AE, D, DC, MC, V.*

Inexpensive

Deli at Killington
Here you can get made-to-order sandwiches and subs piled high with toppings, plus there are soups and hot sandwiches such as turkey or roast beef. It's a quick-grab, no-fuss place, good for buying a lunch to enjoy on the mountain. *Killington Rd., Killington, tel. 802/775–1599. AE, MC, V.*

Kanpei Lounge at the Chinese Gourmet
On the go or on the table: downstairs you'll find standard Chinese fare, with hand-painted, handcrafted tables and cathedral ceilings; upstairs there's Japanese cuisine, with a sushi bar, fish tanks, and a Japanese-style pillow room. Kanpei even delivers to your room, condo, town house, or chalet. *Killington Rd., Killington, tel. 802/422–4241. AE, MC, V.*

Outback Pizza
The Outback serves wood-fired pizza in a funky, eclectic environment that's pure Australian. Mock alligators cruise branches beneath the canvas-awning ceiling. Try the Vermont BLT pizza with cheddar, mozzarella, crumbled bacon, tomato slices, basil, and artichoke hearts. You can eat here or take it with you. *Killington Rd., Killington, tel. 802/422–9885. AE, MC, V.*

Peppers Bar and Grill
Amid Rube Goldberg gadgetry in a steel-and-wood environment reminiscent of a '40s diner, you can enjoy some of the most inexpensive dining on the mountain road—items like stir-fry chicken and broccoli over linguine with a mustard cream sauce, and grilled salmon. Look for the building with the stainless steel facade and neon portholes. *Killington Rd., Killington, tel. 802/422–3177. AE, D, MC, V.*

Powderhounds New World Restaurant
The skylit dining room of this unusual brown-cedar-clapboard restaurant has light-wood booths built of horizontal wooden slats. The light and innovative cuisine here is a mix of Thai, European, and New American vegetarian dishes. Some favorites include the crabmeat and angel-hair fritters and *pahd phak* (Thai noodles with stir-fry vegetables, Thai basil, and chili peppers). *Killington Rd., Killington, tel. 802/422–4141. AE, DC, MC, V.*

Best Bets for Breakfast

Cortina Inn

The setting is formal—white linen and silver—but the style is buffet, with smoked Vermont ham, custom-cooked eggs, fresh fruit, waffles and pancakes, and omelets to order. *Rte. 4, 3 mi west of Killington, tel. 802/ 773–3333. AE, D, DC, MC, V.*

Mother Shapiro's Restaurant

Breakfast is served nearly around the clock at Mother's—monster-sized portions of good old-fashioned ham, eggs, home fries, pancakes, French toast, or bagels and lox. It's fast, fun, and friendly. *Killington Rd., Killington, tel. 802/422–9933. AE, D, DC, MC, V.*

NIGHTLIFE AND ENTERTAINMENT

Après-Ski

Long Trail Brew Pub

The late-afternoon scene hops with live entertainment (either rock or more mellow guitar) and crowds of twenty- to thirty-something skiers, who sometimes dance between the small wooden tables. The look is rustic, with barn board and a large wooden bar. Munchies include veggie roll-ups, mountain bread, chicken wings, and pizzas. Microbrews abound; this place even has the first keg brewed by Long Trail on hand. *Snowshed Base Lodge, tel. 802/422– 3333, ext. 6428. AE, D, MC, V.*

Nightspot

Past the yellow awning on this '60s-vintage chalet-style wooden building, you find a relaxed dance club with oak and brass, as well as the Outback Pizza (*see above*), an enclosed deck where you can get pizza. *Killington Rd., 4½ mi from Rte. 4, Killington, tel. 802/422–9885. AE, MC, V.*

Loud and Lively/Dancing

Grist Mill

The lounge here jumps with rock bands during happy hour and after 9 PM ($3–$5 cover charge). The 30-plus crowd dances and samples Goombay Smashes and other wacky alcoholic drinks at the two bars. There's ice-skating outside for kids, plus a bonfire and hot chocolate when the weather dictates. *Killington Rd., Killington, tel. 802/422–3970. AE, D, MC, V.*

Wobbly Barn

The upper two levels of this barn have been a nightclub since 1963. It's a high-energy place that grooves with duos and trios during happy hour and three or four rock bands nightly. It's filled with twenty- and thirty-somethings out for a good time on the dance floor. *Killington Rd., Killington, tel. 802/422–3392. AE, DC, MC, V.*

More Mellow

Mountain Inn

In this long blue-gray clapboard restaurant with dormers, the lounge has a casual country feel, with wood and carpeting, neutral colors, a large fieldstone fireplace, and small tables and chairs. A guitar duo plays easy music. *1 Killington Rd., 3½ mi from Rte. 4, Killington, tel. 802/422–3595. AE, D, MC, V.*

Summit Lodge

The lounge at this clapboard ski lodge is a good place to cool out after a hard day on the slopes. The carpeted room has small tables, couches, and a large fieldstone fireplace. One or two musicians play quiet music. *Killington Rd., Killington, tel. 802/422–3535. AE, MC, V.*

MOUNT SNOW RESORT

Mount Snow, VT 05356
Tel. 802/464-3333
www.mtsnow.com

STATISTICALLY SPEAKING

Base elevation: 1,900 feet

Summit elevation: 3,600 feet

Vertical drop: 1,700 feet

Skiable terrain: 633 acres

Number of trails: 134

Longest run: 2½ miles

Lifts and capacity: 4 quads, 10 triples, 6 doubles, 4 surface, 2 magic carpets; 38,525 skiers per hour

Daily lift ticket: $52 weekends, $48 weekdays

Average annual snowfall: 153 inches

Number of skiing days 1997–98: 153

Snowmaking: 498 acres; 85%

Terrain mix: N 20%, I 60%, E 20%

Snowboarding: yes

Cross-country skiing: 3 miles

Mount Snow, Vermont's second-largest ski resort, got its start in 1954 when colorful entrepreneur Walter Schoenknecht turned farmer Reuben Snow's upper pastures on Mt. Pisgah into Mount Snow Resort. It quickly became a mecca for serious skiers and '60s snow bunnies from all over the Northeast. Now it draws a diverse crowd of locals, intense hotshots young and old, and families from Connecticut and the New York metropolitan area. There's equally varied skiing on 50 miles of trails on five mountains: you can ski the two peaks of Haystack (the second is called the Witches), then get on a shuttle bus to gentle Carinthia, from which you can wend your way northward to the slopes of the Main Mountain; from its summit you can tackle the terrifying steeps of the North Face or circle around the back of the mountain to sunny Sunbrook. Food and warmth can be found at five base lodges—the weatherboard-modern main base lodge as well as Carinthia, Haystack Lower, Haystack Upper, and Sundance. Mount Snow draws the serious skiers and serious snowboarders; Haystack attracts families, many with youngsters just learning to ski.

If you're renting skis or taking a lesson, you can buy your lift ticket at the rental shop or ski school without having to line up at ticket windows. On weekends, unless you're putting your kids in ski school, don't buy your tickets at the main lodge; instead, turn off Route 100 onto Handle Road and head for the still relatively undiscovered Carinthia. The parking lot is refreshingly compact, lines are short, and if all you need are lift tickets or rentals, you can take care of your business here.

On weekends, when you're ready for lunch, beware: all the cafeterias are crowded, and particularly on holiday weekends it's nearly impossible to find a place to sit; the main base lodge is clogged with people eating standing up, eating in hallways, eating on stairwells—and paying high prices for the privilege. So eat early, BYO, or head for Carinthia or shuttle over to Haystack, whose lodge is also prettier. Condos at Mount Snow Resort are mostly down a ways from the mountain near Snow Lake Lodge— once the resort centerpiece, it's now a bit worse for wear. A spiffy time-share hotel on the southern edge

Children's services: day-care, instruction, tel. 802/464–3333

Snow phone: tel. 802/464–2151

Police: tel. 802/464–2020

Medical center: Deerfield Valley Health Center, tel. 802/464–5311

Hospital: Southwestern Vermont Medical Center, tel. 802/442–6361

Resort services: tel. 802/464–8501

Cross-country skiing: Timber Creek Cross-Country Center, tel. 802/464–0999; White House Cross-Country Center, tel. 802/464–2135

Road conditions: tel. 800/429–7623

Towing: tel. 802/464–2276 or 802/464–2166

FIVE-STAR FAVORITES
Best run for vertical: Free Fall

Best run overall: Uncle's

Best bar/nightclub: Wilmington Village Pub

Best hotel: The Hermitage Inn

Best restaurant: Inn at Saw Mill Farm

of the main base lodge complex is your best bet for ski-in/ski-out convenience. Otherwise, accommodations are in Dover, essentially a strip along Route 100, and in the town at Route 100's junction with Route 9: old-fashioned Wilmington. It's only a couple of miles from the mountain, but the traffic is fierce at day's end, and it can take a half hour or more to get back to your digs on weekends.

HOW TO GET THERE

By Plane
The airports nearest to the resort are **Bradley International** and **Albany County,** both roughly two hours away (*see* Getting to Vermont Resorts, *above*).

By Car
From either north or south, get off I–91 at Exit 2 and pick up Route 9 heading west into Brattleboro. Follow it for 19 miles into Wilmington, then make a right at the light onto Route 100, heading north 9 miles to Mount Snow. From the south you can save about 25 minutes of travel time by taking I–91 to Route 2, heading west at Greenfield, Massachusetts. Watch for the sign to Colrain, Massachusetts; switch to Route 112 heading toward Jacksonville, Vermont; then pick up Route 100 north into Wilmington, Vermont. Turn left onto Route 9 west for a short time and pick up Route 100 again at the traffic light. Make a right and continue to Mount Snow.

You can also take the New York Thruway (I–87) to Albany, New York, then I–787 north to Troy, New York, where you get Route 7 and Route 9 (begins at the Vermont state line) east to Bennington, Vermont. Follow Route 9 east for 21 miles to Wilmington, turn left onto Route 100, and continue to Mount Snow.

Most major car-rental companies are at the Albany County Airport and Bradley International Airport (*see* Getting to Vermont Resorts, *above*).

By Bus
Vermont Transit (tel. 802/864–6811) has scheduled service into Brattleboro.

By Train
Amtrak (tel. 800/872–7245) serves Brattleboro, 19 miles from Wilmington.

GETTING AROUND

With so many of the area's attractions, accommodations, and restaurants spread around the rolling countryside, it's nice to have a car. However, it's not a necessity at all, as the **Moover** (tel. 802/464–8487)— a fleet of buses painted in cow motif—will take you anywhere in the area. It provides regular free shuttle service between Haystack and Mount Snow every half hour from 8 AM to 4:30 PM weekends; 9 AM to 4:30 PM weekdays. The shuttle takes between 10 and 15 minutes. A free local shuttle runs between Snow Lake Lodge and every base lodge at Mount Snow and Haystack, including Carinthia, running continuously from 8 AM to 4:30 PM.

THE SKIING

Mount Snow Resort's skiing ranges from dead-easy to drop-dead difficult, with enough in between to keep a skiing family of widely different abilities happy. Here, black-diamond is correctly labeled MOST DIFFICULT, no doubt about it. What you see is what you ski. You can start the day on a long and winding beginner's run, follow the sun to a south face, then head north and work your heart and thighs on one of the steepest, gnarliest, narrowest, and occasionally iciest bump runs anywhere. And that's all before lunch.

Where to begin? If you're a beginner, intermediate, or crowd-hating advanced skier, consider starting at relatively uncrowded Haystack. It has 44 short trails that add up to 12½ miles of mainly intermediate, mainly sunny skiing with a few diminutive

diamond runs thrown in to keep you on your toes.

Haystack is unusual in that it has two base lodges, one serving only a beginner's area below and entirely separate from the intermediate and expert trails. The rest of the area is composed of two peaks, the Witches and Haystack Mountain. The Witches is by far the steeper, with a number of short but reasonably steep trails that become less difficult as you progress from south to north on the peak.

On Haystack Mountain itself most of the terrain ranges from high beginner to low advanced. You can enjoy a stunning and almost guaranteed solitary view of the surrounding mountains if you remove your skis at the ski patrol hut at the summit of Haystack and then walk a few hundred feet down a pretty wooded trail—using your poles for balance—to a cliff top overlooking the ice-covered Haystack Pond. Bargain hunters can pick up substantially cheaper tickets if they're willing to ski only Haystack—ideal if you like sun and don't need a lot of terrain. (The resort sells an even cheaper Haystack-only family ticket.)

Carinthia is a novice-intermediate mountain with a few short and rather unterrifying black-diamond runs. Most trails are straight shots from the top of the new Nitro Express High Speed Quad to the base lodge; with its ample parking and easy access to the quad, the lodge is a good place to start your day on busy weekends.

The Main Mountain, catering mostly to intermediates and experts, is the most crowded section of the Mount Snow complex. Still, there are ways to beat the crowds. When the trail you're skiing suddenly fills with other skiers, move over to the next trail. Time after time you'll see masses of skiers fighting for space on, say, Sundance, while the equally salubrious Hop, Ridge, and Uncle's are all but empty.

The same goes for lifts. Mount Snow has duplicate lifts for almost every part of the area. When one is backed up, switch to the one next to it. (There is one exception to this rule. Both the line and the ride on the Summit Express Quad move much faster than on the much slower Summit Local. When the weather's cold or windy, stick with the Summit Express Quad.)

Novices

Haystack, Carinthia, and the Main Mountain have an abundance of beginner and intermediate terrain. You'll find plenty of options from any of the base lodges, and except for Haystack, all the mountains are connected by trails and lifts.

First timers and still wobbly folks love the Covered Bridge Magic Carpet lift, a sort of moving sidewalk like those you see in many airports. The Children's Learning Center, on the Main Mountain, is served by two novice lifts, a rope tow, and a handle tow. Both Long John and Deer Run—which you reach from the top of the Clipper, the only detachable quad at the resort—are long, gentle, narrowish beginner runs that wind down the mountain. Deer Run is easier, but it snakes across some more advanced trails, so watch your back because when it's busy, speedy skiers often barrel through much faster than they should. Sweet Sixteen is a bit wider

and steeper and will take you to Carinthia by way of Seasons Pass, another wider, steeper trail.

The Ski Baba chairlift, serving the beginner's area by the Carinthia base lodge, has a vertical rise of exactly 50 feet and gives access to a wide, gentle slope perfect for very young new skiers.

The most interesting trail on Haystack is Outcast, a 125-foot-wide beginner's trail that wanders for almost a mile through deep woods, revealing lovely vistas of the area as you go. Between Haystack and the Witches is a beginner's trail—Flying Dutchman—that runs from the top of Haystack to the upper base lodge. The final and northernmost Witches run, Shadow, is fine for beginners.

Intermediates

Carinthia is your best bet, with slopes such as the forested, beautiful, and narrow Prospector. The terrain on Carinthia won't give strong intermediate skiers anything to worry about, with one small exception—when the blue-square Upper Iron Run turns into Lower Iron Run, it becomes a narrow black-diamond bump trail. If you find yourself suddenly sweating as you stare down the last 100 yards to the base lodge, you'll know you've found it. But fear not. Instead, back up 10 yards and take Detour down to the bottom.

From Carinthia, less-than-advanced skiers can move in two directions: They can cross the ridge from the top of the Nitro Express on Sun Spot to the warm intermediate trails of Sunbrook or keep heading northwest to the Main Mountain on Long John.

Over on the Main Mountain, most of the trails are labeled MORE DIFFICULT, but in fact they are for the most part good, solid intermediate runs. The Sundance chair and the Summit Express high-speed quad take you to several runs down the front of the mountain: narrow Ego Alley, Sundance, and Sapbucket—long, straight, and not too steep.

Don't leave the Main Mountain without at least one run on Snowdance, reachable from the Summit quad or the Canyon quad. This is the ultimate intermediate cruiser, wide enough for the QE2 to tack from one side to the other. With its breadth and moderate pitch, it would be hard to have a bad time here. Then, for variety, take a run on One More Time, a narrow woods trail and the last one before North Face, Mount Snow's most ferocious area.

Not tired yet? Take the Summit quad and blast down Exhibition, a trail wide and varied enough to bring pleasure to skiers of all abilities. If Clipper is superbusy, move over to the next lift, the Sundance triple, and take Uncle's, a winding trail of multiple pitches varying between fairly steep chutes and nearly flat plateaus—it may be Mount Snow's best-kept secret.

After lunch head for sunny Sunbrook, which has its own quad and the most sunshine in the area—perhaps the most in Vermont. Sunspot, Moonwalk, and Big Dipper all are relatively wide, relatively mild runs down heavily wooded south-facing slopes. Ski Thanks Walt, which is gradual at the top and steep in the middle, and Cloud Nine, which goes straight down the fall line, continuing to play on their easy backs for a few more runs. The two trails tend to be less crowded and open up a different, south-oriented vista.

If you want to try the Witches, on Haystack, take the short Spellbinder, an honest intermediate that's more or less straight, more or less wide, and not too steep. Last Chance from the summit is a narrow, winding run that takes you to the base of the Oh No lift. Next time down, traverse south and wind your way down Dutchman to the top of Needle, which is not steep enough for black-diamond designation but will give you an adrenaline surge nonetheless.

Experts

For the expert, the North Face is where your tour begins. To get to the North Face, either take the main lift, also known as Lift 11, also known as the Summit detachable quad, to the summit. Or take the Canyon quad to River Run, which gives an easy cruise to the bottom of the North Face. It's best skied in the morning; the light is better, and the snow hasn't yet been skied off.

The North Face is laced with good, challenging expert trails. Olympic is winding and fairly steep, with moguls on top followed by lips to catch air, followed by flatter terrain near the bottom. It's a sweetheart of a trail but definitely not for sleepy cruising; it demands attentive skiing the whole way down. Olympic's next-door neighbor, Fallen Timbers, is flat-surfaced and very fast, with a lot of different pitches. Challenger winds through a forest, then flattens out near the bottom. When Free Fall, which runs right under the lift, has moguls, it's perfect for showoffs and masochists who crave public humiliation. Chute has killer bumps, but only part of the way down.

The toughest runs at Mount Snow are Jaws and Ripcord. If you want to study them without actually skiing them, take River Run from the Canyon chair. It runs along below the steep stuff, permitting a cool and considered judgment before you take the plunge. Ripcord, Mount Snow Resort's signature double-black-diamond run, is a 1,300-foot mogul field tilted like the back of an unloading dump truck—one of the toughest expert runs in New England. Should you find yourself at the top and suddenly remember that you hate being dumped, there is an alternative route to the bottom. Just to the right of Ripcord is the aptly named Second Thoughts, which will give you a kinder, gentler, and considerably slower descent.

The best strategy for advanced skiers and boarders on Mount Snow is to start at the far north and work your way south. This way you minimize crowds and maximize snow conditions. Start on Fallen Timbers or on Chute for the warm-up run, up the ante on Olympic, and then play your hand on the serious bumps of Plummet. If you're feeling really lucky, have a run at Ripcord.

Next, head over to the toughest trails on the all-intermediate Main Mountain for a descent of the fairly steep and narrow Upper Choke, followed by a turn on untrammeled and snowy Ledge, followed by the pleasure of wide-open giant-slalom cruising on Standard (though it's sometimes crowded).

If you're ready for another bump run, try your legs on Sunbrook's Beartrap, an expert slope that comes equipped with an eight-speaker, 900-watt sound system that plays music all day long. You ski wall-to-wall bumps and listen to wall-to-wall rock and roll.

At the bottom of Ripcord is a snack shack (open when weather permits) that saves you the long circle back to the front of the mountain. And since you're skiing one of the least crowded (and certainly the sunniest) spots on Mount Snow, you may never want to leave. Ripcord is also the site of the annual Glade-iator of the Year contest. Despite its name, it's not a tree run but a bump-skiing freestyle competition for telemarkers, boarders, and skiers. If you're at the resort at the end of March, be sure to catch it.

If you want to ski only expert trails all day, start on the North Face, then jump on the shuttle and ski Haystack's Witches; here the steepest and southernmost trail is Gandolf; by the time you work your way across Cauldron, Merlin, and Wizard, you'll be up for the challenge.

SNOWBOARDING

Mt. Snow's five terrain parks are all accessible by the Nitro Express Quad on Carinthia. Carnival Park, on the Main Mountain near the Covered Bridge Magic Carpet lift, has a funhouse maze design and thrills for young riders (12 and under). El Diablo, on Carinthia, offers banks and spines perfect for intermediate and freestyle riders, and Un Blanco Gulch gives boarders the opportunity to hone their skills on eight acres of freestyle terrain. For advanced boarders, there's Inferno, with extremely challenging freestyle terrain, and PalmerX Park, chock full of banks, berms, hits, and turns. On Carinthia, you'll find a mini-pipe, Bantam, and the Gut, a 460-foot competition-size half-pipe, which is served by its own lift. Mount Snow also provides snowboarding instruction at the Discover Center, to the north of the Clock Tower Building in the Main Base Area.

OTHER SNOW SPORTS
You can go **skating, tubing,** and **sledding** nightly at the Main Base Area. **Snowshoeing** expeditions leave from the Grand Summit Resort at the base of the mountain. Mt. Snow also has snowcat rides, a children's theater, and special family events. The town offers sleigh rides and snowmobiling. Call 800/245–7669 for information about all activities.

WHERE TO STAY
Condos are the mainstay accommodations closest to the resort. Within a 10-mile radius there are distinguished inns, classic B&Bs, and homey lodges. All accommodations can be booked through **Mount Snow central reservations** (tel. 800/245/7669).

Expensive
Grand Summit Hotel & Conference Center
The hotel has a flexible assortment of rooms and condo units. If you want the permanence of a second home without the maintenance headaches, the units are especially convenient. They range from studios to three-bedroom layouts, all with kitchen. The furnishings are cheerful, the rooms comfortable and spacious. For ski-in/ski-out convenience, this is the place. *Rte. 100, Mount Snow, 05356, tel. 800/451–4211, fax 802/464–4192. 200 rooms. Facilities: restaurant, pool, hot tub, sauna, exercise room, concierge, child care. AE, D, DC, MV, V. $139–$800.*

Greenspring at Mount Snow
These extra-large two- to four-bedroom condominiums are just across Route 100 from the resort and have an exceptional view of the mountain. Reminiscent of Vermont farmhouses, they are built in traditional New England style with vertical pine board and batten. Units are individually decorated, many in early American style and some surprisingly modern. All the units have three levels, a spacious living and dining area, and a fireplace with free firewood. *Box 540, West Dover, 05356, tel. 802/464–7111 or 800/247–7833, fax 802/464–1114. 140 units. Facilities: pool, hot tub, sauna, exercise room, video games, shuttle. AE, MC, V. $260–$495.*

Hermitage Inn
Imagine a 24-acre mountainside country retreat with a stately dining room, intimate bar, exquisite wine cellar, decoy collection, and art gallery. All rooms have fireplaces; four are in the main building, four are in the carriage house, and seven more are in the wine house, which has a wine shop on the first level. Also on the property are a hunting preserve, a sugar house, and 50 kilometers of cross-country ski trails. *Coldbrook Rd., Box 457, Wilmington, 05363, tel. 802/ 464–3511. 15 rooms. Facilities: restau-*

rant, bar, cross-country skiing. AE, D, DC, MC, V. $225, including full breakfast and dinner.

Inn at Saw Mill Farm

Architect Rodney Williams transformed this old farm complex into a tasteful and stylish inn. Rooms may have canopy beds and comfortable armchairs—some come with a fireplace and a balcony (no phones or televisions, however). *Mount Snow Valley, Crosstown Rd. and Rte. 100, Box 367, West Dover, 05356, tel. 802/464-8131, fax 802/464-1130. 20 rooms. AE, MC, V. $330–$470, including full breakfast and dinner.*

Seasons Condominiums

These ski-in/ski-out painted-clapboard condos managed by Mount Snow Resort offer a choice of one-, two-, or three-bedroom units, all with plenty of space. Each unit has its own individual style, everything from traditional country to ultramodern, with original art and brightly colored bed covers. All units come with a fireplace, a dining area, and a washer-dryer. *Mount Snow Lodging, 299 Mountain Rd., Mount Snow, 05356, tel. 802/464-7788 or 800/451-4211, fax 802/464-3808. 70 units. Facilities: indoor pool, hot tub, sauna, recreation room, ski-in/ski-out. AE, D, DC, V. $103–$700.*

Moderate

Inn at Mount Snow

This small white-clapboard country inn is right next to the ski area. Half of the rooms have spectacular mountain views. Every room is decorated differently, many with floral patterns. The comfortable living room has a large fireplace and big windows. In the billiards room is an antique pool table with leather pockets. The inn's 30-room lodge next door is ideal for families and groups. *Rte. 100, Box 1546, West Dover, 05356, tel. 802/464-3300 or 800/577-7669, fax 802/464-3396. 45 rooms. Facilities: ski storage, shuttle. AE, D, MC, V. $95–$360, including full breakfast.*

Nutmeg Inn

This handsome 1770s farmhouse on the west side of Wilmington was turned into a country inn in 1957. The rooms, which have woodwork and selectively exposed brick, are furnished with brass or iron beds, Laura Ashley–style bed covers, handmade quilts, colorful throw rugs, and antique or reproduction furniture. *Rte. 9, Box 818, Wilmington 05363, tel. 802/464-3351 or 800/277-5402, fax 802/464-7331. 12 rooms, 2 suites. Facilities: library, lobby lounge. AE, D, MC, V. $95–$200, including full breakfast.*

West Dover Inn

This traditional Greek Revival building in a quiet setting was built in 1846 and is on the National Register of Historic Places. Some rooms are decorated with antique lamps, armoires, and brass beds with hand-pieced quilts; the suites have fireplaces and whirlpool tubs. *Rte. 100, Box 1208, West Dover, 05356, tel. 802/464-5207 or 800/732-0745, fax 802/464-2173. 8 rooms, 4 suites. Facilities: restaurant, bar, library, meeting rooms. AE, MC, V. $80–$200, including full breakfast.*

White House

On a grassy knoll just east of the village of Wilmington is this stately

Colonial-style mansion. Rooms, some with handsome brick fireplaces, are done in Early American style, with polished hardwood floors, rich area rugs, and well-crafted wooden furnishings. Next door at the farmhouse are seven additional rooms, decorated in the same elegant style, though a bit smaller. *Rte. 9, Wilmington, 05363, tel. 802/464–2135 or 800/541–2135, fax 802/464–5222. 16 rooms. Facilities: restaurant, bar, indoor pool, sauna, hot tub, cross-country skiing. AE, DC, MC, V. $115–$190, including full breakfast.*

Inexpensive

Four Seasons Inn
This hotel outside Wilmington, 2 miles from Mount Snow, offers colorful rooms with bright wallpaper and cheerful print bedspreads. All rooms are carpeted; deluxe rooms come with a refrigerator. *Rte. 100, Box 6, West Dover, 05356, tel. 802/464–8303. 24 rooms. Facilities: dining room, bar, sauna, ski storage. AE, D, MC, V. $45–$85.*

Gray Ghost Inn
This inn a mile from Mount Snow has a comfortable family feel. Some rooms are paneled with tongue-and-groove cypress; local pottery and art embellish others. Handmade quilts, maple nightstands, and lace curtains in the rooms and the fireplace in the main lounge lend a real country-inn flavor. *Rte. 100, Box 938, West Dover, 05356, tel. 802/464–2474 or 800/745–3615. 26 rooms. Facilities: dining room, sauna, library, piano. AE, D, MC, V. $45–$67, including full breakfast.*

Old Red Mill Inn
This 19th-century structure on the creek near the intersection of Route 9 and Route 100 in Wilmington used to be a sawmill, and it shows: As you put your feet up on the huge open hearth, you can study the original machinery (check out the huge old bellows), the massive beams, and the slightly lurchy wide-board floors. The rooms upstairs are fairly basic, with sturdy wooden furniture and beds that—like many in the hostelries in these parts—will have you longing for your own. But the price is right. And the restaurant downstairs is downright pleasant. *Rte. 100, Wilmington, 05363, tel. 802/464–3700 or 800/843–8483, fax 802/464–8513. 26 rooms. Facilities: restaurant. AE, D, DC, MC, V. $40–$80.*

Snow Creek Inn
This gray-and-white barn-board motel, 1½ miles from the mountain, offers large, clean rooms with homemade pillows and quilts and a small refrigerator. Efficiencies with kitchenettes are also available. *Rte. 100, Box 1008, West Dover, 05356, tel. 802/464–5632, fax 802/464–0829. 19 rooms, 2 units. Facilities: lobby lounge, laundry facilities. AE, D, MC, V. $60–$100.*

WHERE TO EAT
In and around the resort there's an excellent choice of restaurants. Wilmington and West Dover offer a wide variety of cuisines.

Expensive

Hermitage Inn
Just above the Haystack ski area, this secluded country inn serves elaborate

dinners in several distinctly different dining rooms. The inn's owner raises deer, pheasant, and wild turkey on the premises. The menu includes such delectable dishes as roast pheasant with hunter's sauce (mushrooms, tomatoes, tarragon, and Madeira) and venison sautéed with bourbon, shallots, and cracked pepper. The wine cellar houses some 40,000 bottles. *Coldbrook Rd., Wilmington, tel. 802/464–3511. Reservations essential. AE, DC, MC, V.*

Inn at Saw Mill Farm
The chef here is Brill Williams, son of the inn's owner-architect. The dining room, part of an old barn, has wide-plank floors and toile wallpaper hung with 19th-century portraits and landscapes in massive gilt frames. The linen, sterling, and crystal on the table set a perfect stage for such complex fare as pheasant breast *forestière* and steak *au poivre. Mount Snow Valley, Crosstown Rd. and Rte. 100, West Dover, tel. 802/464–8131. Reservations essential. AE, MC, V.*

Le Petit Chef
Charming and unpretentious, this French restaurant occupies an early 18th-century white farmhouse. Laura Ashley wallpaper decorates the walls above the wainscoting. The menu, which changes seasonally, may feature chicken breast with pine nuts and grapes and roast beef with green peppercorn sauce. *Rte. 100, Wilmington, tel. 802/464–8437. Reservations essential. MC, V.*

Two Tannery Road
Fireplaces warm each dining room of this 18th-century house, formerly a Roosevelt summer residence. The quiet, attentive staff serves traditional fare such as seafood stew, shrimp scampi, steak *au poivre,* and fresh Long Island duckling in black cherry sauce. *2 Tannery Rd., West Dover, tel. 802/464–2707. MC, V.*

Moderate
Dover Forge
This family restaurant has a blacksmith theme, complete with a brick floor and a fireplace flanked by bellows and forges. You select your base entrée—pasta, fish, pork, chicken, or veal—and then choose from a spectrum of sauces and preparation styles. *Andiron Lodge, Rte. 100, West Dover, tel. 802/464–0661. D, MC, V.*

Fannie's
A cathedral ceiling towers above the dining room of this rustic restaurant built as a house in 1838. Among the steak, chicken, and fish dishes are such entrées as Yankee grilled chicken and barbecued St. Louis ribs, and more. *Rte. 9, W. Main St., Wilmington, tel. 802/464–1143. Reservations essential. AE, D, DC, MC, V.*

Poncho's Wreck
This architectural anomaly in the middle of quaint Wilmington is a strange cross between Victorian San Francisco, a beachcombers' Hall of Fame, and the medal room of the New York Yacht Club. The food, as imaginatively whimsical as the decor, includes not only familiar south-of-the-border specialties, but also steak, chicken, ribs, and seafood dishes that shift with the ocean breezes. Sunday brunch is a monster. *S. Main St., Wilmington, tel. 802/464–9320. AE, D, MC, V.*

Inexpensive

Dot's Restaurant

Dot is renowned locally for her great home cooking and baking, not to mention her daily specials, which include baked stuffed sole, chicken stuffed with jack cheese and broccoli, pasta, homemade soups, sandwiches, and burgers. Nifty movie stills and other memorabilia adorn the knotty-pine walls. *Main St., 8 mi south of Mount Snow, Wilmington, tel. 802/ 464–7284. MC, V.*

The Silo

This landmark silo, hay barn, and 19th-century windmill is a good bet for steaks, chops, and burgers from the grill, homemade meat loaf, fried chicken, New York cheesecake, and chocolate mousse. *Rte. 100, West Dover, tel. 802/464–2553. AE, D, DC, MC, V.*

Tony's Pizza

You can either eat it in, take it out, or have it delivered—the *it* being hot and cold subs, pasta, homemade soups, salad bar, and of course, pizza. *Rte. 100, West Dover, tel. 802/464– 8669. No credit cards.*

Best Bets for Breakfast

The Bakery

For the absolute best selection of breakfast baked goods, come here. There's room to sit down and enjoy, or you can choose and go. There are excellent muffins, sweet breads, croissants, and fruit-filled pastries, plus some of the best coffee in the area. *Rte. 100, West Dover, tel. 802/464–5914.*

White House

This marvelously formal, sun-filled dining room is in the stately, Colonial-style hotel of the same name. The atmosphere is quiet and contemplative. Blueberry pancakes, eggs champignon, and French toast made from homemade honey-wheat bread are signature items. *Rte. 9, Wilmington, tel. 802/464–2135. AE, D, MC, V.*

NIGHTLIFE AND ENTERTAINMENT

Après-Ski

Deacon's Den

When you've had your fill of the slopes and want to warm up, you can come here for free soup and a drink. There are airplane props, a carousel horse, and other paraphernalia on the walls and live rock or blues on weekends. Or you can shoot pool, shoot hoops, or just shoot the breeze. *Rte. 100, West Dover, tel. 802/464–9361. AE, D, MC, V.*

Loud and Lively/Dancing

The Silo

This sprawling entertainment emporium has two dance floors, loud music (occasionally live), and two large fireplaces surrounded by big comfortable chairs. In the early evening it's a family crowd, but later on the average age plummets. *Rte. 100, West Dover, tel. 802/464–2553. AE, D, DC, MC, V.*

Wilmington Village Pub

Busy and lively, this sports-bar-cum-dance-hall is decked out in all the appropriate jock memorabilia. There's pool and pinball and multiple satellite-linked TVs. Upstairs is calmer, with a large fieldstone fireplace. *7 S. Main St., Wilmington, tel. 802/464– 2280.*

STOWE MOUNTAIN RESORT

5781 Mountain Rd., Rte. 108
Stowe, VT 05672
Tel. 802/253-3000
www.digitalfrontier.com/smr

STATISTICALLY SPEAKING

Base elevation: 1,280 feet

Summit elevation: 4,393 feet

Vertical drop: 2,360 feet

Skiable terrain: 480 acres

Number of trails: 47

Longest run: 3.7 miles

Lifts and capacity: 1 gondola,
1 quad, 1 triple, 6 doubles,
2 surface; 11,465 skiers per
hour

Daily lift ticket: $54

Average annual snowfall: 250
inches

Number of skiing days
1997–1998: 154

Snowmaking: 350 acres; 73%

Terrain mix: N 16%, I 59%,
E 25%

Snowboarding: yes

Cross-country skiing: 150 kilometers (accessible from
Stowe Mountain Resort Touring Center)

Stowe Resort covers two mountains, Mt. Mansfield and Spruce Peak. Geographically, Mansfield and Spruce look like siblings of different ages and, perhaps, different fathers. Mansfield is big—by Vermont standards, very big. At 4,393 feet, it is the highest peak in the state and by far the most renowned. When northern Vermonters talk about a day on Mt. Mansfield, they say, "Wanna go ski the Mountain?" Mansfield is a hill among hills, high as the sky, broad as a Vermont barn, and as laced with ski trails as a summer cottage in March is with cobwebs.

Spruce Peak is a comparatively diminutive 3,300 feet, and its one skiable face gazes southeast toward Mansfield as if looking up at a big brother. Spruce forms the southern gate of Smugglers Notch, a narrow, winding gap through the Green Mountains that used to be the lair of rum and cattle smugglers and is now, at least in winter, the exclusive domain of cross-country skiers, snowshoers, and peregrine falcons soaring the thermals above their heads.

The first recorded descent of Mt. Mansfield was in 1914. One of the earliest ski resorts in the East grew almost organically—because people kept on skiing down the mountain. The first Stowe winter carnival was held in 1921; it marked the beginning of skiing as a tourist attraction in the area, long before lifts were built. Events included ski jumping, snowshoeing, skating, and bobsledding. During the Depression, Perry Merrill (a skier and director of the Vermont Forest Service) convinced the federal government that ski trails were roads, and so the Civilian Conservation Corps built the first ski trail on Mt. Mansfield in 1932. In 1934 they cut Nosedive, which is still in use (*see* Experts *in* The Skiing, *below*). In 1940 the longest chairlift in the United States opened on Mansfield and broke down on its first run, stranding the governor and other dignitaries. Nowadays the lifts on both mountains are considerably more reliable.

Stowe the town, a much-photographed symbol of New England village life, looks like a Currier & Ives engraving, complete with white-steepled church and old-fashioned general store. Discreetly tucked away in this 19th-century setting are such 20th-century amenities as four golf courses, 50 tennis courts, 51 restaurants, 64 lodgings, and 75 shops. If it's not typ-

Children's services: day-care, instruction, tel. 802/253-3000

Snow phone: tel. 802/253-3600 or 800/247-8693

Police: tel. 911 or 802/253-7126

Hospital: Copley, tel. 802/888-4231

Stowe Area Association: tel. 800/247-8693

Road conditions: tel. 800/429-7623

Towing: Willy's Auto, tel. 802/253-8552

FIVE-STAR FAVORITES
Best run for vertical: Goat

Best run overall: National

Best bar/nightclub: Bert's Place

Best hotel: Green Mountain Inn

Best restaurant: Cactus Café

ical Vermont, Stowe conveys the air of Vermont—the Vermont of Laura Ashley wallpaper, of Swiss fondue restaurants, and of shops called Nothing But Cows, all domiciled in wooden clapboard houses built before the Civil War.

The village is the hub of Stowe, the visual and historic heart of the town. Two major roads meet here, each with a distinctly different character—Route 100, the highway that connects most of the state's ski areas, and the Mountain Road. Route 100 is the classic American strip, but with antiques stores instead of used-car dealers. The Mountain Road and its environs, the newest commercial development in the area, is yuppie heaven, with a colorful mix of inns and eateries, sport shops and boutiques, wine stores and gift emporiums strung out between the highway and the frozen West Branch of the Little River.

Accommodations at the resort include one on-mountain lodge and range from a youth hostel and simple bed-and-breakfasts to lush spas and upscale inns nearby. All are sprinkled on or just off the Mountain Road and up and down Route 100 from the center of town.

HOW TO GET THERE

By Plane
The Burlington International Airport is a 45-minute drive west of the resorts (see Getting to Vermont Resorts, above).

Shuttle Services
Transfers from Burlington Airport to Stowe are available from **Lamoille County Taxi** (tel. 802/252-0204, ext. 3) and **Peg's Pick-up** (tel. 802/253-9490). Advance reservations are required for both services.

By Car
Stowe is 45 minutes east of Burlington Airport (see Getting to Vermont Resorts, above) and 15 minutes from I-89. Get off at Exit 10 (Stowe/Waterbury) onto Route 100. Follow Route 100 north to the intersection of Route 100 and Route 108, in Stowe village. Take Route 108 north (the Mountain Road) for 6 miles to the Stowe Mountain Resort. Stowe is six

hours' drive from New York City and less than four hours from Hartford, Boston, and Albany. From Montreal, Stowe can be reached in approximately 2½ hours.

Car rentals are available in Stowe at Stowe Auto Service (tel. 802/253–7608).

By Bus

Vermont Transit Company (tel. 802/864–6811) and **Greyhound Lines** (tel. 802/864–6811) provide daily service to Burlington and Waterbury. If you arrange it in advance, some inns offer pickup service from Waterbury. Otherwise, taxis are available.

By Train

The **Amtrak** (tel. 800/872–7245) station in Waterbury, Vermont, is 15 minutes from Stowe, and round-trip transfers are available to most hotels. Many lodges in Stowe will arrange to meet your train. Stowe Preferred Round-Trip fares are available on Amtrak's Vermonter from Washington, D.C., Philadelphia, and New York.

GETTING AROUND

By Shuttle

The $1 shuttle bus (tel. 802/253–7321), operated by Stowe Mountain Resort, runs continuously all season long between the village of Stowe and the resort, with stops along the way. You can pick it up roughly every 15 minutes during peak hours and then every hour until 10 PM at key locations, including the Gondola Barn, the Midway Base Lodge, the Spruce Peak Base Lodge, the Vermont State Ski Dorm, and H. H. Binghams, the restaurant at the Toll House lift.

By Taxi

Stowe Taxi (tel. 802/253–9433) serves the town.

By Car

When traffic is heavy on the Mountain Road, as it almost always is on holiday weekends, you'll crawl the 6 miles between the village of Stowe and the parking lots for Mt. Mansfield and Spruce Peak. Your best bet at these times is to use the shuttle service.

THE SKIING

On the ski area map, Stowe is two mountains, Mt. Mansfield and Spruce Peak. On the skier's internal map, Stowe is numerous mountains, each serving different types of skiers. Although most of the areas are on Mt. Mansfield, there's little geographical and even less functional overlap among them. Spruce Peak is a mountain devoted entirely to beginning and intermediate skiers. The pace is slower here than on Mansfield, and so are the skiers and the lifts (the Big Spruce Double was built in 1954). Mt. Mansfield accommodates skiers of every type, from never-evers to the most fearless in North America. The bottom of Spruce is a broad expanse of practice slopes ranging from the fairly precipitous Slalom Hill to the aptly named Easy Street. In addition to slow pace and gentle terrain, Spruce has the advantage of afternoon sun. In December and January, when the sun leaves Mansfield's north-northeast-facing slopes early, Spruce is the place to be. Unfortunately, all that sunshine added to a complete lack of snowmaking on Upper Spruce means that in snow-lean times the Big Spruce lift is roped off, with a CLOSED sign dangling from the rope.

Stowe is great for cruising; there are great runs for everyone from novices to experts. Another skiing mode at Stowe is night skiing, which began here in 1991. The resort has lighted the top of Perry Merrill, the length of Gondolier, and the breadth of the beginner slopes by the Midway Café. The gondola gives access to the lighted slopes and, for beginners, the surface lift at its base. Dress warmly and wear goggles with clear lenses.

To get the most out of your ski time at Stowe, consider these tips: the best the resort has to offer begins on the gondola or quad at 7:30 AM holidays and weekends and at 8 AM during the week. This is when you'll find the best light, the smallest crowds, and every peak and trail on both mountains bathed in sun. At 11 AM Nosedive begins to lose light, and those around it soon follow. Start working your way to the right toward Toll Road.

When the lines at the quad and the gondola go on into next Tuesday, the triple chair is virtually empty. Yet it gives access to a long beginner's trail (Lullaby Lane), wonderful intermediate trails (Gulch, Standard, North Slope), and the lower half of an expert trail (Hayride).

Another Stowe specialty is Stowe Hosts, volunteers who know and will show you where the day's best skiing lies. Stowe Host tours start daily at 10:30 AM and 1:30 PM at the top of the Forerunner quad.

One final bit of insider's information: at the top of the Spruce Peak lift is a closely guarded Stowe secret: a little-known trail (not on the ski area map) that gives you access to the Smugglers Notch Resort, on the north slope of Mt. Mansfield. You reach Snuffy's, the groomed and patrolled connecting trail, by skating over Sterling Pond. Stowe and Smugglers let one another's customers have one ride free. The views from the top are spectacular, and the trail across Sterling Pond is still an adventure that 99% of Stowe visitors never even hear of.

Like most of the mountains of northern Vermont, Stowe is scrupulously honest about its trail categories. If signs say, MORE DIFFICULT, you need to make linked stem turns to enjoy the trail. If they say, MOST DIFFICULT, expect steepness and/or moguls. If a sign says, EXPERTS ONLY, believe it. Snowboarding is a major sport here as well.

Novices

If you're a first-time skier who's going to be spending some time in these parts, has Stowe got a deal for you! You take a beginner's lesson (for $65), and when you're good enough to ski down from Stowe's two easiest lifts, the Mighty Mite (9) and the Easy Street double chair (8), you're given a season pass good for the Toll House double on Mt. Mansfield.

On Mansfield, start with the gentlest run, Toll Road. It's beginner's bliss, novitiate's nirvana. To reach it, take the Forerunner quad from the main base area. Toll Road is Stowe's easiest trail, 3.7 miles of wide curves slowly meandering through the woods down to the Toll House double.

Toll House, the easternmost lift at Stowe, gives access to the bottom third of Toll Road and the straight and deliberate Easy Mile. It is the lift closest to the village and may be the best-equipped beginner's area in the world, with its own restaurant (H. H. Binghams), tavern (the Broken Ski), hotel (the Inn at the Mountain), and condos (the Lodge and Mt. Mansfield Townhouses). It also has its own parking lot, so if traffic is heavy, you can stop here and use the chair to reach the rest of Mt. Mansfield.

When there's natural snow, beginning cruisers can try Main Street on Spruce Peak. The least crowded areas for beginners are Spruce Peak and Toll House.

Intermediates

On Spruce Peak you have a choice of three winding trails through the woods—Sterling, Whirlaway, and Upper Smugglers—plus one wider ski highway, Main Street. All are true intermediate trails, with no unexpected ultrasteeps or nerve-racking narrows to ruin your day.

On Mt. Mansfield, when you graduate from beginner to intermediate status, it's time to ride the Toll House double for the last time and ski down Lullaby Lane to the Mountain triple. Lullaby Lane is nearly as gentle as Easy Mile, but from the triple you can get to the low intermediate Tyro and the solidly intermediate Standard and Gulch. As you ski them, you (and your knees) will feel the difference in terrain. Stowe's trails are laid out so that intermediate skiers have a safe way down from any lift. But bear in mind that as you leave Toll House and work your way left across the mountain section served by the triple and the Forerunner quad (the area known as the Main Mountain), the trails grow progressively steeper.

You can continue left on Rimrock to "the world's fastest eight-person gondola." This technological marvel, separated by a deep, forested bowl from most of Mansfield's trails, rockets out of the Gondola Barn, past the Midway Lodge and Café, and up a steep pitch to the Cliff House Restaurant. From there the intermediate Cliff Trail leads back to the main mountain, or you can cruise straight back to the barn on Gondolier. Other good cruisers are Sunrise (gentler) and the lower half of Nosedive. The least crowded runs for intermediates are Upper Spruce, Lower Standard, Gulch, and Lord.

Experts

The Front Four are the trails that gave Stowe its fierce reputation. Usually groomed, Lift Line starts with a steep drop-off, briefly levels off midway, and plunges straight down at the end. National is even steeper and more challenging, and the remaining two members of the Front Four go well beyond challenging. If you ski Starr or, worse, Goat, make certain that: there's plenty of snow cover, you really are an expert, and your insurance is paid up.

The oldest and best-known expert trail is Nosedive, built in 1934 and widened and somewhat tamed in 1966. It's still a steep and exhilarating challenge at the top and a fine cruising trail lower down.

From the gondola three expert trails lead back to the barn: the hardest is Chinclip; the two others are winding, frolicking Perry Merrill (1½ miles) and Switchback. Depending on what's been groomed that day, any one of these trails could have gentle moguls, but none is allowed to turn ferocious.

From the quad, Lord and North Slope are good warm-up runs. Hayride gives you some more challenge. For experts, the least crowded trails are any that are away from the quad and gondola lifts.

Stowe's worst-kept secret is the glades. Stowe has no shortage of trees and no shortage of glade skiing. Yet except for one short dogleg of a trail labeled Slalom Glades, cut in the mid-1930s, and two trails—Tres Amigos and Lookout Glades, cut recently—they don't appear on the trail map. This is because officially they don't exist. To find these "nonexistent" woods, follow the experts between Chinclip and Gondolier, through gaps in the trees off Cliff Trail, and anywhere else you see skiers darting into the forest. Note well that as these glade trails don't officially exist, you ski them at your own risk. Your ticket won't be pulled by the ski patrol, but you are not encouraged to go in. If you do, go with a buddy. Nonexistent woods are terrible spots to get lost in alone.

SNOWBOARDING

Snowboard Life magazine rated Stowe number one in the east for snowboarding in 1998, and it's no wonder. Snowboarders have access to the entire mountain and to all lifts, a half-pipe, and three terrain parks off the Forerunner quad, the Mountain triple, and the Easy Street double. The terrain park known as The Jungle has walls and obstacles and bumps to keep boarders on their toes all day. The half- and quarter-pipes are groomed daily by a state-of-the-art pipe dragon (a machine for cutting half-pipe). The half-pipe was moved to the North Slope trail in 1998 to make it steeper and longer, and a yurt was erected to give boarders their own comfortable hangout pipe-side. Stowe offers riding lessons for everyone from six years old to any age, plus special clinics for boarders who want to do better on the slopes. Daily advanced riding clinics focus on freestyle, freeriding, and carving. One-on-one coaching sessions are available for $55 an hour, a great way to move up a level quickly. If you're truly industrious, there's the Stowe Boarding Freestyle Camp, where Stowe pros teach ground and air tricks that will wow your friends.You can wow yourself too: the pipe now has a video system that allows you to get out, go big or burn, then watch the replay on film.

OTHER SNOW SPORTS

Snowshoeing, snowmobiling, **ice-skating,** sleigh rides and **cross-country skiing** are available in town. Call the **Stowe Area Association** (800/247–8693) for information; they can find your activity and make your reservation all in one call.

NEARBY

Stowe's biggest competitor is also its Siamese twin: **Smuggler's Notch** (tel. 802/644–1156 or 800/451–8752), considered family nirvana, is connected to Stowe. In summer, you can drive a quick (albeit hairy) 15-minute pass to get there. In the winter, the closed pass means a 40-minute loop out and around Stowe to get to Smugs. You can also ski from Stowe to Smugs using Snuffy's trail.

The side trip is worth it: Smugs offers traditional New England skiing and family fun, including skiing costumed characters and slope-side bonfire sing-a-longs.

WHERE TO STAY

Few resort areas in New England offer the variety of accommodations that you'll find at Stowe, although precious little of it is actually slope-side. There are large resort hotels, modern condo complexes, smaller lodges, basic inns, and motels, plus a wide selection of typical bed-and-breakfast establishments. When choosing where to stay, consider that the town is 5 miles from the ski slopes on Route 108 and that traffic to and from the village and the mountain can be terminally slow and frustrating. All reservations can be made through **Stowe Central Reservations** (800/247–8693).

Be sure to inquire about package rates: most establishments will offer multiday packages that in many cases include meals and lift tickets for considerably less than the posted daily rate. All accommodations in this section are in Stowe and have a zip code of 05672.

Expensive

Green Mountain Inn
This classic three-story inn, built in 1833 right in the middle of Stowe village, is one of five in Vermont named a Historic Hotel of America by the National Trust for Historic Preservation. The character is obvious when you enter the lobby—polished pine floors, comfortable sofas, soft lighting, and classical music. The rooms have modern facilities, but the historic

theme continues with period wall coverings and stencils, four-poster or canopy beds, and watercolors by a local artist. Afternoon tea is served in the lobby. *Main St., Box 60, tel. 802/253–7301 or 800/253–7302, fax 802/253–5096. 50 rooms, 14 suites. Facilities: 2 restaurants, bar, sauna, steam room, health club, shuttle, laundry service. AE, D, DC, MC, V. $89–$189.*

Inn at the Mountain and Condos
If you must ski in and ski out, this 70-year-old three-story hotel and the condos nearby are your only choices. Original Grandma Moses artworks and dark-wood fixtures decorate the inn lobby. The inn rooms are spacious if uninspiring. For the space and privacy of condo living, the tree-shrouded minivillage surrounding the inn is a good bet. The units have one, two, or three bedrooms. Each has a fireplace, a full kitchen, a dining area, a washer-dryer, and a deck. *5781 Mountain Rd., tel. 802/253–3000 or 800/253–4754, fax 802/253–3604. 28 rooms, 7 suites, 13 town houses, 23 units. Facilities: 2 restaurants, health club, cross-country skiing. AE, D, DC, MC, V. $150–$350, including full breakfast and dinner.*

Topnotch at Stowe Resort and Spa
One of the top-rated resort hotel/spas in the Stowe area, the Topnotch exudes old-world substance and style. Its 120 acres of grounds are ringed by mountaintops. Dark woods and Tudor furnishings set the tone; rooms are individually decorated in hunter green and maroon with antiques, original art, and well-crafted mahogany furniture. In addition to the hotel, the sprawling complex has town houses and a full-service health spa. In the

two- and three-bedroom town houses, which are as luxurious as the hotel, decor varies according to the owner's taste. *Mountain Rd., Box 1458, 2 mi from mountain, tel. 802/253–8585 or 800/451–8686, fax 802/253–9263. 90 rooms, 3 efficiencies, 17 town houses. Facilities: 2 restaurants, lounge, spa, indoor pool, cross-country skiing, ski shop, guided tours, baby-sitting, laundry service. AE, D, DC, MC, V. $188–$525.*

Trapp Family Lodge

On a hilltop, surrounded by 2,200 acres of pristine, rolling meadows and woodlands and built (and rebuilt after a fire in 1980) by the legendary Trapp family, who inspired *The Sound of Music,* the lodge is wonderful, elegant, and Austrian in style. The rooms have dark-wood furnishings, bright and stylish accents in rich colors, and nice touches such as fluffy goose-down bed covers. If you want more space, you can try getting one of the private houses on the property, which are available for weekly rental on a limited basis. *42 Trapp Hill Rd., tel. 802/253–8511 or 800/826–7000, fax 802/253–5740. 86 rooms, 5 suites, 100 houses. Facilities: 2 dining rooms, indoor pool, sauna, massage, fitness center. $85–$340.*

Moderate

Edson Hill Manor

This brick and finished-log manor house was originally a private mountaintop estate fashioned after an 18th-century French country house in Québec. It sits on 225 acres of woodland, open to cross-country skiing, horseback riding, and sleigh rides. Rooms are in the manor house and in four newer satellite guest houses; all

are decorated with antiques, elegant wooden furnishings, and area rugs and tapestries. Most rooms have a fireplace. *1500 Edson Hill Rd., tel. 802/253–7371 or 800/621–0284, fax 802/253–4036. 25 rooms. Facilities: restaurant, bar, cross-country skiing, horseback riding, snowshoeing. AE, D, MC, V. $55–$105 per person.*

Golden Eagle Resort

Since 1963, this family-oriented facility has evolved from a modest motel to today's 80-acre, 10-building hospitality and recreational miniempire, complete with mountain and pond views. There are standard hotel rooms with a double or queen-size bed and slightly larger efficiencies with limited cooking facilities. The condos sleep six and have a full kitchen, a living room, and two baths. There's nothing exceptional about the decor or the furnishings here, but everything is spotless and well maintained. *Mountain Rd., Box 1090, tel. 802/253–4811 or 800/626–1010, fax 802/253–2561. 71 rooms, 12 efficiencies, 5 units, 3 houses. Facilities: 2 restaurants, indoor pool, sauna, whirlpool, exercise room, fitness center, cross-country skiing, ice-skating, billiards, laundry, nature trails. AE, D, DC, MC, V. $79–$299.*

Mountain Road Resort

This wonderfully modern and stylish resort complex is nestled in the trees and meadows just off Mountain Road. Accommodations range from basic single rooms to suites to two-bedroom condos, and all rooms are no-smoking. Regardless of size, everything is well furnished—brass beds, attractive fixtures—and well equipped. All units come with a small fridge. *Mountain*

Rd., Box 8, 3 mi from resort, tel. 802/
253–4566 or 800/367–6873, fax 802/
253–7397. 25 rooms, 6 suites. Facilities: indoor pool, sauna, Jacuzzi, outdoor hot tub, gym, wine bar. AE, D, DC, MC, V. $89–$325, including full breakfast and après-ski snacks.

Siebeness

Nestled in the foothills of Mt. Mansfield, this place is homey without feeling cloistered. The main, two-story Colonial building is distinguishable by the stenciled drawings lining each shutter. Though not especially big, rooms in the main building are decorated with tasteful pine and maple antique furnishings, small artifacts, pieces of art, and such personal touches as duvets or quilts. The main inn has a comfortable sitting room with a large fireplace. There is also a full-service cottage that sleeps four. 3681 Mountain Rd., about 2½ mi from resort, tel. 802/253–8942 or 800/426–9001, fax 802/253–9232. 11 rooms, 1 cottage. Facilities: lounge, outdoor hot tub, game room. AE, D, MC, V. $70–$180, including full breakfast.

Inexpensive

The Gables

This rustic, comfortable B&B is housed in a classic, rambling 1856 farmhouse complete with a front porch. Barnboard, exposed beams, and antiques set the tone in the large sitting area warmed by a giant fireplace and filled with overstuffed chairs and couches. The room furnishings are a bit patchwork and vary wildly from room to room, but they're comfortable without being overly fussy. 1457 Mountain Rd., tel. 802/253–7730 or 800/422–5371, fax 802/

253–8989. 13 rooms, 2 suites, 4 carriage house rooms. Facilities: outdoor hot tub, game room, snowshoeing. AE, D, MC, V. $100–$175, including full breakfast and après-ski snacks.

Innsbruck Inn

A Bavarian handcrafted bell tower and Austrian-style murals set this inn apart from other big motels. The rooms are exceptionally large; most have a queen-size bed and a living area complete with a sofa and comfy chairs. Each efficiency sleeps eight and has a kitchenette; the house has five bedrooms, two baths, a full kitchen, a sauna, and four more bunks in the basement. 4361 Mountain Rd., tel. 802/253–8582 or 800/225–8582, fax 802/253–2260. 20 rooms, 4 efficiencies, 1 house. Facilities: restaurant, bar, spa, hot tub, sauna. AE, D, MC, V. $29–$69 per person, including full breakfast.

Ten Acres Lodge

This charming New England–style clapboard lodge in a pastoral setting is warm and inviting. Rooms are stylish and elegant, with colorful print wall coverings. Some rooms come with a fireplace. The cottages have more sleeping space, a kitchenette, and a fireplace. 14 Barrows Rd., tel. 802/253–7638 or 800/327–7357, fax 802/253–4036. 16 rooms, 2 cottages. Facilities: restaurant, bar, outdoor hot tub. AE, D, MC, V. $40–$70 per person, including full breakfast and après-ski snacks.

Vermont State Ski Dorm

This former Civilian Conservation Corps site camp offers bunk-bed accommodations. Not only is it the lowest per-night price in the area, it's the closest to the mountain—less than a half mile. The common room is warmed by a fireplace. There is a surprisingly good breakfast and a dinner that varies depending on who is the current manager. *6992 Mountain Rd., tel. 802/253–4010. 24 bunk beds. Facilities: dining room, lounge, sauna, game room, guided tours. AE, D, DC, MC, V. $20 per person; $24 with full breakfast; $29 with breakfast and dinner.*

WHERE TO EAT

Although there's no shortage of restaurants in the Stowe area, there's definitely a lack of innovative dining spots. Good, hearty, wholesome dining seems to be the mainstay, with a few exceptions. Stowe Mountain Resort is unique because it purchased a Maine seafood company, complete with lobster pound to ensure quality seafood at low prices through the lean winter months. It supplies the restaurants at the Inn at the Mountain with lobster, crab, mussels, steamers, littleneck clams, oysters, shrimp, and other fresh fish.

Most of Stowe's restaurants are strung out along the Mountain Road (Route 108) between the resort and the village, but there are many right in town as well.

On the Mountain

Broken Ski Tavern

It's a bright, cheery tavern with ski memorabilia decorating the walls, a blazing fireplace, and sit-down service with sturdy stews and chili, mountain-size burgers, and a variety of daily specials and sandwiches. *Inn at the Mountain, tel. 802/253–3000. AE, D, DC, MC, V.*

Cliff House Restaurant

This is the most refined dining on the mountain—linen, silverware, tableside service, and a spectacular view. The lunch menu includes a selection of daily entrées, soups, and salads. *Top of gondola, tel. 802/253–3000, ext. 3365. Reservations essential. AE, D, DC, MC, V.*

Expensive

Blue Moon Café

This stylish restaurant in the middle of Stowe Village headlines innovative Vermont cuisine. In a restored village home, the intimate café offers light jazz and original paintings by local artists as a setting for the masterpieces that arrive from the kitchen. Good choices are braised Vermont rabbit with wild mushrooms and roasted garlic or marinated leg of lamb with pine-nut crust and braised sweet onions. There's also an excellent pan-roasted bluefish with lime glaze, roasted peppers, and pine nuts. *35 School St., tel. 802/253–7006. Reservations essential. AE, D, MC, V.*

Cliff House Restaurant

This restaurant atop Mt. Mansfield also serves dinner, and you still have to take the gondola to get there. When you call for a reservation, leave your phone number so restaurant personnel can call back in case high winds or lightning storms prevent the gondola from running. The prix-fixe menu is $39.95, including the gondola ride, appetizer, salad, entrée, and dessert. Entrées may include sautéed salmon in fresh herbs, rack of lamb with Dijon mustard, or marinated Vermont venison with cherry port-wine sauce. *Tel. 802/253–3000,* ext. 3365. *Reservations essential. AE, D, DC, MC, V.*

Edson Hill Manor

Dark knotty-pine wainscoting and walls and ceiling adorned with hand-painted ivy contribute to a tranquil and somewhat formal atmosphere in the dining room here. The menu is heavy on game—local, of course—and may include grilled rabbit or barbecued quail with black bean ragout. *1500 Edson Hill Rd., tel. 802/253–7371. Reservations essential. AE, D, MC, V.*

Foxfire Inn

The Foxfire is a restored country farmhouse complete with wainscoting in its dining room and a living room warmed by a cozy fireplace. Both Northern and Southern Italian dishes are served here, many with a country flavor. There are several veal dishes—including parmigiana and marsala—a good selection of pastas, and an excellent eggplant Parmesan. *1606 Pucker St., 1½ mi north of Stowe Village on Rte. 100, tel. 802/253–4887. Reservations essential. AE, D, MC, V.*

Île de France

The only French restaurant in town is a good place for a special night. There are two dining rooms, both done in the style of Louis XIV, with high-back chairs and crystal wall sconces, crystal and linen place settings, and ever-so-attentive service. Such haute-cuisine specialties as chateaubriand (for two) with a rich béarnaise sauce, frogs' legs sautéed with garlic, butter, herbs, and white wine, and English fillet of sole with lemon butter and white wine head the menu. *1899 Mountain Rd., midway between village and mountain, tel. 802/253–7751. Reservations essential. AE, D, DC, MC, V.*

Moderate

Cactus Café

In an early 19th-century brick house, this Mexican restaurant does a good job of imitating a Southwestern pueblo, right down to the soiled patina on the walls and woodwork. It's a local favorite and can be a tad cacophonous at times, but if you like basic Mexican dishes, you'll find nachos, guacamole, enchiladas, and burritos. If you crave something a bit American, there are baby-back ribs, fresh stone crab, and chicken breast stuffed with roasted red pepper and goat-cheese boursin. *Mountain Rd., ½ mi outside village, tel. 802/253–7770. MC, V.*

Gracie's Restaurant

This place has a fun and funky feel to it, with its dog theme and casual and lively atmosphere. The decor features light butternut wood, with a large wooden bar off to the side of the dining area, and a blazing fireplace. The mainstay of the menu is the lineup of "Just Doggone Good Burgers." There are more than a dozen varieties offered, including the Chihuahua, with tomato and guacamole, and the Blazing Beagle, with spicy Cajun seasoning. There's also a strong lineup of fresh fish (swordfish, scrod, salmon, scallops, and shrimp), which can be broiled, char-grilled, Cajun spiced, or served with different sauces, and a wide array of steaks trimmed on the premises. The baked goods are also available for takeout. *Rte. 100, behind the Carlson Bldg. in Stowe Village Ctr., tel. 802/253–8741. Reservations essential for 6 or more. AE, MC, V.*

The Shed

If you haven't been to the Shed, you haven't been to Stowe—it's one of those Stowe institutions that seem to have been around forever. It opened in 1965, but the original building dates from the 1830s. Old barn timbers are still evident in the bar, and there's also an atrium filled with knotty pine, skylights, and plants. The menu offers something for everyone: seafood strudel, country chicken stew, surf and turf, scallops with spinach, lamb with bourbon sauce, a varied array of burgers, and innovative salads. The original bar next door serves the same food, and it's usually less crowded, with a microbrewery offering golden to dark mountain ales. *1859 Mountain Rd., tel. 802/253–4364. Reservations essential. AE, D, MC, V.*

Whip Bar and Grill

Authentic early 19th-century decor is the name of the game here. The restaurant has been decorated along a tack-room theme, with a remarkable collection of buggy whips aligned to form a partition between the bar and the dining room. The walls are covered with a rich dark green Scottish plaid and accented by wood trim, carriage lamps, and 19th-century horse prints in gilt frames. The menu offers upscale pub food, with sandwiches, soups and salads, shepherd's pie, steaks, ribs, burgers, and trout, and even tofu-vegetable stir-fry. *Green Mountain Inn, Main St., tel. 802/253–7301. AE, D, MC, V.*

Inexpensive

Depot Street Malt Shoppe

At this 1950s-type diner you'll find burgers (try the La Bamba with chili and cheese), hot turkey and roast beef sandwiches, cherry cokes, ice cream, and egg creams. *57 Depot St., next to post office, Stowe Village, tel. 802/253–4269. No credit cards.*

Moonman Pizza

When you're too beat to go out, call Moonman. They'll deliver to your condo, hotel, or RV. The pizza is highly regarded by those in the know, and salads, pasta dishes, subs, and calzones are also available. You can also eat in the restaurant. *Stoware Common, Rte. 100, Lower Stowe Village, tel. 802/253–8931. No credit cards.*

Mr. Pickwick's Restaurant

From bangers and mash to wild boar, Britannia rules through and through at this antiques-filled, dimly lighted pub amid authentic brass-, copper-, and stonework. Other Brit favorites, served with astonishing authenticity, include fish-and-chips, beef Wellington, and Cornish pasty. There is also entertainment, including a resident table-side magician. If you're not a beer lover, try one of the Australian wines. *Ye Olde England Inn, Mountain Rd., ½ mi from village, tel. 802/253–7064. AE, D, DC, MC, V.*

Olives Bistro

This intimate restaurant is just the place for Mediterranean cuisine. Candlelight, linen settings, and tasteful burgundy-and-green tones set the atmosphere. Consider Greek lasagna, with layers of spinach, onion, feta cheese, olives, pine nuts, tomatoes, ricotta, and mozzarella; or a pan-seared sea bass topped with sautéed red and green bell peppers; or shrimp sautéed with sun-dried tomatoes, artichoke hearts, and kalamata olives, served on tomato and basil linguine. *Mountain Rd., Stowe Ctr. Complex, tel. 802/253–2033. AE, D, DC, MC, V.*

Best Bets for Breakfast

Midway Café and Bakery
This is a good, convenient location to grab breakfast at the mountain. It has a large selection of freshly baked croissants, muffins, and pastries. *Next to gondola at main base area, tel. 802/253–3000. AE, MC, V.*

Mother's Village Deli
This homey breakfast nook lives up to its name with its lace curtains and Cape Cod blue walls, not to mention the baked goods—fresh-baked muffins, pastries (try the cinnamon twist), sweet breads, and fresh bagels. You'll also find the best cappuccino and coffee in town. *Depot Bldg., Main St., Stowe Village, tel. 802/253–9044. MC.*

NIGHTLIFE AND ENTERTAINMENT
Après-Ski

Broken Ski Tavern
Conveniently located at the bottom of the Toll Road Run, the Broken Ski is also the first après-ski stop on Mountain Road as you head for the village. It's a classic, woodsy Vermont tavern offering a wide selection of beers, with a blazing fire, a pool table, a jukebox, and an antique popcorn

maker. *Inn at the Mountain, tel. 802/253–3000. AE, D, DC, MC, V.*

Jose's Cantina
This is a must after the last run, especially if you are skiing from the main base lodge area. It's loud, bustling, and filled with après-ski energy. There's music and a full Mexican menu. *Main base lodge area, next to gondola, tel. 802/253–3000. AE, D, DC, MC, V.*

Loud and Lively/Dancing

Bert's Place
Here you'll find a true mix of Stowe visitors and natives. The perfect place to meet, eat, drink, and play, it has the usual Vermont old-building feel. Beneath the exposed beams and ample lighting, you can play pool while choosing your favorite hits on the jukebox. There is, of course, a wide variety of hard spirits and beer, including two Vermont brews on tap (that change regularly), and light fare. *Mountain Rd., tel. 802/253–6071.*

More Mellow

Mr. Pickwick's Polo Pub
It's all Brit pub stuff: lots of dark and mysterious ales, stouts, and lagers (more than 150 kinds), a vast selection of port and Australian wines, good-natured barmaid banter, and the requisite dart boards. Local blues and jazz bands perform as well. *Ye Olde England Inn, Mountain Rd., ½ mile from village, tel. 802/253–7064. AE, D, DC, MC, V.*

STRATTON MOUNTAIN RESORT

R.R. 1, Box 145
Stratton Mountain, VT 05155
Tel. 802/297–2200 or
800/787–2886
www.stratton.com

STATISTICALLY SPEAKING

Base elevation: 1,872 feet

Summit elevation: 3,875 feet

Vertical drop: 2,003 feet

Skiable terrain: 583 acres

Number of trails: 90 (90 acres of glades, 10 terrain parks on existing trails)

Longest run: 3 miles

Lifts and capacity: 1 gondola, 1 high-speed 6, 4 quads, 1 triple, 3 doubles, 2 surface; 21,020 skiers per hour

Daily lift ticket: $48 weekdays; $52 weekends

Average annual snowfall: 190 inches

Number of skiing days 1997–98: 172

Snowmaking: 85% of terrain

Terrain mix: N 35%; I 37%; E 28%

Snowboarding: yes (snowboard park)

Stratton Mountain opened to skiers in December 1961 with 7 miles of trails, two lower lifts, and one upper lift. It was designed as a destination resort, not a drive-in/drive-out ski area. It wasn't until the mid-'80s that ground for the master plan was finally broken and the centerpiece of the resort—the Stratton Village Square—took shape at the base of Stratton Mountain. The winding, street-lamped shopping arcade, with its chic boutiques, four-level parking garage, Stratton Village Lodge, and more than a hundred villas, is now the hub of Stratton's off-slopes action.

Top-quality instruction has been a Stratton hallmark just about from the start. In the '60s Emo Henrich was hired as director of the resort's ski school, and since then his name has become almost synonymous with Stratton Mountain. A native of Innsbruck, Austria, and an expert skier, Henrich had three rules: The ski school should concentrate on novice skiers with the goal of getting them onto the lifts and trails as soon as possible; all instructors should ski and teach the same way; and there should be live music in the base lodge every day. Not long after Stratton's lifts began carrying skiers up the mountain, Tyrolean oompahs began to float through the base lodge. The musicians? Austrian ski instructors, of course. These singing ski experts still step out of their skis and pull on their lederhosen for après-ski at Grizzly's a few evenings every week.

Just as Emo Henrich brought music to Stratton, so Jake Burton Carpenter brought snowboarding. While working as a bartender by night, J.B.C. spent his daylight hours in Henrich's garage designing and building his boards. Under cover of darkness he'd hike the mountain for test runs. In 1983 Burton convinced Stratton's director of mountain operations to open the lifts and trails to snowboarders. Since 1985, Stratton's snowboard park has been the site of the U.S. Open Snowboarding Championships.

In the late 1990s, Stratton built a series of terrain parks and glades that add to the diversity of skiing and snowboarding possibilities on the mountain. Plans over the next 10 years include increasing snowmaking coverage to 100%, building a mountaintop

Children's services: day-care, instruction, tel. 802/297–4000 or 800/787–2886

Snow phone: tel. 802/297–4211

Police: tel. 802/254–2382

Hospital: Carlos Otis Medical Clinic, tel. 802/297–2300

Manchester Chamber of Commerce: tel. 802/362–2100

Taxi: Manchester, tel. 802/362–4118

Road Conditions: Vermont, tel. 800/429–7623

Towing: Coleman's Inc., tel. 802/297–1950

FIVE-STAR FAVORITES
Best run for vertical: Bear Down

Best run overall: Liftline

Best bar/nightclub: Red Fox Inn

Best hotel: Equinox

Best restaurant: Mistral's

restaurant, and creating more high-speed lifts, glades, and terrain parks.

HOW TO GET THERE

By Plane

Albany Airport, in Albany, New York, is 1½ hours away, and **Bradley International Airport,** in Hartford, Connecticut, is about 2½ hours away by car. (*See* Getting to Vermont Resorts, *above.*)

By Car

From New York City and points south, take I–87 (the New York Thruway) to Albany and I–787 to New York Route 7 east to the Vermont border, where it turns into Vermont Route 9. Follow it to Bennington and pick up U.S. 7 north to Manchester. Turn east onto Route 11 and then south onto Route 30 to Bondville, where you take Stratton Mountain Road (the access road) on the right. Alternatively, from New York City you can take I–95 east to I–91 in New Haven, Connecticut, and follow I–91 north past the Massachusetts Turnpike (on which you can connect from Boston) to Brattleboro, Vermont. Take Route 30 north 38 miles to Bondville and then follow Stratton Mountain Road 4 miles to the resort. New York City is 235 miles away, Albany 81.

By Bus

Vermont Transit (tel. 802/442–4808) has scheduled service from major centers into Manchester (25 miles away) or Brattleboro, Vermont (35 miles away), but nothing closer to the mountain.

By Train

Amtrak (tel. 800/872–7245) has scheduled service from major centers to Albany or Brattleboro.

GETTING AROUND

By Shuttle

Big white shuttle buses (tel. 802/297–2200) run a free service continuously from the parking lots to the skier drop-off area on the upper level of the parking garage. The wait is no longer than five minutes. A shuttle bus also runs about every half hour in a loop from the Stratton villas to the parking garage skier drop-off area.

By Car

If you're skiing Stratton just for the day and approaching the mountain on Route 30 from Bondville, park in the four-level garage. If it's full, try Lot 3 just across the road. Another option, especially on busy days, is Sun Bowl. Its parking lot is almost never full, and the walk to the lift is no more than 250 yards. If you're staying at the mountain, leave your car at your condo and take the shuttle bus.

THE SKIING

Stratton, at 3,875 feet, is the highest peak in southern Vermont. With 54 of its 90 trails falling into the intermediate/upper intermediate range and with many of these wide-open, relatively straight, fully groomed "supertrails," Stratton is definitely a cruiser's mountain. Stratton is also a one-mountain resort with no hidden ridges or peaks, so it's an easy place to get around. Its four areas are the Upper and Lower mountains on the main, north face, Snow Bowl to the west, and Sun Bowl to the east.

Although Sun Bowl has its own parking lot and base lodge, you can easily hop on the Sun Bowl quad and hightail it back across the mountain to the main base lodge. Sun Bowl is the place to be when it's cold or windy because it's the most sheltered section of the mountain. The Sun Bowl lift also stays open a half hour longer than the upper lifts (until 4 PM) during the early season (until late January); this means you can grab a last run on the gondola at 3:30 and still have time for one more run at Sun Bowl. If you're an intermediate skier, take Black Bear (from the summit) to the Sun Bowl Express, then hook up with the Sunriser Supertrail to the bottom of the lift. Experts can use any way down they like, but a nice penultimate run is Black Bear to the short, steep double-diamond upper Downeaster, which empties right into the Sun Bowl area. Only private lessons are offered at Sun Bowl, so if you are interested in group lessons (for kids or adults), or if you plan to use the resort's day care, head for the base lodge and the Stratton Mountain Ski School at the bottom of the main mountain.

Stratton's 12-passenger (if they squeeze) Summit gondola is the only bottom-to-top lift on the mountain, moving 2,400 skiers each hour. It's the most popular and most crowded, with the longest lift line, but even on the busiest days the wait is no more than 10 minutes. A good alternative if you want to ski the top of the mountain, especially on warm, sunny days, is to take the Tamarack lift to the bottom of Grizzly or to the North American quad. However, when it's cold and windy, there's no question that the eight-minute gondola ride is pure pleasure.

If you want to beat the crowds, buy your lift ticket and pick up rental equipment any time after 3 PM the day before at the information desk or at the Welcome Center, which is open 24 hours. Save money by buying multi-day tickets.

Novices

The Ski Learning Park, at the base of the lower mountain, was created in 1993 so beginners could learn to ski or snowboard without feeling intimidated by fast-moving objects. It has 45 acres of gentle terrain served by two surface lifts: Cub, a slow-moving platter, and Teddy Bear, a slow, low-to-the-ground handle tow, both of which allow you to keep your skis on the snow at all times. The boundaries of the park are clearly signposted to keep advanced skiers out. Inside the park is a terrain garden with a gentle bobsled run (the Flume) that has banked sides to teach the steering and pressuring movements of the turn; whale-shaped humps (Bear Backs) to encourage flexing, extending, and absorption (skills necessary to ski the moguls); and a 7-foot spiral tower (Treetops) for edging and giving a taste of the steeps. A special lower-priced ticket is good only for lifts inside the park.

The first step up from the park is to take one of three chairlifts: the Villager double (the shortest chairlift); the Tyrolienne double; or for a longer ride that drops you off at the top of Lower Tamarack, the Tamarack triple. They're all slow moving and easy to get on and off, and they lead to tame beginner trails such as Lower Tamarack, Mark's Run, Daniel Webster, and the glades Daniel's Web and Rosie O'Gladey, as well as to the short intermediate trails Duck Soup and Spillway.

To get a taste of Sun Bowl, too, try Lower Middlebrook and Churchill Downs, two of the sweetest beginner trails on the mountain. Both have an easy combination of very mild pitches and near flats meandering through a beautifully wooded setting—in short, a novice's delight. To reach Sun Bowl from the Ski Learning Park, take the Tamarack triple and ski down the long, gentle 91 to the base of the Sun Bowl quad.

If you're at the Sun Bowl and want to get back to the main mountain, it's easiest to take the Sun Bowl Access Trail to Way Home, past the Grizzly lift to Run Away, which leads directly to the top of the Ski Learning Park. From there take any of several lower mountain trails to the main base lodge.

Even a novice can ride the gondola and ski down from the top of the mountain. Begin on Mike's Way, a short trail (while you're here, check out some of the best views on the mountain) that leads to the East and West Meadows. The Meadows are two wide-open, side-by-side cruising trails separated by islands of trees. There are no steep pitches, sudden drops, or otherwise threatening obstacles along the way. If you're heading back to the gondola, take Lower Wanderer, a narrower but still peaceful run, right to the bottom. Following this route, you'll have skied the longest run on Stratton: 3 miles.

For a shorter run, cut from Meadows onto Drifter Link to Old Log Road back to the gondola. A third alternative for novices is to ski Meadows to Drifter Link, then take the Snow Bowl quad back to the summit. Skiing just the top two-thirds of Meadows is an especially nice way to capture the afternoon sun.

Intermediates

Stratton is an intermediate skier's dream. Virtually the whole upper mountain is a mix of wide, groomed cruising trails interspersed with some easy-to-avoid double-black-diamond runs. Many single-diamond advanced trails are perfect for high-intermediate skiers.

If you like making long, curving turns, take one of Stratton's super-trails: the Meadows (East and West), on Snow Bowl, and Kidderbrook and the Sunriser Supertrail, on Sun Bowl. The Sunriser Supertrail is Stratton's widest trail and can be skied many ways. As you're skiing down, hang to the left for some gentle bumps and a nice pitch on the bottom. If you want to cruise in and out among the trees, ski smack-dab down the middle. The Eclipse intermediate glade off to the left of the trail connects with Lower Downeaster for a sylvan run to the bottom.

Another classic Vermont trail for intermediates is the Drifter trio—Get My Drift, Upper Drifter, and Lower Drifter, in Snow Bowl—which you reach on the Snow Bowl quad. Snow does drift and collect on them, and gentle bumps may form, but the trails are wide enough to give you room to maneuver around the bumps if you're so inclined.

One of the most popular high-intermediate/advanced trails is Upper Standard, under the gondola. It's wide, with ungroomed bumps on one side only—the perfect trail if you want to practice in the bumps but don't want to commit to a double-diamond run with no option for bailout. You can also try the single-diamond Shred Wood Forest glade run just to the left of Upper Standard.

Running parallel to Upper Standard is North American, a single-diamond trail under the North American quad that's made just for show-offs. It's also the trail most often used for races.

The single-diamond Kidderbrook is a delight. A broad, expansive trail with surprising drops to keep you on your toes, it is pure fun. Lying on the easternmost shoulder of the mountain, it does pick up the wind, so you may want to avoid the Kidderbrook quad in cold weather.

Experts

There are six expert double-diamond trails spread out across the upper mountain. Bear Down and Free Fall can be reached from the summit or from the Kidderbrook quad, which also aims you for the new double-diamond Moon Dance Glade, off Polar Bear. Bear Down, at 3,000 feet, is the longest expert trail, so don't take it if you're not prepared to stay—once you're on it, there's no escape. The steepest bump run? The prize goes to World Cup; Upper Downeaster is a close second. World Cup is never groomed; the bumps spread from side to side and get really big; it can be seen from the Snow Bowl quad, so you can check out the action before you commit.

Be on the gondola when it opens and head to Kidderbrook for the first run of the day. Ride the Kidderbrook quad to ski Bear Down. Work your way to the Grizzly double and ski Tamarack to the North American quad. By this time you'll be ready for the banquet of bumps on Upper Spruce, Lower Slalom Glade, and finally, World Cup. After another run or two on single-diamond Liftline to rest the knees, you can take a break.

SNOWBOARDING

The Stratton Mountain Ski and Snowboarding School, next to the base lodge, provides daily snowboarding instruction. The resort has a state-of-the-art, 3,000-foot snowboard park full of hits, tabletops, spines, and elbows, a 380-foot half-pipe, and one of the biggest pipe dragons in the east. The park, conveniently lit for night riding, is home to a vintage 1939 diner with a deck, perfect for catching a bite or eyeing competition on the hill.

OTHER SNOW SPORTS

Stratton offers **ice-skating, snow-tubing,** moonlight **cross-country** tours to the Pearl Buck cabin, horse-drawn sleigh rides, and **skiboarding** (a cross between skiing and snow-boarding, involving the use of short, twin-tipped skis that move forward, backward, and in circles). Call 800/787–2886 for information.

NEARBY

Bromley Mountain (tel. 802/824–5522) caters to beginners and children, and for good reason: The accessible hill slopes gently and catches the sun most of the day.

WHERE TO STAY

There's some excellent lodging in and around the Stratton resort, mostly condominiums but also some very good hotels. All have the advantage of access to the lifts in the morning without getting into your car. If you prefer a luxury hotel, a small intimate lodge, a classic Vermont country inn, or a designer bed-and-breakfast, the surrounding area, particularly Manchester, is a better choice. All bookings can be made through **Stratton Central Reservations** (tel. 800/787–2886).

All guests at Stratton-operated accommodations have free access to the Stratton Sports Center, which has two indoor tennis courts, a 75-foot indoor pool, racquetball, aerobics, a fitness center with circuit training, a Jacuzzi, massages, and a steam room. Extra charges for certain services may apply. Some properties are individually owned and decorated, so although quality is consistent, styles vary.

Expensive

The Equinox

The historic, luxurious Equinox opened in 1769. Its white Federal and Greek Revival architecture sets the tone for the picturesque community of Manchester Village. Rooms and suites are decorated with sophisticated bleached-pine country-style furniture and muted colors accented by bedspreads and draperies in deeper colors. In the public areas are antiques such as grandfather clocks and writing desks. *Historic Rte. 7A, 17 mi from mountain, Manchester Village 05254, tel. 802/362–4700 or 800/362–4747, fax 802/362–4861. 144 rooms, 28 suites. Facilities: 2 restaurants, fitness center, health spa, indoor lap pool. AE, D, DC, MC, V. $179–$899.*

Ober Tal

These slope-side ski-in/ski-out one-bedroom units all have a wood-burning fieldstone fireplace, a complete kitchen, a washer-dryer, and a private deck. The units are comfortably decorated in a practical fashion, with Berber broadloom, big comfortable chairs and couches, and a nice blend of exposed brick and wood accents. There's a choice of one-bedroom or two-bedroom units. *Stratton Corp,*

Stratton Mountain Village, Stratton 05155, tel. 802/297–2200 or 800/ 787–2886, fax 802/297–2939. 50 units. AE, D, DC, MC, V. $90–$320.

Stratton Village Lodge
A California designer attempted to replicate an Austrian Alpine village here, but the result is more West Coast than Old World. This ski-in/ski-out lodge has units designed to accommodate four people comfortably. Each has a microwave, mini-refrigerator, sink, and coffeemaker. They are decorated in a modern New England style. All amenities at the Stratton Mountain Inn, just down the hill, are available to lodge guests. *Stratton Corp, Stratton Mountain Village, Stratton 05155, tel. 802/297–2260 or 800/777–1700, fax 802/297–1778. 90 units, 1 suite. AE, D, DC, MC, V. $99–$239.*

Village Watch
This five-story contemporary wooden condo complex comes with both mountain and valley views and has an elevator. The two-, three-, and four-bedroom condos are also ski-in/ski-out—they are between the Tamarack triple chairlift and the Village lift. Each unit has a complete kitchen, a fieldstone fireplace, and a sundeck. *Stratton Corp, Stratton Mountain Village, Stratton 05155, tel. 802/297–2200 or 800/727–2886, fax 802/297–2939. 35 units. AE, D, DC, MC, V. $130–$480.*

Moderate

Birkenhaus
This is the oldest inn on the mountain. The atmosphere is Old World Austrian—cathedral ceilings, stucco walls, and diagonal cedar paneling.

The rooms are spacious and bright, with traditional Austrian handcrafted wood furnishings, floral patterns on drapes and bed covers, and Tyrolean bric-a-brac. The hotel is within walking distance of Stratton Village and the slopes. *Middle Ridge Rd., Stratton 05155, tel. 802/297–2000, fax 802/ 297–2002. 17 rooms, 1 suite. Facilities: restaurant, fireplace lounge, bar. AE, D, MC, V. $69–$159.*

Liftline Lodge
The classic European-style chalet is directly across the access road from Stratton Village and the lifts. It has steep, sloping white stucco walls embracing sturdy timbers, paneling, and wrought-iron fixtures. The rooms are bright and white, with artfully placed wood accents, well-fashioned furnishings, and dark, richly colored carpets. Each unit has a fireplace, stove, refrigerator, and sink. *R.D. 1, Box 144, Stratton 05155, tel. 802/ 297–2600 or 800/597–5438, fax 802/ 297–2949. 80 rooms, 6 units. Facilities: restaurant, bar, café, 1 outdoor and 2 indoor hot tubs, 1 sauna, fireplace, living room, library, fitness center, game room, massage. AE, MC, V. $85–$275.*

Red Fox Inn
This inn and restaurant has quaint, homey rooms in an early 19th-century farmhouse. The decor is country Colonial style, with farming antiques and collectibles and sensible furnishings. *Winhall Hollow Rd., 1½ mi from access road, Bondville 05340, tel. 802/297–2488 or 800/870–2434, fax 802/297–2156. 8 rooms, 2 suites. Facilities: dining room, tavern, game room. AE. $85–$150.*

Stratton Mountain Inn

Just a short walk from shopping and slopes, this large full-service hotel has lots of amenities, from a 24-hour concierge to room service to a health spa. The decor is traditional New England, with exposed brick and beams. The rooms are modern and well maintained, with solid wood furnishings. *Middle Ridge Rd., Stratton 05155, tel. 802/297–2500 or 800/777–1700, fax 802/297–1778. 117 rooms, 3 suites. Facilities: 2 restaurants, bar, lounge, indoor and outdoor hot tubs, sauna, exercise area. AE, D, DC, MC, V. $79–$169.*

Three Mountain Inn

This 1790s country inn with fireplaces in the common rooms and some bedrooms integrates the feel and charm of the 18th century with modern conveniences. Rooms are in the main inn and next door at the early 19th-century Robinson House. The rooms are bright and comfortable, with chintz wallpaper, wooden sconces, ruffled curtains, and Colonial-style furnishings. *Rte. 30, Box 180, 10 mi south of Stratton, Jamaica 05343, tel. 802/874–4140, fax 802/874–4745. 16 rooms, 1 suite. Facilities: restaurant, pub. AE, MC, V. $110–$165, including full breakfast.*

Inexpensive

Haig's

This Early American–style lodge, opened in 1973, is a good deal. The rooms are large and well furnished in a thrifty, Yankee style. Most have a fireplace. One of the restaurants is a Black Angus steakhouse. *Rte. 30 at foot of Stratton Mountain Rd., Bondville 05340, tel. 802/297–1300 or 800/897–5894, fax 802/297–1301. 26 rooms, 3 suites. Facilities: 2 restaurants, sports bar, indoor golf course. AE, D, MC, V. $95–$150.*

Inn at Bear Creek

This practical, all-purpose hotel complex has large, clean, comfortable rooms in the hotel and upscale two- and three-bedroom condo units with kitchens. There is a two-night minimum for the condos. *Rte. 30, 4 mi south of Stratton, Rawsonville 05155, tel. 802/297–1700, fax 802/297–1701. 18 rooms, 20 units. Facilities: restaurant, lounge, shuttle. AE, MC, V. $59–$350.*

WHERE TO EAT

There's a variety of interesting dining establishments in and around nearby Bondville and Manchester, and it's worth the drive to experience them. There are also a number of solid if not spectacular eateries at the resort.

Expensive

The Colonnade

The dining room of the Equinox Hotel is named for the hotel's architectural claim to fame—the more than 285 feet of fluted columns added to the front in 1839. The restaurant has a hand-painted and -stenciled vaulted ceiling, crystal chandeliers, detailed floral rugs, starched white linen tablecloths, and richly colored velvet and brocade drapes. Dinner includes such classic Vermont dishes as maple-mustard-glazed lamb chops on roasted shallot wild rice or apple-roasted pheasant with wild rice and fresh berries. *Equinox, Manchester Village, tel. 802/362–4700 or 800/362–4747. Reservations essential. AE, D, DC, MC, V. No lunch.*

Mistral's
In the woods and on the way to Manchester from the mountain, this low-key, chef-owned restaurant overlooks a stream. The fresh, understated country French feel of the two dining rooms is reflected in a menu that offers such dishes as sautéed native trout stuffed with scallop mousse and medallions of venison with sauce *au poivre,* accompanied by wines from an award-winning list. *Toll Gate Rd. off Rtes. 11 and 30, Manchester, tel. 802/ 362–1779. Reservations essential. AE, D, DC, MC, V. Closed Wed.*

Ye Old Tavern
Stepping through the yellow-and-white Federal and Greek Revival facade into this roadside inn is like stepping into a museum; parts date to 1760. The tavern serves lunch daily by the blazing hearth. The two adjacent dining rooms, open for dinner, offer such traditional American standbys as duck with blackberry sauce, lamb with cranberry-orange sauce, and salmon hollandaise. *214 N. Main St., Manchester Center, tel. 802/362–0611. Reservations essential. AE, MC, V.*

Moderate
Haig's
The dining room is bright, airy, and bustling, with two levels, a wall of glass, and hanging plants. It offers a complete salad bar and such basic entrées as surf and turf, barbecued chicken, lasagna, and baby-back ribs. Black Angus steak is the highlight of the menu. *Rte. 30, Bondville, tel. 802/ 297–1300. AE, D, MC, V.*

Laney's
An antique two-wheeler presides over the dining room, and the bar bristles with vintage sports equipment. Owner Laney Davis's collection of posters, famous caricatures, and other memorabilia decorates the walls, while an old player piano tinkles in the background. The emphasis is on quality and freshness, from the homemade bread to the barbecue ribs to the selection of pizzas. The portions are enormous and the atmosphere is 1,000-watt fun. *Rtes. 11 and 30, Manchester Center, tel. 802/362–4456. Reservations essential. AE, D, DC, MC, V.*

River Café
The restaurant has a beautiful view of the Winhall River, as well as hand-blown lamps, fresh flowers, and antique furniture. Italian specialties include seafood *possillipo* (clams, mussels, and other seasonal sea fare in marinara sauce) and veal *piccata* (sautéed in white wine with lemon, capers, artichoke hearts, and cream), as well as St. Louis-style spareribs and linguine with fresh whole clams. *Rte. 30, foot of access road, Bondville, tel. 802/297–1010. MC, V.*

Three Mountain Inn
The food served in this 18th-century inn's two fireplace-warmed dining rooms is well worth the drive. It's traditional New England, with homemade breads, salad dressings, and soups; filet mignon, fresh fish, venison, and chicken; and a fine selection of wines. *Rte. 30, 6 mi south of mountain, Jamaica, tel. 802/874–4140. Reservations essential. AE, D, MC, V.*

Inexpensive
Mulberry St.
For pasta, pizza, and other Italian specialties in Stratton Village, try this simple restaurant with a sports bar

next door. You can order take-out as well. *S. Village Sq., Stratton, tel. 802/297–3065. AE, DC, MC, V.*

Partridge in a Pantry
Amid charming antiques and miscellaneous cow paraphernalia, there's no shortage of great sandwiches, salads, soups, wine, beer, and cheeses at this deli and gourmet shop. Call in your lunch order in the morning, and just pop in during the noon rush for a quick pickup. *Village Sq., Stratton, tel. 802/297–9850. AE, MC, V.*

Best Bets for Breakfast
Double Diamond Café
This place serves the best coffee (in all its variations) in the area, plus a wide choice of muffins. *Village Square, Stratton, tel. 802/297–3431.*

Sage Hill
You can start the day with a generous buffet breakfast in a large, airy room with a window wall overlooking the valley. *Stratton Mountain Inn, Middle Ridge Rd., Stratton, tel. 802/297–2500. AE, D, DC, MC, V.*

NIGHTLIFE AND ENTERTAINMENT
Après-Ski
Grizzly's
There's live entertainment, dancing, free munchies, and a lot of strutting in a highly charged atmosphere. *Stratton base lodge, tel. 802/297–0012. AE, D, DC, MC, V.*

Mulligans
This is the heart of off-slope fun and frivolity in Stratton Village. You can't miss the moose sporting a derby, who hangs over the fireplace, the imperial elk trophy on the wall, and the black bears (all stuffed) in the rafters. There's good bar food, too. *Village Square, Stratton, tel. 802/297–9293. AE, MC, V.*

Loud and Lively/Dancing
Haig's
This is where you'll find the hottest rock and dance music in the area, usually with a younger crowd. Deejay-driven and video-enhanced, the place sends the crowd to the dance floor in droves. *Rte. 30, Bondville, tel. 802/297–1300. AE, D, MC, V.*

More Mellow
Taverne
This Colonial tavern has a great stand-up bar, a fireplace, and a billiards table, all fostering its warm and laid-back atmosphere. *Stratton Mountain Inn, Middle Ridge Rd., Stratton, tel. 802/297–2500. AE, D, DC, MC, V.*

SUGARBUSH RESORT

SUGARBUSH RESORT

R.R. 1, Box 350
Warren, VT 05674-9500
Tel. 802/583–2381 or
800/537–8427
www.sugarbush.com

STATISTICALLY SPEAKING

Base elevation: 1,535 feet

Summit elevation: 4,135 feet

Vertical drop: 2,650 feet

Skiable terrain: 432 acres

Number of trails: 112

Longest run: 2½ miles

Lifts and capacity: 7 quad
chairs (4 high-speed),
3 triples, 4 doubles, 4 surface
lifts; 24,363 skiers per hour

Daily lift ticket: $52

Average annual snowfall: 350
inches

Number of skiing days
1997–98: 201

Snowmaking: 285.5 acres;
67%

Terrain mix: N 22%, I 46%,
E 32%

Snowboarding: yes

Sugarbush opened for business on Christmas Day 1958, when a lift ticket cost $5.50 and the three employees rotated between selling tickets, tending bar, and washing dishes. There were one mountain, a gondola, a poma lift, and 10 trails. Since then a number of owners have come and gone at the Mad River Valley resort. So have the celebrities—the Kennedys and author Gay Talese, among others. The glitz and glitter inspired the nickname Mascara Mountain.

Having overwhelmed neighboring Glen Ellen, Sugarbush now is two mountains—North and South. Currently under the aegis of Les Otten's American Skiing Company, it is the state of the art among American ski resorts, with a focus squarely on the quality of the skiing. In place of the gondola are 18 chairlifts, including four high-speed detachable quads—one of which swings high above the valley between South and North. Snowmaking covers more than half the resort, with plans for 80% coverage.

The original Sugarbush, now known as Sugarbush South, has formidable steeps toward the top and in front of the main base lodge, with a vertical of 2,400 feet. Sugarbush North, off Mt. Ellen, offers what South has in short supply—beginner runs. North also has steep fall-line pitches and intermediate cruisers off its 2,600 vertical feet.

Accommodations mountainside and in the surrounding valley and such towns as Warren and Waitsfield range from deluxe hostelries and inns to low-budget ski dorms. Sugarbush Village, near the base of South (the original Sugarbush), is where the ski school, the restaurants, and the shops are. Nearby is the Sugarbush Sports Center, which has posh indoor and outdoor pools, a Jacuzzi, indoor tennis courts, a fitness center, massage, a sauna, and a games room (all free to guests at Sugarbush Resort lodgings). The resort's new Winter Wonderland area offers fondue dinners and a coffee bar, snowshoeing, horse-drawn sleigh rides, night-lighted skating, and snowtubing. A car is a must.

HOW TO GET THERE

By Plane

Burlington International Airport is 45 minutes from the resort (*see* Getting to Vermont Resorts, *above*).

Area code: 802

Children's services: day-care, instruction, tel. 802/583–2385, ext. 378

Snow phone: tel. 802/583–7669

Police: tel. 802/496–2262

Medical center: Mad River Valley Health Center, Waitsfield, tel. 802/496–3838

Hospital: Central Vermont Hospital, Barre, tel. 802/229–9121

Chamber of Commerce: tel. 802/496–3409

Resort association: tel. 802/583–2301

Taxi: Morf Transit, tel. 802/864–5588

Road conditions: tel. 800/429–7623

Towing: Hap's service station, tel. 802/496–3948

FIVE-STAR FAVORITES

Best run for vertical: FIS and Lower FIS

Best run overall: Organgrinder

Best bar/nightclub: Mad Mountain Tavern

Best hotel: Sugarbush Inn

Best restaurant: Common Man

By Car

From Burlington take I–89 south to Exit 10 (Waterbury), then Route 2 east to Route 100 south to the Sugarbush Access Road. From New Hampshire, Connecticut, Massachusetts, and New York, take I–89 north to Exit 9 (Middlesex), then Route 2 east for a half mile to Route 100B south to Route 100 south to the Sugarbush Access Road.

By Train

Daily **Amtrak** (tel. 800/872–7245) service is available to Waterbury, Vermont, which is just a 20-minute drive from the resort. Shuttle service or rental-car pickups are available in Waterbury.

THE SKIING

Bowl-shaped South is the expert's expert mountain that also has great beginner trails. Nine lifts—three triples, four doubles, and two surface—serve the mountain. The trails in the Castlerock area, accessed from the Lincoln Peak base area on the south side of the mountain, are among New England's most challenging expert runs. Counterpoint to these narrow steeps are some good, wide intermediate cruisers such as Glades and Snowball.

North is 4,135 feet at the summit of Mt. Ellen, the highest peak in the Green Mountain National Forest. It is the cruiser mountain; the intermediate runs at North are generally wider. North is served by seven lifts—one high-speed quad, two quads, two doubles, and two surface lifts.

Trails on the two mountains are now connected by a high-speed quad that's strung high above a valley. Drop a ski pole, and it's gone forever—and watch out for frostbite when it's chilly. To get from one to the other, you can also take a shuttle bus. North (true to its name) is north-facing, so the sun hits the trails early and leaves early. South stays sunnier longer during the day. If it's a powder day, however, South is the place to get the first chair for fresh tracks on rock.

Novices

South offers a learning area not intruded on by other lift systems. Here, never-evers are able to go from walking to taking the poma lift for a try down a low-pitched hill appropriately named First Time. The Village chair takes you to the wide Easy Rider. The third lift in the beginner's trilogy is Gate House Express, which takes you to Pushover, where you can let those muscles talk, and perhaps to a first blue-square run down Slow Poke.

On North, first-time skiers take the ski-school chair, Sunshine Double, to runs like East Street and Graduation; both trails are great if you're still finding your edge but looking for more variety. With a diploma you can head up the superquad Green Mountain, for a run down the winding Northstar Trail.

Intermediates

It gets busy on the central corridor of South, accessed via the Sugar Bravo Express high-speed detachable quad. Most people take the quad to get to the center of the mountain. Use it between 10 and noon and then after 1:30. Try heading to the Valley House Base Lodge and concentrating on the two lifts to your left, Valley House and Spring Fling. These provide access to blue-square terrain like Snowball, Lower Snowball, Spring Fling (half groomed, half bumped), and Moonshine. Take Reverse Traverse, off Snowball, and ski Murphy's Glade, which brings you back to the bottom of Sugar Bravo. Lower intermediates can start on the trails from the Gate House Express. You'll also find lower intermediate trails off the Valley House chair. The Heaven's Gate triple reaches the summit of one of the four peaks at South: Lincoln Peak. Jester snakes down from the top of Heaven's Gate and provides access to

the center of the hill via Birdland or Lower Jester. For a winding run 2½ miles down, take Jester to Snowball. At North the main corridor is along the Green Mountain quad. Ride it early to the Summit Quad, which brings you to the top of Mt. Ellen, and ski Panorama to either the wide Elbow or the slinky Lower Rim Run. The North Ridge Express also gets you to Elbow (which can become crowded) but provides access to Cruiser, another wide-open trail, and Which Way, the site of Fat Bob, one of Sugarbush's snowboard parks. Sneak over to Inverness via Northway for some time on Brambles, Inverness, and Semi-Tough. If you want to try bumps go to the Cliffs, at the lower end of the black-diamond scale.

Experts

Extreme skiers traditionally head to the Castlerock double chair. Respect the people who are there, and if you're not an expert, don't even think about it. Trails in this area were cut to the natural contours not bulldozed, and this fast and undulating terrain demands concentration and skill. Chutes and narrow spots like Rumble, only 15–20 feet wide, challenge speed lovers. The Valley House chair goes above the Mall, where exhibitionists showboat, to the narrow double-diamond Stein's Run. Paradise (which goes through a tree-speckled bowl) and Spillsville are narrow tests from the Heaven's Gate triple. Organgrinder drops 2,400 feet from top to bottom along the old gondola line. Toward the bottom, advanced intermediate skiers can handle it.

At North, double-diamond Black Diamond is steep and narrow, and Exterminator is wider, with Volkswagen-size bumps. People line up at the top of FIS to tackle the moguls on this short, wide, steep pitch. At the bottom, where it meets Rim Run, another set of skiers congregates to watch and eavesdrop on the expletives of those who have just made it down. Tumbler and Hammerhead leave no room for bailing out. Advanced intermediate skiers might want to try Encore, under North Ridge, where the consistent pitch leaves some room to recover and the bumps are negotiable.

Between South and North is Slide Brook Basin—2,000 acres between Lincoln and Mt. Ellen—where 1½-mile-long trails wiggle down 1,600 vertical feet of completely natural double-black-diamond terrain with completely natural snow cover. These trails are open only to tours, with two guides per eight skiers, but it's the kind of wilderness skiing that's not often available in the East.

SNOWBOARDING

Sugarbush has its own pipe dragon and a staff snowboard coordinator to direct board terrain maintenance and oversee snowboard events. In 1999, Sugarbush debuted its new Mountain Range snowpark at the top of the Gatehouse Express, which joins Godzilla and Fat Bob snowparks on Mount Ellen. The high elevation of Mountain Range allows it to open earlier in the season so you can get right into its gap jumps, tabletops, spines, and half-pipe. In Slow Poke Park, on South, a learning snowpark that has less threatening obstacles,

there is a snowboard development program. Snowboarding on a smaller scale is scattered around the resort at miniparks and playgrounds, which are reconfigured as the season goes on.

OTHER SNOW SPORTS

There is **snowshoeing, cross-country skiing,** and **snowmobiling** at Winter Wonderland. Lincon Peak base offers **snowtubing**; at Slide Brook Wilderness you can go **snowshoeing and touring**; and there is **ice-skating** at the Sugarbush Health and Racquet Club. For information or to make reservations for any of these activities, call 800/537–8427.

NEARBY

Just around the bend from Sugarbush lies one of the bastions of American skiing: **Mad River Glen** (tel. 802/496–3551). The bumper sticker reads "Mad River Glen. Ski It If You Can." And they're not joking. Refusing groomed slopes and bowing in reverence to their old single-person chairlift, Mad River Glen lovers are a breed of their own.

WHERE TO STAY

There are more than 6,600 beds in the area, most in condos and inns.

Expensive

Bridges Family Resort and Tennis Club

These are the best condos in the area, very well maintained and managed. The privately owned one-, two-, and three-bedroom-with-loft units with white wooden exteriors come in six different floor plans. Decor and design vary from unit to unit, but all are spacious and bright, with lots of windows and complete kitchens, fireplaces, and decks. It's about a half mile from the village center. *Sugarbush Access Rd., Warren 05674, tel. 802/583–2922 or 800/453–2922, fax 802/583–1018. 100 units. Facilities: indoor pool, outdoor hot tub, sauna, 2 indoor tennis courts, fitness center, recreation room. AE, MC, V. $175–$350.*

Inn at the Round Barn Farm
A unique B&B away from the hustle and bustle of the Sugarbush Access Road, this early 19th-century farm complex created around a round barn offers luxurious rooms with antiques, fireplaces, and views. On a frosty January night you'll appreciate the down comforter on your bed. *R.R. 1, Box 247, E. Warren Rd., Waitsfield 05673, tel. 802/496–2276 or 800/537–8427, fax 802/496–8832. 11 rooms. Facilities: indoor lap pool, game room, ski storage. AE, MC, V. $115–$220.*

Sugarbush Village
When snow conditions are right, you can ski into and walk/ski out from most of the several hundred condos that make up Sugarbush Village (managed by two companies). All privately owned and decorated, they range in size from one-bedroom suites to four-bedroom villas. They all have a complete kitchen, many have a fireplace, and most have other standard creature comforts such as a washer/dryer, a sauna, or a Jacuzzi. *Sugarbush Village Association, R.R. 1, Box 68–12, Warren 05674, tel. 802/583–3000 or 800/451–4326, fax 802/583–2373. 155 units. AE, D, DC, MC, V. $80–$535. Sugarbush Resort, R.R.*

1, Box 350, Warren 05674, tel. 802/583–3333 or 800/537–8427, fax 802/583–2301. 200 units. AE, D, DC, MC, V. $140–$520.

Moderate
1824 House Inn
Listed on the National Historic Register, this white house is noticeable for its 10 gables and traditional big-house, little-house New England ramble. The rooms all have private baths, and the kitchen serves as a focal point, where you can sip wine, sample food, or rub the backs of the two house dogs and the cat. The 22 acres of woodland and hillside pasture provide plenty of opportunity for wild sledding and cross-country skiing. *Rte. 100, Box 159, Waitsfield 05673, tel. 802/496–7555, fax 802/496–7558. 7 rooms. AE, D, MC, V. $100–$140.*

Mad River Inn
This bed-and-breakfast in a renovated wooden farmhouse with a slate roof has a Victorian interior that's well organized although a bit overdone with dust ruffles, lace, and Laura Ashley. The rooms, however, are comfortable, individually decorated, and come with antique featherbeds. *Tremblay Rd., Box 75, off Rte. 100, Waitsfield 05673, tel. 802/496–7900, fax 802/496–5390. 10 rooms. Facilities: outdoor hot tub, library with fireplace, lounge, pool table. AE, MC, V. $69–$125.*

Millbrook Inn
This blue Cape-style farmhouse with white trim has wide, worn pine plank floors in its entrance. The rooms, all with private baths, are individually decorated with period furniture and

subtle finishing touches, such as hand stenciling, antique objets d'art, and handmade quilts. The hearty breakfast and dinner in the great dining room are well worth the cost of the MAP. *Rte. 17 (533 McCullough Highway), Box 62, Waitsfield 05673, tel. 802/496–2405 or 800/477–2809, fax 802/496–9735. 7 rooms. Facilities: restaurant. AE, DC, MC, V. $50–$70 per person, including MAP.*

Sugarbush Inn
This charming yellow inn with pillars and white trim is the accommodations flagship for the area—the only true full-service hotel. It has a great sitting room that's formal but comfortable, with a fireplace and a cozy library. The rooms are decorated with floral-print wall coverings, matching quilts, and first-rate antique reproductions. *R.R. 1, Box 350, Warren 05674, tel. 802/583–2301 or 800/537–8427, fax 802/583–3209. 46 rooms. Facilities: 2 restaurants. AE, D, DC, MC, V. $115–$180.*

Inexpensive

Hyde Away
This family-friendly renovated farmstead with red tin roofs offers rooms ranging from quaint and romantic with a private bath to bunk rooms with shared baths, which surround this 1832 Greek Revival farmhouse-turned-B&B, painted gray with red and green trim. Inside, rooms are countrified and antique, with period wallpaper, hand-me-down collectibles, and the odd shapes and corners that century-old buildings tend to have. There are horses here on the farm, and sleigh rides are available. *Rte. 100, Box 563, Waitsfield 05673,*

tel. 802/496–4949. 13 rooms. Facilities: restaurant, sleigh rides. MC, V. $60–$125.

Tucker Hill Lodge
Rooms in this blue clapboard hillside inn are simple, clean, and cozy. The mountain-cabin charm is evident throughout the inn—from the knotty-pine living room with its fieldstone fireplace through its two dining rooms to the cute and cuddly couch by the basement fireplace. *R.R. 1, Box 147, Waitsfield 05673, tel. 802/496–3983 or 800/543–7841, fax 802/496–3203. 21 rooms. Facilities: restaurant, lounge. AE, MC, V. $70–$130, including full breakfast.*

Waitsfield Inn
This 1825 inn in bustling downtown Waitsfield is within walking distance from shops, restaurants, and nightspots. It's done in Federal style, with ornate woodwork and lots of country antiques. *Box 969, Waitsfield 05673, tel. 802/496–3979. 14 rooms. AE, MC, V. $79–$129, including full breakfast.*

WHERE TO EAT
There are a number of good restaurants in and around the Sugarbush village area, plus a larger selection on the road between the resort and Waitsfield.

Expensive

Chez Henri
The restaurant, bistro, and nightspot is slope-side on the edge of the Sugarbush Village, which means you can ski in for a stylish lunch, brunch, or après-ski meal. This romantic little French restaurant with a fireplace and white marble bar offers such lunch specials as cheese fondue or Cajun

calamari. For dinner there may be frogs' legs or rabbit in red wine sauce or a scrumptious bouillabaisse. *Village at Sugarbush, base of ski area, tel. 802/583–2600. Reservations essential. AE, D, DC, MC, V.*

Common Man

Just off the Sugarbush Access Road is a quaint dining emporium situated in a mid-19th-century barn that was moved and reconstructed here in 1987. The atmosphere at Common Man is casual, but the fare is not so common. The candlelighted table settings, the crystal chandeliers, and the large fieldstone fireplace are a fit setting for the presentation of such dishes as fillets of trout steamed in parchment paper or medallions of beef tenderloin. *German Flats Rd., Warren, tel. 802/583–2800. AE, D, MC, V.*

Tucker Hill Inn

There's an understated Vermont style to this restaurant with a skylighted terrace section. One of the culinary centerpieces of the Sugarbush area, it has wonderful ways with Atlantic salmon, wood-grilled swordfish, and Long Island duckling. *Rte. 17, Waitsfield, tel. 802/496–3983. AE, MC, V.*

Warren House

Dark wood, plants, wood-burning stoves, and white tablecloths with forest-green napkins set the stage here for the eclectic contemporary American cuisine: tender cuts of steak, unique pastas, and fresh seafood. Despite the elaborate menu, the place is casual enough for children. *Sugarbush Access Rd., Warren, tel. 802/583–2421. Reservations essential. AE, DC, MC, V.*

Moderate

American Flatbread Kitchen

In the barn complex at the Lareau Farm Country Inn you can get what is known as Pizza with Integrity, baked on native Vermont soapstone inside a low, wide, hardwood-fired earthen oven. The dining room is rustic, with wide-plank floors and walls and a wood-burning stove. You can expect such creative toppings as their Medicine Wheel tomato sauce with onions, mushrooms, cheese, and herbs. *Lareau Farm Country Inn, Rte. 100, Waitsfield, tel. 802/496–8856. MC, V.*

Bass Restaurant

Right on the Sugarbush Access Road, this eclectic 1959 building originally designed for theatrical presentations today offers three separate levels for dining. The restaurant's central focus is a massive circular fieldstone hearth vented through a large brass-and-iron cone chimney. The cuisine is American with a hint of the Mediterranean; try the New England fisherman's stew, which includes lobster, shrimp, scallops, and black mussels in an herb-infused tomato broth. *Sugarbush Access Rd., Warren, tel. 802/583–3100. No lunch. AE, D, MC, V.*

China Moon

This takeout restaurant offers Cantonese, Mandarin, Szechuan, and Hunan dishes as well as such nontraditional choices as lobster with spicy Szechuan sauce that capture not only your eye but also your palate. *Sugarbush Village, Warren, tel. 802/583–1024. AE, MC, V.*

The Den

A giant old bank safe is on the right as you enter this ever-so-popular eatery near Waitsfield Center. The main dining room is full of knotty pine, with a scattering of booths and tables. Lunches of burgers, pork chops, and sandwiches such as grilled avocado and cheese are offered. The local dinner favorites are the Texas rib appetizer and the steaks. *Rtes. 100 and 17, Waitsfield, tel. 802/496–8880. AE, MC, V.*

Murph's Steakhouse

Named for Sugarbush founder Jack Murphy, Murph's has true family dining, with steak and fresh seafood as the specialties. The ambience is created by thick, dark tables and pine board floors. Outside the window stands Sugarbush's giant holiday tree. *Sugarbush Village, Waitsfield. tel. 802/583–6861. AE, D, MC, V.*

Inexpensive

Grill Down Under

The grill is the central and highly visible component of this warm and friendly brick-and-wood bistro. The lighting is subdued, and small table groupings give a sense of intimacy. On the menu you'll find everything from plain grilled burgers, chops, and fish to dishes with interesting flourishes like a mustard-maple-syrup topping or lime-cilantro butter. *Sugarbush Inn, Warren, tel. 802/583–2301. No lunch. AE, D, DC, MC, V.*

Hyde Away Restaurant

This Route 17 restaurant is comfortable and casual, with a woodstove, lots of plants, and a menu that ranges from nachos and pasta to tuna, steak, and prime rib. *Rte. 17, Waitsfield, tel. 802/496–2322. AE, MC, V.*

Jay's Restaurant and Pizzeria

In this comfortable local hangout, with oak tables, plants, and an eclectic array of original local art, you can get a great deal on wholesome fare. Chicken comes Southern-fried, parmigiana style, or sautéed with artichokes, mushrooms, and white wine. Or you could go for sautéed pork medallions, stir-fried duck, swordfish puttanesca, fish-and-chips, pizza, buffalo wings, or T-bone steak. The lasagna is excellent. *Mad River Green Shopping Center, Rte. 100, Waitsfield, tel. 802/496–8282. MC, V.*

Miguel's

At the area's only Mexican restaurant, you'll find your favorite authentic south-of-the-border fare among cantina-style stucco and beams, bright posters, and wall hangings. Fajitas, tacos, and enchiladas are on the lineup—with a wickedly hot salsa—along with an interesting chicken breast stuffed with cornbread and pecans and a delicious vegetarian chili. *Sugarbush Access Rd., Warren, tel. 802/583–3858. AE, MC, V.*

Best Bet for Breakfast

Little Grocery and Deli

This takeout emporium with a counter offers a selection of ham, egg, and cheese combos on a choice of English muffin, bagel, biscuit, or croissant. The excellent home-baked muffins come in a variety of flavors. *Sugarbush Access Rd., Warren, tel. 802/583–2757. MC, V.*

NIGHTLIFE AND ENTERTAINMENT
Après-Ski

Green Mountain Lounge
This rustic ski-in/ski-out bar overlooking the mountains has high vaulted ceilings, a fireplace, and a huge deck. On weekends and holidays there is live music. *Sugarbush North Base Lodge, Warren, tel. 802/583–2381, ext. 464. AE, D, DC, MC, V.*

Wunderbar
This modern three-room bar has wooden shutters and a large mural of the local towns. There is live music on weekends, anything from Rockabilly bands to solo guitarists. *Valley House Base Lodge South, Warren, tel. 802/ 583–2381, ext. 464. AE, D, DC, MC, V.*

Loud and Lively/Dancing

Blue Tooth
Built in 1963 to resemble a Vermont sugar house, the Blue Tooth boasts the longest bar in the valley. The interior is blond board, open beams, antiques, and hanging plants. High-decibel live bands perform on weekends. *Sugarbush Access Rd., Warren, tel. 802/583–2656. MC, V.*

Mad Mountain Tavern
At this post-and-beam barn, locals and visitors can eat, drink, dance, play pool or darts, and watch big-screen TV any night of the week. Live bands play Thursday–Saturday. *Rte. 100 and Rte. 17, Waitsfield, tel. 802/ 496–2562. AE, MC, V.*

More Mellow

Grill Down Under
In this comfortable, relaxed place, there is plenty of brass trim and a granite-top bar; 35 wines and five local microbrews are on tap at any given time. *Corner Sugarbush Access Rd. and German Flats Rd., Warren, tel. 802/583–2301. AE, D, DC, MC, V.*

Rumble Rock Tavern
Named for the rock in the Castlerock area known as Rumble, this new tavern features a variety of entertainment and is decorated with artifacts highlighting 40 years of fun at Sugarbush. *Sugarbush Village, tel. 802/583– 1172. AE, D, MC, V.*

Wyoming is a marvelously wild slice of America that is home to the most impressive range of mountains on the continent. The 40-mile-long Teton Range, thrusting toward the sky in a dazzling array of jagged peaks and spires, is composed of the youngest mountains in the Rocky Mountain system. Seven of these giants top the 12,000-foot mark, and the tallest of them all, Grand Teton, reaches 13,770 feet. Circling this tight concentration of ice- and water-sculpted peaks are glacier-fed lakes and rivers shimmering like jewels on the flat plain known as Jackson Hole. Forming the walls of this scenic valley are the Yellowstone Plateau to the north; the Absaroka, Washakie, and Gros Ventre mountains on the east; and merging to the south, the Hoback and Snake River ranges.

Glacially sculpted from some of the oldest gneisses, schists, and granites on earth, the central peaks and pinnacles known as the Cathedral Group have been described as "Chartres multiplied by six." The spectacle of the Tetons is made even more dramatic by the absence of foothills. The Tetons shoot skyward with no geological preamble, resulting in some of the most stunning mountain vistas on the continent.

Beneath this riveting wall of stone, the Jackson Plain, dissected by 40 miles of the snow-fed Snake River before it winds its way 1,000 miles farther to the Columbia River, is home to ranchers and elk, the latter outnumbering the former, with as many as 10,000 elk wintering in the area annually. This high-elevation plain is an extension of the ecosystem of Yellowstone National Park, which occupies the northwest corner of the state, and the major part of both the Teton Range and Jackson Hole are inside the boundaries of Grand Teton National Park.

Created in 1929 predominantly from land acquired by John D. Rockefeller, Jr., the park attracts more than 3 million visitors annually, including those who come to ski. There are a dozen ski resorts in Wyoming, but by far the best known and most spectacular is the Jackson Hole Mountain Resort.

JACKSON HOLE MOUNTAIN RESORT

JACKSON HOLE MOUNTAIN RESORT

Box 290
Teton Village, WY 83025
Tel. 307/733–2292
www.jhsnow.com

STATISTICALLY SPEAKING

Base elevation: 6,311 feet

Summit elevation: 10,450 feet

Vertical drop: 4,139 feet

Skiable terrain: 2,500 acres

Number of trails: 65

Longest run: 4.5 miles

Lifts and capacity: 1 63-passenger aerial tram, 1 8-passenger gondola, 1 high-speed quad, 2 fixed-grip quads, 1 triple, 2 doubles, 1 surface; 10,896 skiers per hour

Daily lift ticket: $51

Average annual snowfall: 402 inches

Number of skiing days 1997–98: 121

Snowmaking: 152 acres; 6%

Terrain mix: N 10%, I 40%, E 50%

Snowboarding: yes

Cross-country skiing: 17 kilometers groomed, plus mapped tours, guided backcountry tours, and trail system of Yellowstone National Park.

Technically speaking, Jackson and Jackson Hole, though closely related, are distinct entities. Jackson Hole is the name of the valley—or hole—that sits surrounded by the peaks and pinnacles of the Tetons, the youngest and arguably the most spectacular mountains in the Rocky Mountain system. Jackson Hole is also the name of the ski resort, though the resort center at its base is called Teton Village. Twelve miles to the southeast is the community of Jackson, a bona fide Western ranching and tourist town that reflects the spirit of the entire region. The resort, the town, and the ski area are all usually lumped together under the name Jackson Hole, but that's okay. The important thing is the way they fit together so perfectly, meshing beautifully with the surrounding mountains to form a whole greater than the sum of its parts.

This harmony of setting, town, and skiing sets this unique, isolated resort in the northwest corner of Wyoming apart. It just feels right. The town is authentic enough to be real but funky enough to be fun. Behind its facade of wooden sidewalks and movie-set storefront buildings, Jackson is in fact more grit than glitz; and yet the town also has a lively and cosmopolitan dining, entertainment, and cultural scene. The skiing at Jackson Hole Mountain Resort is big and bold enough to spawn legends of derring-do but diverse enough to give us all a shot at the Jackson mystique. As for the surroundings—well, the Tetons have to be seen to be believed. They rise abruptly in jagged spires, glistening with deep snows and at once overshadowing and protecting the ranch land of the valley floor, which is a winter home to the largest elk population in the world.

The 12 miles separating town and resort are an easy drive, facilitated by regular shuttle bus service. Teton Village itself is a curious blend of Western and Tyrolean styles, with a half dozen slope-side hotels, a central mall with restaurants, bars, and shops, several condominium buildings, and all the other trappings of modern ski-resort life without the crass overdevelopment that blights so many other resort villages. It's neat, compact, easy to get around, and offers enough variety in accommodations and dining to keep you quietly happy for more than a few days.

Children's services: day-care, instruction, tel. 301/739–2691

Snow phone: tel. 307/733–2291 or 888/333–7766

Police: tel. 307/733–2331 or 911

Hospital: St. John's, tel. 307/733–3636

Jackson Hole Chamber of Commerce: tel. 307/733–3316

Cross-country skiing: Jackson Hole Nordic Center, tel. 307/739–2629; Spring Creek Resort, tel. 307/733–1004; Teton Pines, tel. 307/733–1005

Road conditions: tel. 888/996–7623

Towing: Teton Towing, tel. 307/733–1943

FIVE-STAR FAVORITES
Best run for vertical: Hobacks

Best run overall: Rendezvous Bowl

Best bar/nightclub: Million Dollar Cowboy Bar

Best hotel: Spring Creek Resort

Best restaurant: The Range

If you like to be on the mountain first thing in the morning, it's definitely the place to stay.

If you prefer a little more action in the after-ski scene, you're likely to opt for the town of Jackson. Jackson has a bustling nightlife, with plenty of bars and saloons, a decent and ever-improving array of restaurants, and a number of cultural activities. Most of the action takes place along a six-block section of Old Town, an area that incorporates the Town Square and its four massive elk-antler archways (don't worry: the elk shed their antlers naturally, and the discards are gathered by local Boy Scouts, who auction them off to raise funds to maintain the elk wintering grounds).

Jackson is family-friendly, with diversions for those who don't want to ski every day. Yellowstone National Park is just 60 miles away, and numerous tour operators will give you guided tours of the park on everything from snowshoes to snow coaches. For 30 years the ski area survived with few real changes in lifts or facilities. In fact, that's what appeals to some people about Jackson Hole—it's a down-home, no-glitz kind of place. But under new ownership now, the mountain is beginning to undergo some significant improvements. In 1996 the resort's first high-speed detachable quad was added, and in 1997 the Bridger Gondola was completed. The 8-passenger gondola whisks skiers from the base to Headwall to access much of the same terrain as the tram, minus Rendezvous Bowl. This was a much-needed addition, as tram lines can be up to an hour long on busy days. The gondola enhanced the intermediate skiing opportunities on the mountain.

HOW TO GET THERE

By Plane

Jackson Hole Airport, 10 miles north of Jackson, is the only airport inside a national park anywhere in America. That necessarily restricts its volume, but even so, there are daily flights from Chicago via American, from Salt Lake City (*see* Getting to Utah Resorts, *above*) via Delta and SkyWest, and from Denver via United.

By Car

From Jackson Hole Airport it's a 10-minute drive to Jackson and 25 minutes to the resort. You can also drive from Salt Lake City, 300 miles southwest of Jackson. It's a five- to six-hour drive, 200 miles of it on interstate that is generally free of snow. Follow I–15 north to Idaho Falls and Routes 26, 31, and 33/22 east to Jackson. The following car-rental companies are available at Jackson Hole Airport: **Alamo** (tel. 800/327–9633), **Budget** (tel. 800/533–6100), **Eagle** (tel. 877/568–2045), **Hertz** (tel. 800/654–3131) and **Thrifty** (tel. 800/367–2277).

GETTING AROUND

A public shuttle bus runs between Jackson and Teton Village, and many of the hotels and resorts provide their own private bus service, but even so, a car is an advantage here. **Buckboard Cab** (tel. 307/733–1112) and **Cowboy Cab** (tel. 307/734–8188) serve the town.

By Shuttle

The **START Bus** (Southern Teton Area Rapid Transit; tel. 307/733–4521) makes frequent stops throughout town and at the Teton Village area. It operates daily from 6:15 AM to 10:50 PM. The fare is $2 one-way between Jackson and the resort, $1 one-way within Jackson. **Jackson Hole Express** (tel. 307/733–1719) offers twice-daily shuttles to and from the Salt Lake City and Idaho Falls airports, and twice weekly shuttles to Montana's Big Sky Resort. **Downhill Express** (tel. 208/354–3386), based in Driggs, Idaho, makes regular runs between Jackson Hole and Grand Targhee Resort.

THE SKIING

If you go solely by its reputation, anyone but an in-your-face expert would steer clear of Jackson Hole. Tall tales about its staggering vertical abound. While it's true Jackson Hole has the second-highest vertical drop in the United States and the fourth-highest in North America, behind Big Sky, Montana, and Blackcomb and Whistler mountains, in British Columbia, Canada, it is also true this is a good all-round intermediate-and-up ski mountain. Up is the key. Rendezvous Mountain, the higher of the two peaks that make up the broad-shouldered mountain hulk, is the one that gives the resort its savage reputation, for the terrain here is a mass of vertiginous chutes, couloirs, bowls, and gullies. But between the 4,000-foot-plus vertical of Rendezvous and the substantially lower and less precipitous groomed cruisers of Après Vous Mountain, there are 2,500 acres of varied skiing, including the mostly intermediate Casper Bowl area, which lies between the two summits.

It's a large resort, but it's easy to move back and forth between the three sectors on a well-designed series of cat tracks that actually slope in the direction you're going with no noticeable flat spots. Everybody starts from the compact base area, from which Jackson's aerial tram whips you to the Rendezvous summit: 4,139 feet of vertical in eight minutes; you can't do that anywhere else in America. It's steep, rugged, ungroomed, and uncompromising up here, and sacred areas such as Rendezvous Bowl, Corbet's Couloir, and the Hobacks are always discussed when serious ski addicts gather.

Fortunately, there's a lot more mountain for the rest of us. Just a short distance from the tram's base are the lifts up to the Casper Bowl and Après Vous areas, virtually all of which are long, groomed blue runs with some black pitches and faces. Also at the base begins the lengthy Bridger Gondola, which delivers you below the Headwall at a point just above and south of Casper Bowl. These sections encompass some of the most varied and challenging intermediate/upper intermediate/expert terrain you'll find anywhere. Although experts push their limits on the tough terrain of Rendezvous Mountain, strong intermediates can sample the bliss of Jackson Hole's pure fall-line skiing. Another bliss—for everyone— is the solitude. Jackson Hole Mountain Resort has one of the lowest skier-to-acreage ratios in the country. A busy day at Jackson Hole is maybe 3,000 skiers spread over 2,500 acres.

Novices

Aside from Snowbird in Utah, Jackson Hole is the only resort in the country that seems totally unsuitable for raw beginners or low-end novices. If you fit into one of those two categories, I strongly recommend you look elsewhere and save Jackson Hole for a time when you are at a steady intermediate level. It's not that Jackson Hole doesn't have a fine ski school; and yes, there is a small beginners' area served by a double chair and a quad, so you can certainly get started on skis here. But do yourself a favor and travel to this out-of-the-way mountain when you can enjoy more of it.

If you do by chance end up at Jackson while you're still at the novice

level, your options are limited to either the three short starter runs served by the Eagle's Rest double chair or the trio of slightly longer runs served by the Teewinot quad chair. These meticulously groomed, carpet-smooth extrawide novice trails are the only marked green runs on the mountain.

The next rung up is a fairly sizable one: to move to some of the gentler blue runs that start on the upper part of Après Vous. The Après Vous double chair (from the top of the Teewinot quad) takes you there, and at that point you are immediately dealing with steeper terrain. It's wide, well groomed, and goes in rolls rather than one straight shot, so easy, controlled plow turns will get you down, but you may find it hard work.

If you can't deal with that and want to bail out, you can follow the signs for the Togwotee Pass Traverse, a long, narrow cat track that winds back down to South Pass Traverse and eventually back to the top of the green runs on the lower part of the mountain. Take note: Once you get off the chair at the top, you have to turn left and immediately head down a short, fairly steep section that funnels you to the top of Upper Werner. From there the whole face of the mountain opens up, and you can see precisely what you are in for. The easiest terrain (still blue) is to your right, while the steeper pitches are to the left. You can catch the Traverse bailout about 500 yards down this stretch.

Intermediates

Intermediates will find some heads-up skiing at Jackson, the kind that will stretch you a little, throw you a few more challenges than normal, and even give you a greater sense of confidence at the end of the day. Your warm-up runs should, however, take place on the softer flanks of Après Vous Mountain, where the early sun will appear. Take the Teewinot lift to the Après Vous chair to the top. To the right (looking down) is a superb pair of groomed cruisers—Upper Werner and Moran—that roll and pitch sufficiently to get your legs warm fast. You can repeat them a few times or take the Togwotee Pass Traverse (from the top of Après Vous) over to the Casper Bowl chair, where it's a little steeper, less groomed, and just a little more unpredictable.

There are over 300 acres of intermediate terrain off the Casper Bowl chair, and it's made all the more interesting thanks to the trees and straight-ahead trail cutting that leaves dips, rolls, drop-offs, pitches, and glades as the fall line dictates. Camp Ground, Timbered Island, and Easy Does It, which all start from the right side (looking down) of the Casper chair, are the widest slopes in this area and will give you a good ride back down to the bottom of the Casper Bowl chair. To the left of the top of the Casper Bowl chair (looking down), you'll find narrower, more heavily treed trails. If you go farther to the right and follow the Amphitheater Traverse, you can ride the Thunder chair and ski either the wide-open Amphitheater Bowl area or play in the gladed runs in the Laramie (to the right, looking down) Bowl area. Both areas have good, steep fall-line bowl skiing, a pick-your-own-way-down buffet of options on some of the best intermediate terrain on the mountain.

The new Bridger Gondola has spawned additional opportunities for intermediates. After disembarking just below the Headwall, your many options include following the buffed-out blue Sundance run to the base area, sampling some of the area's off-run tree skiing, or taking Lupine Way to the Amphitheater run or the Nez Perce Traverse.

Above the Headwall and Laramie Bowl areas is the summit of Rendezvous Mountain and the storied couloirs and chutes and rocky gullies that give Jackson Hole its reputation. Good intermediates can push the envelope a little by trying some of the tamer blacks. Only the tram goes to the summit, but from the Laramie Bowl area you can take the Sublette chair to a point just below the summit. To the right of the chair (looking down) is the steep entrance to a trio of tough black runs. You can avoid the drop-off access by taking the blue Hanging Rock, which meets up with the Rendezvous Trail to wind easily down to the bottom of the Sublette chair to give you a sense of the terrain without actually getting you into any trouble. You'll find the black runs steep, treed, and ungroomed, with moguls on the left-hand side, but if you're a good strong intermediate, with some effort you should be able to cut your teeth on them.

Experts

Without a doubt your domain is Rendezvous Mountain with its 4,139 feet of vertical and some of the most demanding and rugged in-bounds skiing in America. You might want to warm up in the Laramie Bowl area first, but eventually you'll head for the summit on the tram. This is where you'll find the stuff that Jackson Hole is famed for: ultrasteep couloirs, chutes, gullies, glades, and wide-open sweeping bowls. The most renowned descent is precipitous, tree-choked Corbet's Couloir, which can only be reached by jumping from a cornice to land 15 feet below. If you're not ready for that, the Upper Rendezvous Bowl is a steep, wide-open screamer that gives you a taste of Jackson's vertical without the impediments of rocks and trees. You can ski this upper part of the mountain from the Sublette chair to avoid going back to the village to ride the tram. Although there are a dozen or so named runs in this area of the mountain, they really do not convey the scale of the terrain; each named run has dozens of free-form options. The lower flanks of Rendezvous Mountain are the home of the Hobacks, a wide swath of steep, powder-packed cruising bowls that again dare you to discover all the different ways down. And when you've tired of this terrain, 20,000 acres of out-of-bounds skiing await you beyond the ski area boundaries. Out-of-bounds gates on Rendezvous Bowl open southward into the Cody Bowl–Rock Springs Bowl complex, and additional gates open onto the Headwall, Granite Canyon, and other precipitous areas. The gates are open only when the forecast for avalanches is low, and their status (open or closed) is well signed at lift facilities.

Skiers and snowboarders assume absolute responsibility for themselves once they pass through the out-of-bounds gates. If they pass through them when they're closed, they risk long-term expulsion from the ski area.

That's the beauty of Jackson Hole for expert skiers: it offers virtually unlimited challenge and a kind of rugged adventure not found at resorts elsewhere. If you like to explore, cut new tracks, push the envelope—then you'll love Jackson Hole.

SNOWBOARDING

You'll find the same advantages on the pair of huge mountains at Jackson Hole as skiers do—rugged, limitless terrain and uncrowded conditions for free riding. Special provisions for boarders at Jackson Hole include a half-pipe near the Après Vous chair in the Deer Flat area, below the Werner run and above the South Pass Traverse. The pipe, which has 10-foot-high walls and is groomed at least three times a week, measures 380 feet in length. It has a cylindrical ramp, open to both riders and skiers, for practicing aerials. There's also a quarter-pipe, along with various terrain features, at the lower end of the Amphitheater run, which can be reached by taking the Bridger Gondola or the Thunder chair.

OTHER SNOW SPORTS

No doubt about it, downhill skiing is the primary focus at the Jackson Hole, but there are other options available at the resort for fun on the snow and ice. Sprawling away from the base area—traversing flat ranchlands and rolling, aspen-studded hills—are 17 kilometers of **cross-country ski** trails groomed for both skate and classic skiing. Rentals and lessons are available at the nordic center's cabin. The Kids' Ranch at the base-area Cody House offers a variety of activities, including **ice-skating** (skate rentals available). A favorite evening activity is the Solitude Dinner Sleigh Ride, which begins at Teton Village. A peaceful excursion in a **horse-drawn sleigh,** with plenty of lap robes to keep passengers warm, stops at a cozy mountainside cabin where a four-course meal is highlighted by a choice of broiled Coho salmon or prime rib. Beyond Teton Village in the greater Jackson Hole area, sleigh rides through the National Elk Refuge, **snowmobiling,** and **dog sledding** are other popular wintertime activities.

NEARBY

In the town of Jackson, **Snow King Resort** (tel. 307/733–5200) is a modest day facility with mostly intermediate and expert runs, an option when the weather is cold and windy at the big mountain or when you feel like skiing for just a few hours without driving far; a new half-pipe opened here in 1999. Beyond Jackson Hole, west of Wilson on Route 22, is **Teton Pass,** one of the most sought-after destinations in the country for backcountry snowboarding; deep powder burying limitless terrain is the chief draw. On the opposite, west, side of lofty Teton Pass from Jackson Hole sits Teton Valley, Idaho, gateway to **Grand Targhee Ski & Summer Resort** (tel. 307/353–2281). Grand Targhee is in the Wyoming Tetons, yet you can't drive here without first passing through this sublime, mountain-ringed Idaho basin. Grand Targhee, with a vertical drop about half that of Jackson Hole's, has garnered a well-deserved reputation for some of the best powder skiing in North America in its glades and basins.

WHERE TO STAY

There's a good range of accommodations at Teton Village and in the town of Jackson, including a variety of resort-style hotels and basic motels. Several small bed-and-breakfasts have sprouted along the 12-mile highway that connects Jackson and the mountain, as well as in nearby Wilson, about 9 miles from the resort. All accommodations can be booked through **Jackson Hole Central Reservations** (Box 2618, Jackson, WY 83001, tel. 307/733–4005 or 800/443–6931).

Expensive

Alpenhof
Just 50 yards from the tram, this is an Austrian-style lodge with a twin-peaked stucco alpine-chalet exterior, and the old-world atmosphere positively oozes from the polished-wood-and-stone decor. The rooms share similar wood trim and pine furnishings; some have stucco and stone walls, fireplaces, balconies, or whirlpools (or all four). *3255 W. McCollister Dr., Box 288, Teton Village 83025, tel. 307/733–3242 or 800/ 732–3244, fax 307/739–1516. 43 rooms. Facilities: 2 restaurants, heated outdoor pool, Jacuzzi, sauna, masseuse, laundry. AE, D, DC, MC, V. $98–$418.*

Rusty Parrot Lodge
This magnificent log-and-stone lodge is one of Jackson's best-known landmarks. Sturdy in its hand-hewn log splendor, with peaks and posts, balconies and beams, yet stylish inside with its handcrafted peeled-log furniture, stone fireplace warming its lounge, Western art, down comforters, and Jacuzzi tubs, the Rusty Parrot is

pure Rocky Mountain elegance. The rooms are all individually decorated with pine and twig chairs and tables, Western-style fabrics and curtains. Half have fireplaces. *175 N. Jackson St., Jackson 83001, tel. 307/733–2000 or 800/458–2004, fax 307/733–5566. 32 rooms, 1 suite. Facilities: dining room, lounge. AE, D, DC, MC, V. $145–$500, including full breakfast.*

Spring Creek Resort
This chic 1,000-acre log cabin resort is high atop the East Gros Ventre Butte 4 miles north of Jackson. It's really a minivillage, with three dozen honey-bronze log cabins and condo structures scattered around two central buildings. The spacious condo suites have hand-troweled plaster walls, handmade lodge-pole furnishings, large stone fireplaces, and down bed covers and kitchen facilities. *1800 Spirit Dance Rd., Box 3154, Jackson 83001, tel. 307/733–8833 or 800/443–6139, fax 307/733–1524. 86 units. Facilities: restaurant, lounge, hot tub, barbecue pits. AE, D, DC, MC, V. $150–$190.*

Wort Hotel
Originally built in 1941 and then rebuilt after a 1980 fire, the Wort (rhymes with "yurt") is a Jackson landmark. A noteworthy Western art collection enlivens the lobby and restaurant. Rooms are decorated in Western style with hand-peeled log beds equipped with comforters, fluffy pillows, and a welcoming teddy bear. The Silver Dollar Bar is a popular watering hole, and the hotel's downtown location is ideal. *50 N. Glenwood Ave., Box 69, Jackson 83001, tel. 307/733–2190 or 800/322–2727, fax 307/733–2067. 60 rooms. Facilities: restau-*

rant, bar, 2 Jacuzzis, fitness room, 3 meeting rooms. AE, MC, V. $135–$450.

Moderate

Inn at Jackson Hole
In a perfect slope-side location just 100 yards from the tram at Teton Village, this inn has some of the most comfortable, spacious, and reasonably priced rooms and suites at the mountain. The units range from standard hotel rooms to loft suites; most of the nonstandard rooms have kitchen facilities, and a few even come with a fireplace. *3345 W. McCollister Dr., Box 328, Teton Village 83025, tel. 307/733–2311 or 800/842–7666, fax 307/733–0844. 71 rooms, 12 suites. Facilities: 2 restaurants, bar-lounge, outdoor pool, 3 outdoor hot tubs. AE, D, DC, MC, V. $120–$275.*

Lodge at Jackson Hole
This massive log building, an easy walk from the Town Square, combines new- and old-West touches: exterior timbers with hand-carved wildlife sculptures, leather-fringed chairs and couches, a log staircase, and antler chandeliers. The rooms, generous in size and amenities and tastefully done in soft pastels, with matching accessories and coverings, are a good choice for families. *80 Scott La., Box 7478, Jackson Hole 83001, tel. 307/739–9703 or 800/458–3866, fax 307/739–9168. 154 rooms. Facilities: restaurant, heated indoor-outdoor pool, sauna, hot tub, games arcade, shuttle bus service. AE, D, DC, MC, V. $89–$150, including Continental breakfast.*

Resort Hotel at Jackson Hole
Nestled against the base of the Tetons, this hotel offers ski-in/walk-out lift access, on a heated, snow-free

walkway. Tastefully appointed rooms have snuggly down comforters. In the Western-theme lobby, a great place for reading and relaxing, are two large stone fireplaces and hand-crafted leather furniture. Try for a mountainside room with a balcony. *3245 W. McCollister Dr., Box 348, Teton Village 83025, tel. 307/733–3657 or 800/445–4655, fax 307/733–9543. 101 rooms. Facilities: 2 restaurants, 2 lounges, heated outdoor pool, indoor and outdoor hot tubs, sauna, laundry. AE, D, DC, MC, V. $90–$260.*

Snow King Resort

This hotel and condominium complex is just six blocks from the Town Square, at the base of the Snow King Mountain ski area, Jackson's "town hill." The largest full-service property in town, the hotel has a soaring atrium-style lobby with massive rough timbers and a 40-foot rock fireplace. The units range in size from standard hotel rooms to three-bedroom condos, and most are modern, with Berber rugs, textured walls, and Southwest-style furnishings. *400 E. Snow King Ave., Jackson 83001, tel. 307/733–5200 or 800/522–5464, fax 307/733–4086. 192 rooms, 12 suites. Facilities: 2 restaurants, lounge/nightclub, indoor ice-skating rink, outdoor heated pool, sauna, Jacuzzi, exercise room, ski shop, conference center. AE, D, DC, MC, V. $90–$345.*

Inexpensive

Angler's Inn

A few minutes from the Town Square, the rooms here are simply furnished and clean. Each has a morning coffee setup plus a microwave and a refrigerator. *265 Millward St., Box 1247,*

Jackson 83001, tel. 307/733–3682 or 800/867–4667, fax 307/739–1551. 28 rooms. AE, D, MC, V. $60–$70.

Bunkhouse

In the basement of the Anvil Motel, this is good, clean, and basic bunkhouse-style lodging, with a central dormitory accommodating both sexes, a common living room with TV, and a kitchen area. *215 N. Cache St., Box 486, Jackson 83001, tel. 307/733–3668 or 800/234–4507, fax 307/733–3957. 25 beds. Facilities: outdoor hot tub. MC, V. $18 per person.*

Elk Country Inn

This is a no-frills but clean and well-maintained motel and log cabin complex just a block off Jackson's Main Street, about a 10-minute walk from the Town Square. There's a variety of motel rooms plus some larger cabin units with kitchen facilities and some lofts. *480 W. Pearl St., Box 1255, Jackson 83001, 307/733–2364 or 800/483-8667, fax 307/733–4465. 23 rooms, 7 suites, 13 log cabins. Facilities: indoor hot tub, laundry. AE, D, DC, MC, V. $38–$110.*

The Hostel

This has to be one of the best hostels in ski country, with its spiffy private rooms, all with private baths and maid service, and its furnishings a definite cut above the rustic style typical of hostels. In fact, the only typical hostel feature here is the price. You can choose from king rooms or twin rooms, which sleep four comfortably in a bunk arrangement. It's just 100 yards from the lifts. *3325 McCollister Dr., Box 546, Teton Village 83025, tel. 307/733–3415, fax 307/739–1142. 55 rooms. Facilities: 2 game rooms,* *play area, library, ski-tuning area, laundry. MC, V. $47–$60.*

WHERE TO EAT

Jackson is not the culinary epicenter of Western skiing, but it does have an interesting collection of restaurants, dominated by traditional Western fare—beef and lots of it, plus various game dishes. It mostly has medium-priced places to eat, by ski-country standards, and the atmosphere is definitely blue-jean casual, with a few exceptions. There are a good number of restaurants in and around the Town Square area, plus others on the road to the resort, and, of course, at the ski village itself. Even if you're staying at the ski area and enjoy the convenience of walking from your accommodation, you would be remiss in not going into Jackson at least a couple of times a week.

On the Mountain

Casper Restaurant

Warm up by the big stone fireplace or kick back at the beer and espresso bar here. For food, the choice is pasta dishes, burgers, chili and stews, as well as barbecue on the outoor deck, weather permitting. *Mid-Mountain Lodge, near base of Casper chair, Teton Village, tel. 307/739–2624. AE, MC, V.*

Nick Wilson's

The Café serves hearty breakfasts, a varied lunch menu, and, on sunny days, outdoor barbecue on the deck. For après-ski, the Watering Hole has a rousing atmosphere with live music on weekends. *Tram Building, Teton Village, tel. 307/739–2626. AE, MC, V.*

Expensive

Blue Lion

Since 1978 the Blue Lion has been serving creative cuisine in an elegant, yet casual atmosphere. Spread over two floors of a renovated house, the interior is intimate and homey, with white walls, low-beamed ceilings, plants, and warm accents. Begin with southwestern pheasant cakes or the best Caesar salad in Jackson Hole, and proceed with a house specialty, such as sliced roast rack of lamb with a peppercorn–rosemary cream sauce and jalapeño mint sauce. Other favorites: mixed grill of elk medallions in a brandy green peppercorn sauce or grilled fresh trout in herb butter. For dessert, sumptuous pastries are created daily. *160 N. Millward St., Jackson, tel. 307/733–3912. AE, DC, MC, V.*

Cadillac Grille

This hopping art deco bistro located front and center on the Town Square has been a favorite of locals since 1983. The granite, chrome, and glass decor complements the walls bedecked with avant-garde art. The fare is eclectic American with Tuscan accents and organic produce. There's always a great selection of fish, game, pasta, wood-fired pizzas, and Black Angus steaks and chops. Menu samplings include lamb with Niçoise olive demi-glace, elk in shallot–Pinot Noir sauce, and fresh Chilean sea bass. *55 N. Cache St., Jackson, tel. 307/733–3279. Reservations advised. AE, MC, V.*

The Granary

It's a large, softly lighted modern room with a spectacular starlit view over the valley. Linen and crystal place settings set a quietly formal tone here. The cuisine is an interesting mix of Continental, Western, and modern Southwestern. Game choices abound on the menu—from panfried Rocky Mountain trout to sautéed medallions of elk. Other entrées may include cedar-planked salmon and rack of New Zealand lamb. *Spring Creek Resort, off Spring Gulch Rd., Jackson, tel. 307/733-8833 or 800/443-6139. AE, D, DC, MC, V.*

The Range

This is popularly considered one of Jackson's two best restaurants. The upstairs restaurant has an open kitchen and striking East-meets-West decor, with black lacquer chairs and rice paper lights. The menu emphasizes regional American cuisine in original combinations. You might start with grilled scallops in Parmesan cheese cups with tomato-vodka sauce or a salad of fresh cactus, red pepper, purple onion, mango, and cilantro in a blue-corn tortilla cup. Entrées include daily game and seafood specials. *225 N. Cache St., Jackson, tel. 307/733-5481. Reservations essential. AE, MC, V.*

Snake River Grill

Just off the Town Square on the second level of a plaza complex, the award-winning "SRG" serves fresh fish, wild game, free-range veal and chicken, pizzas from the wood-burning oven, and organic produce. The wine list runs to more than 200 selections. An interior of lodgepole pine walls, rock fireplace, and leather booths is complemented by a private dining room and outdoor deck seating. There's also counter dining for singles or couples in a rush. *84 E. Broadway, Jackson, tel.*

307/733-0557. Reservations essential. AE, DC, MC, V.

Moderate

Mountain Skillet

This delightful small restaurant in the Inn at Jackson Hole has a casual and cozy atmosphere. You'll find seared yellowfin tuna seved on a bed of sautéed spinach and shiitake mushrooms, grilled chicken with a Cuban garlic-ginger marinade, and beef and pasta dishes. *Inn at Jackson Hole, 3345 McCollister Dr., Teton Village, tel. 307/739-0244. AE, D, MC, V.*

Nani's Genuine Pasta House

Hidden away on a side street, this gem of an Italian restaurant is a tiny clapboard cottage with about a dozen small tables, all covered with red-and-white checked tablecloths. The changing menu may offer items such as fresh handmade ravioli, a spicy white wine broth linguine *con vongole,* and veal *Valdostana,* as well as specials that emphasize a different region of Italy each month. *El Rancho Motel, 242 N. Glenwood, Jackson, tel. 307/733-3888. MC, V.*

Sweetwater Restaurant

This is a marvelous turn-of-the-century log cabin whose character is provided by exposed logs, hand-hewn beams, sloping wooden floors, and wrought-iron lamps. Although small, it provides a touch of elegance with linen and crystal. Pleasantly shaded outdoor seating is an option in summer. Appetizers such as steamed mussels and smoked buffalo carpaccio precede main-course offerings such as roast pepper pork, mesquite chicken, and Cajun lamb loin. The Sweetwater also offers a good selection of wines and desserts. *Corner King and Pearl Sts., Jackson, tel. 307/733–3553. AE, D, DC, MC, V.*

Vista Grande

This pink adobe between the ski area and town has been a favorite après–ski gathering spot since 1978. The margaritas are excellent, and the food is a step up from traditional Mexican fare, with specialties like crab enchiladas, blackened chicken tostadas, and blackened tuna with pineapple salsa. *Teton Village Rd., Jackson, tel. 307/733–6964. AE, MC, V.*

Inexpensive

Billy's Giant Hambugers

On the Town Square, this casual diner-style eatery serves the biggest, fattest, juiciest burgers in Jackson. If it's too crowded you can order from the adjoining bar. *Adjacent to Cadillac Grille, 55 N. Cache St., Jackson, tel. 307/733–3279. Reservations not accepted. AE, MC, V.*

Bubba's Bar–B–Que

You go to Bubba's mainly for the major portions of spareribs and baby-back ribs, hickory smoked and smothered in Bubba's secret special sauces and served with garlic bread. The decor is simply lots of beams, Western artifacts, separate booths, and brick floors. *515 W. Broadway, Jackson, tel. 307/733–2288. Reservations not accepted. AE, D, MC, V.*

The Bunnery

Part bakery and part restaurant, the Bunnery dishes up hearty lunches of thick soups and scrumptious sandwiches made with the Bunnery's locally legendary oat/sunflower/mil-

let bread. It's a good choice for breakfast or an informal dinner. *Hole in the Wall Mall, north of Town Square, Jackson, tel. 307/733–5474. MC, V.*

Lame Duck Chinese Restaurant

This all-purpose Asian restaurant manages to serve the major cuisines—Japanese, Thai, and Chinese—without ruining any of them. The Japanese offerings are sushi and sashimi, limited in selection but fresh and well presented; the Thai dishes carry the spicy peanut and lemon-grass accents of that country; and the Chinese selections run the full gamut from chow mein to sweet and sour chicken to *moo goo gai pan. 680 E. Broadway, Jackson, tel. 307/733–4311. AE, MC, V.*

Best Bets for Breakfast

Jedediah's House of Sourdough

Mountain-size portions of light, fluffy flapjacks, a variety of sauces and toppings, and crisp golden-brown waffles with fruit toppings are the mainstay lure, but there are also the breakfast standbys of ham, bacon, sausage, eggs any style, home fries, and omelets. *135 E. Broadway, 1 block east of Town Square, Jackson, tel. 307/733–5671. AE, D, DC, MC, V.*

Nora's Fish Creek Inn

It's the log cabin with the huge fish on the roof beside Route 22. The pancakes and French toast are a local legend, plus there are monster-size portions of egg and meat dishes, lots of homemade biscuits, and great home fries. *Foot of Teton Pass, Rte. 22, 6 mi west of Jackson, Wilson, tel. 307/733–8288. D, MC, V.*

NIGHTLIFE AND ENTERTAINMENT

Après-Ski

Alpenhof Bistro

This bustling, yet cozy and sophisticated après-ski bar is a touch European in tone. There's always plenty of conversation, and live music is performed twice weekly. Big windows open onto the base of the ski area, and the roaring fireplace becomes an irresistible people magnet after the lifts close. *Alpenhof Lodge, 3255 W. McCollister Dr., Teton Village, tel. 307/733–3242. AE, D, DC, MC, V.*

Mangy Moose

This crazily decorated place offers some potentially crazy times. Two levels of controlled mayhem are surrounded by some of the most bizarre antiques, collectibles, and junk that ever adorned one building—from trophy heads to antique sporting equipment. There's even an entire stuffed moose suspended from the ceiling. You'll find live entertainment on weekends, loud recorded music at other times, and definitely a younger crowd. *Teton Village, tel. 307/733–4913. AE, MC, V.*

Loud and Lively/Dancing

Million Dollar Cowboy Bar

This is Jackson's place to see and be seen. Inside, it's part electric cowboy, part Vegas glitz, and part Western rococo. Two parallel 75-foot bars on either side have saddle bar stools, mirrors, and backlighted art. The enormous dance floor is flanked by a stage with live Country-and-Western entertainment. Swing-dance lessons on Thursday nights are designed to get neophytes dipping and twirling in respectable fashion. *25 N. Cache St., Jackson, tel. 307/733–2207. No credit cards.*

Stagecoach Bar

Each Sunday night in the red building, the Stagecoach Band gets things kicking country style, while Thursdays see a return to the '70s with disco night. The rest of the week the 'Coach is a fairly low-key, but still very popular hangout that has an old brick-and-wood funkiness, a long, handmade wooden bar with log bar stools, and pool tables, a juke box, and darts. *Rte. 22, Wilson, tel. 307/733–4407. MC, V.*

More Mellow

SilverDollar Bar

In Jackson's historic hotel, the Wort, the SilverDollar is a cheerful lounge, regularly energized by an acoustic guitarist and Lynne Wright playing ragtime piano. The bar is inlaid with 2,032 uncirculated 1921 silver dollars, a reminder of the Wort's earlier days as a gambling house. *Wort Hotel, 50 N. Glenwood Ave., Jackson, tel. 307/733–2190. AE, D, DC, MC, V.*

Snake River Brewery

The hand-crafted beers of Jackson's first brew pub have won seven awards at the Great American Beer Festival, along with three World Beer Cup medals. A no-smoking environment, live jazz Tuesday nights, English-style ales and traditional German lagers, and wood-fired pizzas and other tasty food items all add up to a pleasant place to meet and socialize. Up to seven beers are on tap daily. *265 S. Millward, Jackson, tel. 307/739–2337. AE, MC, V.*

NOTES

NOTES

NOTES

Fodor's

Looking for a different kind of vacation?

Fodor's makes it easy with a full line of specialty guidebooks to suit a variety of interests—from adventure to romance to language help.

Fodor's. For the world of ways you travel.